D0402724

NO LONGER PROPERTY OF
SEATTLE PUBLIC LIBRARY

TO BUILD
A BETTER
WORLD

TO BUILD
A BETTER
WORLD

Choices to End the Cold War
and Create a Global Commonwealth

Philip Zelikow
and
Condoleezza Rice

TWELVE

New York   Boston

Copyright © 2019 by Philip Zelikow and Condoleezza Rice

Cover design by Jarrod Taylor. Cover photograph by Alamy Images.
Cover copyright © 2019 by Hachette Book Group, Inc.

Hachette Book Group supports the right to free expression and the value of copyright.
The purpose of copyright is to encourage writers and artists to produce the creative
works that enrich our culture.

The scanning, uploading, and distribution of this book without permission is a theft of
the author's intellectual property. If you would like permission to use material from the
book (other than for review purposes), please contact permissions@hbgusa.com. Thank
you for your support of the author's rights.

Twelve
Hachette Book Group
1290 Avenue of the Americas, New York, NY 10104
twelvebooks.com
twitter.com/twelvebooks

First Edition: September 2019

Twelve is an imprint of Grand Central Publishing. The Twelve name and logo are
trademarks of Hachette Book Group, Inc.

The publisher is not responsible for websites (or their content) that are not owned by the
publisher.

The Hachette Speakers Bureau provides a wide range of authors for speaking events. To
find out more, go to www.hachettespeakersbureau.com or call (866) 376-6591.

Library of Congress Control Number: 2019939105

ISBNs: 978-1-5387-6467-1 (hardcover), 978-1-5387-6466-4 (ebook)

Printed in the United States of America

LSC-C

10 9 8 7 6 5 4 3 2 1

For Paige

To the Rices and Rays, who believed in American democracy
even in the toughest times.

Contents

TO BUILD
A BETTER
WORLD

Catalytic Choices

Two East German Success Stories

One of the new countries created by the Cold War was called the German Democratic Republic (GDR), or, more informally, East Germany. It was the communist Germany.

With its sixteen million inhabitants enjoying some of the highest living standards in the socialist world, as the year 1989 began the GDR seemed solid as a rock. The standard text on East Germany said that it "is apparently one of the world's most stable regimes."[1]

To pick one kind of GDR success story as 1989 began, consider a scientist, a woman who had established her position in a field founded and dominated by men. She was a researcher working in the GDR's Central Institute of Physical Chemistry, a part of the country's Academy of Sciences. She had received her doctorate in physics a few years earlier.

In some ways it was not a difficult job. She did not have to teach. Hardly anyone outside a small circle of fellow scientists could even understand what she did or evaluate her work. Her field was the study of the quantum characteristics of subatomic particles.

The scientist was the daughter of a small-town Lutheran pastor and a former schoolteacher. Her friends used to call her "Kasi" (her last name was Kasner). The communist government did not care much for pastors. But Kasi's father—who had moved from a parish in West Germany to

East Germany in loyal obedience to the Lutheran Church hierarchy—had stayed out of politics. He eventually headed a Lutheran seminary.

Kasi's father had always been carefully monitored by the efficient and omnipresent East German secret police (the Stasi, short for "State Security" in German). Informers reported that Pastor Kasner appeared to adopt the Communist Party line in the internal politics of the Lutheran Church; he was certainly willing to critique capitalist greed and consumerism.

Life was not always easy. Kasi's hardworking, "meticulous" father would tell fellow seminarians how "he had left the West out of free will and about how hard he had worked and he nevertheless was convinced that all was in vain and that the Church—even in his lifetime—would shrink and most parishes would lose their pastor."

Kasi's mother could not take up a teaching job. She knew how to teach English and Latin. The East German government had little interest in hiring women to teach those subjects, especially not in a small town.

The government-set income was below average. But Kasi's family made their way, occasionally getting gift packages and money from their relatives in the West.

Kasi was a gifted student in school. As expected from a star student, she had joined the Communist Party's youth organization. She wore its uniform, with its instantly recognizable indigo blue colors, to school. She won prizes. She studied all the time.

The only foreign language taught was Russian. Kasi devoted herself to becoming fluent in it, enjoying Russian culture. Her other star subject was mathematics, where she was good enough to do well in national competitions.

While Kasi was young, the family could vacation and visit relatives in West Germany. That changed when she was seven years old. When she returned from an August 1961 holiday in Bavaria, East German soldiers were unrolling the barbed wire to fence off the border for good behind what the government called its "antifascist protection wall."

Kasi remembered how, in church that Sunday, "people cried. My mother cried too. We couldn't fathom what had happened." Later, in 1968, her parents were upset by the Soviet-led invasion in Czechoslovakia, a country her family had visited. The invasion crushed that country's experiment with "socialism with a human face."

As a schoolgirl, Kasi was no athlete or social standout, but she had friends. She was well organized and helpful to her classmates. Her skill in the Russian language won her a trip to Moscow. She received a place in an elite high school. Again, her grades were excellent. She was invited to go on to a university and receive a rare, prized higher education provided by the state.

At the last moment, though, the precious opportunity to go to a university almost collapsed. With her graduating high school classmates, Kasi joined in staging for the school an anti-imperialist school play. The expected theme would attack the American war in Vietnam. Instead, the students, in a sort of end-of-school rebellious way, performed a play praising the anti-Portuguese liberation movement in Mozambique. They even worked in a quote from a satirical writer who vaguely alluded to a "wall."

Those in charge were not amused by this play-acting about liberation and references to a "wall" (like the one that now enclosed the East Germans). The school authorities planned to punish all the students by taking away their university admissions. They had used such a punishment before.

Kasi's father, and other well-connected fathers, all desperately pulled strings to get the decision turned around. They succeeded. The students' teacher lost his job, but Kasi was able to go on to the University of Leipzig.

She had originally thought of studying medicine. Instead, she decided to concentrate on physics. This was a field as far from politics as she could possibly get. Naturally she had to take her required classes in Marxist political economy. She also did a little work on the side as a barmaid in the student watering hole, the Thirsty Pegasus.

Ninety percent of her classmates were men. One became her boyfriend, then her husband. As a married couple, it was easier to persuade the state housing office to assign them an apartment. She and her husband both pursued advanced studies. His field was optics. She stayed with physics.

At an initial job interview, the Stasi recruited Kasi to become an informant. She would have become one of millions planted in practically every workplace. Kasi dodged this duty. She found a way to put the Stasi recruiters off without getting in trouble. "My parents always told me to tell Stasi officers that I was a chatterbox and someone who couldn't keep my mouth shut. And I also told them that I didn't know if I could keep this secret from my husband."

She did manage to keep at least one secret from him. It was a big one. He was quite surprised when "suddenly one day she packed her bags and left the apartment we shared." The couple had grown apart after a few years together.

Kasi kept her husband's last name, by which she was now known. She completed her doctoral work in 1986 after eight years of not-too-hurried postgraduate research. She published an article in a peer-reviewed Western journal, *Chemical Physics*.

Again a single woman, childless, she made a quiet life for herself. The GDR did not have much resources and infrastructure for lab research in subatomic particles. She and her friends at the research institute, including a skeptical fellow physicist with whom she became close, would frequently talk politics. They were not "political" people, but they were attentive.

Kasi was not outspoken. But she was observant. She was careful. And she had a dry sense of humor. Being scientists, she and her friends had unusual access to books and travel, although their activities were carefully monitored. She was even allowed to make a trip to the West, to visit West Germany.

In the late 1980s, in private conversation, she and her friends would analyze the arguments of East German dissenters. These dissidents were usually in prison or exiled to the West. Their books were banned in the GDR but illegal copies were smuggled around. Kasi and her friends also would discuss the unrest and martial law in nearby Poland, which they had visited. They would discuss the fascinating news coming out of Moscow, about the reform plans of the Soviet Union's new leader, Mikhail Gorbachev. With her Russian, Kasi could herself read the Soviet newspaper *Pravda* to dissect the latest developments. She and her friends could usually tune in to a West German radio station or TV, if they were lucky enough to share a TV.

As 1989 began, the thirty-four-year-old scientist had her usual routines. She took bike rides on country roads. She had her weekly sauna and drinks with a friend. She did nothing to worry the Stasi, nothing to call attention to herself. The head of her department at the research institute thought she was a good worker. "One gets the impression," he said, that "she is on to something, she works diligently toward a goal but she is also a woman who has a mind of her own."

* * *

As 1989 began, another young professional was carving out a successful career in East Germany. He was an intelligence officer. He worked on the Stasi's side of the street. He and his Stasi friends were making a good living watching the East German people and any foreigners who happened to be passing through, including the Soviet troops and civilians based in the country. Though he was not German, this particular watcher was fluent enough in the German language to be able to pass as one. "I have two natures," he would say, "and one of them is German."

With his wife and two baby girls he was living in the East German city of Dresden, in the southeastern corner of the country, not far from the border with Czechoslovakia. The watcher lived in an apartment complex shared by Stasi families.

He was Russian, a citizen of the Soviet Union. He was a lieutenant colonel in the Soviet secret service, then called the KGB. The lieutenant colonel was living the dream.

When he was a boy of fifteen, young Volodya had been entranced by the most popular movie in the Soviet Union that year, called *The Shield and the Sword*. He had watched it again and again. The movie's fictional hero was a Soviet secret agent, a major. The major had pretended to be a German in order to infiltrate the ranks of the enemy forces. There the secret agent changed history, a heroically successful spy and saboteur. Decades later, Volodya could still remember the lyrics of the movie's theme song, "Whence Does the Motherland Begin." He recalled being inspired by the film's story of how "one man's effort could achieve what whole armies could not."

Volodya was a child of the working class. His family was from a great city once called St. Petersburg, renamed Leningrad by the new Soviet Union.

Volodya's parents' lives were molded by war. In 1941, the Germans had invaded the Soviet Union. Their armies reached the outskirts of Leningrad. Returning to military service, Volodya's father had barely survived the initial months of fighting. Badly wounded, he made it back to a hospital in Leningrad. There he was reunited with his wife.

The Germans besieged Leningrad for nearly three years. Volodya's father and mother both almost died. They endured some of the most extreme experiences humans can suffer—of shelling, bombing, and near-starvation. Two of Volodya's uncles, on his father's side, died in the war. Another of his uncles, on his mother's side, lost his life in the war too—but not at the hands of the Germans. Like many thousands of others, he disappeared after being tried by a Soviet military tribunal for alleged dereliction of duty.

Volodya's eldest brother died before he was born, succumbing to illness before the war. His other brother also died before Volodya was born, a victim of malnutrition and illness during the German siege. Volodya was born after the war. The father, still limping from his wound, became a factory worker and loyal Communist Party member. The mother did all kinds of menial labor. The parents doted on their only surviving child.

Volodya's childhood was poor, rough-and-tumble. But as he entered his teenage years, everything started turning for the better for him, as he found a focus pursuing two passions.

One of these life-changing passions was sports, specifically judo. He joined a sports club and became a skilled competitor, staying with it through his college years. It could be rough, he remembered, as "people would break their arms or legs. Matches were a form of torture. And training was hard, too." If Volodya could avoid serious injury, he might go on to compete regularly at the national and Olympic level.

His other passion took precedence, however. That was his determination to find some way to get into the security services. His dream was to get into the KGB itself.

Having disciplined himself through his sports training, Volodya studied hard to get into the prestigious local school, Leningrad State University. Most of the places at the university were reserved for army veterans. There were few chances for kids straight out of high school. But Volodya made it. His favorite subjects in high school had been German and history.

At university, he studied law. He had heard that this was a favored subject for KGB aspirants. As he was completing college, his dream came true. A KGB recruiter asked him, "How would you feel if you were invited to work in the agencies?"

Volodya's answer was ready. The KGB's background, and the memory of the massacres and purges of the Stalin era, meant nothing to him. "My notion of the KGB came from romantic spy stories. I was a pure and utterly successful product of Soviet patriotic education." He joined in 1975.

Volodya quickly found that the work "wasn't what I had imagined." His first assignments were in counterintelligence in Leningrad. That meant his job was to watch fellow Soviets and foreign visitors. He remembered once asking whether an operational plan followed the law.

His supervisor "was taken aback. 'What law?' "

Volodya cited the law.

" 'But we have instructions,' his supervisor said.... The men in the room didn't seem to understand what Volodya was talking about.

"Without a trace of irony, the old fellow said, 'For us, instructions *are* the main law.' And that was that."

Volodya remembered that he "was never a dissident. My career was shaping up well." He was able to get training in foreign intelligence work at an elite KGB school near Moscow. His fluency in German was a clear plus.

At the KGB special school, he was rated as a good officer, but not a star. So back he went to Leningrad.

Finally, Volodya did get a posting outside of the Soviet Union, and it was to Germany! But it was inside the Soviet bloc, to the GDR. There, he was assigned to a relatively minor post out in the provinces, to join the half dozen KGB men in Dresden. They were well away from the main action in the capital, East Berlin.

Arriving in 1985, Volodya went about his work in partnership with the hundreds of East German Stasi officials covering that region of the country. As 1989 began, he had been in Dresden for nearly four years. He had been in the KGB for almost fourteen. He was thirty-six years old.

Though his office was always on the lookout for traveling foreigners or others who might offer information about the NATO adversaries, an important part of the work was to follow up possible security issues in his part of East Germany. He and his colleagues could look for possible foreign spies (they found none). Or they could try to recruit interesting foreigners at one of the universities in their region, or track misbehaving Soviets who were stationed or traveling in their area. Or, working with the Stasi, they could follow activities among the East Germans themselves.

"Everyone thinks that intelligence is interesting," Volodya recalled. "Do you know that ninety percent of all the intelligence information is obtained from an agent's network made up of ordinary Soviet citizens? These agents decide to work for the interests of the state." In East Germany, the only big difference was that "a large part of our work was done through citizens of the GDR."

Volodya's work record was satisfactory. He was promoted. By 1989 he was the deputy head of the KGB's small *rezidentura* in Dresden. He had a medal for "outstanding services" to the East German army, not an unusual award for someone in his position.

He was more uneasy about developments back home in the Soviet Union. Sometimes a fellow KGB officer would visit and tell disturbing stories, like the ones he heard from a veteran of KGB operations during the Soviet occupation of Afghanistan. The disillusioned veteran confided to Volodya, " 'You know, I judge the results of my work by the number of documents that I did not sign.' That really stunned me," Volodya remembered.

Volodya's boss had been outraged at the end of 1986 when the new Soviet leader, Gorbachev, had released the famous dissident scientist Andrei Sakharov. Volodya was not so bothered. To an office mate, he confided that it might take the "military superiority of the West" to "bring the unconstrained masters in the Kremlin to their senses." To another friend, he even voiced support for the idea that the next Soviet president should be elected.

Volodya and his wife liked life in the GDR. Their second daughter had been born there. His wife, Lyudmila, remembered, "The streets were clean. They would wash the windows once a week. There was an abundance of goods—not like what they had in West Germany, of course, but still better than in Russia."

It did seem to Volodya that the GDR was "a harshly totalitarian country," like the Soviet Union had been a generation earlier. He wondered, "If some changes in the USSR begin, how would it affect the lives of these people?" On the other hand, at the time he thought "it was hard to imagine" any abrupt changes coming to the GDR.

* * *

It was indeed hard to imagine. The Cold War had created the GDR. As the Second World War came to an end in 1945, in first Europe, then much of Asia, and then around the world there were warring camps of rival ideological systems. For generations, divided Europe was also an armed camp, partitioned by barbed wire and minefields, with millions of soldiers readied for war, massing tens of thousands of armored fighting vehicles and thousands of nuclear weapons, regularly conducting large exercises to prepare for apocalyptic confrontation. It was hard to imagine great change, hard to envision just how the Cold War might end. If it did end, then one would have to dream up some notion of what might happen after that, including in the "harshly totalitarian" GDR.

No one could see how the Cold War might end in a way that extinguished East Germany, the entire socialist system of which it was a part, and then even the Soviet Union itself. It was hard to imagine how a divided world would disintegrate and a different one would take its place.

As their world fell apart, Kasi and Volodya would have to build new lives in this different world, along with millions of others. A handful of leaders might change the surrounding structures. Then it would be up to people like Kasi and Volodya to remake and rechart their lives.

They did. In fact, these two onetime East German success stories would eventually meet and get to know each other. By that time, they were among the handful of leaders making the big choices.

Kasi is now better known by her full married name: Angela Merkel. She made choices that would eventually bring her to the summit of political power—in a new, united Germany.

Volodya is now better known by his formal name: Vladimir Vladimirovich Putin. He too made choices, choices that would eventually also bring him to the summit of political power—in a new, diminished Russia.[2]

One is a chancellor in reunited Berlin. The other is a president in the Kremlin in Moscow.

Ups and Downs

History can seem like it has its ups and downs. People try to solve problems. Sometimes they do. All the solutions eventually have problems too, some old, some new.

Perhaps, when we succeed, the new problems are not as terrifying as the ones that went before. Perhaps, when we succeed, the new problems offer more scope for people to realize more of their human potential, more scope for freedom and the pursuit of happiness.

The Cold War certainly had its ups and downs. As it recedes into history it looks like it was a frozen standoff. But lived at the time, it was more like a frightening roller-coaster ride. The West had its scares in the late 1940s and early 1950s.

In the mid-1950s, after the 1953 death of Soviet leader Joseph Stalin, the communist world was riven by doubt and fierce debate. There were huge protests and even violent revolts in East Germany, Poland, and Hungary. The revolts were crushed.

Communism evolved. By the late 1950s it again seemed to be on the upswing, reaching new frontiers in science and new adherents in Asia, Africa, and Latin America.

By the end of the 1950s it was the freer, capitalist part of the world, referred to in shorthand as "the West" (though it very much included countries like Japan) that was full of doubt. Western leaders were alarmed. The communists—first into outer space—seemed to have both know-how and might on their side.

In the early 1960s, some of this gloom dissipated. Capitalism and the West seemed to revive. The peak of Cold War confrontation seemed to have passed.

Yet by the end of the 1960s and the early 1970s, the West felt it had descended into an even more profound, pervasive crisis. There was the awful war in Vietnam. A pro-democracy movement in Czechoslovakia was crushed by Soviet tanks. Once-flourishing capitalist economies sputtered with inflation and unemployment. Riots burned city centers in America. Terrorism plagued countries across Western Europe.

Yet by the late 1980s, the Atlantic world and East Asia had once again regained much of their confidence. That is the story we begin with in chapter 1. Some of these choices were made by leaders in Europe, China, and the United States. Others were made by judges and civil rights lawyers or activists on both sides of the Atlantic; still more were made by American innovators who pioneered a liberating idea of personal computing.

The communist world seemed to have been riding high during the 1970s. More states—in Africa, Latin America, and Asia—came under communist rule, welcoming troops or advisers from the Soviet Union or its allies.

Yet their roller coaster dipped down again. By the 1980s it was the communist world's turn to go through another of its phases of disappointment and doubt. The crisis of communism became general.

What then changed, more profoundly, was the whole system itself. Instead of a seesaw tipping back and forth between the rival sides, a truly global system replaced the divided world that had gone before. Most of the crucial design choices for this new system were set between 1988 and 1992.

This book is about how Kasi and Volodya's world collapsed. It is about the design of the new world in which they would become leaders. Unlike some other "end of the Cold War" books, even one that we wrote nearly twenty-five years ago, this book is less about endings and more about acts of creation.

What to call this new system? To call it a "post–Cold War system" says, literally, almost nothing. Dry references to a "liberal international order" are not much better.

Instead of a system designed for rival blocs to compete in a divided world and prepare for a third world war, the new system designed at the beginning of the 1990s was meant to be truly global. Its designers hoped they were laying the foundation for a global commonwealth of free nations. They sought an open and civilized world, where people everywhere might find a sense of identity, security, and material well-being.

All the principal leaders who dominate much of this book, men and women like Mikhail Gorbachev, Helmut Kohl, François Mitterrand, George H. W. Bush, Jacques Delors, and Margaret Thatcher, were part of a "postwar" generation. They never forgot that. To them, the shadow of war was always there.

Imagine the hopes and fears of this generation. To most of these men and women, words like "tyranny," "freedom," "war," and "security" were not empty abstractions. They brought back very real traumas.

Wounded at the start of the Second World War, Mitterrand had escaped from a prison camp, and then later had to literally run for his life, dashing breathlessly through alleys to escape Gestapo agents hunting him in wartime Paris. As a young political leader in the late 1950s, he was forced by France's internal war over Algeria to again be on the lookout, this time watching for French assassins.

When he was a teenager, Delors's best friend was arrested running messages for the Resistance. That friend was sent to Auschwitz. He died there, as did his father.

When she was a teenager, Thatcher had walked by the blasted shells of bombed-out streets and grown up with the end of empire. Even when she was a young member of Parliament in the early 1960s, her country was still struggling to recover from the deprivation and damage of past wars, full of obsolete housing, "derelict" dockyards, and antiquated factories, its railways in "ghastly shape." France's leader had just brusquely refused to let Britain join the new European Economic Community. As Thatcher attended her party's annual conference in 1964, the leading Conservative newspaper headlined a speech in which a minister pledged "to keep Britain a first-class nation."[3]

Thatcher's West German counterpart, Kohl, had grown up in a country far more devastated than England. In Kohl's childhood, ruins were part of the landscape. His friends scavenged for food. He was named Helmut after his father's brother, dead in an earlier war. He came of age mourning another brother, his own, who never came home from the last war.

Gorbachev's foreign minister, Eduard Shevardnadze, also mourned a brother who had not come home from war, one among millions. Other memories were kept quieter. Gorbachev's family remembered when their region was briefly overrun by German troops during 1942. The Germans were not there long enough to do much harm. But afterward, both of Gorbachev's grandfathers had been arrested by Stalin's secret police. Although they were fortunate and eventually released, the family remembered.

Bush had piloted a plane off aircraft carriers. Shot out of the sky during a Pacific island raid, he had to bail out into the ocean. He counted himself lucky, saved miraculously by a nearby American submarine. His crewmen did not survive.

One could go on and on with such examples among many of the top officials in these governments, men and women who spent much of their lives living in the shadow of wars past and the next war to come. They had become successful and prominent. They were politicians, worldly wise, often cynical. Yet, across the years, they still bore the marks of their memories.

None of these leaders were nostalgic about the postwar, Cold War world. They did not yearn to recover the broken world of their youth. They wanted to build something new and different, dramatically and profoundly different, so that future generations would inherit a better world than the one in which they had grown up.

In 1988 and 1989 they saw their supreme chance. The Cold War was ending. Another era was beginning. At such times, leaders with a vision for the future can make a difference.

An overall vision was essential, but abstract hopes were not enough. Leaders had to make concrete choices and design solutions.

Like a stream that narrows and rushes faster and faster as it approaches a channel and a waterfall, crucial choices began accumulating during the late 1970s and the 1980s. In 1989 the cataract began and leaders all had to shoot through the hole and navigate the rapids. There, no guide wielding an oar has full control. The guide tries a few key moves; the team paddles hard. Gasping, pushing, they try to miss the big rocks and find smoother water.

* * *

Most of this book looks back at recent history, but it is not a conventional narrative of all the major events. It is written as an analytical history of the major choices.

Our approach focuses on leaders and their teams, but the views of ordinary citizens remain an essential part of the situation. For example, in chapter 4 we describe a series of choices and running arguments about when and how to unify Germany. What evolved were two basic sets of positions, with both sides consciously, constantly reacting to popular sentiment. The leaders, interacting with publics, were trying to steer and channel what citizens wanted, expected, or thought might be possible.

The leaders could not settle the matter on their own. Instead they set up two large alternatives being put to the vote in the East German election of March 1990. That election was being powerfully affected by West German opinion, which was also split, as was opinion across Europe. Each side used diplomacy to influence public opinion. Until the votes were counted, it was not at all obvious which side would win.

History is path dependent. Once people have made certain choices, other possibilities fade away, lost among the speculative might-have-beens. We have tried to zero in on the moments of important choice. At those moments, we call out the other possibilities plausibly available at the time. We invite readers to notice and reflect on whether they would have made those choices. We try to recover some sense of the situations and concerns that people could perceive at the time.

One value of this approach is to help demystify some of what policy-making is all about. We do think several leaders performed skillfully. Rather than just say so, we help show what that means. Readers can judge for themselves.

Another value of this approach is that it does a little more to unpack the relevant mix of judgments that interact in choices. These are a mix of beliefs about values (what do we care about?), reality (what's going on?), and action (what can we do?).[4] Here is what went into the deconstruction of one system and the creation of another. Thus readers who wonder about what to do now can better relate the judgment calls of the past to those to be made today.

Operating Principles for a Different World

Leaders inherit their circumstances. Facing those circumstances between 1988 and 1992, some leaders chose, quite deliberately, to transform the basic operating principles of whole societies. They chose to abolish countries and create new ones. They chose to roll back and substantially disarm the largest and most dangerous military confrontation in the world.

But, like all human creations, their new system made trade-offs, had flaws, and set up new issues. A series of crises that we review in chapter 7 bring us forward to the present. We wrote this book because, as we approach another time of rethinking the global system, it is worth studying how and why we got the one we have.

Phrases like "international system" can seem very academic. In this book, what we mean by a "system" boils down to a set of a half dozen or so basic operating principles for how states and communities interact.

The basic operating principles for the old Cold War system were about:

- How the leading opponents (the United States, the Soviet Union, and sometimes China) viewed each other and their struggle;

- How each side organized its military alliances and armed forces for a possible war;

- How they carried on their struggle for the ideologically uncommitted regions of the world;

- How they ran their home economies;

- And how they viewed norms for international finance and trade.

Applying those basic Cold War operating principles in Europe, that meant there had to be operating principles about:

- How to think of the future of Germany ("the German question");

- How to conceive the future of Western Europe;

- And how to envision the future of communist-controlled Eastern Europe (then usually defined as the area between Western Europe and the Soviet Union, although much of the Soviet Union was also in the eastern part of Europe).

For example, the German question noted above actually stayed open, debated, for a while after 1945. By the early 1950s it had been provisionally settled. Germany would be much reduced in size. It would be divided into two separate states, one communist and one not. This division was not abstract. Watchtowers, machine guns, minefields, and barbed wire defined the contours; diverging ways of life defined the interiors.

Much of the politics of the early Cold War was about whether to make that provisional settlement permanent. A series of treaties in the early 1970s, capped by a 1975 "Final Act" signed in Helsinki by thirty-five states, seemed to make it permanent, its borders "inviolable," to be changed only "by peaceful means and by agreement." By the late 1980s the great powers regarded the German question as having been scratched from the list of open questions in the Cold War system, off the table. A divided Germany with two German states was not only a historical fact, it was a historical necessity. The basic future of Eastern Europe was also thought to have been scratched off the list of open issues.

These principles may seem abstract. But they filter into dominating, everyday realities for ordinary people: Putin going to work at his KGB office, watching the West and possible internal dissidents; Merkel a state employee contributing to government science, wary about who was listening to what she was saying, wondering about new research in the West or how to arrange a rare foreign trip.

The Cold War system assumed a world divided between two fundamentally opposed sets of ideas for how to organize modern societies. In each, believers sincerely thought their way of organizing society was imperfect but essentially good. They thought that the alternative model was essentially bad, even profoundly evil.

These beliefs were not lightly arrived at or lightly held. They had been developed and refined as systematic ideologies since the late nineteenth century. The consequences of such beliefs molded lives, just as communism had molded the lives of Merkel and Putin, their families, and many millions more.

* * *

As the Cold War system began to disintegrate in 1988 and 1989, the old questions resurfaced and then began turning into a whole new set of questions. We show how leaders started framing and making choices that accumulated into a new operating system for the world.

At the beginning of the 1990s, the crucial choices set vectors, general directions, about:

- How to provide security? What should be the roles of the superpowers?

- How should a global economy work?

- How should Europe evolve? More European integration? For which parts of Europe?

- How should "the German question" be resolved?

- What about the future of Eastern Europe?

- What about the future of the reforming Soviet Union?

The basic approaches for all these questions were largely set by the end of 1992.

We invite readers to look over the shoulders of those who were making these choices. Consider what might have happened had another plausible path been chosen. To help, at each stage we offer a running map of the big issues and the key choices in play.

The Blindness of Hindsight

Macro-changes often arise from micro-choices. The crucial choices are not always obvious. The historian's microscope can help.

For instance, in chapter 4 we retell the story of the opening of the Berlin Wall during the night of November 9–10, 1989. The East German government did not choose to do this. Nor had protesters organized to assault and force it open. Then why did this momentous result happen? It was set off by a bureaucratic screwup, which we detail. But the Berlin Wall story, taken alone, can mislead. It creates an illusion of accident, of chance.

In the story of the collapse of the East German dictatorship, a real choice, the choice that drove all the others, was not on that confused night in November. It came a month earlier. In early October the East German leaders had to decide: Should we try and accommodate the rising outpouring of East German dissenters? Or should we arrest them, beat them, wall them in, and crush them?

The "crush them" option was certainly plausible. Some East German leaders wanted to use what they called the "Chinese solution." Repression was what the East German government had been doing, quite effectively, for generations. That alternative path of violent repression was vivid to all in East Germany.

That October 1989 choice was no longer just a matter for East Germans alone. They had to deal with an exodus of their citizens through other, formerly allied, countries. The East Germans were also carefully gauging the attitude of the Soviet government. They were also attentive to the West Germans, and the West Germans had been noticing signals from the American government.

*　*　*

There were many such choices between 1988 and 1992. To understand them, we try to guard against hindsight. Hindsight is not 20/20. It is blinding. The path of what happened is so brightly lit that the alternatives are cast more deeply into shadow.[5]

Writing about the coming of the American Civil War, a great historian named David Potter agreed that, with hindsight, the causes of the Civil War seem obvious. Yet Potter pointed out that at the time, in 1861, few people had seen the war coming. They did not anticipate its character or its consequences.

The "supreme task of the historian," Potter said, the only way to combat the "fallacy of reading history backward," was "to see the past through the imperfect eyes of those who lived it." Another great historian of the coming of the Civil War, Ed Ayers, makes a similar point. The war "did not approach...like a slowly building storm." Instead "it came like an earthquake, with uneven and unpredictable periods of quiet between abrupt seismic shifts that shook the entire landscape. It came by sudden realignments, its tremors giving no indication of the scale of violence that would soon follow. People changed their minds overnight, reversing what they had said and done for years."[6]

In this book, we too are recalling an earthquake, with sudden realignments and changes of course. It is hard to reimagine roads not taken. Such roads disappear. They dissolve along with the fading memories of what might have been.

* * *

After a catalytic episode, people naturally try to make sense of what happened. They quickly throw together stories that help them make sense of it. So the end of the Cold War quickly got its few big stories. Democracy and capitalism had prevailed. Communism had failed and was discredited. For some this is an easy and satisfying story. Others prefer tales of incompetence or treachery.

There are more simplifications. There is a triumphalist American story. It goes about like this: Americans stood strong, led the free world to confront the communists. The communists, realizing how decrepit they were, quailed and buckled.

The triumphalist narrative provokes a counterattack. Those who prefer their stories of America and the world to be cautionary tales have a story that goes about like this: It is the communist leader, Gorbachev, who is the singular visionary, joined by ordinary people. The power-obsessed Americans never quite get it. Suspicious, timid, and unimaginative, the Americans just react. Unsupported, Gorbachev becomes a tragic figure.

We resist both of these simplifications. They are not true enough, not insightful enough. Real life is not so inevitable and predetermined. And in those stories about endings, all the new acts of creation tend to go unnoticed.

Another way we complicate the story is that we center it not in U.S.-Soviet global relations, but in Europe. In this period of history, Europe was the most important theater of global choice. Chinese leaders play a vital part, but in 1989 they took their country in a different direction. Later they would return to history's central stage.

The crucial partnerships in our story always involve European leaders, not just American or Soviet ones. It is an ensemble drama. There were several leading players. Each took turns in the spotlight.

Americans do not need to be insecure or defensive about the role their government played in ending the Cold War. That role will become clear enough. But to the extent the Americans succeeded, they only succeeded as part of effective partnerships, first with key West European governments, and then beyond.

No one leader, no one country can fashion a global commonwealth.

Anglo-American cooperation was an old and valuable pattern. But in this story the core of the creation was a partnership between an American team and a European one—a triumvirate centered in Germany, France, and the European Commission.

They all then interacted with a set of vital choices made inside the communist world, and then beyond it. Leaders in the East had agonizing decisions to make about the future of shattered societies. They had to decide whether or how to join in a new system, and if so, on what terms.

* * *

A number of leaders contributed to results that, at the outset, none of them had planned. All were improvising, coursing through the rapids, trying to keep certain aims in view. Some of the improvisations turned out brilliantly. Some did not. Meanwhile, the leaders tried to bring it all to calmer waters, crafting agreements, new or transformed institutions, and new or transformed countries.

Beyond the simplifications, we hope Americans—and others—will learn more about just how their government, or any government, actually influences large events. Little influence came from direct orders, telling others what to do. Nor was the outcome a victory of brute force, the triumph of a bloody war of conquest.

Governments often influence events by creating possibilities—or not. They can create a way to work on a problem. They can table inducements or suggest possible solutions.

If the analysis or suggestions are attractive, people join together and make common plans. They take common action. And common, concerted action can indeed change the world.

Consider, for instance, just one of the great changes: the creation of a new, unified Germany. "For decades a thick closed blanket of clouds obscured the star of German unity," Germany's former foreign minister Hans-Dietrich Genscher recalled. "Then for a short time the blanket of clouds parted, allowed the star to become visible, and we grabbed for it."

"Grabbed" is a good word for what happened. It captures the sense of a frantic lunge, what the British scholar Timothy Garton Ash has called a "hurtling and hurling together, sanctioned by great-power negotiations."

It was, he wrote, a time when "more happened in ten months than usually does in ten years."[7]

A renowned German commentator called the outcome "the greatest triumph of diplomacy in the postwar era." A former Soviet foreign minister called it "one of the most hated developments in the history of Soviet foreign policy."[8] Although now the outcome may seem almost preordained, those closest to the events—whether former Soviet foreign minister Eduard Shevardnadze or political figures from East and West Germany—marveled that this tumult did not lead to a "bloodbath," a war, or another new phase of cold war.[9]

The period between 1988 and 1992 became a catalytic episode in world history. We call it so because a number of ingredients came together, like a new sort of chemical compound, to produce a different system.

Catalytic episodes on a worldwide scale are rare. During the last 250 years there have only been about five of them. This period was one. And among all such global upheavals of such scale in the history of the world, this was the most peaceful one.[10]

Together, the leaders in this episode did help build that different world they had dreamt of. For all its faults, they helped build a world almost inconceivably safer and more prosperous than the one in which they grew up.

Slouching Toward a Systemic Crisis

Amid a general impression of net global success, through the 1990s the global commonwealth was extended, and extended some more. Finally, it reached its limits. So, what happened? What went wrong?

The essential elements of the global commonwealth leaders created in the early 1990s are not well understood. One reason why their acts of creation get less notice is because much of what was new seemed so familiar.

True, there were some new institutions, like a new global trading system with a new World Trade Organization. But mostly there were names people knew, like NATO or the EU or the IMF or the UN. Yet the appearance of familiarity was deceptive.

Sometimes a builder wants to keep a handsome historic building in place, because it looks good in the neighborhood. But because the actual building is obsolete, everything behind the attractive edifice is gutted and renovated. A decrepit mansion keeps its genteel look on the outside, but becomes a modern hotel.

Consider the case of NATO. It retained its historic name. It kept the U.S. commitment to Europe. But in chapter 5 we describe how members of the alliance promised Soviet leaders that, as NATO remained, it would be transformed into a different kind of organization. The allied leaders kept this promise. They dismantled most of what the old NATO used to do, which was to organize a highly prepared military alliance ready for large-scale nuclear and conventional war.

Allied leaders turned NATO into something else. In the background of general American reassurance, the transformed NATO coordinated a program of Europe-wide disarmament, including the withdrawal of most of the American forces, aided by an extraordinarily ambitious and far-reaching Europe-wide arms control treaty. The organization worked on civil-military transitions in post-communist states. Its enlargement to some of those states was consequential politically, not militarily. It actually did relatively little to extend tangible U.S. political or economic influence.

NATO's remaining kernel of military capability was reoriented mainly toward painful and modest security and peacekeeping missions in the Balkans. The United States approached these missions with great reluctance. It did persuade some Europeans to join in "out-of-area" global work, in faraway failed states like Afghanistan.

The extension of the NATO system began reaching its limits in the mid-2000s. This extension did not cause the estrangement of Russia, which had much deeper and more tragic sources. But as Russia did move into an adversarial relationship against "the West," NATO absolutely became a part of that story. That alliance now finds itself ill-adapted for the problems of the twenty-first century.

As we will show, the NATO illustration is not alone. There are other versions of this story of extension, limits, and maladaptation. Leaders are still looking to the United Nations, the European Union, the WTO, the IMF and the World Bank, and other elements of the global system to handle problems they were not designed to solve.

Some parts still work. The much-derided UN, for example, has actually played a quite important role in dealing with challenges from countries like Iran and North Korea, and in helping to end some conflicts like the 2006 Israeli war in Lebanon.

But there are some large new global trends, like the implosion of much of the Arab and Muslim world or the digital revolution that is transforming economies and societies everywhere. The original system had assumed the persistence of a Soviet Union, but that union broke up into fifteen countries, and Russian leaders eventually came to regard the system as a foe.

Two giant countries, India and China, had not originally been fully integrated with the global commonwealth. In the 1990s, leaders tackled the China problem, with mixed results as China tries to straddle a position that is both part of an open world and yet hostile to it. Leaders, and the two of us in our later work, also turned to the problem of integrating India into the system. That has had somewhat better results, though still very tentative.

The global economic crisis of 2008–12 delivered a tremendous shock. The confrontations with Russian and Chinese aggression since 2014 have delivered more. Especially in 2015, the Syrian civil war, on top of other unresolved conflicts, created a massive eruption of refugees and migrants. Then came the Brexit vote and the Trump election of 2016. The U.S. president has questioned fundamental elements of a system that much of his own government still tries to lead. We discuss these developments in chapter 7.

The global commonwealth is beleaguered. But it is too soon to pronounce its doom. Leaders did respond to the economic and migration crises. Little noticed, the system managed huge transfers of funds from American reserves to Europe at desperate moments and saved Europe's financial system. The European Union successfully administered giant transfusions of help to battered states in Eastern Europe. European states also have managed a substantial containment of the migration crisis, for the time being. Some of the bleeding has been stopped. But the patient is still very much in danger.

For more than ten years, a generation-long worldwide trend of growing political freedom and democratic government has been drifting the other way. The global economic recession joined and accelerated a "democratic recession." In the mid-2010s—2014 to 2016—there were more shocks, as war returned to Europe, established liberal democracies began tearing at themselves, and China consolidated a return to one-man rule.[11]

As one of us put it in a recent book, in 2016 the Brexit and American presidential votes were angry voters yelling, "Do you hear me now?" The votes, as Rice wrote, were "a revolt against political and economic elites, their institutions, and their globalizing and sometimes moralizing views [that] has upended the status quo." It has "left all to wonder, *What comes next?*"[12]

What Comes Next?

To answer that question, one also must ask, "How did we get here?" That is why it is so useful to revisit and reflect on the choices that created the world we live in today. The great settlements are back on the table. The great issues about how best to organize modern society have been reopened.

We do not think the world can return to the past. But we can learn from it. No settlements in history are permanent. This generation is coming up on another great time for choosing.

At the beginning of chapter 1 we introduce the story of two prophets of the future of freedom, James Burnham and George Orwell. Burnham was darkly prescient about the appeal of technocratic, all-powerful managerial states. Galvanized by Burnham's dark pessimism, Orwell saw the danger, saw it more clearly than most. Yet he hoped that free societies could pass the test of ultimately being better at tackling society's problems.

We again face such a test. We argue that the goal of a global commonwealth is still the right one. It is still right and wise, including for Americans, to seek a more open, civilized, and democratic world.

One of the oldest and wisest traditions in American statecraft, from its earliest days, is the conviction that for Americans, and for a great many others, an open world is better than one that is closed. A civilized world is safer than one where, as Bob Kagan puts it, "the jungle grows back." A system geared for business opportunity is more prosperous for more people, including more Americans, than a world system designed for crony capitalism and state-owned enterprise.

The system we helped create at the beginning of our careers is becoming obsolete, ill-fitted for today's world. This generation's dominant problems are also very different from the great challenges at the end of the postwar era. Now the problems are more transnational than they are international. They cut across societies and may challenge aspects of our existence, whether they stem from energy use and climate change or new kinds of disorder, or the hopes and fears that come with another great revolution in commerce and culture, the digital revolution. In our epilogue we offer some suggestions about how to envision a changed global system. We retell the story of an earlier generation's acts of peaceful creation in order to inform and inspire new acts of peaceful creation, still to come.

* * *

Like Angela Merkel, that quiet young physicist going about her work in East Berlin, at the beginning of 1989 we too were young professionals. Like her, we were thirty-four years old.

Philip Zelikow was a relatively junior foreign service officer. He had been detailed from the State Department to work at the White House on the National Security Council (NSC) staff of the newly elected American president, George H. W. Bush.

Condoleezza Rice arrived in the same White House office, the NSC staff office for European and Soviet Affairs, on the same day. She came to Washington from Stanford University, where she was a promising professor of politics and a specialist on Soviet affairs.

As with Angela Merkel and Vladimir Putin, the next two years changed our lives. In 1991, Rice returned to Stanford and was asked to become one of the university's leaders, its provost. Zelikow left the Foreign Service to accept a professorship at Harvard.

As we reflected on what we had just experienced, it began turning into a book. It originated as an internal historical study. Zelikow began the work, which turned from an internal study into a full, international history of German unification. Rice joined the book project. We complemented research in the American archives with a careful study of all materials available in German and Russian, as well as in English. (At that time the available French material was limited.) We consulted some papers that had emerged from East German and Soviet records, including many of Gorbachev's papers. We could do this because in 1992, working with Rice, Gorbachev arranged privately for a large number of his papers to be sent to the Hoover Institution at Stanford for safekeeping amid the turbulent and uncertain times in Moscow.[13] We also talked to key decision makers in a number of countries, most of whom we knew. We cited all of our sources. Many were then still secret, but the citations themselves were not. Our original book was published in 1995 by Harvard University Press, entitled *Germany Unified and Europe Transformed: A Study in Statecraft*. Nearly twenty-five years later, scholars still rely on that book and it has plenty of still-valuable detail that we frequently cite in our notes in this book.

Yet, while leaning occasionally on that foundation, we decided to write this new book with a much wider perspective. The scope of this book is much broader. The style is different too, focusing on the critical choices. We also now have far better access to the records of the other governments. Crucial documents have been released and published on the inner workings of the West German, East German, Soviet, British, and French governments, among others. This evidence has hugely enriched, enlivened, and sometimes amended what we thought we knew.

Our own perspectives are now enriched too, with much more experience. We have lived with the consequences of the events in which, as younger policymakers, we had played a small part. When our earlier book came out in 1995 we were still early in our careers. Since then one of us has been secretary of state and national security adviser. The other has been counselor of the Department of State and director of the 9/11 Commission, among other jobs. We have also done a lot of other writing and thinking as scholars.

We have taught generations of students who didn't experience the events we describe. We have read a generation of commentary and scholarship about the end of the Cold War and the events in which we took part. Some of this work is splendid. Our debts are apparent in our notes.

Naturally, we sometimes thought that the scholars had not understood us or that past world. That has challenged us to try to be perhaps a little more understandable. Sometimes, of course, critiques of our past work are spot on the mark and we have had to revise our earlier views. Other times we disagree and welcome the chance to explain why. For instance, we discuss the controversy about NATO enlargement, whether a "deal" was broken to take advantage of a weakened Russia, or how these perceptions have been fostered or manipulated.

We also welcome the opportunity to take on the question: *What comes next?* What has happened to the European and global system put in place at the end of the Cold War? We suggest how history set the stage for the great changes—and what kind of choices we should get ready for now.

CHAPTER 1

The Renewal of the Free World

The Two Prophets

In the 1940s, two prophets made lasting predictions about the future of freedom.

When he first made his mark, James Burnham was a well-bred, well-mannered, neatly dressed, bespectacled young man, a gracious intellectual from a wealthy family—railroad money. He was a star student at Princeton, then at Balliol College, Oxford. In conversation or writing he could move fluently from literature to philosophy to politics.

And young Burnham was an ardent communist. He remained one through most of his thirties, which were also the 1930s. In 1940 he publicly broke with his icon, the exiled rebel communist Leon Trotsky.[1] Burnham still thought democracies like that in America were doomed. But he was developing a different sort of prophecy to explain why.

His first great book, published in 1941 during the Second World War, offered a distinctive and powerful view of future society. It was called *The Managerial Revolution*. A runaway bestseller, widely discussed on both sides of the Atlantic, the book was translated into more than a dozen languages and made Burnham a celebrity. He followed this success in 1943 with another, *The Machiavellians*.

Burnham argued that ideologies like "socialism" or "capitalism" were already outmoded. Class warfare was so old-fashioned, so early twentieth century. The more complex societies of the midcentury powers would be led neither by men of great wealth and property, nor by the proletariat. They would be steered by the increasingly efficient dictatorships of the elite managers and technocrats—the planners, administrators, generals, engineers, financial operators, and scientists.

At the height of World War II, as total war demanded total control over all of a country's mobilizable resources, these predictions seemed to be coming true. Victory, Burnham predicted, would go to the best and most ruthless managerial dictatorships, like those in the Soviet Union, Nazi Germany, or Imperial Japan. They seemed best at warmaking. Burnham expected them to dominate all of Europe and Asia.

As for the United States, which Burnham regarded as a more primitive case of "managerialism," it was better off just staying out of the war, as doing so would be the only way it could preserve what was left of its democracy. Before Pearl Harbor, Burnham was against American entry into World War II.

However, the United States did join the war. Burnham then elaborated a theory that would blend both democracy and dictatorship. The dictatorship had to limit liberty and the rule of law. There could be no alternative centers of power or independent constraints on core authority that would compromise the dictatorship's effectiveness. The rulers would do what they had to do; the law would be for everyone else.

Democracy would therefore be largely symbolic, a veneer of democratic forms for the ruling elite. They would hold plebiscites or managed elections to show off public support. Such support would duly exhibit gratitude, even love, as the ruling elite built and sustained a good society. Burnham's label for his vision was "democratic totalitarianism."

The dictatorial elite would cement their public support with mass appeals to irrational myths. These could evoke nationalism or nativism, fascist style. Or they could use equality of material wealth, socialist style. Whatever worked.

Burnham freely confessed that the elite rulers, so scientific in their approach to wielding power, also had to "profess, indeed foster, belief in the myths, or the fabric of society will crack and they be overthrown. In short, the leaders, if they themselves are scientific, must lie." In practice, he observed, "The tendency is for the deceivers to become self-deceived, to believe their own myths."[2]

Burnham expected the whole world to fall under the sway of about three managerial "super-states." He was philosophical about this. It seemed inevitable. Burnham's characteristic style was stoic pessimism.

Such pessimism was common among the leading political thinkers of the 1940s. Others, like Joseph Schumpeter or Karl Polanyi, also doubted the viability of free societies. Similarly gloomy was Friedrich Hayek, who really believed that once-free countries were on the "road to serfdom." Burnham took the logic further.[3]

* * *

During and just after the Second World War ended, another prophet decided to challenge Burnham. He is best known as George Orwell, the pen name of Eric Blair.

Orwell was about the same age as Burnham. There the similarities diminish. Orwell was English, not American. He grew up in poverty, not wealth. His formal schooling was just enough to get him a job in the empire's colonial service, as an imperial policeman. He detested it, quit, and tried instead to make a living as an obscure writer. Tall and lanky, he dressed shabbily. His health was bad. His lungs were rotten and he would not live long.

During the Depression decade of the 1930s, Orwell, like Burnham, was a man of the left. He knew he was against capitalism and imperialism. Acting on his convictions, he (and his new wife) made their way to Spain at the end of 1936. They volunteered to fight for the new Spanish Republic, which was allied with the Soviet Union, in its civil war against the Spanish fascists and their German and Italian allies.

Orwell served on the front lines. He miraculously survived being shot through the neck by a sniper. Recovering, he found himself a target from his own side, running from Spanish communists and Soviet agents. Orwell and his wife barely escaped. "He went to Spain to fight fascism, but instead wound up being hunted by communists."[4]

Orwell came to hate the distortions of truth that had become so common in the age of extremes. He also hated overweening state power, whatever its ideological guise. He despised the "amoralism" of a good party man who could call abstractly for death and suffering. It was only possible, he wrote, to be that kind of intellectual "if you are the kind of person who is always somewhere else when the trigger is pulled."[5]

Thus Orwell found Burnham's work compelling, yet deeply disturbing. He noticed Burnham's idea that the elites would manipulate myths in order to gain a veneer of democratic consent. Orwell would later make up a word for this deceiving self-deception. He called it "doublethink."

As Burnham developed his vision of the new superstates and their demigod rulers, to Orwell this seemed like Burnham had surrendered to "a sort of fascinated admiration." He wrote that Burnham thought that "Communism may be wicked, but at any rate it is *big*: it is a terrible, all-devouring monster which one fights against but which one cannot help admiring."

To Orwell, Burnham's mystical picture of "terrifying, irresistible power" amounted to "an act of homage, and even of self-abasement." This attitude revealed "a major mental disease, and its roots lie partly in cowardice and partly in the worship of power, which is not fully separable from cowardice."[6]

This power worship, Orwell thought, "blurs political judgment because it leads, almost unavoidably, to the belief that present trends will continue. Whoever is winning at the moment will always seem to be invincible."

In his 1941 book, Burnham had predicted Nazi victory. Later, he had predicted the Soviet conquest of all Eurasia. By 1947 he was calling for the United States to launch a preventive nuclear war against the Soviet Union, as the only way to head off the coming disaster.

It was typical, Orwell thought, for "writers like Burnham, whose key concept is 'realism,' . . . [to] overrate the part played in human affairs by sheer force." He was not "wrong all the time. . . . But somehow his picture of the world is always slightly distorted."

Orwell thought Burnham underrated the qualities of open and civilized societies. Orwell thought they were more resilient. He also believed in "the fact that certain rules of conduct have to be observed if human society is to hold together at all."[7]

Orwell's attacks on Burnham appeared in publications hardly anyone read. So he decided to try and make his case against Burnham in a more indirect and literary way. Orwell had just published his first really successful book in 1945, a fictional allegory of Stalinist communism called *Animal Farm*. He tried out that form again to make his anti-Burnham argument.

Orwell decided to call his anti-Burnham novel *Nineteen Eighty-Four*. The novel came out in 1949. As the book's fame grew, Orwell did not live to see it. He passed away the year after it was published.[8]

The world of the novel, the world of *Nineteen Eighty-Four*, is Burnham's vision. There are three superstates: Oceania, Eurasia, and Eastasia. The British Isles are part of Oceania—"Airstrip One." The superstates conduct an indefinite, unending, small-scale "warfare of limited aims between combatants who are unable to destroy one another [and] have no material cause for fighting."

The actual fighting involves "very small numbers of people, mostly highly trained specialists, and causes comparatively few casualties." The superstates fight "on the vague frontiers whose whereabouts the average man can only guess at.... In the centres of civilization war means no more than...the occasional crash of a rocket bomb which may cause a few scores of deaths." The main fact is that there is a war, a perpetual state of war against perpetual enemies.[9]

The government of Oceania appears to be popular, to the extent anyone can tell. People have enough to eat. They have heroes and enemies. The state subtly, and occasionally not so subtly, guides them. The main character's job is to rewrite history to accord with the current ruling line, dropping old facts into the "memory hole."

Obviously, Orwell himself was very uneasy about the prospects for humanity. In 1947, in a nonfiction essay about the future of Europe, he speculated that the world would indeed divide into the spheres of two or three Burnham-type superstates. These would have "a semi-divine caste at the top and outright slavery at the bottom, and the crushing out of liberty would exceed anything that the world has yet seen." Orwell had written his novel as a dying man's last warning.

Had Orwell given up hope? He did not place great faith in the United

States, a country about which he was ambivalent, a country he had never visited and did not know well.

He did still nurture the hope that somewhere, perhaps in Europe, some states might develop a successful alternative. Freedom would not prevail just because it was right. Being "good" was not good enough. Countries had to show that freedom worked.

The ideas had to work in practice, work so well, so vividly, that history might then flow a different way. Leaders who sought to preserve freedom had to fashion "the *spectacle* of a community where people are relatively free and happy and where the main motive in life is not the pursuit of money or power."[10]

* * *

At the beginning of 1950, when Orwell died, Burnham was a consultant to the CIA. He was giving advice to that new agency's new office for covert action. That was how he met the young William F. Buckley. The two men had much in common. Buckley too had been against American entry into World War II. He too was preoccupied with the danger of communist tyranny and the rule of elites.

Burnham mentored Buckley. Together, the men became editors of a new magazine, called the *National Review*, that would become a flagship for the ideas of a generation of American conservatives. Burnham was a major figure at the magazine for decades, usually helming its foreign policy commentary.

Not that his core vision had changed. In 1964 he published another book of prophecy, *Suicide of the West: An Essay on the Meaning and Destiny of Liberalism*.

In this book Burnham defined "liberalism" in many ways (nineteen criteria and three corollaries). They all boiled down to a belief in human progress, in the possibilities of rational action to make society better, and in the power of truth and reason.

Burnham still did not share these beliefs. He thought his more tragic view of human possibility was more realistic. There was an inevitable struggle for power. Nonrational factors usually held sway. And he thought "the West" would fail.

The West would fail, he argued, because it disarmed itself. Facing

Soviet communism, Western "liberalism" would not confront it decisively enough with force overseas. As the "Third World" rose, as less developed countries drained away the West's power and wealth, again the "liberals" would not use decisive force. They would not confidently defend their superior civilization.

At home, given its ideals about liberty, the West would not crush communist subversion. Facing the challenge of crime in the United States, a growing "anarchy," again liberals did not have the will to defeat it.

In sum, the Soviet Union and its allies had the will to power. Liberalism and its defenders did not. So, Burnham concluded, "Liberalism is the ideology of Western suicide."[11]

* * *

The 1970s and early 1980s were a battle about whether Burnham's dark prevision was right. What about the "alternative" of free societies in which Orwell had rested his dying hopes?

During the second half of the 1960s, protest movements challenged managerial elites all over the world, from Washington to Paris to Prague to Beijing. The established order fought back.[12]

From the start, one of the problems with Burnham's theories was that they understated or ignored the tendency of tyrants to regard managerial elites, this "new class," as their enemy, a rival source of authority. In 1937–38, Stalin and his creatures had murdered most of the Soviet civil and military elite. In 1966–69, China's Mao Zedong organized a populist "Cultural Revolution" against his own country's managerial elite. He rallied mobs of young Red Guards to overthrow experts of all kinds, at all levels. Planners, professors, or generals—most were humiliated or brought low, if they were not abused to death.[13]

Elite intermediaries between rulers and people, intermediaries to manage the principal "social systems," had in fact long been a safeguard for liberty, a major source of checks and balances in a stable democratic society.[14] Nonetheless, visions like Burnham's have thoroughly worked their way into popular culture across the world. It is the vision in all those science-fiction dystoplas. Everyone has seen it in the movies or on television, all the stories in which the gilded masterminds rule from their swank towers, video screens, and conference rooms. Indeed, Burnham's vision, including his vision of state-directed capitalism, seems—much more than anything in Karl Marx—to be the guiding ideological bible for China's present-day rulers.

During the 1970s, free societies certainly did not seem to be working well. In 1975 a widely discussed report by the Trilateral Commission (representing leaders from the United States, Europe, and Japan) was entitled *The Crisis of Democracy*. The authors of this prestigious report opened by describing what all their readers were observing every day, a crisis born in the "disintegration of civil order, the breakdown of social discipline, the debility of leaders, and the alienation of citizens."[15]

By comparison, the communist world seemed orderly. It was expanding. Soviet allies extended new beachheads of influence in Africa and Latin America. The Soviet bloc rapidly modernized its military forces. In China, Mao's death in 1976 seemed likely to bring about a return to a more stable model of Soviet-style socialist rule.

In 1983, when President Ronald Reagan honored the elderly Burnham with the Presidential Medal of Freedom, there was therefore some irony in that award. In that year, Burnham's gloom about the West might still seem farsighted. To one admiring commentator on his work (writing, coincidentally, in 1984), "the dark prescience of *Suicide of the West* is profound."[16]

But it was Orwell's prophetic hope, that future generations might build a compelling and appealing alternative of free societies, that was making a comeback. Few, in fact, spoke more eloquently of such hopes than Ronald Reagan.

* * *

Amid trauma and strife, the capitalist West redesigned and rebooted its operating system. The dramatic new thinking in the West and in China emerged in fits and starts, concentrated in a set of choices made between 1978 and 1985. During the mid-1980s the results of those choices started becoming evident to the world.

The new thinking in the West did not fit neatly under any one nation's agenda or party program. Yet there was a common theme. It was a message of *more* individual freedom and opportunity. That theme, in essence, was the antithesis of Burnham.

Those who embraced this new thinking pushed to extend individual rights. They trimmed back or scrapped state economic controls. They lowered barriers to the flow of money, people, goods, and services. They lent new spirit and resolve to the denunciation of communist dictatorships.

By the middle of the 1980s it felt like much of Europe and Asia was coming together with a sense of growing confidence. Meanwhile, it was the communist world's turn to feel that history was leaving them behind.

The "Rights" Revolution

During 1968, as protesters overturned cars in Paris and burned neighborhoods in Washington, DC, the West felt defensive about civil and human rights. Western leaders who claimed that their side clearly stood for liberty would be met with counterarguments about systematic racial discrimination, or police brutality, or oppression in the rule of colonies, or association with vicious right-wing tyrannies in places like Greece or Guatemala. And as the capstone for all the denunciations, there was the omnipresent argument that shadowed all the others: Vietnam.

By the end of the 1970s the dynamic felt different. America's war in Vietnam was over. European colonies were becoming a thing of the past. Inside the United States, in 1974, the president had been forced to resign for acting as if he was above the law. During the 1970s, the civil rights laws of the 1960s were finally applied countrywide and on a massive scale. A move to amend the Constitution to add an Equal Rights Amendment for women failed, but it did so because the U.S. Supreme Court interpreted another part of the Constitution (the equal protection clause of the Fourteenth Amendment) to provide essentially the same protections.[17] Landmark decisions had transformed institutions, from a case that had rebuffed presidential power to curtail the freedom of the press (the Pentagon Papers case of 1971) to cases changing routines everywhere in the treatment of criminal suspects.

Inside Europe, landmark protections of rights were being extended by national governments as well as by the European Community. Beginning in 1978, the European Court of Human Rights began strongly asserting the rights of criminal suspects, allowing individual petitions (with

France finally accepting such jurisdiction in 1981), and in general reflecting a sense of "European standards," less about economics and more "derived from sociopolitical developments of the more permissive and less patriarchal society that was taking form in many European countries."[18] Laws that outlawed abortion, for example, became a test of women's rights and the right to privacy. Such laws were struck down or repealed across the Atlantic world, in the United States (1973), in France (1975), and in Italy (1978).

These changes were not subtle. Elites might also talk about international human rights, but those were not the changes that had a huge cultural impact.

Guarantees of press freedom were very important. What also touched the lives of ordinary citizens was a broader discourse about "rights"— rights against discrimination in private employment, rights of criminal suspects, rights of reproductive freedom. These debates riveted the attention of ordinary citizens everywhere. Comparisons and precedents went back and forth across the Atlantic and then extended across the Pacific and into Latin America as well.

For instance, when governments began banning employment discrimination based on race or gender, moves that started getting applied en masse to private businesses on both sides of the Atlantic during the 1970s, the effects were enormous. Tens of millions of people sought new opportunities.

At one level, these antidiscrimination mandates could be, and were, portrayed as "big government," authoritarian and antidemocratic, imposed by judicial decrees. Yet the old discriminatory systems had been quite authoritarian too, in a different way. The net effect of the changes was liberating: Power was redeployed to take the side of individual opportunity against institutions that sought, indefensibly, to thwart it.

Some in the West thought all the new rights went too far. Some thought they did not go far enough. But everyone had to acknowledge that some very significant changes were happening in their societies.[19]

These changes created a public discourse about "rights" that had greater reach than ever before. So in the early 1970s it seemed natural for Western diplomats, mainly from Western Europe, to insist that any solemn document about Europe's future, negotiated between East and West, had to include commitments to respect human rights. The Soviet bloc went along with these requirements for the agreement that became known as the Helsinki Final Act of 1975.[20]

The Soviet government and its Eastern European allies were confident that they could handle any dissenters who seemed to take these "Helsinki" rights too seriously. And when the dissenters did arise, in countries like the Soviet Union or Czechoslovakia or Hungary or Romania, those governments did indeed handle them. The dissidents were jailed and tormented. Neither the Helsinki process nor the dissidents were able to become especially influential in the East bloc.

The net effect was not that communist dissidents were empowered. It was to sharpen the contrast between "West" and "East." The "rights" revolution dramatized the difference between cultures that did or did not respect individual rights.

Recall that during the 1960s the essential argument of the left in Europe or the United States was not that the Soviet Union and its allies were good. It was not so much that communism was superior. The essential critique had been that both sides were similarly abhorrent. It was that the establishments on both sides were domineering, militaristic rights abusers. It was that ordinary people everywhere were victims.

By the 1980s, in an age full of discussions about rights, now one side seemed to stand far more clearly for individual rights than did the other. By the 1980s, an ordinary citizen in the East bloc who had never heard much about "international human rights" would nonetheless know that in the West there was a lot more talk and emphasis on individual rights and opportunity. Democracy enjoyed a "third wave" of popularity (after the first in the late eighteenth and nineteenth centuries and a second after the Second World War), as authoritarians yielded power in countries like Greece, Portugal, and Spain.[21]

In the West, by the beginning of the 1980s, the cause of human rights was embraced by parties on the right as well as the left, in both America and Western Europe. For the fate of Europe, what was more important were the swings in intellectual opinion in West Germany, in France, and elsewhere in Western Europe.

These trends had slowly been gathering strength through the 1970s and on into the early 1980s. Intellectuals, politicians, and organized movements of young people led a counterattack, a trend (in German, a *Tendenzwende*) against the old talk of equivalence between East and West. They rallied fresh resolve to oppose a totalitarian enemy.

In December 1973 the Soviet dissident Aleksandr Solzhenitsyn's massive smuggled history of Soviet slave labor camps, *The Gulag Archipelago*, had been published in the West. The reviewer of the English translation wrote, in the *Guardian*, "To live now and not to know this work is to be a kind of historical fool, missing a crucial part of the consciousness of the age."[22]

For Europeans, as for many Americans, the people of Poland were once again a blazing symbol of heroic struggle to the rest of Europe. Economic strains had brought impoverished and desperate workers out into the country's streets, joined by a Catholic countryside inspired as one of their own, Cardinal Karol Wojtyła, ascended to the papacy as Pope John Paul II in 1978. In 1981 the Polish government finally declared martial law to crush these protest movements, which had sought the right to form an independent union and demand a better life. West Europeans led in denouncing the Polish military rulers and those in the Soviet Union and Eastern Europe who had applauded such repression.

As countries in southern Europe like Portugal, Greece, and Spain shook off their dictatorial regimes in the 1970s and early 1980s, even the establishment figures who took charge in those countries—and these were still men of the old regime—felt the influence of this new current in Europe. The new governments in southern Europe felt that they too had to follow the trend toward individual rights, a riptide drawing their new governments into the work of building democracy.

The identification of the West with "rights" also had a powerful influence on thinkers inside the Soviet Union. For some, who regarded themselves as more cultured and reflective, the "rights" discourse affected the way they thought of themselves, of what it meant to be a civilized European in this era. These reflections visibly affected the way they talked and felt about their personal values and norms of political behavior. After 1985 some of these individuals came into positions of great authority.

A perfect example of such an emergent cultivated and thoughtful Soviet couple would be Mikhail and Raisa Gorbachev.[23]

Reconstructing Global Finance (But Not Global Trade)

In the West the 1970s were "a decade of crisis." Economic difficulties were "part of a general sense of meltdown, whether measured in family stability, criminal statistics, or Western military capacity," the historian Charles Maier recalled. The problems of the decade were "comparable to the earlier period of twentieth-century economic hammering in the 1930s and to the geopolitical meltdown that preceded World War I."[24]

What was at stake in this crisis was the viability of the experiment in social democracy. Beginning in the 1930s with New Deal America and experiments in Sweden, and reaching fruition after the Second World War, social democracy answered the critique of capitalism that had emerged during the previous hundred years. Social democracy rejected Marxist socialism and it retained the core elements of a capitalist economic system. But it balanced this core with government commitments to "stabilize the business cycle, provide social insurance, and reserve a central place for organized labor in politics and society."[25]

The Cold War economic system in the capitalist world had two basic dimensions: global finance and global trade. By the late 1970s both of these systems were breaking down. The United States had lost the postwar economic dominance to manage the Cold War economic system.

The global financial system had used the dollar, backed by gold, as a main reserve currency (the use of a dollar-gold standard being more flexible than a purer gold standard). The old "Bretton Woods" international financial system, set up in 1944–45, had maintained the stability of the dollar-gold system by prioritizing national control over money. It strictly controlled movements of capital across borders, then fixed exchange rates in relation to gold and American dollars. That system collapsed in 1971. The postwar system of fixed exchange rates among the leading capitalist countries quickly eroded and collapsed too, in 1973. It has never been restored.

What followed this collapse were years of financial instability, alarms, unpredictable exchange rate fluctuations that discouraged trade, and high inflation as countries simply printed more money to pay their bills.

In global trade, the postwar system had also been fashioned with American leadership. Strongly influenced by the view that international protectionism had been a major source of the awful and destabilizing conditions of the 1930s, and that the United States had been a major culprit, after the war the U.S. government led a general effort to open up international trade. Back then, U.S. leaders were confident about their country's global trading position. They were eager for Cold War allies to be able to sell enough goods so that their economies could recover and flourish. They led the way in negotiating a General Agreement on Tariffs and Trade (GATT) to lower tariff barriers among the developed countries.

By the late 1970s "the liberal world economy that was conceived and built during the 1950s gradually broke up."[26] The Europeans were building a regional trading bloc in their European Economic Community. Protectionism was gaining strength, exacerbated by the global financial turmoil. The Japanese and other Asian capitalist countries had taken advantage of their tolerant treatment in the GATT system and the backlash in the United States was growing.

The less developed world had been largely left out of the system. They demanded a new system that helped them too. The GATT system itself was "crumbling." In 1978 a leading expert on it observed that "almost every rule of GATT is inadequate to the present problems of world trade."[27]

Between 1978 and 1983, leaders in Western Europe, the United States, and Japan successfully rebuilt part of the global capitalist system, for global finance. The foundation was unsteady, but it held together under great strain. This new system for global finance restored price stability to the developed world. It enabled a return to economic growth and reduced unemployment.

These leaders were not able to rebuild the other part of the global capitalist system, for global trade. In fact, the new system of global finance actually made the trade problems worse, especially in the United States. During the late 1980s, Reagan's second term in office, his activist treasury secretary, James Baker, tried heroically to manage the economic and political fallout from the reconstruction of global finance.

The reconstruction of global capitalism from the postwar Cold War system to something new had begun. Part of the design, for global finance, took form. But the rest, global trade and the broader future of the global capitalist system, was still very much unsettled when Reagan's successor, George H. W. Bush, took office.

* * *

Among the economic problems of the 1970s, constant double-digit inflation was the worst. It remorselessly eroded purchasing power, discouraged saving, and forced workers to protest constantly for higher wages, even as mass unemployment also became endemic. The shocks from huge increases in oil prices in 1973–74, then again in 1979, made the problems much worse.

Governments and companies tended to try to solve the problem with more spending to keep up with prices and wages and to provide more welfare support, while experimenting with government controls on wages or prices. Since a lot of the spending was with borrowed money, the U.S. central bank, its Federal Reserve Board, kept interest rates down.

For a long time, a number of Europeans and some Americans had favored an alternative approach. These thinkers were skeptical about government intervention to manipulate the economy and also doubted whether governments had the political will to make the tough choices about either spending or interest rates. They, especially the Germans and Austrians, had deep historical memories and worries about inflation dating back to times when their countries' currencies had been practically worthless. Many of them also feared that growing government intervention to patch up more and more problems would turn into socialist and authoritarian rule.

These thinkers were sometimes known as "neoliberals." They reflected a classical European liberal caution about the scope of government

(Americans often use the term "liberal" in just the opposite sense). Today "neoliberal" is often used as an epithet to describe an affirmative agenda to shift power to global capitalists. But that is a present-day reaction. It is not necessarily the way these people thought about their agenda back then.[28]

The neoliberal alternative welcomed the relaxation of government controls on the movement of capital across borders. They thought investors would naturally put their money where it would hold its value (low inflation) and earn a profit (encouraging to business), and would lend money to governments that seemed solvent.

After Bretton Woods collapsed, these neoliberals found an American supporter in the U.S. treasury secretary, George Shultz (in that job from 1972 to 1974), and Shultz's key deputy, Paul Volcker. These Americans joined efforts to roll back national controls on the movement of capital. Such a relaxation of capital controls would make it easier for international holders of dollars, or other currencies, to accumulate and move their money back and forth across borders.

But these growing money flows became a major source of instability, rushing to wherever bank rates or inflation prospects were best. Exchange rates fluctuated. The dollar tended to depreciate, aggravating American inflation. To dampen speculative rushes from one currency to another, the key players—especially the holders of the most valued "reserve" currencies like the dollar (above all), the Japanese yen, and the main European currencies—would have to present a coordinated set of incentives to money managers.

The credible, coordinated front was not there. During the crisis, the West German economy held on relatively well. The relatively tight money policies of its central bank, the Bundesbank, became an anchor.

Led by Helmut Schmidt, a brilliant and abrasive finance minister, then chancellor, West Germany became a focal point for organizing European economic crisis management. As France moved away from its recent Gaullist patterns of fierce independence, Schmidt forged a powerful partnership with the centrist and pro-European French president, Valéry Giscard d'Estaing.

In 1975, Schmidt and Giscard then worked with Shultz, whom they liked (Shultz was then out of government but working as a private emissary for President Gerald Ford and Secretary of State Henry Kissinger), to work out a new kind of partnership among Western leaders. They built on a recently created habit of regular meetings among leading finance ministers.

Giscard hosted the secret meeting of the three men at a small house near Versailles. Schmidt walked in, looked over the little living room with its blazing fireplace, and promptly asked Giscard, "Who built this for his mistress?"

In this cozy setting the partners worked out a group to try and do a better job of coordinating their policies. This eventually became a Group of Seven, or G-7, made up of the heads of government of the United States, West Germany, France, Britain, Italy, Canada, and Japan. The president of the European Commission became a formal member in 1981.[29]

Yet the new American administration of Jimmy Carter argued for more spending to stimulate growth. Disagreeing, despairing of the Americans, Schmidt and Giscard again took the lead. Britain could not help much: Britain's financial crisis was so grave that in 1976 London had to seek humiliating and conditional debt relief from the International Monetary Fund. Schmidt and Giscard set up a scheme that could at least try to stabilize exchange rates within Europe itself. During 1978 the West German and French leaders sponsored the initiative to create a European Monetary System.[30]

In July 1978, European leaders unveiled this new system to coordinate their exchange rates, anchored on the "hard money" inclinations of the Bundesbank. At first, Britain was outside this system. But in 1979, led by Britain's new conservative prime minister, Margaret Thatcher, the Bank of England informally joined the hard money consensus.[31]

The growing European determination to tighten controls on spending, both directly and through hiking interest rates, created more runs on the dollar, aggravating America's inflation. The crisis was nearing its peak.

The Carter administration gave in and changed course. During July 1978 the G-7 (meeting in West Germany's capital, Bonn) developed a package of real policy coordination. In November 1978, Carter's Treasury officials launched a carefully prepared package of emergency measures relying on strong monetary discipline and coordinated currency interventions, working with the Europeans to restore faith in the dollar.

The following year, Carter made Volcker (then head of the New York

Federal Reserve Bank) the new chairman of America's Federal Reserve Board. Volcker then joined his European and Japanese colleagues in a conscious hard money approach, coupled to decontrol of capital markets.[32]

Under Volcker's leadership the United States drove up its interest rates to hitherto unthinkable levels and kept them there for three years. To avoid runs on their own currencies, the Europeans and Japanese had to follow suit.

The short-term result of these policies was the most severe economic recession in the United States, and much of the world, since the Great Depression. Interest rates skyrocketed. Unemployment hit new heights.

Debtor countries around the world, especially concentrated in Latin America and Eastern Europe, entered a prolonged debt crisis. Mexico's crisis led the way; Mexico defaulted on its debt in 1982.

Yet by the end of 1983, the Western economies began to turn around. Inflation was finally tamed. Exchange rates were not nearly fixed, but the fluctuations began to settle down. The flows of capital and trade surged.

By the mid-1980s the basic operating system of global finance had been redesigned. The old system had put government economic control first, along with exchange rate stability. That system therefore deemphasized the free flow of capital.

In this new system, unlike the Cold War Bretton Woods system, free movement of capital was given top priority. Such a system still relied on government power, above all on the choices of central bankers and finance ministers who set key market conditions. But, to gain more stable exchange rates, leaders had to sacrifice some of their national monetary autonomy, to be coordinated enough so that investors would not have great incentives to switch their investments from one side of the Atlantic to the other. That coordination also yielded significant economic authority to "market discipline" imposed by private bankers and investors.[33]

The new system for global finance relied on the dollar as its principal reserve currency, along with a group of European currencies that were now more tethered to each other, and the Japanese yen. The G-7 governments—including the once-dominant United States—accepted an unprecedented level of true economic interdependence.

To reassure investors, Reagan reappointed Volcker in 1983. When

Volcker left in 1987, his long-serving replacement, Alan Greenspan, also exemplified the hard money commitment (at least until the last years of his service, in the 2000s).

The new system could not fix exchange rates, although Volcker and others never stopped trying. Especially after 1985, the new system tried at least to dampen the range of fluctuations and keep markets relatively stable.

For the new system to work, it required an active partnership among finance ministers, central bankers, and their heads of government. G-7 summit meetings were focal points for this partnership.

A consequence of the new system was the central role in it of West Germany. Within Europe, this meant a core partnership of the West Germans with the French. The British tracked the European Monetary System's guidelines but they were not formal members and did not steer the system.

The economic turmoil of the hard money system tested the politics in all three of these countries. The severest test, the most important test, was in France.

* * *

In 1981 the French people voted out the centrist government that had gone along with the European Monetary System and had cooperated so closely with the West Germans. They voted in the left: the first Socialist president in the history of the Fifth Republic, in a governing coalition in which the Socialists would rule together with the Communists.

The supporters of the new president, François Mitterrand, expected a radical transformation. In its first year, the new government nationalized dozens of banks and five of France's largest companies, raised wages, and reduced working hours.

Mitterrand then faced a financial and political panic. Firms, people, and money were leaving the country. To maintain these policies, France would have to detach itself from those being pursued by its two large neighbors, West Germany and Britain. Elected in March 1979 after a winter of paralyzing labor strikes and discontent, British prime minister Thatcher was an ardent and idea-driven proponent of rolling back the scope of government control over the economy.

To sustain his policies, Mitterrand might even have to pull France out of the European Economic Community itself. If France had to run the currency printing presses to finance its ventures, it would break out of the hard money constraints it had accepted. The French would have to accept the requisite inflation.

Other Europeans were watching closely what was happening in France. The American secretary of state, Shultz, visited Madrid in December 1982, and met with its new democratically chosen leader, Felipe González. González led a large socialist majority in Spain's parliament.

González explained to Shultz that his policy program now owed a great debt to Mitterrand.

"How is that?" Shultz asked.

"President Mitterrand," González answered, "came in with a big majority on a Socialist ticket, just as I did. He put the Socialist program into place, and the result was a catastrophe for France. Therefore I have learned something: don't implement the Socialist program. Use the marketplace. Encourage investors. That is what I am going to do."[34]

During 1982 and early 1983, Mitterrand and his advisers struggled. Mitterrand buckled first in June 1982. Then he fought to hold on to an independent economic policy, telling his prime minister, "I did not appoint you to carry out the policies of Mrs. Thatcher. And if, for some extraordinary reason, I intended to follow in her footsteps, I would not choose you to do so."[35]

Yet "follow in her footsteps" is what Mitterrand did by the end of March 1983, though he relied on taxes on the rich to help do it (which Thatcher most certainly would not have advised). France and Europe could see that Mitterrand had firmly gripped the wheel and swerved into a hard U-turn. The entire direction of government economic policy was reversed. Public spending would be cut; taxes raised.

Talk of a "French path to socialism" was abandoned. Instead Mitterrand's finance minister, a pro-European former banker named Jacques Delors, was put in the driver's seat along with a new, young prime minister appointed in 1984, Laurent Fabius. The Communists were out of the government.

The French government began to deregulate capital markets and privatize enterprises across the economy, not nationalize them. One historian of global finance looks on this period in France as "one of the most consequential turning points in modern economic history."

It was not a simple right-left issue. French conservatives tended to prefer nationalist protectionism, not open markets. "When it comes to liberalization in France there is no Right," one top French economic adviser observed. "The Left had to liberalize because the Right would not."[36]

The French people approved of the liberalization. By 1984, French leaders emphasized the theme of "modernization." And there were the Americans with their microelectronics and entrepreneurial dynamism. "America, even among the Socialists, that's what's chic," declared *Le Nouvel Observateur*.[37]

The drive to privatize had its biggest proponent right across the English Channel, in British prime minister Thatcher. One of her signature moves was to privatize the nation's telephone and telecommunications company, British Telecom (BT).

Thatcher's biographer recalled how in 1981 he bought his first home. It had no telephone and he wished to install one. He called the government phone company, BT, and was told, sorry, to get a telephone "would take six months because of a 'shortage of numbers.'" But, he was told, if his newspaper's editor would just call the chairman of BT, then matters might be fixed up. His well-connected editor made the call. The phone was promptly installed.[38]

Anyone living in the East bloc in the 1980s would recognize such a story. It illustrates how a highbrow concept like "privatization" could easily connect to the everyday experience of ordinary citizens.

On the other hand, the Western governments and Japan had done all this without abandoning the original postwar bargain at the foundation of social democracy. Although the power of organized labor weakened across the Atlantic world, these governments held on to their commitments to provide a significant level of individual economic security. Deregulation and privatization of government services was tried and sometimes it worked. But none of the countries tried to strip away their core commitments to provide social insurance of various kinds. None of them radically pared back their government spending on such programs. In most cases, such spending actually *increased* during the 1980s.[39]

* * *

Partly because of such spending, especially in the United States, the new system of global finance created new problems for global capitalism. It had restored price stability and economic growth in the developed world, which was a great tonic in the 1980s and thus greatly influenced the political tone in the socialist world during the crucial years from 1988 to 1991. But the new system of global finance delivered a hard blow to the future of global commerce.

For many less developed countries, easy loans dried up and it was hard to repay or even service their debts. They desperately sought ways out, trying harder to profit from a global trading system undergoing great stress. Their plight had global geopolitical consequences as it played out in Eastern Europe, as we will detail in chapter 2.

The new system of global finance delivered a shock to America's trading position in the world. The Reagan administration had cut taxes and increased spending. In the short term this helped growth, as inflation was held down by the Fed's tough policies. But the high interest rates, combined with huge budget deficits, meant that America established a huge market of buyers for its high-yield dollar bonds. Investors were happy to buy. The United States thus sucked in a disproportionate share of global capital to finance its consumption-led growth. Although the Federal Reserve Board tightened money on traditional banks, the U.S. savings and loan industry went on a domestic lending spree that would eventually send much of that industry into bankruptcy. The painful politics and economics of addressing the fiscal deficits and the savings and loan debacle would fall on Reagan's successors.

Meanwhile, the American need to sell such high-yield bonds meant that the value of the dollar went up and up. By 1985 economists regarded it as overvalued by at least 30 percent. Every American export thus carried, in effect, a kind of price surcharge of 30 percent or more. American exports and trading businesses were devastated. Imports flooded in.

In Reagan's first term, the Treasury Department took a laissez-faire, hands-off view of this. Politically, the result by 1985 was a tremendous surge of protectionist sentiment in the country and in Congress. In 1986 the Republicans lost control of the Senate (which they had taken over in 1980) and the Democrats increased their majority in the House. The question was no longer whether protectionist legislation would advance; the issue was how far it would go.

Reagan and his top officials still believed in free trade, in principle. The Reagan administration supported the 1986 launch, in Uruguay, of negotiations to replace the tattered GATT system (hence the talks were called the "Uruguay Round"). The work stalled.

The Reagan administration had trouble with the trade issue. At first, they could not follow through on commitments to reduce America's spending, so they still had to offer all those high-yield bonds. The Reagan officials then had little choice but to try some protectionism. On trade, their mix of managed exchange rates and partial protectionism was meant to head off much more radical protectionist proposals, moves that would have demolished even the crumbling postwar free trade system.

In Reagan's second term, his new treasury secretary, Reagan's former chief of staff, James Baker, took a much more activist approach than his predecessor. Tax reforms at least kept the budget problem from getting worse. Baker succeeded in driving down the value of the dollar with coordinated interventions on both sides of the Atlantic, urging Europeans to raise their own interest rates to keep investors from bidding up the dollar, while everyone still tried to keep inflation in check. In the bruising diplomacy he became accustomed to orchestrating deals with the West Germans, French, British, and Japanese.

Meanwhile, in sectoral and bilateral trade talks, the United States added more trade restraints than it removed, a turnabout for the first time from the long-standing postwar pattern. As one Reagan adviser later put it, the administration's strategy was "to build a five-foot trade wall in order to deter a ten-foot wall [that would have been] established by Congress." These measures did reduce the trade deficits enough to avoid the ten-foot wall. Stepping in at the request of the White House, Baker was even able to rescue a free trade agreement with Canada, a precedent that would become important later.[40]

Overall, on balance, to the socialist world, and to European publics in the late 1980s, capitalism seemed to be working far better than it had in the 1970s. Although the conventional wisdom was that the United States itself was overextended and in relative decline, the dark general pessimism about capitalism's future had dissipated. The social democratic model again seemed like an attractive alternative.[41]

Lowering Barriers: The Momentum of Three Examples

Beyond "rights" or the recovery of global finance, the West came to symbolize something more. It then also seemed to stand decidedly for a freer flow of people, goods, and ideas. By the mid-1980s three powerful illustrations of this freer flow and lowering of barriers were China's opening, the advent of personal computing, and Europe's "Single Market."

China's opening

This came after Mao's death in 1976 and with the rise of Deng Xiaoping to the height of power in 1978. The Chinese leaders developed a very clear assessment of the outside world of the late 1970s, and about themselves. They believed that they had learned a lot from the Soviets during the 1950s, but they now regarded the Soviet Union as the "main enemy."

They took an especially hard look at Europe. Deng had spent time in France in his youth. He returned there in 1975, the first state visit ever by a senior Chinese communist official to a Western country.

In 1978 the Chinese organized an astonishing set of foreign study tours. Beijing dispatched hundreds of senior officials, including more than a dozen of the most senior ministers, to nearly fifty countries. The most important sets of trips were to Eastern Europe (Yugoslavia and Romania), to Hong Kong, to Japan, and above all to Western Europe.

The West European trip had an especially powerful impact. The officials visited fifteen cities in five countries. They studied harbors, transportation, factories, power plants, farms, and much more.

"The more we see," Deng summarized, "the more we realize how backward we are." The head of the State Planning Commission remarked,

"We thought capitalist countries were backward and decadent. When we left our country and took a look, we realized things were completely different."

The Chinese were also taken aback by how friendly and open their hosts were, how much flexibility their local governments and enterprises had to operate. The West European models, and the neighboring ones in Japan, South Korea, Singapore (with whose leader Deng developed a particular friendship), and even Taiwan all seemed to show an alternative pathway for China.

Deng turned all these reflections into policy guidance. "Our nation's system...is basically taken from the Soviet Union. It is backward, deals with issues superficially, duplicates structures, and advances bureaucratism.... If we can't grow faster than the capitalist countries then we can't show the superiority of our system." Chinese leaders "embarked on a process of learning from abroad on a scale that has few parallels in human history."[42]

At first this openness to new economic ideas seemed to have a political corollary. In December 1978, Deng announced the new party line, to "emancipate our minds, seek the true path from facts." The party had to be open to critical discussion. "Centralism can be correct only when there is a full measure of democracy," he explained.

By March 1979, Deng had to quickly clarify that "democracy" only meant more open debate and choice within the ruling party. Some who took such words too literally had to be arrested to set an example. As a party official put it, "Lord Ye loved looking at a book with pretty pictures of dragons, but when a real dragon appeared, he was terrified." Deng did not care for the reality of the democratic dragon. The rule came down: No one should challenge the dictatorship of the proletariat through the leadership of the party.

Meanwhile, China would now open itself to the world and the world economy. In January 1979, Deng made a historic visit to the United States. He toured the length and breadth of the country. In Texas, he went to a rodeo. A young girl on horseback gave him a big cowboy hat to wear. He theatrically put it on. One reporter observed that "in this one simple gesture, Deng seems not only to end thirty years of acrimony between China and America, but to give his own people permission to join him in imbibing American life and culture...arresting China's historic resistance to the West."[43]

The advent of personal computing

Adding to that sense of openness and new vistas was the rise of personal computing. In the 1980s there was not yet an Internet. It was the dawn of the digital revolution, like the 1820s were in the first industrial revolution, just as the first steamships and steam-powered factories were coming into use but before the railroad.

It was then called an "information revolution," before its broader significance became apparent. This revolution enabled and accelerated the more globalized financial markets. But it was also "a very antiestablishment revolution, born in the California youth culture of the Vietnam War era."

In the 1980s it seemed that, for the first time, the power of large computers was now available to businesses of any size, even to many individuals, combined with software that could allow ordinary people to use the machines. One of the revolutionaries, Steve Jobs, promoted the motto of "one person—one computer," with the goal of democratizing and personalizing computer power.[44]

In 1980–81, IBM began developing a "Personal Computer," using software designed by a new company called Microsoft. On the horizon were PC "clones" united more by the software than the hardware and new kinds of graphical user interfaces. But people were already realizing that they had vastly new capacities to communicate and process information.

If knowledge is an element of power, the PC revolution was empowering, and it was decentralizing. In 1982, *Time* magazine, for the first time in its history, did not name a man of the year. Instead it designated the personal computer as "machine of the year." Most Americans, *Time* reported, believed that "in the fairly near future, home computers will be as commonplace as television sets or dishwashers."[45]

Young people living in communist countries were aware of the PC revolution. Computers became one of the few industries that really interested them. Homegrown models were usually inferior imitations of earlier Western models. By 1986 one Czechoslovakian computer innovator reported:

In Czechoslovakia there are at present several tens of thousands of Western-made microcomputers, and each summer their number increases by about 10,000. With these computers comes not only technology but also ideology.... Children might soon begin to believe that Western technology represents the peak and that our technology is obsolete and bad....

One of these days I will record on the tape for you what the children say and how they laugh when they see how we are unable to meet our plans for computer production, how they laugh when [the casings on] our computers have to be opened periodically to prevent them from burning out.... We must look at it from the political point of view, because in 10 years time it will be too late to change our children. By then they will want to change us.[46]

It did not take ten years.

The single European market

As the West seemed even more to symbolize new technology to empower individuals, Europe was embracing a whole new dimension of political and economic openness. For leaders and people living in Central and Eastern Europe, or in the Soviet Union, perhaps no development was more vivid, on their doorstep, than the final 1986 adoption of the Single European Act that was on track to create, by 1992, a single European market with free movement of goods, services, and people largely unhindered by special national barriers.

The story behind the Single Market was itself a miracle of policy entrepreneurship. Although West European political leaders had declared themselves in favor of moving toward a European Union, their path to do so was incremental and traditional.

By 1984 a remarkable operating partnership had been formed in the heart of Europe. Its core was a triumvirate of three leaders and their respective teams.

There was a new West German chancellor. In 1982, Schmidt had been deposed by his Social Democratic Party (SPD) for being too conservative on defense and economic issues. The SPD then fell from power, replaced by the centrist conservative Helmut Kohl, in partnership with the small liberal (Free Democrat) party headed by Schmidt's, now Kohl's, foreign minister, Hans-Dietrich Genscher.

Kohl had been a teenager when World War II ended in his home state of Rheinland-Pfalz, close to the French border. Mentored by Catholics from Germany's old Catholic "Center" party, Kohl completed a doctorate in history but he prided himself on his connection to ordinary people. He thought the new Germany had to find a new normalcy, a comfort with its German identity, tolerant, partnered with America, with European integration at the "center of his political desires."[47]

As Mitterrand completed his economic U-turn in 1983, he became Kohl's core partner in Europe. This veteran of World War II and the French Resistance, a political survivor too, was committed—much more than France's Gaullists—to the cause of European integration. The belief in European integration was a view he and other French socialists had fostered from the start of the project at the beginning of the 1950s. He and Kohl cemented their operational partnership in coordinating policy during frequent battles within the European Community, including a formative one in 1984 in which they schemed together to contain and manage Thatcher's effort to renegotiate Britain's financial contributions.[48]

The third member of this triumvirate was another Frenchman, Jacques Delors, who became the new and much more activist president of the European Commission in 1984. The European Economic Community had a governing board, its council made up of the heads of government. Its day-to-day executive entity was the Commission, with nationally selected commissioners heading the major departments.

The image of Delors is of the bespectacled former finance minister and central banker, the stereotype of the "Brussels technocrat." In fact he came from rural roots, raised as an observant Catholic in a family whose politics were centrist. He had been a very good basketball player in his youth, an ardent devotee of American movies and jazz, and had gone to work for France's central bank more from parental pushing than personal inclination. World War II had disrupted his education. He had never gotten the kind of formal college training some of his colleagues had, and he became known for his ability to articulate technical ideas in a plainspoken and often passionate way.

Delors and Mitterrand respected each other but were not really close. To Mitterrand, Delors, an overtly Catholic and idealistic minister, "smells of the sacristy." As Delors's biographer put it, "Delors is direct. Mitterrand sibylline. Delors reads books about economics and social problems while Mitterrand prefers literature and history." Delors had gotten the Commission job as the French candidate on whom Mitterrand, Kohl, and Thatcher could agree.[49]

As Delors took the job, the European Commission was a passive entity, administering its programs. European leaders had recently pronounced that they hoped someday to create a European Union, but there were no operational plans for how to do it. The European leaders had decided in 1984 to proceed with letting Spain and Portugal join the EEC. Delors had the opportunity to try to convert these Union goals into action.

Delors decided to concentrate on a "big idea" that would relaunch the European enterprise. What he chose, where he thought he could gain maximum political convergence, was the idea of a truly common European market. It could not be done within the existing treaty. It would need a new treaty that, Delors announced, would be done and implemented by the end of 1992.

His crucial teammate was a British conservative, Arthur Cockfield (pronounced "ko-field"), later Lord Cockfield, who was the commissioner for the "Internal Market." A former chairman of Britain's Boots chain of drugstores, Cockfield had long held jobs at the intersection of business and government. He had been a favorite of Margaret Thatcher, and had helped her spearhead the privatization moves.

Cockfield was no politician, but he was a clear thinker who knew how to cut to the root of a matter and relate ideas to concrete action. Thatcher used to say, "half-admiringly, half-teasingly," that "Arthur can't walk past a row of pigeon-holes without wanting to fill every one of them." The combination of Cockfield's "cool" logic with Delors's intuition and vision turned out to be extraordinary.[50]

Thatcher pushed Cockfield for one of Britain's two "spots" on the European Commission in 1984, to be the internal market commissioner. Thatcher liked the idea of a European market that would lower barriers to free commerce. What she got was even more than she had bargained for.

Cockfield, backed by Delors and aided by his own talented multi-national team, proceeded within six months, during the first half of 1985, to produce "a massively detailed—yet elegantly shaped—programme of no fewer than 279 measures that they considered necessary to the operation of a 'frontier free Europe.'" By clearly and precisely delineating how to do it, more by taking structures down or harmonizing them than by requiring construction of elaborate new castles, the Cockfield team had in effect called the bluff of the European leaders.

As Cockfield put it, "The proposals in the White Paper programme are a coherent whole. You cannot pick what you like and discard what you do not. Unless the internal frontiers and frontier controls are abolished, the benefits of the Single Market cannot be achieved." The leaders were now faced with an up-or-down choice of a plausible, concrete plan to do exactly what they had vaguely promised to achieve.[51]

That was not all. For the system to work, the old requirement of unanimous decisions by all member states of the European Economic Community had to go too. It would be replaced by "qualified majority voting" among the members to create an organization far more able to act, an organization that now would just be called the "European Community."

The leaders ratified the plan, some with a good deal of reluctance. They realized that if they reopened some of the package, the whole thing would fall apart. Then the Single Market 1992 target would have to be abandoned. The European project would seem derailed. So they said yes.

Thatcher herself felt obliged to go along, while being surprised and annoyed by Cockfield's skill and insistence on harmonizing British taxes as well. She did not reappoint him to the Commission when his term expired in 1988. As his estrangement from Thatcher became evident, that only added to his influence with the other Europeans.[52]

Nothing since the original Treaty of Rome in 1957 did more to transform the economies and societies in the revamped European Community. As Greece and Spain joined the EC on this path to create a European Union, it was a decisive signal that a new Europe seemed to be coming into being. Those in the East were being left out, left behind.

The Renewal of Anticommunism

During the 1960s and well into the 1970s, anticommunism seemed tarnished and frightening. It was associated with forces of reaction, preservation of privilege, imperialism, and the dehumanizing violence of the Vietnam War. The United States seemed to be waging wars to contain communism, overt and covert, all over the world. The Soviet Union and its allies were not doing so much, except to police their own bloc, as with their brief and decisive invasion of Czechoslovakia in 1968.

By the mid-1980s the situation seemed very different. There were still plenty of people who believed the United States was threatening and were worried about the policies of its president, Ronald Reagan. But the war in Vietnam was over. The United States had quit waging big wars of containment.

Elsewhere in the less developed world, the Americans did not seem very scary. During the 1970s the American defeat in Vietnam helped inspire a new generation of decolonization movements and "liberation struggles" in Africa and the Middle East, as well as in Latin America. The United States did not invade Iran after the 1979 revolution there, settling for a hostage rescue mission that failed badly.

The United States considered military intervention to contain the left-wing revolution in Nicaragua in 1979 that was supported by Cuba and the Soviet Union. But the Carter and Reagan administrations both decided against it. The CIA's programs for covert action were largely wound down, accompanied by public revelations and recrimination. The Reagan administration tried to subvert the Nicaraguan government and assist neighboring El Salvador, but these efforts were not very effective and were visibly hamstrung by the U.S. Congress and other domestic opponents.

The American humanitarian intervention in Lebanon in 1982 had turned into an effort to help pacify that country. This failed disastrously in 1983. Outmaneuvered and defeated by the Syrians, the Soviets, and their allies (which included a militia linked to Iran), the Americans gave up and withdrew early in 1984. A meaningless intervention to restore order in the little Caribbean island of Grenada (after a violent military coup overthrew a left-wing government there) did not seem to count for much.

The most dramatic Western foreign intervention of the early 1980s did not come from America at all and it was not against communists. It came from Britain. In the spring of 1982, Thatcher dispatched a task force that successfully reversed the Argentine dictatorship's invasion of the small Falkland Islands in the South Atlantic, which Argentina claimed. The Reagan administration had wavered for months about how to respond, before it finally lined up in support of the British.[53]

In Africa, the Cuban and Soviet bloc military intervention in southern Angola was winning. The Cuban and Soviet bloc military intervention in Ethiopia was winning. The Soviet invasion of Afghanistan had taken over the country; the Soviets and their Afghan allies were fighting continued resistance.

In other words, from the 1970s on into the mid-1980s, in the Third World it was the Soviets and their allies who seemed more active and menacing. In the critical swing states of Europe and East Asia, the 1970s were a time of increasing worry about Soviet military modernization and momentum. The swing states reacted by drawing closer to the United States.

* * *

On both sides of the Atlantic, anticommunism came to stand for principles more associated with classical liberalism: limited government; individual rights; lowered barriers to the free movement of goods, ideas, and people; and defenses designed more to reassure than to threaten. The key states of Europe and East Asia did not plead for American wars of containment. Instead they urged the United States to build up more military power in their regions in order to reassure them that they were safe.

This the United States did. In these core regions the U.S. response, diplomatic as well as military, was competent and effective.

The Chinese leadership had stopped worrying about American aggression in 1969. By 1979, when China's leader took his triumphant tour of the United States, he was attacking American leaders—for not being tough enough on the Soviets! He said that American policy seemed to amount to the appeasement of the Soviet Union. An editorial in the Chinese government's *People's Daily* warned, "Certain leading figures of the U.S. monopoly bourgeoisie have forgotten the lessons of Munich."[54]

In 1979 the Carter administration resolved its earlier doubts and reaffirmed American security partnerships in East Asia. The Reagan administration strengthened these commitments. Amid all its internal squabbling on other matters, the administration had a cohesive and purposeful team working on Asia policy. Led by Secretary of State George Shultz, the United States "set in place a sustained forward strategy in the Pacific that resulted in significantly diminished Soviet ambitions; improved ties with all the other major powers—particularly Japan, but also China and India; movement toward an integrated economic vision of an Asia-Pacific community; and democratic transitions in South Korea, the Philippines, and Taiwan."[55]

* * *

But the prime military confrontation was not in Asia. It was in Europe.

It is difficult now to remember the scale and intensity of the military rivalry in Europe, readying for war between the opposing alliances, NATO and the Soviet-led Warsaw Pact. In all of recorded history, as one well-informed American official noticed, "No other war has been so thoroughly planned and well prepared, yet never fought."[56]

As the Vietnam War ended, the European and American forces deployed in the NATO alliance were hollowed out, and their cohesion and morale sagged. More and more reliance was placed on "flexible response," the U.S. readiness to use nuclear weapons if Soviet conventional forces began overrunning Germany.

Well informed by their intelligence sources in the West, the Soviets understood NATO's problems. During the mid-1970s both sides initiated massive efforts to modernize and improve their forces in Europe, conventional and nuclear.

At all times the American and NATO side felt they were starting from a position of relative weakness. If they could build up their conventional forces and at least slow a Soviet conventional advance, perhaps, their strategists thought, they could reduce the danger of nuclear escalation. If they could match Soviet nuclear weapons targeting Europe with better U.S. weapons of their own, based in Europe, perhaps their nuclear deterrent would also be more credible. That way they would not have to lean so much on threatening to set off a global thermonuclear war by relying on the American weapons based in North America or at sea.

In the mid-1970s the Soviet side built up and added to its military advantages in Europe. Presuming that the capitalist system was inherently aggressive, "Soviet strategy betrayed an inherent sense of insecurity that was to be offset by overwhelming military power. The Soviet military, whose ideological commitment remained strong while the political leadership was faltering, were increasingly influential in shaping the Warsaw Pact's military planning although it was their Kremlin superiors who controlled it."[57]

As NATO was responding to its obvious weaknesses, the Soviet bloc elaborated and began implementing a breathtakingly ambitious military strategy. Using a highly capable theater-range missile based in the Soviet Union, the SS-20, to deter NATO nuclear use and "hold all of Europe hostage" (as a key Soviet war planner later put it), the Soviet military's "strategy of deep operations" planned to be able to advance at least three hundred miles in the first week of an offensive after war broke out.[58]

American and West European governments could see the staggering scale of these Soviet and Warsaw Pact military developments. A small number of officials also had access to key Soviet strategic documents provided by two well-placed agents, one a general in Soviet military intelligence and the other a senior staff officer in the Polish military.[59]

Both sides sought a conventional military advantage that would avoid any nuclear war. The conventional arms race was thus the most costly and dynamic aspect of the rivalry.

The military confrontation in Europe from the mid-1970s until the end of the 1980s spurred "the greatest renaissance of military thinking in the 20th century. High-quality intelligence, in both senses of the word, shaped the actions of the two sides, and each was often very quick to adopt the other's innovations." Yet, the analyst added, "In the arms race that followed, Central Europe gained the disturbing distinction of having the heaviest concentration on earth of conventional and nuclear weapons."[60]

In 1978–79, NATO decided it also needed a better nuclear deterrent, based in Europe, to offset the SS-20s. The leadership for this defense initiative, the most consequential and controversial defense move in Europe since the 1950s, had come from Western Europe. The central figure was West German chancellor Schmidt, whose pressure for American reassurance was one more facet of his unease about American reliability during the Carter administration. The key policy development was done by West German, British, and Norwegian officials, allied with supporters inside the American government. The Carter administration decided to accept the European challenge and provide the nuclear missiles for this NATO deployment.[61]

NATO coordinated a plan to deploy new American missiles in West Germany, Britain, and three other NATO countries, while offering to negotiate an arms control agreement to limit them. After Carter was voted out of office, the Reagan administration followed through on this "dual-track" commitment, balancing military and diplomatic moves.

The United States also turned to a strategy that tried to leverage American technology against Soviet brute strength and numbers: the creation of precision-guided munitions and new weapon systems that depended on sophisticated technology Moscow could not hope to match.[62] At the end of his term President Carter requested the sharpest increase in U.S. defense spending since the height of the Vietnam War.

For Ronald Reagan that was not enough. He believed that the West had been soft on communism and had paid dearly for it as Soviet power and influence spread across the globe. He came to office determined to confront and convert his foe.

Reagan's confrontational style was evident in the way he thought and talked about nuclear weapons. Convinced that the Soviets believed nuclear war to be winnable, he redirected American nuclear strategy toward "warfighting" as the basis of deterrence. In doing so he frightened many Europeans and made many Americans uneasy.

That style was evident in arms control too, which the Reagan administration was certain had codified Western weakness and Soviet strength. Reagan assumed an all-or-nothing negotiating stance, insisting on a "zero option" for U.S. and Soviet intermediate-range nuclear forces in Europe. He made clear that the United States would deploy its own nuclear missile forces in the five NATO countries if Moscow did not remove every single one of the more than four hundred SS-20 intermediate-range missiles that appeared to pose a distinct new threat to Western Europe. The deployment of the U.S. missiles was to begin in 1983.

The Soviet government used every available political and diplomatic asset to prevent the deployment of the American missiles. The standoff in Europe was tense, the most dangerous period of U.S.-Soviet confrontation since the 1961–62 crises over Berlin and missiles in Cuba.

The governments in Western Europe were trying to maintain a delicate balance. They wanted to preserve cordial political and economic relations with the East, but they also wanted to address their fears about security. The governments were assailed by a huge and growing movement of peace activists. The activists argued that the military policies of both sides were insane and endangered everyone.

* * *

By 1982 and 1983 the security and economic debates converged in a great debate over Europe's future. The enormous political battle in Western Europe over NATO deployment of what were called the "Euromissiles" joined the already high tensions over the painful economic adjustments of the "hard money" era. It was a tipping point in a "global election" between alternative systems.

As we mentioned earlier, the socialist-led French government made its choice on the economic issues. In 1982, reacting to the nuclear and economic issues, the West German Social Democrats withdrew their support from their own chancellor.

The small centrist liberal party that had been part of West Germany's ruling coalition, led by foreign minister Hans-Dietrich Genscher, was determined to hold the line on both economics and the Euromissiles. Genscher joined a new governing coalition led by Helmut Kohl. West Germany became the supreme political battleground.

In January 1983, Mitterrand decided that he felt so strongly about the Euromissile question that, although France had not taken a direct part in the NATO nuclear decision, this was a debate France had to join. He and his circle worried that a set of beliefs were developing "with great speed" that excused Soviet behavior and inclined toward pacifism.

With his own sense of history, the sixty-six-year-old Mitterrand "rebelled against this state of mind vehemently, spontaneously, and viscerally." He journeyed to Bonn and, in a remarkable move, spoke directly to the West German parliament, the Bundestag. He asked the West Germans to stick by the Euromissile choice.[63]

The Soviet foreign minister visited West Germany too. Also intervening in West German politics, he urged the German people to reject the missiles. In July 1983 the G-7 nations decided, for the first time, to join together to address a noneconomic topic: a statement of support for the missile deployment.[64]

In elections later in 1983, the West German people voted decisively to support the Kohl-Genscher coalition. The missiles were deployed.

Thatcher was overwhelmingly reelected the same year. Reagan was easily reelected in 1984, as were Thatcher and Kohl in 1987, and Mitterrand in 1988.

Although it was four years before Moscow accepted Reagan's "zero option," NATO had taken the Soviet Union's best shot at derailing Western policy and won. The failure of that confrontational approach had a lasting effect on the Soviets' thinking about their policy toward Western Europe. As Mikhail Gorbachev later acknowledged, this setback weakened faith in a purely military approach to Soviet security problems.[65]

More upbeat economic news was important. But where it mattered, the West had also strengthened its association with "security."

"Security" was not just a matter of the West-East military balance. Publics were greatly disturbed by the host of terrorist incidents in the 1970s and 1980s, whether carried out by mainly radical left groups in Italy and West Germany, or the Irish Republican Army in Britain (including a serious attempt to kill Thatcher), or the spectacular acts of terror associated with radical groups supporting the Palestinian cause.

The images of terrorism and disorder tended to rally citizens more toward anticommunism, toward the conservative parties. Some of the East bloc governments, like that in East Germany, actually seemed to have secret connections with some of the terrorist groups.

The Carter and Reagan administrations' reluctance to mount large foreign interventions turned out in this period to be an asset, not a liability. With "imperialism" and "Vietnam" off the table, America seemed less ogreish, more reassuring. It was Soviet activism that grabbed the most attention and worry. In Western Europe and in East Asia, American help was sought, not forced.[66]

* * *

By the late 1980s it seemed that the metaphorical "West" had gone a long way toward crafting the "alternative" Orwell had desperately hoped for in the dark days of 1947. It was creating "the *spectacle* of a community where people are relatively free and happy and where the main motive in life is not the pursuit of money or power."

The pursuit of money and power was certainly still there. Most people did not quite separate it from the pursuit of happiness. Still, it seemed clear that something deep had changed from the old class struggles of the mid-twentieth century.

Some thought the age merited a new label like "post-materialist." In this emerging post-materialist age, public concerns were shifting away from material necessities or physical security. People were more concerned about the wider environment and their quality of life.[67]

Meanwhile, the Soviet Union still seemed to epitomize Burnham's vision of a "managerial state." As its top leaders had aged, the managerial elite in the ruling party seemed decaying and dangerous, not awe-inspiring. In September 1983, Soviet air defenses had dispatched an interceptor that destroyed a South Korean airliner which had strayed accidentally into Soviet airspace. The Soviet government ardently defended this action.

Also in 1983, and more secretly, the Soviet military and intelligence complex nurtured greatly exaggerated fears about a possible U.S. nuclear attack. These fears elevated the danger of a major war in ways the West only discovered later.[68]

In April 1986 an ill-managed Soviet nuclear reactor in Chernobyl, near Kiev, exploded. The disaster forced a mass evacuation. The tragedy was concealed by the Soviet government for weeks until Western sources detected what had happened.

The West had changed. Arguments about rights and expressive freedom had taken the place of Jim Crow and race riots. Disputes about nuclear arms control had taken the place of "imperialism" and "Vietnam." Speculations about the new Europe or personal computers or Chinese growth had taken the place of hand-wringing about capitalism in crisis.

The East had not changed. Its symbols were the leaders for the last ten years from 1975 to 1985: Leonid Brezhnev, senile and dying; Yuri Andropov, sick and dying; Konstantin Chernenko, sick and dying.

So the biggest symbol of change, at least at first, was the new leader named in 1985: Mikhail Gorbachev, smiling and vigorous.

CHAPTER 2

Perestroika

The "Great Man"?

In February 1980, the new British prime minister, Margaret Thatcher, was trying to do more to understand the Soviet Union. Two of her most experienced diplomats came over to the warren of offices behind the unassuming doorway of No. 10 Downing Street. These men, fluent in Russian, had served in Moscow.

Thatcher started off the meeting by reviewing some of the reasons she was so worried about the Soviet threat.

These "Moscow hands" heard her out. They were sympathetic. They then explained why, although there certainly were causes for concern, the Soviet system actually had some serious problems of its own. The giant was not ten feet tall.

If things were so bad, Thatcher asked, was the system on the road to collapse?

"No, no," the diplomats assured her. "It's not like that at all."

The two men regarded the Soviet system like doctors watching the symptoms of a long-term and debilitating illness. "The germs of change are at work inside Soviet society," they said.

What sort of change? "The system may eventually become more democratic and less expansionist." For now, though, its core was still too strong. Change "will not easily happen while the Soviet Communist Party and its apparatus of repression are still intact."[1]

* * *

Later in 1980, that Soviet apparatus of repression was tested again, but in communist Poland.

Struggling to pay its external debts, the Polish government had to keep raising the price of food. The economy was breaking down. Millions of Poles began to organize themselves into groups outside of the communist system. Workers organized waves of peaceful strikes.

At first the Polish government made concessions. So the Soviet watchers wondered what that might portend for the whole communist system.

Another watcher was a military aide to the U.S. national security adviser, a Soviet expert and Air Force colonel named William Odom. In September 1980, as the Polish crisis got worse, Odom added a provocative aside to a weekly update he prepared for his White House boss, a Polish American named Zbigniew Brzezinski. Odom mused that perhaps, just perhaps, the symptoms were now showing that the illness might be mortal. Perhaps "the dissolution of the Soviet Empire is not a wholly fanciful prediction for later in this century." Odom ventured further. He suggested that, perhaps, U.S. policy might "set its sight on that strategic goal."[2]

During 1981 the Polish government finally cracked down, hard. Military rulers took over. In December of that year, the government declared a "state of war" against the protest movements. It imprisoned thousands of Poles. For some in the party and police, this did not go far enough. Their cells murdered a few especially outspoken figures, including priests.

The apparatus of repression could still work, it seemed. What was left in Poland, though, was a stalemate. The opposition had no power. The government had no legitimacy. The economy was a mess.

* * *

In Moscow, sitting atop the center of communist power in Europe, the Communist Party of the Soviet Union was not panicked by the troubles in Poland. To party leaders this was just one more symptom that it was time to make some adjustments, to renew their system.

Party leaders guided communist governments. They did not actually have to hold the state offices themselves. They could just tell the state officials what to do.

In the Soviet Union the party was led by the "general secretary" of the party's governing committee, the Politburo. By 1985, three aging and sick general secretaries had died in less than three years. The Politburo did not need much genius to figure out that the fourth man should be younger and healthier.

The Politburo leaders wanted a new man to rejuvenate the party, the country, and the cause of socialism. They got one. His name was Mikhail Gorbachev.

He had been a hardworking peasant, a genuine man of the farms. As a boy he had driven combines along with his father from dawn to dark.

A bright student, Gorbachev found that his path out of the fields was to become a star party man, a well-read student of history and law. He chose a wife—his sweetheart in college—who could quote Dickens and taught philosophy.

Gorbachev had been a child during the Second World War, when his home was occupied for four months by German troops during the high tide of German conquest in 1942. The occupation of his region had been brief and relatively benign.

For him, the memories of Stalinism were more searing. His family had suffered hardship and hunger as a result of Stalin's collectivization of agriculture. He remembered the Stalinist deportations that followed after the Germans had retreated. Both of his grandfathers had been arrested and imprisoned by Stalin's secret police.[3]

Gorbachev's rise through the party ranks had been rapid, yet unremarkable. He earned a reputation for unpretentious competence. His direct, no-nonsense style attracted powerful patrons in Moscow, particularly Yuri Andropov.

Gorbachev's biography read like those of scores of other party apparatchiks of the period. There was little in his background to suggest that this general secretary of the Communist Party would be so unlike his predecessors.

As he gained power, however, it did not take long for Gorbachev's distinctive personality to emerge. He had an attractive demeanor, and he displayed obvious intelligence, self-confidence, and courage. In 1985 he was fifty-four years old. His alert, flashing, and intense eyes were the physical attribute that most stood out, contrasting with his rather stocky build. He greeted people warmly, with a broad smile.

Gorbachev was self-aware at all times, projecting different sides of his persona—sometimes within a matter of minutes—for calculated effect. He could turn steely in direct exchanges, speaking from notes that he himself had prepared by hand. During internal debates he could savagely denounce his opponents, a side foreigners almost never saw.

In March 1985, when the ruling Politburo of party bosses placed Gorbachev at the head of the party, he was the man of the next generation. For all the leading camps—party loyalists, military innovators, and would-be liberal reformers—he was the vessel for their hopes. Muted calls to change fundamentally the Soviet Union's relations with the West had filled the halls of Soviet academic institutes and the pages of scholarly journals for years. Now there was a Soviet leader who was prepared to explore the possibilities.

* * *

During the four years between 1985 and the end of 1988, no world leader riveted the world's attention as much as the new man chosen to lead the Soviet Union, Mikhail Gorbachev. Rarely in history has so much of the burden of systemic change fallen on a single individual and his choices. In the Soviet bloc, as in China, so much of the story in these socialist regimes seems to turn on individuals.

In the Soviet case, that was Gorbachev. In the case of China it was Deng Xiaoping.

Both men, Gorbachev and Deng, shared a desire to get at the real facts. They shared a sense that their countries needed to change in comparison with nearby alternatives in Europe and East Asia. Both wanted more "democracy" as a way to encourage more debate and accountability—as long as democracy was handled inside the ruling party.

Both men also still believed in socialism. They believed the state, guided by the disciplined elite in the party, had to be able to direct most or all national resources for the public good. They believed it could plan with coherent, coordinated purpose. This, they thought, gave their system a great advantage when compared to anarchic capitalism and quarreling, divided Western societies.

There were also some important differences between Deng and Gorbachev. The Soviet leader ruled a vast empire that stretched from Central Europe to the Pacific Ocean. The Soviet Union was the other "superpower." Gorbachev's country was very advanced in many ways. It had been the first into outer space. It was second to none in pride about its scientific skills. It deployed thousands of terrifying intercontinental missiles. It oversaw a military that could inspire awe and fear, and that had played a major part in the Allied victory during World War II. In the 1950s the Soviet Union had been China's teacher.

As we mentioned in chapter 1, Deng and his colleagues had concluded that China was relatively backward. It needed to modernize, mixing ideas borrowed from outsiders with their own insights, patiently experimenting their way forward.

Gorbachev and his allies did not regard their country as backward. They and their postwar generation believed that socialism had been effectively constructed in an advanced way.

Their diagnosis was more that the system had grown sleepy and corrupt. It was resting on its laurels of postwar rebuilding and accomplishment.

The supreme state planning entity, Gosplan, "was characterized by calm and inertia." It "worked in low key without any great ambitions.... Naturally, the bosses were not happy about plans not being fulfilled, about the shortages and poor quality of consumer goods, but this dissatisfaction was low-key and matter-of-fact." The planners' view, one of them recalled, "was that the Soviet system was inefficient but stable."[4]

To Gorbachev and his allies, the last decade had felt wasted. The West now seemed dynamic, moving forward. They felt they were stuck, standing still. That was unacceptable.

Reform Communism

When Gorbachev took power, he and his advisers could review a rich menu of ideas for socialist reform. There were no standard ideas. Communist Hungary had experimented with some market reforms. Poland was trying some possibilities. The communist parties in Western Europe, especially in Italy, had been trying out some interesting concepts. Soviet academic economists had a few of their own. Above all, the Soviets could study and reflect on what Deng's patient experiments had accomplished in China since 1978.

Any solution had to start by understanding the system. On the surface, one could say that these were planned economies. So if there were problems, in theory it was time to change the plan.

Yet the theory was wrong. To call the Soviet system of 1985 or the Chinese system before 1978 "planned" would be too great a compliment. It is more useful to think of them as "command" economies.

The state owned practically everything. Planning set targets for production and distribution. It set prices, set wages, assigned housing, and guaranteed jobs for all. The plans would then break down in a thousand ways—fertilizer not showing up at planting time, needed parts not being available. The inevitable problems were addressed with command methods. When things went wrong, as they inevitably would, the relevant boss just gave orders to fix it.

These orders might collide, to be resolved by a bigger boss, and so on. Through such trial and error, the plans could be corrected so that, finally, everything seemed to run smoothly. Imagine: Once the commotion settled down and the bosses found they had a somewhat stable relationship of inputs and outputs, who would want to decree any changes that would mess everything up again?

Outsiders, such as experts in the West, had few realistic notions about how to reform such a system. It was incredibly complex and alien to their experience. To say that such a system could be fixed by using "market forces" was about as practical as suggesting to a friend that if she wanted to, she could jump out of a skyscraper window and fly by using "aerodynamic forces."

In the West, "market forces" took effect through an array of private and public institutions. These institutions were then organized and fenced in by a functioning rule of law and supported by some safety nets, like bankruptcy rules or deposit insurance to supervise or close local banks.

In the communist system, the issue was not whether prices could change behavior, any more than the issue is whether air can lift a wing. The problem was how to engineer a system, to build ways of doing business that workably used these forces, where so many parts depended on others.

For instance, suppose a farmer on a farm enterprise wanted to raise the price of his wheat. Could he then refuse to fill the state ministry's food order, with its set price?

The farmer was constrained. His farm enterprise did not own the farmland. It relied on the state to provide it with fuel for the tractors and the combines. It might rely on state credit, from the state bank, in order to buy seeds from another state enterprise, with its fixed seed prices.

Finally, suppose the farmer's enterprise saved his best apples to sell at a market at higher-than-normal prices. These might be above the state price. Who would protect the farmer and his colleagues from being criminally prosecuted for "speculation"?

There were ways to address such problems. But just this little example shows how many interdependent decisions might be required to "reform" the system.

*　*　*

Soviet experts paid close attention to the Chinese experiments. "Let's be mature," Gorbachev told his colleagues. "China's path in recent years deserves serious analysis."[5]

Deng was not really the mastermind of the major reforms. He "did not have the patience to study all the details." Deng relied on other senior officials, especially Zhao Ziyang, who was more of a Gorbachev-like figure in China.

Those top officials then nurtured experiments in some local region or economic sector. The real designers were people like the party boss in Guangdong province, who oversaw the creation of a special economic zone near, and often partnering with, allies in British Hong Kong. Or, there was an innovative party boss in the agriculture sector. He oversaw an experiment with an arrangement, a bit like in feudal Europe, with the state lending land and equipment to households. In exchange, the state would get a quota of the produce and the farmer was left free to sell the rest in slowly developing markets.

The Chinese experiments were carefully controlled. Throughout, the Chinese maintained rigorous overall budget discipline.[6]

What Deng did was create a political environment in which these energetic and entrepreneurial officials could try out their experiments. He or his key allies would protect the beleaguered experimenters just barely enough to shield them when the inevitable backlash came from those powerful officials who hated the experiments. Little was said about the experiments, to avoid a big political struggle. If one or another of them caught on, it would be allowed to spread, still with little fanfare.

In this quiet space the experimenters sorted through the early problems. Leaders had to learn how to make real plans, instead of just commanding that this thing be produced or that quota be filled. "Therefore," one expert noted, "it is an apparent paradox that in the transition from a 'planned' economy, a central condition of success is the ability of the state to plan effectively. In fact, this ceases to be a paradox once one recognizes that the communist economic systems were not planned economies at all. Success in the transition was conditional upon learning how to plan, as opposed to giving orders."[7]

* * *

After taking office in 1985, Gorbachev and his allies wanted to wake up and clean up a system where "everything is rotten."[8] They first tried the old command methods. Gorbachev gave orders for "acceleration." That failed.

Then he and his Moscow allies tried writing new central laws, more of a top-down approach than the way reform had been nurtured in China. Gorbachev tried to defeat his political opponents in pitched political battles waged from the center.

From the Politburo, Gorbachev and his team could write new laws, but these were so sweeping that they often had to be compromised to allow ministries the discretion they wanted. Gorbachev himself could not master every detail. His authority was not absolute; his most reliable allies were a minority in the ruling Politburo.

There were a few significant experiments. A few daring officials had tried some small ones in the early 1980s, but "the ministries that controlled the Soviet economy obstructed experimentation."[9]

Soviet agriculture was an important example. Gorbachev and his key allies, including his domestic chief minister, Nikolai Ryzhkov, noticed what the Chinese were doing. They grasped the Chinese idea of leasing out land to farmers and letting the farmers keep and sell most of what they grew. They tried to enact this.

But the other ministers fought back. Were the old collective farms to be allowed to go bankrupt? If not, then the government would need to subsidize the old collectives so that they could offset the competition from these liberated farmers.

And anyway, the ministers argued, the real problem was that not enough money was being given to them to buy more tractors and fertilizer. They argued for more command solutions: Give us more money to buy the inputs we need.

Finally, when the deals were made to get the law passed, the ministries obstructed the process to hand out leases to the new, supposedly liberated farmers. Thus the new farms remained miniscule.[10]

What the ministries could agree on was that they needed more money to produce more or innovate. Then they just used this money in the old ways. Central spending and budget deficits grew, to patch up problems. The main sectoral interest groups of the economy—like the military— seemed immovable.

As the spending grew, and more rubles were printed, ruble inflation became a serious problem. The central government could print money, but—since there was no free market—the government could not supply enough things that people wanted to buy. Oil could earn billions of dollars for the government, but in a city at the center of the oil production tens of thousands of people lived in metal wagons turned into temporary housing, with several families often sharing an outdoor toilet in a place where the temperatures frequently fell below zero. In this Siberian city of three hundred thousand people, Nizhnevartovsk, Gorbachev saw for himself in a September 1985 visit that there was not even one public movie theater. A Communist Party youth club sometimes showed movies, but tickets were hard to get.

Revising his prepared remarks to local party workers, Gorbachev began by saying, "It is embarrassing for us to talk about the millions of tons of oil and cubic meters of gas when a drilling foreman says to us that the greatest incentive in Nizhnevartovsk is to be given a ticket to see a film."[11]

The net result of the initial wave of reforms was another paradox, the great paradox of Gorbachev's early years in power. Everything seemed to change. And nothing seemed to change.

To Change the USSR, Change the World

During the first few years, Gorbachev and his team worked hard to enact serious economic reforms. Having been to Western countries, Gorbachev and his team believed that the Soviet Union was not just losing a technological competition with the West. It was even falling behind, as one of his former advisers put it, in providing "more decent living conditions for the 'working masses.' "[12] As their efforts had so little effect, he and his allies began concluding that their problem was structural. The economy was too centralized, isolated, and militarized.

This character was rooted in choices made in the late 1920s. The old Soviet system had worked well for industrialization and militarization. Since its creation, the basic premise of Soviet existence was the inevitability, the necessity, of a colossal global struggle between the socialist world and the rest. In days past, the Soviet Union had taken pride in being a pariah—neither an accomplice to nor a victim of global capitalism's exploitation of the world. This is how Soviet leaders understood Marxist-Leninist ideology. And ideology mattered, not as a blueprint for action but in defining the range of the possible.[13]

Soviet policy from the time of Joseph Stalin had been ideological in precisely this way. It had one central tenet—that the long-term interests of the Soviet Union could not be reconciled with those of an international economic and political order dominated by capitalist democracies. The world had to be divided until the day when socialism would triumph. Marxism-Leninism was at once both the foundation for the internal organization of the Soviet Union and the basis of its place in the world.

Successive Soviet leaders believed that the West would ultimately try to destroy socialism. It would try to do this either by war or, after nuclear weapons seemed to rule this out, by subversion. The first obligation of Soviet leaders, since the success of the revolution and the 1919 creation of the Communist International, was to prepare to fight and win that war.

Stalin structured the Soviet Union as a country that would go it alone until a "ring of socialist brother states" could provide additional resources and security.[14] He made it absolutely clear that the survival and prosperity of the Soviet Union was the first priority for any good communist.

The Soviet-led socialist commonwealth could not tolerate deserters. Therefore, countries that had joined the Soviet bloc could not be allowed to leave it, could not be allowed to fall prey to the forces of capitalist subversion and counterrevolution.

The policy demanded self-sufficiency for the economy and provided insulation from an international economic order that the Soviets feared. The system successfully made maximum use of the resources of its multinational empire to support Moscow's goals and prepare the Soviet state for world war. But this isolation from the world economy, almost from the Soviet Union's inception, doomed Moscow to live with its peculiar economic structure.[15]

* * *

The "new thinkers" decided to reconsider the class basis of international relations. This was at the very heart of Marxist thought. It is in this sense that Gorbachev was truly a remarkable historical figure. He understood his options differently. He concluded that Soviet domestic problems were inextricably bound up in its approach toward the world. In other words, an economy that always put top priority on preparing for war would always have trouble preparing for peace.

Gorbachev and his advisers had met foreign leaders. They judged that the "imperialist world" was in no way preparing to attack or invade the Soviet Union. One of Gorbachev's early priorities was to end the Soviet intervention and occupation effort in Afghanistan. More than a hundred thousand Soviet troops were still trying bloodily to pacify the country, without success. He made an initial effort to settle the conflict with escalation. That failed. During 1985 and 1986, as the Chernobyl disaster seemed to signal one kind of crisis of the old way of doing things, Gorbachev decided that the Soviet Union would have to cut its losses and get all its troops out within the next two years—which is what happened. This decision went down relatively well with the military, many of whose leaders were disillusioned with the Afghan war. The military was much more concerned about Gorbachev's wish to reform the whole size and influence of the military at home.[16]

By 1987 and on into 1988, Soviet leaders seemed to be clustering into two camps. On one side there was Gorbachev and the cause of "perestroika," which can be translated as "restructuring" or "renewal."

On the other side were the obstructionists, the "conservatives." More and more, the "conservatives" were identified with the party bosses of the old system and the managers of the gigantic military-industrial complex. Gorbachev and his allies correctly regarded that complex as a "state within a state."[17]

To defeat the "conservatives," Gorbachev's structural solutions had two main directions: "glasnost" (openness) and a new approach to security.

* * *

Openness meant openness to public criticism, to discussion of the past and the troubling issues of Soviet history. Openness was meant to open up honest discussion of problems, past and present. Openness could bring wider political and public pressure to bear against the party bosses who were blocking reform.

The floodgates rapidly opened in a literate country with millions of people eager to read and comment on every new disclosure about past and present. By early 1988, this deluge of exposure and criticism triggered a strong conservative backlash, a sense that the whole legacy of Soviet achievement was being attacked, belittled, and undermined from within.

Gorbachev did not back down. After his bitter experience with the Chernobyl disaster, after the repeated failures of incremental reform, the challenge to glasnost became a vital test for his rule. In April 1988, he convened a key conference among about 150 party leaders to debate the party's future direction. He lashed out.

What the conservatives were saying, Gorbachev said, was, "Don't touch Stalin! Don't touch bribe-takers! Don't touch party organizations that have long since rotted!"

Such people "don't love their country or socialism," he declared. "All they want is to make their little nest a little warmer."

He turned again to Stalin's legacy. Stalin, he said, had been "a criminal, devoid of any morality. Let me tell you on your own behalf: one million party activists were shot, three million sent to the camps to rot.... That's who Stalin was." Even Nikita Khrushchev, who first acknowledged the crimes of Stalin, had not told the full truth about them "because his own hands were covered with blood."[18]

* * *

Gorbachev himself was so different from his predecessors—relaxed, confident, tireless, engaged. He built up a core team to help him.

When Gorbachev took power it was as the leader of the party, served by party staff. There was no "presidency" or "presidential staff" then. In foreign policy this meant using the staff of the international department of the party's Central Committee. Gorbachev drew from such Central Committee experts, along with help from the Foreign Ministry and a few close aides chosen not only for their substantive specialties but also for their loyalty.[19]

He was difficult to help, according to those who worked for him, given to placing his own phone calls from his dacha and organizing his own calendar. Western officials found the Kremlin apparatus somewhat chaotic, having difficulty even in small matters, such as knowing how to locate Gorbachev for a phone call.

Gorbachev's closest personal aide was Anatoly Chernyaev. Chernyaev was a veteran party theorist who had served as a propagandist in the international department of the Central Committee. Sixty-eight years old in 1989, Chernyaev was rarely far from Gorbachev's side. He was the notetaker at almost all of Gorbachev's private meetings with foreign leaders. He was the man most often designated by Gorbachev as his point of contact for U.S. officials.

Another key adviser was Alexander Yakovlev, a veteran diplomat and party ideologue known for his unconventional thinking. Yakovlev had been ambassador to Canada when Gorbachev recalled him to Moscow, soon put him in charge of the Central Committee's international department, and eventually elevated him to membership in the Politburo.

Yakovlev had a reputation for being anti-American, but the most important thing about him was his commitment to the "new thinking." He was, in fact, its intellectual father and a principal architect of this novel way of defining Soviet national interests.

The most important man in Gorbachev's entourage was, like him, an outsider with no foreign policy expertise. This was Eduard Shevardnadze, the foreign minister.

Growing up in Soviet Georgia, Shevardnadze had been too young to serve in World War II. But his elder brother was killed defending Brest-Litovsk in the first days of the German invasion. Shevardnadze reflected later that "the war with fascism became a personal battle for me" and "the victory in that war became the victory of communism." The war, he wrote, "formed my convictions and purpose in life."[20] Yet, growing up in Georgia, a part of the Soviet Union that is closer to Iran than to Germany and that was never occupied by the Germans, Shevardnadze never seemed to share the deep anti-German feelings sometimes found among Russians scarred by the war.

Shevardnadze had risen through the party ranks in Georgia to leadership of the republic. He first met Gorbachev during the 1950s; the two became friends. Shevardnadze had replaced a notoriously corrupt party boss in the freewheeling Georgian republic. In the 1970s he acquired a reputation for vigilance and honesty. In many ways he was much like Gorbachev.

When the new general secretary thought he wanted to bring a gust of fresh air to Soviet foreign policy, he called on Shevardnadze. Thunderstruck, Shevardnadze recalled that July 1985 call as "the greatest surprise of my life."[21]

He replaced Andrei Gromyko, a rigid figure of the past who had been involved in Soviet diplomacy since the time of Stalin. Shevardnadze spoke Russian with a Georgian accent. He brought a sharp change in perspective and style. The younger diplomats admired his energy, integrity, and openness.

In 1989, Shevardnadze approved the installation of a large memorial book in the front hall of the Moscow Foreign Ministry building. It listed the hundreds of diplomats whom Stalin's tyranny had slaughtered as spies during the great purges in 1937–38, victims of the terror.

That was the kind of ministry Shevardnadze tried to run, an institution willing to look history square in the eye, discard the past, and turn to the future with hope and, sometimes, resignation. In that sense he was a true believer in the "new thinking." He was less of a political tactician than Gorbachev. He was habitually candid, even emotional, as he worked his way through the problems.

Yakovlev, Shevardnadze, and Chernyaev took dead aim at hostile isolation, at proletarian internationalism, as an outmoded basis for foreign policy. For them, global interdependence was now the dominant factor in international life.[22]

* * *

A new approach to security meant taking on the most powerful and autonomous institutions in the Soviet state: the Soviet military and its associated industries. To help do this, Gorbachev used the international diplomacy of arms control.

The Soviet military had become essentially self-governing. State planners could set some broad limits on budget and resources. But after that, everything else that was done was under military control. Top leaders had little insight, or even knowledge, about military programs and force posture.

The civilian leaders therefore had no easy ways to regulate the military internally. So one instrument was to use the negotiation of arms control agreements. Civilian leaders could sign such treaties and use them to limit and reduce the arms buildup.

Many Soviet generals had welcomed the ascension of Gorbachev. They hoped he would revitalize the country and make it more competitive. They worried about the American emphasis on new military technology.

In public there was much debate about Reagan's much-discussed

1983 announcement that his government would seek to build space and ground-based defenses against nuclear missile attack, an idea formally called a Strategic Defense Initiative (SDI) and informally derided as his "Star Wars" idea. The idea seemed to imply that nuclear threats, and with them, nuclear deterrence, might be erased. At the time, the idea was technologically far-fetched and, though publicly the Soviets attacked the plan, secretly the Soviet military had trouble figuring out whether there was any real danger from it. What bothered them the most was not an imminent threat to their nuclear capabilities, but instead that the new American capabilities seemed to threaten the Soviets' greatest and most costly asset, their conventional forces.

Already worried about the emphasis on "smart" munitions with sensors to find their targets, Soviet generals argued that the real impact of SDI-related research was that it might harness the sophisticated technology of the West, such as lasers, optics, and real-time information processing, to render Moscow's vast conventional forces obsolete. American high-performance aircraft married to smart weapons and computer-aided guidance became the Soviet General Staff's worst nightmare.[23]

The worries of Soviet military leaders may seem way overblown. But it is hard for outsiders to appreciate the world of Soviet military estimates in the 1980s.

The head of the assessment department of Soviet military intelligence later reflected that in the case of estimated American tank production in wartime, "our plans were based on forecasts that were off by a factor of more than 100. Such errors were not unusual. We were off target by a multiple of ten in the estimated U.S. wartime output of aircraft.... I know for a fact that these figures were taken literally in planning our defense strategy and preparing the country for the arms race."

It was difficult for anyone to check or debate the military's estimates, however fanciful they were. After the Cold War, this intelligence expert talked to Americans and looked at their estimates. He envied their quarrels and their think tanks. "The Americans also made serious errors, particularly in those areas where the USSR was weak. Still, the order of magnitude of their mistakes was much less than ours."[24]

The exaggerated worries of the professional officers had to concern the political leaders of the Soviet Union. Military strength had first claim on the country's resources and on its finest human and physical assets. It is no accident that military parades became more grandiose as the Soviet Union's internal decline accelerated. Military power was a source of pride, the country's best and brightest achievement.

In 1985, when Gorbachev was looking for big ideas to reduce tensions and cut back the military, the generals suggested that it would be nice to eliminate all nuclear weapons. Gorbachev captivated the world when he made this offer in January 1986.

It might seem surprising that the military would propose such a thing. But to the generals, this radical idea had three virtues: (1) It seemed in the realm of fantasy; (2) if it happened, it would eliminate the West's main hedge to offset Soviet conventional military superiority on the ground in Europe; and (3) the Soviet military was alarmed by (and had greatly overestimated) the scale and dangerousness of the U.S. nuclear buildup and Reagan's new Strategic Defense Initiative program.[25]

Gorbachev sought to reduce tension with a series of high-profile summit meetings with Reagan. They made no breakthroughs to eliminate or even radically reduce the arsenals of nuclear weapons. A key obstacle was the SDI issue, on which Reagan had placed ill-founded hopes and the Soviets had ill-founded fears.

Yet, even if they did not agree to eliminate or radically reduce nuclear weapons, both men did accomplish a fundamental relaxation in tension. We already mentioned that in 1986 the Soviet government decided to pull all its troops out of Afghanistan within two years.

Also, thanks to the persistence of Reagan's secretary of state, Shultz, working with Shevardnadze (both men holding off the conservative political factions in both of their countries), the two countries were able to negotiate a 1987 treaty (the Intermediate-Range Nuclear Forces, or INF, Treaty) that eliminated the intermediate-range nuclear missiles, such as SS-20s and Pershings. This INF treaty resolved the big public and political confrontation of the early 1980s over "Euromissiles."[26]

Still, none of this had a significant effect on the structure of the Soviet economy. The relaxation of tension and the INF treaty did not do much about the size or scope of the defense establishments on either side.

Cutting back some categories of missiles might hopefully be a stabilizing thing to do. But such cuts do little to affect the underlying spending on missile R&D, nuclear weapons R&D, or intelligence and satellite systems. And, most important, the number of soldiers or sailors in nuclear forces made up a small fraction of the military establishments built up by the United States and its NATO allies, or the Soviet Union and its Warsaw Pact allies.

It was the standoff in conventional arms that dominated spending and military planning. Gorbachev and his team realized this. They wanted to talk about large reductions in Soviet forces, both conventional and nuclear. But the Soviet military insisted that these needed to be negotiated with limits that were reciprocal.[27]

Hardly anyone knew anything about or paid any attention to conventional arms control. So it was not much noticed, then or even now, that in June 1986 Gorbachev took the initiative to offer an extraordinary new approach. Instead of the old talks, which had been dragging on inconclusively for fourteen years with a narrow scope on Central Europe, he suggested sweeping reciprocal controls on conventional arms "from the Atlantic to the Urals."

Gorbachev's initiative did lead to the creation of a new conventional arms control negotiation, called CFE (on Conventional Armed Forces in Europe). In 1988 these new talks were finally getting under way. But, as 1989 began, the two alliances (all twenty-three member states in NATO and the Warsaw Pact took part in these talks) could not even agree on what categories of arms should be controlled.[28]

Gorbachev's "Turning Point" in 1988

By early 1988, the whole reform program was tottering. Budget deficits were becoming a quite serious problem. As one sharp observer noted, "Perestroika was closer to collapse in 1988 than at any time before and probably any time after."[29]

Writing to his colleagues in March 1988, Yakovlev said that so far the economic reforms had produced "no effect whatsoever in many workplaces, no much-touted boost to 'self-management and independence.'" The people had no confidence in the economic system. Ministries were "trampling" (Gorbachev's term) on the new laws that were supposed to give enterprises more autonomy.

Outside experts agreed. One commented, "The service sector is incredibly primitive by Western standards, indeed by world standards. Consumer durables are scarce. The underlying technology dates from the early postwar years, and the quality is frequently poor. This economy seems unable to produce a cheap, reliable automatic washing machine, radio or phonograph, and cheap powerful hand calculators and personal computers are still no more than a distant hope. Decent fruits and vegetables... are seemingly out of reach even though twenty percent of the labor force works in agriculture."[30]

Gorbachev and his colleagues decided they had to reexamine the whole guiding ideology and structure of the Soviet government. They had to ask themselves: What was the core of a communist system? What was the irreducible "Leninist" foundation?

Preparing for the summer 1988 party conference, Gorbachev asked working groups—headed by key aides such as Yakovlev and Chernyaev—to examine thoroughly the relationship of Leninism to perestroika. Chernyaev describes Gorbachev in this period (late 1987 and the first half of 1988) reading papers that had been written for Lenin, histories of Marxist thought, and the writings of the "old Bolsheviks," most of whom had been executed by Stalin.[31]

This period became a turning point in the "new thinking." Gorbachev took from his studies the conclusion that there were many roads to socialism. It was permissible to be guided by the historical conditions in a given place or time, especially circumstances that Lenin himself had not foreseen. Gorbachev settled for Lenin's vague endorsement of the need to be guided by practice.[32]

The conservatives launched a major counterattack against perestroika in April and May 1988. Gorbachev and Yakovlev struck back by accelerating the pace of change.

They decided to embrace movement toward "democratic socialism." They would ensure "solidarity and social justice," as one ally put it, while also embracing ideals of freedom and democratic institutions.[33]

Gorbachev and his team deployed their new offensive on two major fronts. First, they would bring democracy into the Communist Party. Second, they would decisively turn communist ideology away from eternal preparation for war.

* * *

During 1988, Gorbachev and his allies developed a revolutionary program of democratization. To understand it, it is important to look harder at the way the Soviet Union was set up.

When the pre-1917 Russian Empire was converted into a Union of Soviet Socialist Republics, imperial provinces became national republics. Each of these had its own national tradition. They were no longer joined by an imperial monarch. Instead the binding agent, the disciplined core, was the Communist Party of the Soviet Union. The Union was a multinational federation glued together by the common Communist Party.

"Soviets" were councils, supposed to be the seeds of a workers' democracy. Gorbachev's new program developed in the spring and summer of 1988 would make the local soviets in the republics into genuinely democratic institutions. Contested elections would be held in the spring of 1989. Party bosses would then chair these elected national soviets.

The people would also elect representations to an all-Union council, a Congress of People's Deputies, more than two thousand in number. About one-third of the seats in this Congress would be reserved for public entities like the party.

The Congress would then pick representatives to turn the Union's moribund "Supreme Soviet" into a working parliament. Gorbachev himself would chair it. He thus began planning to make himself a Soviet president, not just a party chief.

In this new system, legitimacy would thus start draining away from the party. The democratically organized soviets would be seen as the sources of popular authority.

For some time, Gorbachev had seen "personnel as the root of all our problems." The status quo leaders were "philosophically impoverished." They knew no other way to do things. "We won't see new cadres come up," Gorbachev remarked, "unless we create an atmosphere of glasnost and criticism."[34]

To further weaken the party and his potential conservative opponents, Gorbachev reorganized the party's executive entity, its Secretariat. He centered power more and more on the ruling Politburo itself, and on himself. He was preparing a slow transition into becoming more of a traditional state ruler, giving direction to the state ministries and agencies.

In this process Gorbachev and his team purged more of their former conservative allies. He replaced the defense minister, top generals, the head of the KGB, and others of the old guard with less distinguished but more trusted men.[35]

The conservatives had now clearly become an internal enemy. By 1988, however, the political contest was no longer just one of reformers versus conservatives. A third, more radical faction was gaining strength. This group called for more democracy and said Gorbachev was not moving fast enough, that his change agenda was not radical enough.

Gorbachev struck against this faction too, what he called these "ultra-leftist loudmouths." The lead example of such a "loudmouth" was the former Sverdlovsk and Moscow party chief, Boris Yeltsin.

The elections were set for the first half of 1989. It was the internal side of the great turning point. All the powerful players in the system began to calculate next moves, including the leaders of the national republics inside the Union.

* * *

The other side of Gorbachev's 1988 offensive was a further challenge to the generals and military-industrial barons. He planned to take on the basic doctrines guiding Soviet military posture in Europe, including the giant conventional forces.

In Gorbachev's last major summit with Reagan, in Moscow at the end of May and early June 1988, they had made no progress on arms control. The American side complained that the Soviet government had not yet made any real changes in the defense posture, especially its conventional forces in Europe.

Privately, Gorbachev and his key allies admitted that these complaints had some force. They too were frustrated by their inability to effect real change in the scale and spending of the enormous Soviet military-industrial complex. They also believed their own military was misleading them about some of the facts.

In October 1988, Gorbachev invited West German chancellor Kohl to a summit meeting, their first. The sessions in Moscow went well. Right after that summit was done, Gorbachev went off with a small team to a resort on the Black Sea. There they deliberated about what to do next.

If leaders want to accomplish anything substantive, they need help from others who have the time and specialized concentration to develop ideas, formulate concrete objectives, and choreograph all the movements that go into a large initiative. In all the key governments in this period, the core team at the center of policy design and adaptation comprised usually about five to ten people.

Gorbachev's core team in dealing with the world was still a select group of party staff, based in the Secretariat of the party's Central Committee. Chernyaev and Yakovlev were still the leading advisers from the CC Staff. Below them were their top regional experts.[36]

Over at the Foreign Ministry, Gorbachev trusted the minister, Shevardnadze. The former longtime Soviet ambassador to the United States, Anatoly Dobrynin, was still a source of valued counsel. On the military side, Gorbachev had fewer allies. He had overhauled the leadership of the Defense Ministry the previous year. He did look to his new chief of the general staff, a leading advocate of military modernization and reform, Marshal Sergei Akhromeyev, a veteran of the World War II siege of Leningrad.

On October 31, out on the shores of the Black Sea, Gorbachev met with his team. His team had already suggested that Gorbachev not wait for the CFE talks to get going, that he could start off with some unilateral cuts in Soviet military strength. The next five-year plan for the economy was to be rolled out in 1989. If there were going to be big changes in military posture, it was time to start considering them.

The group agreed that Gorbachev should make a substantial move to cut back the size of the Soviet military. The upcoming December speech at the UN would be a good occasion to announce it.

* * *

A few days later, Gorbachev laid this idea before the Politburo. He was "clearly nervous," which he overcame by being "agitated and tough." The INF treaty had just been a "little step," he explained to his fellow leaders. Now it was time to make a big step.

He acknowledged the enormous scale of Soviet military deployments in Europe. With "all this hanging over them," how could the West believe that Soviet intentions were defensive? No one spent as much of their national income on the military as the USSR did. They had to make cuts.

Gorbachev asked for questions.

There were none.

His prime minister, Ryzhkov, bearing the burden of economic management, his voice "very tense," backed his boss. If there were no major defense cuts, he said, "we can forget about any increase in the standard of living."

The Politburo then duly agreed to Gorbachev's proposal.

Next, Gorbachev confronted his Defense Council with this decision. He asked them to come up with a plan. In the next few weeks one was finalized and approved.

The process seems to have been very stressful. We know little about the details. We do know that, as the plan was approved, Marshal Akhromeyev resigned his post as head of the Soviet General Staff (though agreeing to continue as an adviser to Gorbachev). He said later that he had been "distraught," that it was "incomprehensible" that Gorbachev had acted before getting reciprocal concessions from NATO.

Within weeks, the top two Soviet commanders in the Warsaw Pact were also relieved of their commands. We also know that the Soviets had little time to consult their East bloc allies before the move was announced. Shevardnadze remained quite suspicious that the high command might not actually implement the announced plans.[37]

As scheduled, Gorbachev rolled out his initiative in a speech to the UN General Assembly in December 1988. He said the Soviet armed forces would be reduced overall by about half a million. This would cut about one-seventh of the active-duty forces.

He promised that in the coming two years, 1989 and 1990, the Soviets would withdraw 20 percent (six of thirty divisions) of the forces they then had stationed on foreign bases in Eastern Europe. He promised, giving some suggestive numbers, that the Soviet army would also reduce the proportions of tanks and assault equipment deployed forward in Europe.[38]

If implemented, the announced plans were significant. They would not eliminate concerns about the Soviet military. But they plainly moved into a new direction, a level of change no one had seen in a generation. Also, by announcing them publicly in this way, Gorbachev and his team had effectively pinned the Soviet military to a set of measurable targets.

* * *

There was more. Gorbachev also announced that other socialist countries—the countries of Eastern Europe—would be permitted to find their own path without interference from the Soviet Union.

These military and political initiatives were linked inextricably in Gorbachev's mind. His aide, Chernyaev, lamented the widespread failure—even in the Soviet Union—to appreciate fully its ideological significance. It was not the first time that, from the Soviet point of view, the West had missed the point.[39]

The Soviets had tried to get Reagan's attention at the June 1988 summit in Moscow. They had stressed the importance of a declaration on the mutuality of interests between states in an interdependent world and the principle of noninterference in the affairs of others.

It is not hard to see why Reagan's advisers had viewed the statement as a stock set of slogans. The Reagan administration was focused on incremental steps to advance its own four-part agenda: human rights, arms control, bilateral relations, and regional security, as in Central America.

Gorbachev, however, was trying to convey a theoretical and philosophical message that, in his world, carried enormous significance. His December 1988 UN speech emphasized what he had been saying for months: Eastern Europe was free to go its own way, leaving no ideological barriers to a more demilitarized Europe, tied together by interdependence and common values.

Months before the UN speech, Yakovlev had declared that "class struggle" had lost its meaning in the international politics of an interdependent world. Shevardnadze elaborated at a "scientific-practical conference" of the Foreign Ministry, saying that class interests had given way to those of one interdependent world.[40]

Yegor Ligachev, one of the last old-style theoreticians remaining on the governing Politburo after the 1988 party conference, fought back. He appealed for reaffirmation of the fundamental nature of class struggle in international life.[41]

Gorbachev and his advisers did not agree. The Soviet Union would be a member of a "common European home."

As Gorbachev would tell the Council of Europe in July 1989, "It is not enough now simply to state that European states share a common fate and are interdependent.... The idea of European unity must be collectively rethought, in a process of creative collaboration among all nations—large, medium, and small."[42] Two different social systems would exist side by side in this common home. Their differences would be overcome by shared human values. Gorbachev talked about European socialism and Soviet communism as if they were cousins.[43]

When asked if he was a Leninist, Gorbachev always answered yes, forcefully and without hesitation. He did not accept Western notions of private property. He once told George H. W. Bush that he simply rejected the idea of people working for other people as a form of exploitation. But he saw no contradiction between that Leninist basis for the Soviet state and a set of common international values.

He and the new American president, Bush, had a revealing exchange on just this point when they met at Malta in December 1989. The American president asserted that the division of Europe could be overcome only on the basis of "Western values."

Gorbachev took that opportunity to rail against this formulation. This was something he had "heard many times." He proceeded to lecture the American president for almost twenty minutes. "We share the values of democracy, individual liberty, and freedom," he declared.

A beleaguered Bush tried to respond. Then Yakovlev and Shevardnadze joined in the argument.

Rather than argue about the place of ideals such as democracy and individual liberty in Russian or Soviet history, Secretary of State James

Baker asked if it would be more acceptable just to characterize all of these ideals as "democratic values."

The Soviets settled down and agreed with that formulation.[44] They were still committed to socialism. But it was a socialism that was ready to be interdependent with the international system rather than independent and isolated from it. They intended to join this transformed Europe on full and equal terms.

They did not believe they were abandoning the communist dream. They believed they were modernizing it.[45]

What Would All This Mean for Eastern Europe?

During 1988, the leaders of Moscow's Eastern European allies had plenty of urgent questions about what all the new ideas would mean for them, the heads of the six member states of the Warsaw Pact: East Germany, Poland, Czechoslovakia, Hungary, Bulgaria, and Romania.

In the postwar era, Stalin put in place his "ring of socialist brother states." The military side of the alliance was under Soviet command.

When the communists took over these Eastern European countries after World War II, they took charge of deeply scarred societies, divided throughout the twentieth century by violent internal struggles, usually between fascists and antifascists, in addition to the wars that raged across their territories. Particularly in Poland, but also in Hungary and Czechoslovakia, national feeling had also been practically synonymous with being anti-Russian.

By the 1950s the old class and fascist enemies were purged and defeated. Many in Eastern Europe refocused their resentment on Stalinist tyranny and the Russian domination. There were revolts in East Germany in 1953, in Poland and Hungary in 1956, and in Czechoslovakia in 1968. All had been put down. The Soviets and their East European allies had crushed the 1968 "Prague Spring" with two hundred thousand troops and two thousand tanks.

Soviet leaders tried to harness Eastern Europe's economic power toward the goal of building a stronger Soviet Union. This was done principally through the Council for Mutual Economic Assistance (CMEA), an institution that had to manage all the trade and barter arrangements in a system where trade relations could not be regulated by the market or convertible money.[46]

As the Soviet leaders built up this countersystem, it isolated them further from the economic and political order dominated by the West. The Western policy of containment reinforced Soviet isolation. East-West trade was constrained. The West formed an organization, COCOM (Coordinating Committee for East-West Trade), to coordinate controls on the export of militarily useful technologies to the Eastern bloc.[47]

* * *

The socialist ruling elites in Eastern Europe enjoyed their new, high social status. They believed in their systems. They were proud that they had sustained socialism.

But by the 1980s their pride had ebbed. Why? The communist rulers had to "normalize" their countries in two stages. They had to, first, "crush the society into utter defeat and submission; and (2) gratify and tame it with economic rewards and material satisfaction." Since 1956, Hungary under the rule of János Kádár had become a model for how to do both.[48]

During the 1970s the socialist rulers had exhausted the economic growth gains from postwar rebuilding and the construction of old-style heavy industry. They decided to rely on loans from the West in order to keep pace with Western standards of living.

The Eastern European leaders had a theory for their borrowing from the West. In addition to buying desired consumer goods, like decent coffee, they would also use these Western loans to build up top-quality industries. The improved industries would then supposedly produce the exports to repay the loans. Meanwhile the East European countries would dump their inferior products on their Soviet trading partner in exchange for precious Soviet raw materials, like oil, at the kind of non-market subsidized prices that could be set among socialist brothers.

The theory did not work out. What happened instead is that the loans were used to subsidize imports of foreign goods and perks for the elite. Poland, Hungary, and East Germany led the way. Such borrowing became known as the "Polish disease." But it was not unique to Poland. In East Germany, "it was hardly visible then [in the early 1970s], but that was when the switches were set," one of that country's planners later acknowledged in 1989. "From then on the train traveled millimeter by millimeter in the wrong direction. It traveled away from the realities of the GDR."[49]

These countries could have just accepted their limits, as Romania did. That country's dictatorship simply imposed a bleak lifestyle on its people. Wielding a powerful and ruthless security apparatus, the dictatorship made people live with it.

The East Germans, Poles, Hungarians, and Czechs—all from countries with histories of anticommunist and anti-Russian revolts—did not think they could make Romania's choice. They had to promise a better life.

Then came the first oil crisis of 1973–74. The Soviet Union decided to reduce its oil subsidies. It forced the East European satellites to make it more on their own. For example, in the old barter trade arrangements, in 1974 the USSR would give Hungary a million tons of oil in exchange for eight hundred Hungarian buses. In 1981 the same amount of oil had to be paid for with twenty-three hundred buses, and a few years later, four thousand buses. This was while the Soviet Union was still willing to trade oil for buses.[50]

The first crises in Poland arose in 1970, then 1976. As the borrowed money ran out, the regime sharply increased the prices of imported necessities like food and fuel. The workers began organizing and striking for more wages so they could pay. Thus the Polish economic crisis turned into a political one. Society, led by strikers in Baltic shipyards, began organizing itself into a broad protest movement, called Solidarity, that brought together many factions in their hatred of the communist government.

The Soviet Union itself was not immune. It was increasingly dependent on huge amounts of imported grain and foreign technology. But for a long time the USSR was less vulnerable. Until the end of the 1980s it could rely on commodity exports, especially of oil or gas, in order to earn the hard currency to pay for these imports.

From 1979 on, to make ends meet, the East European countries relied even more on continued borrowing from Western banks, mainly in Western Europe and Japan. Then came the global financial overhaul of the late 1970s and early 1980s that we described in chapter 1. Interest rates on debts went up. There was another trebling of energy prices. The Soviet Union could handle the crisis; it had the oil and natural resources it could sell. The East European satellites did not.

* * *

In the United States and Western Europe the tight money crisis at the beginning of the 1980s meant sharp recessions and harsh "austerity" programs. In the rest of the world, debtor nations faced more difficult choices. They could radically curtail consumption. Or they could default on their debts, which would also cut off the flow of funds. This was the global debt crisis. Some governments toppled under the strain. Others, like Brazil, had to transform their political and economic system.

The East European states were neither liked nor admired by most of their people. So, they felt too precarious politically to impose painful austerity programs. Their rulers could be a feared tyranny or a weak tyranny, but they would be seen as a tyranny either way. " 'There is no socialism with a human face,' the [Polish dissident] Adam Michnik liked to say, 'only totalitarianism with its teeth knocked out.' " The Princeton historian Stephen Kotkin wrote that "the competition in living standards all but bankrupted the Communist systems economically, because [to their people] they were politically and morally bankrupt."[51]

Rather than force their people to cut their standards of living significantly, the East European states desperately tried to mix less painful austerity programs combined with even more borrowing from the European and Japanese banks.

In 1983 and 1984, Kohl's conservative West German government went along with this. It deliberately decided to lend billions of deutschmarks to East Germany. The loan eased political tensions in the short term and gained political leverage in the long term.

In April 1987, a periodical that tracked East bloc economies commented about the case of Hungary, "We may sound very cynical, but it is not far from the truth to say that *Hungarian economic fortunes in the near future do not depend on anything done in Budapest, but will be determined in Tokyo [by Japanese bankers].* We doubt very much that Mr. Kadar yet understands this and the implications of such a situation for Hungarian economic sovereignty."[52]

When world oil prices finally dropped during the mid-1980s, it was not such a great relief to countries like Poland and Hungary. By then their debt holes were just too deep.

The mid-1980s drop in oil prices did hit the Soviet Union hard, because it deeply cut the foreign earnings the Soviets were getting for their oil. Then the Soviets started confronting their own challenges to maintain imports of desired foreign goods, including necessities like food. During 1988 the Soviet Union began borrowing much larger sums from Western banks than it had before. This borrowing too was almost entirely from banks in Western Europe and Japan.[53]

During the late 1980s, America and the Reagan administration were running fiscal and trade deficits too. But the Americans could manage their problems through the market, leaning on the financial resources of allied countries in Western Europe and Japan.

The Soviets could not lean on their allies. "While the Western Europeans and Japanese developed robust economies of their own from which the United States could draw, the Eastern Europeans increasingly became a burden to the Soviets, not sources of economic strength."[54]

* * *

During 1986, Poland negotiated an end to the Western sanctions placed on it because of the martial law crackdown on Solidarity and public protest. Poland agreed to wind down martial law and grant amnesty to political prisoners. The Polish government still felt able to contain domestic unrest with its well-tested security methods. But it had no answer to the economic problems, and these kept igniting more unrest.

In 1987 the Polish foreign minister was received in Washington and the U.S. vice president, George H. W. Bush, visited Poland. Above all, the Poles wanted to talk about Polish access to Western credit and finance.[55]

Bush offered U.S. help with Paris Club rescheduling of Polish debt (a promise kept later that year). But that only made new loans possible. It did not provide fresh money to alleviate Poland's grinding economic crisis.

When it came to credits or loans from the IMF or World Bank, Bush introduced conditions. Such credit, he said, would depend on more "institutionalized pluralism." That fancy phrase meant allowing elections with independent voices. It meant allowing the creation of independent trade unions. "Free elections and free trade unions, that is your concern, but the more Americans are able to identify themselves with your solutions the more they will be able to help."[56]

Hungary and Poland started working with the IMF on a loan program, which would also open the way for more private credit. There were those conditions again, because Poland could not pay back the loans if it did not solve its political problems.

By 1988 leaders in these two countries, Hungary and Poland, found themselves coming back again and again to three core points. Consider their problem.

- *First*, they could not count on the Soviet Union to bail them out.

- *Second*, the Western countries and outside lenders would not bend over backward to help them unless their systems became less tyrannical.

- *Third*, the only way to become creditworthy was to inflict more pain at home. The only way to inflict a lot more pain, without a lot more violent repression, was to strike a bargain with the opposition.

Suppose then that leaders face up to that third point—the necessary political bargain. There was only one possible bargain with the opposition: Share the choice for pain in exchange for sharing power.

The IMF managing director put it this way in talking to one Polish leader in June 1988: The government needed a "social consensus"; "increased popular participation in political decision-making might . . . reconcile the population to the sacrifices required for economic stabilization."[57]

During the spring of 1988 the reform communists in Hungary chose to accept this logic. They deposed the old tyrant, Kádár. They decided they would deal with a "Roundtable" among the opposition to negotiate a bargain, one that would maintain a leading role for the Communist Party but allow a loyal opposition.

The situation in Poland was worse than in Hungary. But the Polish rulers were also more stubborn than the Hungarians. The former U.S. national security adviser, Zbigniew Brzezinski, was worried about how "highly polarized" the situation was. "I fear that the combination of political and economic deterioration could create a revolutionary situation."

Finally, during the second half of 1988, after new hardships triggered another series of strikes, the Polish rulers reluctantly also chose to open Roundtable talks. In both countries difficult negotiations began. Where these talks would go would become clear in the new year, sometime in early 1989.[58]

* * *

For Gorbachev, by 1988 there had not been much change in the operation of the Soviet Union's empire in Eastern and Central Europe. In fact, when he first took office in 1985, Gorbachev warned the Poles to be wary of "traps" in their attempts to seek more trade with the West. He derided market-style economic reform.

"Some of you," he said, "look at the market as a lifesaver for your economies. But, comrades, you should not think about lifesavers but about the ship, and the ship is socialism."[59]

The Soviets fiddled endlessly trying to rationalize trade among the states without converting Eastern currencies. But theirs was a closed system, sustained by the exchange of shoddy products that had little value on the world market and constant gaming by the East Europeans to get more de facto Soviet subsidies. The Soviet negotiators knew what was going on, but they usually went along in order to preserve a façade of unity.[60]

Although the Soviet leadership had encouraged its allies to take care of themselves, the allies still expected and received guidance and control from Moscow. Yet, under Gorbachev, Moscow was giving "meager attention" to these countries. It had no coherent strategy toward them.[61]

In June 1988, as part of the preparations for his historic party conference, Gorbachev finally more fully engaged the Eastern Europe issues.

Building on arguments prepared for him by his advisers, his keynote address referred to "the sediment that has accumulated on our relations" with the Soviet allies in Europe. From now on, he said, "The external imposition of a social system, of a way of life, or of policies by any means, let alone military, is a dangerous trapping of the past."[62]

The Soviet government realized that the processes of political change that had begun in Poland and Hungary might spin out of control. Gorbachev's main Central Committee staff expert for Eastern Europe, Georgi Shakhnazarov, wrote him a secret memo in October 1988 warning that "social instability and crisis might well engulf the whole socialist world simultaneously."

The Soviet government did not wish to tell the Eastern European governments what to do. Moscow did not really know what they should do.

Gorbachev and his team were sure about one thing. The worst thing they could do was intervene massively with force the way their country had in the past. Then they would own the East European problems. Such an intervention might destroy perestroika at home too. So their secret preference, as they deliberated these issues on into early 1989, was to rule out Soviet military intervention, even before anyone asked for it. Instead they encouraged the Roundtable processes, like those under way in Poland and Hungary, so that these countries could fix themselves.[63]

When Is the Cold War Over?

In November 1988 the most warlike of Cold War leaders in the 1980s, Prime Minister Thatcher, declared publicly, "We're not in a Cold War now." Secretary of State George Shultz too wrote that at the end of 1988 the Cold War "was all over but the shouting."[64]

Was it? Between 1978 and 1988, there had indeed been another big shift in the momentum of world history. Think of it as a kind of global election.

In this global election, there were "swing states," the vital states where the basic direction and alignment in 1978 was up for debate and whose choices would be decisive. In 1978, these states were not the U.S. or the Soviet Union. They were states in non-Soviet Europe and in East Asia—there the main state in play was China.

Between 1978 and 1988 there was new thinking in the "West" and new thinking in the "East." Burnham's kind of vision of the future, dominated by the most ruthless managerial superstates, seemed notably less appealing. Orwell's kind of vision, for freer and more humane alternatives, had come to seem much more promising. The global election seemed to be tipping toward a broad systemic crisis of the communist world and the old Cold War system—with some large new outcome.

But what would be that outcome? *What comes next?*

* * *

As 1989 began, the world was still divided by the core issue of what the Cold War had been about, at least since 1919: profoundly different conceptions for how to organize modern society. The communist world still believed that the state should entirely dominate commerce, society, and political life. The apparatus of repression was still very much on the job.

Core principles had been put on the table, though. Great storms were gathering. Either the managerial superstates would mutate into more powerful and perhaps menacing forms, or they might give way to something else—but what, and how? Opposing sides were mobilizing their forces for battle—in ornate conference rooms or out on the streets. They were mobilizing in cities like Moscow, Beijing, Warsaw, and beyond.

The old guard held firm power in much of Eastern Europe, most of the Soviet government, and most of the Chinese government. Perhaps the coming battles over the future of socialism would be peaceful; perhaps not. No one then knew how these battles would turn out, or what would happen then.

As 1989 began, the Soviet Union had about forty thousand nuclear weapons and the United States had about twenty-three thousand. Both countries deployed thousands of possible delivery systems, including ballistic missiles ready for launch from land or undersea, aircraft, and shorter-range rockets and artillery. Both countries were proceeding with the planned modernization of their strategic nuclear forces. Britain and France each had hundreds more weapons ready for possible use.[65]

As 1989 began, in Europe, from the Atlantic to the Urals, the rival alliances fielded almost eighty thousand tanks, over sixty-three thousand artillery pieces, over nineteen thousand combat aircraft, and more than five million soldiers and airmen. Germany, West and East, was the most heavily militarized area of real estate in the history of the world.

Let us try to put these numbers in perspective. There were more than twice as many tanks fielded in Europe in 1989 were in Europe in the autumn of 1944, when the fighting in Europe during World War II had been at its absolute peak of intensity and scale.

The majority of these troops and weapons were in the Soviet-led Warsaw Pact countries. Soviets made up two-thirds of the strength of the Warsaw Pact. Though this is often forgotten on both sides of the Atlantic, Americans were a minority part of NATO forces in Europe. The majority of the ground troops readied to fight in Germany were European.[66]

On the night of February 5–6, 1989, a twenty-year-old man, Chris Gueffroy, tried to cross the border from East Germany to West. Border guards riddled him with bullets. He would not be the last person to die that year trying to leave East Germany.

* * *

In other words, it is worth reflecting a little more on just what it would mean for the Cold War to end. As 1989 began, Gorbachev's country had just been staggered by a tremendous earthquake in Armenia that took tens of thousands of lives. In his New Year's Eve message he offered the hope that "a new vision of the world was being established" and that "the Cold War is starting to retreat."[67]

What might all that mean? For the outgoing Reagan administration in the United States as for British prime minister Thatcher, an end to the Cold War was being defined as:

1. Stabilize and reduce any danger from U.S.-Soviet rivalry in nuclear forces.

2. Defuse any major areas of tension in the U.S.-Soviet competition for influence or advantage in the Third World.

3. Persuade Moscow to respect the fundamental human rights of its citizens as a basis for full Soviet participation in the international community.

By these standards the results at the end of 1988 seemed impressive. The Reagan administration and its allies believed that the 1987 signing of the INF treaty and some progress toward a treaty on strategic nuclear forces (START) were accomplishing the first goal. They had finally persuaded Moscow to accept on-site inspection as a basis for verifying arms control.

Soviet withdrawal from Afghanistan and negotiated settlements in southern Africa were signs that the second goal was moving toward fulfillment. There had also been substantial though still uneven progress in the USSR's recognition of human rights.

But what about the basic issues at the core of the Cold War? What of overcoming the division of Europe? There were some soaring words. In 1982, President Reagan had told the British Parliament that his goal was to lead a "crusade for freedom" that would end only when it left "Marxism-Leninism on the ash heap of history."[68] Reagan also used the annual occasion of "Captive Nations Week" to launch rhetorical missiles against communist control and Soviet influence over the states of Eastern Europe, including the Baltic republics of the Soviet Union. His vice president, George Bush, appeared particularly convinced, delivering a provocative 1983 speech that denounced the postwar division of Europe.[69]

Yet Reagan's policies did not act on this rhetoric. In general, the Reagan administration and the Thatcher government avoided direct clashes with the Soviet government over the political division of Europe.

Reagan did give a memorable 1987 speech in Berlin, standing at the Brandenburg Gate and challenging Gorbachev to "open this gate" and "tear down this wall!" It was a speechwriter who had come up with these words, not the foreign policy professionals. One of the key aides to Shultz, a former U.S. ambassador to East Germany, remembers Reagan's speech as "unnecessary showboating," with its big words that "we fought as hard as we could." Reagan liked the way the words sounded and kept them in. It had no effect on policy. Shultz, in an eleven-hundred-page memoir, simply ignores Reagan's speech.

Reagan regretted what he had said. Unprompted, in September 1988 he told Shevardnadze that, "It had perhaps been unrealistic to have suggested [in 1987] that the Berlin Wall be torn down in its entirety." Reagan "realized that the division of Germany and of Berlin was a product of World War II, and the feeling on the part of the Soviet Union and many others that Germany should never again be allowed to be the strongest and most dominant power in central Europe." He just hoped that the two parts could work better with each other. "His proposals represented no attempt to interfere with anyone."[70]

None of this is meant to suggest that Reagan, Shultz, and Thatcher did not care about the division of Europe and Germany. They did.

But to them the postwar realities seemed fixed. Western defense should remain firm. The United States maintained a tough approach in the strategic nuclear arms talks. The NATO alliance had also just agreed, in May 1988, to modernize its shorter-range nuclear missiles in Europe.

Meanwhile the allies would try to make the tragic postwar system more livable, relaxing tensions amid the barbed wire and massed tanks. By those lights they were succeeding. Shultz left office in January 1989 worried that his successors in the Bush administration "did not understand or accept that the cold war was over."[71]

* * *

Nearly seventy years ago the English historian Herbert Butterfield criticized the tendency to write a "whig interpretation of history." What he meant was that historians all too often array the past before us with almost godlike powers, placing events into an order that seems to march logically from where we were to where we are, interpreting the past through the eyes of the present. "The total result of this method," wrote Butterfield, "is to impose a certain form upon the whole historical story, and to produce a scheme of general history which is bound to converge beautifully upon the present," preferably demonstrating "an obvious principle of progress."[72]

It is easy to fall into a "whig" interpretation of the end of the Cold War. As 1989 began, huge political forces had been set in motion across the socialist world.

But most of the choices that would determine the endpoints for those changes were still contested and incalculable. Gorbachev did want to "end the Cold War" and create a "common European home." He used those phrases. But he attributed a particular meaning to them. Events did not turn out in accordance with his plans. The "whig" historian, wrote Butterfield, "too easily refers changes and achievements to this party or that personage, reading the issue as a purpose that has been attained, when very often it is a purpose that has been marred."[73]

In 1989 all the key governments would begin making concrete choices about what to do. The Soviet leadership, more than any other, had put the ball in motion, making the first truly catalytic set of choices during 1988. What would come next?

In December 1988 the American president-elect George Bush asked Gorbachev what the Soviet Union would be like in three, four, or five years. The Soviet leader responded with a quip: "Even Jesus Christ couldn't answer that question!"[74]

CHAPTER 3

Hopes and Fears

"Dream Big Dreams"

In September 1988, Henry Kissinger wrote a long and public "memo to the next president." Back then there were not many Americans who could ask a national newsmagazine (*Newsweek*) to clear the space for a nearly five-thousand-word "memo" about the fate of the world. Kissinger could.

"The postwar era in international relations is coming to an end," Kissinger began.

This was much bigger than Gorbachev. "A new era cannot be based on ephemeral personalities," he explained. It would not be the first time that "the West deluded itself by basing its policies on favorable assessments of Soviet leaders." Moreover, Gorbachev "seems intent on weakening the Western Alliance" because the Soviet policy was "to diminish American influence, if not to expel us from Europe altogether."

The big issue was that Europe was about to be transformed. "The political structure of Europe—East and West—will thus emerge as the central issue of the '90s."[1]

Eastern Europe might again become a battleground, a "re-emergence of the competition between Teuton and Slav that produced two world wars." In some crisis Moscow might use force. If it did, "even as an act of desperation—Western euphoria will switch to hysteria."

Kissinger was dubious about more arms control. What Kissinger emphasized instead was the need "to create a *political* framework" to manage change, with a real political strategy behind it. He speculated about U.S.-Soviet arrangements that would give the Soviets "security guarantees (widely defined)."

Kissinger suggested, for example, "a drastic reduction of all outside forces in Europe—including those of the U.S.—might revolutionize present concepts of security." As these "outside forces" left, there could be "rapid progress toward West European integration."

"The time has come," Kissinger concluded, "for the first comprehensive discussion about the political future of Europe since the outbreak of World War I." And not just Europe. He foresaw the development across the world of "a new international order."

Weeks later, Reagan's vice president, George H. W. Bush, was elected as the new American president. Kissinger pressed his argument again.

"Empires do not disintegrate without convulsions," he warned. Without a full political understanding, "the two sides are working themselves—in the name of peace and arms control—into a classical European crisis of the kind that produced World War I." Any sustainable solution for Europe "must either include both the Soviet Union and the United States or exclude both." Again he suggested, as just one idea, that, at most, only small outside forces should remain in Europe.[2]

The "postwar" era was coming to an end. The whole political structure of Europe, West as well as East, was now back on the table, as it had not been for generations.

* * *

In Moscow, sitting with his Politburo colleagues as the year 1988 came to an end, Gorbachev wondered what the Americans would do next. Shevardnadze spoke up. He alluded to Kissinger's warning about Gorbachev. "Look what remained of [Kissinger's] theory after your [UN] speech," he said.

"Nothing remained," Gorbachev replied.[3]

Gorbachev expected conservatives in America and Europe to try to keep the Cold War going. They would either do nothing or take new steps that would "contribute to the arms race."

More "liberal circles," he said, welcomed the Soviet efforts to rescue socialism. He analogized what he was doing as comparable to the way the American president Franklin Roosevelt had rescued capitalism with his New Deal program in the 1930s.

Gorbachev expected the incoming Bush administration to be "centrist." It would probably not make matters worse. Nor would it do much to make them better. To Gorbachev, the new Bush group looked like "traditionalists" who "still do not have any foreign policy alternative to the traditional post-war course." They were still worried "that they might be on the losing side."

What, exactly, did the Soviets want the Americans to do? In his UN speech Gorbachev had stated three hopes. All had to do with arms control. He wanted the United States to move forward in the talks on strategic nuclear arms (START), chemical weapons, and conventional forces (CFE).

The arms control situation was not encouraging. Nothing had happened on either side that seemed likely to close the difficult gaps in the START talks. The discussions on banning chemical weapons were in an early stage and would depend on quite complex verification issues.

The CFE negotiations were just about to get under way and were on an enormous scale, with all twenty-three NATO and Warsaw Pact states participating in talks that covered Europe from the Atlantic to the Urals. Meanwhile NATO was planning to open up a whole new set of issues, with its plans to modernize short-range nuclear missile forces (SNF).

None of this, though, really spoke to the broader vision for the future of Europe, and the world.

* * *

At the end of 1988, as Gorbachev was comparing notes with his Politburo colleagues, Bush and his newly designated secretary of state, James Baker, were musing about Kissinger's big ideas. Baker asked for comments on Kissinger's arguments from the State Department's European bureau and the aide who would be his new policy planning director, Dennis Ross.

The bureau counseled that the United States should just stay on course. Ross, though, had a different view.

Ross had already worked with Bush, during the Reagan administration and in the election campaign. He had heard Bush say that it was time to "dream big dreams."

Ross agreed. "We're entering a period that is really unlike any we've seen throughout the whole post-war era," Ross wrote to Baker in December 1988, "and this is not the time to put our thinking in a strait-jacket."

He scorned the European bureau's advice as "more of the same." That would just "be content with the current trends, fostering them but not having to do much to fuel them."

Ross argued instead that the full potential for change could be more radical, as radical as Kissinger imagined. It really was a crossroads in world history.

But Ross did not like Kissinger's recommendations. First, he thought Kissinger was too negative about Gorbachev, that he "probably exaggerates the dangers."

Nor did Ross like the idea of seeking a U.S.-Soviet understanding about how to handle change in Europe. "We certainly don't want to create a new Yalta." Here he was referring to the argument that at the Yalta conference, in February 1945, Stalin and Franklin Roosevelt had disposed of the fate of Eastern Europe over the heads of its inhabitants.

The United States should have its own agenda for Europe's future, Ross argued. In the American agenda, the future of Eastern Europe and the rest of Europe should be front and center.

"The division of Europe symbolizes the continuation of the cold war. If we are entering a new era and if there is a great new potential, we ought to be willing to deal with that key symbol—and we ought to tell Gorbachev this."

Just because "we aren't prepared to accept or promote the 'Grand Design' in Europe as Kissinger has defined it, we ought not to be too constrained in our thinking and not simply reject new ideas. That's not the way to dream big dreams."[4]

* * *

Just before Bush took office, Kissinger offered to help set up the sensitive U.S.-Soviet political dialogue that he thought was now so vital. He suggested to Bush that, while in Moscow for another reason, he might meet with Gorbachev and explore a channel for secret discussions. Bush, Baker, and Bush's newly designated national security adviser, Brent Scowcroft, went along with this.

In his Moscow meetings, Kissinger repeated his argument for a political understanding about the future of Europe, "conditions in which a political evolution could be possible but a political explosion would not be allowed." He did not repeat his idea of a mutual U.S. and Soviet withdrawal from Europe. To Yakovlev, he said the U.S. presence in Europe was vital, if just as "a guarantee against the adventurism of Europeans themselves."

Gorbachev told Kissinger, "My view is that we should both keep an eye on Germany and by that I mean both Germanies. We must not do anything to unsettle Europe into a crisis."

On Eastern Europe, Gorbachev was philosophical. Life brings certain changes that no one can stop. But both sides should be careful not to threaten the other's security.

Kissinger proposed a secret U.S.-Soviet channel. In this channel, Scowcroft (also a former Kissinger aide) would represent Bush. On his side, Gorbachev designated former Soviet ambassador Anatoly Dobrynin. The plan was that the "political dialogue" in the channel could get going as early as March 1989.

It would be like old times, when Kissinger was President Richard Nixon's national security adviser and Kissinger-Dobrynin was his prime, secret connection to the Soviets, usually cutting out the secretary of state. Now it would be Scowcroft-Dobrynin.

Gorbachev pledged secrecy. Only he, Yakovlev, Dobrynin, and Shevardnadze would know about the channel. Dobrynin mentioned the Soviet desire to talk about China. "In 30 years they will be a nightmare."

As the meeting was wrapping up, Gorbachev became "pensive." He took a moment to reflect on what was happening at this moment in history. "I lead a strange country. I am trying to take my people in a direction they do not understand and many do not want to go.... But one thing is sure—whatever happens to perestroika this country will never be the same again."

Kissinger replied that if he were a historian, he would wonder why Gorbachev, a product of the old system, was so determined to change it.

Gorbachev answered, "wistfully," that "it was easy to see what was wrong. What is harder is to find out what works. But I need a long period of peace."

Kissinger's comment on this was that Gorbachev "was treading water with perestroika. He is looking to foreign policy as a way out. He will pay a reasonable price to that end."[5]

* * *

Two days after Bush received Kissinger's written report, Gorbachev phoned Bush to congratulate him on his inauguration. Bush promised to hear Kissinger's report in person. He added that we "would not necessarily believe everything [Kissinger said] because this was, after all, Henry Kissinger."

Bush then brought up the proposal of a secret U.S.-Soviet channel. There would indeed be a channel, but his spokesman in it would be James Baker.

Bush said that he hoped Baker, after he finished his consultations in Europe with all of America's allies, would establish the kind of tight relationship with Shevardnadze that Shultz had forged. He stressed that "Jim Baker was very close to him."

That ended any notion of a special Scowcroft-Dobrynin channel. It also effectively concluded Kissinger's role as a facilitator. The Baker-Shevardnadze discussions got under way on about the intended schedule; their first meeting was on March 7.

Baker apparently took care to be sure that Bush established that he, Baker, would be the point person in the U.S.-Soviet relationship. The point was not just about reaffirming Baker's primacy. Baker and his team also wanted to stay in the lead because they regarded Scowcroft and Scowcroft's new deputy, Robert Gates, as too cautious and conservative. For Baker, as for Bush, it was time to "dream big dreams."[6]

The Vectors of Change

During the next few months, between February and May 1989, the new American leaders conferred intensively with their counterparts in Western Europe, Canada, and Japan. Among them, an agenda emerged for a new

Europe and a different world. An operating partnership also began to emerge between the U.S. leaders and key counterparts in Western Europe who actively planned together.

What leaders did was to catalog their key problems and, reasonably systematically, start making choices about how to try and solve them. These choices would set vectors of change, providing a sense of direction and magnitude.

Just after taking office, before Baker set off on a flurry of trips to Europe and Asia and back to Europe, Bush met privately with Baker to go over their thinking about U.S.-Soviet relations.

To Baker, what was essential was that the changes in the Soviet Union were real. Gorbachev really was different. The jury was still out about how it would turn out.

Bush had noticed the public prediction from the Soviet dissident scientist Andrei Sakharov that Gorbachev might soon be overthrown.

Baker did not think the Soviet outcome depended on U.S. actions. But, he noted, even if the United States could only affect Gorbachev's prospects "on the margins," it did not want him to fail.

The U.S. could help frame the hard choices Gorbachev would have to make. It could do this with negative incentives, making it clear that military competition would not work. It could also use positive incentives, by "offering him the hand of partnership and by challenging him to give his slogans real content."

The United States, Baker thought, would soon have to muster its own initiatives, for instance on conventional arms control or on chemical weapons. "Let's honestly probe, and let's challenge him to be bold in actions, not only words."[7]

On this point, as on almost all others in foreign policy, Bush's and Baker's instincts were about the same. Although the media at the time and historians later would make much of a so-called pause early in the Bush administration, these commentaries misunderstand what was really going on. While there were a couple of doubting voices about Gorbachev in the new Bush administration, Bush and Baker were not among them. They agreed that they wished to find a way to help Gorbachev in a constructive way.

What they wanted to do was put their own stamp on U.S. policies. Bush and Baker did not think the policy positions they had inherited from the Reagan administration on next steps with the Soviet Union or on Europe were very interesting or promising. They had not inherited any pending breakthroughs or novel ideas in arms control, for example.

One of Baker's earliest priorities was in fact to distance the new administration from the Reagan administration's stance in Central America. He tried to achieve an early win by persuading Congress (done with great difficulty) to fund nonlethal assistance to the resistance in Nicaragua, then use the emerging peace process there to press the Nicaraguan government toward a solution.

* * *

Less than three weeks in office, Bush offered a revealing outline of his thinking in a relaxed meeting held in Ottawa with his friend, the Canadian prime minister, Brian Mulroney. Baker and Scowcroft were there too.

Bush underscored to Mulroney that this was an important phase for all of Europe. His plan, he said, was to think, consult with allies, and then "take the offensive, to save the Alliance, not just be seen as reacting to yet another [Gorbachev] move." Baker was about to visit with every NATO ally.

Maybe, Bush added, Eastern Europe was the key, to "get in there in *his* end zone! Not stir up revolution." The United States was right on human rights, on democracy, and on freedom. "There is a big opportunity for us in dealing with Eastern Europe," Bush explained, "if we can get our act together. There is a potential for economic cooperation, but there is also the danger," he added, "of pushing too far in Eastern Europe and causing the situation to get out of control, at which point the tanks might come in."

In addition to Eastern Europe, what, Mulroney asked, were Bush's priorities for the Western alliance?

Bush ticked off three. First, there was "Alliance solidarity," with particular concern about Germany. The urgent issue there was a hot emerging one about whether or how to go through with the 1988 NATO decision to modernize U.S. short-range nuclear forces in Europe, which above all meant in Germany.

Next was "moving ahead with the USSR." Baker had already flagged the need to come up with initiatives, at least in arms control.

Third, the United States needed a policy to deal with West European integration. The single European market was to take full effect in 1992.

Mulroney knew very well how strong protectionism had become in the United States, amid the general erosion of the Cold War trading system. Mulroney had just gone through the near-failure of the new U.S.-Canada trade agreement. Called in to save the deal by the Reagan White House, Baker (then the treasury secretary) had rescued it in the waning months of the administration. It had been a very close call.

Now the Europeans seemed, with the Single European Act, to be creating what could become a "Fortress Europe," the largest integrated market in the world. This could redouble protectionist pressures on both sides of the Atlantic. Bush said he wanted to find a way to sustain an open economic system.

Baker brought the discussion back to Gorbachev. He stressed that the administration did not want Gorbachev to fail. This was the Bush administration's position, even if there were some people in the United States who might disagree.

Perhaps feeling called out, Scowcroft added that he too wanted to "move forward" with the Soviet Union. But he wanted to think of ways to do it that could be reversed quickly if something happened to Gorbachev. He wondered what could be done to preempt Gorbachev strategically.

"That's the big issue," Baker chimed in, "and what we're seeking but don't yet have." The Americans would work on this. But, echoing the point he had made to Bush, "we *do* think that it's what happens in the USSR that will determine his success or not—not what the U.S. or the alliance does."

Mulroney had some advice that resonated with Bush and Baker. "Some smart politics by the President of the United States is in order—a trip, a statement, and an initiative in the near-term, at least by May or June."[8]

* * *

Bush and Baker started off at the run, as Baker visited all the NATO allies, then joined Bush in East Asia. Bush, the former World War II pilot who had flown missions against Japan, was going to the funeral of the emperor who had led that nation in wartime, Hirohito. Then Bush and Baker would head on to South Korea and China (a return to a country where Bush had been America's envoy in 1974–75).

Bush is often portrayed as a cautious, prudent "realist." A less schematic but more accurate assessment would find something different.

Bush was an intelligent and almost peripatetically restless man, a competitive college baseball player in his younger days now reduced to tennis, golf, fishing, horseshoes, or competing at anything else that came to hand. Unlike Reagan, a self-taught intellectual who loved thinking and writing about political ideas, Bush was more action-oriented than reflective.

Bush was never comfortable with prepared, public speeches. Here again he was unlike Reagan. He came across better in person than he did on television.

Though he was conversant on the issues, Bush's judgments about basic direction were often intuitive. His conversation and his correspondence (he was a frequent and faithful note and letter writer) are full of expressions like—later explaining how he and Gorbachev came to be able to "go around the world on issues"—"I thought I had a feel for his heartbeat."[9]

Bush's characteristic way of operating was to read, listen, and try to get to the essence of the tone or position he thought he should adopt. Once he thought he had the essence of it, he would then reach out to counterparts and talk it through with them in his own way.

* * *

When it came to hammering out the details, Bush would often turn that over to "Jimmy."

Few but George Bush would refer to James Baker that way. But, except for the pairing of Thomas Jefferson and James Madison, no president in American history had ever been this close to his secretary of state.

At the end of 1988, Bush and Baker had been almost brotherly friends for more than thirty years. They had gone through a lot together, from personal tragedies to political campaigns.

During the eight years of the Reagan administration, when Baker had been White House chief of staff and treasury secretary while Bush was vice president, Baker's political power on a given day had often been greater than Bush's. At one level they regarded each other as peers, with an undercurrent of rivalry that was part of their makeup. Yet Baker carefully separated two George Bushes in his mind, one the longtime friend and the other the person Baker would address even in small meetings as "Mr. President."

Like Bush, Baker was oriented toward action. Where Bush would look for an essential theme or stance, Baker would try to convert it into a practical strategy, mapping out and negotiating the details.

In history books, Baker often comes across mainly as a kind of political lawyer, acknowledged as tactically gifted, expert at negotiations, but not regarded as a policy strategist in the way outsiders perceive someone like Kissinger. Such an appraisal of Baker might be close to the mark when he was Reagan's chief of staff during Reagan's first term. But by the end of that term, and certainly by the time he had finished another term as a very active treasury secretary, Baker was accustomed to mapping international strategy on a large scale.

If strategy consists of charting just how to connect means and ends to get something done, including on a grand scale, Baker was the Bush administration's principal strategist. Most comfortable when focused on action, Baker, aware of some of his own strengths and weaknesses, constantly interacted with a small team mapping out ideas and sizing up practical ways to apply them in upcoming trips, meetings, or phone calls.

Integral to that small team were two veterans of the 1988 election campaign, which Baker had managed for Bush: Robert Zoellick, who had been the campaign's overall issues director, and Dennis Ross, the foreign policy lead.

Zoellick had worked for Baker at Treasury. Ross, who in the mid-1980s had been at UC Berkeley running a center on Soviet international behavior, was also a specialist on the Middle East. He had already served in government at State and Defense. In the Reagan White House, on the NSC staff, since 1986, he had worked closely with Bush. He knew Bush much better than he did Baker.

After Bush chose Baker as his secretary of state and Scowcroft as his national security adviser, Bush invited the forty-year-old Ross to take his choice of jobs. He could be the deputy either to Scowcroft or to Baker.

Ross chose to work with Baker. He knew he liked Baker's operating style and wanted to be closer to the fieldwork of diplomacy. Zoellick also turned down a top position on the White House staff in order to work on Baker's team. But the point is that Baker's team, like Baker, had good personal relationships with Bush.[10]

Zoellick and Ross then became Baker's two chief strategists at the State Department, Ross focusing on the Soviet Union and the Middle East and Zoellick on Europe and practically everything else. Zoellick was thirty-five, raised in the Midwest, near Chicago, and had earned joint degrees from Harvard Law School and the Kennedy School of Government before going into full-time government work.

Baker relied heavily on Zoellick and Ross. Until he brought in a new team during the second half of 1989, he had little confidence in the leadership of State's European bureau, believing that they had no new ideas about future strategies.[11]

The Bush-Baker relationship was practically symbiotic. To one former governor who later joined Bush's cabinet, Bush and Baker "seemed connected telepathically; each man appeared perennially aware of what the other was thinking and doing." Each was conscious of the other's strengths. Even when they had played tennis doubles together as winning club players, Baker remembered that Bush was "great at the net and I was great at ground strokes. We were both weak as servers."

When it came to foreign policy, Baker recalled simply that "there was no daylight between us. We really saw everything pretty much the same way."[12]

Baker would frequently see Bush alone, discussing what they would do next. Scowcroft would often be invited to sit in. When Baker later made a move, he could count on Bush to back his play.

Because Baker, Zoellick, and Ross had already worked so much and so recently with Bush, unlike Scowcroft or his staff, Scowcroft was, at first, a bit of an outlier. Bush and Baker had first worked with Scowcroft (and soon-to-be defense secretary Dick Cheney) nearly fifteen years earlier in the Ford administration.

Scowcroft was hardworking, discreet, and cautious. He had served most recently as a member of the Tower Commission, which investigated the Iran-Contra mess in the Reagan administration. The investigation had left Scowcroft deeply uneasy about the way Reagan ran his White House. Scowcroft looked for top-quality staff work, another deficiency he had observed in the Reagan White House.

After Ross turned down the job as Scowcroft's deputy, that concern about the quality of the staff work was a factor that drew Scowcroft to choose Bob Gates, a CIA career officer who had spent considerable time on the NSC staff. Gates was the CIA's deputy director during Reagan's second term. Well organized, disciplined, and extremely skilled at the day-to-day operations of government, he ran the deputies committee of top subcabinet officials so efficiently that full meetings of the National Security Council were rarely needed to clarify issues before they were presented to President Bush.[13]

Gates had been relatively outspoken in voicing skepticism about Gorbachev. In October 1988 he had given a speech that had so infuriated Secretary of State Shultz that Shultz directly confronted him about it and then tried to get him fired. Knowing this, during those early months in 1989, Baker and his staff kept a wary eye on Gates, to make sure the administration spoke with one voice.

The NSC staff office for Europe and the Soviet Union was led by Robert Blackwill. A career diplomat who had worked on Kissinger's staff in the 1970s (but did not share Kissinger's policy prescriptions for Europe), he was probably hired because Bob Gates remembered him well from their common service on the Carter administration's NSC staff. Scowcroft recalled Blackwill's "reputation for brilliance, laced with irascibility," a "forward-looking original thinker who reveled in finding ways to take advantage of the rapidly changing European scene." Some of the office's ideas turned out to appeal more to Bush (and Baker) than they did to Scowcroft.

Joining Blackwill were the authors of this book. Condi Rice, then a young (thirty-four-year-old) Stanford professor, was an expert on Soviet affairs. Scowcroft and Gates were both acquainted with Rice. She also knew and got along with Ross; they had both been part of the Berkeley-Stanford center on Soviet international behavior. To help on Western Europe and European security, Blackwill brought in Philip Zelikow, a thirty-four-year-old former trial lawyer who was then a career diplomat and a veteran of the conventional arms control talks.[14]

* * *

On March 7, Baker and Shevardnadze opened their channel with direct talks in Vienna on the margins of a conference of foreign ministers of all thirty-five European nations participating in the "Helsinki process," the Conference on Security and Co-operation in Europe (CSCE) that had been founded in 1973. They agreed on an agenda and exchanged their positions on the range of issues.

Shevardnadze stressed Soviet readiness to move on conventional arms control. The Soviets had shown their readiness to do something about armored forces. They pressed the United States to put aircraft, helicopters, and troop numbers on the table too.[15]

On strategic nuclear arms control, the START talks, one of Bush's first acts had been to replace the Reagan administration's START negotiator (Edward Rowny) with Richard Burt, who was transferred from his post as Reagan's ambassador to West Germany. The Burt pick was a loud signal, to those who remembered the battles over arms control in the Reagan era, that Bush was siding with those who wanted rapid progress in the START talks.

The issues holding up progress were difficult and technically complex, mainly about whether to ban strategic defense systems and how to handle cruise missiles. The important moves to break these logjams began later in 1989.

The new national security adviser, Brent Scowcroft, had launched a series of formal policy reviews that might develop a distinctive Bush administration approach. Historians have given these too much attention. Baker had gone along with Scowcroft's wish to have these reviews, but they made no difference for what Baker and his team were doing. "We treated that exercise as something to monitor and manage so it wouldn't bind us," Zoellick recalled, "but not to treat it in a serious way."[16]

Just before Baker's March 7 meeting with Shevardnadze, Scowcroft sent Bush a memo on "Getting Ahead of Gorbachev." Scowcroft's tone was wary. He warned against "early and dramatic proposals." He instead argued for "a sound strategy," laying out a set of sensible, conservative principles. The American ambassador in Moscow also had just sent back a set of similarly conservative policy suggestions.[17]

Meanwhile, Scowcroft's staff, like Baker's team, had already given up on the formal reviews. Both of us joined in a memo to Scowcroft telling him that the reviews "were not proceeding well."

We thought the analysis part of the Soviet work was fine, but "the policy half . . . is largely a restatement of last year's agenda, vague and unfocused." It "lacks any clear guide as to how the future may differ from the past and what we can or should do to shape it."

While the European bureau's work on Eastern Europe was more constructive, we thought the Western European work was even worse than the Soviet effort. We pointed out that, over at State, Ross and his aides "fully shared our negative assessment."[18]

Returning from his March 7 meeting with Shevardnadze, Baker also had a quite different sort of approach in mind. Baker sat down with Bush on March 8. He argued in favor of just the sort of early and dramatic proposals on Europe and the Soviet Union that, a week earlier, Scowcroft had warned against.

To Baker, all the debates about whether Gorbachev would succeed or fail seemed like "academic theology." Each side had their case. "What mattered to me were what actions we could take in the face of these two different possibilities."

The Soviet "new thinking" was not well defined. The United States should suggest some of the "content."

On the plan to modernize U.S. short-range nuclear forces (SNF), Baker had listened to the Europeans. He wanted to reconsider the U.S. position.

The worries about nuclear deterrence were linked to the conventional force position in Europe. On that key subject, "I'm less convinced we have ideas, much less the analysis to support them." Baker wanted Bush to ready a major conventional arms control move for the historic NATO summit meeting, celebrating the alliance's fortieth anniversary, scheduled for the end of May.

Baker thought a "small, reliable group" had to come up with really big ideas about the future of U.S. forces in Europe. He warned Bush that the bureaucracy would probably hinder or leak about any such bold effort. He stressed that the pace of change in Eastern Europe seemed to be picking up, "both political and economic," and the United States also needed to step up the pace in thinking about how to encourage those developments.[19]

Bush liked Baker's activist approach. Scowcroft too had to admit that his formal policy reviews did not seem to be producing any interesting ideas. In the second week of March, the word came down to us that it was time to disregard the formal reviews. We should go all out to develop a menu of ideas on all fronts concerning the future of Europe. This was not just about the Soviet Union. The wider future of Europe was in play.

In the flurry of policy development that followed, it is hard to follow all the moves without a map. So we offer an issue map.

With each issue there was a basic choice to make. These were not theoretical choices. They were actual, plausible ones debated at the time. Like switches that control the course of an aircraft, they would set the vectors of change.

This list roughly corresponds to the chronological sequence in which these issues were tackled during the spring of 1989, but that does not mean that one was necessarily more important than another. As policies evolved, new issues and new choices would emerge.

Issue Map

Ending the Cold War in Europe (Spring 1989)

Future of Eastern Europe	• Set goal of toppling the ruling Communist Party?
	• Offer Western aid?

Future of Soviet Union	• Another stage of confrontation or is this a new era?
	• Openness (glasnost) – how best to test this?
	• Nuclear arms control? Chemical weapons control?
European Integration	• Create an Economic and Monetary Union?
	• "Fortress Europe" or open global trading system?
Security in Europe	• Keep lots of foreign-deployed U.S. and Soviet forces?
	• Short-range nuclear forces? Modernize or withdraw?
	• What to do about the conventional military confrontation?
Future of Germany	• Put the German question back on the table?

To force the pace of new policy moves, Bush, Baker, and Scowcroft decided to create a series of action-forcing events. The White House and State teams mapped out a plan for two major European trips by the president in 1989. First, in the late spring, Bush would go to Western Europe, and there would be a NATO summit. Second, in the summer, Bush would concentrate on Eastern Europe, and this would culminate in the G-7 economic summit, to be held that year in Paris. The White House also planned a series of speeches in the spring in order to set the new vectors.

Because it would be months before Baker had a new team in place to run State's European bureau, in this early period Blackwill's NSC staff office became a critical engine room for churning out ideas. Along with Zoellick and Ross on Baker's team, they would become the "small, reliable group" that Baker had wanted.

* * *

Over in Western Europe, the prevailing mood was similar to that in Washington. Officials speculated about Gorbachev's future. French president Mitterrand had followed Kohl's October 1988 visit to Moscow with one of his own in November. He, foreign minister Roland Dumas, and their advisers regarded Gorbachev's nuclear arms control ideas as "romantic." They emphasized conventional arms control instead. They said they "were not subject to the 'Gorby-mania' they observed in Germany."[20]

Western leaders waited to see what would happen in the Roundtable talks in Hungary and Poland. They debated about the emerging single European market and emerging proposals to intensify an economic and monetary union. They worried about what it all meant for the Atlantic alliance. West European leaders joined in setting the vectors for change, driving much of the agenda. They did this through development of a different kind of direct operating partnership with the Americans.

* * *

In the early 1970s, bargaining between the U.S., the Soviet Union, and Western Europe sometimes seemed like a triangle in which each of the three sides would play off the others. Baker never tried to run a triangular game. He and Bush preferred an orchestrated, coordinated partnership.

Rather than operating that partnership mainly through a British-American transatlantic bridge, Bush and Baker consulted broadly and deeply with West European counterparts, especially with the West Germans. A Washington-Bonn nexus began to supplant the traditional Washington-London one. This came naturally to Baker, from his experience in working with economic issues and the Bonn-centered European Monetary System.

Though it is now practically forgotten, the NATO modernization debate about SNF (short-range nuclear forces, usually referring to missiles with ranges of zero to five hundred miles) was the great security issue in Europe in the first months of 1989. As part of the bargains surrounding the INF treaty of 1987, NATO had formally agreed that it would plod ahead with freshening these short-range forces, which would be the only U.S. nuclear missiles that would remain in Europe (in addition to the nuclear bombs that could be carried on aircraft). This commitment to modernize SNF had become one more token that, as tensions relaxed, America would not "decouple" its nuclear deterrent from European defense.

British prime minister Thatcher had no doubts. She devoted her first call to Bush after his inauguration to the "urgent" need to modernize SNF.

But, especially in West Germany, the prospect of another huge debate about putting in new American nuclear missiles was disheartening, especially with West German elections coming in 1990. These proposed new missiles would have so short a range that the most likely targets would be in places inhabited by Germans. Such a push seemed more and more bizarre in the age of Gorbachev.

To Gorbachev, getting reports on the allied debates, it seemed that "Baker traveled around Europe and he is in a panic: Europe is breaking away from their [American] control. Their society is reacting powerfully to our work."[21]

The Future of Eastern Europe

Early in February 1989, Gorbachev retreated from Moscow's snows to a well-earned vacation at Pitsunda, on the Black Sea coast, a longtime resort spot for Soviet leaders. He was in that pensive mood that Kissinger had sensed in mid-January, that perestroika was "treading water." The same day that he had met with Kissinger and wondered aloud about his "strange country," Gorbachev had confided to his aides, "We're walking on the razor's edge."

It is hard to avoid the impression that at some level, Gorbachev felt he had shot his bolt and now the future was starting to move out of his hands. He went to work on a new book, dictating main ideas and turning over the drafting to a team of writers led by Chernyaev. In early March the resulting four-hundred-page manuscript was ready for Gorbachev's review. It was to be entitled *1988: The Turning Point Year*. The book was never finished.[22]

During March, in Moscow the party leadership was getting ready for the democratic reforms that we described in chapter 2, the election of a reconstituted Supreme Soviet. The leaders had to select the "Red Hundred," the party members who would be guaranteed seats.

During March, in Warsaw and Budapest, Poles and Hungarians were hammering out their first moves toward some more inclusive and democratic government. Those agreements were to be implemented during the early summer.

Watching Poland and Hungary, the Soviet government ran a very secret policy review about how to get ready for possible changes in Eastern Europe. Remembering the Polish crisis in 1980–81, the Soviet government and the military were not at all eager to send in the tanks, shoot civilians, and crush new revolts, as they had crushed them in the old days.

The threat of Soviet tanks might help local communists who wanted to scare the dissidents. But Moscow did not actually want to send in the tanks. It did not want to assume the burden of having to fix or subsidize states that would not fix or finance themselves.[23]

As we mentioned in chapter 2, since October 1988 a few of Gorbachev's key advisers on this subject, like Georgi Shakhnazarov, had been urging leaders to get ready for upheaval. But to Shakhnazarov, this meant Moscow should get ready for restraint, to *not* send in the tanks.[24] In late January 1989, another senior aide on the CC Staff and America watcher, Vadim Zagladin, asked Gorbachev to authorize a "painstaking review" of Soviet policy on military assistance to foreign states in "extreme circumstances." Gorbachev had agreed.

On March 25 the review's conclusions were presented to Gorbachev in a ten-page report from Shevardnadze, Defense Minister Dmitry Yazov, and the head of the state foreign economic commission. They recommended that the Soviet Union assist its East European allies militarily only if there was an external, foreign attack. Gorbachev had already come to the same conclusion.

Zagladin suggested that the Soviet Union might wish to let the United States know about these important decisions. Moscow could reassure the United States, confidentially, that it did not plan to send in the tanks if there was a crisis.

On this point, the ministers disagreed with Zagladin. Such assurances to Washington would be leaked. Then "we would appear in the eyes of our allies to be conspiring behind their backs with the Americans regarding our obligations."[25]

Gorbachev had another policy review under way, also in secret, to review Soviet policy toward Western Europe. The new policy should develop Soviet ideas about a "common European home," turn them more toward a European focus, what he and Chernyaev thought of as "Mitterrand's approach." The goal was to have that new policy ready for a trip and speeches in Western Europe in July 1989.[26]

* * *

In late March the Washington press had been diverted by talk about Kissinger's supposed "Yalta II" plan for U.S.-Soviet management of change in Eastern Europe. That idea had been quashed secretly months earlier and was now dismissed publicly. Baker warned that no one should see some "signal that somehow we are getting together with the Soviet Union and carving up Eastern Europe."[27]

Like the secret group in Moscow, Bush and his team were getting ready for some new democratic process in Hungary and in Poland. The Bush team did not know about the policy review in Moscow. They did know that the Roundtable agreements would test Soviet tolerance.

In April, Bush delivered the first in the planned series of policy statements, this one on Eastern Europe. When Bush went to Poland and Hungary that summer, after the Poles held their first free elections, it would be the first visit by an American president to Poland since 1977 and the first such visit ever to Hungary.

The occasion of the speech was memorable for Bush, partly because it was his first foreign policy speech since his inauguration, and partly because he later learned that an assassin had been in the crowd hoping to kill him. Deterred that time by metal detectors, the would-be assassin tried to intercept Bush at two other locations before he was eventually arrested and jailed.

Speaking to a Polish American community in Hamtramck, Michigan, Bush quoted his inaugural address: "The day of the dictator is over.

The totalitarian era is passing, its old ideas blown away like leaves from an ancient leafless tree." The West, he said, "can now be bold in proposing a vision of the European future."

As Ross had argued back in December 1988, Bush looked beyond more arms control. Arms, he added in a conscious echo of Czech dissident Václav Havel, "are a symptom, not a source of tension. The true source of tension is the imposed and unnatural division of Europe."[28]

Should the U.S. offer aid? Internally, the Bush administration was divided about what aid the United States might offer. His administration felt constrained, dealing with the hangover of unsustainable public and private debt incurred during the Reagan years. Bush started with some moves on export credits and again rescheduling and writing down Polish public debt. No president had ever offered major economic assistance to a Warsaw Pact state and Soviet military ally.

But, in his speech, Bush held out the hope that America and international financial institutions, like the IMF, could do much more. As he had told the Poles in his vice-presidential visit, aid would be conditional. "Help from the West will come in concert with liberalization," he declared. "We're not going to offer aid without requiring sound economic practices in return."

Bush, Baker, Scowcroft, and Treasury Secretary Nicholas Brady had already started arguing about the size of possible aid to Eastern Europe. Brady stressed, accurately, that Poland had already gotten itself in deep trouble by borrowing and squandering money.

"Baker and I argued that the policy this time was different.... The dispute was emotional and irreconcilable," Scowcroft remembered.

Bush finally "directed that [he] wanted to see aid proposals—[and] hoped that, in a pinch, [the budget director] could find money." Since that budget director, Richard Darman, had been Baker's longtime deputy, there was a good chance that Baker could find the money he wanted. What eventually emerged was a substantial American aid program that was developed with Congress, turned into legislation, and passed into law during the next seven months.[29]

The truth was that in the summer of 1989 neither Bush nor any other Western leader was ready to tell the changing governments what exactly they should do. None of the Western governments had developed substantial plans that presumed to tell them how to go about transforming the whole economy of a communist country.

The United States looked to Western Europe for help in developing a wider agenda for assistance to Eastern Europe. They jumped into that common planning during the late summer of 1989, as the election results in Poland and Hungary electrified the world.

The Future of the Soviet Union

Since Scowcroft had agreed with his staff (and Baker) that the formal policy review on U.S.-Soviet policy was "going nowhere," late one March evening he told Blackwill and Rice, "See if you can write something that has more bite." Rice took the better part of a weekend to rough out a notional policy statement and then went over it with Blackwill and with Ross.

The essence of the paper was to throw the switch away from the grand strategy of "containment" that had guided policy toward the Soviet bloc during the Cold War. "For forty years" that was how the United States "had committed its power and will," but "a new era may now be upon us."

In the new strategy, "We may be able to move beyond containment to a U.S. policy that actively promotes the integration of the Soviet Union into the existing international system."

The paper then listed military and political conditions "that will support a cooperative relationship between Moscow and the West." These included a "smaller and much less threatening" force posture, renunciation of the principle of permanent international class conflict, permission for self-determination in Eastern Europe, a more pluralist and humane domestic political life, and at least a willingness to cooperate on other issues.

That document became the centerpiece of the president's first speech on policy toward the Soviet Union, an address at Texas A&M on May 17. "Beyond containment" became a catchphrase for Bush.[30]

The American concept was that the Soviet leadership was clearly moving toward or considering such fundamental changes. So the American stance was to spotlight the hope and spell out a set of goals, or tests, that could set clear, reasonable benchmarks for a Soviet shift to a cooperative world system.

Some Soviets disliked Bush's tone, with its Cold War concerns about Soviet behavior and posture. Others liked the basic thrust, which lined up with their new thinking, to end the Soviet Union's isolation from the international system.

Bush also made it clear, both in the speech and through Baker (who had just returned from Moscow, where he met with Gorbachev and Shevardnadze on May 10 and 11), that he hoped for Gorbachev's success. Bush's defense secretary, Dick Cheney, sought to offer a more skeptical and hawkish view.

The White House censored portions of a speech Cheney had prepared. Then Cheney gave a press interview indicating that Gorbachev could well fail. Baker felt great regard for Cheney from their work together in the Ford administration. But as he later recalled, "I picked up the phone. I called the President, and said, 'You can't have this.'"

Bush and Baker decided that the White House would put out a statement disavowing Cheney's comment. "And they [the White House press office] went out there and they cut the ground out from under Dick quicker than you could imagine."

Later in the year, in October, when he thought Gates was trying to voice a distinct view about Gorbachev, Baker would step hard on that too, and make a point of having done so. Bush and Scowcroft backed Baker up.[31]

* * *

In his speech, Bush proposed a specific test of Gorbachev's commitment to openness, to "glasnost." He revived an idea called "Open Skies." He proposed that the United States, the Soviet Union, and their allies should be willing to open their skies to multinational teams that could fly over and surveil military sites. Dwight Eisenhower had first tried out this idea in 1955, to head off an era of thermonuclear fear. Bush thought it was time to try again, and the new idea would include all the NATO and Warsaw Pact states.

Even though it had been developed by Blackwill and Zelikow on his own staff, Scowcroft thought the idea was old and "smacked of gimmickry." This dismissive view was echoed by Bush's political opponents and the press.

Bush did not agree with Scowcroft or the critics. "I thought we had a lot to gain" from Open Skies, he said. Although it was commonly believed that satellites already provided abundant information, there were many advantages to aerial imagery compared to satellite imagery, especially in that era.

Also, Bush's proposal would open up such access and transparency to at least twenty-three states, not just the superpowers. The initiative later led to a treaty. As this book goes to press, Open Skies flights continue in the United States and across Europe.[32]

Bush did agree with Scowcroft that it was best to delay a summit with Gorbachev until there was something "concrete" to do or announce. The press would place high expectations on what such a meeting might produce. But in July, Bush decided the time was right for the summit with Gorbachev, as soon as possible.[33]

The Future of European Integration

While the Americans were working on their policy ideas, the leading West European governments were busy too. On the subject of Eastern Europe or the Soviet Union, their views were similar to those in the United States.

What occupied a lot of their attention, though, was the future of the European project. Their issue, in the spring of 1989, was whether to take European integration to another stage, beyond the single European market, and develop a plan for European monetary union. The key initiative again emerged from the triumvirate of Kohl/Genscher, Mitterrand, and Delors.

Drawing on his life experience, especially out of the Second World War, Mitterrand was committed "to a peace-enabling rebirth of Europe in the process of its unification." This "was the great political passion of his life."

It was to preserve this cause of Europe that Mitterrand had made one of the most difficult decisions of his public life, in 1983, when (as is detailed in chapter 1) he had reversed his whole economic program in order to preserve the partnership with Germany and Europe. It had been his crucial "act of faith." He would remember it, and remind other Europeans of it, later in 1989.[34]

As for Delors, in Brussels, still the president of the European Commission, he had already achieved a stunning accomplishment in the Single European Act that had been signed in 1986. He had not rested on these laurels.

With the particular help of an Italian adviser, Tommaso Padoa-Schioppa, Delors pushed for another stage. They believed that a unified European commercial system had to be accompanied by allowing easy movement of capital across borders too. Thus, Delors and Padoa-Schioppa argued, a single European market had to deepen into some kind of economic and monetary union (EMU). The logic was strong that if countries had free capital movement and fixed or tightly coordinated exchange rates, they should move away from independent national monetary policies.

The West Germans liked the idea of free capital movement; the plan was less appealing to French finance officials and banks. Once more, the triumvirate guided change. Mitterrand's broad vision was shared to an exceptional degree by the West German coalition leaders, Helmut Kohl and Hans-Dietrich Genscher. They decided to join the EMU cause.

Pressed hard by his French counterpart, Roland Dumas, in February 1988 Genscher produced a memo that outlined the "Creation of a European Currency Area and a European Central Bank." He proposed that a committee of wise men develop the idea. A few months later, in June 1988, Mitterrand and Kohl came to an unwritten understanding that they would go ahead with a plan for free capital movement within Europe, in a wider plan for economic and monetary union. They persuaded other European leaders to at least let the work begin on the idea.

Delors would be in charge of working up the plan. Kohl insisted on the key role for Delors.

* * *

This plan for monetary union, surrendering West German control over their currency, was a huge step for Germans to consider. The stability of their D-Mark was a symbol for their pride in their whole economic success story since the war.

Kohl decided to help Delors confront the Bundesbank, the West German central bank. In July 1988 Kohl personally appeared before the bank's governing council.

He offered the central bankers a broad historical perspective. The EC might enlarge further, he predicted. There was also "great interest" in the EC in Eastern Europe (a remarkable statement to make at the time). Kohl also stressed how important it was to preserve the Franco-German partnership, which "went beyond the economic."

Mitterrand understood the German concerns. To his cabinet, in August 1988, he explained that "Germany is divided even though it remains a great country, a great people. It is deprived of the attributes of sovereignty. It insists on its power. Yet its power is the economy; the deutsch mark is its atomic force." Mitterrand did not know if he could integrate this power into a European union, "but I hope so."[35]

Many of the French did not share Mitterrand's pro-European vision. "It represented a cultural image that, within the Socialist Party, was particular to Mitterrand. In no sense did it embody the characteristic image and rationale of Franco-German relations and European unification to be found in the Foreign Ministry, the Finance Ministry, or even the Elysée." But, thanks to Mitterrand, the EMU project went forward.[36]

The British finance minister regarded this Delors-led planning process as a "disaster." He and Thatcher hoped that, since the West German Bundesbank's president and the head of the Bank of England were both on Delors's committee, they would torpedo the idea.

By the spring of 1989, this "Delors report" was being finished. Delors had eased the fears of his opponents by promising that the new European Central Bank would be "a Bundesbank-type" central bank: independent, an inflation fighter. The Bank of England head decided to be constructive and he did not sabotage the enterprise.

The plan very much envisioned that "a monetary union also requires some measure of fiscal union" of common budget policies. It did not necessarily require a single currency. But the plan would at least set up tight coordination among the national currencies.

Details leaked to the press in April 1989. The political debate went public. Dissenting, the Bundesbank's leader claimed the proposal was "completely unrealistic." The head of the Bank of England worried that others in his government were "going to clamp down on me because of all this independence stuff."[37]

The French finance minister was unhappy too. He attacked the plan as "too Germanic." France's central banker, who was helping Delors, stubbornly explained that he was doing his work directly for Mitterrand.

Though Delors kept him informed, Mitterrand was not interested in the details. What he wanted was enough political momentum to keep the process moving forward. His staff coordinated the maneuvers among the triumvirate (Paris, Bonn, and Brussels) and with Madrid, since the Spanish were chairs of the EC process during the first half of 1989.[38]

In the spring of 1989 there were two basic choices for what the West Europeans would do next about EMU. Either the governments would adopt the report or they would "shelve it and make it material for doctoral theses."[39] The first choice, adoption, meant that a new committee would get to work on writing a treaty.

Kohl was now uneasy and wanted to delay the work, at least until after his 1990 reelection effort was done. Mitterrand was against delay.

The triumvirate came up with a middle option. At their June 1989 summit in Madrid, European leaders adopted the report as a "sound basis for future work." They set up an intergovernmental conference to write the treaty, but then put off deciding when this conference would start or finish its work.[40]

Thatcher felt powerless to veto this result. It had not fixed an outcome. Having chosen to still stay outside of the existing European Monetary System, Britain had less leverage to tell others inside that system what they should do to improve it.

* * *

At this interesting time in the development of the European project, in the spring of 1989, Bush invited Mitterrand to come to his family's retreat on the Maine coast, in Kennebunkport. He also offered to speak about Europe's future, together with Mitterrand, on the same dais at Boston University.

The American administration had played practically no part in the advancing European argument about economic and monetary union. The Bush administration was awakening to the full significance of the way Europe was changing. Bush made a conscious effort to improve relations with Mitterrand and with France. Blackwill had pressed him to reach out to Mitterrand, and Bush had helped persuade a reluctant Scowcroft to go along.

It worked. Bush and Mitterrand renewed their acquaintance. They had known each other since 1981. The atmosphere in Bush's home was warm.

But their friendliness could only go so far. Bush asked Mitterrand to go out with him for a ride on Bush's cigarette boat, a racing-style motorboat.

"Mitterrand took one look at the boat and firmly said, 'Non.' "

Bush then asked Blackwill to go. A loyal civil servant, Blackwill did not feel quite able to decline. The ride, he recalled, "scared the bejabbers out of landlubber me, as the President drove like a maniac."[41]

Safe on dry land, Bush and Mitterrand reassured each other about their support for European integration. The two leaders found that their strategic outlook converged on other European issues too. The American vision for Europe's future as a whole was that the Cold War might end as all of Europe converged on shared fundamental principles. The European Community had become a magnet and precedent for this approach.[42]

Looking to institutions that embraced all of Europe, the Bush administration soon proposed that the pan-European political organization, the Conference on Security and Co-operation in Europe (CSCE), could do more too. It could promote pluralism by setting guidelines for how to hold free elections in Eastern Europe, as the Hungarian and Polish Roundtable talks were agreeing on their own tentative democratic experiments.[43]

In his policy address with Mitterrand, on May 21, Bush called attention to the coming single European market. This fed protectionist fears in the United States, as the world trade system seemed to be falling apart and Europe was now forming into an economic superpower.

From the start of the administration, Baker had warned the rest of the cabinet that European integration was "a major challenge; we need to make sure the result is outward-looking, not inward." This would require a "well-coordinated, consistent, active effort" by the U.S. government.

The Boston speech became the occasion for Bush "to make the strategic case for not letting our economic agencies declare war on the [European Community] at this point in history." Another part of that strategic case was that European integration was a powerful magnetic force "drawing Eastern Europe closer toward the commonwealth of free nations."

So, Bush told his Boston audience that "the postwar order that began in 1945 is transforming into something very different." In language that was heard loud and clear on the other side of the Atlantic, the American president declared that, whatever others may say, "this administration is of one mind. We believe a strong, united Europe means a strong America."[44]

Later that month, Bush had a chance to reiterate this message directly with Delors in Brussels. Two weeks later, in Washington, Delors returned the visit. Delors told the Americans that the monetary union could follow the huge work associated with the single European market ("EC 92"). The Americans expressed no concern about the "Delors report."

Instead, what Bush and Baker wanted was an understanding about where all this would go. They wanted to head off the danger of an integrated European economy becoming an economic Fortress Europe. That meant they wanted a hard linkage to link completion of EC 92 to a new agreement on global trade.

The negotiations to create this global trading system were called the "Uruguay Round" in the framework of the old GATT system. This round of global trade talks, ultimately involving more than 120 country signatories, was the most ambitious ever launched since the original framework was created in 1947.

It was called the Uruguay Round because, after four years of exploratory work, the round had been launched in 1986 at a meeting at Punta del Este, Uruguay. It had the most ambitious negotiating mandate ever attempted. The new global trade agreement was, in theory, supposed to conclude at the end of 1990.

Delors agreed. A single European market and a conclusion of the Uruguay Round had to run together. He agreed that Europe should not have one without agreement on the other.[45]

Security in Europe

On March 30, sitting around the Oval Office with an informal group of his top advisers, President Bush chaired a meeting to brainstorm about the whole future of Europe—the list on our earlier issue map. This meeting set a pattern of informal sessions among just a small group of principals.[46]

Scowcroft kicked off the meeting with an initial presentation. One of the big questions they took up was the vision for the future of U.S. and Soviet forces in Europe. Associated with that was the concept for what conventional arms control in Europe might achieve.

Scowcroft had been intrigued by Kissinger's original idea of a mutual withdrawal, perhaps of all foreign forces at least in Central Europe. He asked Blackwill about it, who was appalled. Scowcroft liked the idea as a way of getting Soviet forces out of Eastern Europe. His staff had warned that such Soviet forces would still be in the European USSR, while U.S. forces would be going back over the Atlantic Ocean.

Undeterred, Scowcroft broached the idea in the Oval Office session on March 30. He recalled that "Dick Cheney looked stunned, and replied that it was too early to consider such a fundamental move."

Baker tried a different tack. He wondered about just withdrawing all tanks, since they were so essential to an offensive military posture.[47]

After that first skirmish, there was a burst of further work. The United States and its allies kept going back and forth during April about how to address the European security issues, both SNF and conventional forces. West German, British, and U.S. envoys crisscrossed the Atlantic searching for common ground. The Dutch foreign minister also played a helpful role.

Back to Moscow in early May, where he met with Gorbachev and Shevardnadze, Baker encountered more Soviet offers about what they were prepared to do about their short-range nuclear forces. Baker came back to Washington feeling fed up. He was now determined to find some way to pull back from the controversial 1988 NATO decision to modernize SNF.[48]

Baker's impatience was matched at the White House. Gorbachev would be making a triumphant visit to West Germany and France in June. Bush's staff had the sense that here he was, the toast of Europe, and they were fighting over whether to deploy more nuclear missiles there.

* * *

Blackwill and Zelikow had developed a plan for a major move on conventional forces. Armed with these ideas, Scowcroft and Baker talked about how to move forward. Together, they arrived at a key insight.

They agreed to fuse two problems—SNF and conventional forces in Europe—into one solution. A breakthrough on conventional arms control would help Gorbachev. It would enlarge and accelerate the withdrawal of Soviet tanks and troops out of Eastern and Central Europe. It could also defuse the quarrel over the short-range nuclear forces.[49]

The SNF part of the idea was to put off *both* modernizing and negotiating about the shorter-range nuclear forces. U.S. nuclear forces were supposed to offset the Soviet advantage in conventional forces. Very well. Then, first complete the CFE treaty. That would reduce and equalize conventional forces in all of Europe. Then the specifics of the nuclear deterrent would not be quite so vital.

That strategy required a plan to finish the CFE treaty very soon. To make that credible, the NSC staff proposal was that the United States would move toward the Soviet position in the talks.

The Soviets and their allies had offered to go along with reductions to common ceilings in tanks, artillery, and armored fighting vehicles. These were potentially huge reductions, involving the elimination of tens of thousands of weapon systems.

In return, what Moscow insisted on was that the NATO side reciprocate and put its strengths on the table too. If the Soviets would reduce these key ground force weapons, they insisted on Western agreement to similar reductions in two categories of weaponry where the West had at least a qualitative edge: combat aircraft and helicopters.

This Soviet proposal was quite controversial in Western capitals. Bush went along with his staff's proposal. He decided he would agree to include the proposed ceilings on aircraft and helicopters, as the Soviets had proposed. He would lead the NATO alliance to agree to offer such a deal.

Bush approved another U.S. move. The United States would offer to set a common ceiling on American and Soviet troop numbers on foreign soil in Europe. Bush personally pushed the Pentagon to come up with a manpower number that would represent a significant cut by the United States. The final number they came up was 275,000. This ceiling was about 15 percent below the existing U.S. troops deployed in Europe, then about 320,000.[50]

Bush, Baker, and Scowcroft were not trying to implement Kissinger's idea of a withdrawal of both U.S. and Soviet forces out of Europe. They thought their proposal would greatly reduce the Soviet forward presence while retaining a strong anchor for the United States to stay coupled to Europe's defense. They were not trying to abandon forward defense. By offering ways to adapt, they could preserve the essence of it.

Since the Soviets had so many more forward-deployed troops, this common ceiling would require a much larger drawdown of the Soviet troop presence in Eastern Europe than anything Gorbachev had proposed so far. Gorbachev's well-known proposal of December 1988 announced a unilateral plan to withdraw about 20 percent of Soviet divisions from Eastern Europe. The American (and NATO) proposal would require withdrawal of more than half of the Soviet forces stationed in their forward, foreign bases in East Germany, Czechoslovakia, Poland, and Hungary.

The Defense Department opposed these CFE moves. Cheney argued that the proposal would "unhinge the Alliance" and that the "British and French would go crazy." The Joint Chiefs of Staff chairman, Admiral William J. Crowe, joined the opposition. He called the proposal "PR" moves that would put "forward defense" at risk.

Bush overruled the objections. He sided with Baker and Scowcroft. Those in the meetings remembered that Bush "was the most forward leaning of all." "I want this done," he said. "Don't keep telling me why it can't be done. Tell me how it can be done."

* * *

Baker's deputy, Lawrence Eagleburger, and Scowcroft's deputy, Bob Gates, were secretly dispatched to Europe to tell allies what the United

States had in mind. Their trip was bracketed by presidential phone calls and more envoys exchanged with the Germans.

Thatcher did not care for the plan. Gates recalled, "We both felt like schoolchildren called before the principal for committing some unspoken dastardly act."

Kohl, on the other hand, was "ecstatic." All the allied leaders ultimately went along.[51]

Baker and Zoellick hammered out an agreed document at the NATO summit codifying the deal among the sixteen allied presidents and prime ministers. SNF decisions would be deferred to later negotiations with the Soviets, with a "zero" solution ruled out. The CFE proposal would be advanced. As Bush privately explained at the time, "Some say we're cold warriors, that we don't want Gorbachev to succeed. I've made clear that's not the case."[52]

Gorbachev and Shevardnadze welcomed the NATO moves. Such a CFE treaty would drastically change the whole defense posture of the Soviet Union, in the context of a mutual agreement. If achieved, CFE would be the most ambitious arms control treaty ever concluded. The CFE talks did in fact take off and made rapid progress.[53]

Bush's conventional arms control/SNF joint initiative came as a complete surprise to the gathered journalists. The episode, along with the way the huge SNF shadow had suddenly dissipated, lifted the way Bush was perceived in Europe and also boosted the new Bush team's self-confidence.

Bush and his team tended to rely thereafter on the improvised and secretive policymaking processes they had used in the spring of 1989. A bit bemused by the acclaim that greeted the summit outcome, Bush reminded reporters three days later, "I'm the same guy I was four days ago."[54]

The Future of Germany

In mid-March 1989, Blackwill and Zelikow drafted a deliberately provocative memo that declared, "Today, the top priority for American foreign policy in Europe should be the fate of the Federal Republic of Germany."

The Kohl government was expected to go to the polls the next year, in December 1990. It was expected to be a very close election.

Bush's advisers urged him bluntly to do what he appropriately could to "help keep Kohl in power." Kohl's "government is now lagging in the polls behind an opposition that, as currently constituted, has too little regard either for nuclear deterrence or for conventional defense."

The NSC staff argued that the broad goal of U.S. policy in Europe "should be to overcome the division of the continent through acceptance of common democratic values." Gorbachev was proposing a "common European home" divided into different rooms by social systems, alliance structures, and historical realities. Instead of that, the United States would propose a vision for a "commonwealth of free nations."

In the same memo to Bush, Scowcroft signed off on a principle, though he was uneasy about it, that the United States should be willing to put German unification back on the table. The United States should "send a clear signal to the Germans that we are ready to do more if the political climate allows it."

The State Department's European bureau, headed by a former ambassador to East Germany, had been scornful about ideas to jeopardize the hard-won Cold War status quo. Zoellick later recalled that when, in early 1989, he had asked a visiting West German colonel about German attitudes toward unification, the bureau chief sharply observed that unification was "the subject that all Americans are interested in and no German cares about."[55] Scowcroft too shared some of these doubts. But Blackwill and Zelikow pushed the point.

Bush marked up the memo and noted to Scowcroft that he had "read this with interest!" He liked the forward-looking tone. He regarded himself (in his words) as "less of a Europeanist, not dominated by [that] history."[56] He noticed when Scowcroft flagged the issue of German unification at their March 30 brainstorming session. Baker too, urged on by Zoellick, was open about possible German futures.

Bush began saying publicly, as he put it in a May interview, that he would "love to see" Germany reunified. He added, "Anybody who looks back over his shoulder and then looks at the present and sees a country ripped asunder by division, a people ripped asunder by political division, should say: 'If you can get reunification on a proper basis, fine.'"

When then–Vice President Bush had visited the German city of Krefeld in June 1983, at the height of the mass demonstrations against Euromissile deployment, the new Federal Republic chancellor, Helmut Kohl, had taken time to get to know the American. Bush recalled demonstrators slinging rocks at his car without any security counteraction ("Our Secret Service would have shot them!") and sitting in a garage with Kohl waiting for a route to clear.

West Germany, Bush remembered, was a society willing to pay the price for free speech. Though the first to admit he was not clairvoyant and "can't claim to have understood everything that would happen in Europe from Day One," he had concluded that West Germany was a solid democracy. It had done penance for its sins, and "at some point you should let a guy up."[57]

The NSC staff advice helped encourage Bush to feel that it was okay for him to support possible German unification. Scowcroft was slower to come around to this view.[58]

* * *

With Bush already thinking and talking about German unification, when Bush met with Mitterrand in May, he asked the French president what he thought about the prospect of German unification.

"As long as the Soviet Union is strong, it will never happen," Mitterrand replied. Perhaps such a thing might be possible "after ten years" and a "disruption [*dislocation*, in French] of the Soviet empire." But at this time the Soviets would oppose this "with force." They have other problems and "won't take a chance on reunification."

Bush pressed. What was Mitterrand's own view?

"If the German people wished it, I would not oppose it," he answered. "But not enough has changed since World War II to permit it."

In any case, he said, he could not see how it would happen. The Soviets would not permit it and "Gorbachev is very happy that East Germany is the most reactionary [government in the East bloc]."[59]

This quizzing of Mitterrand about German unification set a pattern. In his meetings at the end of the month in Europe, Bush kept asking European leaders what they thought of the idea of German unification. None were quite as forthcoming about German wishes as Mitterrand had been. All were at least as cautious about any immediate moves.[60]

Talking with the press after the NATO summit, Bush reaffirmed that he would define the end of the Cold War as an end of the division of Europe. "Our overall aim is to overcome the division of Europe and to forge a unity based on Western values."[61]

Reporters talking to Bush on the final stop of his trip in London were struck by his emphasis on the potential for change in Eastern Europe. Although the region was relatively quiet at the moment—a week before the Polish parliamentary election and shortly before other states in the region would experience serious unrest—Bush called Eastern Europe "the most exciting area for change in the world." According to one journalist, he "came back to [Eastern Europe] time and again in response to questions on other subjects."

What did "beyond containment" mean? the reporters asked. Bush answered, "It means a united Europe. It means a Europe without as many artificial boundaries."[62]

In a follow-on visit to West Germany, Bush gave a major speech at the Rheingoldhalle in Mainz, the capital of Rheinland-Pfalz, where Kohl had risen to political prominence. The West's goal now, Bush proclaimed, was to "let Europe be whole and free."

"To the founders of the Alliance, this aspiration was a distant dream," Bush added, "and now it's the new mission of NATO. The Cold War began with the division of Europe. It can only end when Europe is whole. Today it is this very concept of a divided Europe that is under siege."

Alluding to Gorbachev, Bush observed that "there cannot be a common European home until all within it are free to move from room to room." He called for the Iron Curtain to come down: "Let Berlin be next."[63]

Having introduced the volatile language of unity to his German audience, Bush then used carefully phrased language. "We seek self-determination for all of Germany and all of Eastern Europe," he declared.[64] Bush's remarks delighted many Germans, who were quick to infer that he hoped the seemingly frozen German question might thaw.[65]

West German officials hoped that the GDR might begin a process of internal reform, like that in Poland or Hungary. They also believed that such reform might be "easier if the GDR was not challenged by the question of territorial unification." Once the East Germans had democratic rights, anything might be possible. But for the time being they preferred not to talk about unification. Instead they wanted to emphasize human rights for East Germans.[66]

For the moment, the West German government was not ready to take on Bush's May hints of support for unification. In July 1989, Horst Teltschik, Kohl's foreign policy adviser, repeated the point West German president Richard von Weizsäcker had made years earlier, namely, that "for us, the German question is not primarily a matter of seeking a territorial solution."[67]

Bush's rhetoric was duly noted by diplomats and commentators in West Germany, but one reporter quoted the prominent West German professor Karl Kaiser's comment: "You Americans have taken our reunification debate far more seriously than we have." The Soviets, Kaiser said, simply would not allow a political reunification of Germany.[68]

Teltschik recalled later that the United States "was far ahead of the Germans at this time" on the issue of unification. He did not necessarily mean far ahead in wisdom or in desire for unification. It was just that some Americans were readier to raise a subject that West German leaders, for reasons that varied from person to person, judged they still needed to handle with reticent care.

This reticence masked real differences among West Germans. Some no longer even wished for unification, regarding it as a dangerous illusion that might inflame older German pathologies. Others felt strongly about holding on to the possibility of unification, but did not think the time was right to press the point. Latent German attitudes about unification therefore remained beneath the surface, unexpressed, unexamined, and uncertain, until circumstances changed dramatically during the second half of 1989.[69]

* * *

In his Mainz speech, Bush had also described the West Germans as "partners in leadership." This was not an empty expression. The spring 1989 diplomacy cemented a true core partnership between the U.S. and West German governments, in the sense of joint planning and coordination of policy moves.

Since the United States first began learning the habits of true coalition planning, in 1941–42 and beyond, the usual habits of core partnership were Anglo-American. Washington and London also shared intelligence to an unusual degree, routines that were extended to Canada, Australia, and New Zealand as well.

The Anglo-American core had been the default pattern of the Reagan administration. Reagan and Shultz got along well enough with Mitterrand and his ministers, or with Kohl and Genscher, but the relationships were not close enough to become policymaking partnerships.

In the first half of 1989, Bush and Baker had changed this pattern. There is no evidence that they deliberately set out to do so. It evolved that way as they worked to orchestrate common views about Europe's future. The American-German partnership became central and remained so for years.[70]

The routines of interaction with London remained strong, especially at the working level. But British diplomats assigned to Washington and to Bonn quickly sensed "a shifting balance of power in the alliance as between US/UK/FRG." They reported that "we are no longer regarded as necessarily the best interpreter between the US and Europe."[71]

Later in 1989, as the great issues of Germany's and Europe's future became acute, Blackwill delicately shared his concern, with a senior British diplomat and friend, that Thatcher's estrangement from other European leaders undermined the White House's ability to work with Britain. Thatcher's hostility to the French and dismissiveness about the Germans made Bush uncomfortable. Blackwill's friend, who had worked for her, doubted that anything could be done to "change her basic views and reactions."

The friend thought the United States might help manage German issues "by strengthening the European structures within which this might be done." Blackwill confirmed Bush's personal commitment to "the development of 'Europe'" and added that he thought the "White House was ahead of the State Department in this regard."[72]

Bush's good relationship with Mitterrand complemented the strong relationships with the West Germans. The Americans were therefore now linked firmly with the Kohl-Mitterrand-Delors triumvirate shaping broader policies within Europe and in the EC. By the middle of 1989 all these governments were therefore unusually well positioned to pull together as they entered the rapids.

* * *

Gorbachev and Bush were both soon back in Western Europe. Breaking away from his consuming domestic troubles, Gorbachev had a triumphal visit to West Germany in June and another to France early in July.

During Kohl's visit to Moscow in October 1988, the chancellor had spoken publicly, as he always did, about his hopes for the ultimate unity of the German nation. Publicly Gorbachev had repeated that history had divided Germany and that any attempt to change the situation with "unrealistic policies" would be "unpredictable and even dangerous."[73]

Kohl and Genscher each debriefed Bush on the meetings with Gorbachev. Bush asked Genscher specifically about whether unification had come up. Genscher replied that "Gorbachev had asked the West Germans not to talk too loudly about reunification but rather to let events take their course—toward a more cooperative and integrated Europe, not a reestablishment of the German Empire."[74]

The elderly East German party boss, Erich Honecker, traveled to Moscow two weeks after Gorbachev left Bonn. Gorbachev reassured him that he had adhered to traditional principles. Gorbachev did not want to destroy the East German state; he hoped it would reform. He believed that socialism had put down deep roots in East Germany and could weather its own version of perestroika.[75]

Gorbachev had insisted to Kohl that outsiders should not meddle in what was going on in Eastern Europe. "If anyone tried to exert influence from the outside, this would lead to destabilization and a loss of confidence and would endanger the understanding between East and West."[76] He complained that some of Bush's statements amounted to such meddling, though he declined to identify which ones. When Kohl debriefed Bush, he did not mention Gorbachev's complaint.

Gorbachev's visit to Paris a few weeks later (July 4–6) was another kind of victory tour. Mitterrand treated him as a great statesman. Even more flattering, he treated Mikhail and Raisa Gorbachev as kindred spirits, fellow intellectuals. Mitterrand even confided to Gorbachev that he did not think Bush was a very "original thinker." Gorbachev came away feeling that Mitterrand proved that "at last Western leaders believed in perestroika."[77]

Gorbachev gave his long-planned speech to the European Parliament, in Strasbourg. He elaborated on his concept of a "common European home" as a place that would "replace the balance of forces with a balance of interests."

But what would this mean? Gorbachev envisioned an all-European system of collective security, the emergence of a vast economic space from the Atlantic to the Urals, concern for the common environment, and respect for human rights.

He called for another CSCE summit of all thirty-five European member states, the first such meeting since the summit in Helsinki in 1975. The United States agreed with this initiative. The CSCE summit was scheduled for November 1990, in Paris.[78]

The Chinese Solution

On May 15, 1989, as the Bush administration was completing its internal debates on the SNF-CFE policy move in Europe, Gorbachev descended into the noisy epicenter of a vast and public debate about the future of the socialist world. His airplane landed in Beijing.

The Chinese leadership had to conduct the welcoming ceremony at the airport, instead of the more traditional location outside the Great Hall of the People, because they feared that demonstrations would disrupt the ceremony. China's people were in the midst of a massive confrontation with their government. Mass protests had been getting larger and larger for a whole month. Hundreds of thousands of mostly young demonstrators had come out into the streets, many of them students, centered in Beijing but also gathering in cities all over China. Their demands, their challenge, was for a freer press, more rule of law, and more democracy.

Obviously, Gorbachev could understand such demands. His visit was inspirational for many of the protesters. He had led the way with introducing such ideas about openness, accountability, and democracy into hitherto closed communist systems.

The new Polish elections would be held in June. Also in June, the Hungarian government would begin negotiations about the political future with a Roundtable of other representatives from Hungarian unions and civil society.

The initial Soviet elections, the ones Gorbachev and his team had set in motion during 1988, had just concluded at the end of March. The thousands of newly elected delegates to the Congress of People's Deputies would soon meet for the first time, a week after Gorbachev returned from China.

For Gorbachev, the new Soviet experiment had certainly complicated his politics. In 1988 it had seemed that there were two main camps. There were the reformers (aligned with Gorbachev) and there were the conservatives, the party apparatchiks who resisted change and openness.

Now, in the first half of 1989, Gorbachev's reform faction watched opposition come at them from three directions. There were still the conservatives, who had used the way the election had been structured to retain a majority in the new Congress of People's Deputies. But now the critics who thought the reform movement was much too slow, who called themselves "democrats," had gained much more strength. They were led by the aging dissident scientist Andrei Sakharov, and Boris Yeltsin, who had won an at-large district in Moscow and returned to the national stage.

Finally the national groups, seeking to detach themselves from Moscow's rule, were walking on stage. Representatives of the three Soviet Baltic republics (Estonia, Latvia, and Lithuania) were leading the way.

Just a few days before he arrived in China, Gorbachev had assured his Politburo colleagues, "We shouldn't identify the popular fronts [in the Baltics], which are supported by 90% of the population, with extremists." We have to "think, think, think how in practice to transform our federation. Otherwise everything will really collapse." But of course, he said, "the use of force is out of the question."

As Gorbachev knew well, the use of force had already come back on the table. In early April nationalist protests had been held day after day in the southern USSR, in Tbilisi, the capital of the Soviet republic of

Georgia (and Shevardnadze's home). On April 9, Interior Ministry troops, joined by regular army soldiers, attacked the demonstrators. Hundreds of civilians were injured and about twenty of them were killed. Finger-pointing had already begun about who was to blame, with some even saying that Gorbachev had acquiesced.[79]

* * *

Gorbachev had not come to China to offer advice about reform. He had come to turn a page in Sino-Soviet relations. The two communist powers had definitively split apart since 1960 and, as Deng told Gorbachev, China had regarded the Soviet Union as its most dangerous enemy for much of the 1960s and 1970s. That era had now passed. Now it was time to "normalize" relations. That was the main purpose of the visit.

Yet in the Chinese city of Taiyuan, on the day of Gorbachev's arrival, more than ten thousand students had gathered from around their province of Shanxi. One of their slogans was, "Where is China's Gorbachev?"[80]

* * *

China did have its own "Gorbachev" among its leaders, at least two of them in fact. Its current party general secretary, Zhao Ziyang, and his predecessor, Hu Yaobang, held views about their countries and socialism that were very similar to Gorbachev's.

Imagine that when Gorbachev came to power in 1985, his mentor from the "old guard," Yuri Andropov, had still been alive. Suppose Andropov, regarded by all as the senior statesman, had just chosen to step back from day-to-day authority in order to let the younger reformer, Gorbachev, take over the day-to-day work. Imagine too that Andropov had supported Gorbachev but also kept key conservatives in their places on the Politburo as the debates over reform heated up during 1988 and on into 1989.

Such was the scenario in China. Deng had stayed in the background, yet was regarded by all the leaders as the paramount authority.

Deng was eighty-five years old in 1989. He had empowered the reform leadership of Hu Yaobang. Zhao Ziyang, working for Hu as an economic reformer, recalled him as a "generous and tolerant man" who wanted to open up China to intellectual argument and believed, as Hu put it in a draft doctrine, that "the most important [negative] lessons learned during the development of socialism were: first, neglecting development of the economy, and second, failing to build real democratic politics."[81]

Amid an initial wave of protests and controversies from China's reforms, Hu had been forced to resign in 1987, accused of "bourgeois liberalization." He had stayed on the Politburo and Zhao Ziyang took his place. When Hu died in April 1989, it was public sorrow about his passing that had set off the first wave of protests that had now grown to such an enormous scale by the time of Gorbachev's visit.

At first, Zhao had been happy to put issues of political reform to one side. But by the time Gorbachev visited, amid the enormous and growing protests, Zhao had come to believe that some sort of structural program of political reform was a necessary companion to the economic liberalization.

As he and Gorbachev sat down to talk, the discussion quickly turned to the student protests (a topic Deng had ignored). They quickly saw eye to eye.

Zhao said the students often looked at things "naively, simplistically," but clearly should be heard and understood.

Gorbachev commented that "we, too, have hotheads." Both attacked the forces that refused to consider change.

Zhao opened up. "Here we speak the same language with you. I think that at the present time the socialist movement has really entered a decisive stage." He continued, "Many young people are asking: who has the advantage now, socialism or capitalism. The youth has a hard time imagining the degree of backwardness of pre-revolutionary China or of old Russia. Besides, even under the socialist regime, mistakes of subjective nature were made," including in China. "The advantages of socialism can manifest themselves only through reforms; only they can increase its attractive force."

The two men again agreed. They discussed the difficulties they had encountered with enacting price reforms that would introduce market incentives (Zhao called them "the law of value"). They exchanged views on how to secure the rule of law and sustain an independent judiciary.[82]

It might have been the start of a beautiful friendship.

* * *

The next day, Deng chaired a Politburo meeting and told his colleagues that the situation in the streets had become intolerable. "Especially in Beijing, the anarchy gets worse every day.... If we don't turn things around, if we let them go on like this, all our gains will evaporate, and China will take a historic step backward.... If things continue like this, we could even end up under house arrest." The Chinese had been tracking developments in Europe and wanted to contain the virus.

The Politburo decided to bring in the army and declare martial law. "The aim of martial law," Deng declared, "will be to suppress the turmoil once and for all and to return things quickly to normal." Zhao objected to the plan. He was overruled, Deng told him. "The minority yields to the majority." Zhao accepted party discipline, but the next day drafted his letter of resignation, complaining of ill health.[83]

By May 17, the day after Deng and Zhao met with Gorbachev, security authorities estimated that 1.2 million people in Beijing had joined the demonstrations, coming from all walks of life, calling for a change of leadership. Students on hunger strikes were collapsing one after another.

The government declared a state of martial law on May 19. Troops moved in. The protesters did not disperse. Zhao and his supporters were purged from their posts. The fighting began on June 3 and escalated on June 4.

There were protests and confrontations in cities throughout China. In their initial internal exchanges as the fighting subsided, party leaders referred to about seven thousand people being wounded and about four hundred dead or missing.[84] No reliable final statistics about the losses are available.

By June 6 the party leaders congratulated themselves that they had "put down the counterrevolutionary riots" and defended party power everywhere. Deng hoped that China would stick with economic reform and its opening to the West, but political reform had to be strictly controlled to avoid any more instability.

Zhao Ziyang remained opposed to the violent crackdown. He was eventually placed under house arrest, where he remained for the rest of his life.

* * *

The Chinese crackdown left Bush frustrated and disheartened. He had served in China and had been hopeful about the developments there. He saw how the promising wave of changes could go all wrong, very quickly.

In the United States, Bush's domestic opponents attacked him for preserving relations with such a brutal Chinese government. Bush, Baker, and Scowcroft believed that it was best to limit but hold on to the relationship and ride out the political attacks. They were making a long-term bet that China would still evolve in a positive direction.

Gorbachev's reactions to the Tiananmen Square crisis were different. Soviet relations with China continued to improve. Gorbachev "clinically separated his personal aversion to the use of force and his sympathy for the students' cause from the exigencies of power politics." Talking to the Indian prime minister, he even appears to have imagined a possible future alignment cementing ties between the Soviet Union, China, and India.[85]

The Chinese crackdown did not alter Gorbachev's still-secret wish to avoid Soviet intervention in Eastern Europe. There, he still thought those communist governments had good options for internal reform, and he still did not want Moscow to have to shoulder the burden of fixing them.

Gorbachev was also fully preoccupied with his political problems at home. The new Congress of People's Deputies was incredibly fractious, with riveting and publicized spectacles from one day to the next.

Later in October 1989, told that the death toll in China might be as many as three thousand, Gorbachev commented to the Politburo, "We must be realists. They, like us, have to hold on. Three thousand...so what?"[86]

* * *

The Chinese solution was on Bush's mind as he visited Poland and Hungary and then came to Paris for the G-7 economic summit. Poland's elections produced a stunning vote against the government and for Solidarity in the seats that were up for grabs. It seemed clear that a new government would probably have to be formed soon.

In his July visits to both countries, Bush welcomed the changes in Poland and Hungary. He was exhilarated by the crowds at his speeches and by the exciting changes under way.

At the G-7 summit Scowcroft noticed something interesting. The press was "grousing" that Bush had not dominated the G-7 work, as he had the NATO summit. He "had accepted ideas from his colleagues. It was beginning to appear to me that the press definitely was not receptive to his collegial style.

"The reporters seemed to thrive on flamboyance and fireworks," Scowcroft reflected, "rather than on friendly persuasion—and results." He was frustrated. He and Bush believed that allies "appreciated a cooperative rather than an imperious approach."[87]

The G-7 coordinated a common approach on China. Bush, with Japanese support, successfully held out for a balance that maintained all relations but restricted new World Bank loans and offered asylum to Chinese student-refugees.

On a late summer afternoon, Bush and Mitterrand sat together in Mitterrand's ceremonial office in the Elysée Palace. No one else was present but one aide for each man (Scowcroft and Jacques Attali) and interpreters.

Bush shared his impressions from Hungary and Poland. On Poland, he mentioned that the "labor demands will make it difficult to introduce reforms." But "another state crackdown would lead to chaos and possible [Soviet] intervention."

Bush had also tried hard not to create more problems for Gorbachev. He acknowledged that "the Poles cannot move away from their alliances." He was happy to work, at least for the time being, with Wojciech Jaruzelski, whom much of the world regarded as the face of Poland's brutal former martial-law regime but whom Bush saw as "battered but experienced."

Bush wanted to hear Mitterrand's impressions of Gorbachev.

"Gorbachev is very disturbed about his domestic problems and a little disturbed about his external problems," Mitterrand told him. "He dreads having to stop the political liberalization. He does not want to do something like what the Chinese have done with Tiananmen. But he fears he will be dragged into it." Gorbachev had said, "It's hard. I do not sleep."

Mitterrand sympathized. Gorbachev seemed "tired, harassed, but he still pursued his policies in the same direction. We need to encourage him."

Bush said it might now be time for him to talk with Gorbachev. Mitterrand agreed. He urged Bush to schedule a summit meeting.

Bush had been considering this for months. He wondered aloud to Mitterrand: Would the meeting be useful even if none of the arms control agreements were ready? He was concerned that there was not yet anything "concrete to do" at such a high-profile meeting.

Mitterrand said the important thing now was to talk. Gorbachev was "nervous." A "policy of letting things get worse" (*politique du pire*) could mean "the failure of perestroika." Gorbachev wanted a personal relationship with Bush.

As for Poland and Hungary, Mitterrand argued that "the USSR will accept a lot of things." Western economic action might be fine.

In other matters "there are limits, or it will be Budapest in 1956" (when the Soviets and their allies intervened massively to destroy a dissident Hungarian government). For the time being, Mitterrand urged that "we have to give [Gorbachev] the impression that we will not cross those limits." As an example, Mitterrand said that the Soviet-led military alliance, the Warsaw Pact, "might have to exist to the end of the century for stability."[88]

* * *

Still in Paris, Bush, Baker, and Scowcroft sat together on a terrace in the American embassy's garden. Bush reflected on Mitterrand's advice. He told the other two men that it was time to meet with the Soviet leader.

Baker had not been against it. Scowcroft no longer was. Anyway, as Scowcroft recalled, Bush "put it in that way he has when his mind is made up."[89]

Bush sent a secret message to Gorbachev to begin work on the arrangements. "Up until now," he wrote, "I have felt that a meeting would have to produce major agreements so as not to disappoint the watching world. Now my thinking is changing." He was open to any suggestions about where to get together, ready to open his home in Maine to Gorbachev or meet anywhere else they and a few advisers could be comfortable.[90]

Later Bush remembered how "moved" he was at this point "by the hope I saw in Eastern Europe." He saw dangers ahead. "I would have to respond with even greater care as Eastern Europeans pushed their own way to the future. We could not let the people down—there could still be more Tiananmens."[91]

American Decline? Soviet Decline?

Early in September 1989, the well-informed British embassy in Washington, led by Antony Acland, prepared a careful, cold-blooded analysis of the new Bush administration and the situation in America. The British diplomats granted that Bush and Baker were "non-ideological" and very politically minded practical men.[92]

Yes, their foreign policy team was unusually cohesive. The "interagency warfare which was the hallmark of foreign policy-making in the [Reagan] Administration (and others) has been conspicuous by its absence."

Yes, Baker's deputy had said back in March that they would put alliance togetherness first, that "West/West is the key to East/West." The British had duly noted all the "general pointers" in the speeches. They grudgingly granted credit for the CFE initiative that had, for the moment, quieted some of the critics.

But the British still felt bruised by the way some of the moves had been handled. The secretive administration was like Bush: "His style is rather easier to identify than his beliefs." Acland wrote that he thought "there is more to it—and to him—than that. But it is on his policies that he will have to be judged, and the jury is still out." So far, the British saw "little sign of a coherent overall approach to policy."

The basic problem, the British embassy thought, was American decline. The prevailing response in Washington was "economic nationalism." The Bush administration had not yet shown that it had a policy answer for either.

The British diplomats observed "a widespread feeling in the United States that American dominance of the industrialized world is eroding, perhaps irrevocably." Americans had helped foster the emergence of a successful Europe and Japan, yet were now ambivalent about both. "And, within the Alliance, the Americans (but not only the Americans) have yet to assess the implications of a restive and more assertive Germany."

"This sense of decline in their country's place in the world is the more painful" because it was such a blow to Americans' image of themselves. The British had been following "the national debate" about American "over-stretch" and decline, amid unchecked federal budget deficits and high trade deficits. Any American policies had to assume an "economy of resources."

American concerns about decline, the British stressed, "have resulted in a new mood of economic nationalism." Many of the congressional Democrats represented this movement. Bush was the first president in more than a hundred years to start his presidency without his party holding a majority in either of the houses of Congress.

Bush, they said, "is well aware of the problem." In his May speech in Boston about Western Europe he had said, "What a tragedy, what an absurdity it would be if future historians attributed the demise of the Western Alliance to disputes over beef hormones and wars over pasta."

Yet the British saw "no clear sense of direction in the Administration's trade policy," raising doubt about the U.S. will to uphold free trade and an open world economy, especially against "a protectionist Congress."

In sum, the British argued, "the mood of economic nationalism, lurking just beneath the surface [in America], and waiting to be exploited by any unscrupulous politician (or Presidential candidate), is stronger and deeper than at any time in recent years." Meanwhile, the changes in the world were "calling into question many of the assumptions on which [the Americans]—and we—have based key aspects of our foreign and security policies since the end of World War Two."

The Bush administration faced problems that were "dauntingly complex," and its policies were still at a "formative" stage. Still, Acland hedged, we "should not underestimate a man who is competitive as well as cautious."

In the summer of 1989 the British argument about American decline very much reflected the common wisdom. A year earlier a former U.S. official had announced that "the American Century is over. The big development in the latter part of the century is the emergence of Japan as a major superpower."[93]

A prominent political scientist tried to buck this trendy view. Harvard's Samuel Huntington observed, "In 1988 the United States reached the zenith of its fifth wave of declinism since the 1950s." Huntington argued that the coming period could actually turn into an era of American renewal. But his seemed like a contrarian voice.[94]

* * *

Within the U.S. government, a few important officials also were focused on the danger of decline. But they were not as concerned about American decline. They were watching the Soviet Union.

Gates warned Bush about rising unrest, as more foods were being rationed, and violent outbreaks (as had just happened in Soviet Armenia) could become more common, with cycles of upheaval and repression. A senior Soviet analyst at the CIA who had worked closely with Gates, Grey Hodnett, developed a provocative assessment. He did not necessarily want Gorbachev to fail. But he believed he probably would.

Hodnett's argument was that Gorbachev had undertaken a set of "gambles" about nationality issues, postponing marketization and deep economic reform, and his partial democracy experiment. But these gambles were "based on questionable premises and wishful thinking."

Hodnett's main point was about what might happen next. One possibility was general repression, like the Chinese solution. If this happened, Hodnett forecasted that Gorbachev would lose his natural constituency and "his entire political program."

If Gorbachev did stay in power, he could try more democratization, loosen the Soviet Union, and accept the short-term pain of financial stabilization and market reform in exchange for long-term gain. If he did not make the needed and painful financial and market reforms, he might ease his way for a while. But fairly soon, "in the near and medium-term," unrest would rise. Hodnett warned of "likely movement of the Soviet system toward revolution, a hard-right takeover, or 'Ottomanization'— growing relative backwardness of the USSR and a piecemeal breakoff of the national republics."

Gorbachev thus needed a foreign policy that reduced external dangers. But, Hodnett warned, Western actions that appeared to "'take advantage' of Soviet instability could hurt Gorbachev."

In August 1989, Rice added her own analysis, for Scowcroft. She tended to share Hodnett's very worrying assessment (although his was not the majority view in the U.S. intelligence community).

Her particular take was that Gorbachev and his few key advisers were stirring up the people to confront local officials, making them the "goats." It was a populist approach (Rice called it "Peronist," referring to Argentina's former dictator), to make Gorbachev and Moscow the source of solutions.

Rice believed this approach might work for a little while. Soon Moscow would run out of solutions.

Then the crunch would come. After that, "whether Gorbachev survives personally or not, the system has already been weakened enough that, short of an all-out crackdown, unrest will continue whoever occupies the Kremlin."[95]

Rice agreed that the Soviet leadership would become increasingly preoccupied with their internal problems. Since so few people were handling so much, the leaders would have difficulty engaging constructively on foreign policy issues. Signs of this were already becoming evident in Baker's work with Shevardnadze. "'New thinking' in foreign policy—to the extent that it exists—does not have deep roots in the Soviet bureaucracy."

What did this mean for policy? Rice doubted that the United States could do much to help the Soviets solve their internal problems. The United States should "be clearer and more focused in pushing a few core issues." She went on, "We need to decide what we really can and must achieve during this window of opportunity—a window whose duration is increasingly uncertain."

CHAPTER 4

The Pivot: A New Germany in a Different Europe

In February 1989, Bertrand Dufourcq, a French career diplomat and political director of the Foreign Ministry, circulated a note to his colleagues on the journey from the Europe of "today to that of tomorrow." "Everyone has the feeling," he wrote, "that the organization of Europe as it resulted from the Second World War is about to give way to something new without anyone knowing clearly where we are going."[1]

Had Dufourcq returned to his February note only six months later, in August 1989, he could already have cited five developments of shattering proportions.

• Poland and Hungary were conducting negotiated revolutions. Gorbachev-like reform in the region was giving way to the end of communist regimes and the establishment of multiparty systems through democratic elections.

• The world's foundational communist state, the Soviet Union, had begun an experiment with partial democracy—ripping away the authority of the Communist Party in favor of "normal" governance. A continent away, China crushed a large pro-democracy movement. The leaders in Beijing had no intention of following Gorbachev's lead.

- In Europe, the largest military confrontation in the world seemed to be unwinding. For the first time in history, the great armed camps on the continent converged on a framework for Europe-wide reduction and limits on conventional armed forces.
- The epicenter of the Cold War—Germany—was about to explode onto the international agenda. Massive refugee flows challenged the communist regime in East Germany. The "German question" was back on the table.
- West European leaders were contemplating economic and monetary union. These plans could also be linked to the creation of a new system for global trade.

In the last months of 1989, Dufourcq, like his counterparts around the world, would be forced to write, tear up, and rewrite new guides to "where we are going."

The Revolutions Begin

After his pleasant visit to France, Gorbachev traveled to Romania, to Bucharest, to sit down with the other leaders of the Warsaw Pact on July 7–8, 1989. The meeting became an argument about the future of traditional communist rule in Eastern Europe. Gorbachev and the new, reform-minded leaders of Poland and Hungary were on one side; the conservative communist leaders of East Germany, Czechoslovakia, Bulgaria, and Romania were on the other.

"We are receiving letters of panic from everywhere, written by those who believe that socialism is seriously threatened," Gorbachev said. Well, "these fears are not founded and those who are afraid had better hold on, because perestroika has only just begun." He added, "We are going from one international order to another."[2]

In the last days of August 1989, Poland's leader agreed to form a noncommunist government. Hungary's leaders decided to open their borders to Austria, allowing growing numbers of East German refugees to flee west. These two choices were more parallel than connected. The Hungarian choice—and its significance—was especially unexpected.

East European communists were saddled with bad economic conditions, and the hapless and unhappy citizens of the region faced shortages of goods and valueless money. Those circumstances were not new.

But it was different this time. Polish and Hungarian rulers were not willing to crush opposition with the usual instruments of beatings, arrests, and imprisonment. Some of the reasons were specific to Poland and Hungary—a loss of confidence in the communist system and a culture in which overt political violence seemed more abhorrent than it had in the "old days" earlier in the twentieth century.

The crucial difference, though, was that Moscow was now led by a reformer who wanted the people to have legitimate confidence in communism—not a grudging obedience imposed by force. The Poles and Hungarians took their cues from Gorbachev. Earlier, Hungarian conservatives had warned that the Soviets would be angered by democratic reforms, and "each time, those reactions did not materialize, and the conservatives' position kept weakening."[3]

It could have gone very differently. Poles could have turned on each other—communist against noncommunist, drawing on the deep-seated hatred between them. Or the economic transitions in Hungary and Poland could have failed, giving the communists new life, particularly if there had been violence as a result. But the worst did not happen, thanks to cool heads and considerable skill in Warsaw, Budapest, and Moscow— and in the international community as well.

When Bush had visited Budapest and Warsaw in July, the memory of the "Chinese solution" was very fresh. Bush's public speeches sounded the trumpet call for freedom. In private, he urged care. To the Hungarian reformers, Bush and Baker seemed overly cautious.[4]

In Warsaw, though, Bush's step-by-step approach seemed very well judged. Following the advice of his State Department experts and the very influential American ambassador to Warsaw, John Davis, Bush encouraged Poland's leader, General Wojciech Jaruzelski, to run for president in the upcoming elections. Jaruzelski had been the hated leader of the martial law regime. Yet in a communist country, his role was a strange one.

Generals were not supposed to run a communist government. During the 1980s, Jaruzelski had turned a party-led government into a military junta. Though allied with the Polish communists and using state institutions, a "core group of generals" really ran the show. They made decisions outside of the usual party apparatus and helped drain legitimacy away from the party.[5]

On June 23, Ambassador Davis had cabled a blunt warning. "Most Solidarity leaders are apparently convinced that Jaruzelski must be elected president if the country is to avoid civil war."

It was his conversation directly with Solidarity leader Lech Wałęsa that impressed Bush most. Wałęsa wanted to avoid a "Chinese" outcome. He believed that the terms of the Roundtable agreement with the communists needed to be respected. That would calm nerves in Moscow because Gorbachev trusted the general.[6]

Jaruzelski, though, was a proud man and was concerned that his unpopularity might lead to an embarrassing outcome: He might be spurned by his fellow citizens in the elections. In the end, the Americans succeeded in getting him to take on the presidency, keeping intact the bargain that Solidarity and the communists—and by extension Moscow—had made. He was elected in mid-July.

* * *

Though he was the president, Jaruzelski then had to form a government. Once again, he confronted his old foe, Wałęsa. Since 1988, for more than a year, neither side had felt strong enough to overrun the other.

Jaruzelski could not do much about the economic problems without Solidarity's support. Solidarity was not yet sure it could run the government—or that it even wanted to take responsibility for the current mess. One of Wałęsa's chief allies, Tadeusz Mazowiecki, believed that Solidarity might wish to stay in opposition, or at least stay out of a leading role, for a transition period that could take years.

Poland badly needed a functioning government. Jaruzelski tried and failed to form one. After weeks of tension, Wałęsa suddenly decided that Solidarity should make its move to power. It should take the lead in forming a government. Mazowiecki himself was to be the prime minister.[7]

To do this, Wałęsa and his core allies decided to compromise. Mazowiecki and Wałęsa chose a peaceful transition, in partnership with the communists. For that very reason, these choices are still very controversial in Poland.

At the time, this compromise worked. It did reassure Gorbachev. And Gorbachev responded constructively. From his vacation spot on the Black Sea, the Soviet leader intervened personally, on August 24, to help persuade the Polish communists to go along.

He sent his KGB head to Warsaw for consultations with the new prime minister and the communist leadership. Mazowiecki announced what the Soviets wanted to hear most: Communists would retain the Defense and Interior Ministry portfolios. Poland would remain in the Warsaw Pact. Satisfied, Gorbachev went along with establishment of the first noncommunist government in Eastern Europe since 1948.[8]

Gorbachev had stuck with the nonintervention policy. The Brezhnev Doctrine was not just rhetorically dead now—it was in reality no longer a factor in Soviet policy toward the Eastern bloc.

Fresh from his triumphal trips to Western Europe, Gorbachev was aware that his openness to change in Eastern Europe had become a defining test of his promised "new thinking." It was the test of his commitment to a "common European home." It was also a test of how Gorbachev saw himself, of his sense of what it meant for him to be a humane citizen and leader in Europe and the world.[9]

* * *

Wałęsa too was aware of the international environment that favored compromise. He and Jaruzelski also knew that the West was gearing up to provide some substantial assistance to Poland.

Polish leaders had been speculating about aid based on analogies to the scale of Marshall Plan aid for European recovery that the United States had offered between 1948 and 1952. No one using the Marshall Plan analogies had looked hard at exactly how that program had worked.

None of the Western nations had identified large amounts of money they could offer as incentives or grant programs that made sense. As to the existing Polish and Hungarian debt, American banks actually held little of it. Most of the debt, and most of the relevant experience with East European finance, was in West European and Japanese institutions and in the IMF.

In any case, Western governments could not do much until they saw what kind of regimes might emerge and what economic program they were prepared to adopt. Since any such program was bound to be painful, at least in the short term, Bush had been careful throughout his visit and the surrounding talks not to promise any "blank check" that would deflect the Poles from making hard choices.

Bush had scraped some U.S. aid to offer in his visits. Although the move included a novel idea that turned out to be productive, "Enterprise" funds to stimulate small business, its scale was initially modest.[10]

At the G-7 summit in Paris in July, the Americans and the West Germans argued for two main steps. First, they pushed to relax and reschedule the foreign debt, especially Polish debt. This had been high on the Polish list of concerns. Eventually, in 1991, the arguments would get down to which banks and which countries would accept major losses, an issue that would be especially painful for the Germans.

Second, the West Germans and the Americans proposed a multilateral conference to develop a significant aid and reform program for Poland and Hungary. The idea appears to have originated with Kohl, in a secret set of suggestions that he sent to Bush in June.

Kohl was especially focused on Poland. He remembered that 1989 was the fiftieth anniversary of the outbreak of the Second World War with Germany's invasion of Poland and the Hitler-Stalin partition of the country.

Everyone could begin to see that their various bilateral aid efforts had to be coordinated somehow. There were also debt discussions among government creditors (the Paris Club) and private creditors (the London Club). The governments also quickly realized that most of the experience with planning economic transition on this scale was in the international financial institutions, especially the World Bank and the IMF. Also, most experience in trading with Eastern Europe was in the European Community.

The leaders created a new ad hoc body to get all the concerned states and organizations together. This new Group of 24 (G-24) would move on urgent matters, like quick food aid, and also on longer-term transition plans and assistance.

Baker wanted the West Germans to organize the G-24 work. The

Germans preferred to give the job to the European Commission. The Americans agreed to this. That result also pleased the French.

The G-24 quickly got to work, holding its first meeting two weeks later, on August 1. Just in the rest of 1989, Poland received 359,000 tons of food aid, most of it from Western Europe, amounting to about 20 pounds of food for every person in the country.[11]

Wałęsa thought the aid plans should be much larger. But he also knew that disorder and violence would hurt Poland's chances of receiving any significant aid at all.

Both Jaruzelski and Wałęsa were focused on a key Western institution for them, the International Monetary Fund. In chapter 2 we introduced the significance of the IMF role in Poland and Hungary.

The IMF had a French managing director and a mostly non-American staff, headquartered in Washington, DC. Created at the end of the Second World War, the old IMF had played an important but relatively limited role, helping governments manage balances of payments in a highly regulated international financial system where cross-national capital flows were modest.

During the 1980s the IMF began to transform into a very different kind of organization. As capital began flowing freely, some borrowers built up large debts. When money became tight and interest rates went up in the early 1980s, the profligate borrowers of the 1970s and early 1980s could not pay. This was the debt crisis we mentioned in chapter 1.

In that crisis, the IMF turned into the institution that took the lead in reestablishing the terms of creditworthiness in the debt workouts. It thus became a kind of standard-setter for access to foreign capital. The support of the IMF would be vital if Poland wanted to get on top of its debt crisis and sustain access to Western credit.

The IMF would not do anything significant for Poland unless the new Polish government undertook restructuring of the economy. That would require an inclusive government able to carry the political burden of the dramatic and very painful changes that would be required. That was a big part of the reason why the Roundtable process had taken place at all, why the Poles had opened up their politics. The next step, then, was that Jaruzelski ended up having to appoint a non-communist-led government, one that might undertake a dramatic, market-oriented reform program.

Yet Mazowiecki's new government inherited an economy "in free fall." The IMF, like Western governments, suggested that the only way out was for his government to take a leap, with a program of "genuinely radical and comprehensive reform." His government did this. They did it with lightning speed.[12]

Theirs was a daring and difficult leap. No one really knew exactly what to do. There was no established playbook for radical post-communist economic transition. Some experts and politicians might wave at analogies to the Marshall Plan or to reform plans in East Asian countries like South Korea. But these analogies were actually not terribly useful for a country in Poland's circumstances.[13]

A little more useful was the experience accumulating with developing-country debt crises during the 1980s. Western experts, mainly in the IMF and World Bank, were fashioning a paradigm for thinking about the reform of communist economies. But the new cases in Eastern Europe, led by Poland, presented this challenge in an extreme form.

Mazowiecki and his ministers called the West's bluff. Aided by Western advisers, they came up with a credible program for economic transition. Their approach is known, for good reason, as "shock therapy." It was an immediate transition to a convertible currency with the prompt elimination of price controls and nearly balanced public budgets.

In exchange, in September 1989 the new Polish government asked for some big, quick help from outside governments. It asked, in several forms: a billion-dollar stabilization fund to sustain a convertible currency, credit lines from the IMF and the World Bank, suspension of debt servicing, and a program of debt relief that would write down and reschedule loans without damage to Poland's future access to credit markets. Poland also would need specific technical help and some targeted foreign money to make structural adjustments.

The West, led by the United States and Western Europe, delivered on its part of the bargain. As the Polish government adopted the internal plans by the end of 1989, the Stabilization Fund was created (with contributions from seventeen countries, 20 percent from the United States). The international financial institutions played their part. The desired process of debt restructuring was under way.[14]

The G-24 also helped organize a new institution, a European Bank for Reconstruction and Development, to provide more varied, longer-term support. The United States and other governments added significant bilateral aid programs, in which Poland (which had plenty of supporters in the U.S. Congress) received especially generous priority.[15]

The transition was difficult, with very high inflation and great turmoil. But it was successful—at least measured against the original objectives of the Poles who led the program.[16]

* * *

The Polish crisis had come on very visibly, with plenty of advance warning at each stage. The crisis in East Germany crept in through the side door.

Bolstered by relatively greater affluence than his country's Eastern European neighbors enjoyed and a fantastically elaborate system of internal controls, East Germany's longtime leader, Erich Honecker, seemed secure in his position. An English observer, Timothy Garton Ash, visited the GDR in July 1989. Opposition activists were deeply pessimistic about any chance for change. "The State Security Service—the 'Stasi'—still seemed all-powerful, the population at large not prepared to risk its modest prosperity. Above all, the ranks of the opposition had been continuously thinned by emigration to West Germany."[17]

Western observers had long known that many East Germans despised and even hated the regime, but their bitterness seemed to lapse into passive, cynical resignation. There were a tiny number of open critics, thinly tolerated with the watchful bemusement of the secret police, their ranks honeycombed with informers. There were leaders of peace movements, feminists, and ecological groups; a few figures in East Germany's literary establishment; and a handful of dissident Marxist intellectuals. Many of these individuals found shelter in the highly influential Protestant churches and their reformist ministers who enjoyed a modicum of freedom from the state.

If there was a threat to the regime in East Berlin, it appeared to come from reformist elements within the ruling Communist Party, called the Socialist Unity Party (SED). Reformers, such as Dresden party chief Hans Modrow, seemed ready to take their cue from Gorbachev and begin East German perestroika. But the GDR's rulers held fast. In June the East German parliament applauded Beijing's bloody crackdown.

To Gorbachev and the Kremlin, the East German reformers were the solution. Honecker was the danger. The more stubborn and reactionary he was, the longer he put off needed reform, the more danger of an explosion.

And then the side door opened.

Hungary was a popular travel destination in the communist bloc. Some East Germans had noticed a May announcement that Hungary's border with Austria, and thus the West, would open. The new Hungarian prime minister, an admirer of Gorbachev, thought the old barbed wire border was a "gruesome anachronism." When Bush visited Budapest, the leadership proudly presented him with a piece of the barbed wire. It was a nice and symbolically meaningful gesture. But almost all Hungarians were already permitted to travel freely to Austria, with which Hungary had built "a masterpiece of European détente."[18]

The Hungarians had not expected ordinary East Germans to take much interest. Only those with valid GDR exit stamps in their passports could leave. Illegal crossers would be arrested and sent home, as in the past.

Citizens did take an interest, and rising numbers of East German travelers, mainly East Germans traveling in Hungary but also some traveling in other East European countries, attempted to push through the Hungarian exit. Hundreds, then thousands, of them were detained in Hungary or stranded in other ways, now purposefully trying to get to the West through the side door.

The East German leaders felt growing alarm. It reminded them of the terrible days before they had built the Berlin Wall in 1961 and closed off the border with West Germany. One Politbüro member recalled "this unspeakable and unbearable manifestation of desertion" that created a spontaneous, if usually unspoken, sense of "concern and malaise."[19] By the end of August the refugee problem became a significant international crisis. A cartoonist in a South Carolina newspaper later portrayed it in the drawing we reproduce on page 168.[20]

West Germany was not encouraging anyone to flee the GDR. In August, Kohl assured Honecker that his only wish was for the East German refugees to return to a worthwhile life back in the German Democratic Republic.

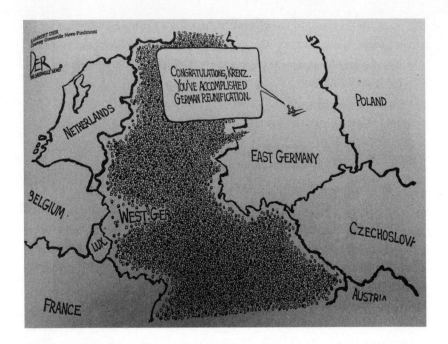

But legally, and politically, the West German government felt obliged to help East German refugees who wanted to find their way to the Federal Republic. Other West Germans accused Kohl of doing too much to help, saying he was destabilizing the situation. Mainly his government was just improvising. Genscher's Foreign Ministry was "absolutely taken by surprise."[21]

The Hungarian authorities met secretly with Kohl and Genscher. They cut a deal to allow East Germans detained in Hungary to come to the FRG. One reason Hungarian leaders were willing to cut their deal to facilitate refugee flight to West Germany was that they were preoccupied with their foreign debts, an issue that was still mostly secret.[22]

East Germany had to close its border with Hungary. Then, in September, East Germans began trying to get out through Czechoslovakia. Failing, they sought refuge in the West German embassy in Prague. The East German government now had to close practically all its exits in order to hold its citizens in the country.

By the middle of September, the East German refugee problem had come home. Though the secret police had seen scarcely any visible dissident movement, the landscape was like dry brush after a long drought. The refugee crisis provided the spark that ignited a mass movement of protesters, practically overnight.[23]

The regime, then still led by its seventy-seven-year-old longtime head, Honecker, did have the plans and the means to implement a massive crackdown. In East Berlin, more than a thousand people were arrested on October 7–8. Police told them they would end up in "the garbage dump." The protesters were not deterred but they were angered.

Demonstrations broke out in more than fifty cities. A massive demonstration in Leipzig on October 9 was pivotal. Robert Darnton, a historian living in East Germany at the time, recalled that "everyone present at that demonstration was convinced that the government had prepared to commit something comparable to China's Tiananmen Square massacre."

Yet, at the last minute, the troops withdrew. The communist officials in Leipzig had been unable to get any final guidance from their leaders in East Berlin. Those officials were too paralyzed by indecision to order a violent "Chinese solution."[24]

This paralysis effectively became a crucial choice, between October 4 and 9, 1989, that East Germany would not choose the "Chinese solution." The East German Politbüro was undecided because many of the leaders could see an alternative to mass killing and arrests. The alternative—serious internal reform—had not yet been tried.

With encouragement from Gorbachev, who had just been in East Berlin to celebrate the GDR's fortieth anniversary, the East German Politbüro deposed Honecker. The new leader was Egon Krenz.

* * *

The new East German government of Krenz confronted crises at every turn—but perhaps none more urgent than the crushing debt burden. Right after Krenz took power he flew to Moscow. He talked in depth with Gorbachev on November 1. They spoke in Russian without interpreters present and with only two other people in the room.[25]

Gorbachev said that he was aware of the true economic condition of the GDR, that production figures had long been exaggerated.

Krenz heard Gorbachev out. Then he told him the real story. The GDR owed the West $26.5 billion as of the end of 1989 and had a current account deficit for the year of $12.1 billion.

The notetaker recorded, "Astonished, Comrade Gorbachev asked whether these numbers are exact. He had not imagined the situation was so precarious."

There was no mistake. In fact, Krenz explained that just to pay the interest on the GDR's foreign debts would require $4.5 billion, or about 62 percent of all the foreign currency earned by the country's exports.

East Germany had been living well beyond its means, starting in the early 1970s. If it based its standard of living only on its own output, then that standard would immediately drop by 30 percent.

To avoid that, Krenz needed to get financial credits. He had considered going to the International Monetary Fund, but giving the Western-dominated IMF an influence over the economy would create an extremely difficult political situation.

Gorbachev advised Krenz to tell the East German people the truth, that they had been living beyond their means. The Soviet Union would supply vital raw materials. The GDR would also have to continue a "principled and flexible" policy toward West Germany. "Naturally," Gorbachev remarked, "one must handle things so that decisions will be made in Berlin and not in Bonn."

What Gorbachev had in mind, as he explained to Krenz and shrewdly explained to his Politburo two days later, was that the Soviet Union would help strike the balance in managing both Germanys. He would not let the West use him as the bad guy, to oppose German aspirations. Instead, "we should proceed in a triangle, with the participation of the FRG and the GDR, and do this openly."[26]

Krenz understood. After all, he said, "the GDR is in a certain sense the child of the Soviet Union, and one must acknowledge paternity for his children." On November 6, Gorbachev telephoned Ambassador Vyacheslav Kochemasov in East Germany and had told him emphatically, "Our people will never forgive us if we lose the GDR."[27]

Gorbachev needed a stable and successfully reformed GDR. But with his own deteriorating economy at home, it was not at all clear that he could keep his promise to help the failing client state. Perestroika, launched with such hopeful enthusiasm in 1985, was stalling. The republics of the Soviet Union were becoming restless. Moscow too was confronting chaos.

The Soviet Agenda: Beyond Containment—and Beyond Communism?

With all the excitement in Central Europe, it is easy to lose sight of the choices that the international community still had to make about another crucial vector of change, the future of the Soviet Union. By the last months of 1989 the seriousness of the problems within the borders of the USSR were becoming obvious.

The Baltic republics were claiming national autonomy. In the southern USSR there were more strikes and struggles between Armenians and Azerbaijanis. There was unrest in the Moldavian Republic, bordering Romania. And at the end of August ethnic violence swept the Abkhaz region of the Georgian Republic. The security forces cracked down in a decision that Gorbachev would later say he regretted. In Ukraine, nationalist demonstrators demanded independence.

In September 1989, Gorbachev had a difficult trip to Lithuania. He called a special party plenum (a full meeting of the Central Committee) to deal with mounting problems. The session, held on September 19–20, led to more personnel shakeups, including the replacement of the longtime party chief in Ukraine. This Band-Aid did not deal with the underlying problem. The multiethnic Soviet empire was fraying badly.

The economic situation was deteriorating too. To meet all the demands, the Soviet government had been printing billions of rubles, flooding money into the economy. In a free market system, experts would expect sky-high inflation. But this was a system where prices were set by decree. So the money was out there, with few ways to spend it, in what was called a "ruble overhang." Incomes began going up by double-digit amounts but goods disappeared from the shelves

The Soviet Union was running short of food, and also of the foreign currency to buy it, since rubles were not a convertible currency. The Soviet Union had to engage in more foreign borrowing. For the first time, during 1989 and into 1990, the Soviet government began to feel threatened by the size of its growing foreign currency debts.

Even in the best case, a thoughtful U.S. administration had to at least imagine and plan for scenarios in which Gorbachev was deposed. These would obviously include a takeover by conservative forces, and they could extend to violent upheavals approaching civil war.[28] In fact, Gates commissioned just such a study—not from the intelligence community, however. Fearful of leaks, he asked Ross, Rice, and Bob Blackwell (of the CIA, not the Bob Blackwill working on the NSC staff) to think through these scenarios. Their work was so closely held that there were no calendar entries for their meetings. A leak that the United States was even considering such scenarios would have been disastrous.

The United States was faced with crucial choices about Gorbachev and his country. Conditions in the Soviet Union seemed to confirm those CIA analyses that were pessimistic about Gorbachev's chances for success. In October, Bob Gates attempted to give a speech saying this publicly. Baker angrily quashed the Gates speech. He refused to go along with Gates's attempts to edit it. Baker had no particular quarrel with the intelligence assessment, though he thought that assessment should remain secret. To Baker, the question instead was, "What should the U.S. do?"

Bush and Gorbachev had arranged to meet in a harbor off the island of Malta, in the Mediterranean Sea, on December 2–3. Early in September, Baker framed the issue for Bush and the rest of the cabinet. Rather than the standard sort of Cold War question about how to manage the Communist threat, now he described the issue as: How do we manage the "crumbling of Communism—not the threat of Communism but [the] consequences of its failure?"[29]

* * *

After all, pessimism is not a policy. Appraising attitudes in the Bush administration in the last months of 1989, Scowcroft recalled a nice little group portrait in which "everyone" agreed that Gorbachev's chances of pulling off a comprehensive reform agenda "were not good."

Beyond that assessment, there was no consensus about what to do.

There was Baker, on one side. He was "the most optimistic concerning [Gorbachev's] sincerity about reform." Scowcroft placed himself as being more suspicious, but also eager to see what was possible. Eagleburger was close to this position, finding the debate about whether to support Gorbachev "academic and sterile."

Gates emphasized pessimism about Gorbachev's prospects. He worried that any reforms could easily be reversed. Cheney was still more negative. The new chairman of the Joint Chiefs of Staff, Colin Powell, avoided contradicting Cheney but seemed "on the moderate side." Vice President Dan Quayle was even more negative than Cheney.[30]

But Bush did not try to find the median point in this group. His views were practically identical to Baker's.

Moreover, Bush was determined to use the thaw in U.S.-Soviet relations to make big progress in arms control, in part because—as he confided to his diary—"we've got to do less in the way of defense spending."[31] He was determined to carry out a general fiscal retrenchment to deal with the hangover from the Reagan era and cut the public deficits.

If "everyone" was pessimistic about the prospects of Gorbachev's program, Bush and Baker also believed in his sincerity. Even if Gorbachev and his circle were sincere, however, the United States and its allies were uneasy about how deeply these changes were accepted in the rest of the Soviet government. At his December summit meeting with Gorbachev, in Malta, Bush raised a recent discovery of Soviet/Cuban arms supplies, including surface-to-air missiles, in Nicaragua and El Salvador. It was not at all clear that Gorbachev had ordered or was even aware of this.

Bush and Baker therefore answered the "what to do" question with a strategy that had two dimensions:

• Moving "beyond containment," the United States would try, as best it could, to help Gorbachev. The U.S. role might be marginal, compared to what Soviets did. But such a course might improve the odds that the Soviet leader's program would succeed. Good on the merits, the effort would also demonstrate at least that the United States wanted to help. That itself was vital.

• The United States would hedge against failure, and against the disconnect between Gorbachev and his security establishment, by trying to cement objective achievements as rapidly as possible. Since May–June 1989, the arms control tempo had already accelerated on all fronts, mainly in the Baker-Shevardnadze work. Bush would redouble pressure, including on officials in his own government, to turn this into a full-court press to reduce strategic nuclear arsenals, achieve a worldwide ban of chemical weapons, restrict underground nuclear testing, establish Open Skies, and push the radical downsizing and redeployment of conventional forces in Europe.

Bush wanted to get most of this work done in only about one year, by the end of 1990. That rushed timetable would also later figure in the push to accelerate the unification of Germany. No one knew how long the "Gorbachev window" would be open.

Preparing for the Malta summit, Baker suggested that rather than wait and react to a presentation by Gorbachev, Bush should lead off the whole set of meetings. Bush should outline a comprehensive program with these ingredients. Scowcroft was hesitant. But Bush liked the idea. He pushed his staff to redraft presentations and be as forthcoming as possible.

* * *

American and Soviet leaders arrived in Malta along with one of the Mediterranean's violent winter storms. They had intended to meet aboard cruisers of the respective navies. Instead, as the winds howled outside, the talks on Marsaxlokk Bay were confined to the wardroom of a support ship, the Soviet cruise liner *Maxim Gorkii*.

Amid the waves, Bush, old sailor that he was, climbed aboard the Soviet vessel for the first full meeting. He moved right into outlining a "framework of areas in which we want to move forward with you."[32]

After Bush finished, Gorbachev said he had been looking for a tangible demonstration of American support. "During your presentation, I heard it. I was going to ask you today to go beyond words. But you have done so."

Where Bush had tabled initiatives, Gorbachev spoke about his political philosophy. "The emphasis on confrontation based on our different ideologies is wrong." Those "methods of the Cold War were defeated."

The Soviet leader knew that some Americans thought Eastern Europe was falling apart and the United States only needed "to keep its baskets ready to gather the fruit." But he did not think that Bush believed this.

Bush assured Gorbachev—and it was a recurrent theme—that as Europe had changed, "we have not responded with flamboyance or arrogance. . . . I have conducted myself in ways not to complicate your life. That's why I have not jumped up and down on the Berlin Wall."

Gorbachev said he had noticed that and appreciated it.

Bush and Gorbachev agreed on the goals and urgency of the arms control agenda. Baker and Shevardnadze would follow up (and spent a fair amount of time at Malta, while the leaders were in their small meetings, on a U.S. move in the chemical weapons talks).

* * *

On no subject was the new agenda "beyond containment" more evident than on economics. Bush had offered a series of proposals that were, in essence, about how to bring East and West economic systems closer. The U.S. and Western side would have to lift old sanctions. They would have to open more trade and investment. They should offer whatever advisory help might be welcome and bring the Soviet Union—at least as an observer—into the new global trade system that was being worked out in the Uruguay Round negotiations.

One of the Malta meetings was devoted to discussion of the Soviet economy. With Bush's support, America's chief central banker, Fed chairman Alan Greenspan, had gone to the Soviet Union in October 1989 (accompanied by Zoellick) to survey the Soviet economic situation. Never before had Soviet economic officials opened up this way to such an American economic inspection.

Greenspan came away "skeptical" that the Soviet leadership would be able to develop and execute a difficult, coherent program to attain any "quick takeoff into a rapidly growing market-oriented economy." Market pricing alone was not an answer unless there were competitive enterprises and competitive pricing, thoughtful sequencing of the needed changes, and more institutional capacity to handle the disruption. Analyzing various scenarios, Greenspan saw serious dangers of disorder and violence.

Greenspan did not think the Soviet military was the big obstacle. The soldiers were worried about the economy too. He found that his Soviet counterparts were "surprisingly open to our ideas," but had trouble seeing how to carry them into practice.

Despite his unease, Greenspan supported U.S. help "to improve the performance of their economy which is in our longer-term interest. The odds on the success of such activity are long; but the potential payoff is large."[33]

The Soviet economic problems were enormous. No one had easy answers for how to do a post-communist transition. Government as well as academic expertise was thin. The IMF was one of the few places that had relevant experience on the financial side; the World Bank one of the few that had serious institutional knowledge about all the microeconomic and sectoral changes that might be needed. But it was a giant undertaking and the transition was bound to be painful.

The United States simply did not find the kind of economic policy partners in the Soviet leadership that the U.S. had found among the new leaders in Poland. The Soviet system was far less flexible and much more burdened by the huge claims of monopoly industries and the military complex.

Gorbachev's aide, Chernyaev, took some time during the autumn of 1989 to read over a set of Western writings about possible Soviet reforms. Two points stood out to him about how Westerners saw his country. One was that the Westerners thought that "Gorbachev needs to finally decide to make a breakthrough, he cannot linger and play on the safe side any longer, he has to step away from half-measures, time is working against him." More and more, Chernyaev had come to share this view. During 1990, Gorbachev's unwillingness or inability to "make a breakthrough" became Chernyaev's greatest single frustration with the boss to whom he was so devoted.

Yet Gorbachev could not do this alone. The other point Westerners kept making was that "Gorbachev" needed to make this or that choice. "Everybody appeals to the personality," Chernyaev noted in his diary. "But the problem," he added in this personal journal, "is that Gorbachev no longer has the power to do anything decisive, even if he makes up his mind."

Why? "This is not because, as the West thinks, he is hindered by Ligachev [a 'right'-wing opponent], the apparatus, or the bureaucracy. It is because Gorbachev does not have a mechanism through which he can implement his decisions. There is nobody to enforce them. The Party is no longer recognized as a governing body."[34]

Whatever the specific policy proposals, in retrospect a modest start on an ambitious agenda, Malta had done what Bush intended. Chernyaev was "simply astonished" at the cooperative approach Bush and Baker adopted, as if they were colleagues at a Politburo meeting trying to solve common problems. To his diary, he noted that "M.S. [Mikhail Sergeyevich] acted like he and Bush were old pals—frank and simple, and openly well-intentioned." He thought the meeting made "a big impression" on Gorbachev too, "convincing him on an emotional level that the U.S. administration had made a choice."[35]

Putting Words into Action

Throughout the turbulent winter of 1989–90 and on into the spring of 1990, the U.S. government maintained this dual approach: Help Gorbachev politically and economically and raise his odds for success; at the same time consolidate the Soviet withdrawal from Eastern Europe and lasting arms control.

As Scowcroft put it to Bush, this was a "rare period in which we can seek to achieve a fundamental shift in the strategic balance, especially in Europe," with the opportunity to gain "freedom for Eastern Europe," a "significant reduction of the Soviet military threat to the West," and "the demilitarization of Soviet foreign policy in the regions." The United States would help perestroika as much as it could, "as long as Gorbachev continues to tolerate the diminution of Soviet power in Eastern Europe."

Within a few years the change would be irreversible; the USSR would not be able to restore its military domination of Eastern Europe without a "full-scale invasion." The United States had to do all it could, since it expected that Gorbachev's power would face even more serious challenges during 1990.[36]

The arms control work was running through five different sets of negotiations. Bush and Baker were pressing for all of these to produce mutually satisfactory results within a year.

Bush's instrument for managing this staggering agenda within his huge national security machinery was a special interagency group, called an "Ungroup" because it was outside the usual interagency system. This was run with great skill by one of Scowcroft's staffers, Arnold Kanter, and ramrodded with superb staff work by Gates.

If the combination worked, if Gorbachev could manage change and the changes could be consolidated in all these military spheres, the result would be a different kind of global system. It would be one in which the United States and the Soviet Union would have a fundamentally more cooperative relationship, in a system with new structures for such cooperation, even as national interests occasionally diverged. Gorbachev told Bush flatly that he believed, and would say, that the United States and the USSR were no longer adversaries.

For the Soviet military the CFE talks on conventional forces in Europe were always the most consequential and threatening. Most historians have paid little attention to the details of CFE; many hardly mention it, even though it was the most ambitious arms control agreement of all time. CFE was negotiating ceilings from the Atlantic to the Urals, among twenty-three states, on tanks, armored fighting vehicles, artillery, combat aircraft, and helicopters. The 1989 add-on of limits on foreign-deployed U.S. and Soviet forces was another item.

But the main focus in CFE was on reductions and limits of equipment, which were vital and more verifiable. The planned reductions would have a fundamental impact. Soviet combat power west of the Urals would be cut by about half. The crunch time for those choices would come during 1990. The conclusion and difficult implementation of this agreement put more strain on Gorbachev during 1990 and 1991 than any other set of arms control problems.[37]

Himself a combat veteran who had fought against the Germans during the Second World War, Chernyaev had a jaundiced view of the Soviet military brass. He privately noted that Gorbachev "knows that nobody will start a war against us. There is no real military threat. We need the army for the superpower prestige, and internally because there is nothing we can do with it right now. It has turned into an organic burden on society."[38]

* * *

Bush did want to help Gorbachev, but it was hard to know what to do. At least on economic matters and in matters of arms control, the United States could offer constructive ideas—and in the case of security policy, push ahead with forward-leaning agreements. But on the nationality problem it was harder to find the right balance between wanting Gorbachev to succeed (and stay in power) and America's long-standing support for self-determination in the Baltic states.

It was also hard because Gorbachev himself did not seem to really have a strategy for dealing with the problem. It often seemed as if he was temporizing.

The Baltic republics of the Soviet Union—Lithuania, Latvia, and Estonia—had once been part of the tsarist Russian Empire. They had gained their independence after World War I. In 1940, while Hitler and Stalin were dividing up Eastern Europe, the USSR had forcibly annexed these short-lived republics. The United States had never recognized the annexations.

Early in 1990, the Lithuanian leaders demanded full independence from the USSR. After narrowly heading off demands for immediate use of force against the dissident republic, Gorbachev canceled all his foreign appointments and headed a delegation that flew to the Lithuanian capital, Vilnius, on January 11. The results were inconclusive. The Lithuanians formally declared their independence in March 1990.

Also in January, a little more than a week after the talks in Lithuania, there was interethnic violence in Azerbaijan. Gorbachev sent defense minister Dmitry Yazov to the scene. Yazov ordered the use of force.

Hundreds were killed during fighting in Baku on January 20. As one top aide bitterly remarked, "Trans-Caucasus became Soviet Lebanon."[39]

* * *

Gorbachev was a complex man who had often responded to challenges by trying to leap ahead of them—even if he didn't seem to know quite where he was going. In early 1990, the Soviet leader took another such leap. He decided to revolutionize the structure of executive power in the Soviet Union.

The USSR had a dual structure on paper. Government officials were in charge of administering the country. But any decision that mattered was up to the party apparatus itself, not the government structures. The party told the Soviet government what to do. Gorbachev owed his power to his position as head of the party.

As the changes that Gorbachev himself launched gained momentum, the power and legitimacy of the party eroded. Gorbachev became more and more frustrated with party officials and the structures that supported the status quo.

His risky alternative, his leap forward, was to create a normal government that no longer ruled through the party. During January 1990, he appears to have decided to make himself a direct state ruler. Yakovlev urged him to concentrate "the real, plenipotentiary State power in your hands, removing the Politburo and even the talkative Supreme Soviet from the levers of power."[40]

In the first months of 1990, Gorbachev and his team developed a plan to turn him into a president. A president of the Soviet Union would gain his legitimacy through election. Then he might wield broad executive power directly over the government officials across the Union.

To design this new presidency, Gorbachev chose a model with elements drawn from both American and French experience, with ministers looking toward both the president and the parliament. He would be advised by a newly created Presidential Council, a kind of cabinet of ministers and leading intellectuals, and a Federation Council, representing the different republics (and reminiscent of the Bundesrat model in German history). Gorbachev's team secured this massive revision of the Soviet constitution in March 1990. They then sought and received advice and help in this work from the American and French governments.

Conservatives were willing to support the new moves, which sounded like a way to strengthen executive power and restore some order.

Liberals were suspicious. But they liked the multiparty democracy the reforms seemed to invite. The constitutional guarantee of a ruling monopoly for the Communist Party was repealed.

Rather than risk a divisive Union-wide election campaign and a possible conservative coup, Gorbachev took one step back. Rather than run for election to the presidency, he instead sought an indirect election to his new office. The new Congress of People's Deputies—the legislative body of the government—would choose the president, not a popular election. Not surprisingly, he was chosen as the Soviet Union's first president on March 14; he took his oath of office the next day.[41]

Gorbachev was very proud of his new title. When he visited Washington three months later, his aides told the Americans to refer to him as President Gorbachev, not General Secretary Gorbachev. The Soviets landed at Andrews Air Force Base in a plane bearing the Soviet flag on the tail—Air Force One, Soviet-style.

As Gorbachev took office, the Russian republic had just run its own elections. These were popular elections on a more open and democratic model, with a range of parties.

Almost half of the elected deputies followed a coalition called "Democratic Russia," and about another 40 percent were "Communists of Russia," with the rest swinging back and forth. Yeltsin led the "Democratic Russia" camp. He, like other leaders in the republics, could now claim legitimacy from having been directly elected, and he was a dominant figure in the newly elected Russian parliament. He was elected its chairman at the end of May 1990.

A New Germany?

The new Krenz government in East Germany tried desperately to fulfill the promise to Moscow to reform and tell the people the truth. This resulted largely in ridicule and an increasing sense that the GDR was beyond help. Still, many wanted to believe that East Germany would survive and that the reform of the country and the question of eventual unification could be separated. Some wanted to contain even any talk of unification.

No one expressed herself more clearly on this point than Margaret Thatcher. She visited Moscow late in September. At one point in the conversation, she asked the Soviet notetaker (Chernyaev) to put his pen down. He did.

"Britain and Western Europe," she said, "are not interested in the unification of Germany. The words are written in the [May 1989] NATO Communique, but disregard them. We do not want the unification of Germany."

Such a development, Thatcher explained, "would lead to changes in the post-war borders, and we cannot allow that because such a development would undermine the stability of the entire international situation and could lead to threats to our security.

"We are not interested in the destabilization of Eastern Europe," she added, "or the dissolution of the Warsaw Treaty either."

"What a woman!" Chernyaev confided to his diary. Later, Thatcher praised Gorbachev for an hour on Soviet television.[42]

The Soviet government certainly agreed with Thatcher. Shevardnadze, in America, had complained privately to Baker and said publicly, in a speech to the UN General Assembly, "It is to be deplored, that fifty years after World War II some politicians have begun to forget its lessons. . . . It is our duty to warn those who, willingly or unwillingly, encourage those forces."[43]

When he met with Krenz on November 1, Gorbachev confidently listed all the West European leaders and other prominent people, including Americans and West Germans, who had pronounced that German unification was anathema.[44] Gorbachev admitted, however, that Bush's government was making some troubling noises.

* * *

Bush did indeed have a different view. On September 7, Baker's deputy, Eagleburger, told Kohl's chief of staff, Rudolf Seiters, that "one thing needed to be clear about U.S. policy: although it does not make much sense for the U.S. to talk a lot about the subject of reunification, when President Bush says that he favors reunification, he means it. The U.S. private position on reunification is the same as our public one—we favor it."[45]

If that point was not already clear, Bush made it again, in public, on September 18. Reacting to a couple of columns that morning, a reporter raised the subject. Bush said, "I would think it's a matter for the Germans to decide. But put it this way: if that was worked out between the Germanys, I do not think we should view that as bad for Western interests."

He went on, "I think there has been a dramatic change in post–World War II Germany. And so, I don't fear it.... There is in some quarters a feeling—well, a reunified Germany would be detrimental to the peace of Europe, of Western Europe, some way; and I don't accept that at all, simply don't."[46]

Helmut Kohl was rethinking the possibilities too. As a young politician in the postwar Christian Democratic Union (CDU), he had been a follower of then-chancellor Konrad Adenauer. Back then the CDU view was that the GDR was illegitimate. Change would come from Western strength and Western pressure.

That hope faded as years of division hardened into a modus vivendi to support two separate states—both UN members, both internationally recognized. Annually on the "day of German unity," the German chancellor would say something vague about the hope for one country again. But it was just that—a hope, with no operational implications at all.

By October 1989, Kohl was reverting back to the old ideas of his political youth. The communist regime was illegitimate. Western firmness and pressure was the way to get results.

Kohl was careful. "Now a clear head is necessary, not excitement," he told his party colleagues. A political revolution was brewing inside the GDR, he believed. The Krenz government would not last.

So Kohl pushed for free elections in the GDR that could end the communist monopoly on power. As for what would happen after that, it would just be left open. At the time, this short-term agenda was radical enough.[47]

To ask for help, Kohl called Bush on October 23. Bush promised he would help, and he did. The next day he gave an interview to the *New York Times*. He said, "I don't share the concern that some European countries have about a reunified Germany."[48]

Kohl sought and received similar support from Mitterrand, who saw the matter in broad historical currents. To him, the German nation was a historical force. Reunification was a possibility, not to be ruled in or ruled out.

Secretly, Mitterrand's cabinet had held a quite farsighted discussion about Germany's future on October 18. So Mitterrand's position was considered and deliberate. After meeting with Kohl on November 2–3, Mitterrand announced that "I am not afraid of reunification. I do not ask myself that kind of question as history advances.... The answer is simple: insofar as Eastern Europe is evolving, Western Europe must itself grow stronger, strengthen its structures and define its policies."[49]

Kohl then took his stand to demand free elections and change in the GDR. As for the long term, he emphasized "free self-determination."

But he went on, "Our fellow Germans do not need lectures—from anybody. They themselves know best what they want. And I am sure: if they get an opportunity, they will decide in favor of unity." After quoting, significantly, Konrad Adenauer ("We strive for both—for a free and united Germany in a free and united Europe"), Kohl concluded, "We have less reason than ever to be resigned to the long-term division of Germany into two states."[50]

There he left if for another day—one that would come sooner than anyone, even Kohl, could have imagined.

* * *

As the new East German government prepared to announce its reform program at an upcoming party meeting (called a "plenum"), ordinary citizens poured into the streets to voice pent-up dissatisfaction with decades of hardship and repression. The daily public protests were capped by the rally of an estimated half a million in East Berlin on November 4.

Krenz replaced part of the ruling Politbüro. The plenum reorganized the government and vaulted Hans Modrow, a reformer within the SED exiled as party boss in Dresden, into the Politbüro. The new government promised to legalize the New Forum and other opposition parties. The U.S. embassy in East Berlin reported to Washington that the plenum had demonstrated "a significant shift toward potentially credible reform, primarily because of the dramatic rise of Modrow."[51]

The Soviet government liked Modrow more than Krenz. Moscow had long harbored a friendly interest in the Dresden chief's future.[52] Now that reformist communists such as Günter Schabowski and Modrow were coming to the fore, the USSR felt even more strongly committed to backing a new leadership. The Soviets hoped this group could now stabilize the situation.

The reorganized East German government quickly faced the question of travel restrictions. Should they continue to keep East Germans penned up in their country? On November 4 the GDR had begun allowing East Germans to travel to the Federal Republic through Czechoslovakia. Once again tens of thousands of East Germans crowded the roads into Czechoslovakia, trying to make their way west. Once again, the West German embassy grounds in Prague began filling with refugees.

Krenz had promised Gorbachev that he would allow almost all East German citizens to travel, so long as they took no money with them, and Gorbachev had posed no objection.[53] Shevardnadze's top deputy told the Soviet ambassador to let the East Germans decide this, treat the travel laws as a GDR decision. The ambassador insisted on receiving a written instruction telling him to step back. After a few days, he got one, duly stating that the travel law was "an internal responsibility of the GDR."[54]

The East Germans gave the job of writing the new travel law to the former security chief, Erich Mielke, who had just been forced out of the government and the Politbüro. The text of the law was hastily drafted, the Soviets were later told, by two Stasi colonels and two departmental chiefs from the Interior Ministry.

The draft extended new liberal rules to all trips, even short private ones, and to all of the GDR's frontiers, including those in Berlin. No senior official on the East German side fully grasped that, in theory, the law would apply to the Berlin Wall, a border and a city under Four Power supervision.

"Four Power" controls were the rights of the four occupying powers in Germany—the U.S., the Soviet Union, Britain, and France—in 1945. Since there had never been a formal German peace treaty, these rights over "Germany as a whole" and over the administration of Berlin had never been relinquished.

The poorly drafted text of the travel law read, "Requests for private trips abroad may be submitted from now on even in the absence of special prerequisites." There was certainly no intention to authorize trips abroad without forcing citizens to first get an exit visa. The draft was submitted to the 213 members of the SED Central Committee present for the party plenum. No one objected.[55]

The Central Committee blessed the draft on November 9. Krenz then gave a copy to Politbüro member Schabowski, who had been holding daily press conferences on the activities of the SED party plenum. Krenz was busy with other matters.

One of the notes to the document promised that the new travel regulations would be announced the next day, November 10, *after* exact instructions on how to implement the law had been circulated to East German security authorities throughout the country. Krenz had told Gorbachev that he would submit the new law to the legislature before Christmas.

Schabowski overlooked this detail and read the new law near the end of his hourlong press conference. Reading and extemporizing, he said that interim travel regulations had been prepared that would allow anyone to apply for private travel, that permission would be forthcoming in short order, and that the police had been told to issue visas for permanent emigration "immediately," without application. The new law, he said, would take effect immediately. Then, just after seven o'clock in the evening, Schabowski drove home.

Those watching the press conference were seized with curiosity. But the exact text of the draft was not available, so the journalists reported their interpretations of the law, garbling the language and creating a public sensation during the night of November 9–10. Confused diplomats and West German officials were trying to figure out what Schabowski had meant. During his press conference the West German mission's press representative—clearly more aware of the import of the announcement than Schabowski himself—was seen to grasp his head, moan, and dash from the room to sound the alarm. Officials in Bonn, including the intelligence service, were taken by surprise.[56]

Rumors spread that all travel restrictions were being dropped, including exit visa requirements. Thousands of people began massing near the Berlin Wall. They asked border guards about the new regulations, but the guards had no information and no guidance to offer.

As the night wore on, huge numbers of people crowded at the wall. The guards at their checkpoints still had not received their instructions. They did not know what to do and were uncertain about their legal duty.

Security forces might have been able to handle a planned demonstration, but this was not a demonstration. With hordes of people forcing the guards to give way or shoot the confused and milling throng, local guard commanders gave way. The bewildered interior minister ratified what his guard commanders had already decided. Crowds streamed through into West Berlin. The wall had been opened. November 10 became a holiday in Berlin as masses of East Germans joined their Western brethren in a tumultuous, euphoric celebration.

Krenz immediately put the best face on events and pretended that the opening of the wall had been intentional. That was true in substance. But it was not supposed to happen the way it did. Actually, the government had been so disorganized that it took months before Schabowski himself was able to piece together just what had happened that night.

Krenz had phoned the Soviet ambassador in the morning of November 10, and Kochemasov had told him that the Soviets were confused about what was happening and were angry that he, Krenz, was being so indecisive.

But, Krenz replied, we were planning to open the borders in any case, as your side knew.

Not this way, Kochemasov answered, and on the FRG-GDR frontier, not in Berlin. Matters in Berlin affect the interests of the Four Powers.

Well, replied Krenz, this is now a theoretical question.[57]

In one of the most colossal administrative errors in the long, checkered history of public bureaucracy, the Krenz government abdicated responsibility for the most important decision in its history to the people in the street. The enormous façade of government authority had been devastated. Robert Darnton observed a week later that "in East Berlin especially, the idea has spread that in conquering the Wall the people seized power."[58]

The people never let the government have its power back again. It was a mortal wound to the communist regime.

Schabowski was not worried, however. He was just glad that the government had finally done something popular. "We hadn't a clue that the opening of the wall was the beginning of the end of the Republic," he said. "On the contrary, we expected a stabilization process."

Years of insulation from the feelings of ordinary people had left East Germany's leaders with no instincts for how they should seize this historic moment. In the next few days not a single leader of the GDR appeared at the wall. But every leading figure in the Federal Republic of Germany showed up there. They came to speak both to West Germans and to the new leaders of East Germany—the common people.[59]

* * *

The opening of the Berlin Wall was as electrifying and emotional an event as the world had seen in many years. There were the scenes of families reunited after years of separation. There were the giddy East German citizens encountering the casual prosperity most West Germans took for granted, the bewildering array of material goods that had been nothing more than images on West German television. And there were the feelings of nationhood that welled up in Germans on both sides of the divide—among people who had assumed that those emotions were long dead and properly buried. Upon learning that the wall had opened, the Federal Bundestag broke spontaneously into the national anthem.

The moment did not produce immediate calls for unification of the country. But it did produce an atmosphere in which most understood that the old order was dead. The question would come rapidly onto the international agenda, and events threatened to overrun the ability of statesmen to answer it. What would the new Germany be?

By the end of November, the leaders of the two Germanys offered competing visions for their countries. Then, literally within a week and a half, so fast one could miss it, the French and American governments added their voices.

* * *

In Bonn, policymaking on the German question was dominated by a small number of key personalities. Helmut Kohl has already been a major figure in our story. It may help to recall that Kohl was the first chancellor of the FRG who had not been of military age or older during the Second World War. He represented the first postwar generation. This was the generation that remembered both the pain of German division and the riveting 1948–49 Allied airlift of food and coal into Soviet-blockaded Berlin as formative experiences. Kohl's wife came from a family of refugees from Germany's lost eastern territory.

Never known as a charismatic speaker or party visionary, never the ideological standard-bearer, Kohl had been underestimated throughout his career. A master of party politics, Kohl instinctually perceived the middle ground on an issue before others could discern it. By the time they found it, Kohl might already be standing there.

Kohl's style was more distinctive than his ideology. He had a solid common touch, which was an authentic part of who he was. In private as well as in public, he was dedicated to traditional family values and a deeply felt, sometimes defensive, pride in his German nation. He was like Bush in the sense that underlying principles or convictions were more important to him than the particulars of policy disputes, although he could certainly handle details.

With Genscher and the Foreign Ministry barred from "domestic" inter-German unity negotiations with the GDR and some of the key high-level diplomacy, Kohl became the central figure for the FRG. Kohl's closest aide for foreign policy was Horst Teltschik, forty-nine years old in 1989. Other staff members and relevant cabinet ministers (finance, interior) handled negotiations on internal German issues.

Teltschik had suffered personally from Germany's defeat and division. He was six years old when, with his family, he had fled to Bavaria, refugees from the German-speaking community in the country of Czechoslovakia. The family had a difficult time.

After becoming an army officer, Teltschik trained as an academic. Like the American, Rice, Teltschik's academic work focused on the workings of the communist bloc (his dissertation was on East German–Soviet relations, hers on civil-military relations in the Soviet bloc).

Neither Teltschik's influence nor his brashness won him any friends at the Foreign Ministry, where Genscher had become an institution, and a powerful one. As foreign minister since 1974, Genscher was one of the most enduring and popular figures on the West German political scene.

Genscher had grown to adulthood during the Hitler period and the Second World War. At the age of ten (1937) he had joined the Hitler Youth. He was only sixteen when he found himself manning air defense batteries against the bombers raining explosives down on his country. American soldiers took him prisoner. Released, he rejoined his mother in Halle, in the Soviet zone of occupation.

After the war he studied law. He found life under communism unbearable. In 1952, after seven years of it, he made his way into West Germany (this was before the wall went up in 1961). There he settled into law and FDP politics in Bremen, then Bonn. The FDP, a small European liberal party, favored limited government; it rejected communism, socialism (the SPD), and clericalism (the Protestant CDU or Catholic CSU). Known for his wit and judgment, Genscher rose to become interior minister in 1969, then foreign minister in the 1974 coalition formed by SPD chancellor Schmidt.

As we mentioned in chapter 1, in 1982, Genscher and his party had left the SPD coalition and joined the government headed by Kohl. Genscher, whose wife's family had also fled Germany's former eastern territory, shared Kohl's deep convictions about the nation's larger national identity.

As foreign minister, Genscher had positioned himself as a bridge between East and West, between Germany and France. This stance was popular. So was Genscher's energetic globetrotting style. By 1989 he personified German foreign policy to an entire generation that could barely remember a time when he did not hold the post.

* * *

No one—neither ordinary citizens nor heads of state—knew what would or should happen next in Germany. Years after the event it is easy to assume that the popular pressure for unity was immediate, predictable, and irresistible. It was not.

Even after the first popular voices for unification were heard on November 19 in Leipzig, many East Germans still thought that the GDR should remain a separate sovereign state. Even those who favored the idea of eventual unification wanted to retain "socialism." East German dissidents wanted a better socialism in a separate German state, one that rejected the materialism and exploitation of the West.

At first, the dominant theme was wariness. Everyone was cautioning each other. Bush was criticized, and satirized, for offering what was regarded as an underwhelming public reaction. It annoyed him. He had made a deliberate choice not to humiliate the Soviets. "I won't beat on my chest and dance on the wall."

Telephoning, Gorbachev warned Kohl that every action must now be "carefully thought out." He said that "we cannot allow clumsy actions to endanger this turn or, worse, to push events toward an indescribable path, a path to chaos." Kohl readily agreed.[60]

In the first weeks, the West German line was clear. As the new British foreign secretary, Douglas Hurd, summarized it, "[The West Germans] want to encourage free elections, avoid talk of reunification, and reassure the Soviet Union."[61]

In East Germany, leaders began moving to follow the Polish and Hungarian models for change. This was a Roundtable process to set up elections to be held in 1990.

The East German parliament, no longer a rubber stamp for the ruling party, elected a new prime minister, the one credible communist reform figure, Hans Modrow, the party secretary from Dresden who had been chastised in early 1989 for supporting Gorbachev-style perestroika.

Unassuming, straightforward, Modrow formed a government with several new faces, including some noncommunists. Political reform, he explained, would establish the legitimacy of the GDR as "a socialist state, a sovereign German state." The GDR would reject the "unrealistic as well as dangerous speculation about a reunification."

The two German states would now have a "cooperative coexistence" on all questions, from peace and armaments to culture and tourism, cemented by a "treaty community" (*Vertragsgemeinschaft*).[62] The two German states could form a relationship akin to that of members of the European Community, including harmonization of rules and even, perhaps, a form of economic union.

In mid-November, Modrow's approach won support. For the first time there was a voice in East Berlin to counter Kohl's vision for Germany, backed by many voices in both East and West Germany.[63]

* * *

The new East German government was looking toward multiparty elections that, it then thought, would be held in late 1990 or early 1991.

Public opinion was cautious. Polls indicated that the largest segment of West Germans, 44 percent, foresaw closer relations between the two states along the lines of the Federal Republic's ties to Austria and Switzerland. Another poll showed that most West Germans at least supported unification in principle, and nearly half thought it might be achieved in maybe ten years.

Kohl's likely opponent in his 1990 reelection campaign, Social Democratic Party leader Oskar Lafontaine, had a clear view—against unification. He said that "the conservative right wing" might have "the old national state as its point of orientation." To Lafontaine, "this isn't appropriate anymore, and it certainly has nothing to do with the current wishes and feelings of the people of the GDR."[64]

In the third week of November, after his staff had some initial discussions with the new East German leaders, Kohl decided to announce his preferred agenda for change. It was the most daring and consequential move of his public life.

Teltschik and a constitutional law scholar whom Kohl admired, Rupert Scholz, had urged Kohl to outline a concept of his own. They said he had a historical duty to offer some vision that might lead to German unity.

As we have mentioned, Kohl's attachment to this ideal ran deep. It distinguished him from some of his political rivals, even inside his own party.

Teltschik and Scholz encouraged Kohl to believe that such a program could be outlined as a step-by-step plan. The steps could walk through a confederation (a little like Modrow's "treaty community") and on to unity.

Teltschik had been encouraged by his much too optimistic reading of an informal paper that he had just received from a Soviet German expert. The paper seemed to imply flexibility in Soviet analysis of the situation.

Kohl decided to move fast, gathering his confidants in his bungalow on the evening of Thursday, November 23. They decided that over the weekend they would secretly prepare Kohl's speech.

Teltschik held the pen. Genscher and the rest of the West German cabinet was deliberately excluded from all of these deliberations. If they were included, one adviser counseled, "an hour later" Kohl's idea would be in the press, where "it will fizzle and vanish (*'geht kaputt'*)."[65]

The following Tuesday, November 28, Kohl delivered his address to the West German parliament, the Bundestag. It was a ten-point program for German unity, phased as a series of steps. Kohl mentioned no specific timeline for achieving them. The international status of this united Germany was deliberately left vague. The plan, he said, would involve a "peace order" and arms control, all embedded somehow "in the all-European development and in the East-West relationship."[66]

With this speech Chancellor Kohl defined a path to German unity, both internationally and within German domestic politics. It was cautiously and reassuringly worded, implying a long-term time frame. Privately his advisers had a five- to ten-year timeline in mind.

But the endpoint goal, unity, was the magnetic pole that would attract or repel. Genscher felt he should congratulate Kohl on his "great speech" and stand by the program. The opposition SPD, divided on how to react, offered qualified support for the plan.

Teltschik exulted in his diary about the "giant success!" He wrote, "We have achieved our goal. The Chancellor has taken over the leadership of opinion about the German question."[67]

Fearful of leaks, Kohl had not revealed the contents of his speech to his Western allies either. He could hardly tell foreign governments what he would not tell his own foreign minister.

Some of his advisers foresaw that springing the move without any warning could prove to be counterproductive. Teltschik preferred the "surprise effect." Kohl backed this view, but with one exception. He ordered that the text of the speech be sent to President Bush as it was being delivered, accompanied by a lengthy message explaining what Kohl was trying to do.[68]

In Washington, at first some officials were irritated about the lack of consultation, until experts quickly realized that Kohl had not consulted Genscher either. There was angst about the absence of any specific mention of NATO. But Bush and others were essentially positive. He and Kohl discussed it ("We are on the same wavelength," Bush said), and planned to meet together (without their foreign ministers, at Kohl's request) in Brussels about a week later, after Bush's Malta summit with Gorbachev.[69]

"Every word of sympathy for self-determination and unity is very important now," Kohl said. Bush knew it. Talking to reporters later in the day on November 29, he told them, "I feel comfortable. I think we're on track."

The reporters asked Bush what he wanted for Europe. He replied, "In terms of the 'vision thing,' the aspirations, I spelled it out in little-noted speeches last spring and summer, which I would like everyone to go back and reread. And I'll have a quiz on it [laughter].... You'll see in there some of the 'vision thing'—a Europe whole and free."[70]

* * *

The opening of the Berlin Wall cracked the edifice of communist repression throughout Eastern Europe. In an instant the new leaders in Poland and Hungary felt more secure. People surged into the streets in Bulgaria, then Czechoslovakia, followed finally by a violent revolution that overthrew the Romanian dictatorship in December. The Romanian dictatorship was still willing to shoot its enemies. The revolution therefore ended with the dictator and his wife being lined up in front of a firing squad. The new Romanian government then abolished capital punishment. Communist rule in Eastern Europe had collapsed.

As 1989 drew to a close, the question was no longer whether East Germany would remain communist in the old sense. It was about what would come next, as the former communist reformers now had become democratic socialists.

The choices about Germany's future were no longer theoretical. At this point, in December 1989, the three main options were:

- Continue with two independent, democratic states, the FRG and the GDR;

- Two states in a confederation of some kind;

- Two states merging into a new, unified Germany.

And there was a corollary: How fast should all of this move?

Gorbachev, Thatcher, and many others favored the first option. Their answer to the corollary was clear—as slowly as possible.

Some Soviets and Germans, East and West, favored the second option, partly because they thought the first one was unsustainable.

Kohl, Bush, and Mitterrand all were at least willing to accept full unification, the third option. In this phase they all believed the process would go step by step, over a number of years.

One note about terminology: "unification" or "reunification?" About one-third of the pre-Hitler Germany had been annexed by postwar Poland and the postwar Soviet Union. So "reunification" might seem to imply the re-creation of that prewar Germany with those old prewar borders of 1937. Therefore, U.S. officials (like the authors of this book) usually preferred to talk of "unification" to describe the process of creating a fresh single German state.[71]

* * *

Kohl and Modrow framed the agenda for their opposing views. In December, the Soviet government was privately and publicly furious with Kohl. Several West European leaders were angry too.

The Canadian leaders, who had just come from Moscow, quoted to Bush and Baker a Shevardnadze comment that "all of us who were in the war are against revanchism and neo-Nazis." Brian Mulroney remembered Gorbachev's remark: "People have died from eating unripened fruit."[72]

If Gorbachev chose a confrontational response, he had options. There were nearly four hundred thousand Soviet troops in East Germany. Gorbachev could call immediately for a peace treaty conference that might reassemble all of Germany's Second World War adversaries and would be inclined to cement the status quo. If there was a confrontation, Kohl would be blamed by many in West Germany and in the alliance.

Some Soviets wanted to get ahead of the action with a conciliatory confederation proposal. But the consensus in Moscow, at this time, was that "one could definitely not talk of the disappearance of the GDR. The Soviet Union will not permit it."[73]

Meeting at Malta, Gorbachev and Bush agreed to disagree on the long-range goal. At the post-Malta press conference, Gorbachev stressed the "Helsinki process," involving all the countries of Europe, whose leaders had last met in 1975. That process, he said, "summed up the results of the Second World War and consolidated the results of that war. And those are realities." That "was the decision of history."[74]

* * *

These cautions were quickly being overrun by events in East Germany, however. The more liberated press began disclosing the high living among the communist rulers, scandalizing the East German public. Upper-level officials of the old regime were charged with corruption; the arrests of former top officials began on December 3.

The ability of the government to do anything was waning. At one point, garbage delivery ground to a halt in East Berlin as workers simply refused to work.

Krenz resigned his post as head of state on December 6. Modrow took over. Civil authority began to break down. Some citizens' committees seized public buildings in order to stop secret-police destruction of incriminating government records.

Some crowds attacked East German and then Soviet military installations in the GDR. For instance, in Dresden a crowd marched on the villa where the Soviet secret police, the KGB, had its headquarters. Colonel Vladimir Putin was in charge. The crowd had seized weapons from the East German secret-police armory.

Putin ordered his men to stand at the windows and display their weapons. He pleaded for the local Soviet garrison to send troops.

The general replied, "I asked Moscow but Moscow is silent."

"But what are we going to do?" Putin asked.

"In any event, I can't give you any help," the general replied.

To Putin, recalling the episode years later, "it seemed to me as if our country no longer existed. It became clear that the Soviet Union was in a diseased condition, that of a fatal and incurable paralysis: the paralysis of power." Moscow was silent.

Putin went to the crowd with a small armed escort. Pretending to be a German-language interpreter, he pleaded with the people to leave the building alone, that it was just a Soviet military installation. Some eye-witnesses say he brandished a pistol and said he was prepared to die. Then some other Soviet troops did show up after all, and the crowd eventually dispersed. Scenes like this were replaying around the GDR.[75]

* * *

Gorbachev had reason to worry that a loss of face on Germany might be the final straw in his battles at home.[76] At the end of November he had phoned Mitterrand and reportedly told him that on the day Germany unified, "a Soviet marshal will be sitting in my chair."

One such marshal, Marshal Akhromeyev, later reflected bitterly that Gorbachev's failure to give a "concrete answer" to the German question must have convinced the West that they would encounter no decisive opposition from the USSR. He blamed Gorbachev. He blamed a Foreign Ministry that "was not ready for a serious discussion" of the issues.[77]

But, back in Moscow, meeting with Genscher a few days after the Malta summit, Gorbachev unleashed his anger. In an extraordinary meeting that Chernyaev thought went "far beyond the bounds" of Gorbachev's usual discussions with statesmen, the Soviet leader treated Genscher like an errant child.[78]

Kohl's move had been an "absolute surprise," Gorbachev said. He thought that he and the chancellor had reached an understanding. Or perhaps the chancellor did not need this understanding anymore.

"Perhaps," said Gorbachev, "he thinks that his melody, the melody of his march, is already playing and he is already marching to it." This attitude could not be reconciled with the talk of constructing a "common European home."

Gorbachev attacked the ten-point plan in detail. These confederation ideas, he exclaimed, what did they mean for defense and alliance membership? Would the FRG be in NATO or the Warsaw Pact?

"Did you think this all through?" he demanded of Genscher.

Shevardnadze interjected dramatically, "Even Hitler didn't permit himself this."

The Soviets "left no doubt" that the GDR must remain an independent state and a member of the Warsaw Pact.

With Mitterrand, a day later in Kiev, Gorbachev uncorked his full scorn for Kohl, the provincial, and his deep anger about what he thought Kohl was trying to do with this "diktat." He told Mitterrand that when Genscher pleaded a cooperative desire, he had replied witheringly, "You tell me you agree with me, but your support for the Kohl plan and your whole career contradict that. After this plan you [Genscher] should resign."

But Gorbachev did not yet have an alternative plan to propose. Mitterrand asked at one point, "What should we do concretely?" The meeting ended inconclusively.[79]

Mitterrand was sympathetic to Gorbachev's concerns. He alluded, as he would several times in this period, to the danger of going back "to the Europe of 1913." But Mitterrand, like Bush, was in the midst of an intense effort to link Kohl's plan firmly to a wider vision for Europe's future.

A New Germany in a New Europe?

Of course, the future of the German state also held implications for the alliance structures that had dominated European security for nearly four decades. Several ideas were in play.

- Both alliances could remain and the unified Germany could be neutralized between them.

- Both alliances could disappear and U.S. and Soviet troops would go home.

- Both alliances could disappear and be replaced by an all-European security treaty of some kind.

- The united Germany could remain in NATO. This would go hand in hand with Germany's continued membership in the European Union.

Gorbachev and Thatcher, among others, supported the first option. But with the states of the Warsaw Pact fleeing communism, it was hard to say how long the Soviet-led Warsaw Pact alliance could last.

And while others thought that some combination of option two and option three would work, the Americans were clear from the very beginning. Germany should choose. Washington was willing to bet that a Kohl-led, united Germany would choose NATO.[80]

Kohl, however, tried for as long as he could to avoid giving specific answers to these key international issues. He was still reluctant to go further on European integration. He was reluctant to detail an answer to the NATO issue. He was reluctant to offer a public commitment about the future borders of a united Germany.

Privately, Kohl tended to say the right things, at least in a general way, on all these points. But he did not want to be publicly boxed in. For those who were distrustful, this could be very troubling.

The more trusting tended to believe that Kohl, having already taken a huge political gamble, was trying to hold every possible West German voter that he could. From a domestic political point of view, consider Kohl's problem. None of these commitments on international issues, specifically, were big vote getters. All could antagonize some segment of the voting public.

On the other hand, the overall impression of international solidarity was popular and an essential vote getter. Kohl may well have reasoned that he had to preserve every appearance of such solidarity, while avoiding any unnecessary points of friction. (Genscher had some ideas of his own, but these were not deployed until late January 1990.)

Intuiting much of this, during this initial phase, France and the United States both played crucial roles. Their public support was indispensable for Kohl, especially with so much tension from the Soviet Union. They then leveraged their position, and their sympathy for Kohl's aspirations, to nail down two essential conditions: Germany would unify fully and completely—within NATO and the European Community.

*   *   *

Mitterrand and his team had prepared themselves for this moment. In their sensitive cabinet discussion on October 18, Mitterrand's longtime diplomatic adviser and sometime spokesman, Hubert Védrine, had prepared a remarkable analysis of German possibilities. He broke down all the different unification possibilities. He presumed that some sort of unification was already becoming inevitable.

Rather than try to stop this historical development, which was not Mitterrand's instinct, Védrine argued that "it was necessary to go with the Germans by accompanying them." What he meant was very close to what Bush and Baker would also soon start saying.

Védrine emphasized European integration. "Everything remains manageable if this movement toward the end of the division of the German people does not advance faster than the European construction and the overall removal of barriers between Eastern and Western Europe."[81]

All of Mitterrand's moves stayed with this policy line. He and the key policy advisers on his team, including Foreign Minister Dumas, Védrine, and (on Europe) Élisabeth Guigou, fixed on a litmus test. Would Kohl agree right now to start work on economic and monetary union with an intergovernmental conference that would get to work soon, during 1990?

This was the issue that, earlier in 1989, the leaders had deliberately left open. They had put off a final decision on what to do with the Delors report.

Now Mitterrand was chairing the next European Council summit, in Strasbourg on December 8–9. Beginning in late October, he pressed Kohl hard on this litmus test—to agree to begin work.

Kohl stubbornly resisted. He still preferred to put off such a decision for at minimum another year, at least until after his election campaign was over at the end of 1990. Then came his surprise announcement of the ten-point plan. Now the Franco-German interactions became truly intense.

Mitterrand met with Genscher on November 30. It was a meeting Genscher later remembered as the "most important" he ever had with the French president.

Mitterrand was angry. For him this took the form of becoming icy cold and unambiguous in tone. He did not threaten to oppose unification. Instead, he painted a picture of an alternative Europe, one in which Germany unified on its own terms. It is worth reading carefully what Mitterrand had to say:

> If we want to go forward in East-West relations without risk, then
> it requires the parallel progress in European integration. If the
> West Integration stands still, it goes backward. If it goes back-

ward, then the conditions in Europe would experience fundamental changes and new, privileged alliances would arise.

It is not even to be ruled out there would be a return to the conceptual world of 1913 [just before the outbreak of the First World War]. That Europe of 1913 would, however, be full of threats.

If the future German reunification is accomplished in such a Europe, whose structure had not been decisively further developed, then we will have risked getting back to the old ways. It was [Mitterrand's] opinion that the reunification, if such a day comes, must be embedded in an even stronger, stabilized European Community. Otherwise the European partners would "seek new counterweights to line up against this new body of 80 million people."

Genscher assured Mitterrand that these new counterweights would not be needed—if the European integration went forward "as we have wished."[82]

In following weeks, Mitterrand would return to these warnings, again and again. In late January 1990, meeting with Thatcher, he recounted how he had told the West Germans that they had to "think of the consequences" if the European construction did not keep pace with German unity. "Russia will send a diplomat to London, then to Paris: Let us understand each other. I will say yes. Then we will be in 1913."

Thatcher, who had far less faith in European constructions, had already been thinking about such possibilities. Her private secretary and key foreign policy adviser, Charles Powell, had been musing with her, also using early-twentieth-century analogies, about bilateral British alliances with France, or with Russia, as well as with the United States. These all clearly would be aimed at containing German power in the absence of a NATO framework.[83]

On December 8–9 the EC leaders held their summit in Strasbourg. The confrontation between Mitterrand and Kohl, over whether Kohl would pass France's litmus test for commitment to European integration, had reached its height.

Pressed hard by Genscher, Kohl decided to give in on the core issue.

The leaders agreed, and announced, that in 1990 they would go ahead and convene an intergovernmental conference to draft a treaty for European economic and monetary union.

The European summit in Strasbourg was still very tense. Kohl commented on the "icy climate." Mitterrand and Thatcher were privately commiserating.[84]

Yet Mitterrand had accomplished a major objective. On European integration he had put extraordinary pressure on Kohl to make a concrete commitment. And he got it.

Mitterrand accepted the possibility of unification philosophically. Or, as he drily remarked directly to Kohl early in January, "If I were German, I would be for reunification. That is patriotism. Being French, I do not have the same passion for it."[85]

* * *

Like Mitterrand, the Americans had been imagining an alternative Europe. They could easily envision a Europe in which, no longer needed, both NATO and the Warsaw Pact disappeared as outmoded relics of the Cold War system. A unified Germany's place in the EC might also become uncertain, as East European economies and countries drifted once more between the traditional power centers in Berlin and Moscow.

As NATO disappeared, all the European armies—and above all the German one—would have to develop their own independent high commands, capabilities, and strategies. Outsiders did not fully appreciate that the West German army had no general staff, that traditional seat of German strategic culture, because its general staff was NATO's International Military Staff.

In this different Europe the original, Cold War anchor for an American security commitment in Europe, NATO, would be gone. The United States forces would probably return home and disengage from Europe, as the U.S. had always done before 1917, as it had done in 1919, and as it had started doing again in 1945 before the creation of NATO in 1949.

For Americans, the burdens of a forward, evident security commitment could be quite tangible. Most of the benefits were not. Through history, many Americans had long regarded Europe and its problems with distance, or even distaste.

To Americans, this would not be a return to the world of 1913. It would not even be a return to the world of the 1920s. In the 1920s the United States had at least been a dominant financial creditor in the European economy. America was now a net debtor. Americans could easily find themselves turning inward in ways for which there was no ready historical analog.

* * *

"NATO" then was not just an organization. It was a shorthand symbol of a whole mental map of America in the world, a map in which America was a vital part of an Atlantic world, a member of an Atlantic community, linked by commerce, culture, and shared interests—ultimately including security.

On this point, Bush and his team did embody a distinct personal historical perspective. They believed in America's place in an Atlantic community, right down to their bones.

For them, Europe had been the principal source of the last two world wars, both of which had drawn Americans in. Bush and his generation remembered this personally. As a young Marine, Baker had served in Europe in the early 1950s.

A new Europe without much American engagement, its future politics and alignments all reopened in a time of painful transition, could become another major source of global instability and insecurity. Unlike in 1913, that would play out in an age of missiles and nuclear weapons.

To prevent that world, Bush and his advisers believed it was now the time to stake out a historically controversial position. Mainly to shape the expectations of other Americans, Bush began to say firmly, even bluntly, that, looking back over the stream of history during the last hundred years, America was now and should remain "a European power." It should remain so "as long as Europeans want that."

America exercised that power through partnerships. The NATO alliance was its only anchor.

Shortly after the Berlin Wall opened, U.S. officials began drafting principles to accept German unification, "consistent" with German membership in NATO and a stronger EC, and accepting the CSCE principles that borders could only be changed peacefully. The day after Kohl

announced his "ten-point" plan, Baker publicly announced these principles. The press did not notice. Teltschik did, though, and he passed Baker's
statement to Kohl.[86]

Flying from his Malta summit with Gorbachev directly to Brussels,
Bush had dinner with Kohl on the evening of December 3. At that dinner, Kohl accepted Bush's and Baker's principles.[87] Kohl then still thought
it would take years, perhaps five or more, to work through the stages to
reach the goal of unification.

Bush said Gorbachev was uncertain. That was why "we need a formulation which doesn't scare him, but moves forward."

Kohl referred to a recent Kissinger comment, that the Germanys
might come together within two years. That was obviously impossible,
Kohl said. The economic imbalance between the two states was too great.
But Bush should not misunderstand; the unification question was developing "like a groundswell in the ocean."

West European reactions were mixed, Kohl admitted. "I need a time
of quiet development."

At a gathering of NATO leaders the next day in Brussels, Bush then
deployed a carefully prepared statement. It was about "the future shape of
the new Europe and the new Atlanticism."

He asked all the alliance leaders to agree that the "goal of German
unification should be based on the following principles":

> First, self-determination must be pursued without prejudice to its
> outcome. We should not at this time endorse or exclude any
> particular vision of unity.
>
> Second, unification should occur in the context of Germany's
> continued commitment to NATO and an increasingly inte-
> grated European Community, and with due regard for the
> legal role and responsibilities of the Allied powers.[88]
>
> Third, in the interests of general European stability, moves
> toward unification must be peaceful, gradual, and part of a
> step-by-step process.
>
> Lastly, on the question of borders we should reiterate our support
> for the principles of the Helsinki Final Act.

Bush added, "An end to the unnatural division of Europe, and of Germany, must proceed in accordance with and be based upon the values that are becoming universal ideals, as all the countries of Europe become part of a commonwealth of free nations. I know my friend Helmut Kohl completely shares this conviction."

Then Bush proposed—this was the "new Atlanticism" part—that the basic purpose and character of the NATO alliance should change too. It would make the promotion of greater freedom in the East a basic element of its policy. The alliance's original purpose, defense against the Soviet bloc, was fading. Instead it would evolve into a source of fundamental reassurance about stability in a period of historic transition.

Bush said, "I pledge today that the United States will maintain significant military forces in Europe as long as our Allies desire our presence as part of a common security effort." He concluded, "The U.S. will remain a European power."[89]

After Bush completed his statement, Chancellor Kohl remarked that no one could have done a better job of summarizing the alliance approach. "The meeting should simply adjourn," he said.

There was an awkward pause. Then other West European leaders— led by the Italian prime minister, Giulio Andreotti, and by Thatcher— began voicing their disquiet about German developments.

Kohl responded sharply. The Dutch prime minister, Ruud Lubbers, interrupted the skirmish to rally a consensus behind Bush's approach. One by one, other allied heads of state supported the general thrust of Bush's principles.[90]

Thatcher felt defeated. After the NATO meeting in Brussels, she later wrote, "[I knew there] was nothing I could expect from the Americans as regards slowing down German reunification [and] possibly much I would wish to avoid as regards the drive towards European unity."[91]

Kohl and his advisers, by contrast, were elated. The world leaders would not derail Kohl's plan. "On the contrary!" Teltschik wrote. "The signal stayed green—caution will be admonished, but the railway switches are all thrown the right way."[92]

* * *

A week later, Baker offered the fullest statement of the alternative vision for "a new Atlanticism in a new Europe."[93]

The first element of the new architecture would be a different sort of security structure for Europe. Yes, NATO should be part of it. But this would not be the same NATO. It would be a different kind of organization, a base for an Atlantic community's political vision. It would attend more to nonmilitary aspects of security, such as arms control and the process of disarmament.[94] The security mission, Baker explained, would evolve to address future problems, such as regional conflicts and the proliferation of weapons of mass destruction. It would no longer be an alliance aimed against the Soviet Union.

The second element was, as the French and Americans had stressed, the future development of the European Community. Since the U.S. vision accepted the Mitterrand-Kohl-Delors vision for a stronger EC, Baker then paired the Atlantic vision to it by stressing "a significantly strengthened" American partnership with the EC.

Further, Baker argued that the EC needed to become wider, not just deeper. It should become a base to engage the new democracies of Eastern Europe. This move had already been foreshadowed in the emerging structure of aid programs to help the economic transition in those countries.

A final element of the new architecture was the CSCE. Baker argued that the CSCE had outgrown the pessimistic view in 1975 that it would only codify the postwar status quo. Instead, the organization had set up standards for human rights and consultation that were already helping to overcome the division of Europe.

The CSCE should, then, offer overarching principles for all of Europe and the United States. He thus proposed new agreements in each of the organization's three "baskets" of issues: security, economic transactions, and human rights.

One of the most interesting (and secret) reactions to Baker's "new Atlanticism" came in Paris. The French officials instantly realized that the United States was proposing to transform NATO from an anti-Soviet military alliance into a primarily political entity.

Their initial reaction, which they shared with Mitterrand, was to see this as a battle for political dominance in the future new Europe between an American Atlanticist vision and a Franco-German European vision. A lead Mitterrand staffer called out an analysis that Baker wanted "to entrust the Atlantic Alliance, where American preeminence is guaranteed, with the overall mission of leading the evolution of Europe, in its place, in all areas." Other staffers warned of a NATO that would "straddle" a rising EC. Or they complained that Baker wanted "to integrate the European construction into the Atlantic alliance," a "dangerous" idea.

Their different vision was that the transition should make NATO's role smaller, much more narrowly military. Mitterrand's alternative was to construct a new "European confederation" that would take on broad political and security roles.[95]

This French reaction to Baker's vision was instinctive and defensive. In fact, Baker's vision was genuinely inclusive. It was neither American-centered nor hierarchical. As Zoellick had explained it, writing to Baker weeks earlier, the "architecture of the New Atlanticism should not try to develop one overarching structure. Instead, it will rely on a number of complementary institutions that will be mutually reinforcing."[96]

Bush, Baker, Mitterrand, and Dumas had a chance to reassure each other about these plans. They submerged their differences, at least for a time, at their pleasant December talks on a French island in the Caribbean.[97]

Mitterrand agreed to the linkages with NATO and the EC. But this meant that German developments should go no faster than the EC construction, or the whole thing "will end up in the ditch." He referred again to how Europe could return to the world of 1913, in which case everything could be lost.

* * *

By late December, two basic visions had thus emerged for Germany's and Europe's future. Baker's speech was the broadest articulation of a vision in which Germany could choose to unify, doing so as part of a different Europe, one with a transformed NATO, a transformed EC, and new roles for the CSCE.

The alternative vision was for a modified status quo. This was the view offered by East Germany and the Soviet Union but also with supporters in Europe and in the United States. In this vision, internal reforms and democracy were welcome. But the international status quo of the Cold War system should stay in place. This would preserve both alliance systems and maintain a divided Germany with two German states, even as the Soviet Union and its allies became democratic socialist states.

In a kind of response to Baker, Shevardnadze chose a December 19 address to the European Parliament, in Brussels, to make his major statement of the modified status quo position. Soviet officials in Moscow debated a key point: Should they fight unification inch by inch, which might require some massive help to shore up the transitional East German government? Or should they side with German national aspirations, freely accepting some form of loose German confederation in order to insist on conditions that would protect their international interests?[98]

Shevardnadze leaned toward the latter course. But Gorbachev preferred to fight for the GDR's continued separate existence and continued acceptance of the "postwar realities."

After difficult internal arguments and last-minute rewrites, and without clearing the speech with the Politburo, Shevardnadze ended up with a strange hybrid of old policy and new.[99] He appeared to rule out unification. But at the same time he posed questions about how it could occur. He offered no alternative conception of East Germany's future. The effect was at once puzzling and ominous.

He reminded his audience that the Allied powers had legal rights over Germany, dating back to the occupation agreements of 1945. If that were not enough, Shevardnadze added, the Four Powers "have at their disposal a considerable contingent of armed forces equipped with nuclear weapons on the territory of the GDR and the FRG."

There had been a chance to get a united democratic Germany, Shevardnadze acknowledged. But that time had come and gone. It had passed after the rejection of a Soviet diplomatic offer in 1952 and the Federal Republic's decision to join NATO.

Having denounced German unification, Shevardnadze then posed a list of (seven) challenges that would have to be addressed by anyone who hoped to restore German unity. There were no apparent answers to any of them.

Genscher acknowledged Shevardnadze's challenge. He began suggesting some answers to Shevardnadze's seven questions that might satisfy Soviet concerns. Meeting privately with his own officials, he held up an article from the popular newspaper *Bild-Zeitung* that suggested how Germans should answer Shevardnadze's questions. The article said the Germans would not accept neutralization. But they would consider abolishing both alliances. They would consider reducing the American troop presence to a "symbolic contingent." Genscher told his officials: If you want to know our answers to these questions, read this article![100]

* * *

As 1989 came to an end, Scowcroft gave Bush a memo (drafted by Zelikow) about "U.S. Diplomacy for the New Europe." It had been quite a year. The year 1989 would be remembered as one, like 1848, that "transformed a continent."

But the story of the European revolutions of 1848 had not ended very happily. Looking back, "when the democratic revolutionaries of 1848 were at the peak of their success, cowing kings and toppling princes, they thought the remaking of society would overshadow the old diplomatic rivalries." They thought, as Victor Hugo put it, that "we are a predestined generation." Sadly, the revolutionaries of 1848 soon met violent, overpowering reactions.

In 1989 the "outlines of ancient European antagonisms" were already beginning to reemerge. The still-powerful Soviet government was unsteady and anxious. The German question was back. The European future was under intense discussion in constant EC meetings without Americans there.

The goals set in 1989—"active support for democratic change in Eastern Europe, the search for a new security environment through the CFE process, the continuation of nuclear deterrence, and an American partnership with a more united continent"—were inspiring. The challenge for diplomacy in 1990 now, though, was how "to make these things happen."

Scowcroft's memo was a call to action. "Twentieth century history gives no encouragement to those who believe the Europeans can achieve and sustain this balance of power and keep the peace without the United States." Kohl, in Bonn, had just told Baker the very same thing.

The United States was at a strategic crossroads. It would "either find a way to keep up" or "we will drift away from the inner workings and direction of European politics," leading to a new kind of isolationism: "detachment by default rather than by choice."[101]

Hit the Accelerator

That young theoretical scientist in East Berlin, Angela Merkel, was one of those swept up in East Germany's autumn revolution. She obtained a leave of absence for a few months from the Academy of Sciences and visited the headquarters of some of the new political parties and movements, sampling their wares.

Naturally, Merkel checked out the East German Social Democrats (SPD-East). She noticed that "someone had come in from the West to organize it all." She was put off by the singing of old Russian revolutionary songs ("Brothers, to the Sun, to Freedom") and how everyone, even the Westerners, addressed each other as "Comrade."

Shortly before Christmas 1989, she ended up signing up with a little party, headed by an outspoken lawyer, called "German Awakening." It was fundamentally aligned with the new Kohl agenda, a step-by-step process leading eventually to a unified German federal state.

When she joined, the party manifesto was committed to a "social market economy with a high level of ecological consciousness." It sought "nonalignment" and "demilitarization": If Germany was united, then the FRG must withdraw from NATO, a position broadly supported in the GDR.

Merkel was happy to volunteer what help she could. Her language skills and ability to articulate positions soon elevated her into a role as one of the spokespersons for the little party as it prepared for elections.

It turned out that the lawyer who headed Merkel's party had been one of the countless informers for the Stasi, the East German secret police. When this was disclosed, just before the elections, the party was discredited and received less than 1 percent of the eventual vote.

But because it was fundamentally aligned with Kohl's vision, rather than that of Modrow or the SPD (East or West), her little party had joined a larger coalition, called the "Alliance for Germany." The coalition was led by the CDU-East. In the old GDR, the CDU-East had been a puppet party. Now it was for real. It was headed by a musician (viola for the Berlin Symphony Orchestra) and lawyer, Lothar de Maizière. Like everyone in the GDR, de Maizière was inexperienced in democratic politics, but his party was getting plenty of organizing help from its Western counterpart.

As part of this Alliance for Germany, Merkel made new acquaintances. She did not return to the Academy of Sciences. Her professional life of scientific theory had now become compellingly practical.[102]

Merkel's experience was like that of many East Germans. By the end of 1989 a divide had opened between the civic groups, organized around small cells of longtime dissenters, that had played a leading part in the autumn revolution, and a mass movement of the general population. Unlike the Solidarity coalition in Poland, which had been organizing on a large scale for years, none of the civic groups in the GDR had a mass following.[103]

The whole population of the GDR was now practically forced to pay attention to politics. The civic group leaders were understandably inexperienced in either politics or policy. So a great many East Germans began to identify themselves with one or another of the established West German political leaders in the CDU or SPD. Or they identified themselves with the former communists (now renamed as the Party of Democratic Socialism). Free East German elections were scheduled for May 1990.

* * *

Kohl experienced the volcanic changes in East German politics firsthand. After a difficult meeting with Modrow, in Dresden on December 19, he addressed crowds of cheering East Germans. He spoke emotionally of the German nation. The crowd reacted by chanting for unification. It seemed that the East German people were rallying to the dream he, Kohl, had told them could come true.

At first, the American reports of this clamor were worried. Baker advised President Bush that Kohl's activities "may raise again the question with some, however, of whether the Chancellor's domestic political interest is leading him too far, too fast on the issue of unification; he's tapping emotions that will be difficult to manage."[104]

Genscher's adviser, Frank Elbe, told his counterpart on Baker's team, Zoellick, that the whole issue of speed was turning around. In the middle of November, he had told Zoellick that German moves might need to slow down, that "the tempo of German unification cannot be permitted to endanger the stability of Europe." A few weeks later, in early December, Elbe now felt that unification should take off, and it was Europe that would have to adapt to that. "If German unity doesn't come, *that* will endanger the stability of Europe."

Zoellick replied, "We also see it that way."[105]

New battle lines were starting to form in German politics. Modrow's government had gained some strength. The SPD—West and East—had more sympathy with his views. Kohl's reluctance to talk about a united Germany's future borders seemed to be pandering to a few voters who still resented the 1945 loss of so much historic German territory.[106]

Modrow had weathered the storm of corruption allegations. His biggest challenges were the economic issues and the open borders with West Germany. The freedom of citizens to travel, combined with the artificial East German price system and currency, created huge distortions. Westerners could snap up anything valuable in the East German marketplace. Every week, thousands of East Germans were migrating westward, especially those who were most employable—and therefore also especially important to East German society.

Modrow's government had no good answer to the economic crisis. He had difficulty staffing key positions and was unable to put together a budget. His program at first included only a few market elements. It offered little scope for privatization even as state enterprises, starved for subsidies, were starting to go bankrupt.

Kohl's government was reluctant to subsidize this East German system. As the weeks passed, his government was actively seeking to undermine it. Kohl became convinced that he should have nothing to do with Modrow or any other official of the old Communist Party. By the time

Modrow proposed a draft treaty for confederation, Kohl was no longer interested.

Instead Kohl began preparing to take another risky leap. Seeing the CDU-East, despite its former status as a puppet party of the communists, as the only available Eastern ally for his own party, and also seeing the coming elections in the East as a preview of those in the West, he started to imagine a direct path to the unification of Germany on his terms. He and Teltschik became convinced that the East German elections should be held soon, earlier than May.

Modrow also realized that he could not hold the country together until spring. He and the Roundtable advanced the elections from May 6 to March 18, partly because they thought faster elections would help their parties win.

Kohl welcomed the move, even though he thought that earlier elections would actually favor the communists and the SPD-East since they had the best-known and best-organized parties in the GDR. By dropping any effort to negotiate a step-by-step arrangement with Modrow, Kohl had to put together an entirely new course.

The alternative was a straight line toward unification with no stops in between. That policy made sense on only one timetable—as fast as all the issues could be resolved, as fast as the international traffic could bear (although in late January 1990, Kohl still seemed to think that would be about five years).[107]

In Washington, American officials had also begun to change course in the second half of January 1990. At the White House, Blackwill worried to Scowcroft that "we seem to be proceeding with business as usual—unwieldy...extended interagency disputes too small to be seen without the aid of a magnifying glass.... You will know the quality of exchanges on these breathtaking developments in Europe at your breakfast meetings with Baker/Cheney."

The United States needed a more ambitious policy. Blackwill had concluded that the sooner Germany became unified, the better. There should be a rush toward de facto unification along lines worked out between the United States and the Federal Republic.

The international community would be presented with a fait accompli.

Blackwill advised Scowcroft on January 26 that "reunification is coming rapidly, not gradually and step by step, and the process will not await 'an increasingly integrated European Community.'" Baker and his aides had arrived at the same judgment.

That might mean the Americans would waive their Four Power rights, but Washington should spare no effort to seize the high ground with the German people in becoming the foremost advocate of their national unity.[108]

When Teltschik met Scowcroft at a conference in Munich on February 3, he discovered that the White House had come to the same conclusion as the Chancellery. There should be a direct move, and at the fastest possible pace.

Such a fast pace would endanger all the international assurances that had been offered in late 1989. The Soviets would feel threatened. European integration could not keep pace. NATO issues and the future linkage of the United States to Europe were up in the air.

On the other hand, Blackwill feared that if unification were stretched out for years, the problems would become obvious. The international bargaining would become onerous. The Soviets and others would find too many opportunities to trade their acceptance of unity for concessions from Bonn on Germany's NATO membership, its military participation in the alliance, and the presence of American forces and nuclear weapons in Europe.

* * *

The West German–American convergence on the need for speed became apparent by the beginning of February. As they wanted to hit the accelerator, French and British leaders worried that Europe would not be able to adapt in time. They shared the American worry that the Germans might trade off other issues to get unification done. The American answer was to jump on the fast-moving train in order to help steer it. The French and British had a different idea. They wanted to slow the train down.

For example, on February 2, Dumas told the British ambassador that the FRG was now putting reunification ahead of everything else. "[Dumas] feared that, if neutrality was the price to be exacted for reunification, the FRG Government would be ready to pay it. Similarly, if the FRG Government had to choose between reunification and the continued development of the EC, they would choose the former."[109]

The same day Dumas confided his worries about speed, the British ambassador to Washington sent back word that "the clear US message is that speed is essential if we are to avoid a free fall to German unity."

Thatcher reacted: "The essential thing is to agree with Gorbachev/ Shevardnadze. Then we can try to persuade Germany."[110]

A week later, Thatcher's adviser, Powell, went out to Bonn for a meeting with Teltschik. He was struck by the "heady atmosphere" in West Germany. "Great events are in the air," he wrote to Thatcher, "and for the first time in 45 years Germany is out in front. For the Germans, this is the breakthrough. After decades of sober and cautious diplomacy, and adjusting themselves to fit in with decisions taken by others, they are in the driving seat and Toad is at the wheel. The exhilaration is unmistakeable. This time they are going to take the decisions and others can tag along."

Powell's report inflamed Thatcher's concern about "nationalism with a vengeance."[111] In Washington, though, U.S. leaders thought that speed was still the right choice. Blackwill believed that, at the moment, Gorbachev was still in power. The Soviets wanted the friendship of the West. Their German policy was cautious, even confused. This window of opportunity would not stay open much longer.

What would the Soviets do? Rice's assessment was that "creeping reunification—because everyone is afraid to talk about terms—is probably not very smart."

Of course, Gorbachev would be alarmed if the pace quickened. Yet the Soviets were in a difficult position. Rice thought that the United States should go ahead and hit the accelerator. "I believe (and this is a hunch and I guess if we did this that I would spend a lot of time in church praying that I was right)," she wrote, "that the Soviets would not even threaten the Germans. Within six months, if events continue as they are going, no one would believe them anyway."[112]

Depending on how officials wanted to unify Germany, they argued about a process to negotiate the terms. A strictly Four Power process, with only the former victors of World War II, was now off the table. The United States, at least, would not go along.

A giant international conference to negotiate a German peace treaty, as had happened at Versailles in 1919, was another idea—perhaps organized using the CSCE process and its thirty-five member states. The French and the Soviets seemed to like that idea.

The Americans were against such an unwieldy conference, which they thought would be mostly an excuse to delay or—even worse—try to impose conditions on Germany that neither America nor Bonn wanted. At the White House, Scowcroft and Blackwill advised Bush that the CSCE venue could become an "open-ended negotiation about the future of Europe in about the worst multilateral setting one can imagine."[113] But the NSC staff had no other idea to suggest. During January 1990, it was Baker's team that came up with a constructive answer.

* * *

On the other side, Gorbachev and Modrow were not standing still. On January 26, Gorbachev convened an extraordinary meeting of advisers for four hours of debate about policy toward Germany. He had just returned from difficult talks in breakaway Lithuania.

Chernyaev urged a radical position. He urged Gorbachev to align himself directly with West Germany, with Kohl. Chernyaev thought that Kohl was a reliable partner, that firm FRG ties to NATO were a good thing, and that Kohl would link German unification to development of the "all-European process."

More traditional experts sharply disagreed. Yakovlev backed them.

Shevardnadze and Prime Minister Ryzhkov tried to find a middle ground. All but Chernyaev agreed, as Ryzhkov put it, that "one should not give everything to Kohl." The Soviets should work more closely with those seeking to restrain the West Germans, particularly the British and the French.

Gorbachev summed up. Looking at West Germany, he wanted to balance between Kohl and Kohl's opposition, the SPD. There were "six players" (the two Germanys and the Four Powers). There was Modrow and the former communists ("it is impossible that of 2.5 million party members there is no one to constitute a real force"). His attitude toward Kohl had softened a bit, thanks to Kohl's help in expediting some needed shipments of food to the USSR.

The Soviet leaders opposed any enlargement of NATO and opposed a united Germany's membership in NATO. They were willing to explore withdrawal of Soviet forces from East Germany, as part of a proposal to withdraw all foreign forces from both German states.[114]

The Soviet government coordinated these plans with the East Germans during Modrow's January 30 visit to Moscow. Modrow and his advisers hastily refined their own plan for a confederation of two German states, bound by a treaty that would link them economically and in some spheres of governance while preserving political independence. The Modrow plan would strengthen the alternative German confederation. Eventually it might be possible to imagine both German states transferring sovereign powers to the new confederation. The German right to self-determination would be undisputed.

So Modrow could announce a plan for "unification," but through a confederation that preserved two German states. This was the first time the Soviets were prepared to accept the prospect of some sort of German unification, albeit based on Modrow's confederation plan.

Gorbachev presumed that a future German confederation would be militarily neutral. He could imagine working with the British and the French to develop a plan for all of Europe in which NATO would be transformed and Germany would be neutralized, all sealed by a German peace treaty.

Modrow publicly presented his new plan on February 1. It imagined a set of steps, with a peace treaty, elections, and the establishment of a single German parliament in Berlin. "Germany should again become the united fatherland of all the German nation," he said.

Gorbachev and Shevardnadze enthusiastically praised Modrow's plan. Gorbachev commended it to Bush, asking for Four Power negotiations to discuss it. Their vision was consistently linked to a peace treaty, the "all-European process," and a new Germany that was militarily neutral and disarmed. Moscow finally had a coherent policy coordinated with East Berlin.[115]

* * *

In the space of about a month, from the end of January until the end of February 1990, all the Western countries faced another round of difficult choices in three dimensions. Based on their assessment of the choices and the problems, East German voters would in effect signal their choice in the March 1990 election.

To help see both emerging choices about basic direction, the "vectors," and the choices that had to be made "to keep up," here is another issue map, as of January 1990. As with the one we offered in chapter 3 (for the spring of 1989), we have tried to identify choices that were real at the time.

Issue Map

Building a Better World (January 1990)

Future of Eastern Europe	• Okay for noncommunists and communists to rule together? In GDR?
	• What conditions to place on support for the new, democratic GDR?
Future of Soviet Union	• How to support Gorbachev? Any conditions?
	• How to get ready for the "crumbling of communism . . . and the consequences of its failures"?
European Integration	• Atlantic vision (with North America) or European vision (continentalist)?
	• Within European vision, stall European union or accelerate it?
	• If more integration of Western Europe, what about Eastern Europe? Role for CSCE?

Security in Europe	• Should U.S. forces, including nuclear forces, stay or go home?
	• Should Soviet forces, including nuclear forces, stay or go home? Symmetry with treatment of U.S. forces?
	○ Future of NATO?
	○ Future of Warsaw Pact?
	○ Both alliances stay or both disappear?
	• New pan-European security structures?
	○ Arms control and transparency: CFE? Open Skies? Role of CSCE?
	○ Collective security of all defending all? Including both United States and USSR? Role of CSCE?
Future of Germany	• Slow down process of German change or hit the accelerator?
	• Ultimate outcome...
	○ Confederation—two states, connected as one nation?
	○ Merger—negotiated between two states and in constitutional convention to form a new German republic?
	○ Takeover—West German annexation of the GDR?
	• How to decide?
	○ Big German peace conference (use CSCE?) to prepare final settlement?
	○ None of the above... or something new?

- Germany's international status...

  ○ Modified status quo (two states, two alliances)?

  ○ Unified Germany in NATO (and transformed EC, with enhanced CSCE)?

    – If unified Germany, and in NATO, what about status of former GDR?

    – If unified Germany, and in NATO, what about status of U.S. and Soviet forces there? And nuclear weapons?

    – If unified Germany, and in NATO, Germany stays in NATO integrated military command?

  ○ And unified Germany and the EC/EU?

  ○ And unified Germany's permanent borders?

- Can all this be synchronized? Should or can rapid German unification be coupled to settlement of the international issues?

Time to Decide on German Unity

By the beginning of February 1990, the two Germanys were clearly going to come together in some way. There were three broad possibilities:

- Confederation—two states, connected as one nation;

- Merger—negotiated between two states and in constitutional convention to form a new German republic;

- Takeover—West German annexation of the GDR.

Kohl's and Modrow's governments, and the major German parties on both sides of the border, were all coming toward agreement on at least the goal of creating an economic and monetary union between the FRG and the GDR. To Modrow, if the European Community could keep separate states and negotiate such a union among them, perhaps a German community of separate states could do its own such union. Vast economic support might flow into the GDR.

Inside his own government, Kohl submitted his proposal for economic and monetary union to his cabinet on February 7. To unpack the policy choices just about West–East German economic and monetary union, Kohl's finance minister, Theo Waigel, outlined three possible designs.

The most complex plan envisioned a move toward full currency union, only after the GDR made progress with economic reforms.

A second option was to establish a fixed exchange rate between the deutschmark and the East German ostmark. That fixed rate would have to be propped up by the Bundesbank.

The third option, simplest and yet most radical, would be immediately to make the deutschmark the sole legal currency in East Germany as well as the FRG. This dramatic step would require the Bundesbank to take more responsibility for the GDR's monetary policies as East Germany was absorbed into the West German economic system.[116]

The last option, the offer of the deutschmark, was one of the "riskiest decisions that Kohl had confronted." Kohl's government had decided to hit the accelerator with a "policy of big steps." The common currency decision was a leap into economic unification, with incalculable costs, before the political side of unification had been resolved.[117]

Kohl hoped the offer might slow the flood of East German immigrants into West Germany. This flood of migrants was already becoming unpopular and helping the prospects of his SPD political opponent, Oskar Lafontaine.

But to go ahead with this option, Kohl's government would have to take over at least the economic governance of East Germany too, to control its spending and currency management. This meant he would have to cut off and destabilize Modrow's government, which was pleading for emergency financial help. This would antagonize the Soviets and many West Germans, while also inflaming West German fears about currency inflation from free spending to lift up the standard of living in the GDR.

During the first week of February 1990, Kohl chose this last option, the most radical approach. Doing this, he again put himself in front of the unification process, again staking out a position in domestic politics (looking to the West German election later that year) as well as his foreign policy.

Then his crucial problem was to decide on a position for the governance of the GDR. Modrow's model for economic and monetary union would, like the EC ideas, be more about interstate coordination, not surrendering his government's authority.

On February 13, Modrow came to Bonn for talks with Kohl and others to compare their plans. Modrow did, of course, want West German money—DM 10 to 15 billion worth. He also had just announced his vision for a specific kind of step-by-step, limited economic and monetary union with the FRG. It was not that far from Waigel's first and second options, listed above. In other words, the East Germans wanted to receive the benefits of monetary union while maintaining their basic economic autonomy.

Kohl refused. The talks became bitter. East Germans accused the West Germans of trying to annex them as Hitler had annexed Austria in the Anschluss of 1938. The Westerners were offended. The Easterners were annoyed by what they perceived to be the haughty and peremptory tone of the Western side.[118]

The stalemate with the GDR was not just bad for Modrow. As more refugees poured in from the East, Kohl's popularity was threatened. He needed to settle on a preferred path to unity and also to think through the possible political union.

* * *

The idea of a German confederation was not new in German history. There were a variety of precedents. Even after the original German unification from 1871 to 1918, the actual government was not so unitary. Various kingdoms and principalities retained their own governance (above all, Prussia), and the unitary forms were linked mainly by the person of the Prussian king/German emperor and by a relatively weak all-German parliament.

If it went straight to a unitary state, not a confederation, the FRG had to select between the two paths to unification provided in West Germany's constitution, or Basic Law. The negotiated merger path would create a new state, with a new constitution and form of government, and a new set of rights and responsibilities in the international system.

The West German takeover path would instead use a provision of the West German Basic Law that permitted "other parts of Germany" simply to join the existing FRG. This article had actually been used for the incorporation of the Saarland in 1957, after France agreed to end its military occupation of the province after the Second World War. The GDR would become part of the existing Federal Republic. The constitution, form of government, and rights and responsibilities in the international system of the FRG would remain intact. This was a profound choice.[119]

Yet many West Germans and some American officials were attracted to the annexation/takeover option. They reflected that by 1990, Germany had experimented with a constitutional monarchy (1871–1918) and three "democratic" republics: Weimar (1919–33), Bonn (1949–), and East Berlin (1949–). The track record of these experiments was...mixed. Should Germans (and the world) risk another?

* * *

From the beginning of February, Kohl's circle of advisers started moving toward the takeover option. They feared what would happen if the FRG's constitution were opened for renegotiation. The opposition and East Germans would probably want substantial changes in the founding document of the West German state, especially if the East German SPD won the March elections and established primacy in the constitutional assembly. There was simply no way to tell what the outcome might be, particularly given the external pressures now surrounding German unification from the Soviet Union and others.

A takeover through annexation had another advantage for Kohl's advisers. It would simplify the problem of persuading the European Community to accept East Germany into its ranks. There would be no need to amend the Treaty of Rome establishing the community, if one member just got larger.

In the negotiated merger scenario, the transitional issues, including with the EC, would be more difficult. Thus this scenario would become an obstacle, not an ally, to the forthcoming intergovernmental conference to work up the Delors plan.[120]

Finally, for both the West Germans and the Americans, the "merger" challenge—negotiating a new constitution for the new republic—was so great that this path could actually be used to block unification. The sides would argue about clashing political ideals. The arguments would become bitter. The inevitable reality of economic hardships would hit even harder in an East Germany exposed to West German market forces and open borders. The path to unification might seem long and twisted. A modified status quo might look better and better.

As doubts grew, Kohl's political future would darken. The SPD's political prospects would brighten. These conjectures worried American officials, because they felt that so much about the "new Atlanticism" and the future coupling of American and European security depended on the success of Kohl and his party.

By the beginning of March, only a couple of weeks before the East German election, Kohl decided firmly and said publicly that annexation/takeover was the only acceptable route to unity. An economic takeover with the D-Mark and a political takeover by West Germany. The CDU-backed parties contending for power in East Germany promptly adopted this position.

The East Germans understood what was at stake. An annexation of the GDR would liquidate their whole system of government. Kohl had to win the support of the East German people. He needed a clear mandate for his approach from the March 18 elections.

Unfortunately for him and his hopes, the conventional wisdom in both the West and the East was that he would lose. The East German Social Democrats (SPD) were expected to win the March 18 elections. The SPD-East, like the SPD-West, wanted monetary union without a West German economic takeover. It was sympathetic to the "confedera-tion" approach to unification. If there was to be a single, unitary state, the SPD favored getting there through negotiated merger rather than a takeover.

In other words, the differences between the two main positions were clear and they were significant. Everything would be riding on the outcome on March 18.

Should the Unified Germany Be in NATO?

As the tempo quickened on German unification, the Americans worried that they did not have a firm answer from Kohl regarding NATO. Germany was now firmly planted in the plans for deeper and faster European integration. But there was still a good deal of international debate about the future of the alliance.

There were all sorts of possibilities being thrown about. Take, for example, the prominent views of an American conservative such as Henry Kissinger. He believed that a new Germany might take the form of a confederation linking the FRG and GDR, with a disarmed eastern portion integrated into NATO. The Western allies would cut their forces in Germany to a fraction of their former strength. Not only would NATO forces not move eastward, but the alliance would move westward—back to some agreed-upon line east of the Rhine.[121]

Entering February, the NSC staff rapidly sketched out their preferred blueprint. All of a united Germany would be in the NATO alliance, even if the former GDR territory had some special status. Refining this during the first week of February, the NSC staff specified that the former GDR would not be demilitarized. German forces should be allowed there, still in NATO's integrated military command. But U.S. or other foreign forces would be excluded from the former GDR. Reduced but still substantial U.S. forces, including nuclear weapons, would remain in Germany.[122]

Bush wanted Germany fully integrated into NATO. He hoped to convince Gorbachev of the wisdom of that view—once he had convinced Kohl.

He had his work cut out for him.

* * *

Kohl's coalition partner was producing a very different set of ideas. Genscher had been working on the alliance problem too. He had developed a distinctive vision of his own.

Genscher went along with rapid progress toward German unification. Therefore, to him, the international side had to get a great burst of extra energy to keep up. On January 31 he announced his proposal in a speech, in Tutzing, on "German Unity in the European Framework." He had worked on his plan with just a couple of aides. This time it was his turn to announce a position on his own, which he had not cleared in advance with the Chancellery.[123]

On February 2, he came to Washington. He and Baker had a relaxed and friendly, jackets-off two-hour fireside talk. Genscher presented his core ideas.

Germany would remain a member of the EC and of the Western alliance. "We do not want a united Germany that is neutral," he declared. He proposed that there be "no expansion of NATO territory eastwards." The former GDR would not be incorporated into NATO or NATO's military structures.

Baker went along with Genscher's idea. He appears to have believed, then and for about another eight days, that Genscher's idea was similar to the U.S. idea about German membership in NATO, with a demilitarized status of some kind for the former GDR.[124]

In fact, they were not the same idea. At some level, Genscher's idea would make no sense, since a united Germany could not entirely be a member of NATO yet have part of its territory outside of NATO.

But Genscher was imagining this NATO status only as a transitional stage. Baker may have been relieved that he was not proposing that Germany would rest somewhere between the two alliances. Genscher's vision was that NATO, along with the Warsaw Pact, would become "elements" of new "cooperative security structures throughout Europe."

Genscher's plans were tied to the organization then called the CSCE, the "Conference on Security and Co-operation in Europe," which we have referred to briefly before. It was a forum that then included thirty-five states, including all the NATO and Warsaw Pact members, including, across the Atlantic, the United States and Canada. It also included a dozen "neutral" European states like (the then united) Yugoslavia, Ireland, Sweden, and Cyprus. It was sometimes called the "Helsinki process," because this forum, originally usually called a European

Security Conference, had been used with great ceremony to lay down the principles of postwar Europe in the first CSCE summit, held in Helsinki in 1975.

Gorbachev had proposed convening a "Helsinki II" summit meeting, to be held in Paris, probably later in 1990. France and other states, including the U.S., supported his proposal. Many in Europe hoped that all these issues about Europe's future might be settled at this Paris summit, which might then become another great European peace and security conference, in the tradition of the Congress of Vienna in 1814–15 or the Versailles conference of 1919.

The U.S. government thought the all-European summit might be good for several things. At a meeting of American, British, French, and West German political directors, "We all agreed," the British representative reported, "that the CSCE was becoming more important as East/West relations become more fluid. It is the only body that involves all the key players, European and American. The Western objectives of democracy, the rule of law and human rights are on its agenda."

But the U.S. government did not think this all-European conference was the right place to settle the future of Germany or NATO. Genscher agreed with the Americans on the German point.

But Genscher did think the CSCE process could handle the alliance issues, because the alliances might just disappear—and the foreign troops with them. He was not alone on this. None other than Vaclav Havel, the heroic Czech dissident now helping to lead his freed country, talked of all foreign troops leaving Europe—replaced by "a new European security system, also including links to the United States, Canada, and the USSR, but different from the present one." The new Polish leader, Mazowiecki, had a similar view.

Bush was not a bit convinced that this leap into space would work. He thought the risks were too great. He said so directly to Havel.

Yes, he agreed that NATO had to be transformed into something different. But the existing treaty was the best way to keep the United States in Europe. He argued to Havel that "our presence in Europe—military and economic—has been a stabilizing presence, not a threatening presence."[125]

There was, then, a major difference between Genscher's "Tutzing formula" and the U.S. government's position. Puzzled about how a united Germany could stay in NATO while its eastern portion was excluded from it, journalists pressed Genscher to explain how the Tutzing formula would work. He gave a very revealing answer: "Nobody ever spoke about a halfway membership, this way or that. What I said is, there is no intention of extending the NATO area to the East. And I think you should wait for things to further develop.... That will be the situation at this summit, the CSCE summit."

Genscher was trying to kick the issue down the road, worried as he was about the position of the Soviet Union. Elbe later recalled how "nervous" Genscher was, fearing that even the Tutzing formula's commitment to NATO was on "thin ice."[126]

In their February 2 meeting, Baker went along with Genscher's Tutzing formula, partly because he did not yet understand how it differed from what others in the U.S. government wanted, and mainly because Baker was concentrating on other issues.

Baker and his key aides, Zoellick and Ross, had developed the Two Plus Four negotiating plan, comprising the two Germanys plus the Four Powers with historic legal authority still pending from the military occupation agreements of 1945. In their plan, the Two Plus Four would also have a limited scope and a clear mandate. It would exist "to bring German unity to fruition." It would begin work only after a freely elected East German government could participate, after the March 18 elections.

Others in the U.S. government, including the two authors of this book, had our doubts about the Two Plus Four approach.[127] But Baker was right. The "big peace conference" alternative to handle the German problem was gathering momentum. Baker's alternative helped head this off. His alternative also helped give the Soviets a sense that there would be a meaningful process to engage key issues.

Baker was not opposed to any CSCE summit. But there would be a preparatory meeting in Bonn, in March, to start working up "a set of basic principles to guide the conversion of socialist systems to market economies." Another preparatory meeting, in Copenhagen in June, would advance human rights and the new elections initiative, to get the CSCE into the democracy-building process.

Here, Baker said, were the American preconditions for the large and high-profile all-European summit.

- First, there had to be more progress on human rights, such as agreement to the U.S. initiative on principles for holding free elections at the Copenhagen meeting of ministers in June.

- Second, any CSCE summit had to be preceded by completion of the CFE treaty.

- Third, the CSCE summit should not be turned into a German peace conference.

With advance work by their key aides, Elbe and Zoellick, Genscher went along with these three conditions. He agreed to support Baker's Two Plus Four plan. He agreed that the new forum would not start until after the East German elections.[128] They agreed to Genscher's idea of "no intention to extend the NATO area of defense and security towards the East."[129]

While Baker was meeting with Genscher, Scowcroft and Blackwill were en route to Munich. There they received a report on Baker's meeting and also met with Teltschik. Scowcroft wrote to President Bush that Germany "was like a pressure cooker." It would take America's best efforts, and those of Kohl, "to keep the lid from blowing off in the months ahead."[130]

* * *

First Baker, then Kohl, set off to Moscow to talk about Germany with Gorbachev. Beforehand, Baker had talked over his plans with President Bush. Baker had in mind a straightforward quid pro quo: The United States would help make unification happen. The West Germans should stand with the Americans on the issue of NATO. Scowcroft too advised Bush that "with Kohl traveling to what may be the most portentous foreign meeting of his life, I believe you should both give him all the personal support you can and make clear to him our preferences concerning the future of a united Germany."[131]

On February 9, Bush sent an important letter to Kohl. Bush came straight to the point. German unification was coming soon. That "just means that our common goal for all these years of German unity will be realized even sooner than we had hoped.... In no event will we allow the Soviet Union to use the Four Power mechanism as an instrument to try to force you to create the kind of Germany Moscow might want, at the pace Moscow might prefer."

The NATO alliance did need to become a different institution, one with "more emphasis on its original political role." Then Bush laid out his approach on the status of former East German territory as Germany stayed in NATO. It differed from the Genscher approach.

- Eastern Germany would not be demilitarized; German troops could be stationed there.

- NATO's defense commitment would cover all of Germany, not some of it.

- German troops in eastern Germany, and all other German troops, could thus still be part of NATO's integrated military command.

- Eastern Germany would have a "special military status," with only German NATO troops stationed there in peacetime.

- U.S. troops would remain in western Germany.

Germany would thus stay in NATO, linked to the military commitment of the United States. The Soviets would withdraw most or all of their troops from Central and Eastern Europe. The two sides would not be treated the same way, if that was Germany's choice.[132] A couple of weeks later, Kohl alluded to this letter "on the eve of my trip to Moscow...which will be going down in history as an important document of German-American friendship."[133]

In Moscow, Baker (who had not yet seen Bush's final letter to Kohl) urged Gorbachev to accept a unified membership of Germany in NATO. Baker made the case for keeping German military power embedded in a NATO framework. For instance, "a neutral Germany would undoubtedly acquire its own independent nuclear capability."

He then stressed that NATO itself would have to then become a "changed NATO," one "that is far less of a military organization, much more of a political one." In this context, the U.S. military presence was stabilizing and reassuring." As for America, "we do not necessarily desire to keep troops in Europe.... So if there is any indication that the Allies don't want them we will in no way keep our troops there."

Baker repeated that point again: "[If foreign countries] don't want [the U.S. military], our country is simply not going to be able to sustain a presence in Europe and we will immediately bring our troops home." If Europeans wanted it, NATO would need to become a political alliance "by which we maintain our presence in Germany and elsewhere."[134]

Baker helped sell Gorbachev on Two Plus Four.[135] Gorbachev's team had also been thinking about a "six-power" forum. "I say four plus two; you say two plus four. How do you look at this formula?"

"Two plus four is a better way," Baker answered. It put the German states first.

The Two Plus Four process, Baker explained to Gorbachev, could work on security assurances. It also "could explore" certain assurances, such as "no NATO forces in the eastern part of Germany." Or, as Baker put it in his meeting with Gorbachev, using the Genscher formula, NATO would not extend "one inch to the East."

* * *

When we published our original, detailed account of this diplomacy, we did not try to rebut claims that, in this exchange, there was an agreement never to enlarge NATO. Back in 1994, when we finished drafting that book, we did not think that anyone would make such an argument.

Although new evidence has become available about the exchanges in February 1990, we think our original account is still factually accurate. It can now be supplemented by some even more detailed historical dissections of just what was said then and why, using all sources that have become available in all the relevant languages. The best of these reconstructions is by a European historian, Kristina Spohr, who most fully combines the story behind the scenes in all the major capitals.[136]

A few key points stand out.

First, neither Baker, nor Kohl, nor any of the Soviets could quite understand or explain Genscher's position. This was because they do not appear to have understood, and thus were not able to articulate, the full Genscher vision of how the half-of-Germany NATO jurisdiction was meant to work.

They could not articulate it because Genscher's vision wasn't meant to work in the long run. It was just supposed to be an interim stage, hanging in the air, until a succession of CSCE summits (in 1990 and 1992, he had told Baker) replaced the old NATO and Warsaw Pact structures with the new all-European structure.

Since Genscher himself had not worked out the details of that next stage, or secured any agreement to them, he therefore could only allude to them promisingly and vaguely. No one else could explain it. He regarded the Warsaw Pact and NATO as temporary structures.

Thus the Soviets could not have just locked in this deal in February 1990. They would have had to help develop and agree not only to the partial (temporary) membership idea, but also commit to the all-European half of the design. No one had even outlined how that might work.[137]

* * *

Second, the Soviets themselves neither understood nor came close to accepting the Genscher position, as presented by Baker and Kohl. They heard out this odd assurance and were perfectly noncommittal, if not just puzzled. Baker presented a choice between his formula, on the one hand, and a neutral Germany with foreign forces gone, on the other. Obviously, this was a matter that would have to be hashed out in some further negotiation.

After all, when Gorbachev saw Baker and Kohl (on February 9 and 10), Gorbachev and Modrow had just developed and publicly presented their alternative vision of how the German question was to be solved. Modrow had announced it on February 1, to worldwide notice. Gorbachev and Shevardnadze vigorously defended the Modrow alternative.

They also knew that even this stance was considered far too soft by some in the Soviet government. Germany was exhibit A in an attack that had just been launched against Gorbachev from the right wing of the Communist Party's Central Committee, led by Politburo member Yegor Ligachev, who pleaded with the Soviet leader "to prevent a prewar Munich." Or, as Ligachev put it in an emotional confidential letter sent to Gorbachev the next month, "The socialist commonwealth is falling apart, NATO is gaining strength. The German question has become of primary importance."[138]

The Soviet government was not tempted at this point to abandon the plan they had just so painstakingly developed with their ally. Gorbachev had no intention of dismantling the Warsaw Pact. The notion of Poland or Hungary or any member of the still-extant alliance joining NATO was not yet on the table.

What did impress Gorbachev was Baker's argument about the danger of a situation in which Germany was neutral, outside of any alliance system. Gorbachev added that he could see advantages to having American troops in Germany. "The approach you have outlined is a very possible one. We don't really want to see a replay of [the aftermath of] Versailles, where the Germans were able to arm themselves," he said.

"The best way to constrain that process is to ensure that Germany is contained within European structures. What you have said to me about your approach and your preference is very realistic," he added. "So, let's think about that. But don't ask me to give you a bottom line right now."[139]

* * *

While Baker was traveling, Scowcroft worried that the Genscher formula might cause trouble. While Baker was still in Moscow, Scowcroft explained the matter to Bush. Bush then sent his message to Kohl, cc'ing Baker, that we described above.

Baker, who had already been struggling to explain the position, realized the distinction. As soon as he digested Bush's letter (on February 9, a week after his press conference with Genscher, and just after his meeting with Gorbachev), he snapped into line.

Bush had explained that a former GDR would have a "special military status" to be negotiated. Working on Bush's letter, Zelikow had borrowed the particular phrase "special military status" from a suggestion offered by NATO's secretary-general, former West German defense minister and Bush friend Manfred Wörner. Other officials in other governments, like the British, arrived at the same formula. The specifics of that would be left to another day.

Baker made no commitments about a future in which there would be no Soviet Union and no Warsaw Pact—only NATO and new democracies in Eastern Europe clamoring to get in. In the first half of February 1990, that future was not yet what leaders were discussing.

* * *

The day after he wrote to Kohl, Bush met with Wörner.[140] In his different jobs, as a West German defense minister and now as NATO's secretary-general, Wörner had gained a broad perspective on European security. The Bush-Wörner relationship was important to both men. Wörner was one of those who helped persuade Bush to view the European Community as a partner, not a rival.

Wörner took care to explain why the term "special military status" was important. It meant that all of the German armed forces could remain part of NATO's military command. Having such a command made European defense a multinational effort rather than a national one, and German participation was what made it credible. A special military status for the former GDR did not mean demilitarizing eastern Germany.

Wörner was adamant about the need to keep a united Germany firmly in the NATO alliance. Otherwise, he warned, "the old Pandora's box of competition and rivalry in Europe would be reopened." Neutrality was dangerous, for Germany and for Europe. In that situation, eventual German acquisition of nuclear weapons was quite possible.

To Wörner, a demilitarized Germany was also unacceptable. A neutral or disaffected Germany would be tempted to float freely and bargain with both East and West. Nothing could replace NATO as the only stable security structure.

It was Bush's "historic task," Wörner argued, that he should protect the Germans from temptation, save the new Europe from instability, and safeguard those who had made a new Europe possible. It would assuage the fears of other countries in Western Europe too.

* * *

On the NATO specifics, Kohl did not yet agree either with Bush or with Wörner. He stuck with Genscher's vague formula.

When Kohl met Gorbachev, the atmosphere was friendly. Gorbachev told Kohl that it was up to the Germans to decide for themselves whether or not they wanted to unify. It was also up to them to choose their form of government, the pace of unification, and the conditions under which it would occur.

Kohl and Gorbachev reached agreement on the Two Plus Four process. Gorbachev was persuaded that the CSCE was too unwieldy to be a useful forum for discussing the German question. The Two Plus Four would also elevate the Soviet role.

Kohl, filled with emotion, assured Gorbachev that nothing but peace would ever rise out of German soil. He silently gestured to Teltschik to make sure he was copying all of this down, word for word. Teltschik was jubilant inside. "That is the breakthrough!" he noted in his diary.

Kohl, at Teltschik's urging, portrayed the February 10 meeting with Gorbachev as a historic event. He wanted the German people to know that the Soviet leader had given him the "green light."

Genscher and his aides were appalled. They considered such crowing about a "breakthrough" very risky. They scorned Teltschik as a foreign policy "amateur."[141]

Gorbachev did not believe he had made any great new concession. He saw his position as consistent with the German unification plan he had just agreed to with Modrow, announced on February 1. Modrow was about to undertake another round of his key negotiations with Kohl in Bonn, right after Kohl returned from Moscow. It is thus an error to claim, as some scholars have, that in exchange for Kohl's reiteration of Genscher's NATO proposal, Gorbachev publicly offered agreement to Kohl's plan for unification, or to Kohl's particular plan for economic and monetary union.[142]

Gorbachev and Modrow had just worked out a plan they had presented as an alternative, better form of "unification." Modrow, with Soviet support, had already been advocating another form of economic and monetary union with the FRG, in a confederation. It was not the form of union that Kohl's government wanted. Only eight days earlier, Gorbachev had personally urged Kohl, Bush, Mitterrand, and others to accept the new Modrow plan.

But in crowing about the "green light," Kohl was playing to the crowd: the audience of East (and West) German voters. He was trying to make his cause look realistic and attainable to them, the Germans who would be going to the polls in a little more than a month.

Soviet officials of course understood Kohl's political game. As Genscher and his aides had feared, the Soviets hastily, and angrily, took pains to contradict Kohl's glowing portrait of the decisions made in Moscow. As for Genscher's Tutzing formula, the Soviets claimed that their leaders "couldn't understand such a scheme."[143]

The plan Gorbachev had just worked out with Modrow was still quite plausible. It appeared at the time to have strong support in both East and West Germany. Gorbachev immediately debriefed Modrow on his meetings with Baker and Kohl. Modrow, about to meet with Kohl on the economic issues, pleaded for Gorbachev to press Kohl for help in getting the FRG to immediately transfer billions of marks in emergency aid to the GDR. On that one, Gorbachev did not feel able to help.[144]

Just a day after Kohl returned from Moscow to West Germany, Modrow arrived in Bonn to talk with Kohl about currency, aid, and models of economic union. These were the discussions we mentioned earlier, the meetings that became so acrimonious once the West Germans seemed to refuse emergency help and insisted on a monetary takeover.

Gorbachev then himself detailed his views on Germany on the front page of *Pravda*. Perhaps, he suggested, "history has started working in an unexpectedly rapid way." But that was just "one side of the matter." The other side was that unification concerned "not only the Germans." There needed to be a peace treaty with Germany, he said. "It is this agreement that can finally determine Germany's status in the European structure in terms of international law."

This treaty, Gorbachev explained, would maintain the role of both NATO and the Warsaw Pact. Any change in the "military-strategic balance" between these two organizations was "impermissible."[145]

* * *

When Kohl returned to Bonn, he first had his difficult clashes with Modrow. Then he faced another political battle, this one inside his own government.

Kohl's defense minister firmly opposed the Genscher "no extension eastward" NATO formula. Genscher brusquely maintained that only his formula was "realistic."

The battle spilled into public view. With the East German elections now only a few weeks away, Kohl chose solidarity with Genscher. His defense minister had to back down. It now seemed that there was a real difference between the United States and the West German positions on the NATO question.[146]

Kohl then traveled to Washington. "The time has come," Bush's staff told him, "for an honest and unadorned talk with Kohl about his bottom-line on security issues, despite the difficulty in pinning the Chancellor down."

Kohl met with Bush at Camp David (without Genscher being present, by Kohl's design). The presidential retreat was a pleasant setting for Kohl and Bush to review plans for the months ahead. The Germans were flattered by the invitation; no chancellor had ever before been a guest there. The weather was cold, but a fire was burning in the hearth, and the lodgings were unpretentious but very comfortable.

Both Kohl and Bush were accompanied by their wives, and other members of Bush's family joined them at lunch. The Germans could tell that the atmosphere would be relaxed when Baker greeted the chancellor's party at Dulles International Airport wearing a red flannel shirt and cowboy boots.

Bush's staff had emphasized that the Camp David meetings would be the crucial occasion for settling West German agreement on the external aspects of unification. Kohl was driving the internal agenda and the United States was backing him fully. It was time "to cement a historic bargain: Kohl's pledge not to alter the form and substance of Germany's security commitments to NATO in exchange for a U.S. promise that the Two Plus Four process will not interfere with German unity." The Camp David sessions, on February 24–25, sealed these bargains on all counts.[147]

Kohl was in good form, thoughtful and prepared. He told Bush that he wanted America in Europe, not just for its soldiers, but also to prevent the construction of rival trade blocs, pitting the United States against a Fortress Europe.

Both leaders also agreed that after staying for some limited time, all Soviet troops should leave the territory of a united Germany. The status of American forces would not be equated with the position of the Soviets. You must stay, Kohl told the Americans, even if the Soviets leave Germany.

Bush repeatedly stressed the need to clarify a future Germany's status in NATO. It must have full membership in the alliance.

Kohl wondered aloud if Germany could be handled the way France was handled. France was a member of the alliance but, in 1966, it had withdrawn from NATO's military organizations and command structure. That was when NATO headquarters had left Paris and moved to Brussels.[148]

Bush said that he hated to think of another France in NATO. Germany ought to be a full participant.

Kohl then raised the specific question of NATO's presence in former East German territory. He said that NATO units, including German forces dedicated to NATO, could not be stationed on East German soil.

The U.S. side was determined to persuade Kohl to reverse the position he had just taken in Bonn. Teltschik (who had sympathized with the defense minister) had worked on the matter with Blackwill. They drafted a press statement that would publicly show a common line.

Teltschik urged everyone to agree that the limits would apply only to NATO "forces," but that NATO "jurisdiction" would indeed extend to all of the former GDR.

Baker said Teltschik was right. He admitted that he had used the term only before he realized how it would affect the application of the North Atlantic Treaty to the defense of all of Germany. Kohl and Bush agreed.

As the meeting ended, Bush turned to Kohl. They had come a long way together, but this was now a crucial moment. "We are about to have a press conference," Bush reminded the German leader. "I need you to say that a unified Germany will be in NATO." With Kohl's agreement, Bush afterward told the press, with Kohl beside him, "We share a common belief that a unified Germany should remain a full member of the North Atlantic Treaty Organization, including participation in its military structure."

Immediately after the Bush-Kohl meeting, Baker wrote to Genscher to tell him of the agreement that "all of the territory of a united Germany would benefit from the security guarantee provided by the Alliance." Just to be clear, he added that references to limiting NATO jurisdiction were "creating some confusion" and should be avoided.[149]

Kohl's task had been made easier by Bush's earlier willingness to demonstrate—not just talk about—a different NATO through further arms reductions. Adding to his earlier proposal in 1989, Bush had announced a plan to drop the ceiling of U.S. and Soviet stationed troops in Europe even lower. The cuts would eliminate at least a quarter of remaining American troop strength and the large majority of Soviet deployments outside of the USSR.[150]

Bush brought Kohl along, who loved the idea. Thatcher was less enthusiastic. Bush sent Eagleburger and Gates back out to Europe to talk about it some more, and reassure, and he also presented the proposal to Gorbachev on the same day he announced it in his State of the Union message to Congress, on January 31. Two weeks later, Baker and Shevardnadze hammered out a compromise to set such reduced ceilings.[151]

But many Europeans believed these planned troop cuts were just a first stage in the departure of all the foreign-deployed U.S. and Soviet forces. When Bush had talked through his troop plan with Mitterrand, the French president had been cool to the idea. He said he was worried about a slide to German neutrality.

Bush endeavored to reassure Mitterrand that his goal was just the opposite. He wanted to set a floor, not just a ceiling.

Mitterrand made it clear to Bush, clearer than he had before, that he hoped American forces would stay in place between the Soviet Union and Western Europe. Internally, Mitterrand and his staff believed the phase of foreign forces being stationed in Germany might be coming to an end. He told Bush he was making his own plans to pull French forces in Germany back to France.

Privately, Mitterrand expected all the Americans to leave too. He did not necessarily want that. He just thought that phase of history was coming to an end. Europe, he felt, would be back on its own.

By mid-February, in his public musings, Mitterrand seemed philosophical. The FRG would do as it pleased, he said. France, after all, had nuclear weapons and Germany did not.

"The main thing, for me," he said, "is for Europe to take up its true place in the world again after the self-destruction of two world wars. In short, I expect Europeans to keep in mind, as I do, a paraphrase of that well-known expression, 'Let Europe take care of itself.' "[152]

* * *

In mid-February, with the European transformation accelerating, foreign ministers from every NATO and Warsaw Pact country gathered in Ottawa, Canada. The Ottawa meeting had originally been scheduled to begin serious negotiation of an agreement on Open Skies, the initiative Bush had relaunched in May 1989. That subject for the gathering was now eclipsed, however, by the diplomacy swirling around questions of Germany's and Europe's future.

Baker persuaded his colleagues to accept his conditions for holding a CSCE summit, in Paris, hopefully later that year. The conventional forces agreement (CFE) was no longer simply an arms control negotiation. Now, with the rapidly changing situation in Europe, it would also speak volumes about the underlying political situation.

Dumas of France pushed back. He argued that a CSCE summit might need to be held in Paris, regardless of progress on CFE, in order to deal with the German issues.

Genscher and Baker presented a united front against this argument. Baker stated unequivocally that the United States would not attend a summit unless a CFE treaty was done, ready for President Bush's signature.[153]

The Two Plus Four design was not just about the number of participants. That had occurred to others too. The other half of the design was agreement that this forum was not meant to obstruct but was instead to facilitate "the establishment of German unity."[154]

For the Americans and West Germans, the Two Plus Four announcement was aimed squarely at public opinion in East and West Germany. They eagerly publicized the Ottawa announcement's vivid acceptance "of the establishment of German unity," to help reinforce the impression that the international problems, so often mentioned in the press, were manageable, and were being managed.

At Ottawa, other members of the Western alliance had felt left out. Italian foreign minister Gianni De Michelis was especially unhappy. "We have worked together within the Alliance for 40 years," he complained.

The Americans, British, French, and West Germans all tried to be conciliatory. Baker pledged to consult others about the activities in this new forum.

Finally, however, after De Michelis repeated his concerns, Genscher lost his patience. He turned to the Italian and said sharply, "You are not part of the game." In the stunned pause that followed that remark, the Canadian chairman gaveled the meeting to a close.[155]

The German Election

The Soviets and East Germans hoped to channel unification into a more gradual process. Their hopes rested on a leftist victory in the March 18 GDR elections. This was the outcome that most observers expected.

Amid all his own concerns, about to be voted the Soviet Union's first "president," Gorbachev kept working with Modrow and his noncommunist East German coalition partners. They met in Moscow on March 5–6. The Soviet government turned up the volume, also trying to help their side in the upcoming East German elections. In Ottawa, Shevardnadze had complained in a speech to the Canadian parliament about "politicians...who want to play a game of political speed chess with a time limit of five minutes."[156]

Moscow denounced the annexation/takeover path to unity as unacceptable, even "illegal." Gorbachev said any form of participation in NATO by a unified Germany "is absolutely out of the question." There must instead be stages, tied to the CSCE, as they articulated an ultimate vision practically identical to Genscher's. He scorned those who did not treat such questions seriously.[157]

West Germans rushed to assure the USSR—and the German public—that no harm would come to Soviet interests. In doing this, Genscher announced again that he thought "the alliances will increasingly become elements of cooperative security structures in which they can ultimately be absorbed."

The last phrase brought Genscher close to the position of centrist SPD experts who believed Germany's membership in NATO would be temporary, since the alliance would dissolve within a year or two. More radical thinkers in the SPD were flatly opposed to German membership in NATO at all.[158]

The SPD-East and the SPD-West had also issued a joint foreign policy statement announcing that "a future united Germany should belong neither to NATO nor to the Warsaw Pact."[159] The idea of German membership in NATO was not terribly popular. A February 15 poll showed that an astonishing 58 percent of West Germans wanted a united Germany that was neutral, outside both alliances.

At this time, no senior officials in either Washington or Bonn thought the Soviet and East German positions were hopeless. They knew the USSR still had significant leverage over events in Central Europe. Moscow could force the German people to choose between unification and membership in NATO, channeling the surging tide for unity against the supporters of the alliance.

Moscow could also force the German people to choose between respecting the Soviets' wishes or precipitating a major international crisis. The U.S. government knew that, especially in an election year, Kohl and the West German voters had little stomach for a major international confrontation with Mikhail Gorbachev, a man so widely admired in the FRG.

* * *

In Bonn, Kohl's mood had been shooting up and down. He had gone to the GDR and campaigned directly for the CDU alliance, encountering huge, cheering crowds. In six appearances he had spoken before about a million people, almost 10 percent of the electorate.

Yet the stress was tremendous. He had undertaken an extraordinary gambit by publicly announcing the annexation/takeover plan for the GDR. His coalition partner, Genscher, had forced him into a difficult confrontation with Defense Minister Gerhard Stoltenberg. The mood in the FRG was uncertain and anxious. So much hinged on the election in the GDR.

On March 13, at a rally in Cottbus, Kohl went further. He promised East German voters that after the West German takeover, their ostmarks could be exchanged for the prized deutschmarks at a one-to-one rate. The economic logic of this flowed from the annexation plan, but it was a staggering (and enticing) promise. Economists in both German states (and internationally as well) thought it was also a flawed, financially unsound idea.

But Kohl believed that politics trumped economics at this moment: History's call was too strong and would judge timidity as unwise. The Alliance for Germany had to win. This was the best chance that it would. He had simplified the question for the East German voter: After more than forty years of communist rule, do you want to try new social experiments or join a proven and prosperous democratic state?

The SPD had declared repeatedly for the negotiated merger plan, one that took into account the specific characteristics of the GDR. Its position on alliances clearly now differed from Kohl's.

Most analysts in early March, including the American embassy in East Berlin, thought that the Social Democrats, the SPD-East, were likely to win the March election. The odds seemed long and bleak for Kohl, the CDU, and the Alliance for Germany. Teltschik remembered Kohl feeling so weary and depressed that he wondered aloud whether he could just give up and go home.[160]

Kohl had always seemed to have a "common touch." His political instincts—not his ability to mobilize through great rhetoric—had always served him well. On this fateful choice, those instincts came through for him again. In the first free election to be held in eastern Germany since 1932, the voters chose absorption into the more prosperous West. They voted decisively for Kohl's path to unity.

The turnout was over 93 percent of the electorate. The margin of victory was clear. The Alliance for Germany won more than 48 percent of the electorate, the SPD about 22 percent. The former Communist Party, the PDS, held some 16 percent of the voters, many in Berlin. The dissidents of 1989, New Forum and the like, running as Alliance '90, mustered less than 3 percent of the vote.

De Maizière and his Alliance for Germany colleagues formed a grand coalition in mid-April. They included the SPD as a junior partner in order to have a comfortable two-thirds majority to effect constitutional changes and command a government with the appearance of consensus support. Young Dr. Merkel was doing what she could to help.

If there was a consensus, though, it was not for de Maizière. It was for Helmut Kohl's plan, his promises, and his vision for Germany.[161]

* * *

Shaken by the election results in the GDR, the Soviet Union still stood its ground. Shevardnadze, Baker, Genscher, and other dignitaries gathered in Windhoek, Namibia, on March 20–22 to celebrate the independence of this new southern African state. Shevardnadze's position was unchanged. He was convinced that the matter would ultimately have to be resolved, somehow, "at the highest levels." Baker noticed that Soviet positions on arms control topics were hardening too. The Soviet military appeared to be exerting more influence.

Baker reported to Bush that Shevardnadze's mood, shadowed by developments in Germany and in Lithuania, "was more pensive than I have seen before." He and Gorbachev "seem to be genuinely wrestling with these problems, but have yet to fashion a coherent or confident response. They also have yet to shape their bottom lines." The Americans, Baker concluded, should therefore "not underestimate our ability to affect their choices and perhaps even the formulation of some of their options."[162]

Nearly a month earlier, at Camp David, Bush and Kohl had mused about how to persuade the Soviets to go along. His competitive spirit surging, Bush had said the Soviets were not in a position to dictate Germany's relationship with NATO. "To hell with that. We prevailed and they didn't. We can't let the Soviets clutch victory from the jaws of defeat."

But then they got serious. Kohl thought the Americans would have to carry the burden of persuading the Soviets.

Bush, Baker, and Kohl thought that in the end, Gorbachev would probably accept German membership in NATO. The Soviets should understand that the United States and the FRG were in total agreement. The time for games had passed.

But, Kohl said, Gorbachev would probably make this concession directly with the U.S. president. The Soviets might then name their real price for agreement. He wondered aloud if their compliance might just be a matter of money.

Bush wryly observed, "You've got deep pockets."

The economic issues would be important. But all of them recognized that Soviet security concerns mattered too, a lot. They would have to be addressed seriously.

For Gorbachev to concede, Baker thought Gorbachev would need to see, on the one hand, that the Germans were unshakably behind full NATO membership. But they would also have to see that the West was willing to take legitimate Soviet security concerns into account.[163]

That, Bush commented, was why the United States and Germany ought to have the closest possible consultation. We are going to win the game, he said, projecting an air of confidence. But we must be clever while we are doing it.

The U.S. government was now balancing its ambitious objectives for Germany and Europe with its parallel objectives for the future of the Soviet Union. On that vector the United States was still trying to balance large, rapid achievements in arms reductions and limits with an agenda to help Gorbachev succeed.

The West German–American agenda for Germany was in plain tension with their common hopes to help Gorbachev. Awareness of this tension was something that Baker and Genscher very much had in common. The French and the British were even more worried about Gorbachev's future.

The West was trying to achieve, in peace, a reversal of fortunes for Soviet power in Europe not unlike the results of a catastrophic defeat in a war, without the bloodshed. The United States had decided to try to achieve the unification of Germany unequivocally on Western terms.

It was a bitter pill for Moscow when the East Germans made their choice to throw their lot in with the stronger and more powerful FRG.

An East German intellectual had been prescient when he questioned Gorbachev's ideological pronouncement that the international system was no longer governed by class struggle. "If there is no longer class struggle as an organizing principle," he asked, "what is the argument for two Germanys?"

It turns out there was no argument. There would be one Germany—the Federal Republic of Germany, integrated in NATO and the European Community. Now it was up to America, the allies, and Helmut Kohl to deliver that vision. They wanted desperately to do it in a way that brought Moscow along without bitterness and, perhaps, without an end to Gorbachev and Soviet reform.

CHAPTER 5

The Designs for a New Europe

Back in January 1990, Charles Powell, Thatcher's private secretary for defense and foreign policy matters, was assembling participants and papers for a secret seminar Thatcher was convening at Chequers, the prime minister's country retreat. Powell was the forty-eight-year-old son of a senior Royal Air Force officer. He had received an elite education, majoring in modern history, before joining the diplomatic service right out of college. After twenty years of well-regarded diplomatic work, he had started working directly for Thatcher.

In January 1990, Powell had been in that job for nearly seven years. There was no one whose advice on foreign affairs Thatcher trusted more. So one of the papers Powell added to the compilation for the seminar was his own.

Powell's jumping-off point was a provocative, widely discussed essay by an American political scientist, Francis Fukuyama. Fukuyama had wondered, in print, if the world had arrived at "The End of History."

Fukuyama did not really mean that history was over. He was referring to a philosophical theory of history, associated with Friedrich Hegel (and, following Hegel, Karl Marx), as a dialectic. The dialectic was that every system produced an antithesis which, after a struggle, evolved into the new synthesis, at which point the historical cycle would repeat again. Perhaps the world, Fukuyama thought, was arriving at a new synthesis, modern liberalism, that would end the cycle.

Writing to Thatcher on January 21, Powell offered a different prospect. "Far from being the end of history the next decade will mark the return of history. The period since 1945, with Communism reaching its high water mark of political and military influence and then beginning to ebb, will seem in retrospect a diversion from the norm."

What, then, was this "norm" to which the world was about to return? Powell went on, "As Communism retreats, we shall find ourselves once again confronting nationalism and the conflicts to which it gives rise. Far from eliminating nationalism, Communist suppression of it has only ensured that it will now re-emerge in greater strength than ever. And the greatest risk will be that we and others will get drawn into conflicts between nationalities (in some cases fuelled by Islam).

"We shall have won the Cold War," Powell granted. "But instead of being the dawn of a new, peaceful era, we shall find the next decade altogether more complex, with a multiplicity of dangers and threats rather than the monolithic enemy represented by Communism."

If that was right, what then should be the design of a new Europe? Powell envisioned that Soviet military power would be out of Eastern Europe. All-European institutions should help the former communist countries keep their independence, dependencies of neither Germany nor the Soviet Union.

Powell hoped that German unification could be delayed. If it could not, he hoped means could be found to contain German power.

Powell hoped NATO would remain essential. But he worried about the Americans. He thought the U.S. commitment to Europe, including its nuclear commitment, was likely to erode and the Americans might leave. All the more important, then, to keep British and French forces strong, including their own national nuclear forces.[1]

* * *

By the end of March 1990, two months after Powell wrote this paper, the East German elections had decided that a unification of Germany was plainly going to happen, soon, as a kind of West German annexation of the East. The "internal" unification process was being settled. But all the "external" aspects were still open, as were the wider issues of what Europe would become. Many Americans and Europeans shared Powell's concerns about "the return of history."

Mitterrand, Thatcher, and Delors were conceptual, deductive think-ers. They thought hard about grand designs and tried to make policy conform with an elaborate worldview, preconceived theories, and a grand strategy. Gorbachev quite consciously enjoyed considering the world in theoretical terms too, often in a more abstract way.

Bush and Baker, like Kohl and Genscher, had a different style. They were practical problem-solvers, focused on concrete results, attentive to all the available instruments of national power. They had principles. Baker sometimes called his approach "principled pragmatism." But they did not enter the pivot and design years of 1989 and 1990 with a formal grand strategy.

These leaders focused on choices in front of them, choices that we have outlined in each chapter. Some of their underlings would then knit those choices into conceptual frameworks.

In the spring of 1990 the driving fact was the acceleration toward a German unification that now seemed irresistible. Alone, that fact did not necessarily favor either American or Soviet preferences.

The Soviets had more physical capabilities to interfere. German poli-ticians might pay a high price in domestic support if they seemed to be alienating either side—and the West German elections would be held before the end of the year. Everyone had reasons to prefer an agreed inter-national solution, if one could be found.

To sketch out some of the choices coming into view, we again offer one of our issue maps.

Issue Map

Building a Better World (April 1990)

Future of Eastern Europe	• Now in transition
Future of European Integration	• Atlantic vision (with North America) or European vision (continentalist, Mitterrand's confederation proposal)?

- European monetary union going forward, but...

    ○ Move to single currency?

    ○ With a European Central Bank replacing national central banks?

    ○ With what other conditions? Fiscal convergence? European bank regulation?

- Add push for political union?

    ○ If so, what model? European federation? Confederation? Hybrid?

- How to include Eastern Europe? Role for CSCE?

Future of Germany

- If internal unification going fast, should external aspects be decoupled and handled later?

- Future Germany's borders, settled how and when?

- How to manage future German military power?

    ○ Special regulation of German forces and behavior?

    ○ No unique regulation of German forces, use other institutions and CFE?

Security in Europe

- If Soviet forces are leaving foreign soil, should U.S. forces, including nuclear forces, stay or go home? Related to...

- Alliance status of united Germany

    ○ All in NATO?

    ○ Out of NATO with other international controls?

- Future of the two alliances

  - Both stay?

  - Both disappear?

  - NATO stays and Warsaw Pact goes?

- New pan-European security structures?

  - Get CFE treaty in 1990? Open Skies? Role of CSCE?

  - Collective security: All defending all?

Future of Soviet Union

- Soviet Union versus Lithuania

  - Support Lithuania, retaliate against Soviet efforts to crush its independence?

  - Support Gorbachev even if he cracks down to hold union together?

- Large-scale economic assistance for Gorbachev

  - Yes, large-scale government-guaranteed loans. What bargain or conditions?

  - No, Soviet Union not yet creditworthy or deserving.

  - Limited help, conditions, IMF starts working with Soviets.

- What to do about the secret Soviet biological weapons program?

A New European Union

As agreed in December 1989, the members of the EC had started to draft a treaty to create an economic and monetary union (EMU). This plan would at least consider creating a single currency for all the participating countries, along with a European Central Bank that might take the place of national central banks like the mighty Bundesbank.

Early in 1990, Kohl and his team, working with Delors, developed another major move. They pushed for an expansive vision of European political union to be adopted too.

Again, Delors played a catalytic role. The French European Commission president was quite worried. Without vigorous action, the upheavals in Europe might put all the European Community work on the "garbage heap of history." The ideas of Europe had to adapt. Delors wanted Europe to have a conception of expansion to the east, even if at first this happened in "concentric circles" of integration.[2]

Kohl was sympathetic. From his point of view, Germany was already going down the path toward more integration. The EMU would embed German economic policymaking in European institutions. NATO would embed German security policymaking in Atlantic institutions.

Kohl believed deeply in such transnational integration. He frequently looked back on the history of the twentieth century, and he felt this was one of the absolute core lessons from it.[3]

But Kohl felt, as many other Germans did, that if Germany was going to commit itself so deeply to the European construction, others should step up too. Such a European structure also had to be political. France and others should join Germany in a more integrated, federal, and democratic Europe. The intergovernmental conference to build an economic and monetary union should, he and others concluded, be accompanied by another intergovernmental conference, one to build up Europe's political union as well, and this union should give more power to its European Parliament.

Such a political union, moving toward the ideal of a European federation, appealed to some of the medium- and smaller-sized member governments in Europe, such as Italy, Ireland, and Belgium. The idea was anathema to Thatcher. It was not especially popular in France either. Much of France's political class was proudly nationalistic (like the Gaullists) and prized France's political independence.

* * *

In February 1990, Delors worked up an idea for a special European summit with the Irish prime minister, Charles Haughey (in the first half of 1990 it was Ireland's turn to chair the European Council). This special summit would be in April, right after the East German elections.

The job of the special summit was to explain how Europe would adapt to German developments. The planned agenda had two parts: (1) a move to develop a political union, alongside the economic and monetary union; and (2) efforts to reach out, welcome the East German people, and help address their needs.

As German unification gathered steam, Delors had helped Kohl with constructive advice and support. A host of issues had arisen in figuring how to cope with the possible absorption of East Germany into the EC. Delors used his considerable ingenuity to find solutions in what he proposed to treat as a "special case."

When Delors proposed his plan to Kohl, the chancellor embraced it. He brought it to Mitterrand.

At first, the French reactions were guarded. More than most French leaders, Mitterrand supported European integration. But he also saw the nationalist argument against a "political" union. He knew what kind of criticism he would get from socialist and Gaullist politicians at home.

Mitterrand's main aide for European issues, Élisabeth Guigou, helped persuade the president. Guigou argued for making this a joint Franco-German initiative: France and Germany together would propose that, at the end of 1992, as the single European market came into being, the European Community would become a European Union.

Making this a Franco-German joint initiative was not just an appeal to Mitterrand's ego. With such an initiative, France could help make sure that the Union avoided "federalist excesses." Guigou argued that the Union might contain the powers of Delors's Commission and build up the powers of the national governments working through the European Council. The Commission might take on more "management powers." But it would do so under the Council's authority, and with an improved European Parliament giving legislators more powers too.

Mitterrand signed up. One more time, the triumvirate of Kohl-Mitterrand-Delors and their staffs swung into action, working with Irish prime minister Haughey.

Kohl and Mitterrand announced their joint initiative at the end of March. In April they sent out a joint plan to other EC leaders. The special Dublin EC summit at the end of April went beautifully.

The new Union's creation would now run on two tracks: EMU and European political union. Negotiations on both would begin at the end of 1990. The new union would build up European institutions, including the creation of a common European foreign and security policy.

The April Dublin summit was a pleasant meeting, the tone convivial. Everyone had noticed the results from the East German elections in March. Thatcher's negativity could not dissipate the warmth with which EC members, especially from the smaller states, welcomed this inclusive initiative. It was quite a contrast from the last European summit, the one in Strasbourg in December 1989. Then the atmosphere had been icy, inside and out. Now it was springtime, inside and out.

It now seemed perfectly plain that when Kohl said that German and European development were "two sides of the same coin," he meant it. Genscher liked Thomas Mann's 1952 pronouncement: "We do not want a German Europe, but a European Germany."[4]

At this point, in 1990, the political union proposal had already accomplished its most important objective—to signal a common (not just German) subordination to the European ideal.

The national governments did limit the political scope of this new European Union. The Maastricht Treaty, signed early in 1992, created a Union that was a balance, more than a confederation of independent states, but not a federation, not a United States of Europe.

The Union did set the goal of having a "common foreign and security policy"—if member governments could agree. Little new power was delegated to the Commission or the Parliament.

There was some similar movement toward common policies in "justice and home affairs." But although EC borders opened, national governments still maintained most powers to set migration and asylum policies.

There was a Union "social policy" too. But it had little new content, because the EC already addressed discrimination and work safety issues. Business opposed European regulation of wages or pensions. Britain opted out of what little was agreed on "social policy."[5]

* * *

As planned, the economic and monetary union was also part of the Maastricht Treaty. It was far more significant. In phases of implementation this EMU eliminated national currencies in favor of a new, common euro, to be used by the countries that joined the "Eurozone" within the Union. A new, independent European Central Bank managed this money. Germany gave up its D-Mark and its Bundesbank. In exchange, it gained a euro and an ECB, both set up largely on lines Germany preferred, free of political influence from national governments so it could stick to a low-inflation hard-money line.

In the EMU, the "M" (monetary) ended up being more unified than the "E" (economic). True, to enter the Eurozone a country had to meet strict criteria, with a promise that there would be no bailouts for governments. National governments were supposed to control their spending, but the national capitals still controlled their budgets. Under extreme circumstances the EU could impose sanctions on a profligate spender, but in practice this was hard to do.

Also, since the political union was relatively weak, neither the Commission nor the ECB were given strong powers to regulate private European banks. Banking regulation was left to the control of individual states. This was more like the system used in America before the United States overhauled its banking regulation system during the Great Depression.

In February 1992, when the Maastricht Treaty was signed, these potential problems in the design of the Union were in the background. In the foreground, everyone could see a sustained will to accomplish European integration, especially among the Germans, the French, and Delors. Everyone could see that leaders had set deadlines and worked very hard to stick to them.

As the best historians of the process put it, "Given the difficulties of history, ideology, and political interests involved, what was achieved at Maastricht represented an extraordinary political achievement. It was an image of a Europe far removed from the images of *blocage* and sclerosis that had been so prevalent in the early 1980s."[6]

It was a good thing that the summit of EC leaders in Dublin, in April 1990, had been so harmonious. The Soviet reaction to the East German election results had not been so warm. As we mentioned at the end of the last chapter, the Soviet government seemed to be digging in for a fight. Not only was its position hardening on Germany, progress on the various arms control issues seemed to have stopped, or was even going backward. And then, on top of all those existing issues, there were new crises to consider.

Lithuania, Biological Weapons: Walking a Tightrope

One of the new challenges was a crisis everyone knew about and that forced both Gorbachev and Bush to walk a tightrope. The other new issue was a crisis almost no one knew about.

The crisis everyone knew about was the most serious challenge to the future of the Soviet Union that had arisen so far. Lithuania had declared its independence from the Union in March 1990.

Gorbachev authorized military maneuvers in the republic. He deployed additional troops there, confiscated private weapons and disarmed the local national guard, and seized printing presses and Communist Party property. Most important, the Soviet government imposed economic sanctions—including a cutoff of oil and natural gas.

Privately, Gorbachev was feeling overwhelmed. In February, in a down moment, he had mused to Chernyaev about being ready to leave office. In April, grappling with Lithuania, he had the impulse to cancel all his upcoming meetings with foreigners, even an upcoming summit with Bush (though he soon changed his mind).

Chernyaev could not tell whether Gorbachev was thinking about going back to the old line and maintaining the empire, or whether he would decisively break with the party once and for all. If he broke with the old guard, perhaps he would follow through on his talk about being ready to "go so far that you [Yakovlev and Chernyaev] cannot imagine."

He was under pressure to get much tougher, to crush the Lithuanians with force and set an example. Analysts can argue about whether a "Chinese solution" was still truly feasible in the Soviet Union. In the spring of 1990, we think it still was, maybe for the last time.

Such a move would not have been able to stop with Lithuania. It would, in essence, have been the point where Moscow said: Enough! A full crackdown would probably have extended to other emergency measures, defiance in the diplomacy, a financial confrontation with Western creditors, and the reestablishment of a "socialism in one country" kind of philosophy.

Gorbachev might have been tempted to lead such a counterrevolution. But then, he would say to Chernyaev, a full crackdown on the republics might mean putting a hundred thousand people on trial. "We would be going back to 1937," he said, alluding to the peak of Stalin's great terror.

So far, Gorbachev had tried an economic blockade of Lithuania. He had expected a popular revolt against its breakaway leaders. That did not happen. To his diary, Chernyaev worried that, "[Gorbachev] does not have a Lithuania policy, just pure ideology of power not to allow the breakup of the empire."[7]

* * *

Meeting in Bermuda on April 16, Bush and Thatcher compared notes on what Bush called Gorbachev's "dilemma." Both agreed the situation was getting worse. Thatcher judged that "the military is no longer on Gorbachev's side."

Bush said that "if Gorbachev doesn't get out of the Baltic dilemma, I can't do business with him.... We have come so far, but there is a danger we could slide back into the dark ages."

Gorbachev's partial crackdown in Lithuania in April and May filled the American press with calls for a strong reaction from the United States. Bush noted to his diary that he was in "almost a no-win situation, and I keep hoping that Gorbachev will recognize the disaster this will bring him internationally." He asked visiting senators what they suggested he should do; they had no answers to offer.

Seeing Mitterrand only three days after his meeting with Thatcher, Bush sought the French leader's advice. Mitterrand urged patience and negotiations. "Gorbachev has inherited an empire. It is now in revolt. If the Ukraine starts to move, Gorbachev is gone; a military dictatorship would result."

After an internal debate among his advisers, Bush decided to freeze plans to normalize trade relations with the Soviet Union until the Soviets lifted their economic blockade of Lithuania and resumed dialogue. He personally drafted a letter to Gorbachev on this. The Senate voted its own resolution with the same conclusion.

Meanwhile, Bush indirectly put pressure on the Lithuanians to soften their stance and come to the table. He encouraged an initiative from Kohl and Mitterrand. The French and German leaders wrote to the Lithuanians and urged them to "suspend" their independence declaration and resume negotiations.

The Franco-German work was backed by a similar message delivered to the Vilnius leadership by a senior Republican senator, Richard Lugar, acting with Baker's secret help. Bush and European leaders met with the Lithuanian prime minister in early May. Negotiations resumed; tensions calmed—for a while. Gorbachev (and Bush) stayed on their tightropes. Bush said privately at the time, "I don't want people to look back 20 or 40 years from now and say, 'That's where everything went off track. That's where progress stopped.' "[8]

* * *

Lithuania was the *public* crisis. The *secret* crisis was at least as serious. In October 1989 a Soviet defector had contacted the British government. In the spring of 1990, Thatcher, Bush, and a few of their advisers had to make some very difficult choices.

Back in 1969 the American government had decided to shut down its biological weapons (BW) program; the British had done so ten years earlier. Both governments had concluded that such horrifying weapons were not militarily useful. The Soviet government also said it did not need them. So the superpowers led the way in signing (in 1972) a Biological Weapons Convention (BWC), which entered into force in 1975, to ban the development, production, or stockpiling of any such weapons. It was a historic agreement, eventually signed by more than a hundred countries.

During the 1980s the United States had raised concerns about some possible Soviet BW research, because of a suspicious 1979 outbreak of anthrax in the city of Sverdlovsk. The Soviets heatedly denied the allegations. By the end of the 1980s, most opinion among people who followed the issue tended to believe the Soviet story that there had just been a public health problem from contaminated meat.[9]

Very few U.S. or British analysts still followed BW issues. The U.S. national security community still regarded BW as militarily useless. So the Americans and British worried a little, but not too much, about a Soviet BW program.

The Soviet official who defected to the British in October 1989 had been the head of a key lab in what, he secretly revealed, was a very advanced and active BW program—extensive, extremely secret, and entirely illegal (prohibited by the BWC that the USSR had signed). The program was not only manufacturing large quantities of BW for battlefield use; it was producing about a dozen different kinds of biological weapons, some at scale: quantities of anthrax, smallpox (a disease the world health community had just congratulated itself on eradicating at long last), pneumonic plague, and more. Sophisticated methods for weaponizing the viruses had been developed for possible strategic use in missiles to kill large numbers in a faraway enemy population. Active work was under way to develop viruses resistant to antibiotics (and also to immunize Soviet soldiers).

As these details were digested in early 1990 in the British and American intelligence agencies, at first the analysts could not quite believe what they were hearing. The Soviet BW program was worse than anything they had imagined.

The agencies then did extensive work to verify as many details of the defector's account as they could from other intelligence sources. Verifiable details of the account checked out. But the agencies could not get into the sites to be sure or learn more. (It turned out that the defector had been truthful. In fact, the program was more elaborate than even he knew. The head of the whole BW program defected to the United States in 1992.)[10]

In April and early May 1990, at the very same time they were dealing with the Lithuanian crisis, Bush and Thatcher and their top aides were deliberating what they should do about this startling information concerning the clandestine Soviet biological weapons program. They could not even be sure that Gorbachev and Shevardnadze actually knew all these details.

It is rather astonishing, but true, that Bush and Thatcher seriously wondered whether the top leaders of the Soviet Union were aware of such a large and incredibly dangerous program in the Soviet scientific and military establishment. This is a question no one would have ever asked when Leonid Brezhnev or Yuri Andropov were running the Soviet Union. (In fact, Gorbachev and Shevardnadze did know something about this program. The defection of the lab director had been promptly reported straight to the ruling Politburo.)

If what the U.S. and British leaders now knew was made public, it would be a shock and a sensation. To ordinary citizens, the revelation of such a hitherto secret Soviet arsenal would have been much scarier than anything going on in places like Lithuania. It is hard to imagine what would have happened to all the diplomatic work about Germany, arms control agreements, and everything else that at that moment was still so up in the air.

Thatcher and Bush and their top aides considered this. They assumed that, if confronted in a public and embarrassing way, the Soviet government would instantly go into full defensive mode and deny everything. Evidence about later Soviet behavior reinforces their supposition that denial would have been the order of the day. In such a public confrontation, the American and British leaders could not see how they would be able to get the program shut down—which was their most important objective—while also preserving a relationship with Gorbachev.

On the other hand, if they did *not* make what they knew public, the leaders might later be faulted for not having called public attention to the danger. And there was also a risk that the information might leak.

Thatcher and Bush together decided to keep the information about the Soviet BW program as secret as they possibly could. Bush authorized a briefing for a small number of members of Congress. There were no leaks.[11]

But Bush and Thatcher decided they would present the concerns to Gorbachev and Shevardnadze, in the hope that the Soviet leadership would secretly solve the problem, and do so in a way that U.S. and British experts could verify. On May 14 and 15, the U.S. and British ambassadors in Moscow made carefully prepared and coordinated presentations about their concerns to Chernyaev and the deputy foreign minister, Alexander Bessmertnykh. The two Soviets did not appear to know anything about the program.

According to Bessmertnykh's record of the meeting, the American ambassador (Jack Matlock) emphasized that the two governments wanted to solve this problem "without additional fuss." They "do not intend to raise the given question in a confrontational context and do not intend to make it public.... We [the U.S. and Britain] are absolutely not interested in burdening our relations with a new problem on the eve of the most important negotiations at the highest levels."

In Moscow a couple of days later, Baker delivered the BW message personally, to stress its significance. He made time for a substantial private discussion about the BW program with Shevardnadze.

When Gorbachev came to Washington a couple of weeks later for his summit meeting with Bush, the American president also raised the BW problem personally. He waited until they were at Camp David and then pulled Gorbachev aside for a private discussion about it. He would raise it again at later summit meetings. Thatcher also raised the issue with Gorbachev during her trip to Moscow in June 1990 (her last as prime minister).

The immediate reactions from Gorbachev and Shevardnadze were defensive. They displayed little knowledge (this was only partially truthful) and promised to check into it. Gorbachev pushed back, saying that his government thought that the U.S. also had a secret BW program. He offered to set up mutual inspections and site visits.

The U.S. pursued that, a process that continued into 1991 with more top secret, high-level exchanges. The Soviets discovered that the U.S. was telling the truth. The U.S. inspectors, by contrast, discovered more Soviet cover-ups. Gorbachev himself encountered prolonged difficulties in trying to completely shut down this program, obstacles he never fully overcame. The issue would pass to his successor in 1992.[12]

At the time Bush, Baker, Scowcroft, Gates, and Thatcher wrote their memoirs, the details of what they and their intelligence agencies had known were still secret. Therefore, none of those memoirs discuss the BW issue, the many high-level discussions about it with the Soviets, or the choices the U.S. and British leaders had to make. We have not seen evidence that the BW program details were shared at this time with either the West Germans or the French. The historical literature therefore has so far not touched on this topic and the way it intersected with everything else that was going on.

While this secret crisis was unfolding, the leaders might compartmentalize the concern, putting it in a sort of mental safe, just as the secret information itself was compartmentalized and so closely held. But the leaders did not forget about the Soviet BW program. Even if left unstated, it was the kind of concern that might come to mind in a discussion about whether or not to give the Soviet government large-scale economic assistance, especially since the U.S. leaders knew that some key figures in Congress—who would have to act on any such request—also had this knowledge.

A Plan to Manage German Power

The united Germany would have about eighty million people. For those with historic memories, this was still a reduced Germany. In territory, it was 50 percent smaller than the Germany that fought the First World War, 30 percent smaller than the Germany that Hitler had taken over in 1933. Instead of a population that in 1937 was nearly double that of France, this united Germany would only have about 40 percent more people than France.

Yet the two Germanys were still a well-armed country, both the part that served with NATO and the part that served with the Warsaw Pact. West Germany was an economic and engineering powerhouse. Europeans wanted more reassurance.

During February and March 1990, a complex diplomatic minuet, in which Bush helped play a mediating role, produced suitable West German promises to Poland that there would be no change in the existing Polish-German border.[13]

More difficult than the problem of borders was the question of whether—or how—to put special limits on the German armed forces and German behavior. The new Germany's armed forces would be large and capable. No one was especially worried about the intentions of the country's political leaders in 1990. The question was whether or how to set some special limits on the Germans that were meant to last through the decades.

The stock approach, pressed by some Soviet officials and tempting to some West German diplomats, was to set and agree on unique German limits. The Soviets took a very tough stance on these issues throughout the spring of 1990, what one German participant remembered as a "cold shower" to Western hopes.

The Soviets said that if the Germans wanted to unify, very well then. But the Four Power occupation rights would remain in order to regulate that new Germany. The process of internal unity and external settlement could be decoupled.

Either in a Two Plus Four agreement or in a full-blown peace treaty including a number of other former combatants in the Second World War, Germany would be placed under a set of controls. There would be no extension of alliances. The treaty would place severe restrictions on the size of German forces, both in quantity and quality.

To help enforce these restrictions, the troops of the Four Powers, including Soviet troops, would remain in the united Germany for a transition period of at least five years. Germany would not only be forbidden from having nuclear weapons, it would not be able to participate in decision making about such weapons (thus restricting its NATO activities). Its politics would be monitored to prevent any resurgence of Nazi-like political movements. At the same time, the Soviet government stalled progress toward conclusion of the CFE treaty.[14]

The unhappy precedent for such controls on Germany was the 1919 Treaty of Versailles.[15] That treaty had imposed a ceiling of one hundred thousand soldiers, along with other limits on the quality and placement of German forces. It had also envisioned using foreign occupation forces to enforce those controls, at least for a transition period, and with future rights of intervention.

Hitler had exploited German resentment of the controls in his rise to power, and on seizing power had ostentatiously torn up those restraints. After the Second World War, the Americans had developed an even more draconian, rigorously verified disarmament approach for the planned German peace treaty. But that disarmament plan was put aside, as negotiations over a German settlement broke down early in 1947.[16]

The Americans took seriously the Soviet threat to decouple internal unification from the external issues. Moscow was threatening to maintain occupation powers and leave hundreds of thousands of Soviet troops in Germany, to be maintained at German expense (per East German–Soviet agreements that the Soviets insisted would remain in force).

The Americans quietly discussed contingency plans, in which the United States, Britain, and France would give up their occupation rights when Germany unified, even if the Soviets did not. In early May 1990, the authors of this book wrote that the Soviets "must know that, after a given date, the West will declare the game over, devolve their own Four Power rights, and deploy legal arguments to the effect that all Four Power rights—including the Soviets'—have now lapsed." Moscow and Gorbachev would then have the unpopular task of insisting to the German people that they alone retained the right to supervise a newly united and democratic German state.[17]

Kohl had come to a similar conclusion. Unification had to go ahead. Foreign policy, he told the visiting British foreign secretary, was like mowing grass for hay: You had to gather what you had cut in case of a thunderstorm.[18]

* * *

Yet the Americans and West Germans sought more creative ways to address Soviet concerns without such a blunt, dangerous confrontation. Their ideas would use the institutions of the new Europe.

First, they stressed NATO and NATO's integrated military command. The stock, cutesy quote, constantly repeated, and attributed to Lord Ismay, is that the purpose of NATO was to "keep the Russians out, the Americans in, and the Germans down." This is clever. It is not really right.

The basic genius of the European constructions was to temper all the old national conflicts in a wider political community. The old European Coal and Steel Community, a precursor of the European Community, included the vital industrial resources of France as well as Germany. NATO, then, was similar to the European Community, later the European Union, in that it was not just a control mechanism—it was a different kind of political and economic and even military community. The political community worked because its members were free and democratic.

Like other NATO members, West Germany did not have truly independent armed forces. All of them were assigned to NATO's command structures, so that the higher command and staff echelons were international. By retaining full German membership in NATO, the German military remained enmeshed in this international military structure.

NATO was also a key factor on the question of German nuclear weapons. Before Germany agreed to join the Non-Proliferation Treaty in 1969, governments had been arguing for ten years about whether the Germans needed nuclear defenses. West Germans had their share of national pride and felt very threatened by Soviet military power. The renunciation of nuclear weapons finally made sense to them because of the NATO alliance. They could point to the assurance of British, French, and, above all, American nuclear defense. For the systems in Europe, American nuclear defense was coordinated through NATO.

* * *

The other big constraint on the Germans would be the planned CFE treaty. The Germans were willing to be constrained, but only in ways that did not single them out for special, discriminatory limits. The American mantra on this, publicly announced by the White House (on the occasion of the April meeting with Thatcher) and repeated often, was, "A united Germany should have full control over all of its territory without any new discriminatory constraints on German sovereignty."[19] The West Germans and Americans were happy to limit a future German army, but only if and when other national armies in Europe were limited too.

After the first CFE treaty was concluded in 1990, it would limit alliance totals of military equipment and U.S. and Soviet stationed manpower. These would not necessarily limit *German* force size. The plan was that in the next round of CFE talks all countries would accept national manpower ceilings too. The Germans would then have national limits along with everybody else.

The Soviets did not want to wait for the "next" CFE treaty after this one. The governments worked out a compromise solution, with some particular help from the American side. The plan would still be that all the CFE countries would accept such limits. Rather than be silent and noncommittal until that future agreement was signed, the West Germans would lean forward and simply make a unilateral political statement about the ceiling they planned to adopt in that future negotiation.

Thus Germany would have committed itself to a future ceiling. But it would still stick to the plan that such a ceiling would only be binding when all the other CFE parties went along and joined in accepting limits too. The solution had another key virtue: It kept the pressure on the Soviets to come to agreement on the current CFE treaty and get that done in 1990, a very difficult task.[20]

This plan worked. The Germans made their commitment. They picked a total ceiling of 370,000 on the active-duty strength of their armed forces. This was a meaningful reduction. In 1988 the West German armed forces alone were about 490,000 strong; the East German forces numbered about another 170,000. So, in theory, on unity the combined German armed forces would have been about 660,000 strong, but the Germans were pledging to cut them back to no more than 370,000, along with all the other CFE limits on military equipment.

The Germans complied with these limits, at great expense. They ended up destroying nearly 11,000 items of major military equipment at a cost of about $5 billion.[21]

As planned, the CFE treaty was signed at the Paris CSCE summit in 1990. Also, as planned, the follow-on agreement (CFE 1A) was concluded alongside another CSCE summit, in Helsinki in 1992. It added the binding national ceilings on troop strength for all of the other twenty-nine countries that then were parties to the agreement (as by then the Soviet Union had broken up).[22]

German forces remained in NATO's integrated military command.

This, plus the use of "annexation/takeover" as the vehicle for unification, helped settle Germany's nuclear weapons status as well.

The old FRG's acceptance of the Non-Proliferation Treaty in 1969 remained binding on the enlarged FRG. The Two Plus Four treaty (the Final Settlement with Respect to Germany) reaffirmed Germany's non-nuclear weapons commitment. Further, since the Western approach would not allow American forces to be stationed in the former territory of East Germany (the "special military status"), that area thus also became a nuclear-weapons-free zone.

All these agreements have long been taken for granted. Yet it is worth remembering how much these understandings are intertwined with other structures, like CFE and NATO. If the wider structures disintegrate, long-entombed questions about German security, and that of others, will return to Europe.

* * *

During Kohl's visit to Washington on May 17, Bush and Kohl had a private talk, practically alone.

Quietly sitting in the Oval Office, Bush asked Kohl for his honest opinion about the core question: Did the German public want the American troops to stay, if Soviet troops left, as Bush thought they should?

Bush acknowledged the "isolationist" tendencies on both sides of the Atlantic. "It would be understandable," he said, "if [the German people] didn't want U.S. troops."

Kohl's answer was twofold. "The U.S. troop presence is related to NATO. What sort of NATO would it be, leaving U.S. troops aside? If the U.S. left, NATO would vanish and there might be only CSCE." Where would be the security, including for countries like Norway or the smaller states?

Second, Kohl added, even if the Soviet Union withdraws, "it is still in Europe. If the U.S. withdraws, it is 6,000 kilometers away. That is a big difference."

Looking at the future of Europe even beyond the year 2000, Kohl foresaw the Americans staying in Europe. If the Europeans allowed the Americans to leave, it would be "the greatest defeat for us all. Remember

Wilson in 1918," he said, referring to the failure to keep the United States engaged in Europe after World War I.

Kohl became emotional. Trained in history, he felt deeply about issues and places of national memory. Looking ahead to his next visit to the United States, in a few weeks, he and Scowcroft had already made plans to tour Arlington Cemetery, where many American soldiers, sailors, and Marines rest.

"George," he said, "don't worry about those who draw parallels between U.S. and Soviet forces. We will push this through. We'll put our political existence at stake for NATO and the political commitment of the United States in Europe."[23]

* * *

Germany was not alone in such beliefs. Almost all the NATO member governments positively liked the alliance. Led by some ministers with especially good experiences, like Norway or the Netherlands, the smaller governments felt enlarged and empowered by being part of a greater whole.

Therefore, it is a bit disorienting for us to read contemporary scholarly arguments about these years, accounts perhaps a bit colored by knowledge of what happened after 1990 and 1991, that see in this diplomacy an offensive American master plan to attain "preeminence" or "hegemony" in Europe (or some other imperious-sounding term currently in academic fashion). It should be apparent by now just how complex transatlantic and European power relationships were, and still are even now.

In 1989 and 1990, Bush was in fact planning a gradual but large *downsizing* of the American military and U.S. defense spending, a plan he announced in August 1990 (a historic announcement that coincided, by astonishing happenstance, with Iraq's invasion of Kuwait). With the world changing and the tide of American presence in Europe going out, the Bush administration was trying to anchor a diminished but still reassuring military presence and ensure that America remained a European power. In that sense the administration felt defensive, not expansive.

In 1989–90 the United States was coming off a large national debate about U.S. decline and the powerful surge of economic nationalism so remarked upon by American and foreign observers. A core issue—as Bush opened up about so candidly to Kohl—was whether, and how, the United States would maintain a major presence in Europe at all. On this point, American leaders were extremely attentive to European views and the currents of European opinion, none more important than those in West Germany.

In this context, the true consensus position emerging during the spring and summer of 1990 was that the East Europeans, watching what the Soviets were doing to Lithuania, were losing interest in retaining any defense alliance with Moscow. The West Europeans wanted to keep the alliance they had. Dangers did seem to have diminished for the moment, so there was no pressing need to create any new alliances.

* * *

What was pressing in the spring of 1990 was a widely shared sense of *uncertainty* about the future. On May 4, 1990, Bush used a commencement address in Oklahoma to discuss the need for a new kind of NATO, with a new strategy. He apologized to the graduating college students for dwelling on such a seemingly faraway topic.

The new mission, Bush explained, would be much more political. As for the military side, as he put it, "our enemy today is uncertainty and instability."[24] That phrase seemed like a vague hedge. It was. It also turned out to be an accurate prediction.

Few, if anyone, predicted in May 1990 that the NATO allies would face two wars just in the next year. One would arise in the Middle East: Iraq's August 1990 invasion and conquest of neighboring Kuwait. The other, for which the storm clouds were already gathering, was a set of wars that arose in the Balkans, as the disintegration of Yugoslavia led to conflicts that began in 1991.

The Soviet threat seemed to be receding. But new sorts of conflicts and dangers were already on the edge of bursting into flame. In April 1990 the Soviet government was placing an embargo on breakaway Lithuania, and the threat of violence was obvious.

Leaders liked and generally trusted Gorbachev. But they were already looking beyond him. For instance, by 1990, Kohl and Mitterrand were as close as cousins, or even brothers, including the occasional flareups. In a meeting at Mitterrand's country home in Latche near the southwestern coast of France on a chilly, windy January day, the two men had mused about what might come next in Moscow.

"The Gorbachev experiment will still go on for a certain time," Mitterrand predicted. "What will come after, if he fails?"

"Ultras!" Mitterrand said, answering his own question. "Not Communists, but a tough military dictator." If the military won, Mitterrand thought they would stick with liberalization of the economy. "But the nationalist elements would stand strong in the foreground. Blood would flow in Georgia and other parts of the Soviet Union."[25]

Conjectures like these were common in 1990. They were one reason why the existing allies valued their defense link to America.

Worries like these were also a reason to try to help Gorbachev stay in power. It was why Bush, Kohl, Mitterrand, Thatcher, and others all worked hard to find a way to help Gorbachev with the issue of Germany staying in NATO.

How to Help Gorbachev?

By May 1990 there was no doubt that Gorbachev was interested in getting significant economic assistance for the Soviet Union. The Soviet desire for economic assistance surfaced at last when Shevardnadze spoke with Kohl in Bonn on May 4. It was becoming difficult for the Soviet government to borrow money to import goods, especially food. Their existing creditors (in Western Europe and Japan) would not make new loans.

Shevardnadze asked the West German government for help. Kohl was determined to assist as much as he could.

Without informing his cabinet (but telling Genscher), Kohl contacted the leaders of two major West German banks. He sent Teltschik and the bankers to Moscow, in secret, to explore the Soviets' needs and possible responses.[26] The Soviets asked for a credit line of DM 20 billion (about $12 billion) guaranteed by the West German government. The West German government could not back up that kind of loan.

Teltschik met directly with Gorbachev, who again linked the credit issue to the continuation of his overall program of economic reform and perestroika. But Gorbachev was not interested in compromising on the security issues involving Germany. They at least agreed that Kohl would come back to the Soviet Union in the summer and visit Gorbachev in his home region, the Caucasus.

When Kohl met with Bush in Washington a few days later, the Soviet request for money was at the top of his agenda.[27] Kohl said his government could guarantee about $3 billion in loans. He hoped the United States would guarantee some more.

Bush would not do it. He was still walking his tightrope. He had tried not to be too tough about Lithuania. But with that crisis not yet settled, adding more Soviet debt without real economic reform did not make sense to him.

Kohl urged Bush to change his mind. But Bush stood firm. He did not think the Soviets could repay big new loans under their current circumstances.

Kohl disagreed. He urged Bush to help Gorbachev, not wait for him to be overthrown.

Did Kohl think that there would be a military takeover? Bush asked.

Yes, said Kohl, by a civilian group backed by the military. He urged Bush again to think about the upcoming summit. Gorbachev needed to be able to stand beside the American president as an equal.

Bush promised to treat Gorbachev as an equal, moving forward on political relations and arms control. But the United States would not give Gorbachev money, not unless the Soviets changed their policy toward Lithuania.

The issue of economic assistance was left there for Bush to ponder as the U.S.-Soviet summit approached. Meanwhile, Baker was meeting with Shevardnadze, then Gorbachev, in Moscow.

The meetings did not go well. With Gorbachev, Baker made little headway, but he did deploy a set of nine assurances, about managing Germany and changing NATO, that Zoellick had drafted and tried out earlier in the day.

For weeks, Chernyaev had privately urged Gorbachev to stop what he called this "nonsense," this "false patriotism of the masses," and adjust his position on NATO and not "again miss the train." Gorbachev, however, still seemed adamant.[28]

Gorbachev moved the conversation with Baker to his agenda. He challenged the Americans' real intentions toward the Soviet Union, given the clashes over issues such as Lithuania and Germany.

Then, just as Kohl had expected, he made the same kind of request for money that he had made to the West Germans. Gorbachev said he needed $20 billion in loans and credits to overcome a significant funding gap over the next few years. The United States had to be involved, at least symbolically, in the loan effort. The next few years would be critical in easing the transition to a market economy.

Baker could offer Gorbachev little encouragement. It was hard to justify spending U.S. taxpayers' money if the Soviets were subsidizing the Cubans and blockading the Lithuanians. Baker was essentially making the same points Bush had made to Kohl in Washington the day before.

Reflecting on this meeting in a message back to Bush, Baker's leading impression was that Gorbachev was clearly feeling squeezed and would probably react strongly to any action that compounded his political difficulties at home. "Germany definitely overloads his circuits right now."

* * *

It was one thing for the United States and the Soviet Union to no longer be enemies. It was still another long road for the United States to actually consider giving the Soviet Union large sums of money.

Consider: First, the United States at this point did not even have normal trade relations with the Soviet Union, something that Bush could not do alone. Any such deal would require support from the U.S. Congress, which was controlled by the opposing Democratic Party. U.S.-Soviet trade relations were not yet even on the level the United States had with China (normal status, but temporary, up for renewal each year).

Then, someone would have to make a case about what the money was for—how it would actually be spent. And after that, Bush would have to persuade Congress, which was then embroiled in a taut battle with Bush over his determined efforts to move back toward balancing the budget, that the United States should appropriate large sums of money to a Soviet government that, on the surface, still seemed to be in pretty good shape and was devoting an enormous part of its economy to its military-industrial complex and massively subsidizing governments like those in Cuba and North Korea.

After Baker returned, Scowcroft laid out what he thought was the "strategic choice" for Bush. This was the first time the Soviet Union had asked for help in this way from Western governments. "The decision," Scowcroft wrote, "is not in essence about aid to Soviet economic reform—the chance that we can turn the Soviet economy around is a slim one indeed.

"This is—and you should view it as such—a strategic choice about whether economic assistance is a direct and expeditious means by which to secure the victory of the West in the Cold War by obtaining the unification of Germany in NATO and the withdrawal of the Soviet military from Central and Eastern Europe."

On that question, Scowcroft thought that a big investment, even $20 billion, was worth considering. "Some will say that we would be paying for what the Soviets will have to do anyway—leave Eastern Europe and Germany." But he explained how difficult things could get. The Soviets "could make Central Europe a tense place for the next few years—years that are critical to the solidification of the Western gains of the recent period."

It was true that the money to the Soviets might be wasted. It "would probably be spent on a quick infusion of consumer goods to blunt the impact of half-hearted economic reform measures."

Nor would Congress support help "while the Soviet Union spends $15 billion a year to arm its client states—$5 billion in Cuba alone—and continues to strangle the Lithuanian independence movement." But the United States had to concentrate on the most important problems, even if such an understanding about assistance would be a gamble on both sides.[29]

Free to Choose

Mitterrand did not like to lean on Gorbachev. When he journeyed to Moscow to meet again with the Soviet leader in late May, about a week after

Baker left, the French president's tone was more philosophical. He threw in his weight on the German freedom to make the choice of alliances for themselves. "I do not see," Mitterrand told Gorbachev, "how to forbid united Germany from choosing its alliances as agreed in Helsinki."[30]

The notion of Germans debating about NATO was not idle theory. In election campaign after election campaign, anyone who had followed German politics that year, West or East, could see that their political leaders—West or East—were offering a full menu of options, in or out of NATO.

Free to choose: The Soviet government had said it agreed with that principle when it was codified in the Helsinki CSCE Final Act of 1975. This had always been an argument that had stuck with Gorbachev, resonating as it did so strongly with his other political principles.[31]

By the end of May, as Gorbachev contemplated his trip to the United States, he faced a turning point in the course of East-West relations and perestroika. The stakes in continued cooperation with the West were enormous. Gorbachev and Shevardnadze had stated both publicly and privately that their first priority was domestic reform. That meant cutting military expenditures and avoiding the distraction of a major international crisis.

In the spring of 1990 the Soviet Union appeared to be resigned to the failure of its policy in Eastern Europe. A long document prepared by the Central Committee staff spoke matter-of-factly about the changed political and ideological face of Eastern Europe. The analysis warned Soviet leaders that they currently had no policy to respond to this situation. There was a vacuum, and the West was filling it.

The USSR was withdrawing with "no rational explanation, with no regard for the immense material and spiritual investment that we made there." The policy guidance grasped at straws. There was still a chance to strengthen the Soviet cultural presence, interest in the Russian language, and so forth. Ties needed to be developed with youth, trade unions, feminists, and religious groups. The Central Committee staff even suggested to a leadership desperately short of hard currency that a new policy in Eastern Europe might require a certain financial investment. "We should not economize," the staff told their impoverished leaders, "because this is a matter of capital for the future."[32]

Soviet policy in Eastern Europe—premised on the potential for reformed communism—might be dead. Germany and Lithuania, however, were a different matter. The division of Germany and Soviet dominance of its eastern half could be considered the most important achievements of half a century of Soviet foreign policy. This Soviet emplacement in the heart of Europe was the highest and last remaining measure of meaning from the vast sacrifices endured during the Great Patriotic War. Now the West and NATO were threatening to take over this bastion of Soviet power. It seemed inconceivable that the USSR could submit supinely to such a reverse. Gorbachev's own political survival could be jeopardized by such a concession, and Gorbachev would face a full congress of the Soviet Communist Party in July.

Gorbachev tried new economic reforms. On May 24, Prime Minister Nikolai Ryzhkov announced a major new economic reform program, including liberalizing prices. The cost of bread would triple. A wave of panic buying and public unrest followed. Gorbachev addressed the nation on television on May 27, pleading for calm.

The economic reform measures were eventually rejected by the Supreme Soviet before they could take effect. And, as if to underscore Gorbachev's beleaguered political situation, on May 29 the Russian legislature chose Boris Yeltsin as its president despite Gorbachev's opposition.

* * *

Kohl called Bush just before Gorbachev arrived in Washington. Again, he pressed Bush to commit a lot of money for the Soviets. But Bush had decided against the kind of $20 billion "strategic choice" that Scowcroft had invited him to consider.

There was just too much against it. There were the problems with how the money would be used.

Also, though this would be time-consuming to explain in top-level meetings, under its laws the West German government had much more scope to offer government-guaranteed loans to support its country's exports than was (or is) the case in the U.S. government.[33] Bush and Baker had trouble seeing how to get the federal government to guarantee loans on this sort of scale, and certainly not while Lithuania (and the BW program) were still unresolved.

It would be hard enough just to try and normalize trade relations. As Gorbachev was arriving, Bush had been going through a very hard battle with the Congress over his decision to renew normal trade with China for another year.

So Bush did not expect any breakthroughs with Gorbachev. He hoped to at least maintain forward progress.[34]

On the morning of May 31, Gorbachev was formally welcomed in a ceremony on the South Lawn of the White House. Guns boomed; a fife and drum corps dressed in the eighteenth-century uniforms of the Continental Army paraded for the leaders.

After the opening ceremony, Bush and Gorbachev walked from the South Lawn into the Oval Office for a private meeting, joined only by Scowcroft, Chernyaev, and their interpreters. Gorbachev promptly turned to the issue of American economic help for perestroika. A U.S.-Soviet trade agreement was essential. It was the one matter under discussion that might make a favorable impact at home.

Gorbachev knew that Lithuania was still a problem for the Americans. He pledged to avoid a violent solution by pursuing a peaceful dialogue with the republic's leaders. Bush was noncommittal. In another room Baker and Shevardnadze were replaying the same discussion. Shevardnadze was particularly emotional, admitting that he had rarely spoken like this before, but a U.S.-Soviet trade agreement was "extremely important" for Gorbachev's standing at home, to defend the Soviet leader's policy of cooperation with the West.[35]

Gorbachev returned to the Soviet embassy for a luncheon with American intellectuals and celebrities and then came back to the White House for an additional meeting. The main subject was Germany and the future of Europe.[36]

Bush wanted to tackle this difficult subject right from the start. Naturally he knew that the open question of the trade agreement still lurked in the background. He began the Cabinet Room discussion by delivering a carefully prepared presentation on Germany. He used the "nine assurances" that Baker had just previewed with Gorbachev in Moscow.[37]

Gorbachev presented his alternative. A united Germany could be a member of both military alliances, or it could be a member of neither.

Moscow could live with either possibility. In a rambling presentation, Gorbachev said that letting a united Germany join only NATO would "unbalance" Europe. He repeatedly referred to the need for a long transition period. Perhaps by the end of this period Germany could be anchored in both NATO and the Warsaw Pact. As part of the transition both alliances would be transformed into political organizations. "You are a sailor," he told Bush. "You will understand that if one anchor is good, two anchors are better." He felt that if the United States and the USSR could decide on how to proceed, the Germans would surely agree.

Bush argued that a unified Germany in NATO was the most stable solution for Europe's security.

Gorbachev agreed that the U.S. presence was stabilizing. This presence was linked to NATO. Fine; new structures could come later. But first NATO must change.

After back-and-forth arguments among Bush, Gorbachev, Baker, and Shevardnadze, Bush went back to the "free to choose" argument. Under the CSCE principles in the Helsinki Final Act, all nations had the right to choose their own alliances. So Germany should have the right to decide for itself which alliance it would join. Was this not so?

Gorbachev nodded. He agreed matter-of-factly that it was true.

The Americans were startled. They could see members of Gorbachev's team shifting in their seats. Blackwill whispered to Zoellick, sitting next to him, that he would pass a note to the president. Zoellick agreed. Blackwill jotted down a quick note pointing out to President Bush that, surprisingly, Gorbachev had just supported the U.S. position that nations have the right to choose their own alliances. Could the president get Gorbachev to say it again?

Bush could. "I'm gratified that you and I seem to agree that nations can choose their own alliances," he said.

"Do you and I agree that a united Germany has the right to be non-aligned, or a member of NATO, in a final document?" Gorbachev asked in reply.

"I agree with that," Bush said. "But the German public wants to be in NATO. But if they want out of NATO, we will respect that. They are a democracy."

"I agree to say so publicly," Gorbachev then said, "that the United States and the USSR are in favor of seeing a united Germany, with a final settlement leaving it up to where a united Germany can choose."

Bush then suggested an alternative formula: "We support a united Germany in NATO. If they don't want in, we will respect that."

"I agree," Gorbachev answered.

"With the second part?" Bush queried.

"With both parts."

Meanwhile, many of Gorbachev's aides could not conceal their distress, whispering and gesturing at each other. "It was an unbelievable scene," Bush recalled, "the likes of which none of us had ever seen before—virtually open rebellion against a Soviet leader." Zoellick recalled the scene as "one of the most extraordinary" he'd ever witnessed.

Then Gorbachev appeared to return to the familiar Soviet stance, describing the notion of a prolonged transition period during which Europe would change in order to accommodate a unified Germany. Gorbachev slipped an adviser, Valentin Falin, a note asking him to explain why the Soviets considered a pro-NATO solution unacceptable. Falin scribbled, "I am ready," and sent it back. Gorbachev nodded, and as Falin launched into his presentation, Gorbachev conferred with Shevardnadze.

When Gorbachev reentered the discussion, he proposed that Shevardnadze work with Baker on the German issue. Oddly, Shevardnadze at first openly refused, right in front of the Americans, saying that the matter had to be decided by heads of government. Gorbachev asked him again. Shevardnadze relented and agreed to explore the matter with Baker.

As the meeting ended, Bush and his advisers were in accord. There had been no misunderstanding: Gorbachev had indeed agreed that a united Germany could choose to be a full member of NATO. Back at the Soviet residence in Washington, Falin later recalled, Gorbachev complained about Shevardnadze's passivity, and expressed unhappiness that the foreign minister had done nothing to explore what kinds of variations the Americans might be prepared to accept on the NATO issue.

Perhaps Shevardnadze, having been rebuffed by Gorbachev and others in the Politburo when discussing Germany earlier in the month, was reluctant to stick his neck out. If Gorbachev, who had overruled Shevardnadze then, wanted to make concessions now, let him take the responsibility.

But now Gorbachev had made a concession, and the entire Soviet delegation knew it. Immediately after the meeting, on the lawn of the White House, Akhromeyev practically assaulted Chernyaev, interrogating him about Gorbachev's comments. Had they been written down as part of his briefing papers? Why had Gorbachev said what he'd said? Chernyaev replied that the comments were spontaneous; he did not know why the Soviet leader had chosen to make them on the spot.[38]

Gorbachev's and Shevardnadze's behavior at the meeting seemed, and still seems, quite unusual. It is actually very rare in diplomacy to change one's mind right at the table. The best interpretation consistent with the available evidence is that Gorbachev's resolve had been weakening little by little, even before he arrived in Washington. Nothing that the Soviet Union suggested about Germany seemed to be working. The Soviet leader had made all the old arguments again and again.

Finally, as he faced Bush in Washington, something snapped. Bush's invocation of the right to choose one's alliance system (the same argument Mitterrand had made a week earlier) may have caught Gorbachev off guard. Chernyaev recalled later that it would not have been logical to reject this idea since Gorbachev had already granted that a united Germany would be fully sovereign. Indeed, Gorbachev had often adopted the rhetoric of free choice and national self-determination. So when Bush struck the wall of resistance from this new angle, it suddenly cracked.

Gorbachev went on with his schedule: a formal dinner at the White House in the evening, breakfast with congressional leaders the next morning, June 1. He explained his economic difficulties and asked the congressmen to back a trade agreement. The agreement would not bring quick results, he said, since "the trade relationship between us now is so primitive," but "I think it is very important that you make this gesture mostly from a political standpoint."[39]

Gorbachev returned to the White House later that morning, and he and Bush talked further about the trade agreement. Bush had checked views around his administration and on Capitol Hill. Opinions were divided, but Baker recommended going ahead with the deal. The administration should try to negotiate some links to Soviet behavior in Lithuania, but the United States had to deliver this visible support to reform. Shevardnadze had been persuasive on this issue.

Bush agreed. It is probable that Gorbachev's apparent move on Germany contributed to the president's decision to help the beleaguered Soviet leader.

The White House had scheduled a ceremony at the end of the day on June 1 to announce the agreements that had been concluded. Gorbachev arrived. A few top officials on both sides huddled privately outside the East Room, where the ceremony was to take place. "Are we going to sign the trade agreement?" Gorbachev asked.

Yes, Bush replied. Shevardnadze and Baker had worked out a plan under which the deal would be signed, to take effect as progress was made on liberalizing Soviet emigration and talking to Lithuania. And the leaders signed.

Later that night Bush's aides thought of a way to capitalize on Gorbachev's concession on Germany. The NSC staff drafted a statement for the president to deliver at the joint press conference that would close the summit on Sunday morning, June 3. The statement repeated that "we are in full agreement that the matter of alliance membership is, in accordance with the Helsinki Final Act, a matter for the Germans to decide." To make sure that Gorbachev was "in full agreement" with this statement, Rice passed the draft to the deputy foreign minister, who later confirmed that there was no objection.

At Camp David for more relaxed and private discussions, Gorbachev, as Bush had expected, raised the question of U.S.-government-guaranteed loans.

Bush said that he wanted to help but needed to see more economic reforms, movement on Lithuania, and a reduction of subsidies to Cuba. Progress on Germany would also create the right political climate for Bush to seek money from Congress.

Bush did pledge that the G-7 would consider a broad multilateral assistance program, including substantial credits, at the Houston summit in July, to be held right after the NATO summit in London.[40]

At dinner Gorbachev looked untroubled, serene. With the trade agreement signed, the atmosphere was warm and friendly.

None of the reporters at the press conference appeared to notice the significance of Bush's press statement. Nor did American officials call attention to it. They sensed that Gorbachev had finally turned a corner in his approach to the German question, but the situation was tentative and shaky. Indeed, later in June, Shevardnadze continued to present a doctrinaire line in the discussions about Germany.

Bush carefully reported on his press statement in phone calls to Kohl, Thatcher, and Mitterrand. He did not dramatize the concession. He instead emphasized the need to follow up with a successful NATO summit in July.

None of the other leaders appeared, at least at first, to grasp the significance of the Soviet move; none even inquired about it. (Teltschik, however, noted that this was "a sensation.") Mitterrand did remark shrewdly that Gorbachev would be counting on achieving his security objectives through West Germany's domestic politics.

Bush then followed up with written messages. Again, his tone was cautious: "We, of course, will have to see whether this reflects real flexibility in the Soviet position."[41]

But, as Chernyaev recalled, the Americans were correct to take the exchange on Germany's right to choose very seriously. When asked later when the Soviet Union agreed to membership of a united Germany in NATO, Chernyaev "unhesitatingly" answered, "On May 30 [sic], at the Soviet-American summit in Washington."[42]

A New Atlantic Alliance

In the spring of 1990, the Soviets put forward their ideas for pan-European security structures, designed mainly to handle the German problem. At first these seemed, to the Soviet diplomat charged with deploying them, like a "surrealistic jumble of ideas."

The most polished set of Soviet suggestions, deployed in May–June 1990, looked about like this:

• NATO and the Warsaw Pact would remain. They would evolve into friendlier, cooperative structures.

• The united Germany would be in both alliances, or neither. But it would be under control measures for some transitional period, overseen by the Four Powers, perhaps involving the CSCE.

• The CSCE would develop into a pan-European organization that could help manage disputes with a conflict prevention center. To illustrate, in one conversation Shevardnadze mentioned disputes like those between Hungarians and Romanians, or between Czechs and Slovaks, or among the contenders in Yugoslavia. The CSCE's conflict prevention center might be similar to the European Security Commission suggested by the new Czech foreign minister.[43]

There was another possibility. Neither CFE nor CSCE offered an all-European alliance, a promise to come to another member's defense in case of attack. In theory, then, a country could have proposed a thirty-five-nation alliance in which every member promised to come to the aid of the others. In such an alliance, the United States and the Soviet Union and Germany would promise to defend each other, or Yugoslavia, or any other member. Some of the Warsaw Pact member state leaders, like Czech president Vaclav Havel, were—in these early days—naturally taken with just such a concept.

This particular all-European idea was never seriously developed. It is not at all clear that the Soviet government actually wanted such a collective security alliance across all of Europe.

Also, in the spring of 1990, the Soviet Union was on the verge of possible internal wars, including a real danger of imminent conflict with breakaway Lithuania. It would have been hard to muster much enthusiasm around Europe to figure out how to handle all the possible scenarios that could arise from signing mutual defense pacts with Moscow.

What the Soviets instead began floating, as we mention above, were the ideas about a CSCE center for risk reduction and arms control verification. This might be attached to a pan-European peacekeeping force to help with resolution of civil conflicts. The risk reduction center idea was very close to ideas that, quite independently, the United States was also developing at that time, ideas that eventually all would agree to adopt as a complement to the CFE system.[44]

* * *

Instead of some new alliance, perhaps old-style defense might no longer be necessary at all. Those alliances had been created in the 1940s and 1950s for Cold War dangers.

In this argument, alliances would go away altogether. The CFE/CSCE system would be there, regulating arms. Eastern European countries no longer seemed quite so interested in wanting a defense guarantee from Moscow.

The Soviet government was coming close to this position. Yet neither Moscow nor Genscher were willing at this point to go all the way to explain and defend this argument either.

In the spring of 1990, the Warsaw Pact members had not yet firmly decided to dissolve their alliance. Some, including Poland, were still musing about whether they needed some sort of Soviet defense relationship, maybe even a bilateral one, to hedge against a German threat. But they were all trending away from wanting a Soviet alliance.

The situation was quite different among the fourteen NATO member countries on the European side of the Atlantic or bordering the Mediterranean Sea. During 1990 or 1991 it would have been hard to find a single one of those governments that even wanted to talk about severing its defense guarantee and relations with the United States.

* * *

Gorbachev's main problem with Germany staying in NATO, and the United States staying in Europe, was not rooted in solid arguments about the military balance or strategic necessity. NATO would help manage German power. The Germans should be free to choose. The CFE system would address the military balance of power.

The reduced Soviet military forces would still be enormous, relative to the others. The Soviet Union would not be vulnerable to a Western attack.

Gorbachev and Shevardnadze's main problem was political. It was the imagery of Germany joining the enemy side. Their generation had been taught and reminded that NATO was an implacable foe, a dangerous bloc.

After four hours of talks with Shevardnadze early in May, Baker wrote back to Bush that the Soviet leaders "don't know how to square the circle. They're wrestling with it." The core problem was that "I suspect that Gorbachev doesn't want to take on this kind of an emotionally charged political issue now, and almost certainly not before the [July 1990] Party Congress." Genscher, also deeply engaged in working the issue, saw it the same way. Shevardnadze was trying to change NATO's "demonic" image at home.[45]

To help him, the Americans promised real progress at a special NATO summit to be held in London early in July, before the Party Congress. Bush's May 4 speech had set high expectations for this NATO summit. Since February, for five months Bush and his team had led the way to put meat on the bones of their promise to make NATO more political and change its military approach.

Back in February the White House had created an ad hoc "European Strategy Steering Group" to work the whole set of issues. It was chaired by Gates, Zelikow was the executive secretary, and it included Zoellick and Ross from State in addition to the usual line officials. An unusual set of interagency debates within the U.S. government was followed by extraordinary, rushed, and intense arguments in the alliance.

With Wörner's support at NATO headquarters, the United States bypassed the usual working-level process. Bush took his ideas directly to his counterparts, to be negotiated on-site by Baker and ministers, or directly by the leaders. This risky strategy produced a turning point for the alliance at its London summit of July 5–6, 1990.[46]

The leaders publicly agreed, in their declaration on a "transformed" alliance, that they were no longer adversaries of the Warsaw Pact states. That military purpose was gone.

The CFE system and related confidence-building measures would reset and regulate defenses. It would be followed by new conventional arms reductions that would go even further with "far-reaching measures" during the 1990s to "prevent any nation from maintaining disproportionate military power on the continent."

The reduced national forces (including U.S. forces) would be integrated more into multinational commands. "Forward defense" would become a "reduced forward presence."

The old NATO nuclear strategy of "flexible response" would also become history. In the new strategy, nuclear forces would be turned "truly into weapons of last resort." All nuclear artillery and most other U.S. nuclear forces would be removed.

The summit planned for new arms control talks on these forces. In September 1991, the United States and Soviet Union jumped over that process. To get the work done faster, they proceeded with reciprocal unilateral reductions of almost all of their nuclear forces in Europe (outside those in the Soviet Union itself).

The U.S. approach thus followed through on Baker's December 1989 promise that NATO would return mainly to its political mission. It was already evolving into a place where all NATO members could discuss political and security concerns.

Another major initiative from London was to welcome the Soviet Union and all the other former Warsaw Pact states to NATO. They were invited to establish permanent diplomatic liaison missions in NATO, with ambassadors accredited to the alliance.

This particular U.S. initiative, which the two of us developed in March and April 1990, anticipated the decay of the Warsaw Pact, which was formally abolished in 1991. We, and the leaders who then adopted this initiative, sought a way to welcome these countries to NATO, without having to get into issues of formal membership or alliance status.

We did not see any need to prejudge or get tangled up in those issues in 1990 or 1991. We just thought it was more important and useful to turn NATO into a community where representatives from the former enemies could start working directly with other representatives and staff at alliance headquarters on issues of common concern. As time passed, and everyone got to know each other and work together, they could make decisions about any further steps.[47]

This move proceeded about as planned. A year later, at another special NATO summit held in Rome in November 1991, NATO created a more formal structure to include Soviet and East European ministers, a North Atlantic Cooperation Council (NACC).

As we will discuss below, NACC was not just empty symbolism. Using it as a key forum, governments from across Europe did vital work during the early 1990s to adapt the CFE system and the European military balance after the breakup of the Soviet Union. The NACC, in turn, evolved by 1994 into a "Partnership for Peace," bringing the former adversaries even closer to NATO's security deliberations.

The London NATO summit helped Soviet leaders with their NATO image problem. In his memoirs, Shevardnadze described how "in the extremely inflamed atmosphere of the [July Party] Congress it was difficult to breathe." So, "when the news came out about the NATO session in London, I knew there had been a response." Gorbachev and Shevardnadze quickly found ways to laud the move in the Soviet press. NATO's move paved the way, they said, "for a safe future for the entire European continent."[48]

A Final Settlement for Germany

Between April and late July 1990, diplomatic attention centered on the allied effort to persuade Gorbachev and his government to accept the Western approach for settling the German question. At the time, we believed that this would probably work out somehow. Just the same, we were very anxious about it.

Gorbachev had indicated a degree of acceptance—the "free to choose" point—at the end of May. It took more effort, including the indication of the "transformed" NATO that came out of the London summit, and Gorbachev getting through his Party Congress, until the main deal was closed by Kohl and Genscher after many hours of meetings in Moscow and in the Caucasus on July 14–16.

Relaxing with his team on the evening of July 15 at the lodge where they were staying, Kohl sighed delightedly and said, "Never in my life have I had to work so hard. But never in my life have I also been so happy." The treaty for a final settlement of the German question was negotiated rapidly in the following two months among the six countries in the Two Plus Four (with a July visit from Poland's foreign minister).[49]

We have often reflected on this historic agreement, focusing especially on the turning points in the spring and summer of 1990. Five observations, taken together, help explain that final outcome.

* * *

First, the West Germans and Americans did put together a serious and adequate package of assurances about how to address future German military power. These reassurances were probably more important to Moscow than the NATO membership issue itself. Germany's NATO membership was essential to this control concept. It, along with the planned CFE arms control system, allowed such controls to make lasting sense for the Germans.

As we mentioned, in Moscow in May, Baker and Zoellick had started using and sharing a set of "nine points" to summarize all the ways that the West was already addressing, or moving to address, Soviet concerns. These points, frequently reiterated, had real substance. And the United States, the West Germans, and their allies followed through on every one of these points.[50]

* * *

Second, therefore neither Gorbachev nor Shevardnadze could really come up with a truly persuasive, plausible alternative to the West German and American approach on the question of German NATO membership.

Gorbachev and Shevardnadze would later be attacked for having done a poor job in the diplomacy. It is true that they could have orchestrated a more powerful counterattack, especially in the early phases. They could have done much more to disrupt and delay the unification process, decouple the external aspects, create a major crisis, and polarize West German politics.

As tacticians, at the time we were keenly aware of, and still see, their lost tactical opportunities. One can then argue, as many have, that Gorbachev and Shevardnadze struck a poor deal for their country.

We do not agree. Is this just a product of our American bias? This was not a game. Those who levy the criticism bear the burden of making an argument about alternative Soviet strategic objectives and posture in the new Europe. Those making that argument must then link it to their proposed alternative conception of the future of the Soviet Union itself.

Gorbachev and Shevardnadze could have chosen an alternative grand strategy, one of forceful dictatorship and empire. Such a strategy might have required different leaders of the Soviet Union. But would such alternative leaders, such an alternative strategy, really have made the Soviet Union better off? Or Europe?

* * *

Third, by the spring of 1990 the quality of coordination among U.S., West German, French, and British diplomats was very strong. They did not agree on everything. Yet the net orchestration was detailed and effective.

Thus Gorbachev encountered a reasonably united front. Whether it was the American-Soviet summit in May, or the West German–Soviet summit in the Caucasus in July, in both cases the allies worked from a common script.

The Americans were pleasantly surprised by the July breakthrough. The press commented in predictable ways about whether Kohl deserved the credit, not Bush.

Bristling about such commentary, Blackwill, as he was about to leave the NSC staff at the end of July 1990, gave a talk at a Washington think tank in which he described the Soviet-German result as the product of a U.S.-directed policy. It had been, he said, "the most intensive application of US diplomacy of all time. Anyone who thought that the Administration had been upstaged by [the Caucasus breakthrough] must have been living on the planet Zarkon."[51]

We understood our colleague's irritation. But in fact, we all knew that the West Germans had a vital and difficult role to play in all this too. We also knew that the West German diplomacy with the Soviets had its own special character.

As our account makes clear, the allied partners were not robots, marching in perfect sync. There were plenty of strains and suspicions and sotto voce comments. They persisted right up to the very last hours of talks in Moscow in September 1990.[52]

These were all proud, powerful governments of great countries whose leaders and officials very much had minds of their own. What was remarkable was not that there was disharmony and tension. That is the norm. It is mitigated—at best—only with constant effort and well-understood common policy designs.

What was remarkable was the extent to which the partners actually did function effectively as a team. A close examination of the diplomacy that culminated in the German-Soviet talks shows the constant interaction, coordination…and teamwork. Bush and Baker were not too troubled. They knew and they acknowledged, as did Kohl and Genscher, what a team effort it was.[53]

* * *

Fourth, in the spring and summer of 1990, Gorbachev was terribly preoccupied and beset by his internal problems. We have noted how the "NATO" issue had already become more about image, and the struggle he was facing at home.

* * *

Fifth, Gorbachev pushed hard to get Western money, leaning especially on Kohl and on Bush.

We mentioned that Bush was not yet convinced. The G-7 countries agreed that an IMF-led team of international agencies would do a crash study of Soviet needs (which it did). The United States and other G-7 governments, including Delors, did not see how massive transfers would do much good, even if the money could be found or appropriated by legislatures, without much more far-reaching reforms in the Soviet Union itself.

Germany did transfer a lot of money to the Soviet Union. In May, Kohl had agreed that his government would guarantee further private bank loans to the USSR. In September, he agreed to a large cash transfer to offset the costs of withdrawing Soviet forces from Germany. Some refer to this as a successful "bribe" to seal the deal.[54]

The money was important. But the "bribe" label is not fair to anyone involved. Even before Kohl arrived in Moscow in July for the historic meetings that would conclude in the Caucasus, Chernyaev and Gorbachev had already planned to confirm Soviet consent to full German membership in NATO.

Chernyaev was therefore worried about the *appearance* that German assistance had caused the Soviets to give way on NATO because, as he noted to his diary, "After all, the world does not know about the agreement made with Bush in Washington, so it could appear that Bush was not able to convince Gorbachev, but the German quickly won him over with loans." To Chernyaev, writing the day after Gorbachev confirmed the agreement on NATO, "it is not the bait (loans) but the fact that it is pointless to resist here, it would go against the current of events, it would be contrary to the very realities that [Gorbachev] likes to refer to so much."[55]

The largest later Soviet claim on the Germans, in their tough negotiations in September 1990, was for help offsetting the costs of maintaining and rapidly relocating the hundreds of thousands of troops, families, and stocks of equipment from installations that had been in East Germany for generations, and effectively subsidized there.

These relocation costs were real and they were large. It was quite reasonable for Moscow to ask for West German help in offsetting those costs, since West Germany wanted the troops to leave the unified Germany as rapidly as possible. There was plenty of room to haggle over the right numbers, since there were no good ways to calculate them objectively.

In September, Gorbachev drove a hard bargain about German compensation for the troop withdrawals, probably amounting to the equivalent of about $9 billion in grants. In these talks, the Soviets had a bargaining advantage, and they used it.

Kohl's offer of the D-Mark to East Germany, plus the rapid dissolution of the East German economy, meant that every day the West Germans were effectively losing more money, until they could get full political control over all the institutions. If the Soviets chose to delay political unification, the West Germans would lose much more money. By that time, a quick resolution, even at a relatively high price, was actually in West Germany's economic interest, as Moscow knew.[56]

The other big source of German aid to Moscow was huge sums of credit guarantees, private loans guaranteed by the German government. By the spring of 1991 the German government had extended credit guarantees and other credits for a total of about $25 billion (which Moscow was supposed to pay back).[57]

In theory, the Soviet Union had enough export income to manage its debt.[58] The big issues were internal: State entities had borrowed the foreign money, but as the Soviet economy was starting to fall apart amid a mismanaged "reform" process, those entities no longer ran the firms or earned the money to repay the debts.

A year later Gorbachev admitted to Baker, "Things disappear around here. We got a lot of money for German unification, and when I called our people, I was told they didn't know where it was." Baker was a bit staggered by this. He checked later with Yakovlev, who told him, "It's just gone."[59]

First Tests for a Transformed NATO

The United States and NATO followed through on the commitments to transform the alliance into something else. Like any protected historic landmark structure, NATO kept the same reassuring shell. The interior was gutted and completely renovated.

During the next few years, as all Soviet troops returned home and the Soviet Union itself broke apart, most U.S. troops also left Europe. A core remained. This numbered about 100,000 by 1993, less than one-third of the 1989 strength. By 1999 that number—down to about 69,000—had been reorganized for entirely different missions.

What was left was a core commitment to a continued guarantee of U.S. nuclear defense with a small remaining force of American bombs that could be delivered by allied and American aircraft kept in Western Europe. The old wide deployments to resist territorial aggression from the East were gone. Diplomats from all those countries now went to regular meetings at NATO.

The London Declaration promised that the new alliance would replace older force structures with "smaller and restructured" forces, "highly mobile and versatile so that Allied leaders will have maximum flexibility in deciding how to respond to a crisis," and relying "increasingly on multinational corps made up of national units." And this is what happened.

These restructured forces would be designed to be able to use European bases for two kinds of purposes:

- Agreed joint military actions outside Europe; or

- Agreed crisis management/peacekeeping efforts inside Europe.

Sooner than anyone had expected, both of these contingencies moved from the world of theoretical communiqués to problems of real action.

Agreed joint military actions outside Europe

That contingency arose in August 1990, with Iraq's conquest of Kuwait. People at the time argued about whether the United States and other countries should confront Iraq and go to war in 1990–91. Both of us entirely agreed with the policies of the Bush administration in which we then served.

But, whatever one thinks about the policies, governments might at least want to have the *option* of being able to organize a decisive international response. NATO—as an institution—showed how valuable it could be in such a crisis, even one that originated outside of Europe.

British and French combat forces joined the military coalition, based in Saudi Arabia, assembled for the main campaign against Iraq (along with Arab forces from Saudi Arabia, Egypt, Syria, and the UAE). Beyond those national choices, though, the NATO alliance structures turned out to be highly useful.

> First, early in August 1990, the United States asked Turkey, an alliance member, to risk an Iraqi attack by cutting Iraq's oil lifeline as part of the global sanctions to persuade Iraq to withdraw from Kuwait. To help the Turks, the United States sought and obtained an unprecedented NATO commitment that the alliance would defend Turkey from Iraqi attack, if Turkey took the risk.
>
> Second, in late 1990 and early 1991, NATO structures, well rehearsed and operating 24/7 on a large scale, provided the essential planning and logistical capability for the very challenging redeployment of an entire U.S. corps, with its equip-

ment, from Germany to Saudi Arabia. This corps became
the principal attack force for the "left hook" part of the war
plan against Iraq. Also, as U.S. naval forces redeployed to the
Middle East, allied naval forces helped pick up the slack in
the Mediterranean.[60]

Third, early in 1991, NATO deployed a multinational mobile
force (made up of German, Belgian, and Italian aircraft,
along with Dutch air defense units) to defend Turkey as it
also became a base in the imminent war against Iraq.

Fourth, NATO was involved in the deployment of a Dutch
Patriot air defense unit to Israel in 1991, along with U.S.
forces, to help defend Israel from Iraq's missile attacks on it.
This military aid in Israel's defense was part of the effort to
keep Israel itself from joining the war against Iraq (which
Iraq was trying to provoke). This was only the second time
in Israel's history that foreign troops had been deployed on
Israeli territory to aid in that country's defense.[61]

Crisis management and peacekeeping inside Europe

This other main contingency for NATO's future role also surfaced soon
after the NATO leaders issued their July 1990 London Declaration. The
country of Yugoslavia began disintegrating during the second half of
1990.

By late 1990, the U.S. government judged that the breakup was
inevitable. The intelligence community accurately forecasted that the
breakup would probably lead to widespread violence, including possible
wars among the contending nationalities. Scowcroft and Baker's deputy
secretary, Lawrence Eagleburger, had served in Yugoslavia earlier in their
careers and had some feel for the situation there. The lead NSC staffer for
Europe at the time (who had replaced Blackwill) recalled concisely that
"the Bush administration was well aware of the potential of a violent dissolution of Yugoslavia." The problem was that "it simply knew of no way
to prevent this from occurring."[62]

The crises and wars in the former Yugoslavia revealed how institutional choices for the new Europe could matter a lot, or not matter much at all. Some people thought the United States or European countries should have done much more to contain or pacify the Croatian, Bosnian, or Kosovo wars. Some thought they should have done less. Whatever one's view, the failings were not because of institutions.

Governments or publics might use institutions as an excuse for failure, blaming NATO or the EU. But they were not the cause. The main problem, from 1990 to 1995, was that no sufficiently powerful group of outside countries could agree on what to do.

They could not agree to ignore or just contain the conflict. They could not agree to intervene decisively to help settle it. In Europe, as in the United States, there was loud disagreement within the governments, as well as with each other.

From the start, the United States was ready to let Europeans guide the way. The United States preferred to support European leadership in sorting out a coordinated policy. But the major European powers were themselves divided. This was not a case where some small European government blocked consensus. At the very core, France and Germany could not agree on what to do.

At this time, the Germans felt they were blocked from doing anything at all militarily, for legal and historical reasons. The French were reluctant to organize and dominate a European military intervention. They were also reluctant, at least in the early years, to forcibly confront the Serbs. The British did not want to act outside of NATO. But, really, they were reluctant to act at all. Foreign Secretary Douglas Hurd told French foreign minister Roland Dumas, "No British soldier will ever fight in Yugoslavia."[63]

European and American forces found themselves, then, supporting ineffectual United Nations efforts. Finally, after years of agony, in 1995, once the atrocities mounted to newly horrifying magnitudes and the humiliation of the UN was complete, the United States decided to take a more forceful lead.

At that point, decisive coalition action was possible, and NATO was used to help organize it. After NATO had organized an initial peacekeeping force in Bosnia, the European Union took the lead in organizing a follow-on force.

In other words, depending on the political commitments, there were several institutional possibilities. Whether a UN-organized force or a NATO-organized force or an EU-organized force, or some mix in which the United States supported an EU force, all might have been effective.

The Balkan crises and wars revealed something else. All the alternative all-European "security architectures" would have been no more effective. They could very well have made matters worse.

* * *

At the pivotal London NATO summit of July 1990, the most outspoken dissents against the reinvention of NATO had come from Thatcher and from Mitterrand. Thatcher's opposition was relatively predictable. Her approach to NATO was more conservative. Like some in Washington, she thought and argued that Bush's proposed changes in defense posture were too radical, too soon.

Both Mitterrand and Thatcher were unhappy that the U.S. was downplaying its nuclear weapons and nuclear deterrence. They feared that such moves might go too far. Then British and French nuclear forces would be on the spot, either to make up the gap or join in the cutbacks. But their fears turned out to be overdrawn. The United States had rightly judged that adaptation could become an anchor, not a slide down a slippery slope.

Mitterrand, though, had a bigger, more fundamental objection to the American plans for NATO. The French were conservative in another way. As Scowcroft put it, the French leader "wanted to keep NATO confined to its traditional role—defense against a massive Soviet attack on Western Europe." This "traditional role," Scowcroft stressed, "was precisely what we did not want."[64]

To Mitterrand, all the talk of giving NATO this new political role, giving it a new military role, was all going in the wrong direction. He and his team believed the Americans would probably be leaving Europe. The French did not push for this, but they expected it. So the Europeans should build up new institutions of their own.

Grudgingly, Mitterrand went along with the London outcome. He could abide the goal of trying to make NATO less threatening to the Soviets. But he showed his pique by announcing that French troops stationed in Germany as part of alliance defense would soon return to France.[65] More than a year later, when NATO leaders in Rome ratified their new Strategic Concept in November 1991, Mitterrand pronounced, "The Alliance is good, but it is not the Holy Alliance."

Through the rest of 1990 and 1991, France posed a choice: In addition to having the transformed NATO, which allies were moving rapidly to put in place, did Europe really want a multinational defense structure of its own, answering to the European Council, one that could act autonomously without the United States?

In principle, the argument for this was strong. It was a good idea to empower Europeans to act on matters the Americans did not wish to address. For example, as civil wars began in the former Yugoslavia during 1991, the American government did not want to get militarily involved. Perhaps a "European security and defense identity" might be good. Baker said so, even though some of his officials tended to want to stick with NATO.

It was in practice where the French argument ran into trouble. As European countries cut back their military forces in a new Europe, there was not a lot of surplus to be able to stand up *two* effective command systems and sets of multinational units.

The Germans wanted to please both the Americans and the French. Most other European governments—and certainly the British—did not think a standalone European entity would be militarily viable. Pushing it too hard might just spur the Americans to leave the Europeans on their own, which most European governments did not want.

Finally, in practice, the French theory was embarrassed by the two formative crises of the early 1990s. In the Gulf crisis in the Middle East, NATO had been quite valuable and no hindrance to selective European involvement. In the Yugoslav crisis, the leading European powers were themselves split about what to do—including a deep split right at the center, between France and Germany. Rather than empowering Europe to act, the European Union's leaders exemplified its paralysis.

One of the best historians of the argument, himself French, concluded that by the end of 1991, the United States was far from being just a "last resort against an otherwise diminishing threat, as the French had anticipated." Instead, "under the leadership of a United States resolved to remain a 'European power,' NATO was emerging in the immediate post–Cold War period as the pivot of European security." He notes, "The net result" was "a re-Atlanticization of European security to a degree unprecedented since the origins of the Cold War."[66]

* * *

Americans should take no great satisfaction in this result. It was not the ideal outcome. The ideal solution was, in fact, for groups of concerned European governments to be able to act *either with or without* the United States, depending on the circumstances and the level of American interest (or insight).

Mitterrand stressed this point during a particularly unnecessary argument in July 1991, at a time when the United States was devoted to the transformation of both the CSCE and NATO. Mitterrand still believed, as he told Bush, that "in the years ahead, your country will pull away from Europe." So, as Mitterrand explained to Kohl, he did not want to "enclose Europe in a structure that is totally dependent on Washington and stifle any desire for European defense."[67]

Bush and Baker were defensive because, as they told Mitterrand, they feared his stance would be a self-fulfilling prophecy, one that would trigger the American withdrawal from Europe. But the French president was also right. Indeed, in the Balkan case, the American government would have very much preferred to play a supporting role, not a leading one.

Fortunately, the institutions eventually evolved in just this more flexible direction. In 1990 the French and Germans created a multinational "Eurocorps" that also attracted troops from other countries, like Spain and Belgium. This new Eurocorps was a focal point of the 1991 quarrel. Years later, the Eurocorps became active once the French agreed, on German insistence, that the unit could operate under NATO command if there was a fight.

After a new French president took office in 1995, after NATO—that same year—became the instrument for firm coalition action in Bosnia, the French also began a process of slowly rejoining all of NATO's organizations. By the end of the 2000s, France had rejoined NATO's integrated military command.

By the end of the 1990s, the European Union was well launched. The authority of its governments, in the European Council, was enhanced. All the institutional structures were put in place for EU interventions, with EU-organized multinational battle groups beginning to take the field during the 2000s.[68]

The 1990–91 visions for the transformation of the European Union and the Atlantic alliance turned out to be reasonably sound and durable. The problems were more eternal and immutable: to decide what was important, what capabilities to have, and how to solve the problems.

The largest of these problems also emerged right away: What to do about the rest of Europe, post-communist Europe? And how would all those countries fit into these emerging political, economic, and security visions?

Creating a Better League of Nations

The great and tragic precedent was in 1919. In that year, the established governments from Berlin to Vladivostok, from Riga to Belgrade, were all up for grabs. Their futures were sorted out in awful civil wars and revolutions that wracked practically every country. Millions lost their lives.

With borders patched together by treaties signed between 1919 and 1923, the nations remained bitterly divided among revolutionary communists, ruthless anticommunists, and armed nationalists. Within about ten years democracy had disappeared in every state from Germany to the Soviet Union, except for Czechoslovakia.

In 1990 and 1991, established governments from Berlin to Vladivostok, from Riga to Belgrade, were back on the operating table. This time the settlements were remarkably peaceful and remarkably durable.

Despite terribly painful economic and social upheavals, only Yugoslavia descended to full-scale civil war. That awful example helped encourage others not to follow it. In general, the futures were sorted out peacefully. Although Czechoslovakia itself broke in two, the Czech and Slovak republics chose a peaceful divorce. Ten years, even twenty years later, democratic norms still governed in almost all of Europe.

We opened this chapter with Charles Powell's ominous prediction to Thatcher, in January 1990, about a return to cycles of national struggle and violence. Powell's predictions seem prescient—from the perspective of the 2010s. But in the 1990s, most Europeans in fact did *not* follow that downward cycle.

Even in Russia, when the Soviet Union collapsed in 1991 and Gorbachev finally lost power, it was not the "ultras," not a steely military dictatorship, that took his place. The "ultras" tried and failed.

The "ultras" were defeated by a democratic revolutionary. This revolutionary leader claimed legitimacy from the ballot box, and he—Boris Yeltsin—and his followers, his Russian allies, promised freedom.

Some of this, including in Russia, would later go wrong. Yet it is also worth noticing what went right.

* * *

In 1919, the main institution for Europe had been a new creation, a League of Nations, headquartered in Geneva. The League of Nations had not included the United States (by America's choice). It had not included the Soviet Union (that center of world revolution). In its first years it also did not include the recently defeated countries either, like Germany, Austria, or Hungary.

The League had been a Eurocentric institution, dominated by Britain and France. Those two powers used the League (if they could agree) to tackle a number of lesser problems with "arbitration, mediation, and conciliation," sorting out some border issues, organizing plebiscites.

In its first ten years the League intervened in seventeen such disputes. It successfully sorted out about half of them without military force or economic sanctions. In this early phase it handled the " 'small change' of world affairs. It dealt with minor disputes and limited issues and not with the fundamental problems of reconstruction."[69]

In 1990 and 1991 the structures put into play for the new Europe were much more enveloping and ambitious. This time both the United States and Germany would play very large roles. The Soviet Union was there at the founding too, but its implosion would soon test the new structures.

* * *

As 1990 began, Mitterrand was still focused on his idea of a European confederation. He did not see how all the other countries in Europe could be absorbed into the European Community. Talking with Kohl, Mitterrand emphasized that the EC had to integrate further. This deepening ruled out adding new members anytime soon.

What then should be done with the countries that had just been "freed" from the Soviet bloc? "What will they do?"

They might form new groupings of their own, Mitterrand speculated, like a federation of Italy with Yugoslavia, Austria, and Hungary. "Others with other states. It would be a dangerous path."

One had to find, the French president argued, "a status and structures for the European countries that one cannot leave outside." There had to be political agreements with them, eventually also with the Soviet Union, so that it would not be isolated. "Then there will be a new situation by the end of the century."

Thus Mitterrand thought a European confederation of democratic states might be a plausible alternative. The CSCE was there, but it included the United States and Canada.

He wanted a confederation that would include Europeans, to build up a common legal area with the countries on an equal basis, the large and the small. It would be a loose structure, with few mandates, but the countries would all be there.

Kohl agreed that the EC could not play this all-European role. He stressed that there had to be preconditions. Any member countries had to be free (*freiheitlich*), respecting the rule of law.[70]

What Mitterrand was talking about, however, was really a substitute for the CSCE, a substitute that would exclude the United States (and Canada). Kohl never really believed in this. The Germans preferred to focus their efforts on the CSCE. But they cordially let the French try to persuade others.

The French tried to recruit East European governments to support their confederation plan. As those governments came to understand that Mitterrand's idea would include the Soviets and exclude the Americans, they lost interest. During 1991 the French government made a high-profile launch effort. It crashed.[71]

The Soviet government also had pan-European ideas, dating back to Gorbachev's concept of a "common European home." These were consciously similar to Mitterrand's idea, and drew a similarly pallid degree of European support.

As the French and Soviet visions faltered, the Americans and West Germans, with support from the British and several other European governments, clarified an emerging consensus. As we mentioned, NATO would be transformed. This started with an anodyne joint statement of cooperation with the Warsaw Pact. More important was the invitation to the Soviets and other Warsaw Pact states to send ambassadors to NATO.

The Americans and West Germans planned to build up CSCE too. The formative work occurred mainly during the first half of 1990.[72] The Americans included a draft set of CSCE institutional proposals among the initiatives they sent to allied leaders for endorsement at the NATO London summit. Baker previewed them in detail with Shevardnadze even before NATO allies saw the full plan. Some Soviet ideas for the CSCE, like the idea for a conflict prevention role, converged with the ideas coming out of Washington, Bonn, and London.[73]

With the final German settlement signed in Moscow in September 1990, the all-European part of the design was signed in Paris in November 1990 with two main pan-European pillars, the CFE treaty and the Charter of Paris.

* * *

The completion of the CFE treaty in November 1990 was an arduous diplomatic achievement. The Soviets did help clear away the last obstacles in the final months, especially since the treaty had been firmly linked to Soviet goals both on Germany and for a CSCE summit.

The treaty reduced and limited the conventional armed forces of at least twenty-three countries in Europe from the Atlantic to the Urals (every then-member of the NATO and Warsaw Pact alliances). Not only were there real limits on key items of military equipment (tanks, other armored fighting vehicles, artillery, aircraft, and helicopters), but there were also regional limits in specified zones to prevent threatening buildups of forces. The treaty created a thorough regime of intrusive transparency and inspections. Despite the stress and adjustments caused by the

Soviet military's large-scale effort to circumvent the CFE treaty reductions, the treaty attained its objectives.[74]

The Soviet military deeply resented the CFE treaty. The required reductions were large (about fifteen thousand items of equipment just in Russia) and costly to implement. Nonetheless, the Soviet government, and later the Russians too, took the treaty very seriously.

After the Soviet Union broke up at the end of 1991, the CFE treaty had to be significantly revised and updated to take account of the new situation. There were now eight countries in formerly Soviet territory covered by the treaty, some very suspicious of each other. New kinds of national and regional limits were needed to adjust to all the new kinds of security concerns.

Using the new North Atlantic Cooperation Council (which included all these countries, the evolution from their having set up diplomatic missions at NATO) and a NATO working group, the new national limits were successfully hammered out in 1992 in another difficult but successful negotiation, sometimes called CFE 1A.[75]

The other states in the CSCE joined the CFE system. It thus became a truly all-European security structure. The CSCE became a permanent OSCE ("O" for Organization) with a secretary-general and a permanent secretariat (in Vienna), the "world's largest regional security organization" (now with fifty-seven member states).

Using both NATO and OSCE structures, revised CFE limits in regional zones (sometimes called the "flanks") then had to be worked out. Russia now saw its main concerns lying more to its south, not the west.

Rather than the whole treaty being torn up and renegotiated, which might have been impossible, Russia's concerns were effectively addressed and the necessary revisions in the existing treaty were agreed upon in 1996. Because the massive CFE system functioned reasonably well, few noticed what "proved to be a highly adaptable and flexible instrument of European security."[76]

The OSCE has a conflict prevention center, picking up on the original ideas from the United States, Germany, and the Soviet Union. The center does not conduct military operations. It monitors conflict situations, offering information and a site for diplomacy and mediation. The center has played a useful role in a number of European disputes. It still runs significant field operations around Europe, including near the current battlefields in Ukraine.

Beginning in Paris in 1990, the OSCE members added further transparency measures to build confidence. On top of all this, all the OSCE members joined the new Open Skies system. That system of aerial surveillance has offered significant further transparency and reassurance. Amid various stresses and challenges, it also continues to operate to this day.

* * *

In the Charter of Paris, the CSCE members (transitioning into the OSCE) agreed that they would be democratic republics with the rule of law. They even agreed on a set of governing norms. To help put them into practice, they institutionalized the American-British initiative to create an office to offer advice and monitor the conduct of free elections in all the member states.

Based in Warsaw, this institution is now called the Office for Democratic Institutions and Human Rights. It has effectively monitored scores of elections. At the follow-on Helsinki summit in 1992, the leaders added a small but active office for a High Commissioner on National Minorities.

The OSCE members also agreed on common principles of greater economic freedom. The Paris process included specific commitments to respect property rights, allow private businesses, share economic data, and help small and medium-sized enterprises grow. It followed through on hopes to establish "a set of basic principles to guide the conversion of socialist systems into market economies."[77]

The Charter of Paris also called for the creation of an all-European parliament, which was then established. The OSCE still has such a parliamentary assembly. It overlaps with the better-known parliamentary assembly of the Council of Europe. The CoE's parliament has forty-seven member countries but does not include the United States, Canada, or the former Soviet states of Central Asia that are part of the fifty-seven-member OSCE's parliamentary assembly. The European Parliament of the EU only includes EU members (so not Russia, Ukraine, Turkey).

Put in historical perspective, the OSCE/CFE/Open Skies system had most of the positive attributes of the old League of Nations, but turned out to be much broader in scope. It also proved to be more impactful, more inclusive, and more lasting. Looking back, Gorbachev was rightly satisfied that, as he put it, "The Paris conference [in November 1990] heralded a new, post-confrontational era in European history."[78]

But these designs for a new Europe were not braced for the upheavals of post-communist economic transition, the breakup of the Soviet Union, or the most brazen act of international aggression in a generation. The works of creation were not nearly complete.

CHAPTER 6

The Designs for a Commonwealth of Free Nations

President Bush first spoke of his hopes for a "commonwealth of free nations" in speeches he gave in Boston and Mainz in May 1989. Occasionally shortened to "commonwealth of freedom," the phrase became part of the boilerplate. Bush repeated it in a number of his speeches and in his administration's formalistic national-security strategy documents. It was an aspiration. In his January 1990 State of the Union message, for example, he referred to the "great and growing commonwealth of free nations."

The origins of this particular phrase lie, as so many do, in an effort to find evocative language for a speech. Zelikow was trying to find some coinage for Bush that would compete with Gorbachev's much-publicized ideal of a "common European home." He bounced the phrase "commonwealth of free nations" around the office, and it stayed in the draft for the May speeches.

The ideal of a "commonwealth of free nations" was different from a "common European home." It was not geographical—Gorbachev's phrase rankled, for instance, some of us interested citizens in North America. Bush's expression was open-ended.

Bush's phrase was explicitly built on a foundation of "nations." Yet the nations are bound together in a "commonwealth." That was a very old word, one that for centuries has evoked some broadly based community. "A common wealth," wrote one Englishman in 1583, "is called a society . . .

of a multitude of free men collected together and united by common accord and covenants among themselves."[1] It was a word found in the formal names of various states whose founders liked that sort of definition, states like Virginia, Massachusetts—or Australia.

And Bush's phrase, unlike Gorbachev's, did have this politically charged word in it: "free." At the end of 1990, speaking to audiences in Prague and in Brasília, Bush spoke of his ideal commonwealth having "four key principles": "an unshakable belief in the dignity and rights of man, the conviction that just government derives its power from the people, the belief that men and women everywhere must be free to enjoy the fruits of their labor, and, four, that the rule of law must govern the conduct of nations."[2]

These were lofty principles. At the end of 1990 they were already being tested in some unprecedented ways. The choices made at the beginning of the 1990s laid down some basic design ideas not only for Europe, but also around the world.

Issue Map
Building a Better World (1990–91)

Future of Soviet Union

- Any window for giving major aid to Soviet Union?
- Breakup of Soviet Union
  - Actively support?
  - Actively discourage?
  - Neutral? What else to do?
- Future of Soviet nuclear weapons?
  - What could the United States do that could radically, rapidly reset the situation of all the thousands of widely deployed nonstrategic weapons?
  - Which of the new republics would become nuclear weapons states?

- What, if any, institution could help reduce, consolidate, and secure the vast post-Soviet nuclear (and biological) weapons complex?

- Should Western aid for Russia and Ukraine (and others) be major or minor?

- What kind of conditions and policy preferences should accompany such aid?

  ○ Radical reform?

  ○ Partial reform?

- What kind of institutions could make this work?

Future of Eastern Europe	• Integration with NATO and EU?
	• Should Western aid be major or minor?

	• What kind of conditions and policy preferences should accompany such aid?
	
	  ○ Radical reform?
	
	  ○ Partial reform?

	• What kind of institutions could make this work?
Integration—European and Global	• How to develop the European Union?
	• EU in new global trade system and World Trade Organization?
	• U.S. stance on new global trading system? New regional trade blocs—NAFTA?
Security in Europe Shifting to Global Security	• What to do about outlaw states? Iraqi crisis of 1990 as key test
Future of Germany	• Largely settled, now huge internal German work

Last Chances for the Soviet Economy

Late on the last Saturday afternoon of July 1989, Shevardnadze met with
Baker in Paris. The occasion for the meeting was itself a sign of the times.
They were there to work together and with others on sorting out the
future of Cambodia. They were slowly winding down some of the usual
hotspots of global rivalry—talking about how the Soviets were disengag-
ing from Afghanistan and how the United States was trying to end proxy
fighting in Central America.

Then they changed the subject. It was a point in the meeting, "a few,
focused minutes," Baker remembered, when Shevardnadze "fundamentally changed our relationship."

They started talking about what had happened in China and what it
meant for the Soviet Union. Shevardnadze was glad Baker had raised this.
Shevardnadze then opened up, and spoke for nearly an hour.

The situation was very difficult, he began. The changes were "affecting every part of our society, and every person and every family, too. We
are now in the most crucial stage in what we call our revolution." He
continued, "Indeed, we are having a revolution. The old mechanism and
the old machine have been abandoned, and unfortunately the new one is
not yet able to function at full strength. We are at a most difficult time,
because our renewal of the political system is running well ahead of the
renewal of the economic system."

The discussion eventually ended with a common understanding
about the need to avoid a "Chinese solution" in the Soviet Union. The
immediate concern was about how Moscow would deal with a miners'
strike in Siberia. But the issues were much bigger than that.

"We won't allow destabilization in the Soviet Union," Shevardnadze
said. "Destabilization in such a huge country with enormous military
and economic potential would be a grave thing for the Soviet Union and
the world. The same is true for Eastern Europe. It is one thing to speak
of renewal (perestroika), but destabilization is harmful, and it could be
catastrophic."[3]

* * *

Signing of the final settlement for Germany, Moscow, September 12, 1990. Seated from left to right: James A. Baker III, Douglas Hurd, Eduard Shevardnadze, Roland Dumas, Lothar de Maizière, and Hans-Dietrich Genscher. Mikhail Gorbachev can be seen standing behind Dumas, listening to Soviet deputy foreign minister Yuly Kvitsinsky. A state department lawyer, Michael Young, is standing next to Baker as he signs the document. Robert Zoellick and Condoleezza Rice are standing behind Baker. *(Bundesbildstelle Bonn)*

Mikhail Gorbachev and George Bush, Camp David, June 1990. From left to right: Baker, Barbara Bush, George Bush, Raisa Gorbachev, Mikhail Gorbachev, Shevardnadze, Brent Scowcroft, and Sergei Akhromeyev. *(Bush Presidential Materials Project)*

Bush and advisers at his summer residence, Kennebunkport, Maine, July 1990. From left to right: Treasury Secretary Nicholas Brady, Dan Quayle, Philip Zelikow, Bush, Robert Blackwill, Baker, Raymond Seitz, Dick Cheney, Zoellick, and Colin Powell. *(Bush Presidential Materials Project)*

Erich Honecker and Helmut Kohl, Bonn, May 1987. *(German Information Center)*

Horst Teltschik. *(German Information Center)*

Margaret Thatcher and Bush, Camp David, November 1989. *(Bush Presidential Materials Project)*

Bush and advisers review talking points for meeting with Gorbachev in Helsinki, September 1990. From left to right: White House chief of staff John Sununu, Marlin Fitzwater (seated against wall), Dennis Ross, Rice, Scowcroft, Baker, and Bush. *(Bush Presidential Materials Project)*

George H. W. Bush and François Mitterrand at Kennebunkport, May 1989. *(George Bush Presidential Library and Museum)*

The "G-7," Paris, July 1989. From left to right: Jacques Delors, Ciriaco De Mita, Helmut Kohl, Bush, Mitterrand, Thatcher, Brian Mulroney, and Sōsuke Uno. *(George Bush Presidential Library and Museum)*

Hans Modrow and Helmut Kohl. *(German Information Center)*

James A. Baker III, Eduard Shevardnadze, and Bush, September 1989.
(George Bush Presidential Library and Museum)

Kohl and Gorbachev at the Kremlin, February 1990. Seated left to right: Teltschik, Kohl, Anatoly Chernyaev, and Gorbachev. *(Private collection)*

Kohl, Bush, and Baker relax at Camp David, February 1990. *(Bush Presidential Materials Project)*

Delors and Bush, April 1990. *(George Bush Presidential Library and Museum)*

Gorbachev and Bush in the Oval Office, May 31, 1990. *(Bush Presidential Materials Project)*

The dismantling of Checkpoint Charlie, Berlin, June 1990. *(Private collection)*

Genscher, Gorbachev, and Kohl in the Caucasus, July 1990. *(Private collection)*

The Day of German Unity, October 3, 1990. From left to right: Genscher, Hannelore Kohl, Helmut Kohl, Richard von Weizsäcker, and de Maizière. *(German Information Center)*

That was in July 1989. By March 1990, as Gorbachev became the first president of the Soviet Union, "destabilization" had arrived.

It had already swept Eastern Europe. It was rising in the Soviet Union. The implications of a post-communist, post–Cold War world ran right to the heart of the Soviet state that Lenin and Stalin had built.

Gorbachev led a Soviet Union that had replaced the old Russian Empire, a multinational dynastic monarchy, with another kind of empire, a multinational union of communist republics ruled from party headquarters in Moscow. The communist glue was dissolving. What principle of governance would take its place?

He led a Soviet Union that had an economy built to be a communist Sparta, overwhelmingly dedicated to heavy industry and a giant military. The military leviathan was no longer needed; the Soviet people could not eat the millions of tons of steel rolling out of the mills. What economy and society would take its place?

* * *

The decisive variables were Russian and Ukrainian policy choices, the quality of their governance, and respect for local conditions. These were well-endowed countries. They had tremendous natural resources and well-educated people. Their assets were badly misallocated into unproductive uses, including a colossal defense establishment and related heavy industry. But the great issues were about how they would reset their policies and institutions.

One reason that Soviet or post-Soviet reform could not readily imitate Chinese models is that China had been, and then still was, a very poor, mainly rural society at a low stage of industrial development. Its reform program was more one of construction and greenfield development, not of massive conversion and reconstruction of an already fully urbanized and industrialized society.

While there was still a Soviet Union, the last great window of opportunity for radical economic reform opened and closed during August and September 1990. The contest was over the rise and fall of an agenda for radical reform called the "500-day plan."

The late summer of 1990 was Gorbachev's opportunity to make another series of major moves, on a scale with the choices he made during

1988, which we described in chapter 2. In foreign policy, Gorbachev had done it. He *had* made a big move. He had waited until late in July 1990, after beating back the conservatives at the Party Congress, and then moved decisively to settle the German question and complete the agreements concluded later that year. Perhaps now he would make his big move on economic reform too.

If Gorbachev made a radical move to transform the Soviet economy, he would have to share economic management with leaders of the emerging national republics. Of these, the most important was the newly elected leader in Russia—Boris Yeltsin. There was really no way to separate such a huge economic move from a basic political shift. Gorbachev, if he wanted to lead the next wave of reform, would also have to step out to lead the growing liberal and democratic forces in the country in a direct confrontation against the communist old guard. As of August 1990, those democratic forces were looking more to Yeltsin as their standard-bearer.

Using a team of informal economic advisers headed by Stanislav Shatalin and Grigory Yavlinsky, Gorbachev took the first step. He authorized the development of a radical program for economic change, meant to be implemented on the schedule implied by its name: the "500-day plan."

Yeltsin backed the radical reform. At first, it looked like Gorbachev and Yeltsin might indeed reconcile in support of this "500-day plan." They seemed excitedly supportive of this new, joint strategy.

But Gorbachev still thought there was some better way to reconcile all the ideas, old and new. He asked Chernyaev to write an essay on the "Market and Socialism." Chernyaev struggled. To him the basic problem was that "the cat loves fish but hates water. More importantly, the combination of the two words in the title doesn't work."

The more conservative communists heading Gorbachev's government, led by Prime Minister Ryzhkov, hated the radical plan. Prime Minister Ryzhkov told the reformers that he was "not about to bury the state with my own hands." He promised to "fight you, its gravediggers, as long as I have the strength."[4]

He put forward an alternative, more conservative plan, another partial reform. Some of Gorbachev's top advisers urged him to "say goodbye to Ryzhkov. He unites the Military-Industrial Complex, the directors (including the military men), and he unites them on anti-Gorbachev positions."

Gorbachev disagreed. He told his advisers, "You are little kittens. If in this situation I create another opposition front here, it will be the end." He believed a natural development of the market might happen later in the year, and that this would take care of Ryzhkov and the party.

His advisers "agreed verbally, but not in our hearts, because we are again losing time. An economic program needs to be accepted not at some vague point in the future, but this September."[5]

After Ryzhkov's bitter confrontation with the reformers, accompanied by threats of overthrowing the government and more, Gorbachev stepped back from the radical reform plan. He put both plans—the reformer's and Ryzhkov's—before the Supreme Soviet in September 1990.

* * *

The top American leaders were now preoccupied with the crisis arising from Iraq's August 2 invasion of Kuwait. The Germans, and the Americans too, also were intently focused on the endgame of the German diplomacy.

Yet both governments were certainly following the emerging debate in Moscow about fundamental economic reform. On July 13, the U.S. ambassador in Moscow, Jack Matlock, sent in an extraordinary cable predicting a dire future for the Soviet Union and for Gorbachev. Bush asked Rice to comment. She thought the cable's diagnosis was insightful and, while disagreeing with some of the policy suggestions, concurred with the bottom line: "Control is slipping rapidly out of the hands of the central authorities and most especially Gorbachev."[6]

Gorbachev did not seek advice or help from Western leaders in his internal decision about whether to lead another revolutionary change in his country, joining forces with the democratic and pro-market reformers. The Soviet government still regarded itself, understandably, as a superpower. It was only beginning to invite in outsiders from the West to look around and give advice. The IMF-led research team authorized by the G-7 at their July 1990 summit was just starting its work.

If the Soviet government would have talked to any Westerners about economics and finance, they would likely have first spoken to the West Germans, who were their principal creditors. In early September, Kohl and Gorbachev, and their subordinates, did wrap up their hard bargaining about money to compensate for Soviet troop withdrawals from Germany. But they do not seem to have had a really serious, wide-ranging discussion about the fundamental choice Gorbachev was prepared to make about the Soviet future.

Gorbachev and Bush also had a good chance to discuss Soviet economic plans when they met again, in person, in Helsinki on September 9, 1990. Baker would be following up in Moscow a couple of days later to join other ministers in wrapping up the German settlement.

Bush and Baker had just organized and dispatched a group of American CEOs to arrive in Moscow, as a business mission to follow up on the buildup of U.S.-Soviet economic relations begun with the trade deal at the Washington summit back in May. They knew that the IMF-led team of experts from the international financial agencies were rapidly conducting their review of the Soviet economy as a preliminary to possible future help during 1991.

Preparing Bush for his Helsinki meeting with Gorbachev, Scowcroft and his staff called attention to the "critical juncture" now in front of Gorbachev at home. "Gorbachev's own authority, popularity and power are in precipitous decline." He had to work with Yeltsin and radical reformist mayors, like Gavril Popov in Moscow and Anatoly Sobchak in Leningrad. (Sobchak had added to his entourage a KGB officer who had just returned home to Leningrad from an assignment in East Germany, named Vladimir Putin.)

Scowcroft flagged how important this "500-day plan" was. Of all the problems Gorbachev had to face in the autumn of 1990, "the most serious is structuring a coherent and workable economic reform program which can successfully lead the country through the transition from a command economy to one based on free market principles." He told Bush about Gorbachev's "tactical" alliance with Yeltsin.

But the United States was no longer sure how much Gorbachev supported this plan. Bush's staff thought Gorbachev "has waffled [on the economic reform program] in recent days, angering Yeltsin and confusing everyone else." But Gorbachev would have to act soon, "which will signal whether he is indeed committed to deep and speedy reforms advocated by Yeltsin and many of his personal advisors, or the more gradualist approach of Ryzhkov which the Supreme Soviet rejected [in the spring of 1990]. If he cannot reverse the now pervasive sense that he is indecisive, he risks irrelevancy as bolder leaders emerge."

Scowcroft concluded, "The message on economics [Gorbachev] may really need to hear yet again in Helsinki is that our ability to assist him in any meaningful way depends very much on the scope and pace of his own reforms in the months ahead."[7]

* * *

In Helsinki, Bush worked through tough discussions with Gorbachev about the most urgent business, the Iraqi crisis. Once that was out of the way, he raised the topic of economic reform.

Gorbachev replied that on economic reform, they had "reached the decisive phase." He described some of the issues. He said he would make his decision by October 1.

Bush wanted to understand how the process would work. Gorbachev said they would need the republics to agree. There would then be three to five months to "stabilize the market" and then start relaxing price controls during 1991 and 1992. "The transition period will come only then, and it will be long and hard." Yet, he added, "if we do not act radically, it will be dangerous."

Bush alluded to the various things the United States was doing to build up commercial ties. He warned that his government did not have the cash "for large economic assistance." He was in the midst of high-stakes negotiations with Congress to cut American budget deficits. He did not lecture or lay down conditions for future support. "Out of this new order," he said, "we can find a way."

That was their discussion. Little more emerged during Baker's talks in Moscow.

At the same time in Moscow, the American business executives on the presidential mission heard upbeat messages from Gorbachev and others. They were a bit bewildered by what they were told. They could not tell what the economic program would be. Nor could they figure out where authority would lie, although they were impressed by Popov and Sobchak. "None of the Soviets asked for any form of aid."[8]

* * *

What ended up happening was that Gorbachev flirted with all the economic ideas, then rejected them. At first, beset by "paralyzing doubts," he stalled and criticized the new ideas. Making their case to the Supreme Soviet, the reformers explained that it was no longer a choice between socialism and capitalism, but between life and the grave.[9]

Gorbachev asked for a compromise solution between the two alternatives. Then, once that was prepared, he abandoned that too. In the end the government took no meaningful action at all. Gorbachev again broke with Yeltsin.

Chernyaev, Yakovlev, and other key insiders believe that Gorbachev's September 1990 choices about the economic reform program were, as Yakovlev put it, his "worst, most dangerous mistake." It was Gorbachev's last chance to prevent the collapse of public confidence along with the USSR's monetary and fiscal structures. In his heartfelt and detailed memoir, Chernyaev puzzled over this episode at some length. He finally concluded, "In the end, it was emotions, fear of risk, and an unwillingness to break with the old ways of ruling that won out."[10]

By the end of October 1990, French analysts in Paris judged that the Soviet crisis was now terminal, "the prospects for a rapid exit from the doldrums seeming virtually nil." Their diplomats saw three possibilities: (1) Yeltsin would sideline Gorbachev as the USSR broke up; (2) there would be a turn to dictatorship to restore order and an adequate standard of living; or (3) the Soviet Union would recover. What about the chances for a recovery? "This scenario," they wrote, "is unfortunately the most difficult to imagine."[11]

Gorbachev's constant rearguard actions in 1989 and 1990—partial democracy, partial economic reform, grudging national concessions—turned out to be paths to ruin. In 1990, while his authority and the cause of reform remained relatively strong, he could have tried to get ahead of the situation with a decisive agenda of political and economic reform. This could have included a voluntary federal union with an elected president (Gorbachev was never elected to his office as head of the party or as president in a popular vote) and parliament, linked to an agenda of radical economic reform. Instead, in the last months of 1990, as he celebrated the receipt of a Nobel Peace Prize, Gorbachev reshuffled the government.

The Breakup of the Soviet Union

In December 1990, Shevardnadze resigned, warning of a coming dictatorship—a shock. In January 1991, after Ryzhkov had a heart attack, Gorbachev installed a new prime minister, who was bewilderingly incompetent. "By the turn of the year the original Perestroika team had gone," the British ambassador recalled. "To replace them Gorbachev looked to the men of the right—conservative hacks in the old Soviet mould."[12] Practically all these people would join the coup against him seven months later.

Gorbachev had already begun warning Bush that he would have to use his executive authority to restore order. Lithuania became a test case.

The negotiations during the spring of 1990 had persuaded the Lithuanians to suspend their independence moves for a few months. Without having settled their differences, the Soviet government began moving some elite troops into Lithuania, followed in January 1991 by an ultimatum demanding that Lithuania abandon its independence moves at once. As Gorbachev made these demands, Soviet troops began occupying government buildings in Lithuania's capital.

From Washington, Bush condemned these moves and called Gorbachev to ask him to stop. In Moscow, Yeltsin also condemned them, suggesting that Russian draftees would not serve in such operations. As Yeltsin explained to the American ambassador, "If they are successful against the Balts, we will be next on the list!"[13]

After an elite Soviet military unit stormed the Lithuanian TV facility, killing sixteen and wounding many more, thousands of Lithuanians

ringed their government buildings, defying Soviet tanks. Gorbachev vac-
illated and then blamed local commanders. Yeltsin went on the radio to
tell Soviet soldiers in Lithuania, "You are a pawn in a dirty game, a grain
of sand in the Kremlin's building of an imperial sand castle." Amid a
general outcry, including from the United States, Gorbachev called off
the military moves (which he might not even have authorized in the first
place). Gorbachev asked the American ambassador "to help your president understand that we are on the brink of a civil war." He might have
to do things that would be hard to understand. The U.S. should expect a
period of "zigs and zags."[14]

* * *

This ominous confusion and crisis at the top was the context as, during
the first half of 1991, the Soviet economy slid into collapse, hyperinflation
(mainly in the growing black market for scarce food and other goods),
and looming state bankruptcy. Gorbachev pushed hard for more foreign
assistance. There was no credible reform program.

One of the economists involved in the 1990 effort, Grigory Yavlinsky,
worked with prominent Western academics, including Graham Allison
and Blackwill (then at Harvard), to persuade Western governments to
offer a "grand bargain" of massive aid for the kind of reform proposed in
1990. Bush knew very well that the Soviet Union was in what he and his
colleagues called "a prerevolutionary condition."

But Gorbachev was still blending old-guard enemies of reform with
the reformers, just as he had tried to do in September 1990. The U.S.
government, and even Yavlinsky, could see that there was not much of
a political base for reform. And the Soviet government's authority itself
was up in the air, as the national republics asserted themselves and started
negotiating the terms of new union.[15]

Though still kept secret, the Americans and Soviets were also still trying to settle the biological weapons problem. They had arranged visits of
experts on both sides. But, as Baker noted, the site visits "didn't resolve
our questions, [they] heightened them."[16]

Meanwhile, despite the difficulties, Baker tried to develop some sort
of assistance package to help the Soviets. "We want to work with you,"
he stressed. But "we honestly don't believe the current 'Anti-Crisis' [eco-

nomic] program will work." Baker presented a lengthy list of suggestions for Gorbachev's representative, Yevgeny Primakov, who was coming to make the pitch for the G-7 grand bargain.

Primakov's May 1991 presentation of the Soviet government's "anti-crisis" economic program to American leaders degenerated, Gates recalled, into "as sharp and unfriendly an exchange as I could remember, as our side asked hard questions and the Soviets had no answers. Yavlinsky might as well have sat on our side of the table for the critical observations he made and his obvious lack of support for his government's program."[17]

Seeking aid, Gorbachev came to the G-7 summit meeting in London in June 1991 still without a good reform program. Delors had been to Moscow before the meeting, trying to gauge the situation for himself.

The Soviets worked hard to get ready for him. The meetings were difficult. Delors was allowed to meet with Gorbachev's cabinet. He spoke to them in terms "so harsh," Chernyaev noted, "that their jaws dropped."[18]

At the G-7 meeting itself, in London, Delors peppered Gorbachev with some of the toughest questions about what he was trying to do. The G-7 responded cautiously to Gorbachev's pleas, offering technical assistance in various sectors and waiting until the future of the Union was sorted out.

Kohl met with Gorbachev soon afterward, in Kiev. When Kohl's finance minister pleaded for the Soviet government to work with the IMF, Gorbachev lost his patience. "The USSR is not Costa Rica! 'Your' [the West's] behavior toward the USSR will affect the direction of history."[19]

Soon after the G-7 summit, at the end of July 1991, Bush traveled to Moscow and Kiev. His summit meetings in Moscow were dominated by arms control work (success), more private discussions about biological weapons (not much success), and discussions of economic reform (inconclusive).

The exchanges on economic aid were painful for both sides. Gorbachev pressed for help and guidance. Bush had little to offer.

At one point, Gorbachev blamed Bush for not making up his mind about what kind of Soviet Union he wanted. What was he waiting for? Gorbachev asked. The Americans had found money to fight a regional war against Iraq. Here, with the fate of the Soviet Union in the balance, they were talking about a much greater project.

Bush colored at this challenge—"his eyes darkened." He then spoke "with restraint," Chernyaev recalled, "suppressing his agitation, in a measured tone."

He said he would make his vision clear. "We would like the Soviet Union to be a democratic country with a market economy, dynamically integrated into the Western economy." Without meddling in Soviet internal affairs, some understanding between the center and the republics was fundamental for private investment. "So: firstly—democracy; secondly—market; thirdly—federation."[20]

Throughout 1991, Bush not only did not see any credible Soviet reform program, his basic conviction was that, under the circumstances, "we [Americans] simply did not know enough to design any detailed aid programs." That was an unsatisfyingly modest judgment. But it was true.

Bush and his G-7 colleagues did want to help somehow. Thatcher's successor (since November 1990), John Major, played a helpful coordinating role. The G-7 states committed food, medicine, and credits to help Soviet agencies buy humanitarian goods. In about a month and a half the G-7 countries corralled emergency food aid and other credits worth about $4 billion, $10 billion during all of 1991, along with some debt rescheduling.[21] Beyond that, they developed a broad program of "technical assistance" for various sectors of the economy, to help the Soviets come up with a plan.

* * *

It was hard to contemplate a more systematic effort until the future governance of the Soviet Union became clear. With the USSR entering a terminal economic crisis, Gorbachev finally made headway in negotiating the terms of a new, federal Union that would have included most of the old Soviet Union.

Yeltsin, now the elected leader of an emerging Russian nation-state built on the hitherto powerless Russian Soviet republic, was willing to go along. So was the leader of Ukraine.

Rather than definitely trying to destroy the Soviet Union, Yeltsin may well have hoped to take Gorbachev's place and lead the reconstructed Union. Yeltsin and Gorbachev secretly planned to reshuffle the top security officials of the new Union.

Hearing about that plan to take away their power, the "ultras" decided to make their move. A central figure in the coup attempt was the leader of the KGB. Spying on Yeltsin and Gorbachev, he had probably learned that he and other key officials were about to be turned out of office. The August 1991 attempt to take over the Soviet government completely backfired. Not only did the coup fail, it killed any prospect for survival of a Soviet Union.[22]

Gorbachev refused to go along with the plot. Yeltsin led a courageous resistance. Foreign governments—led by the United States—turned decisively against the coup plotters. Finally, the army, divided, would not go along.

After the coup collapsed, both Russia and Ukraine decided to emasculate, then discard, the Soviet Union and go their independent ways. In December 1991 the Russian and Ukrainian leaders, then joined by others, replaced the Union with a Commonwealth of Independent States.

What About the Nuclear Weapons?

In 1991, neither Bush nor Baker, nor any of the allied leaders, were in any hurry to get rid of the Soviet Union. At the time and later, some—both in and out of government—criticized that position.

The critical argument goes something like this: The Soviet Union was an enemy superpower and oppressor of subject nationalities. The United States would be better off if its enemy broke up; the subject peoples would be better off if their oppressor was gone.

One part of this logic was not controversial. The United States and most other West European governments had supported the independence of the Baltic republics and hoped their separation could be arranged peacefully.

Nor was there much controversy about the possibility of a breakup. As we mentioned in chapter 4, since September 1989, Rice had quietly been leading a small group looking at a wide range of contingent possibilities.[23] The thinking about that contingency only intensified the conclusion of Bush and his aides in late 1989: Help Gorbachev, but also—as Kohl had put it in 1990—gather as much hay as one could before the storm.

That was part of the reason for all the urgency on Germany and arms control. The CFE treaty was done. Bush and Gorbachev signed the Strategic Arms Reduction Treaty (START) in Moscow at the end of July. Some, even some Americans who should have known better, hooted at Gorbachev for having given up too much in the START treaty. Those reactions were themselves part of a Cold War mentality. With only a little hindsight, it is hard to find any serious Soviet, or Russian, interest that really ended up being harmed by that treaty.

At the *beginning* of August 1991, there was an issue about whether to encourage breakaway independence for Ukraine. At that time this was not so controversial among responsible officials. The consensus answer, in the United States and other allied capitals, and even with Yeltsin and the Ukrainian leader at the time, Leonid Kravchuk, was: No, don't interfere. Let Gorbachev, Yeltsin, and Kravchuk close the deal on a new Union treaty.

That new arrangement, to create a more federal Union, was actually looking quite promising at the *beginning* of August 1991. That was when Bush visited Moscow, then Ukraine's capital, Kiev.

On August 1, 1991, Bush gave a speech to the Ukrainian parliament, an elected body in which a majority favored staying with the Union and a large minority favored complete independence. Bush praised freedom, but he then added that "freedom is not the same as independence. Americans will not support those who seek independence in order to replace a far-off tyranny with a local despotism. They will not aid those who promote a suicidal nationalism based upon ethnic hatred."[24]

This speech has been the source of significant comment and, indeed, criticism, particularly since the Soviet Union would collapse and Ukraine become independent four months later. It is important to understand the context at the time. What were Bush's choices?

He could have supported, openly or tacitly, those who were pushing for independence. He might have remained silent on the question. But instead he decided to take a course that appeared to be trying to restrain those forces seeking independence, a position that seemed to many to be making Moscow's case.

However, Bush knew that a new Union treaty was in the works, viewed positively by key republic leaders. He was also affected by the experience of coping with the crisis of Yugoslavia dissolving into civil war. He also knew that since 1989, violence had come repeatedly to parts of the Soviet Union itself.

The new Union might well have come into being. In fact, it was fear of the new Union treaty, and the shakeup in Union leadership that would go with it, that caused the KGB and military ultras to organize the August coup to overthrow Gorbachev. Bush felt close to Gorbachev and quickly denounced the coup, a stance that was helpful—as Yeltsin and Gorbachev both acknowledged.

The coup attempt, in the last week of August, is what destroyed any hope of rehabilitating the Soviet Union. In St. Petersburg, Vladimir Putin was still a KGB colonel working with Mayor Sobchak, in the process of resigning from the service. The coup did not rally him to the side of his boss, the KGB head at the center of the plot. Instead, he told an interviewer in 1999, "In the days of the putsch all the ideals and goals that I had on going to work in the KGB collapsed."[25]

It was at the *end* of August, on August 30, *after* the coup attempt had fatally damaged Yeltsin's and Kravchuk's hopes for a federal Union, that a conservative *New York Times* columnist, William Safire, advantaged by his hindsight, went back to Bush's August 1 speech, to deride it as a dish of "Chicken Kiev." Back then, Safire mocked, Bush had had the chance to endorse Ukrainian independence and had chickened out.

In fact, as August ended and September began, as the possible breakup of the Soviet Union accelerated, some of the most difficult choices were just coming into view. On September 4 and 5, Bush discussed the possible breakup with his cabinet, then the next day with his usual ad hoc small group of top foreign policy advisers. Their discussion was lively, with an argument about whether the United States actually wanted the Soviet Union to break up. Secretary of Defense Cheney wanted the United States to support a breakup. Baker emphasized, "*Peaceful* breakup is in our interest, not another Yugoslavia." He preferred to see the Union continue, including as a focal point for the assistance flows from the United States and other G-7 countries. Cheney thought that was "old thinking." Scowcroft leaned toward Cheney's view. Bush seemed to lean toward Baker's.

A gradual transition would have been better. The military and monetary issues were just too large and difficult to handle overnight. But all the Americans could agree that the United States should not actually do anything to meddle or take sides one way or another, other than to ready deliveries of humanitarian aid.

On September 4, Baker had already announced a set of principles that were relatively simple and could "set the philosophical and practical framework within which the process of Soviet dissolution can occur peacefully and orderly." They were: (1) peaceful self-determination consistent with democratic values and principles; (2) respect for existing borders, "both internal and external," with any changes occurring peacefully and consensually; (3) respect for democracy and the rule of law; (4) human rights, particularly minority rights; and (5) respect for international law and obligations, especially the CSCE's Helsinki Final Act and Charter of Paris.[26]

It turned out that the United States would face a breakup occurring practically overnight. The monetary issues in fact did become a cause of ruinous trouble. But the military issues were even more serious than that, almost incomprehensibly dangerous. What the United States had to do was come up with basic policy directions, vectors, to cope with the likely breakup of a nuclear superpower.

* * *

In 1991, the Soviet Union had the largest stockpile of nuclear warheads of any country in the world—about 35,000. Of those, aside from weapons in storage facilities of some kind, nearly half were operationally deployed in strategic (long-range) forces in four republics: Russia, Ukraine, Belarus, and Kazakhstan. The majority were nonstrategic, shorter-range tactical nuclear weapons of many kinds. The Soviet government had been withdrawing these from Eastern Europe and the Baltic republics, but as it broke up, the thousands of such weapons were probably deployed on the territory of at least nine republics. This was a profoundly dangerous situation that had no precedent in world history. As Cheney put it in a December 1991 press interview, "If the Soviets do an excellent job of retaining control over their stockpile of nuclear weapons—let's assume they've got 25,000—and they are 99 percent successful, that would mean you could still have as many as 250 that they were not able to control."[27]

There were three basic issues: What could the United States do that could radically, rapidly reset the situation of all the thousands of widely deployed nonstrategic weapons? Which of the new republics would become nuclear weapons states? What, if any, institution could help reduce, consolidate, and secure the vast post-Soviet nuclear weapons complex?

What could the United States do that could radically, rapidly reset the situation of all the thousands of widely deployed nonstrategic weapons?

On this issue Bush himself kicked off a crash, proactive effort to get ahead of the problem. At the informal meeting of top officials on September 5, he wanted to use this opportunity to make large further changes in U.S. defense strategy and further cuts in defense spending. He asked "impatiently" for the group to come up with something ambitious.

It was Scowcroft, working first with Cheney and then with JCS chairman Colin Powell, who—in days—developed a sweeping, creative answer that Scowcroft then went over with Bush. On the nonstrategic forces, they would bypass arms control. The United States would act on its own, unilaterally, to withdraw and eliminate almost all of the nonstrategic nuclear arms in its forces around the world—on ground, sea, and air.[28]

Bush would then challenge Gorbachev to do the same, trusting that he would. If Gorbachev did follow suit, then the Soviet (and successor governments) too could make a crash effort to concentrate these weapons, storing and eventually getting rid of most of them. On the strategic forces, Bush would also invite another round of major arms cuts, following on the START treaty he and Gorbachev had just signed.

In just three weeks, the proposal was ready. In a September 27 speech to the nation, Bush announced what he rightly recalled as "the broadest and most comprehensive change in US nuclear strategy since the early 1950s."

Gorbachev's response was everything Bush wished for, a striking demonstration of the trust the two men had developed, amid many strains. Gorbachev counterproposed ideas of his own. Yeltsin too was enthusiastic. The end result was successful. Tens of thousands of U.S. and Soviet nonstrategic nuclear weapons were redeployed, stored, and destroyed, A START II treaty was quickly negotiated and signed in January 1993, just before Bush left office.

Other arms control targets were met. After great progress with the Soviet Union in 1990 and 1991, in 1992 the U.S. and its allies launched a completed convention to ban chemical weapons (it now has more than 190 signatories). Secretly, Yeltsin eliminated what was left of the illegal biological weapons program, though concerns linger about continuing Russian research.

The START II treaty was worked out with only one leader—Russia's Boris Yeltsin. The United States had decided that only one country should inherit the Soviet nuclear legacy and did all it could to make that happen.

Which of the new republics would become nuclear weapons states?

At first, Scowcroft thought "there was positive benefit" in distributing command and control over the thousands of Soviet long-range, strategic weapons among the four republics that had them on their soil. Such a result might reduce the size of an attack any one country could mount against the United States.

Others offered different arguments for Ukraine, at least, to become a nuclear weapons state. Carter's former national security adviser, Zbigniew Brzezinski, worried about Ukraine's ability to defend itself against Russia. A political scientist, John Mearsheimer, also thought Ukrainian nuclear weapons would be a stabilizing force.[29] Ukraine's leader, Kravchuk, was also clearly tempted—at the least—to retain nuclear weapons in his country.

The Bush administration, and the Clinton administration after it, made a different choice. By the end of 1991, Baker could add a sixth principle to his original five—central control over nuclear weapons. He and his State Department colleagues took the lead in pushing for the "Russia only" outcome.[30]

By the beginning of 1992 the policy was clear: Russia would take on the whole debt burden of the entire Soviet Union. And it would also take on many of the Union's unique assets—its nameplate on the UN Security Council, its diplomatic missions, and every one of its nuclear weapons.

During the last months of 1991, before the Union disintegrated and before the United States had established diplomatic relations with Ukraine, a Harvard group, including Zelikow, worked informally with the Ukrainians and U.S. officials to get Ukraine to give up its nuclear weapons. In 1992 the U.S. government, led by Baker, pressed this point hard.[31]

The Germans were not directly involved, but they and other West European states entirely backed the American position and said so to the Ukrainians. If they wanted international sympathy and support, Ukraine, Belarus, and Kazakhstan had to sign the Non-Proliferation Treaty and agree to give up their weapons. In the spring of 1992, Ukraine stalled on withdrawing tactical nuclear weapons. In April, NATO's new North Atlantic Cooperation Council (where Russia and Ukraine were both members) then placed united pressure on Ukraine to get rid of them. Ukraine relinquished the weapons; the transfer was completed the next month.

A Russian political adviser recalled how, once the United States made the nuclear issue a test of cooperation with the West, "it was solved in a week." Another Russian said bluntly, "Baker solved the nuclear problems with Ukraine."[32]

All the other non-Russian republics went along too. Kazakhstan, fearful about the dangers in its region, also hedged. Bush and Baker persuaded the Kazakh leader, Nursultan Nazarbayev, to stick to the nonproliferation commitments, an understanding capped in May 1992. But, as Nazarbayev explained to Bush when they met in Washington, "It's not clear what will happen in Russia. In China some of their books show part of our territory as Chinese. To the south is fundamentalism. That is why we wish to be close to the United States. This is why we wanted temporarily to remain a nuclear state."[33]

The Clinton administration, upon taking office, followed up with its full-court press. The Ukrainians and others sought security assurances against Russia. What was worked out, and concluded in a CSCE framework at the beginning of 1994, was a trio of memoranda signed by the United States, Britain, and Russia. The memoranda promised Ukraine, Belarus, and Kazakhstan that none of the three countries would use force, the threat of force, or economic coercion against any of them. If there was an act of aggression, the memorandum only promised that the signatories would seek UN Security Council action against the aggressor. The other open nuclear weapons states—France and China—offered even weaker assurances.

Twenty years later, Russia violated the pledge in this memorandum, as it also violated other international agreements with Ukraine, with fellow OSCE members, and in the UN Charter. The United States and Britain did seek Security Council action against Russia, which, predictably, Russia blocked.

Since Russia's aggression in Crimea and the Donbass, Ukrainians and others have said that Ukraine was wrong to give up the seventeen hundred to nineteen hundred strategic weapons still on its territory and that it was wrong for the United States and others to insist that it should do this. This argument is only superficially appealing. Neither Ukraine nor the world would have been safer if such a large and deadly arsenal remained in a country undergoing a complete economic collapse and extreme corruption, which was Ukraine in the first few years of independence.

Nor, because of their long range, would these former Soviet ICBMs have been especially useful against Russian targets. Nor is it likely that the infiltration of Russian conventional forces into Crimea and the Donbass could have been deterred by threatening nuclear attack and the mass killing of Russians. The outcome of such a nuclear confrontation might more likely have been the end of the Ukrainian state itself, and perhaps much else. What Ukraine really needed was the political, economic, and military strength to be able to defend itself—without nuclear weapons.[34]

What, if any, institution could help reduce, consolidate, and secure the vast post-Soviet nuclear weapons complex?

The post-Soviet republics outside of Russia had few resources to maintain, secure, or transport nuclear weapons or special nuclear material, including large quantities of plutonium and highly enriched uranium left at various sites, particularly in Kazakhstan, a longtime site for weapons development and testing. Especially during the early 1990s, Russia itself was desperately short of means to handle its own gigantic nuclear complex, which had reached peak size during the 1980s. And there was also a large biological weapons complex. It was especially secret because the complex had been developed in violation of the 1972 treaty the Soviet Union had signed that abolished biological weapons.[35]

No one had really imagined the creation of a whole new institution to help address these costly and extremely dangerous legacies of the Cold War. The United States took the initiative: Specifically, in the fall of 1991 a Democratic U.S. senator, Sam Nunn, stepped up to try and fill this void. Nunn worked closely with a group at Harvard, led by Ashton Carter, along with Graham Allison and others. He later brought in the expertise of an analogous group at Stanford, led by William Perry, that had a larger quotient of scientists and engineers as well as excellent contacts with leaders in the American nuclear laboratories.

Nunn chaired the Senate committee that oversaw the Defense Department, and he proposed to tap the defense budget to find help. In November 1991 his effort to find a billion dollars for such a denuclearization initiative came up for a vote. One of Nunn's aides recalled that just before the bill came to the Senate floor, "a Democrat [Harris Wofford] won a formerly Republican [Senate] seat in a special Pennsylvania election, largely on the basis of an 'America first platform.'" This "sent an anti-foreign aid shock wave through the House and Senate." The Democratic leadership pulled Nunn's legislation.[36]

Yet, right after that defeat, Nunn found a new ally, the senior Republican on the Senate Foreign Relations Committee, Richard Lugar of Indiana. Providing intellectual ammunition, the Harvard group also issued its first report spotlighting the new nuclear dangers and what could be done.

Baker and Bush got on board. The new "Nunn-Lugar" bill passed at the end of 1991. Baker then worked closely with Nunn and Lugar and their congressional allies to plan more aid of this kind. Another package went into an omnibus former-Soviet aid bill (called the FREEDOM Support Act) they developed and passed during 1992.[37]

All through 1992, Bush and Baker had been pressing Ukraine's Kravchuk to give up on nuclear weapons. Ukraine had made the general political commitment. The tactical nuclear weapons were gone.

But the strategic weapons that had been deployed in Ukraine were still there. In September 1992, Kravchuk said his country needed $174 million in U.S. assistance to eliminate the large arsenal of strategic nuclear arms still in his country. In December, the new aid bill passed, and Bush could write to Kravchuk and pledge "at least" $175 million for Ukraine. "Of course, before we can do so," Ukraine had to complete the Non-Proliferation Treaty obligations.[38] The aid helped break the logjam. The Clinton administration then followed through.

When the Clinton administration took office in 1993, Perry, Carter, and Allison all got top jobs in the Defense Department. They made sure that the "cooperative security" program took root and grew. Ultimately the United States spent billions of dollars and, with its partners in the former Soviet Union, built trust and made astonishing progress in cleaning up sites, discovering and containing frightening threats, and destroying weapons—beating the Cold War's swords into plowshares.[39]

By the late 1990s, enriched with enormous technical experience in doing this work, the programs had evolved into a broader mission of preventive "cooperative threat reduction" of many kinds around the world. This was a timely evolution, in a world where technologies for weapons of mass destruction and organizations of transnational terrorists were evolving too.

The Shock of the New: Building Different Economies and Societies

The "new Europe" forced post-communist countries to transform their economies and societies if they wanted to maintain reasonably open borders and open economies. In chapters 3 and 4 we also explained that the West chose, starting with the Polish case, to offer substantial aid if countries would make the leap in a rapid transition from communist to market economies.

The real choices in 1990 and beyond were not about whether to provide *some* help to the new democracies in Eastern Europe. Any set of governments would have tried to be helpful.

The choices were at three levels: Should the aid be major or minor?

What kind of conditions and policy preferences should accompany such aid? What kind of institutions could make this work?

It is hard to track and assess all of the aid. In every case, it flowed through several kinds of channels, bilateral and multilateral, and it took several kinds of forms. There were humanitarian deliveries of food or energy supplies. There were grants or credit lines to transfer or lend money to import goods. There was technical assistance—a fancy term for aid that helps people learn how to perform certain tasks or set up institutions. There was macroeconomic aid to help new central banks have more foreign exchange, often in the form of loans or credits, and microeconomic aid (including "Enterprise Funds") for sectoral help or lending to new businesses.[40]

The aid could and did help, some. But the shock of transition was not just economic. Much of it went much deeper, as the transition rocked the whole structure of society itself.

"'Joining Europe,' the leading slogan of the time, meant adopting the Western lifestyle, freedom, consumerism, and value system." A whole new middle class started slowly to emerge, beginning with many new small businesses and professional offices.

An astute Hungarian observer of the process added, "The doors opened widely, but most of the people were frightened of entering an unknown world.... They had to learn an entirely new life strategy.... In the old regime, there were only a few paths to success; now several ways opened and required mobility, flexibility, entrepreneurial attitude and risk taking. All of these new behavioral patterns were difficult to learn. Most of the adult population was unaware of how to behave appropriately in this situation, and became paralyzed and bitter."[41]

On top of this, the small-scale corruption that was a standard part of communist life took on a whole new meaning. The hectic reforms created many new chances for those who had or could buy connections.

"The reforms were like a pool of cold water that everybody jumped into without knowing how to swim." Where else to jump? Gorbachev's gradualism and partial reforms had failed. The West European models were too expensive and required institutions that these countries had not yet built. "The only life buoy floating in the pool was neoliberalism. The reformers saw no other choice than to cling to it."[42]

* * *

The Western plan for Eastern European reconstruction was more ambitious than anything that had been done before. Many people pointed to precedents in the postwar American European Recovery Program, better known as the Marshall Plan. In 1989 and the early 1990s analogies to the Marshall Plan were everywhere. Such analogies were not very useful.

"One of the great challenges in replicating the Marshall Plan," a recent historian of the plan concluded, "aside from the sums involved, is making conditionality effective." The Marshall Plan setup forced European governments to work together and drop trade barriers with each other. A special effort was made to restart Germany as a source of goods to help the rest of Europe get going, and other European governments had to accept this too.

The aid also could not take the place of good local government; it could only empower it. In their Marshall Plan partnerships, the Americans ended up supporting right-wing and left-wing governments, but they all shared core principles. In France, Marshall Plan aid had the task "essentially to fix the (many and large) potholes caused by war and occupation." Paris would usually do this the way it wanted. "That Paris might prefer asphalt, and Washington concrete, was never going to make the difference between ultimate recovery and stagnation."[43]

The post-communist reconstruction project had to be different from the Marshall Plan in practically every way. The basic economic machine was not functional in market terms. It could be rebuilt on communist terms, with closed economies dealing with each other through negotiated barter arrangements. Or it had to be redesigned, with the new structures and institutions then built to a large extent from scratch, on some market basis, with open economies allowing more open (if not necessarily free) trade using world prices.

At the time and later, citizens and scholars bitterly criticized the human cost of "shock therapy" and resented the "Washington consensus" that caused so much hardship. Market reforms created plenty of short-term pain. The leading market reformers, like those in Poland, underestimated how bad the pain would be. The post-communist economies went into full depression, usually suffering declines of at least 30 percent of their GDP.

But if countries chose to have open economies rather than closed ones, this painful transition was unavoidable. It had taken a long time to destroy the old market economies and thoroughly replace them with communist ones. It would take a long time to construct another system.

Not all countries accepted radical reform. Russia and Ukraine did not. Russia tried the path of partial reform; Ukraine tried to hold on to the status quo system. But experience showed that a gradual or partial approach did not reduce the pain. It only prolonged it. Partial reform did not ease the income inequality produced by market reform. It made the inequality worse.[44]

* * *

To understand why the Western push for radical reform was so important, it is worth explaining more about the politics and economics of *partial* reform. To begin, no Western government would subsidize the communist status quo. Western taxpayers would not appropriate money for factories to make things no one wanted to buy. Nor would they pay taxes so that Eastern Europeans could buy cheaply what their Western or southern European neighbors had to buy at market prices.

Partial reform might look better. But it could be even worse. We can start with a simple example of a common form of Western aid in these years: credit guarantees to buy food. Here is the way this might work. Suppose that a German bank loaned money to the Russian government so it could buy Western food, with the loan guaranteed by the German government. The credit guarantees were politically popular. The German government could tally it up as humanitarian food aid. The European farmers made money. The hungry Russians got food.

What might then happen was that the Russian government would get the food through a trading or food agency. The government agency would then sell the European food to local Russian firms, who would then retail it to consumers. Under *partial* reform, Russian food prices might still be set artificially low, so people could buy cheap bread, and in rubles that had a similarly artificial official exchange rate. The Russian firms could thus buy the European food very cheaply, at Russian prices with official exchange rates, from their government trade agency. But the Russian firms would then take advantage of *partial* reform to resell some or all of the European food at real market prices. They would rake in huge profits.

These profits would, of course, not go back to the Russian government that had borrowed the money to buy the food, although some officials might privately get their cut. The profits, converted into foreign currency (hopefully again at a contrived rate), might instead end up in a bank in Cyprus.

The Russian government was then saddled with a loan it could hardly pay (with the local currency it got for the food), and the German government that had guaranteed the loan might end up paying the bill. One can see how "food aid" that might sound great would in practice enrich the wrong people and also become unsustainable.

In the Soviet Union and later in Russia and Ukraine, some of the ways "partial reform" could be abused became truly epic. People could buy three tons of oil for the local black market street value of a pack of Marlboro cigarettes.

Or you could take the aluminum quota being supplied to keep your defense plant in business making Sukhoi combat aircraft. You could transfer the aluminum somehow to the new "cooperative" you or your friends had set up. You could then sell the aluminum on the world market for a 10,000 percent profit. Meanwhile the state would end up printing the money to keep the defense plant open and subsidize its employees.

Economists describe such practices with technical-sounding euphemisms like "spontaneous privatization," or "rent-seeking."[45] This was the world of "partial reform." Goods and currency with world value were being bought and sold on the black market; valuable goods at subsidized prices disappeared from stores; more and more money was being printed that could buy less and less. Food was scarce; inflation would skyrocket.

Well-connected groups would make vast profits, much of which would end up in banks in Cyprus and Western Europe. Although the Soviet Union, then the former Soviet republics, offered the most dramatic examples, others can be found across the post-communist world.

Many ordinary people understood how they were being exploited. It may seem surprising, since radical reform had its own price shocks and unemployment, but where people had a real chance to vote for truly radical reform in genuinely democratic elections, they often supported it. This was true even where—as in Poland—former communists came to power and swept out the original reform group. Western insistence on radical reform could help.

The radical reformers needed all the help they could get. The opposing forces were powerful because the politics of partial reform created odd coalitions. It was no surprise that people hurt by market forces would vote against them. "More surprisingly," the political counselor at the European Bank for Reconstruction and Development observed in 1998, "the politics of postcommunist economic reforms has not been dominated by the traditional short-term losers of economic transition—striking workers, resentful former state bureaucrats, impoverished pensioners, or armies of the unemployed.

"Instead," he explained, "the most common obstacles to the progress of economic reform in postcommunist transitions have come from very different sources: from enterprise insiders who have become new owners only to strip their firms' assets; from commercial bankers who have opposed macroeconomic stabilization [that would constrain money supply and spending] to preserve their enormously profitable arbitrage opportunities in distorted financial markets; from local officials who have prevented market entry into their regions to protect their share of local monopoly rents; and from so-called mafiosi who have undermined the creation of a stable legal foundation for the market economy."

What these powerful elites wanted, and often got, was to stall reform in midair. They thrived in a *"partial reform equilibrium* that generates concentrated rents for themselves while imposing high costs on the rest of society."[46]

The key principles in the radical reform agenda were to insist that more open economies had to be combined with firm controls on public spending and regulation of private lending. Shock therapy is usually equated with radical *privatization* of state enterprises. That is not actually an automatic principle. The radical reformers did not need to insist on rapid privatization of those state enterprises that were sustainable and had some value. There was still plenty of scope to decide what should be privatized or how to set up social safety nets. Practice on privatization varied in Western Europe as well as in the East.

* * *

Some, including prominent scholars, have argued that "gradualism" could have worked better than shock therapy. They often cite the example of China. We think the China analogy is misplaced. The evidence that gradualism would have worked better is unconvincing.[47]

Not all prescriptions of shock therapy had the same ingredients. Some were wiser or better tailored to local circumstances, some less so. One of the virtues of a more democratic system with rule of law was that governments would vary their practice and try to find the right balance.

As happened across Western Europe in the Marshall Plan era, citizens debated what sort of society they wanted. All the Marshall Plan aid to Britain, for example, had gone to a government ruled by a democratic socialist party, a party that was bringing major parts of the economy under state control.

In Eastern Europe at the beginning of the 1990s there were nearly violent arguments denouncing shock therapy or "neoliberalism" (an old term then being repurposed as a catchall for capitalist excess).[48] The biggest problem for those preferring a gradualist approach was that they needed a realistic alternative, one that dodged the corrupting quicksand of the "partial reform equilibrium."

Two of the most vehement scholarly critics of the role of outsiders in the Soviet/Russian case acknowledge (in an endnote), "We should note here that Western nonmonetarist forces—whether of the social-democratic or other type—never came forward with a serious program of economic reform. Western leftists simply did not understand the reasons for Soviet citizens' rejection of the old economic system."[49]

* * *

The term "Washington consensus" can mislead. There was a lead institution that arose to articulate and help enforce the "radical reform" conditionality. It was headquartered in Washington. It was the International Monetary Fund.

But the fund was headed by a Frenchman. Its professional staff, drawn from around the world, was mostly non-American. The term "Washington consensus" was invented in 1989 at a Washington conference in which authors from ten *Latin* American countries had gathered to summarize the hard lessons they had learned in their countries during the 1980s.

The man who coined the term "Washington consensus" was summarizing what the Latin Americans had learned, "never dreaming that I was coining a term that would become a war cry in ideological debates." And, as we mentioned earlier, privatization of state enterprises was not even one of the ten recommendations at the core of this "Washington consensus."[50] Even the "silent revolution" of ideas about free international movement of capital was at least as much European as American, as we pointed out in chapter 1, and Ronald Reagan had little to do with their ascent.

The IMF is another one of the institutions at the beginning of the 1990s that, as with NATO, had kept the outward shell of reassuring continuity, while being gutted and renovated on the inside. The IMF had been created to help governments manage balance of payments imbalances in an era of highly regulated capital movements and exchange rates in the Cold War world. The organization's transformation began in earnest during the 1980s.

As global private capital flows took off, governments found themselves in severe debt crises beginning in 1982. The fund's historian wrote, "The debt crisis had a transforming impact on the IMF, catapulting it into the role of international crisis manager."[51]

What eventually happened was that the fund became the base of international expertise on the policy conditions for reform. Its conditions then set the standard not only for its own credits, but also for the much larger sums usually involved in other public and private credit flows.

The IMF therefore emerged as a key institution in post-communist economic transition. It was still quickly staffing up and trying to absorb lessons to play this part.

One of the earliest and most influential outside advisers on post-communist transition, David Lipton, later became a senior IMF official. He recalled how, "looking forward during the inception of reforms, the prospects for transition seemed daunting. In fact, at first, most observers thought the effort would not succeed." At the IMF, Lipton admitted that the institution "had helped countries overcome debt and inflation, but had no experience in designing and executing the sweeping changes needed to convert economies from the communist system to capitalism."[52]

Other institutions were involved too, like the new G-24 coordinating structure in the EU, the World Bank, the OECD, and the new European Bank for Reconstruction and Development. But the IMF had the lead, more and more having to consider issues like corruption and regulatory systems.

The national governments had even less experience or proven expertise to guide such deep transitions. But the problems would not wait.

As some of the veterans later put it, "Interesting and critical as the answers to the questions of the optimal speed and sequencing of reform are, it was necessary to make decisions on how to proceed well before the evidence could be gathered."[53] In other words, as the IMF's historian noticed, "In most cases, the can-do and must-do-now culture of the IMF clashed badly with the must-get-it-right-even-if-it-takes-longer culture of the World Bank and other agencies."[54]

That "can-do and must-do-now" culture of the new IMF ended up playing a vital role in painful but necessary transitions. "With hindsight," one group of scholars found, "it is apparent that radical reform has proved the best way to eliminate subsidy-seeking behavior."

It was true that radical reformers sometimes lost elections. The former communists were strong and often more united. But it turned out that "gradualists are even more likely to lose elections. . . . People want faster reforms." Foreign aid, the authors concluded, "can play a key role, but only when it is highly conditional on policies that break the power of the former elite and permanently reduce the scope for rent seeking."[55]

Russia's Brief Window of Opportunity

As the Soviet Union collapsed at the end of December 1991, the new government of sovereign Russia, led by Yeltsin, developed its own program for radical economic reform. The Russians asked for Western help.

The aid request was for Poland-like help on a Russia-size scale, including about $6 billion in grants for a stabilization fund. There were also requests for tens of billions more for other kinds of support. Aid for "technical assistance" might or might not help, depending on the subject and the kind of outside engagement in working on it with local problem-solvers.

The stabilization fund request was credible. So were requests for help with vital supplies, so long as aid did not swamp or ruin local producers. The Russian government would also face serious issues of debt relief (mainly from German creditors). The Russian reform program was serious. The time available to work on it and develop joint action was not.

Yeltsin himself understood little about the details of an economic reform program. At the start, though, he empowered the lead figure in the reform effort, a thirty-five-year-old economist named Yegor Gaidar.[56]

Gaidar felt his window of opportunity was short, before the inevitable political backlash curbed his work. "The dismissal of the reform government was a foregone conclusion. The only question was when."

His window was perhaps shorter than he and his allies expected. One capable outside adviser, Anders Åslund, later estimated that the effective launch window for radical reform ended up lasting from about October 1991 until March 1992.[57]

Should the aid be major or minor?

The aid would be major.

Bush and much of his remaining team were depleted. It is revealing that Bush and Scowcroft's excellent memoir tails off when the story reaches the end of 1991. Bush was mustering energy for a reelection campaign in which his opponents were accusing him of spending too much time on foreign problems.[58]

Kohl too was distracted. Though reelected resoundingly at the end of 1990, he was preoccupied with the issues of unification and with conclusion of the agreements creating the transformed European Union. He told Bush in March 1992 that he was at his limit for offering any bilateral aid.[59]

Nonetheless, the United States, the Germans, and other allies started scrambling to help the new Russian government. As the Soviet Union disappeared at the end of December 1991, its debt was all assigned to Russia, thus freeing the other new republics of that burden. The creditors pressured the Russians not to default, so that Russia could maintain access to more credit flows. The Germans, who held more of the debt than anyone, did not want to write it off. So Russia's debt was rescheduled with fresh payment terms over the next twenty-five years, and then repeatedly rescheduled later in the decade. (Russia eventually paid it off in the 2000s.)

Baker had already worked hard to put together a humanitarian package for the Soviet Union to get through the winter of 1991–92. This included significant grants, not just more loans. It also included more than a billion dollars in U.S.-government-guaranteed credits to buy food. The United States had also pressured the Saudis to help Gorbachev.[60]

In early December 1991, before the final Soviet disintegration, Baker, energized by work with congressional allies, made another try at putting together a really large Western aid program for Russia and the other former Soviet republics. His tone, including with Bush, was emotional. "We face a great opportunity and equally great danger." He warned that "if the democrats cannot at least build some 'islands' of success, we face the danger of an authoritarian reversal or fascism." He said the case was strategic, moral, political, and historic.[61]

When it came to fresh aid for Russia, as that country started its independent life in 1992, the stabilization fund was a key issue. This needed billions of dollars in straight grants, not loans. In December 1991, Gaidar had warned that he needed such a fund to go with the immediate decontrol of prices, or else inflation would gallop. The British ambassador remembered him remarking, "If the fund was not in place by April the government would not survive beyond June."[62]

At the beginning of February 1992, Yeltsin arrived at Camp David for talks with Bush. Their meeting went extremely well. Yeltsin was at the top of his game. He outlined his economic reform plan.

Baker followed up in Moscow later that month. He pledged that he would personally work on the stabilization fund. Bush's Treasury Department was slower to come around.

Baker met repeatedly with Bush to galvanize the work. To organize

American action, overcome the reluctance of an uncertain president, and defeat his opponents in the administration, Baker joined forces with Nunn, Lugar, and their bipartisan congressional group. Together, Baker and the congressional leaders met with Bush in March 1992. They persuaded him that action was feasible and politically possible.

Baker organized a team working an omnibus aid bill with Congress, while he and the White House spurred Treasury's work with other finance ministers. He and Scowcroft orchestrated a tandem rollout of the U.S. aid legislation and a G-7 aid agreement, both at the beginning of April. Linked to this were announcements from Bush in Washington and Kohl in Bonn, since Kohl was the current G-7 chairman.

The G-7 plan was for a total of $24 billion. The commitments were on a Marshall Plan–like scale.[63] They did include a commitment to raise money for the $6 billion stabilization program, to be disbursed through the IMF, with the United States to provide 20 percent of the grant money.

With help from Democrats in Congress, the Bush administration aid bill, which included the money for the U.S. share in this fund as well as much more American money for the IMF, passed Congress that summer with strenuous lobbying by Baker and by the new U.S. ambassador to Moscow, Robert Strauss. It was signed into law in October 1992. This was fast work, especially in a national election year.[64]

Baker had pushed to at least get the Western offers rolled out at the beginning of April 1992, before the angry Russian parliament (elected in March 1990 under old rules) reconvened that month. But the show of Western support failed to mollify the parliamentarians. Gaidar's political support began to fade.

Gaidar's prediction to the British ambassador had been close to the mark. By April 1992 the stabilization fund was not yet in place; "by the middle of 1992 inflation was beginning to run amok; and at the end of the year Gaidar was forced to resign." This was not all the West's fault. By June 1992, when Yeltsin put a free spender in charge of Russia's central bank, it was clear that the ruinous "partial reform equilibrium" was starting to win the battle for effective control of the spending spigots and the banking system.

Without effective budget and financial control, it was hard for the

IMF to nail down an agreed program with Russia. Large Western grants and credits would fuel the corrupt partial reform machine, not curb it.

In June 1992, the IMF was ready to deliver an initial billion-dollar tranche of support. As Gaidar put it, "by the time the paperwork was finished, our stabilization program [in Russia] was coming apart at the seams."[65]

In 1993, the incoming Clinton administration made a major effort to rejuvenate and enlarge the aid programs ("less shock, more therapy," Strobe Talbott famously commented). So did the Kohl government. In 1993 the G-7 upped its nominal offer of assistance from $24 billion to more than $43 billion. But the Russian commitment to radical reform had fractured and many of these aid plans fractured with it.[66]

What kind of conditions and policy preferences should accompany such aid?

The conditionality with Russia was halfhearted. The essential conditions had to include monetary constraints, market prices, and a sustainable tax/spending balance. The prescriptions of radical reform do *not* require monetary inflation, unregulated banking, premature bargain-basement privatization of valuable state enterprises, selective law enforcement, or corrupted elections.[67]

One valid analogy from China, one which was well noted by Soviet experts but then not followed by either the Soviet or the Russian governments, was in China's tight oversight of spending. "Moscow's China-watchers had long believed that Beijing's fiscal policy was a crucial determinant of the country's success."

The Soviet experts had stressed, including in the advice they gave in the 1990 development of the "500-day plan," that every time the Chinese saw a surge in inflation during the 1980s, they controlled it with "austerity measures that cut credit growth" and careful spending controls, with greater efforts to grow tax revenue and stop off-budget financing and corruption.[68]

Beginning in 1992 and continuing through 1998, G-7 leaders (especially the Americans, Germans, and French) and their top officials frequently put great pressure on the leaders of the IMF, specifically on managing director Michel Camdessus and his top deputy, Stanley Fischer, to relax conditions and just give out the money, especially for Russia. IMF officials understood and often sympathized with the political reasons for the pressure. They shared the genuine concern about the conditions in Russia.

The IMF officials did not surrender their belief that the radical approach was still the best way to ease the pain; they did not openly abandon their conditions. Instead they usually gave way by accepting Russian official assurances and hoping for the best.[69]

The best was not what happened. As inflation wiped out savings and output collapsed, with halting progress in reform of the political institutions, Russians endured years of terrible hardship. Ukraine's experience was similar.

Russians often put the blame on the outside advice. Some prominent scholars in the West joined the chorus of critics. Because the citizens acidly observed that "the post-Soviet system rarely operates according to its proclaimed principles of market democracy," terms like "democracy" and "reform" became terms of sarcasm and mockery.[70]

The large added Western help did not prevent the devastating Russian financial collapse in August 1998. It may even have facilitated it. Only that further awful blow finally led to a durable radical reform measure, a clampdown on Russia's fiscal policies.

In all the continuing quarrels about what went wrong in Russia during the 1990s, the best-informed outsiders and their most vocal critics actually are seeing many of the same things. All see the triumph of the new elites (the rising "oligarchs") and the "informal practices" that were part and parcel of the rigged games of partial reform.

The IMF made mistakes in Russia. In 1992, its experts were divided and they waffled on the crucial issue of whether to keep a common ruble zone among the former Soviet republics. Partly for political reasons, the experts and the United States tended to favor it. Gaidar and his aides were against it. They feared that the banks of all the other republics would keep printing rubles and fueling the hyperinflation. "Why hold down the budget deficit when you've got your own printing press?" said the Ukrainian prime minister. And that is exactly what happened.[71]

The IMF also may have erred in its advice to Russia about exchange rate policy in the mid-1990s. Its experts encouraged Russia to stick too long with a strong ruble in a fixed band of value that, because of its loose fiscal policy, Russia eventually could not defend. That position contributed to the disastrous Russian financial crisis in 1998.[72]

Despite these mistakes, the basic IMF policy prescription for radical reform, not partial reform, had been the right one. In the case of Russia, the IMF did not insist on that policy.

Yeltsin had led a Russian revolution, up to a point. But among those elites who were already seizing informal power and wealth in the declining years of the Soviet Union, there was no revolution. There was no true radical reform. For this power elite, a mix of the old and the new, the chaos of partial reform became their golden hour.

* * *

That was certainly true in Ukraine too, the next most populous country to emerge from the Soviet disintegration. But the Ukrainian case is worth its own brief look. Conditionality did not fail there. It was not as compromised by political pressures. It actually ended up working.

Ukraine started off free of Soviet-era debts and free of assets, laden with military industry to supply the Soviet military and government-run collective farms. The independent Ukrainian government tried the partial reform path, a "soft" entry into the market with large-scale price regulation and its own printing press for money. For three years it resisted radical reform. Or, as one Ukrainian official later put it, "We made all possible mistakes."[73]

In those three years the Ukrainian economy totally collapsed. Russia suffered terrible depression, about a 30 percent drop in per capita GDP. Total collapse is worse: The drop in Ukraine was 54 percent, along with hyperinflation.

At the end of 1994 a new Ukrainian government, led by Leonid Kuchma, changed course. It accepted radical reform. It built a partnership with the IMF. The first wave of reforms at least stabilized a badly traumatized patient.

Then, in 1998, the financial earthquake in Russia threatened to take down Ukraine with it. Working with Kuchma and his team, and with a timely boost from the French president, Jacques Chirac, the IMF made an extraordinary and successful effort to provide money and pressure on other creditors to help. The outside partners helped the Ukrainian people get through that fresh crisis.

In 2000, the Ukrainian government, still helped by the IMF, enacted another round of reforms. The rest of the 2000s was encouraging: strong growth and Ukrainian recovery. Yet in 2007, Ukraine was hit again by a crisis from the outside—the ripple effects from the global financial crisis.[74]

Ukraine's political and economic life was badly scarred by its Soviet legacy and its early years. Wealthy oligarchs dominated the three major political parties. Ukraine's politics was a hybrid of presidential authoritarianism and parliamentary democracy, with neither fully in charge. Its rule of law started out as selective and corrupt. That system, with the usual post-communist thicket of licenses and permits and special tax rules, continues to burden business and political life even after better laws have been enacted and macroeconomic reforms take hold.

As politics in post-1998 Russia became more authoritarian, politics in post-1998 Ukraine slowly became freer and more democratic. This was hardly the usual pattern in the post-Soviet republics (except for the Baltic republics). Nor was it obvious that citizens who had been through so much would still keep trying to make democracy work. But they did.

What kind of institutions could make this work?

In Eastern Europe the institutions to help make changes work came in two waves: international financial institutions, led by the International Monetary Fund, and then the European Union. Various individual governments had bilateral programs and influence, but the international institutions were most important.

In Russia and other post-Soviet republics, the first wave was similar—the IMF and other international financial institutions. The IMF could do some good with all sorts of technical advice about financial management and central banking. But its basic policy influence was weaker, because the conditionality was being relaxed from above.

There was no second wave of outside institutional engagement. There were no EU membership plans. The post-Soviet republics remained loosely integrated with each other in their Commonwealth of Independent States.

National governments frequently dispatched aid workers or advisers, usually contractors hired in aid appropriations to give technical assistance. These efforts often did not turn out well. Such technical assistance programs, offering guidance about how to reshape particular sectors of the economy or manage particular projects, came in for plenty of criticism, much of it well deserved, throughout the 1990s. Sadly, the experience with post-communist transitions ended up providing more ammunition for the critics.[75]

The "Marriott brigades" of consultants and contractors often did not engage deeply enough to adapt their advice to local conditions. Some recipe books for local privatization were ill-adapted, at best. Occasionally, the contractors were even in league with the oligarchical networks, joining in the "informal practices."[76]

The EU's relations with Eastern Europe, annoying as they often were for both sides, imposed year after year of hard, painstaking work as local officials refashioned their institutions, while still often facing democratic accountability at the ballot box. One reason why so many Ukrainians hope for membership in the EU is that they fervently want their country to go through this same constructive ordeal of institutional adjustment, the process they have watched happen next door.

The Integration of Eastern Europe

In 1991 the Warsaw Pact disbanded. Yugoslavia broke up. The Soviet Union disintegrated.

All the former Warsaw Pact and Soviet states were groping for larger institutions in which they could take part. The former Soviet states set up their "Commonwealth of Independent States."

At first, the new East European governments had not put a high priority on trying to get out of the Warsaw Pact. But after April 1990, watching the Soviet government try to coerce the Lithuanians, these countries, led by Hungary and Czechoslovakia, tried to exit the Warsaw Pact and get Soviet troops out of their territory as quickly as possible. They tried to get closer to the EU and NATO about as fast as they could.

Their interest in NATO puzzled some political scientists. One theorist, reviewing a book about NATO enlargement, just shook his head. "Both the theory and history of international politics strongly suggest that NATO should have dissolved, not expanded," he wrote. "No alliance has ever survived victory; and the possession of overwhelming power in the hands of one state typically induces balancing, not bandwagoning, behavior among contenders."[77]

As the East Europeans saw it, their countries had seven basic security options. They could seek: (1) an alliance with the big power to the east—the Soviet Union or, later, Russia; (2) neutrality (à la Austria or Switzerland); (3) regional alliances with others in Central or Eastern Europe; (4) Western integration, in NATO and/or the EU's growing security structure; (5) a pan-European approach in the OSCE; (6) a "balance of power" strategy of switching back and forth; or (7) just unilateral national defense (like Switzerland).

The former Warsaw Pact and former Soviet states sampled this menu. They joined the pan-European structures we mentioned at the end of our last chapter. They flirted with various regional groupings. But eventually all the ones in Europe concentrated on option 4, Western integration.[78]

* * *

The Soviet government thought about that option too. For a brief moment, it even seemed like Gorbachev was toying with the idea of seeking membership in NATO for the Soviet Union itself. In May 1990, meeting with Baker in Moscow, he wondered aloud whether the Soviet Union might join NATO. Baker had the impression that Gorbachev was not joking. He and Zoellick regarded this at least as a theoretical option.

Baker quickly checked with Genscher, who had just met with Shevardnadze, to see if Shevardnadze had raised such an idea. Genscher replied that Shevardnadze had certainly had the opportunity to raise it, but had not. And the Soviet government did not pursue it.[79]

In 1992 and 1993, Russia's new president, Boris Yeltsin, raised the issue of Russian membership in NATO in a more serious way. At the end of 1993 he met with NATO secretary-general Wörner to discuss a possible action plan for Russian membership.

The Americans and their allies found it hard to imagine how Russia's enormous military would relate to NATO's integrated military command. Many Russians also could not figure out how they would fit into NATO, which they regarded as an organization in which the United States played a leading role.

Early in 1994, Yeltsin's view had evolved to one that was more of a "concert" system, in which the United States, Russia, and Europeans cooperated together on global issues. Yeltsin was then opposed to any NATO enlargement. If NATO enlarged, Russia should be first in line. But he admitted, "In truth, Russia is not yet ready to join NATO."

By September 1994, Yeltsin was suggesting to President Bill Clinton that Clinton publicly say that any expansion of NATO "will be gradual and lengthy. If you're asked if you'll exclude Russia from NATO," he advised, "your answer should be 'no.'"

Clinton liked that. By 1995, the general ambivalence on both sides about Russian membership in NATO had gently resolved, without either side formally ruling it out, into a dual-track approach. On one side, NATO was moving toward possible enlargement. On the other track, NATO and Russia would develop an agreement on how to manage their future relations, to respect Russia's influence and role in European and global security. Yeltsin was mainly concentrating on how to push the issue off until after his 1996 election was done.[80]

* * *

The countries in the middle, like Poland, had a rather different perspective. As Lech Wałęsa put it, "Yeltsin and I . . . are like drivers on a strange road at night, without road markings. The difference between us is that I am driving a baby Fiat and he a huge juggernaut."[81]

By the fall of 1991, Czech leaders openly sought an "associate membership" with NATO. The United States and other allies turned that down. They did create the North Atlantic Cooperation Council in November 1991. This very much included the Soviet Union.

At first, as Poland's foreign minister from 1989 to 1993 later recalled, "The position of the Alliance at the time was clear: from its perspective, the admission of new members was absolutely out of the question."

As he recalled, correctly, it was not ruled out that "at some point" the United States would take more interest in this. And Germany "would not want to be forever [the alliance's] eastern outpost."

"However," the foreign minister added, "that was a matter of further developments, which at the onset of the 1990s did not yet appear."[82]

As the Bush administration left office at the beginning of 1993, it was internally divided about next steps. At the top, though, there was little division. Bush, Baker, and Scowcroft were not yet ready to press enlargement plans.

The Kohl government, decisively reelected in December 1990, was not going anywhere. Internally, Berlin too was arguing about next steps. Like Bush and Baker, Kohl and his new foreign minister, Klaus Kinkel, were not ready to press the issue.

Western integration was not just about NATO. In fact, the EU would play a much more important part in the reconstruction of Eastern Europe. After Mitterrand's confederation idea collapsed, Delors "suggested to Mitterrand that the task of integrating Eastern Europe with the West should have been left to EC institutions, as it eventually was. But for that to happen, the [French] president would have had to trust those institutions instead of wanting to supersede them with new ones which would be more readily susceptible to French influence."[83]

But, consumed with many troubles accompanying its own "deepening" into the new Union, it would be years before the transformed EU could take up the question of new members from the former communist world. Before that, the EU did offer membership to the countries of Scandinavia, and Sweden and Finland both chose to join.

* * *

With pressure growing, especially from Poland, Hungary, and the Czech Republic (Czechoslovakia having peacefully split into two countries), the first major public arguments about the NATO enlargement question broke into the open during 1993. The German defense minister, Volker Rühe, publicly advocated this limited enlargement. The new Clinton administration, battered by some early crises and missteps, began trying to make its own mark by defining a foreign policy theme of "democratic enlargement."

Both the German and American governments remained internally divided about how to proceed. A violent struggle for power in Russia in September 1993 between president and parliament provided ammunition to both sides.

The basic philosophical tilt toward eventual NATO enlargement occurred in the winter of 1993–94. It was cemented at a meeting of NATO leaders in January 1994 with a consensus that the issue would not be "whether" but "when." The "when" part would consume a great deal of diplomatic energy during the next five years, until the NATO enlargement added Poland, Hungary, and the Czech Republic in 1999, with more to follow.

The new U.S. administration was anxious to carve out a positive policy of its own on some big subject. This was a period of great strain over what to do about the wars in the former Yugoslavia and reverses in other crises in Somalia and Haiti.

President Clinton declared that his younger generation would go beyond what their elders had done before. "I believe," he said, that "our generation's stewardship of this grand alliance, therefore, will most critically be judged by whether we succeed in integrating the nations to our east within the compass of Western security and Western values."[84]

At all times, however, any choice about the enlargement of NATO depended on German assent. Germany was much closer to the pressures and the dangers. It was very involved in the trade-offs regarding relations with Russia. A number of other allied states would look to a German view on this issue as least as much as they would to one from Washington.

During the early and mid-1990s, one well-informed German observer said, "The governments of Western Europe, to put it bluntly, back NATO's eastward extension because they cannot muster the political will to tackle in earnest an eastward extension of the European Union." EU expansion was much more important, politically and economically. But for a time, NATO seemed like a cheaper and readier instrument for reassurance.[85]

Yet once the positive political signal had been sent, the Europeans were in no hurry to enlarge NATO. There was no pressing strategic concern. The Germans and French were very concerned about Russia's unhappiness. The French were not very interested in pushing the matter at all.

Kohl remained chancellor of Germany until 1998. Since 1989 he had personally taken part in every single major negotiation about NATO's future with all the key leaders, Soviet, Russian, and American. No one knew better than he what had been promised, formally or informally, and he was well attuned to Russian concerns.

Kohl was ready to support further enlargement. On the other hand, though, he emphasized a careful and gradual process, one to which Russia assented.[86]

That is what happened. About three years were spent (1994–96) in the "dual-track" negotiations about setting up criteria for new members and working with the candidates on the one hand, while negotiating a special NATO partnership with Russia, a NATO-Russia Founding Act.

Then another few years passed in order to work on the details of actually bringing in the first three new members (Poland, Hungary, and the Czech Republic). That happened in 1999. NATO announced in that year that it had a new, more political strategic concept. Actually, the 1999 strategic concept was not much different from the one that the transformed alliance had adopted in 1991.[87]

* * *

As Kohl had intended all along, by the time NATO actually expanded, at the end of the 1990s, the EU enlargement process was slowly catching up to it. The EU enlargement process was vastly more intrusive and time-consuming. The EU, along with the International Monetary Fund and the World Bank, and various bilateral aid programs (including that of the United States), played a large part in the hard, painful work of post-communist transition.

The IMF had played a large role in post-communist transition in Eastern Europe, with more rigorous and successful insistence on programs of radical reform and the associated shock therapy. Outside pressure from the IMF or Western governments was not enough. The changes needed were so massive that much more institutional help was needed inside these countries.

Fortunately, by the mid-1990s the influence of the EU in Eastern Europe was steadily growing. Former Warsaw Pact states were soon included in a "Europe" agreement that gave them a kind of associate status. By 1994 some of them had formally submitted the first applications for full EU membership. By the late 1990s the process of EU enlargement was changing the governance of every country that hoped to join the Union.

The enlargement process cut deep. It touched the inner workings of the governments—their personnel systems, their judiciaries, their legal structures, their regulations, their protection of the environment, and more.

Often the applicants angrily resented the ordeal and red tape that accompanied the process. Yet they had to acknowledge the positive side: Billions of euros had already been sent as aid; trade skyrocketed; and private investment also flowed in.

The EU exerted most of this influence, however, *before* the new members joined the Union. Once in, it became harder for the Union to judge or sanction the conduct of its members.

The EU had to adjust too. The old member states had to decide how quickly to adjust their work rules to allow migrants from new members. Britain, Ireland, and Sweden were the first to open their doors.

In the early 2000s the scale of West–East aid of many kinds rose into the tens of billions. By this time the new members (the first major enlargement was implemented in 2004) were ready to make good use of the money.

In sum, as one prominent critic of outside advice conceded, "Europe's unprecedented generosity has paid off: the countries that have joined the EU have outperformed all the others, and not just because of access to Europe's markets. Even more important was the institutional infrastructure, including the abiding commitment to democracy and the vast array of laws and regulations." The Union, another scholar pointed out, "did not merely influence but actually determined the Central European governments' internal policies."[88]

* * *

All the institutions of the new Europe—NATO, the EU, IMF/World Bank, and OSCE—combined pressure on some common themes. All put pressure on post-communist governments to adopt democratic government and open economies, to peacefully settle border issues, to put civilians in control of their militaries, and to respect the rule of law. The treatment of national minorities was a frequent topic.[89]

In some cases, like the breakup of Yugoslavia or the struggle between Armenia and Azerbaijan over control of a region called Nagorno-Karabakh, hardly any peaceful measure could work. Yet in many others such external pressures made a big difference.

For instance, the restored country of Estonia adopted national citizenship laws of blood ancestry. These discriminated against ethnic Russians, especially those who had come there under Soviet rule. European states, the United States, the OSCE, the EU, and the United Nations all put Estonia (and Latvia) under plenty of pressure to revise these citizenship laws. They did. Ultranationalists who rejected EU (and NATO) conditions, like the government of Vladimír Mečiar in Slovakia, were "swept away because people did not want to lose the opportunity to join Europe."[90]

* * *

How far into the post-Soviet space should NATO and the EU go? The year 1997 was one of political struggle over the future of Europe. It began with a general consensus that Poland, and at least a couple of other countries, should join both the EU and NATO by the end of the decade. The question was not about whether these institutions should enlarge, but about the limits of this enlargement.

One of the key issues in both organizations was whether the doors would be open to the Baltic republics. In the United States, the new secretary of state, Madeleine Albright, and her deputy, Strobe Talbott, had a particularly strong view, much influenced by their reading and experience with the history of the region, in favor of an "open door" for the Baltics.

In Europe, the British and the Nordic NATO members (Denmark

and Norway) strongly supported Baltic enlargement. Norway was not a member of the EU, but Sweden and Finland now were (both had recently joined, in 1995), and both countries felt a strong sense of community with the states on the other side of the Baltic.

During 1997, after some heated arguments, both NATO and the EU arrived at a common consensus approach. Both decided on an open door. They would set criteria for the extension of membership to any European country from the Baltic to the Black Sea.

At a NATO summit meeting in Madrid in July 1997, the Spanish secretary-general of NATO, Javier Solana, had crafted a compromise document opening the door to all. The French president and Italian prime minister insisted on a more limited extension, preferring expansion in the Balkans rather than the Baltics.

Kohl asked to speak. "The place was absolutely silent," an American observer remembered. Kohl said that he regretted having to contradict his French and Italian colleagues. But, he said, an open door for all, the Solana compromise, was the only proposal that all the allies would be able to accept. The Dutch prime minister seconded him.

Solana asked for approval. No one spoke and he gaveled the meeting to a close.[91] The EU made a similar decision at the end of 1997, at the European Council meeting in Luxembourg.

Following up on these "open door" decisions and related criteria for membership, between 1997 and the end of 2002 both the EU and NATO proceeded to make their last great wave of positive decisions about enlargement. At the time they did not quite realize that they were hitting their limits, but they were.

Poland, Hungary, and the Czech Republic joined NATO in 1999. The EU decided to accept twelve new members, ten of whom, including Poland, joined the Union in 2004. NATO decided to accept seven new members, all of them joining in 2004. The three Baltic republics were in both groups.

* * *

As the EU and NATO expanded, a diminished Russia had a painful adjustment. Russia inherited many of the legacies of being a Cold War superpower, including the proud historical status of a "great power," however that term is defined, since the eighteenth century. In 1989, few would have challenged the image and reality of the Soviet Union as a super-power. During 1990 and 1991 all that was changing. By 1992 the Soviet Union was gone and Moscow ruled less territory in Europe or Central Asia than it had at any time in centuries.

But during 1990 and 1991 the U.S. and West European leaders continued to deal with Gorbachev as the head of a great power. In the response to the crisis over Iraq's invasion of Kuwait, the Soviet government played a large role. Ultimately the United States and its allies shouldered the main burden of containing, then reversing, the Iraqi conquest. But the United States devoted enormous effort to handling the issue in partnership with the Soviet Union, despite the inevitable tension and suspicion on both sides. As difficult as they were, the choices for cooperation were the right ones, on both sides.[92]

Later in 1991, even though the United States did much of the diplomatic work to set up the first direct multilateral peace talks between Israel and all its Arab neighbors, the invitation to the talks came from both Bush and Gorbachev. Both of them opened the discussions in Madrid in October 1991, the last major diplomatic event of Gorbachev's time in office.

Entering the 1990s, Russia was going through an inevitable period of upheaval. Still, neither the United States nor the West European leaders had written off its importance. Russia was constantly consulted and involved in the diplomacy and peacekeeping efforts in the Balkans, at least through the mid-1990s.

The leaders of the new global system were in effect keeping a seat at the table for Russia to occupy, in substance and not just form, once Russia was able to give constructive attention to European and world problems. The NATO-organized and U.S.-led intervention to end the Bosnian war in 1995 was irritating to the Russians, but Russia remained involved and this was not a breakpoint.

The enlargement of NATO was contentious. But the Clinton administration made a real, conscientious effort to assure Russia, in the NATO-Russia Act, that it would be treated as a peer, its views carefully weighed in any future NATO action.

Therefore, what stands out, especially in Strobe Talbott's careful memoir of U.S.-Russia relations, is the significance of a small war that few Americans now remember—the U.S.-led and NATO-organized war against Serbia in 1999 to force that country to yield in its treatment of the breakaway province of Kosovo. The Serbs tried to hold on to Kosovo, with its persecuted ethnic Albanians.

Russians and Yeltsin vehemently opposed this further war against the Serbs. They believed that their views were simply overridden. Whatever one's view of the merits of the U.S. and NATO strategy to deal with Serbian actions in Kosovo, this has to be counted among the costs.

In that crisis, which occurred in his last year in office, before he was succeeded by Vladimir Putin, Yeltsin told Clinton, "I have never met such a difficult, complicated issue as the ongoing NATO military action in Yugoslavia." In one of several very emotional discussions, he truthfully commented, "Of course, we are going to talk to each other, you and me. But there will not be such a great drive and such friendship that we had before. That will not be there again."[93]

Global Designs and a New World Order

Our story has mainly focused on Europe. The Bush administration's policies in Asia were relatively static. Resisting great pressure at home, it held open a door to normal relations with China; it held off pleas to start a trade war against a Japan that itself was in a passive phase; and it held fast to an American defense presence in East Asia.[94]

The U.S. concentrated on Europe because what happened to Europe between 1988 and 1992 changed the world. To pick just one large example, in 1991 the government of India, watching what was going on, made its historic decision to modernize its economy and open up more to participation in world commerce.

With its global perspective, at the beginning of the 1990s the United States tried to look beyond Europe, and widen the promise of a global commonwealth of free nations. As we mentioned back in chapters 1 and 3, the American leaders were determined to build a new system of global trade, in negotiations called the "Uruguay Round."

The GATT, the General Agreement on Tariffs and Trade, was developed by British and American officials during the Second World War. Once upon a time there had been hopes to create an "International Trade Organization," but in the 1940s that seemed like a fantasy. What the Americans and the British set up with others in the late 1940s and early 1950s promoted freer trade, not free trade, applied selectively to promote Cold War goals.

It was, a historian concluded, "a moderate form of multilateralism. Free trade ideals were left behind, victims of domestic regulatory practices, the influence of protectionism, and, above all, the Cold War."[95]

By the 1980s the Cold War bargains in the GATT were no longer so meaningful. Americans began accepting a narrative that portrayed gullible Americans helping European, Japanese, or Korean allies who were now taking advantage of this American goodwill or naivete. Protectionism was rising, not only in many new trade barriers being created by the United States but also in new ones found in Japan or Europe. The problems with global trade were what led the United States and Canada to carve out a free trade agreement of their own in 1988, itself a very difficult achievement.

The Bush administration gained some momentum to try to expand trade. The U.S. trade position had improved as it took office, and the economy was recovering in the second half of the 1980s. More industries were taking advantage of global openings to obtain steel or semiconductors for their own production lines. Japan entered a prolonged slump.

Using the moment, Bush, Baker and Zoellick, and Bush's trade negotiator, Carla Hills, all worked to reset the "vector" of U.S. and global trade, to switch it from "closing" to "opening." They were no longer relying on the old Cold War narrative. Their argument was that expanded trade would increase business, growth, and employment on both sides of the deals. They also believed that the greater cooperation among these economies would reinforce wider political partnerships across the board.

* * *

The worldwide effort was most important, but what got most of the attention in the United States was the effort to create a North American Free

Trade Agreement (NAFTA). NAFTA was forged during the Bush administration, working with Mexico and Canada. The Clinton administration followed through and, with great difficulty, secured its passage through Congress.[96] But the more important work that the Clinton administration also carried through to conclusion was the Uruguay Round and the creation of a World Trade Organization.

For the first time the United States was leading an effort to conclude a global trade arrangement that would include both the developed and developing worlds. The scope was broad, ranging from agricultural subsidies to intellectual property. In addition to new rules, Canada—with European support—suggested the creation of a new organization to provide expertise and umpire disputes.

After Bush vetoed a quota on textile imports, opening the way to getting rid of the trade restrictions on textiles that hampered poor countries, the United States was able to ask for and get concessions that it wanted. The talks began to make rapid progress.

Since 1989, as we mentioned in chapter 3, the United States had linked its support for the single European market ("Europe 92") to European support for a successful global trade deal. In other words, the newly enlarged and built-up Fortress Europe had to be open to world trade. Although there were problems with several countries, especially Japan and India, the most significant dispute ended up pitting the United States against Europe. The issue was agriculture. The whole agreement stalled over this problem.

In early 1992 the United States retaliated against European agricultural subsidies with high tariffs on a billion dollars' worth of European exports. After very difficult negotiations during 1992 that repeatedly involved Bush, Delors, and other top leaders, the United States and Europe finally struck a deal, the "Blair House agreement" at the end of 1992.

With that deal passed to the Clinton administration, the Europeans pushed hard for establishment of the new WTO (the Canadian name—the Europeans had called it a "Multilateral Trade Organization"). In December 1993 the United States agreed. The final agreements were signed by 117 nations in Marrakech, Morocco. The U.S. Congress approved the deal in November 1994.

This Uruguay Round agreement was "the most ambitious and far-reaching multilateral trade negotiation since the establishment of the GATT in 1947."[97] It did not produce complete free trade. Global trade could still be an obstacle course of local regulations. But the framework was much clearer and more orderly.

The Uruguay Round agreement did not eliminate agricultural subsidies, but those were substantially reduced. Average formal tariffs were cut by about one-third. Some of the old nontariff barriers, like "voluntary" export restraints, were eliminated. There were agreements on trade in services, on intellectual property, and on investment. America was opening its market to much more of the world, but the world was also opening its market much more to America—thus many political constituencies favored the deal. It was the last such global deal.

* * *

In Asia, in 1989, the United States picked up an idea launched by the Australian prime minister, Bob Hawke, for an Asia-Pacific Economic Cooperation forum (APEC). The United States argued that APEC could coexist with the other major multilateral forum, among Southeast Asian states, called ASEAN (the Association of Southeast Asian Nations). APEC had a new configuration, mixing government officials with representatives from the business world and academia. It was a place to discuss common problems, divided by sectors, and try to find solutions.

APEC, for example, became a way to host delegations from China along with Taiwan and Hong Kong. A similar compromise was later used to bring all three into the WTO in 2001, and thus more fully into the global economic system.[98]

The great test, though, was whether the United States would accept China into the new Uruguay Round global trade system, thus giving it normal trading status in the American market without the annual reviews that had happened every year since 1980, often attended by controversy and uncertainty, especially after Tiananmen Square. China had signed on to the agreement, but the United States and its Congress still had to consent.

Clinton's trade negotiator concluded a deal in November 1999. Clinton and Congress engaged in another major battle, like that over

NAFTA. Finally, in May 2000, the House passed "Permanent Normal Trade Relations" (PNTR) with China by a vote of 237–197. Two-thirds of the Democrats opposed it.

The China PNTR deal had a far larger impact than NAFTA or the earlier Uruguay Round deal did. During the 2000s, imports to the United States from China more than tripled. This "China shock" had a very heavy impact on manufacturing employment in the United States, the first such shock that can be substantially linked to trade, rather than a mix of ordinary competition and technological change. Although trade had actually helped manufacturing income in earlier years, none of the trade changes had much effect on income inequality, however, which mainly has other causes.[99]

Because the United States was a big borrower from the world during the 2000s, as it is now, world sellers who accumulate a lot of dollars did not and do not need to use those dollars to buy U.S. goods. Following the pattern first established during the Reagan years (though then on a smaller scale), the foreign dollar-holders can invest in American or any other dollar-denominated assets (which then ups the prices of those assets, including the value of the dollar). Often, they are buying the bonds that lend the dollars back to Americans, who are borrowing so much money from the rest of the world. The Americans then pay the interest on their debts to their many creditors around the world.

At the beginning of the 1990s, for better or worse—but mostly for better—American and other world leaders made a deliberate, planned decision to build a global trade system. Along with the global financial systems that had evolved during the 1980s, these trade and financial structures were core features of global capitalism. That was the plan.

The next part of the global design at the beginning of the 1990s, per-haps the most prominent of all, had not been planned at all.

* * *

Iraq's invasion and conquest of neighboring Kuwait on August 2, 1990, came as a shock to neighboring Arab countries (including Kuwait). It came as a shock to the Soviet government that had thousands of advis-ers in Iraq. And it came as a shock to the United States, which had very much noticed the massing of Iraqi troops on Kuwait's border (and had consulted all the others about what it meant).

The motives of Iraq's dictator, Saddam Hussein, would not have been easy for any outsider to understand. Those who have examined the Iraqi records have concluded that Saddam believed, from escalating tensions and financial pressures, that he and his country were the target of an American-Israeli-Kuwaiti conspiracy to "strangle Iraq and topple his regime." So in Saddam's mind, he would get ahead of the plot, conquer Kuwait, and annex that country and its oil riches permanently.[100]

This precedent-setting case—Iraq and Kuwait—was extreme. It was the most brazen act of out-and-out international conquest since the Second World War. It was even more brazen than the North Korean invasion of South Korea in 1950. In the Korean case neither country had recognized the legitimate existence of the other. The Korean case was also seen, correctly, as related to the larger Cold War struggle already taking shape.

The Iraqi conquest was novel. It was not a Cold War battle. The case asked: How would the emerging global system handle outlaws? The question really had two parts. Was there any international law or norms that should be respected? If there were any, Iraq's conquest of Kuwait violated them.

The other part of the question was: If such law or norms are to be enforced, who should do it, and how? How the world responded to this case would offer a blazing example of how such questions would be answered. Not only had Iraq seized one of the world's larger oil producers, but its military now stood close to the oil-producing region of Saudi Arabia, a country that could not defend itself against Iraq's army.

* * *

Both of the authors of this book were working for Bush when this invasion occurred. Both of us became quite involved in the crisis in the days and weeks to come. On the first day after news of the invasion hit Washington, Zelikow traveled with Bush to Aspen, Colorado, where Bush was planning to visit with British prime minister Thatcher.

In Aspen, by coincidence, Bush planned, and proceeded, to give a speech to announce a large drawdown of America's military strength and a change in outlook. "We're entering a new era," he said, and "the defense strategy and military structure needed to ensure peace can and must be different."

He continued, "In a world less driven by an immediate threat to Europe and the danger of global war, in a world where the size of our forces will increasingly be shaped by the needs of regional contingencies and peacetime presence, we know that our forces can be smaller. . . . I can tell you now, we calculate that by 1995 our security needs can be met by an active force 25 percent smaller than today's. America's armed forces will be at their lowest level since the year 1950."

Bush did not waver from these plans. But he and Scowcroft (Baker was on the other side of the world, rushing home and talking to Shevardnadze) immediately made up their minds, as Bush, in impromptu fashion, told reporters a few days later, "This will not stand, this aggression against Kuwait."

People could, and did, make their geopolitical calculations. Iraq then had one of the larger armies in the world. Ejecting it from its positions on the other side of the world would be an awful task.

But there was a core judgment, which both of the authors of this book immediately saw at the White House and which we shared. Unexpectedly, Bush had to set a precedent for the character of the new world that in August 1990 was dawning.

Baker was exactly right when he later wrote, "The President's statement reflected his instinctive sense, very early on, that this was no ordinary crisis, that it truly would become a hinge point in history."[101] As to how "this will not stand," that was a complicated path. But Bush's determination was fixed. Scowcroft was equally determined.

And as it turned out, many others, including many world leaders, shared this core conviction. They too sensed, in different words and shadings, that a test had come. Especially for leaders of the postwar generation for whom World War II was not just something in books and film, this was a test they decided they would pass. The world was entering a new era, one way or another, and leaders who wanted to build a better one had to step up.

Before the Iraq crisis of 1990, no country had planned any of this. There were no deliberations about a new grand strategy for how best to handle novel global security problems. There were preexisting principles, institutions, and habits of thought. But these did not automatically dictate the choice about the "vectors" we have outlined.

Reasonable people disagreed. New situations forced new choices. Making those choices, often driven by the specific details of what was going on and evaluations of alternative actions, the leaders then began reflecting on the larger meaning and patterns set by what they were doing.

* * *

The "how" part was vital too. Bush decided, amid disagreements (including from Thatcher), that he would offer American leadership through a true global coalition, endorsed by the United Nations. This was a hard road. It required the support of the Soviet Union and China, among others. It was the first time that Franklin Roosevelt's original vision for the United Nations came fully to life.

During the Second World War, while Bush was a young pilot flying missions in the Pacific, Franklin Roosevelt had imagined that the UN Security Council would have at its core a concert of the great powers. He thought of them as "Four Policemen," the United States, the Soviet Union, Britain, and China. At that time France had not yet won permanent membership in the UN Security Council, and the China FDR had in mind was the Nationalist Chinese government led by Chiang Kai-shek (Jiang Jieshi). In this vision the great powers would join forces against future outlaws, like Nazi Germany had been.[102]

The vision had never quite come true. The Korean case of 1950 came close, but the Soviet Union was out of the UN at the time the decisions were made, abstaining because it complained that the wrong China (the noncommunist one that had fled to Taiwan) then had China's seat at the UN.

So the Iraq case in 1990 was the first true test of FDR's original vision. And it worked about as well as he could possibly have hoped it might.

Not only did the United States and other leaders organize a political coalition for UN action, but there was also a multinational military coalition that organized a force more than half a million strong in Saudi Arabia. This included the British and French, but also troops from Egypt, Syria, and Saudi Arabia.

There was also an economic coalition that gave huge sums to countries that suffered from joining economic sanctions against Iraq (like Turkey and Jordan) but also offset the costs the United States incurred, because the Americans were also fighting on their behalf, and they, for various reasons, could not contribute that way. Baker called this his "tin cup" coalition, as he went around and asked them to contribute, which they did—more than $50 billion. The big contributors to this economic coalition were Germany, Japan, Saudi Arabia, and of course, Kuwait.[103]

Across the span of world history, it is hard to find any case of a set of coalitions so intricate, overlapping, and successful. Part of the credit goes to an extreme U.S. diplomatic effort. As one of our key NSC staff colleagues, Richard Haass, put it, "Everything else was secondary. The U.S. government, for better or worse, revolved around this set of issues."[104]

But most of the credit for the construction of these worldwide coalitions does not go to Americans. The overlapping coalitions worked because other countries *shared the objective*. They recognized the test. They *wanted* to join to pass it.

While Bush had been flying missions in the Pacific at the end of 1944, Mitterrand had been helping to liberate France. He had no particular affection for the Kuwaitis. "To make war on behalf of these billionaire potentates will be hard for us," he told his foreign minister. But his immediate instinct, like Bush's, was that "we must be firm.... We have to defend international law and solidarity."

Mitterrand, like Bush, then listened to his advisers debate what to do. They were divided. Some were reluctant, preferring to hang back from the United States, win friends in the Arab world, and concentrate on economic sanctions. After one such debate, a week after the Iraqi invasion, Mitterrand listened, and listened, and then lashed out.

"When you shelter behind those arguments you're just reasoning in a vacuum!...The Americans know that the French and the British are the only ones [in Europe] capable of taking action. If we don't respond, it means we are going to sit on the sidelines....If we evade that problem, we've gathered here to no purpose."

Speaking privately to his cabinet, Mitterrand spoke bluntly. "Iraq is an unscrupulous, bloody dictatorship.... In this case we must be clear about our solidarity. If we have to choose, I consider that we must fight against Hussein, whatever the consequences may be. If we don't, we are false brothers of the West."

Months later, as Bush phoned to say the land offensive was about to begin, Mitterrand would again evoke such comradeship. "We're a very small group of 'happy few,'" he told Bush.[105]

* * *

Saddam Hussein's Iraq would not leave Kuwait unless overwhelming force made them do so. The coalition began fighting in January 1991. To fracture it, Iraq then fired dozens of missiles at Israel, hoping that an Arab-Israeli war would break the coalition. Again, through remarkable coalition work, the world rallied to Israel's defense without Israel itself having to go to war against Iraq and thereby play Saddam's game.

The coalition defeated Iraq, liberating all of Kuwait. The UN imposed an armistice in 1991. In all the UN resolutions on Iraq the United States and the Soviet Union maintained a common front. The cease-fire terms required that UN inspectors be able to police Iraq and be sure the remnants of its advanced nuclear program (and other weapons of mass destruction) were dismantled and destroyed.

"In the first days of the [Iraq] crisis," Scowcroft remembered, "we had started self-consciously to view our actions as setting a precedent for the approaching post–Cold War world... for the Security Council to operate as its founders had envisioned." This would be a new kind of world order. Exercising their usual literary flair, Bush and Scowcroft thus thought of it as, and then began calling it, just that: a "new world order."

The phrase itself was no more than a flat description. They did believe in world order—and what was happening was new. Scowcroft's own description of what it meant to him was characteristically terse. "Our foundation was the premise that the United States henceforth would be obligated to lead the world community to an unprecedented degree, as demonstrated by the Iraqi crisis, and that we should attempt to pursue our national interests, wherever possible, within a framework of concert with our friends and the international community."[106]

The Unipolar Mirage

In the winter of 1990–91, the late Charles Krauthammer coined a memorable phrase in an essay for *Foreign Affairs*, which he entitled "The Unipolar Moment." "The center of world power," he wrote, "is the unchallenged superpower, the United States, attended by its Western allies."[107]

Just one year before Krauthammer wrote this essay, in September 1989, the best-informed foreign embassy in Washington had seen a somewhat different America. As we recounted in chapter 3, the British embassy had privately explained to London that the general wisdom in America was that the country had entered a period of great decline, that it was experiencing a troubling adjustment to its loss of status, and that economic nationalism was the dominant national theme.

The British diplomats of September 1989 had accurately described what they were reading and hearing. Krauthammer, too, was accurately articulating a national mood, self-congratulatory and triumphal—after the collapse of the Soviet Union and even more after the February 1991 victory against Iraq.

* * *

The U.S. government had not suddenly gained magical powers from one year to the next. During the two years from the East German election in March 1990 until the spring of 1992, the United States did seem powerful, and it was. America's was a power gained from combining strengths—political, financial, and military—in networks of partnerships with others. The power was apparent not because leaders bragged about how much of it they had, but because well-designed policy choices produced visible, constructive results.

In a prepared address he delivered to Congress in September 1990, Bush urged his fellow Americans to see a "rare opportunity to move toward an historic period of cooperation," one "freer from the threat of terror, stronger in the pursuit of justice, and more secure in the quest for peace." It would be "a world quite different than the one we've known."[108]

Bush would not be reelected to lead America into that different world. By 1992, he was already being attacked on both sides for having given too much attention to the rest of the world. In his essay, written well before Patrick Buchanan, then Ross Perot, chose to run against Bush in 1992, Krauthammer already foresaw "a resurgence of 1930s-style conservative isolationism."[109]

Thatcher had been a dedicated cold warrior, yet struggled with all the new designs until her own party toppled her from power in November 1990. Kohl helped create a new Germany and a new Europe and stayed in power long enough to endure endless quarrels about both.

Gorbachev's own reflections were especially poignant, mixed with satisfaction and regrets. At one point, in February 1991, he mused to Chernyaev, "It's a new era. Even in our country it is already post-*perestroika*. All revolutions end in failure, even if they change the country, and some change the whole world."[110]

CHAPTER 7

New Challenges Evolve

On December 25, 1991, the flag of the Soviet Union—the hammer and sickle—came down from the Kremlin for the last time. Mikhail Gorbachev called George H. W. Bush that day. Bush assured him that "what you have done will live in history and be fully appreciated by historians."[1]

They both had reason to believe that history would be kind to them. The "commonwealth of free nations" and "new world order" that they had launched would indeed be a firm foundation for prosperity and, yes, for democracy going forward. After a century of war and near-war, at last it seemed possible to build a durable peace.

Twenty-five years later, the powerful antibodies to the new designs were evident. They seemed to emerge suddenly, mostly in one seminal year—2016.

The very states that had begun the revolution for freedom in Eastern Europe in 1989, Hungary and Poland, saw far-right "populist" parties move to center stage. Political scientists reminded readers that populism was a nice word for a political condition in which people vote for a leader who claims to express the national will, to defeat the institutions, elites, and dissenting voices that they think stand in the way of that will.[2]

Elites in Germany recoiled as the right-wing Alternative for Germany (Alternative für Deutschland, or AfD) blew through the 5 percent electoral threshold and took ninety-four seats in the Bundestag.[3] Most of that victory had been won in the regions that had been part of the old East German state.[4] The United Kingdom did the unthinkable—it voted to exit the EU, calling into question the future of a united Europe. The United States elected a president who spoke of America First and questioned the value of the Atlantic alliance. Americans and others learned that Vladimir Putin's authoritarian Russia was up to old tricks in a new form—trying to manipulate elections by stirring discord among disaffected populations within democratic states.[5] One year later, Italy elected a far-right movement called "Five Star." The four horsemen of political apocalypse were back—populism, nativism, isolationism, and protectionism.

While all of these events can be traced to "local" factors, larger long-term trends set the stage. The financial crisis of 2008 delivered a hard blow to confidence about the future and benefits of global capitalism. Just as the world had begun to recover from that shock, chaos in the Middle East—principally in Syria—accelerated a migrant crisis the likes of which had not been seen since World War II. The events irrevocably altered politics in Europe and in the United States—and cast a pall over hopes for the future of a global commonwealth.

The Financial Crisis

"You probably ought to know that Goldman and Morgan Stanley could fail tomorrow." Josh Bolten, chief of staff to President George W. Bush, had called Rice aside at a White House reception in the East Room. It was September 2008. In whispered tones he told her that, as secretary of state, she "might need to make some calls around the world tomorrow to calm nervous friends." Rice had trouble focusing on what he was saying. Frankly, she couldn't get past the words "Goldman and Morgan Stanley could fail tomorrow."[6]

They didn't, but Lehman Brothers did. JP Morgan—at the behest of the U.S. government—had already bought Bear Stearns. Bank of America took over Merrill Lynch. Credit was drying up. The international financial system was—in perception and perhaps in reality—on the verge of collapse.

The origins of the crisis have been analyzed and debated by numerous scholars, as have the measures taken to avert the total collapse of the system. For the purposes of this book, three points about the basic operating principles of the global system that had emerged in the early 1990s stand out.

First, the crisis was fueled by a great strength of the global system: the ability to move giant pools of money across borders, especially within and between America and Europe. Much more money was available for credit and investment around the world. With that also came chronic debt crises, on a pattern of about one every ten years, in the mid-1980s (importantly including Poland and Hungary), in 1997–98 (which so badly affected Russia and with Ukraine caught in the fallout), and this time in the heart of the advanced economies.

Second, from the start, therefore, the crisis was neither American nor European—it was both. The American phase of the crisis hit first, peaking in 2008–9. The European phase hit next, peaking between 2009 and 2012. The Great Depression had followed a similar sequence, with the American panic hitting in 1929, followed by a European panic that began in 1931.

Third, in both America and Europe the crisis exposed gaps between the powerful forces at play in the global system and the domestic policy structures to handle them. The United States set interest rates too low in the early 2000s, and the European Central Bank followed the American example. Countries in southern Europe that needed higher rates could not get them because the ECB wanted a uniform rate in Europe and the Germans would not accept higher rates on themselves. The low rates encouraged overextended mortgages, fostered by the securitization of the mortgages, the breakdown of the ratings agencies, and government encouragement of the overextension of housing debt, financed with the giant flows of capital from global investors looking for yield in a world of low interest rates.[7]

The crisis exposed the two great design flaws in the European monetary union. Going back to the formative Delors report of 1988–89, the best advocates of monetary union, including Delors himself, had emphasized the need for requirements that would help fiscal convergence—which they thought should occur with relatively low debt—and produce Europe-wide banking standards. The final result did not adequately assure either. The EU got a sound currency and low inflation, but these original design flaws opened up other problems.

Of course, what we call "design flaws" others call "design choices," of just the kind we have discussed in earlier chapters. Tough fiscal convergence requirements would have reduced member state autonomy to set their own taxing and spending levels. Strong EU-wide banking governance might foster a smaller number of stronger European banks, but— just as in the American case during the nineteenth and early twentieth centuries—individual states want their own banks, with their own regulations, to be sure those banks are putting the interests of their citizens and their borrowers first.

European bank practices belied the supposed monetary union. They might use a common money and central bank, but their banks were regulated nationally by dozens of authorities. Thus small institutions, often weakly regulated at home in countries like Iceland, Ireland, Spain, Estonia, Italy, or Greece, could eagerly overinvest. To a historian, the European Union's problem—a big economy populated by many weak banks—had some of the same dangers as the American union used to have, before the United States nationalized and modernized its federal banking laws.

Britain, outside of the euro, found no safety there. It experienced the first run on a British bank in 150 years. The UK would eventually announce a bailout package for its banks worth $88 billion.

As countries raced to arrest the rapid decline of the banking system and confidence in it, they took extraordinary measures. They nationalized banks, bailed out companies, and the central banks became bond buyers on a massive scale, in effect putting trillions of dollars in loans on central bank balance sheets.[8]

* * *

The crisis exposed real flaws in the global commonwealth. It also demonstrated real resiliency. In the Great Depression, the fundamental weakness was that the United States did not cooperate effectively with the principal European economic powers (Britain, France, and Germany), and the Europeans did not cooperate effectively with each other. It became a cry of "every man for himself." The 1931 aggravation of the crisis sent economies on both sides of the Atlantic off the cliff.

In the Great Recession that began in 2008, international cooperation was essential to the firefighting. And although the public knows little about it, new and old institutions stepped up to a new challenge in global governance.

The G-20 was not the old G-24 created in 1989 to help post-communist transition with four members thrown overboard. The G-20 is a different and more important entity. It started life at the end of the 1990s among American and German financial officials, working with a Canadian prime minister, to provide a better sort of governance institution after the financial crisis of 1997–98. During most of the 2000s it remained an institution among finance officials.

Why G-20? The idea was to pick some round number of countries that represented a broader, more global group than the old G-7, but to build a more inclusive group without having to use the much more unwieldy and speechifying economic structures of the UN. The G-20 had the virtue of including countries that encompassed at least 80 percent of world trade and 85 percent of world GDP.

The Bush 43 administration that took office in 2001 had been reluctant to elevate the G-20 into a top-level group and add one more set of summit meetings. The global financial crisis changed Bush's mind.

It was in the fall of 2008, with the global financial crisis in full flight, that French president Nicolas Sarkozy visited Bush at Camp David.[9] He impressed upon the president the need for the United States to host the G-20. Bush agreed. G-20 heads of government met for the first time in Washington, DC, on November 14.

The irony may have been lost on the worried leaders gathered at this crucial moment: The G-20 had originally been formed, at lower levels, in part, to assist developing economies that were vulnerable to the Asian financial crisis—including those in the former Soviet bloc. Now it met to try to save the mature economies of the prosperous West.

The G-20 members promised not to adopt "beggar thy neighbor trading policies" or protectionist measures. This was a nod toward their understanding of the catastrophic effects of such policies in the interwar period—actions that had aggravated the Great Depression. Rather than liquidate all their investments, they tried to stay the course.

More important, the G-20, at this Washington meeting and at a follow-up summit held in London in April 2009, now with President Barack Obama, strengthened institutions for the governance of banks. It turned an existing Financial Stability Forum into a Financial Stability Board. The board would help set standards, working in partnership with the IMF to oversee the implementation and enforcement of those standards.

Further, the G-20 agreed to push plenty of money in to help beleaguered countries. Again using the IMF, the IMF member states raised an enormous war chest of money. This was backed by large fiscal stimulus moves undertaken by both the United States and China.[10]

Meanwhile, in 2009–10, as the European phase of the crisis kicked in, the U.S. Federal Reserve gave massive dollar support to help European institutions. This cooperation prevented a European collapse that then would have rippled back across the Atlantic and around the world. Rather than the crisis or the new institutions displacing the dollar or the U.S. role, both the innovations and U.S. performance actually solidified both, but did it in a much wider and stronger global structure.

Protectionism did increase in response to the global financial crisis. But it was not like the dramatic reversals of the early 1930s. The net effect on global trade was not a *reversal* of globalization. Many small protectionist measures, along with technological and business trends that were replacing wholesale outsourcing with more complex global supply chains, *flattened out* economic globalization at about the levels of 2008. That is about where they remained for the next ten years.

As the global financial crisis exposed economic weaknesses in Europe, the economic issues became political. All of southern Europe experienced depression levels of unemployment and hardship. The poster child was Greece.

In 2009, Greece announced that it had underestimated its deficit and debt figures for years. Shut out of international markets, the country was on the verge of bankruptcy. Germany took the lead in organizing a broad response. After tense negotiations and public humiliation, the IMF, the ECB, and the European Commission bailed Athens out with a €240 billion package. Ireland, Portugal, Spain, and Cyprus would eventually receive bailouts too.

As the first to face the crisis—and a country that many in Europe

dismissed as a profligate spender with poor tax collection and lax work habits—Greece became the face of the troubles. Dueling headlines across Europe summed up the anxiety and the anger. On July 11, the German newsmagazine *Der Spiegel* published a provocative cover showing an alarmed German tourist "dancing" with an ouzo-drinking Greek. "Our Greeks—Getting Closer to a Strange People," read the headline.

The German newspaper *Handelsblatt* denounced the cover, calling it "humorous like a German." In a sardonic editorial, it noted, "The last time Greece belonged to 'us' was when the Swastika flew over the Acropolis."[11]

The bailout sparked angrier indignation in Greece. Shortly after the deal was announced, the hashtag #Boycottgermany began trending on Twitter. Citizens in Athens said bailout supporters were "Nazi collaborators." And on social media, individuals shared a doctored image of the EU flag in which the circle of gold stars had been replaced by a circle of swastikas.[12] The newspaper's response captured the larger trepidation Greece felt toward Germany.

Back in Germany, Angela Merkel was forced to answer the question: Why should a hardworking German bail out a not-so-hardworking Greek? She defended the ideal of one for all and all for one in Europe. "It is important—and in this position there will be no change—that our own efforts and solidarity continue to belong together."[13] The German chancellor reminded her citizens that at least some of their economic success was due to membership in the single currency and integrated market. In the end, she and others won the battle—but at a cost—as confidence in European leadership suffered a blow and Euroskeptics began to take center stage.

In time, the economies that had been hard hit by the financial crisis and the follow-on troubles in the Eurozone began to recover, though at varying rates. France and Germany rebounded within two years. Spain, Portugal, and Italy continued to flounder until 2014.

Scholars disagree about the degree to which the global financial crisis sparked the rise of populists in Europe.[14] The better question is whether the crisis weakened the confidence of populations in their leaders, and in the elite groups—including financial leaders—whom they had trusted to make capitalism reasonably safe.

Reviewing the crisis in December 2018, a still very sharp George Shultz, a week before his ninety-eighth birthday, homed in on three fundamental principles. "One is accountability. From the ground up, there was no accountability. Number two is the sense of [in]competence.... Number three: trust. You have to trust that the people doing things know what they're doing, and that was violated. So I think the net of all this was a very bad episode, and we still pay the price for it.... We've got to get back to a day when the bailouts are not in the picture, where competence is rewarded, and trust returns."[15]

The Migrant Crisis

Like all wealthy parts of the world, Europe has experienced migration of peoples for centuries.[16] The mixing of peoples across the great empires—Austro-Hungarian, Russian, even Ottoman—had largely been taken in stride. Concepts of citizenship were more fluid in earlier times.

Then, twenty or so years after World War II, non-European

immigrants found their way to the continent in reasonably large numbers. In some cases—Turks in Germany, for instance—migrants were allowed to work but with no promise of a path to citizenship. Britain and France absorbed dark-skinned peoples from former colonial territories in North Africa and South Asia. Their children would become citizens, but integration was minimal. In fact, it was the espoused policies of these governments to promote "multiculturalism" at the expense of the adoption of European cultural identity.[17] This often led to the "ghettoization" of the populations in confined areas of London or Paris. But they enjoyed full political rights, and by 1992 parliaments and governments began to look a little more like the changing face of the countries.[18]

The issues of emigration, immigration, and asylum of the twenty-first century were different. First, there was the wave of emigration from Eastern Europe to the West. In 1995, the European Union created the Schengen Area, intended to lower barriers to the movement of people across borders in the Union (Table 1).

Table 1.   List of EU and Non-EU Countries in the Schengen Area

EU Schengen				Non-EU Schengen	EU Non-Schengen
Austria	Belgium	Czech Republic	Denmark	Iceland	Bulgaria
Estonia	Finland	France	Germany	Lichtenstein	Croatia
Greece	Hungary	Italy	Latvia	Norway	Cyprus
Lithuania	Luxembourg	Malta	Netherlands	Switzerland	Ireland
Poland	Portugal	Slovakia	Slovenia		United Kingdom
Spain	Sweden				

Differing economic prospects in Eastern and Western Europe led to a large migration of people and concerns about a "brain drain." While the "Polish plumber" would come to signify the concerns of Westerners about low-skilled labor (and become a rallying cry for populists), many East Europeans who left their homes were well educated and more likely to have gone to college than the rest of the population.[19] About eighteen million citizens of Eastern Europe left in the years between 1990 and 2015.[20] The effects were dramatic: In 1997, 7.5 percent of UK employees were from outside the country; by 2008 it was 14 percent.[21]

Second, the wars of the twenty-first century would create an even more critical and neuralgic migrant problem for Europe. The wars in Afghanistan and Iraq sent roughly three million people in search of safety. Many remained within the Middle East, with the migrant population doubling in number between 2005 and 2015. Jordan, Turkey, and Lebanon each took on the immeasurable task of hosting millions of refugees. But the Syrian civil war—with over seven million internally displaced people and refugees—could not be contained within the region.[22] The problem began to spill over.

By October 2015 the countries of the Mediterranean Basin— particularly Greece, Spain, and Italy—were straining under the weight of unprecedented migration from the Middle East and North Africa. That month, 221,454 asylum seekers arrived. To put this in perspective, just this one month's total was more than triple the number of irregular migrants that had reached the EU in all of 2012.[23]

Under an EU law known as the Dublin Regulation, asylum seekers were to be registered and processed in the country where they arrived. This was to prevent "asylum shopping." If a seeker moved to another country for processing, he or she could be forcibly returned to the arriving country through a "Dublin transfer." The EU had already suspended the rule for Greece in 2011 and overhauled the rules in 2013. By 2015, other countries began to unilaterally suspend the Dublin Regulation.[24] Europe needed to spread the migrant burden. Others needed to accept asylum seekers by transfer.

German chancellor Angela Merkel, moved by the horrific circumstances of Syrian refugees (and the strain on the EU's southern members), made a fateful decision: She welcomed the asylum seekers to her country with a hearty "we can do it!" (*wir schaffen das!*).[25] In practice, this meant that Germany would try to absorb roughly one million people. She hoped that her European counterparts would (proportionately) do the same. "If Europe fails on the question of refugees," she warned, "it won't be the Europe we wished for."

Religious and political leaders across the world lauded her compassion. The pope called it a "reawakening of conscience" and challenged states to do more, "to be close to the smallest and forsaken, to give [refugees] concrete hope."[26]

But these leaders were mostly in places that did not have to take the people. President Barack Obama said that the United States would perhaps take 110,000 refugees. But bipartisan concerns over "gaps in our refugee program that terrorists could exploit" prevailed. The United States eventually took just 33,000 refugees.[27]

The European Union split on the matter too. Countries from the Nordic region like Sweden and countries in Eastern Europe like Hungary objected. Bulgaria built a wall. Others flatly refused to take the refugees.

And in Germany itself, the highly controversial decision produced a backlash that helped the AfD find its political footing. Anxiety worsened in November 2015 after a coordinated terrorist attack across Paris by Islamist extremists killed 130. Officials discovered that at least one terrorist had traveled from Syria to Europe, masquerading as a refugee in order to avoid suspicion. Outrage soared. When on New Year's Eve in 2016 a group of revelers was attacked in Cologne by men who had gained asylum, the narrative was sealed: Migrants became the "other" that populists needed to make their appeal complete.

Hungary and Poland Again

In 2012, Rice journeyed back to Eastern Europe to join in ceremonies honoring Ronald Reagan's role in the liberation of the former Soviet bloc. Sitting in Viktor Orbán's ornate office in 2012, the American delegation, including Rice, listened with concern as the Hungarian president dismissed questions about his treatment of his political opposition. "I cannot help it if the opposition is weak and divided," he told Rice and her colleagues. "I have to do what is best for the country."

Orbán had once been the darling of the international community. When he was elected for the first time in 1998, he became the youngest prime minister in Hungarian history, and he was known as a strong proponent of his country's integration into NATO (which Hungary

joined in 1999) and the EU (which Hungary joined in 2004). He champ-
pioned austerity programs that led to lower inflation and acclaim from
free market economists. His Fidesz-Hungarian Civic Party called itself
"center-right."[28]

The government started to emphasize ethnic Hungarian identity, its
ties to ethnic Hungarians living in Romania, Slovakia, Ukraine, Serbia,
Croatia, and Slovenia. It voiced a not too subtle defense of the purity of
Hungarian bloodlines and the need to "defend" their rights wherever they
lived. Still, Hungary seemed well on its way to consolidated democracy.

In October 2008, already weakened by political scandals, Hungary
was hit with the full weight of the financial crisis. The value of its currency plummeted. The IMF, the EU, and the World Bank had to cobble
together a rescue package worth 20 billion euros.

The population felt the brunt of the collapse. In 2009, a Bloomberg
poll found that only 56 percent of Hungarians supported democracy.
Support for capitalism, at 80 percent before the crisis, was down to 46
percent.[29]

Viktor Orbán remade himself into a right-wing populist. His refashioned party, called Fidesz, returned to power in 2010 promising jobs and
law and order, with a huge majority in the Hungarian parliament. The
anti-Semitic and hypernationalist Jobbik party won more than 10 percent
of the seats.[30]

With his supermajority in parliament, Orbán pushed through laws
that burdened foreign investment and allowed the government to punish
news organizations for stories regarded as unbalanced or insulting or offensive to public morality. Amid the criticism, particularly within the European Union, some compared him to Vladimir Putin.[31] Undeterred, in 2011
the Hungarian parliament passed a new constitution that strengthened the
executive and limited freedom of expression and movement.

For the next two years, Orbán played a cat-and-mouse game with the
EU and the international community. Under intense criticism, Hungary
would make changes to the controversial laws, but not substantial enough
to undermine the prime minister's growing power. Hungary's weak but
still active democratic institutions tried to fight back.

Then, in 2014, elections reaffirmed Orbán and Fidesz's grip on the
country, granting the ruling party a supermajority once again. Two

months later, Orbán made clear that he was done with liberal democracy.[32] He announced his plan to turn Hungary into an "illiberal state" because liberal democracy had failed. He quoted "an internationally recognized analyst" as saying that "the strength of American soft power is in decline and liberal values today embody corruption, sex and violence, and as such discredit America and American modernization." He went on to say, "We must break with liberal principles and methods of social organization.... We are constructing in Hungary an illiberal state.... It does not reject the fundamental principles of liberalism such as freedom, and I could list a few more, but it does not make this ideology the central element of state organization.... The stars of the international analysts today are Singapore, China, India, Russia and Turkey."[33]

Orbán found a bigger megaphone, heard outside of Hungary, with his opposition to the European Union's response to the Syrian migrant crisis. Throughout the summer of 2015, he found ways—big and small, symbolic and real—to establish his antimigrant credentials. In July, Hungary began construction of a razor-wire fence along the Serbian-Hungary border. In September, reacting to Merkel's plan, Orbán called the migration crisis a "German problem," not a Hungarian one.[34] And though government measures had slowed asylum seekers to a crawl, the state of emergency was extended. In April 2018, Fidesz and Orbán won enough support to again secure two-thirds of the seats in the parliament for the prime minister's third consecutive term in office.

* * *

Not all of Eastern Europe is infected by Hungarian "contagion." Certainly in Poland, the rise of the Law and Justice Party—a Euroskeptic, anti-immigrant movement—bears some similarities to the Hungarian case. But the situation in Warsaw is not identical.

The popularity of Law and Justice comes from still another source of Euroskepticism in the East. When Andrzej Duda, a forty-three-year-old candidate from Law and Justice, defeated incumbent president Bronisław Komorowski, pundits were shocked. The Civic Platform that had controlled the government since 2007 had led Poland through a period of prosperity and stability. Poland was one of the few states in the European Union to avoid the effects of the global financial crisis. GDP grew at a rate of 3.5 percent between 2008 and 2012.[35] While unemployment spiked in 2008 for most countries, Poland saw its unemployment figures drop to single digits for the first time since 1990.[36]

Still, Law and Justice went on to win a majority in the Polish legislative elections and immediately touched off a constitutional crisis over the independence of the judiciary.[37] Laws abridging the independence of the media followed.

Poland is, outside of its major cities, a deeply religious and conservative country. For instance, though the attempt failed, Law and Justice tried to outlaw abortion—a move that was popular in rural, heavily Catholic areas of the country but resisted in the cities. Many observers of Polish politics note the degree to which Civic Platform was seen as worldly and European—not truly Polish. This has given space for ultranationalists to rally. In 2017 on Polish Independence Day, thousands of far-right nationalists marched through Warsaw with signs saying "White Europe of brotherly nations" and "We want God," a lyric from a nationalist Polish song.[38]

But Poland is not Hungary—not yet. The opposition has continued to press its case in protests big and small. And the government has on occasion backed away from truly controversial laws. Poland is deeply pro-NATO and, ironically, it is a Polish politician, Donald Tusk, who is currently the president of the Council of Europe.

The European Union has made all the right noises about disciplining those countries that seemed destined to fall from democratic grace. Hungary has been censured by every European institution. The European Parliament voted in 2017 to start proceedings against Poland that could strip the country of its voting rights, and the European Commission in 2018 opened a new legal case against Warsaw over changes to the Supreme Court.

So far, both Budapest and Warsaw have successfully deflected these measures—sometimes by ignoring them, and in some cases by making minimal concessions to the EU. As a result, Eastern European populists who affirm their national identity and question Brussels's writ have come into power in Hungary, Poland, and the Czech Republic.[39] In every case they are chipping away at the foundations of democratic institutions, establishing executive power at the expense of parliaments; challenging press freedom; and stoking anti-immigrant fever among their populations.

Young democracies are vulnerable to rollback of the institutional arrangements that protect freedom. That vulnerability is to be expected in democracies that are not well consolidated. The first decades of democracy often produce a tug-of-war between a too strong executive and counterweights to it. Populists who are determined to go "directly to the people" rather than through their elected representatives, the media, or civil society thrive in those circumstances.

What is surprising, and more disturbing, is the echo of this state of affairs in *consolidated* democracies where Europe—once thought to be the answer—has for many become part of the problem. Hungary and Poland—young democracies—were canaries in the coal mines about populism. But one of the most remarkable circumstances emerged in Germany, where so much of our story began.

* * *

In 1990, with a unified Germany, hopes ran high that the integration of the parts—separated by forty-five years of economic, political, and social division—would be achieved, if not seamlessly, at least successfully. By most metrics, it was. But the eastern part of the country has been fertile ground for populists—this time in the form of the AfD, the Alternative for Germany.

The former East Germany is statistically not all that different from the West in absolute terms (Table 2).

Table 2. Socioeconomic Differences Across East and West Germany[40]

Statistic	East Germany	West Germany
Population change, 1990–2017	−11.0%	+8.2%
Single-parent homeownership (2017)	24.9%	17.5%
Average monthly consumer spending (2016)	€ 2,078	€ 2,587
Income spent on consumption (2017)	53.3%	53.6%
Poverty rate (2007)	12.9%	19.5%
Poverty rate (2017)	17.8%	15.3%
Economic growth (2017)	1.9%	2.3%

These measures do not fully capture the sense of being looked down upon that is still prevalent in the eastern part of the country. The chancellor is from the east. But eastern Germans are 20 percent of the population and under 5 percent of the elite in politics, business, science, and media. None of the thirty leading companies listed in the German share index have an eastern German boss. Almost all professors of sociology or political science are originally from the west—even in universities in Leipzig or Dresden. And there were fewer leaders of eastern German origin in the five eastern German state governments in 2016 than in 2004.[41]

And though statistically the population in the east is doing well, there is nostalgia for the old days. People have a tendency to remember what is good—guaranteed incomes and housing, even if they were substandard, for instance. They forget the knock of the secret police at night.

Der Spiegel ran a series of vignettes about this phenomenon in 2017. The experiences of Tino Chrupalla, a painter-decorator from Weisswasser, in eastern Germany, captured a prevailing mood:

When 42-year-old Chrupalla talks, he comes across as friendly, open, frank. He waxes lyrical about Weisswasser's golden years in East Germany, when people worked in the lignite mines and the glassworks, and lived in ultra-modern high-rises.

"I had a lovely childhood," he says. "Very nice, very safe." Doors were left unlocked in the countryside, there were few break-ins and when they did happen, the perpetrators were soon apprehended by the East German police. "My parents never had to worry about where I was playing."

Once the Berlin Wall had fallen, Helmut Kohl—the CDU chancellor who went down in history as the father of reunification—became his new idol. He joined the Junge Union, the youth wing of the CDU, and he and his friend and fellow party member Michael Kretschmer paid a visit to the chancellor. Chrupalla trained to be a housepainter and went on to set up his own business. His company thrived, he got married—reunification brought him nothing but good fortune.

But he felt increasingly alienated from Germany. Thousands of jobs were lost. Half the inhabitants of Weisswasser moved away. Bus routes in the surrounding countryside were cancelled. Stores and schools in local villages were closed. And gangs from Eastern Europe started crossing the open border to steal cars.

The region was changing, and so was Germany. The financial crisis, the euro crisis, the refugee crisis and then same-sex marriage. "No one ever asked us what we thought," says Chrupalla. He took part in the anti-Islam, far-right Pegida demonstrations in Dresden and eventually joined the AfD. Then he stood for election as a member of the German parliament.[42]

Chrupalla won his election in 2017 along with several other AfD candidates.

Whether in Germany or Poland or Hungary, the rise of the populists has called into question one of the key assumptions underpinning the European Union—that national identity could be subsumed in a common European one. For elites, ending nationalism was a positive notion, burying the scars of hundreds of years of war. By granting authority over national affairs to Brussels and Strasbourg, many thought politics was evolving toward a kind of second Enlightenment where national boundaries would mean little.

The French president articulated this hopeful spirit in a speech to the European Parliament warning against a "European civil war." "Our [European] parliament," he said, "is a European miracle. Peacefully bringing together the elected representatives of the peoples of Europe to discuss their differences, empowered by and conscious of their history and that which has sometimes divided them, is unique in the world. We have kept this miracle alive for 70 years."[43]

The United States of Europe That Never Was

As the historic "Brexit" vote in the UK approached, European politicians expressed confidence that the British people would do the right thing. That "right thing" was clear to them—"Remain" would win. For a while, polling data supported their optimism, showing margins that were close but comfortable in favor of Britain's membership in the European Union.[44]

The polls, the pundits, and the politicians were wrong. The British people rejected continued membership in the European Union narrowly but forcefully. Brexit was a reality.

The first reaction of European elites was disbelief, then anger at British leaders and ridicule toward the British people, and finally, a realization that the unthinkable had indeed happened. As of this writing, the most common explanation among European elites is that the British people were somehow duped—they didn't understand what they were voting for, and didn't understand the consequences. Had they been fully competent, the citizens of the UK would most certainly have chosen Europe.[45]

Practically every Briton now knows that the intricacies of remaining or leaving were not fully understood. But that does not explain why 51.9 percent of British citizens decided that they would be better off outside the European Union than in it.[46]

To be sure, Britain had always had a somewhat attenuated relationship with the Union. It was not among the original members of the institution and never joined the Eurozone. And skepticism had always characterized part of the British political spectrum—particularly among elements of the Conservative Party. The long-standing political divisions within the party led David Cameron to promise a referendum in an effort to end or at least quell the debate. This was a monumental mistake—though, to be fair, few thought that it would result in "Leave."[47]

The road to European integration had never been easy. In France, Ireland, and Denmark, the governments held national referenda on the Maastricht Treaty. It passed in all three, although the vote margin was close and it took two tries in Denmark. The vote was so tight in France that it came to be known as the "*petit oui*."[48] Maastricht went into effect.

The Treaty of Amsterdam, passed five years later, introduced additional institutional reforms without much difficulty. It changed voting rules in the European Parliament and Council of Ministers. Member states agreed to coordinate their approach to asylum and immigration issues and relax border checks for members of the Schengen Area.[49]

But the institutions were less consequential in reality than on paper. The Council of Europe sought to coordinate the behavior of sovereign states by gathering leaders together regularly to forge common policies.

Not surprisingly, the outcomes were often least-common-denominator compromises: Integration moved forward at a snail's pace.

The European Parliament and European Court of Justice competed for influence with their national counterparts—rarely gaining additional authority in the process. The gap between sovereign decision making and European policy was thus filled by the European Commission. It sat permanently in Brussels with approximately thirty-two thousand bureaucrats and twenty-one commissioners with competencies covering everything from trade to environmental standards to social policy.[50]

Unlike the other bodies, though, the Commission was not elected by the people—its president picks individuals on the basis of outside recommendations and then presents the entire Commission to the European Parliament for blanket approval. The "unelected bureaucrats," as they were sometimes derisively called, were to many the face of the united Europe. If nothing else, the Commission was by far the most active body in the firmament of European institutions.

In 2014, Jean-Claude Juncker took over as president of the European Commission and announced his plans for the EC to play a more activist role in EU political affairs. It was likely ill-timed, because the EC already had a reputation for overreach. As an example of the kind of minor incident that gets headlines, public anger about an edict to ban refillable olive oil bottles in restaurants (ostensibly to protect customers against mislabeled olive oil), caused the Commission to withdraw the order.[51] Juncker himself never stood for European election and had nothing like the personal prestige or informal authority that his long-ago predecessor, Delors, had enjoyed.

Is this a "democratic deficit"? National parliaments cannot hold politicians operating at the EU executive level accountable. Experts argue about whether the European Parliament has enough authority to check the power and meaningfully oversee the work of the Commission.[52] On big issues, like the migrant crisis, anger directed at the EC is intense.

It is not that European populations fail to see some of the positive elements of European integration. Support for the EU peaked in 1991, but people know that they have enjoyed benefits from it. Not surprisingly, support has been lowest at times of crisis, during the start of the American invasion of Iraq in 2003, the global financial crisis in 2008, and the Euro-zone debt crisis in 2011.[53]

European leaders tried, through constitutional referenda, to put the organization on a firmer, more democratic footing. But the process was unwieldy and constitutional reform proved difficult. In 2004, France and the Netherlands failed to ratify a revised EU Constitution.[54] Four years later, a second attempt succeeded (mostly through parliamentary action, not popular referenda), bringing into force the Lisbon Treaty in 2009.

The Lisbon Treaty created a presidency (not to be confused with the presidency of the Commission) with a two-year term. The office was to be occupied by a politician who did not represent a sovereign member. Prior to Lisbon, the presidency rotated every six months among the members of the Council. Sometimes the post was held by the German chancellor or the French president and carried weight—sometimes it was held by the head of government of a small country with little influence. This change was meant to strengthen the office and give it real power.

But interestingly, when given a chance to elect a president with gravitas, the European Union passed over "big names" and settled on Herman Van Rompuy. When the global financial and Eurozone troubles plunged the continent into crisis, it was sovereign heads of state that mattered—Merkel, Sarkozy, Brown, and Cameron.

The European Union received the Nobel Peace Prize for having overcome centuries of war on the continent. That it had done. But it was not and would not become a United States of Europe.

The process of deepening was hard enough, but it came simultaneously with the decision to broaden as well. In a relatively brief period of ten years, thirteen new members joined the European Union.[55] In the case of the East European states, the EU had been a north star for democracy. As we observed in chapter 6, the accession agreements with detailed requirements for economic, civic, and military reform undeniably accelerated positive institutional trends in the former communist states.

But broadening and deepening the EU at the same time stressed new institutions and new relationships between populations. As noted above, the "borderless" labor policies produced massive immigrant flows from the East to the West, as people sought good jobs in more prosperous countries.

The European passport became a highly valued asset.[56] And populations seemed to mix relatively easily until the financial crisis produced tensions between native and immigrant labor: a harbinger of deeper tensions when the migrants were no longer European, but from the troubled Middle East.

* * *

In choosing a national anthem for a supranational state, the messaging can be a bit tricky. Since the day of German unity in 1990, when the Berlin Philharmonic performed the great "Ode to Joy" from Beethoven's Ninth Symphony, that masterwork has become the EU's anthem. It is entitled "All Men Become Brothers (After Schiller and Beethoven)."

As the first verse croons:

> *O friends, no more of these sounds!*
> *Let us sing more cheerful songs,*
> *More songs full of joy!*
> *Joy!*
> *Joy!*
> *Joy, bright spark of divinity,*
> *Daughter of Elysium,*
> *Fire-inspired we tread*
> *Within thy sanctuary.*
> *Thy magic power re-unites*
> *All that custom has divided,*
> *All men become brothers,*
> *Under the sway of thy gentle wings.*

Europe thirty years later does not look like one in which all men have become brothers.

For the most part, people do not reject European identity. It is just that they feel more strongly about their national one. Since 1994, individuals have been less likely to self-identify as European and more likely to identify solely with their own nationality.[57]

The sociologist Edward Lawler observes that individuals tend to favor identifying with smaller groups over larger ones due to the "proximal" rule—their greater influence over the smaller group.[58] In the more integrated Europe, people identify more deeply with a more proximate social group (the nation-state).

But we are not trashing the idea of a European identity. Some five decades ago another social scientist, Ronald Inglehart, argued that people could hold both a national and a European identity. The latter would grow with education and the appeal of cosmopolitanism—and the acceptance of post-materialist values.[59] In a series of surveys conducted in 1963, he showed that as levels of education went up, so too did the identification with Europeanism.

Both, it turns out, might have been right. Attitudes vary, class and political orientation matter. Anyone who spends much time around the elites of the continent can attest to their devotion to a "European identity." They travel widely, speak several languages, and seem always to be off to a meeting of one kind or another of a European body.

But a significant part of the population undeniably sense that decisions that affect their lives have been taken out of their hands. For them, the "democratic deficit" can be specific and visceral: Why should policymakers from Germany make decisions for individuals living in Greece? People no longer trust the elites who gave them the financial crisis and the migrant mess.

For many, Europe has come to represent the epitome of that loss of control—Brussels is a long way away. Nationalism is not the problem—it is their protection.

We do not know how Brexit will work out. But one thing is certain: Britain will never feel like or really be a full partner in Europe again, at least for a long time. We do not know whether populists will continue to win elections or whether they will just force centrist politicians to take more populist stands.

Immediately after Brexit, the election of Emmanuel Macron in France was greeted with relief and enthusiasm. After all, here was a politician who was an avowed Europhile and believed deeply in the whole globalist project. He seemed poised to lead and fill the void left by exhaustion in German politics, division in Britain, and American disinterest.

Macron had big ideas like a French-German defense force as a backstop should the United States withdraw. At home, he championed a rapid response to climate change, with a tax on those who drove carbon-dioxide-spewing automobiles into the center of Paris. Who were those people? They were workers who had been forced to live far outside the city by high housing prices. They were the ones who had to drive into the middle of Paris. The elites—if they wanted to—already lived there.

Within weeks yellow vests clogged the main thoroughfares of the capital. Macron was caught off guard and eventually retreated, but the damage had been done. There was no better example of how out of touch elites were with the concerns of common people. Like their fellow citizens in Britain, Italy, Germany, and beyond, the French protesters were angry and looking for someone to blame. The populists had answers for them: Blame the immigrants; blame the big banks; blame your clueless leaders and elites; blame the "other." So far, European elites have failed to give a good retort to that litany.

America: The Politics of "Do You Hear Me Now?"

The election of Donald Trump in 2016 was born of many of the same frustrations that propelled populists to prominence in Europe. For the first time in their history, the American people elected a man whose first job in government was president of the United States.

The loss of confidence in American institutions has been accelerating for some time now. In 2018, distrust of Congress hit a new high, with 46 percent indicating little trust compared to 11 percent with a great deal of trust. Other public opinion polls find the popularity of Congress so low that even cockroaches, Genghis Khan, and traffic jams are viewed more favorably than the legislature.[60]

* * *

Americans had not been immune to class identification, but it was never as significant as in Europe. The American "myth" was one of upward mobility through education and hard work. If you were not rich, your children might be. Wealth was not something to provoke jealousy—it was something to motivate you to do better. And there was a strong enough middle class with enough stories of people who climbed the ladder to sustain the idea. The Horatio Alger ideal was not uniquely American, but it was strongest here.

The financial crisis put a spotlight on failing hope. Scholars had been warning that social mobility in the United States was stalling, wages were stagnating, public education was failing, and indebted citizens were sinking. Between 1980 and 2008, the wealthiest 10 percent of households went from holding 34.6 percent of the wealth to 48.2 percent. Income growth for the bottom 80 percent of households was essentially flat between 1967 and 2008 despite growing 70.3 percent for the wealthiest 20 percent. And American debt-to-income was a staggering two-to-one ratio.[61]

American voters sought "Hope and Change" and voted across economic, social, and even racial lines for Barack Obama. The Obama campaign won nearly every income bracket. He won a majority of both high school and college graduates. White voters who had previously voted for Bush in 2000 and 2004 switched their support to Obama, flipping a number of "red" states for him, including Indiana, North Carolina, and Nevada.

* * *

The American ideal had eroded in another way too. "We the people" had in reality been rather exclusive at the beginning of the Republic: white, landowning, and male. Little by little the franchise was expanded to include others, most remarkably, perhaps, the descendants of slaves. That the U.S. Constitution would be the means for doing so would seem to be a triumph for democratic institutions.[62] The organizing principle remained access to opportunity—not to outcomes.

Over time and perhaps predictably, the line between the two would start to blur. How could one measure access to opportunity for people who were descendants of the oppressed? What about pay gaps for women that were putatively related to job title but might really have been a tautology? Women occupied lower-paying jobs, which were lower-paying because they were occupied principally by women. How could one have a legally recognized, state-sanctioned status called marriage and deny it to two men with equal rights as citizens?

As people sought equal justice, the idea of a common American identity gave way to multiple ones—each with its own narrative and its own grievances. American diversity became the organizing principle. Frank Fukuyama identifies the problem in his excellent study: "Diversity cannot be the basis for identity in and of itself; it is like saying that our identity is to have no identity; or rather, that we should get used to our having nothing in common and emphasize our narrow ethnic or racial identities instead."[63]

Two decades ago, the philosopher Richard Rorty warned that a focus on certain identity groups would ultimately lead everyone to seek their own narrow one. After World War II, the fight for economic justice became the fight for social justice. The "reformist left"—which had championed the rights of unskilled labor for decades—was now the "cultural left." Multiculturalism and diversity became a rallying cry for the left, raising attention to key civil rights issues for these groups. However, this shift had two consequences.

First, politicians began to ignore other characteristics of late-stage capitalism in America—inescapable poverty, stagnant wages, and unequal access to educational opportunities—in favor of the diversity narrative. Economic injustices festered, aggravating wealth inequalities between the haves and the have-nots. Resentment grew as "members of labor unions, and unorganized unskilled workers, will sooner or later realize that their government is not even trying to prevent wages from sinking or to prevent jobs from being exported." The system did not have their back. The politicians who had previously been their greatest advocate had moved on.

Second, it fractured the left. Promoting multiculturalism in the short term produced a lot of good. It gave a voice to communities who had been marginalized for decades: women, African Americans, LGBTQ people. But it also had the unintended effect of encouraging factionalization as individuals tried to define and find their own identity groups as part of these cultural debates.

As in Europe, the push for multiculturalism and integration boomeranged. The coalition for multiculturalism grew too big; everyone had their own identity and set of grievances they needed to address. When the coalition grew too big, it fractured into smaller groups. Individuals sought out more proximal groups based on similar identities. Attempts to push diversity started to backfire. And the larger gains the cultural left hoped to achieve ended up being reversed. Affirmative action, political correctness, and university safe spaces—not to mention the "war on Christmas"—did indeed become exhibits of what a focus on diversity had wrought. "All the sadism which the academic Left has tried to make unacceptable to its students," Rorty predicted twenty years ago, "will come flooding back. All the resentment which badly educated Americans feel about having their manners dictated to them by college graduates will find an outlet."

Rorty predicted that it would not be long before those who had been left out of the identity sweepstakes would seek to join it.[64] When unskilled (white) labor found itself abandoned, it organized itself partially under the banner of white nationalism.

This shift, however inadvertent, undermined trust in our political institutions. Reform movements believed that economic injustices had to be corrected "by using the institutions of constitutional democracy"—by working within the system. Their efforts propelled massive reforms.

However, when social justice movements emerged in earnest in the 1960s, many rejected this premise. The system was too corrupt and unjust to address their grievances. Change could only come about by working outside the system, by rejecting the one currently in place.[65] In other words, revolution.

* * *

Every action does provoke a reaction, and so it has been with identity politics.[66] In 2016, those who sought to define American identity by reference to a time past found their voice. For many, it was the "dominant" group or the "majority" that no longer had representation. That, given America's history, can be a terrifying conclusion. It has helped to produce torchlit marches in Charlottesville and vicious assertions of "white nationalism." Most Americans do not identify with these extremes. But some do—and that has added to the sense that America's long road to justice has taken a wrong turn.

Moreover, it has been almost comical to watch the American

scholarly and journalistic elite suddenly discover "common people." Some national commentators sounded a bit like anthropologists studying remote tribes—trying to glean insights from *Hillbilly Elegy* and road trips to the South to see what "those people believe." The election of 2016 set off alarm bells about American unity. It had been eroding for some time.

The American creed is still alive. The next generation remains optimistic about the future. In 2018 a national essay contest asked teenagers to describe what they saw as America's creed and vision for the future. One young man in Oakland, California, wrote, "Being American is looking at your situation and being able to say, 'It might not be good now, it might not be good for a while, but I'm going to work hard enough so that it can be good for me and hopefully the next generation.'" Another young woman in Chicago wrote, "Being American means loving this country so much that you know it's not in the place where it needs to be. You need to do whatever you can to make sure it reaches its fullest potential."[67]

Still, the divide has to be addressed. There is a deepening belief that elites—in their universities, movie studios, and coastal big cities—have forgotten and even despise large parts of the population. The cultural divide and the gulf between elites and "ordinary" people does not have an easy or ready solution even though it is urgently in need of one. In the meantime, the populists of America, like those in Europe, will continue to define the problem and offer their own, explosive answers.

From the Peace Dividend to Perpetual War

In June 2001, President George W. Bush first met with Russian president Vladimir Putin in the sixteenth-century castle of Brdo, outside the city of Ljubljana in Slovenia. It was a kind of summit of the successor generation. President Bush had of course seen the historic events of his father's administration from close up. Rice now had Scowcroft's old job.

Putin, the former KGB colonel in Dresden, had built a new career and risen to the apex. Rice had met Putin before, for the first time back in 1992, when Putin was just starting on his new path, as an aide to the reformist mayor of St. Petersburg.

This June 2001 Bush-Putin meeting was before the 9/11 attacks. The agenda was still very much molded by the legacies of 1988–92. There were more discussions about how to further control or reduce nuclear arms.

At that time, there were no great issues in European security to discuss. Although it is tempting to see a straight line from the issues of the 1990s to the problems at the end of the 2000s, this is a fallacy of hindsight. As we will explain, Putin adjusted his views in some very important ways during the course of the 2000s.

Of course, Putin—like many other Russians—had very deep feelings about his country's loss of stature and national pride. His views about the Soviet Union were mixed, but his Russian patriotism was very strong. As he and others analyzed what had happened to their country, they sometimes cast blame in many directions—including at former Soviet leaders, for instance sometimes at Gorbachev. The enlargement of NATO up to that point was one of the issues that rankled. But in June 2001 it was not a central issue. The anger over the 1999 NATO intervention in Kosovo was much sharper and more recent.

In June 2001, Putin was open for a fresh start with this American president. His approach to the talks was serious, thoughtful, and businesslike. He did not bother much about recriminations or rehashing of issues of the past. As for George W. Bush, he came to the talks prepared to establish a genuine partnership, to treat Putin exactly as the Russian leader wanted and expected to be treated—as a fellow leader of one of the world's great powers.

* * *

Bush did not foresee that America was about to enter a period of perpetual war. The Clinton administration had continued the defense cutbacks that George H. W. Bush had begun. The U.S. defense budget fell 36 percent between 1985 and 1998.[68] Active-duty military personnel shrunk 22 percent between 1993 and 2000.[69] George W. Bush had campaigned on a promise to rebuild the American military, saying that the cuts had gone too far. But he had entered his office determined to focus mainly on domestic issues.

The great new feature of American national security since 1991 was a unique U.S. role in trying to enforce essential global norms of international safety. As the Cold War progressed, decade after decade, hardly anyone had expected that the UN would ever come close to living up to the original hopes that its Security Council would become an effective center for enforcing international law or norms against the world's outlaws. The institution was content to occasionally authorize deployment of unarmed or very lightly armed forces to supervise cease-fires, but not to fight.

As we explained in chapter 6, the "vector" set by the Iraq crisis of 1990–91 dramatically changed that pattern. Before the Iraq crisis of 1990, other than Korea in 1950, an unusual peacekeeping operation in Congo in the early 1960s, and a small action to enforce economic sanctions against Rhodesia (in 1966), the UN had not authorized any major military operations. After the Iraq crisis, the UN authorized military operations twenty-three times between 1991 and 2007. Many of these were small and short-lived, but some were not.[70]

Such UN action requires great power consensus. Such actions are therefore selective. Most law enforcement is selective, international law enforcement most selective of all, especially since international law itself has such a varied and debated status.

In some ways, the Iraq case of 1990–91 was sui generis, a uniquely brazen challenge of international aggression. But it invited imitation in situations not nearly as clear-cut and in those where the leaders and citizens of the major powers were not nearly as committed to a common cause.

Still, in the ten years since 1991, one constant—with considerable global support—was a global enforcement role against outlaw countries trying to acquire weapons of mass destruction. For ten years, the United States concentrated a great deal of its attention on the same small group of most worrisome countries—Iraq, North Korea, and Iran—with occasional cameo appearances by nations like Pakistan and Libya.

* * *

So when Bush met Putin, and one of their topics was the future of ballistic missile defenses, Bush was mindful of this global enforcement mission. He was anxious to explain why the United States hoped that both countries could now step away from the 1972 treaty banning such weapons. He assured Putin, truthfully, that the defenses were not aimed at Moscow—they were to deal with the North Koreas of the world.

"I don't like it," Putin told him, "but I don't intend to jump up and down either."

Indeed, they did seamlessly handle this issue. When the United States withdrew in December 2001, the announcement was coordinated with Moscow, which, as promised, did not jump up and down. A few months later, the two leaders then signed a new treaty, the Moscow Treaty, which cut their offensive nuclear forces down even further.

Like Bush, Putin was also worried about wider issues. He wanted to talk about Pakistan and Saudi Arabia and their support for Islamic radicals who formed the backbone of groups like Al Qaeda. This was a problem that, in June 2001, Bush and Rice were following too.

Rice, sitting in that meeting with Putin, understood more fully that day a conversation with the Saudi minister of the interior she had had back in 1999. "We offered the Russians money to help with the development of the Caucasus," the Saudi had said. "They turned us down and we said fine—get your money someplace else."[71] What had bothered the Russians was that they thought the Saudi money would build mosques and madrassas in the Islamic south of their country. Pointing to the radicalization of Pakistan after the Afghan war, Putin explained in no uncertain terms that this was the biggest security threat from his point of view. America, he said, had not done enough to address the danger.

On September 11, 2001, Putin could well have said, "I told you so." But he didn't. Instead he offered partnership.[72]

The day after 9/11, George W. Bush and Vladimir Putin had an extraordinary conversation about the task at hand. They created a quite remarkable basis for intelligence sharing and law enforcement cooperation. They sponsored the Proliferation Security Initiative to interdict suspicious cargo destined for nuclear proliferators or terrorists. They sponsored legislation on terrorist financing in the UN Security Council.

As the United States led an offensive to topple the Taliban regime in Afghanistan and hunt Al Qaeda, Bush and Putin were again together, in

Shanghai, when Kabul fell to American forces and their Afghan allies. The Russians had been extremely helpful in providing war materiel to the Afghan fighters in the north with whom they had long been associated.

Bush consulted Putin on whether to allow the Afghan fighters to enter the city and pursue the Taliban. Putin thought it better that they not, given the ethnic makeup of the liberating force (it was more Tajik and Uzbek than Pashtun). They could just "invest" or surround the city until the Taliban surrendered. The issue ended up being moot, since the Afghan forces took matters into their own hands and marched straight for the presidential palace. Nonetheless, given the past history there, it was a remarkable sight to see the Russian and American presidents plot strategy for Afghanistan.

Putin knew exactly what he wanted from the partnership: He wanted support from Washington for his struggle against terrorists in the south of the country. This was difficult for President Bush because Russia's terrorism problem was wrapped up in the Chechen war.

Al Qaeda had embedded itself with local Chechen separatists during the Second Chechen War, which had begun in 1999 and expanded in the intervening years. Russia's brutality in the Caucasus made it an uncomfortable partner for the United States.

Sometimes, though, Bush did side with Moscow. For instance, after a terrorist attack on a kindergarten and elementary school in Beslan in 2004, he said unequivocally that it was an act of terrorism and he tied it to America's own experience. Putin told him later that he greatly appreciated that show of support at a time of great sadness for the Russian people.

The Chechen population as a whole did not deserve the brutal, often horrifying, treatment that Russia perpetrated on them. But the Chechen leadership had undeniably fallen in with bad company. The links between the Chechen rebels and Al Qaeda were close.[73] In fact, when U.S. and Afghan forces liberated the north of Afghanistan, numerous Chechens were there—along with many Pakistanis, several other foreign nationals, an Australian, and an American. The lead 9/11 terrorists who attacked America, including Mohamed Atta, had initially been recruited and journeyed from their homes in Germany to Afghanistan during 1999 in order to fight Russia in Chechnya.[74]

In retrospect, it is therefore easy to see how Putin believed he had found a new basis for a strategic relationship between the United States and Russia. It was a close affiliation and played to Russia's strengths—military and intelligence prowess.

The partnership came at the right time for the United States too. September 11 was the earthquake that fundamentally changed America's concept of its security. The country had not been attacked on its home territory since the War of 1812 (Pearl Harbor was an attack on a military base located on a territory that was not yet an American state). The United States was suddenly at war in a way that its leaders had not imagined.

In time, the ad hoc mechanisms developed in the days after 9/11 would mature into institutions for internal security: the Homeland Security Department; a military command for the continental United States; the director of national intelligence; a National Counterterrorism Center; and the position of homeland security adviser for each state.[75]

America's national security apparatus was quickly remade into one that accounted for both internal and external threats. In his address to the Congress on September 20, President Bush told the country to prepare for a long war. "Our nation, this generation, will lift the dark threat of violence from our people and our future. We will rally the world to this cause by our efforts, by our courage. We will not tire, we will not falter and we will not fail."[76]

* * *

The British prime minister, Tony Blair, was in the gallery that night at the U.S. Capitol. He told the president that he had come to stand by the United States as it had stood by Britain in World War II.

Blair was not alone in standing by the United States. A few days before, NATO had invoked Article V (an attack upon one is an attack upon all) for the first time in its history in support of the United States. When the member states accepted that commitment in 1949, no one dreamt that it would be triggered on behalf of the United States, instead of the other way around.

In so many ways, 9/11 put an exclamation point on the end of an era in which America was preoccupied with the defense of others as the outer shield of its own security. Now every American president's first security concern would be the defense of the homeland, and in that work Russia would be a capable and willing partner in the fight against terrorism. The NATO transformation, envisioned in 1990 and 1991, took the next step in its out-of-area evolution. It sent forces to help with the global enforcement mission, to fight terrorists in Afghanistan and beyond.

When NATO invoked Article V, member states were anxious to join in the fight alongside the United States in Afghanistan. Rice has written that this was a seminal moment that did not work out as it should have. "I felt that we left the Alliance dressed up with nowhere to go."[77]

The problem for the alliance was one of capability. Most of the armed forces were not mobile, let alone flexible enough to take on a role in the remote mountains of Afghanistan. September 11 and Afghanistan brought new urgency to the task of transformation. Looking back, the alliance did a great deal. Operation Eagle Assist provided defensive air support over the United States, with allied countries flying sorties over U.S. airspace. In October 2001, Operation Active Endeavour sent naval forces to patrol the eastern Mediterranean and interdict shipping vessels suspected of terrorist activity.

Then, at the Rome summit in May 2002, leaders committed the alliance to "operate when and where necessary to fight terrorism." This broadened NATO's mandate, enabling it to participate in the International Security Assistance Force in Afghanistan. Eventually, NATO would lead that mission, with twenty-eight countries participating in missions ranging from active combat to humanitarian and development support. When the alliance met in Prague six months later, NATO adopted several new defense measures, the most important being a commitment to create a rapid response force to give the alliance the kind of flexibility that had sidelined it in the weeks after September 11. There was a great sense of pride in the transformed nature of the alliance, which had seemingly found its footing and a crystalline example of new purpose.

* * *

But there was no quick and evident way out of Afghanistan, and America's response to the new security environment did not end with Afghanistan.

The older problem of Iraq had come back. In 1996 and 1997 the old 1991 armistice with Iraq had broken down, as had the disarmament inspection regime there. Intelligence agencies in the United States and Europe became suspicious about Iraqi plans. In December 1998, the Clinton administration launched a small war, a massive air operation, against Iraq called Operation Desert Fox. The results were, at best, inconclusive. And then came 9/11.

In 2002, President George W. Bush decided to seek UN endorsement for action again against Iraq, to insist on the return of effective inspections and enforcement of some of the old armistice terms. In November 2002, the UN Security Council joined together to insist on the return of the inspectors.

But in February 2003, when Iraq appeared to be frustrating the inspectors' work, the majority of the Security Council refused to endorse common military action and an invasion of Iraq. The United States and some of its allies went ahead, with results that are still being debated today.

Neither of us wish to use this book to go over the historical issues about the war in Iraq that began in 2003. In her memoirs of that time, Rice addresses the subject. It is a painful account. She details a great many grim moments and tragic choices about the events leading up to the war and in the years that followed. Beginning in 2005, Zelikow joined the effort to find a successful conclusion to the war.[78]

Suppose, like the majority of Americans, one regards some aspect of the war in Iraq as mistaken and tragic. The question that is relevant for this book is: What should this have meant then, or mean now, for the U.S. role in the world? Should Americans reset the basic "vector," in which the U.S. takes on heavy responsibility for enforcement of essential norms in the global system?

One answer might be that the United States should *not* have assumed this burden of enforcement in a case like Iraq. The vector should be reset. The United States should have left the Iraqi problem, and other such problems, to others to solve as best they could.

Another choice, another vector, would be that the U.S. government was right to assume the burden of addressing the concerns about Iraq. That does not mean all the other choices were also right. The United States and its allies should have done a better job of intelligence assessment. U.S. lead-ers should have made different choices in the way they handled some of the political and military issues that ensued. But an issue now is whether the basic concern was valid, and all the responsibility that goes with it.

We understand and sympathize with Americans who are weary of these burdens. There seems to be no end to war in the Middle East and Afghanistan, or watching the dangers of weapons of mass destruction and global terrorists, especially for those who have actually had to carry those burdens, either in the field or on the home front. So we present the choice.

Our view is that the responsibility has to be faced. But it is useful to go back to reflect on the defining precedent of 1991, the story we tell in chapter 6.

We should carry this burden only for the most essential norms of global safety, the kind of norms that can draw and deserve broad public and international support. And it surely does help to be able to define realistic policy designs and campaign plans with attainable objectives.

In Rice's memoir, she recounts a story about Iraq and "a silly debate inside the administration about how much authority to give the United Nations." Secretary of State Colin Powell had warned that we would need the help. "He was, of course, right," Rice recalled. "Our problem wouldn't be too much UN involvement but too little.... Eventually we would want help from everyone—a *lot* of help—to rebuild Iraq."[79]

The need for help did not end with Iraq. Beginning in 2006, when Rice was secretary of state and Zelikow was the department's counselor, it was the UN Security Council that became the essential institutional foundation for the first major campaign of economic sanctions to deal with Iran's nuclear and missile program. Also beginning in 2006, the Security Council's resolutions became, and remain, the foundation for the economic sanctions to deal with North Korea's nuclear and missile program.[80]

We are not special pleaders for the UN specifically, or any other partic-ular institution, just because it is an institution. Not every established insti-tution is still well adapted to present purposes. We do argue, though, that to have any good chance of sustaining hope for a global commonwealth of free nations, the United States may sometimes have to take on responsibil-ity for tackling big problems. When that time comes, the record—and this book is full of examples—shows that we will "want help from everyone—a *lot* of help." That implies an issue that attracts shared purposes. It implies an open mind about building and using the institutions of partnership that can organize and sustain a challenging common effort.

The Break with Russia

NATO faced another challenge in the 2000s, and that challenge did eventually become part of a confrontation with changing views in Moscow. To pick up where the NATO enlargement story left off in chapter 6, in 2007 the alliance included twenty-six members: Belgium, Bulgaria, Canada, the Czech Republic, Denmark, Estonia, France, Germany, Greece, Hungary, Iceland, Italy, Latvia, Lithuania, Luxembourg, the Netherlands, Norway, Poland, Portugal, Romania, Slovakia, Slovenia, Spain, Turkey, the United Kingdom, and the United States. The Baltic states had been incorporated in 2004, in the most recent class of new admittees. Russia was silent.

The alliance had tried to make good on the promise that Moscow could be a partner with the creation of a rejuvenated NATO-Russia Council in 2002. Although the United States was working well with Russia on other issues in 2002, the Russians were not very interested in this council. They went through the motions—sending hapless diplomats as ambassadors to NATO, some of whom spoke neither English nor French, or regarded their appointment as some kind of punishment rather than an opportunity.

Admittedly, the council meetings could be trying for the Russians. The Poles, Czechs, Romanians, and others could not resist turning the tables on their former oppressors. "Sergei, welcome to NATO," they would intone derisively.

The Russians often returned the favor. In one memorable performance, the Russian foreign minister, Sergei Lavrov, came to the council in Oslo one April, hours after Putin announced that Russia was suspending important aspects of the CFE treaty.[81] He came also to attack NATO's plans for missile defense and propose cooperation between NATO and the Russia-led Collective Security Treaty Organization (CSTO). The latter was an ad hoc organization started by Russia in 1992 to re-create the Warsaw Pact or something like it. By 2007, its members included Russia, Armenia, Azerbaijan, Belarus, Georgia, Kazakhstan, Kyrgyzstan, Tajikistan, and Uzbekistan.

Lavrov's idea didn't gain traction. Instead, he was berated for the CFE decision. He faced an alliance united on the missile defense question. He couldn't wait to get out of the room. But he did deliver one last shot. "I've heard the arguments about missile defense—the same argument, just in different languages."[82] He said something about the importance of coop-eration, but it was pretty clear he didn't mean it.

A more consequential NATO-Russia Council meeting was in the offing, though. On April 2, 2008, Vladimir Putin came to a council meeting of leaders in Bucharest. It was his valedictory as Russia's presi-dent. He was about to step down—temporarily—in favor of his hand-picked successor, Dmitri Medvedev.

He spoke in veiled and dark language about the future—including a bizarre reference to Ukraine as a "made-up country."[83] That speech was one of the warning shots, beginning in 2007, that the hoped-for relation-ship with Moscow was not going to materialize. The efforts of successive American presidents—Bush, Clinton, and Bush—were not going to suc-ceed. Russia was on a different path.

* * *

The Russians as a people have asked a question throughout their history: Who is to blame? They asked it of their tsars, their commissars, and of themselves. It has shaped the national imagination of a country that has always felt under siege in one way or another.

In recent years, certainly since 2007, Putin's answer to the question has been the United States. He blames Washington for the end to the dream of Russia fully integrated into Europe. It is not so hard to see that conclusion from his point of view.

We have seen how, after 9/11, Putin thought that he had a basis for a new strategic relationship with Washington. It would bring the two military and intelligence superpowers together to fight Islamic radicals whether they operated in Chechnya, Afghanistan, or New York.

The Russian president was greatly disappointed when he learned that the war on terrorism had another pillar, however. The Bush Doctrine was indeed "you are with us or against us."[84] But the president also believed that the long-term fight against terrorism could only be won if one of its root causes—tyranny and the damage to human dignity—could be addressed.

Bush was greatly influenced by the 2002 Arab Human Development Report, which identified three gaps as the source of underdevelopment and chaos in the Middle East: the knowledge gap, the women's empowerment gap, and the freedom gap.[85] The last of these appealed to Bush and his advisers as an antidote to the hatred that drove Al Qaeda and its kin. It would address despair and terrorism. Human beings were at their best when they were free. This was the real hope for prosperity and peace. For Bush there was no place—and there were no people—for whom tyranny, not freedom, was the answer.

For a time, it appeared that the call to freedom had been answered. The Rose Revolution in Georgia in 2003, the 2004 Orange Revolution in Ukraine, the 2005 victory of March 14 in Lebanon, and the same year's Tulip Revolution in Kyrgyzstan were evidence that people universally desired freedom.

But for Vladimir Putin, these revolutions called up other kinds of memories, of escalating revolutions in 1989, which he remembered so well and so personally. To him, these revolutions were evidence that the Bush Doctrine was a wolf in sheep's clothing. The antiterrorism message had united Moscow and Washington. This pro-freedom message divided them. The Kremlin was determined that Russia would not be next.[86]

In one of Rice's last meetings with Putin, he talked about Russia and reform. "You know us, Condi," he said. In some ways the reference to her background as a Soviet specialist was endearing—an attempt to establish common ground.[87]

"Russia has only been great when it was led by great men like Peter the Great and Alexander II," he continued. Both tsars had been reformers but by no means democrats. They had been intent on modernizing Russia in order to preserve the monarchy, not to destroy it. Another reformer, Mikhail Gorbachev, had tried to modernize the Soviet Union while preserving communist rule. That had failed too.

Having lived much of the story we tell in this book, Putin was well aware of the difficulty of changing his country without losing control. Moreover, he didn't appreciate Washington's advice about how to do it. In time, he would decide that it wasn't just advice but a plot to undermine him in an American effort to spread revolution to Russia as well.

The narrative of Washington's intentions found confirmation for Putin in NATO's consideration of a NATO Membership Action Plan for Ukraine, just before his arrival in Bucharest for that 2008 meeting.

In 2008, the motion to put Ukraine on the road to NATO membership failed. German opposition—opposition from Merkel—blocked it. Ukraine was also striving to find a way into the European Union. But for Putin, the NATO proposal itself was evidence that the United States intended to integrate Europe right up to Moscow's doorstep.

* * *

When Putin returned to power in 2012, he was even further removed from the leader who had met with George Bush in Slovenia in 2001. That Vladimir Putin had been picked by an exhausted Boris Yeltsin to pull his country out of the chaos and humiliation of the 1990s. The Russian people were tired of falling incomes, meager pensions, oligarchs who "privatized" the assets of the country, and drive-by shootings by criminal gangs on Moscow's main streets.[88]

Putin came to power promising the Russian people respect, security, and order. He delivered that—much to the relief of many even in the West. But by 2012 he no longer trusted the Russian people or anyone else. His election that year was widely regarded as fraudulent, a point of view that was made very clear by the secretary of state of the United States, Hillary Clinton. He would get his revenge, interfering in the American election of 2016 in the hope of defeating her and sowing chaos in her country.

Today, having destroyed Russia's nascent democratic institutions, Putin governs with little organized opposition. The trappings of democracy are there but the Russian president rules with his own brand of populism—one built on "autocracy, orthodoxy, and Rodina" (colloquially in Russian, the motherland)—and a cult of personality that cements his grip.

Putin does face certain perils, most importantly an economy that is under constant pressure from low oil prices and Western sanctions. Regimes like Putin's can be brittle. In recent years he has purged the hard men in the circle around him from time to time—suggesting that he is constantly aware of threats from inside his ruling apparatus.

And there are some signs that the population's patience with shortages and declining standards of living is wearing thin. As an antidote to his people's dissatisfaction, Putin offers pride in their national identity and their global influence. He speaks darkly of those who would encircle or punish Russia. The Western sanctions, he tells them, are meant to bring the great Russian people to their knees. It will not happen, he says, because he protects them and they are strong.

He reminds them that he alone has returned Russia to its rightful place in the world. Crimea is Russian again and the world can do nothing about it. Russia is a player in the Middle East again and America can do nothing about it. The Russian military—for centuries Moscow's greatest asset—is respected and feared again. He loves to burnish his image as a strongman and a military leader with frequent visits to the troops, underground bunkers, submarines, and missile launchers. Russia is great again.

There just isn't much room in his narrative for partnership with the United States—or even with Europe. That would have been a great disappointment to the men and women of 1988–92 who designed the new Europe.

Perhaps the collapse of their hopes for a friendly Russia were inevitable. Some disagree, saying that Putin's sense of encirclement could have been allayed had NATO not expanded. Others say that the breaking point was promoting European integration for Ukraine and consideration of NATO membership for Kiev. The critics are right that these were policy *choices* that successive American and European leaders made. But explicitly to leave these new liberated countries outside of Europe's democratic perimeter was another kind of choice—inconsistent with the values that had united the Atlantic alliance for decades.

The argument assumes that Russia's course toward autocracy was principally a response to the West. That view ignores the internal challenges that Russia faced and how its leaders met them. It also ignores the preferences and values of the young KGB colonel in East Germany whom we met at the beginning of this book, back in 1989.

Is America Done?

As the alliance has struggled to deal with a resurgent and hostile Russia, it has faced another unanticipated challenge. Is America done?

In August 2008, Rice was standing in the Oval Office with President Bush. He was complaining about the polls that showed how unpopular his administration had become. "I don't believe we are this unpopular," he said to Karl Rove. "What were the questions?"

Rice intervened. "Mr. President, they are tired of us. It has been war, terrorism, vigilance. They are just tired of us."

President Barack Obama came to office promising to end the long wars. Americans had had enough and it was time for others to lead. He did bring American troops home from Iraq, only to have to return them there to fight a new threat—the so-called Islamic State of Iraq and Syria (ISIS)—at the end of 2014.

The president's frustration at being unable to lift the burdens of international leadership spilled out in his last interview with Jeffrey Goldberg in the *Atlantic*. "Free riders aggravate me," Obama confided during the interview. The Libya invasion in 2011 epitomized the challenge. Obama recalled the problem where "Europe and a number of Gulf countries... are calling for action. But what has been a habit over the last several decades in these circumstances is people pushing us to act but then showing an unwillingness to put any skin in the game."

Limited airstrikes ousted Libya's aging tyrant, Muammar al-Qaddafi, but they also pushed the country into a civil war, created a refugee crisis in North Africa, and carved out ungoverned spaces for the Islamic State to move in and organize. "When I go back and I ask myself what went wrong," Obama said, "there's room for criticism, because I had more faith in the Europeans, given Libya's proximity, being invested in the follow-up."[89]

* * *

Was America tired? After seventy years of defending the free world, unifying Germany and defeating the Soviet Union, killing Osama bin Laden and pushing back Al Qaeda and ISIS—couldn't someone else do the job?

The first pillar of Donald Trump's populism was an answer to "Do you hear me now?" He told the disaffected that he alone did.

The second pillar of his populist appeal in 2016 was an affirmative answer to that searing question about America's role in the world. He came to power saying that America had been suckered.

While others built great infrastructure—roads and airports—in their countries, the United States built roads and airports in Baghdad and Afghanistan. While others created jobs for their people, Washington exported them to China and Mexico. While the United States defended Japan, Germany, South Korea, and others, they grew rich and didn't pay their fair share. His was not just a critique of specific policies—Iraq or Afghanistan—it was an all-out assault on the premise that America should lead.

Candidate Trump even used language, perhaps inadvertently, that was associated with Americans who had wanted their country to mind her own business in World War II. "America first" was a phrase—a shot—heard around the world.

For all of those who had chafed under what they sometimes called American unilateralism, it was suddenly a real possibility that America would simply stay home. That was an eventuality that the men and women who designed the new Europe, and with it the hope to build a global commonwealth of free nations, had just refused to accept—even if some worried that it might just happen.

* * *

The Olympics often present vivid metaphors for the state of international politics. The 1992 Summer Games were rich with those moments.

Germany fielded a united team. It finished in third place for total medals.

For the first time, professional basketballers were allowed in the Games. So an American "Dream Team" excelled on the court and dominated the headlines.[90] A perfect symbol of the influence and reach of the world's sole superpower.

The Soviet Union's athletes marched under the Olympic flag, not a national one. They received their medals to the playing of a song that most of them admitted they had never heard before. There was no national anthem for the new Commonwealth of Independent States.

East European athletes proudly represented countries with long histories of foreign dominance that were now enjoying a fresh start and a nationalist revival.[91] They knew where they belonged and their leaders did too: They wanted to be fully and completely integrated into the prosperous and democratic West.

* * *

They sat together, sixteen years later—Putin and Bush in the Bird's Nest observing the opening ceremonies of the 2008 Beijing Olympics. The Russians had invaded Georgia the previous day. Bush was peppering Putin with questions about it. The Russian feigned ignorance, saying that Medvedev was in charge.

As the two carried on with each other, they might have missed the spectacle below. On the field, 2,008 Chinese soldiers were rising up from below the surface, drumming in perfectly coordinated rhythm and tempo. China's moment, they seemed to signal, had arrived.

To Build a Better World

When we were young, we were fortunate to be able to play small parts in a great common enterprise to replace a divided world with a better one. This enterprise was successful.

Leaders can only do so much. But sometimes, what they can do is make choices or build structures that channel the countless streams of human endeavor in different directions, maybe more constructive.

This particular set of leaders had grown up with the Second World War. They had lived their lives as part of a "postwar" generation. Think about the shadow that adjective describes. They had lived their lives preparing for the next world war, one that could be apocalyptic. They were not nostalgic for the international system in which they had come of age. They hoped they could leave a better inheritance for their children. And they did.

Of course, it was not perfect. Their solutions engendered new problems, new issues. The world was freer, up to a point. Most superpower nuclear weapons were stored or dismantled, but not nearly all. The scale and burden of military confrontation was greatly reduced, the specter of international aggression diminished, but not nearly gone. The globalization of capital liberated flows of investment and reduced interest rates, while bringing chronic financial crises. The globalization of commerce reduced global inequality at an unprecedented rate, but within some countries—as diverse as China, Russia, and the United States—inequality grew.

We did not write this book because we want to turn the clock back to the world of 1992. The problems are different now. Institutions that handled those problems may not work as well in tackling new ones.

We wrote this book because we believe the world may be drifting toward another great systemic crisis. To prepare for such a crisis, we recall why and how we got through the last one. To redesign the global system, we recall why and how leaders designed the current one.

Principles, Partnership, and Practicality

Looking back, again and again we notice the power of this combination. At different times, across many pivotal choices, a variety of leaders were effective when they brought these elements together.

In chapter 1 we mentioned one example not well known among Americans: the partnership of the Frenchman Jacques Delors and the British official Arthur Cockfield as they created the basic design of the Single European Act in 1984 and 1985. Delors was a socialist, yet also an observant Catholic and banker. He was typecast as a bland, bespectacled "Eurocrat," yet he was well known for his emotional outbursts and his passionate regard for local communities (one reason he fought so hard over European agricultural subsidies during the knock-down and drag-out talks in concluding the Uruguay Round).

Cockfield was in and out of government, a civil servant who also became the managing director of the Boots drugstore chain in Britain, then was back in political life again. He was considered a doctrinaire advocate of privatization and a Thatcher acolyte. But he—a man born a month after his father had been killed on the Somme in 1916—became a key architect of a single European market.[1] He deeply alienated Thatcher in the process, yet attained his objects through his close partnership with Delors—who in turn was constantly working with and through Kohl and Mitterrand and their teams, along with many others.

In this one story the roles of principles and partnership are obvious—but also practicality. Delors and Cockfield related broad ideals to practical solutions, with concrete choices about agendas, trade-offs, and outcomes, even if on a breathtaking scale.

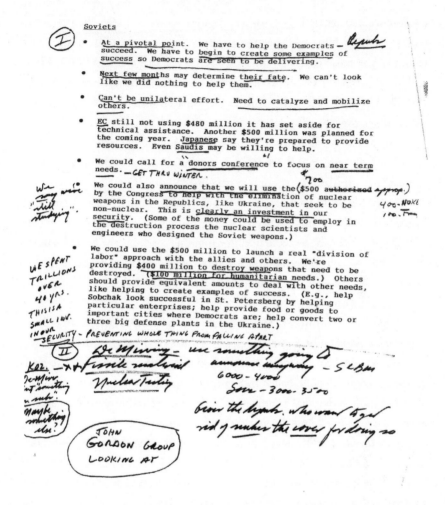

Or, for another very concrete example of what we mean, reproduced above is a copy of a Baker paper for one of his meetings. This particular meeting was on December 4, 1991, as the Soviet Union was about to break up. The paper leads with concern for the fate of would-be democrats in their new post-Soviet republics. This particular paper was drafted by Dennis Ross. The handwritten markup is Baker's, in his usual style.

The paper, and there are scores like it, opens with principles, with an immediate discussion of possible partnerships with Europeans, Japanese, or even Saudis, and then a very specific discussion of pending concrete moves and money. It blends urgent humanitarian needs with longer-term plans. It then ties back to wider institutional moves (e.g., a "donors conference" to set up a "division of labor approach") and then back to core principles. Note too that the paper is not fearful or just oriented to threats—the basic thrust is constructive. What can we help build? How can we help? For instance, Baker notes in the bottom right-hand corner that the U.S. can "Give the [former Soviet] Repub[lics] who want to get rid of <u>nukes</u> the <u>cover</u> for doing so."

This sort of work defies many of the usual bumper-sticker caricatures so beloved of opinion writers and international relations theorists. Is this "realist" or "idealist"? Is it "conservative" or "liberal"?

Since the world so wants such labels, Baker himself would struggle to make one up, trying out phrases like "principled pragmatism." When the authors of this book were in office together again at the State Department, the two of us grappled with this sort of phrasemaking exercise. We first tried out "practical idealism." Rice then fell back on "uniquely American realism."

Whatever one thinks of the catchphrases to describe American policy, some principles can be expressed clearly. At the beginning of this book we introduced two East German success stories: a young physicist at the East German Academy of Sciences and a promising KGB officer working in an East German provincial center. Catalytic choices made by others swept away East Germany and the world they had known.

A different world offered new scope for their talents. The physicist became a politician, then a minister, and then Germany's chancellor. The KGB officer became a political adviser to a Russian mayor, then an adviser to Russia's president, and then he was Russia's president.

They now represent different operating principles for public and international life. Their differences are not far from some of the basic differences that divided Orwell and Burnham during the 1940s, the clashing visions we sketched at the beginning of chapter 1.

The leaders who built a better world at the end of the 1980s and beginning of the 1990s favored open societies over closed ones. They favored freedom over tyranny. They favored a civilized world with at least some rules over a world that had none save force. They thought America and the world would be better off with a great and growing commonwealth of free nations. Those principles seem as relevant as ever.

Yet to apply these principles in action, they must be converted into practical choices that set vectors for change. To understand these choices—and we invite readers to understand and second-guess them—one must reimagine the mix of values, judgments about reality, and analyses of alternative actions that were reasonably available at the time, involving several countries.

At the beginning of 1989 there were many ways to define the problems or opportunities. In economics, freer global finance had created new problems of American debt, East European debt, and West European pressure for a monetary union that might help combat American financial pressure and complete the new Fortress Europe. The Cold War trading system was under stress and economic nationalism was rising.

The Soviet military was questioning its military commitments but was still trying to improve its forces. Western allies were torn by fresh debates about whether to again modernize their nuclear forces, as they had agreed to do in 1988.

Some East European communists sought compromise with their non-communist enemies in order to gain a consensus on how to handle their debts. Preoccupied Soviet leaders wanted them to sort out their problems on their own. Some communist leaders hoped their countries would follow the example set by China, which crushed the largest mass movement for democracy in the world. China, in turn, had suppressed its protests in part to be sure the contagion of European democracy did not spread.

Our story shows how a handful of leaders, West and East, set the vectors for change through a series of very specific choices, which we have mapped. Throw some of those switches differently, and expect different results with chains of actions and reactions that are hard to predict.

There were so many volatile questions. Could change in Poland have turned violent or seemed hopeless? Should or could East Germany have been saved? Would a Soviet leader tolerate a unified Germany? What was the right design for Europe's future security or economic structures? Were the designs for a united Germany the right ones? Did the push for a new European Union go too far, too fast, or not far or fast enough?

Should Gorbachev have cracked down on the Lithuanians, or should he have moved promptly to a voluntary federation and sought to lead the USSR's rising democratic movement? Was there ever a chance for better Soviet or Russian economic reform? Would a different Western approach, including on the size or conditionality of aid, have caused different transitional outcomes for Eastern Europe—or for the Soviet Union? And so on.

What we saw was a constant struggle to assess people, countries, and situations. Practicalities of action were debated; choices were made; principles wrapped around them; dangers and opportunities confronted; and institutions devised or adapted.

The dust settled. Europe and its institutions were being transformed. Outlaw aggression was thrown back by a uniquely united world. Different structures to guide and mold a global security system and a global economy came into view: a revived UN, a transformed NATO, a transformed IMF, a new WTO, a new EU, and more.

As time has passed, scholars, practitioners, and even those who participated have naturally looked to make sense of what happened and to turn those events into grand narratives that simplify the past, gloss the present, and forecast a future. What do all the new precedents now mean? How should they be applied to the next case, the messier case? Do the old institutional solutions still work for the new problems?

The leaders of the late 1980s and early 1990s worked the problems their age presented. When they were most effective, they were always oriented more to figuring out what they could do. They prided themselves on their care and practicality. Later some would say that they had "ended history." We rather doubt that these wise leaders thought that to be true. They were practical people. They did not linger long on issues of blame. They got on with the task of building a new order—leaving the next chapter to those who now meet new challenges.

One thing is certain: Their successors will face a world transformed by a digital revolution. This is not just about technology. It is about new ways of living, new forms of economic organization, and—most challenging for leaders—the emergence of new political communities that may cross traditional borders and allegiances. At this early stage, we can already see the faint outlines of how this technological revolution is affecting political life and the shape of the challenges facing leaders today.

The world will be fortunate indeed if leaders today and tomorrow do as well in the work before them as those discussed in this book did in their day. Today, those responsible will have much to do. But three new vectors demand immediate attention if the global commonwealth is to survive and prosper: the rise of populism and the "rejection" of elites; the emergence of great power rivalry; and rebuilding a confident America that is once again willing to lead.

Balancing the Local and the Global

If indeed people have lost confidence in elites and their leadership, job one is to rebuild it. To be sure, elites deserve some disapproval. But, in most lines of work, from carpentry to computers, elites stand out because of some mix of expertise and experience.

The people who responded to the challenges from 1988 to 1992 did so from a deep reservoir of both. There is nothing wrong with having studied a subject or having met challenges before—and there is nothing particularly laudable about ignorance. Human beings will make mistakes, whether informed or not. The policy answers to international political problems defy scientific method: There are too many factors, personalities, and turns in the road to predict precisely what will work and what will not. Even medicine, which is clearly more scientifically based, cannot avoid the necessity of trained judgment. Most people understand this. It is why they continue to want their kids to be educated, why they want to acquire skills and experience in what they do. They do believe that expertise counts for something.

The issue may not be a rejection of expertise but a sense that elites are losing the competence to solve public problems and have separated themselves from those whom they govern and whose lives they affect: that they do not respect the "common wisdom" of the people. That would mean, for instance, that a gas tax on people who have no choice but to drive because of high housing prices in the city of Paris will come out badly.

In that regard, advocates of globalization are now a bit like those who are speaking to someone who doesn't understand their language. If we address someone who speaks only Italian (which we do not), there is a tendency to speak *louder* and *slower*. Speaking louder and slower to an unemployed coal miner about the benefits of globalization will not get through.

Rather, the new governing contract will have to reconnect governing elites to practical public problem-solving, rooted in local knowledge and understanding. People understand that some of the problems are broad and difficult—inequality, failing public schools (assuring that the elite will never be penetrated by the children of those who are not already a part of it), and a gap between available jobs and skills to fill them. A growing economy is one part of the solution—and an open trading system helps that. But the other pillar is education and skills development. Economic nationalism and protectionism will continue to gain traction if people blame foreigners because they cannot connect their skills to useful work. Both of us have offered ideas about how to adapt America's public agenda to this century's problems.[2]

There are those who would address these concerns by denying the success of free markets in creating prosperity. They do the disaffected no favors. Socialist countries from the Soviet Union of the past to the Venezuela of the present have demonstrated that dismissing the importance of incentivizing work is a dead end. As Soviet citizens used to say, "We pretend to work and they pretend to pay us."

When Russia emerged from communism, the leaders adopted free markets in theory but, in reality, the absence of institutions that could contain the worst of human behavior led to oligarchs and crony capitalism. We told that story in chapter 6. There is a lesson in that. Economic freedom without trustworthy institutions will not answer the problems of the disaffected either.

In Europe more than in the United States, market-based economies exist side by side with belief in a duty to address the well-being of the population through significantly greater government intervention. But this has been done through established institutions that are a part of the ecosystem of democracy.

Now, admittedly, governing institutions are stressed and viewed as failing by many. America's founders understood that the people's preferences could not be ascertained, nor their rights protected, without intermediation: That was the purpose of representatives, courts, and the right of assembly in civic organizations.

Populism is not necessarily antidemocratic, but it is anti-institutional. It encourages a direct line from a leader to the population without regard for the intermediaries, and intermediating structures, that safeguard rights and liberty. The founding fathers also knew that government closest to the people would likely be the most effective and trusted. Federalism and decentralization may be even more important given the complexities of governing today over diverse populations.

Moreover, we should separate the problems confronting consolidated democracies and those of younger ones. Institutions are only as good as the paper that they are written on until people come to trust them. That takes time, as citizens test courts, constitutions, and elections to see if they are fair. Each time they prove themselves, they gain authority.

If the institutional landscape is barren, with weak checks on executive authority, illiberalism will grow when populists take advantage of that imbalance. But if it is rich—as it is in more developed democracies—parliaments, courts, a free press, and others will check the power of even the most determined president or prime minister. Thus one answer to the democratic "recession" is to shore up these institutions, particularly where they are new. The CSCE, later the OSCE, turned out to be a very important place before and after 1989 for civil society and opposition leaders to develop, grow, and find support. That function should be reenergized.

The European Union has a particular problem of distance between elites and the people. Brexit may turn out to have been an epic mistake. But the sentiments that caused more than 51 percent of the British people to reject membership in the European Union cannot be ignored. To date, the EU has not addressed the "democratic deficit." There is a tendency to blame British politicians for the referendum in the first place or the British people for buying "a pig in a poke." The essential question goes unaddressed and unanswered. What really is the right balance between an unelected European Commission and other supranational bodies—not to mention between the EU as a whole and national structures? Is the notion of a United States of Europe viable? Desirable?

Nationalism is going to continue to exist. As Americans, we are somewhat reluctant to tell Europeans this because we understand the negative connotation that it brings. But people do want to feel kinship with those who share their history, culture, language, and traditions. To ignore that is to cede the ground to those who would turn kinship into nativism.

The Emergence of Great Power Rivalry

Each region of the world has its threats and troubles. The men and women who designed a new Europe and a global commonwealth were concerned, above all, with the greatest dangers—a return of great power conflict that could convulse the world. Because they were the children of World War II, they wanted to make sure that such rivalries never dragged them and their descendants into horrific struggle again. They had an added incentive to avoid global war: Nuclear weapons had made it unthinkable to fight at that scale.

After the remarkable events we chronicle in our book, there was good reason to hope that these rivalries would not emerge again. The Soviet Union and its claim to an alternative political and economic system had collapsed. There was at least some hope that the successor states would join the commonwealth of free nations.

China was beginning to emerge, but policymakers would soon rush to encase the economic potential of its more than one billion people in the system of free trade and free economies. Western and Japanese leaders bet that the lure of the global commonwealth would be irresistible to both Russia and China.

That has not been the case. Both Moscow and Beijing, and lesser powers like Iran, seem quite determined to alter or perhaps destroy the global order that emerged after 1989. It is tempting to see the most important ones, Russia and China, as similar in the challenges that they bring. But they are very different.

Russia is a declining power with an economy roughly the size of Australia's. It is based largely on extractive industries.[3] When was the last time that someone celebrated the global dominance of consumer products or technological breakthroughs designed in Moscow? The Russian economy is an oil and gas syndicate with political and personal fortunes inextricably linked to it.

Without the capacity to influence the international economy, except through oil prices, Russia has turned to its historic strength, military power. There is an anecdote that makes the rounds among diplomats. The scene is from the Congress of Vienna in 1815. A British journalist spots the Russian tsar, Alexander I, standing alone in the hall, dressed in his splendid military uniform, the epaulettes on his shoulders and his headgear adorned with the double-headed eagle of Imperial Russia.

"Who is that?" the journalist asks a British diplomat.

"That is the Emperor and Sovereign of All the Russias, of Moscow, Kiev, Vladimir, Novgorod; Tsar of Kazan, Tsar of Astrakhan, Tsar of Poland, Tsar of Siberia, Tsar of Taurian Khersones, Tsar of Georgia; Sovereign of Pskov and Grand Duke of Smolensk, Lithuania, Volhynia, Podolia, and Finland; Duke of Estland, Lifland, Courland and Semigalia, Samogitia, Bielostok, Korelia, Tver, Yugria, Permia, Vyatka, Bolgary and others; Sovereign and Grand Duke of Nizhni Novgorod, Chernigov, Ryazan, Polotsk, Rostov, Jaroslavl, Bielo-ozero, Udoria, Obdoria, Kondia, Vitebsk, Mstislav, and Ruler of all Northern territories; Sovereign of Iberia, Kartalinia, the Kabardinian lands and Armenian province: hereditary Sovereign and Ruler of the Circassian and Mountain Princes and of others; Sovereign of Turkestan, Heir of Norway, Duke of Schleswig-Holstein, Stormarn, Dietmarsen, Oldenburg, and so forth, and so forth, and so forth."

"But who is he?" the journalist presses.

The British diplomat again repeats his answer—"The Emperor and Sovereign of All the Russias..."

After several attempts to get his question answered satisfactorily, the exasperated journalist says, "Okay, I know who he is. But why is he here settling the fate of Europe?"

"Well..." The diplomat paused. "Because his armies are in Paris."

Well, Moscow's legions remain strong and feared.

Russia also enjoys a UN Security Council veto, and the Soviet Union once had a vast network of vassal states. The former remains; the latter is gone. This leaves the Russians largely with the capability to disrupt, and that has been Putin's chosen course for some time now. The latest innovation has been to stir trouble *within* democratic political systems, the 2016 election in the United States being perhaps the boldest but by no means the only example of that strategy.

The United States and its allies have confronted Russia largely through sanctions and, in Europe, through NATO deployments in the Baltic states and Poland. The latter are meant to demonstrate resolve and fealty to Article V of the North Atlantic Treaty, the defense pledge. East-ern Ukraine continues to suffer from Russian military activities that have made that region resemble a failed state. And the West seems to have no answer for Russian influence in Syria and the devastating consequences of Bashar al-Assad's continued rule.

Still, the NATO response to the territory within its jurisdiction has been impressive. The allies have maintained a united front on sanctions. But disagreements over energy policy continue to rise within the alli-ance and the EU, particularly over the Nord Stream II plan, a pipeline intended to run from Russia to Germany while bypassing Poland and Ukraine. Moscow will take every opportunity to sow division between the United States and Europe.

The sanctions have held, but it is important to remember that they are a blunt instrument. One challenge for the West will be to punish and isolate Putinism while keeping an open door for those in Russia who want to take a different course. A lot has changed in the nearly thirty years since the collapse of the Soviet Union. Younger Russians and even some older city dwellers love to travel, spoil their children at McDonald's, and furnish their mortgage-enabled apartments. In the elections of 2012, Vladimir Putin won less than 50 percent of the vote in Moscow, even in a fraudulent election. (He made certain that he would win in 2018 through widely acknowledged fraud.)

There are also many young Russians who have studied in the United States, in law schools and MBA programs. They have worked in Western banks, corporations, and law firms. These young people thought they had found a patron in Dmitri Medvedev, who did seem to want to take Russia in a different direction. He believed that his country *could* be influential in the knowledge-based economy. At Stanford in June 2010, dressed in his Armani jacket and jeans and reading from his iPad, he told a small group of venture capitalists this: "Russia has the best mathematicians and software engineers in the world." It was very tempting to tell him that many of them were now working in Tel Aviv and Palo Alto.

There is no doubt that the Russian people are among the world's most creative and brilliant. The problem is that the system has not allowed them to flourish. Many of them know this, so continuing to find ways to connect to the "other" Russia should be a high priority. There is some evidence that sanctions, and the associated problems with travel and visas, are beginning to harm those whom we should help, in hopes of a better day for Russia.

* * *

If the challenge with Russia is to contain the disruptive activities of a declining power, the issue with China is to channel the significant capabilities of a rising one. Academics have long debated whether a status quo power can accommodate a rising one without war or at least conflict. Graham Allison's controversial book *The Thucydides Trap* concludes that conflict is likely. Kori Schake's insightful history of Britain's reaction to America's rise suggests a different possibility.[4] But in the latter case, the two powers shared values—it was a kind of a handoff of responsibility from one member of the club of democracies to another.

For a time, there were two narratives about China. One—let's call it the security narrative—saw an aggressive China, intent on driving the United States out of the Asia-Pacific region. The exhibits for this view were many: Chinese aggression in the South China Sea, and military modernization aimed at denying American naval forces the ability to protect U.S. allies, friends, and the principle of freedom of navigation. When, in 2007, China tested a sophisticated antisatellite missile, the possibility of denial in space appeared to be a real one. And of course, there were all of the nefarious cyberattacks ranging from industrial espionage to hacking the records of the Office of Personnel Management. China was seen to be a military adversary and needed to be treated as such.

But there was a counternarrative—let's call it the CEO narrative. China was a market too big to ignore, and even if there were challenges in accessing it, companies were making money there. The ability to manufacture in China was an undeniable boon to consumers, who got cheaper goods as a result. The intermingling of the U.S. and Chinese economies was evident in everything from semiconductors to smartphones to goods sold at Walmart. There was shared benefit—China grew dramatically and the international economy drafted on that growth.

In the last two or so years, that second narrative has collapsed, or, more correctly, been absorbed into the first. China, it turned out, was not "joining" the international economy as a full partner devoted to reciprocity. Instead, it was cherry-picking: continuing to close large segments of its market to foreign competition; allowing the creation of joint ventures with the intent of forcing technology transfer; outright stealing intellectual property through espionage; and privileging "national" champions like Alibaba and Baidu over foreign competitors.

Now the Chinese challenge looked different—the new narrative was one of the merger of an economy destined to become the world's largest with military power great enough to one day dominate the Asia-Pacific region.

One question about China remained, however. What was its intent? How would it use this marriage of military and economic prowess?

For years, the Chinese claimed that their interest was only in domestic development. It was sometimes frustrating to hear officials claim that China wanted only "peace and prosperity and a calm international environment. We are still a developing country," they would say. In other words, Beijing steadfastly denied having any ambition for global leadership, let alone global dominance.

Something changed with Xi Jinping. He seemed to crave the mantle that his predecessors had avoided. From Xi's October 2017 speech at the 19th Communist Party Congress in Beijing: In an obvious take-off from Reagan's famous invocation of America's place as a "shining city on a hill" for the rest of the world, Xi praised the "China system" as a new type of "shining city on a hill" for other countries, saying that it "offers a new option for other countries and nations who want to speed up their development while preserving their independence, and it offers Chinese wisdom and a Chinese approach to solving the problems facing mankind."[5]

Said Xi, "No one should expect China to swallow anything that undermines its interests." But he added, "China's development does not pose a threat to any other country. No matter what stage of development it reaches, China will never seek hegemony or engage in expansion."

China's policies have begun to reflect that aspiration. It has been active in Africa in infrastructure development and trade for a long time, a trend that could be chalked up to mercantilism—support for the Chinese economy. But more recently, the Chinese have talked openly about a future in which the renmimbi was a rival for the dollar (even if that was a long way off) and have sought to increase the number of international transactions in their own currency. The decision to launch the Belt and Road Initiative is a marker that China intends to influence other states—and not just those on its periphery.

As a good recent study from a group of scholars at the Rand Corporation observed, "The principal Chinese challenge is not that it will impose authoritarian governments on its trading partners but that, over time, it will skew global standards for trade and investment in its favor to the disadvantage of its competitors."[6]

The Chinese leaders, who study at least their version of history, are very familiar with the way the British Empire worked during the nineteenth century. That empire gained much of its global influence from dominating the basic infrastructure of the nineteenth-century industrial revolution and that age of globalization. Its influence was found in the control of ports, the Suez Canal, shipping, railroads, finance and exchange, mines, insurance, commercial standards, manufactures that drew in the world's commodities, and the telegraph cables that connected it all. In China, the decaying Qing dynasty even relied on British servants to collect the customs revenue that was the kingdom's principal means of paying its debts.[7]

Any student of British imperial history can only smile in studying China's Belt and Road Initiative. It finances land and sea connectivity in a twenty-first-century global system built to Chinese norms and standards of cooperation, financed by a network of Chinese-funded banks and funds. It welcomes trade with everyone; it is indifferent to how others govern themselves, so long as they behave appropriately toward China.

If borrowers cannot pay, the Chinese take over facilities, natural resources, and revenue streams. Ecuador is far from China, in South America, on the other side of the Pacific Ocean. But China now takes 80 percent of Ecuador's most valuable export, its oil, to pay debts, mainly for a failed dam project.[8] The Chinese navy now sails in every ocean; its interests are on every continent. China is the largest contributor to UN peacekeeping forces. Beijing launched an Asian Infrastructure Investment Bank in 2016, a possible competitor to the American-led Asian Development Bank. The pursuit of policies that would cement China's role as a great power is well under way.

China is setting itself up to become the twenty-first-century builder of the Pax Sinica. But its governing philosophies in the 2010s are very different from those that animated Britain in the 1880s.

Great powers, though, have a view of how human history ought to unfold. China has always maintained that it believed in noninterference in the internal affairs of others. It would be a mistake, though, to see noninterference as synonymous with disinterest: It might be possible for Beijing to have its cake and eat it too. There are many strongmen who would love to have a patron who doesn't have a view about matters like individual liberty, press freedom, or human rights. Even better to have a patron whose views are closer to your own.

A new kind of coalition against freedom has emerged. Some suggest that Russia and China will lead it in order to balance and counter the United States. While this is possible, it is well to remember a few facts about these two powers. First, Russia has little to offer China in economic terms. Cheap oil would serve China—it would not serve the interests of Gazprom and Russia's ruling clique. Second, the two have a long history of animosity, in part driven by Russia's irrational fears, bordering on xenophobia, of Asians. Russia has always contended that its wealthy but underpopulated Far East would tempt Asian conquerors. Finally, Moscow as a handmaiden to a rising power doesn't quite accord with Vladimir Putin's illusions of grandeur for the great Russian nation. There may well be shared tactical interests, but it is harder to see the Moscow-Beijing axis as an enduring alliance.

Still, as the United States reacts to the inevitable rise of China, it will be important not to overreact in a way that ensures conflict. China may well want to cherry-pick the international economic order—but it is a policy choice to find ways to prevent that. In fact, the Chinese themselves know that their current economic model has run out of steam. They are no longer the low-cost labor provider. The long-awaited transition to a consumer-oriented innovation economy has stalled time and again.

The problem for Beijing is that it does not know how to move toward greater marketization of the economy without a loss of political control. This has caused the regime to fall back on old tropes about ideological purity. It has also led to clear discomfort with the role of China's biggest private-sector companies. Rumors persist that there will now be Communist Party officials on boards of directors—and that the Alibabas of the world are under pressure to support the party's priorities at home and abroad.

China's pursuit of economic reform has thus been halting and erratic. The United States and the rest of the world would benefit if the Chinese can find a path forward. It is hard to imagine international economic growth without Chinese economic growth—and eventually that will implicate America's prospects too.

So, how to deal with China's rise? Clearly, its military adventurism has to be challenged, and the United States is right to insist (including with demonstrations of the principle) on freedom of navigation. U.S. military modernization will have to account for China's path, attentive to the new challenges—denial on the seas, weapons in space, and in cybersecurity.[9]

One wonders if the Chinese investment will really pay off with countries that are not known for their creditworthiness but are known for their craftiness. There is already a backlash in places like Malaysia about China's demands and willingness to enforce unequal bargains on the indebted. Sometimes the truth is the best defense—the United States should draw attention to these practices.

American leaders might also learn from the wisdom of their predecessors chronicled in this book. First, remember our point in the Introduction about the Cold War's "ups and downs." Second, just as European allies played such a large role in our story, America's powerful Asian allies—including Japan, South Korea, Australia, and those in Southeast Asia—should be partners in the work to be done. And the important friendship with India, which shares our values, can also play a constructive role in Asia's future. And this whole book underscores the possible value and lasting wisdom of an enduring Atlantic partnership among the world's great democracies.

Moreover, when the leaders who were building a better world had a chance, they found ways to accommodate the pride and aspirations of a dying Soviet Union. It is equally important to do so with a rising China when possible. Would it have been so bad to support the Asian Infrastructure Investment Bank? We could have said, "We need infrastructure. Let's start in Afghanistan." And then help to define that organization in ways that are consistent with the global commonwealth that we helped build.

The question of China's challenge to the United States in so-called frontier technologies—artificial intelligence, machine learning, and quantum computing—is more complicated. Xi Jinping, we believe, made a mistake in declaring a frontal assault on the U.S. dominance in these areas. It has provoked an American response that is alarmed, angry, and bipartisan. The Committee on Foreign Investment in the United States (CFIUS) has been transformed into a body to review every Chinese investment in America's technology sector—and that sector is being defined quite broadly.

China's lead horse in telecommunications is under fire from the United States and several of its allies. Not only have counterintelligence charges been brought against Huawei officials, but the United States is in an all-out campaign to prevent its allies from installing its networking equipment.

More troubling, though, is the response that targets Chinese students studying in the United States. It is true that "China's intelligence agencies are expanding efforts to collect information from Chinese students doing research on U.S. university campuses in areas relevant to China's key technology targets."[10] There are those who believe that American universities should limit the access of Chinese graduate students to academic programs in AI, machine learning, and other high-end technologies. This would require universities to renege on one of their most important principles— that knowledge should have no boundaries and no nationality tests.

In our view this would be a mistake. First, it assumes that the Chinese will never innovate on their own. Second, it prioritizes the short-term goal of preventing technology transfer over the longer-term one of influencing a generation of China's best and brightest. No one can guarantee that the latter will bear fruit—but the evidence from the past is that it will.

Can a Confident America Rise Again?

This brings us to the final challenge and one that has no easy answer. The rise of China seems to have pushed Americans and their leaders onto their back foot. So much was invested in a China that would liberalize and play a constructive role in a global commonwealth. Now there is widespread disappointment and frustration. The mistake, though, would be to adopt strategies that try to "out-China China." Denying Chinese students access to America would be just one of the many ways in which we could try to do that.

The United States has been through crises of confidence before. The Soviet Union was going to beat us in the space race. Japan's industrial policy would lead it to dominate the United States in the global economy. Now, China—admittedly with a stronger hand than the Soviet Union and with troubling values, unlike Japan—is going to surpass the United States for global leadership. Of course, Sputnik produced a uniquely American response—make the next generation better at science and math; teach people to speak Russian; support private fundamental research with government funding. Japan would soon learn that its industrial planning was no match for dorm rooms in Cambridge and garages in Palo Alto. Innovation, it turned out, came from distributed excellence, not centralized mandates.

Some will argue that China will bring many strengths, including the ability to feed machine learning and AI with huge amounts of data because privacy will not be an issue. This is one type of authoritarian envy, but it is evident in other arguments about Beijing's "advantages." They can get things done—look at Belt and Road, look at their infrastructure, look at their single-minded response to pollution in their cities.

Authoritarians can indeed get things done. They suffer, though, from the problem that while leaders can be omnipotent, they are rarely omniscient. Thus bad policy is also efficiently delivered. Forty years ago, China had an answer to its population explosion: the one-child policy. It was efficiently—even brutally—delivered. And now thirty-four million Chinese men don't have mates.[11]

The modern-day version of authoritarian efficiency will be to harness the Internet for the purposes of political control. Yet can a country that is so frightened of its people that it insists on loyalty and conformity through social credits also motivate them to create and innovate?

America will—thankfully—never be China. But we do need to regain our confidence that the American way is alive and well. There are new sources for optimism. In many ways, the biggest change from 1989—let alone from 1945—is the pervasive importance of technology as a force in international politics. At its worst, it allows Russia to interfere in elections and China to pursue a strategy that is likely leading to the split of the Internet into two separate entities—one free and one controlled and censored. At its best, technology may help to solve the problems of educational inequality, through online learning that can reach under-served populations. At its most consequential, it can help to change the energy mix in addressing climate change. One thing is clear: The United States is still the most innovative country in the world, whether in educational initiatives or the production of electric cars. That is just one source of confidence as America's leaders seek to reengage with the world.

It took a confident America to declare in 1949 that "an attack upon one is an attack upon all," with Joseph Stalin astride Eastern Europe and having detonated a nuclear weapon in that same year—five years ahead of schedule. It took a confident America to bet on "the democratic peace," and help to build a democratic West Germany so strong that it would absorb its communist neighbor and unify, the U.S. president helping to guide the outcome. It took a confident America to believe that the world's economy did not have to be zero sum, but could grow through free trade and open economies, and to act on that, building the foundation for a global commonwealth that has already made the world more prosperous for a larger fraction of its people than ever before in human history.

America's confidence was rewarded with seventy years of prosperity, and largely with peace. When one looks at China or Russia, they have few friends and fewer allies. When the National War College holds its classes this year, military people from thirty-two countries will participate. No great power in human history has had that many countries who share its interests—and in many cases its values. There is clearly work to do at home to make sure that all of our citizens are included in the positive bargain that the global commonwealth promised. But that should not obscure, or postpone, the work that must be done to make sure that, recalling Burnham's and Orwell's prophecies about the future of freedom, we once again prove that liberty actually works. The alternative would take humanity to a very dark place.

* * *

On August 25, 1943, having met with his team in Canada at another wartime strategy conference with Winston Churchill and the British team, the work of the conference done, Franklin Roosevelt spoke to the Canadian parliament and, through the radio microphones, to millions more. Tens of thousands of spectators cheered him as he entered and left the House of Commons.

He said he knew people were now thinking about the future. "There is a longing in the air," he said. "It is not a longing to go back to what they call 'the good old days.' I have distinct reservations as to how good 'the good old days' were. I would rather believe that we can achieve new and better days."

He and Churchill had announced some high principles toward a greater freedom from want, the freedom that would come from "driving out the outlaws and keeping them under heel forever."

"I am everlastingly angry," he went on with his old vigor, in that slow, rolling, rhythmic cadence of his, at those "who assert vociferously" that these principles "are nonsense because they are unattainable.

"If those people had lived a century and a half ago, they would have sneered and said that the Declaration of Independence was utter piffle. If they had lived nearly a thousand years ago, they would have laughed uproariously at the idea of Magna Carta. And if they had lived several thousand years ago, they would have derided Moses when he came from the mountains with the Ten Commandments.

"We concede," FDR admitted, "that these great teachings are not perfectly lived up to today, but"—and here he paused to measure every word—"I would rather be a builder than a wrecker, hoping always that the structure of life is growing—not dying."[12]

Acknowledgments

This book tends to focus on the doings of a relatively small number of people out of the total array of officials importantly involved in these events. We single out a relatively small number, partly because some were especially influential, but also so that it would be easier for a reader to keep track of the people we mention. So, our first acknowledgment is to our former colleagues in the United States and other governments, diplomats or generals or intelligence officials, whom we do not mention in describing episodes in which they too played their part. In one episode or another they were our teammates, and this book is partly about what teamwork can do.

In preparing this book we are grateful for the support of our home institutions, the University of Virginia and Stanford University. We received valuable research assistance from Iris Malone, Nicholas Mortensen, Matthew Frakes, Grace Anderson, Daniel Begovich, Emma Frerichs, and J. Bradford Morith. We received wise comments and research tips from Daniel Collings, Liviu Horowitz, Mark Kramer, Melvyn Leffler, Dennis Ross, Kristina Spohr, John Taylor, James Graham Wilson, and Robert Zoellick. Kirill Kalinin gave us some translation assistance.

The archivists we worked with at the George H. W. Bush Presidential Library, such as Zachary Roberts and Mary Finch, exhibit a sense of duty and public-spiritedness that would make George H. W. Bush proud of the caretakers of his records. We are also especially grateful to the staffs of the other archival facilities and documentary project leaders whose efforts we acknowledge in our notes. At the National Security Archive, Svetlana Savranskaya deserves special notice for her dedicated work over the years as scholar, editor, and translator.

At Twelve and its parent company, the Hachette Book Group, we are grateful for the editorial work of Sean Desmond and Roland Ottewell, organized by Carolyn Kurek and assisted by Rachel Kambury. We are also grateful for the advice and help we have received from our literary agents, Andrew Wylie and Wayne Kabak.

Notes

Some abbreviated references to collections of documents recur frequently in the notes.

United States

Bush Library—George H. W. Bush Presidential Library, Texas A&M University. In addition to its documentary holdings on site, the Bush Library has placed all of the Bush records of conversations with foreigners (almost all of them now opened) in a well-designed, chronologically organized database accessible online.

Baker Papers—James A. Baker III Papers, Seeley Mudd Manuscript Library, Princeton University.

Bush 41 OHP—Bush 41 Oral History Project, Miller Center of Public Affairs, University of Virginia. The Miller Center also has oral history records, in varying states of openness, for the Carter, Reagan, Clinton, Bush 43, and, soon, Obama presidencies.

Clinton Library—William J. Clinton Presidential Library, Little Rock, Arkansas.

Where U.S. documents are cited without indicating an archive location, Zelikow had access to them, in work on our 1995 book, before they were archived and cataloged. Many of these records may still be classified. We cite them because the citations themselves were unclassified. The earlier citations have facilitated the declassification process for many of these records. We discuss the circumstances of Zelikow's original access to these materials briefly in the introduction to this book and further in the preface to the earlier book.

Soviet Union

Gorbachev papers donated to Stanford—In 1992, in turbulent and uncertain times, Mikhail Gorbachev worked with Rice to place some of his papers at Stanford University for safekeeping and research. Rice studied these papers (which are not translated) in their uncataloged form. They are now cataloged and open for research at the Hoover Institution Library and Archives, Stanford University. Hoover also has records and correspondence related to our earlier research work.

National Security Archive—This invaluable institution, located at George Washington University, collects documents released by the U.S. and other governments, often working with the Cold War International History Project at the Woodrow Wilson International Center for Scholars, In Washington, DC. The Wilson Center also has its own Digital Archive of opened international documents, usefully organized.

Chernyaev diary—Anatoly Chernyaev (often also transliterated as Chernyayev) donated his diaries to the National Security Archive. Translated by Anna Melyakova and edited by Svetlana Savranskaya, they were published online twenty years after they were created (1989 in 2009, etc.).

Federal Republic of Germany

DzD-Einheit—Dokumente zur Deutschlandpolitik: Deutsche Einheit Sonderedition aus den Akten des Bundeskanzleramtes 1989/90, research supervision from Klaus Hildebrand and Hans-Peter Schwarz with Friedrich Kahlenberg of the Bundesarchivs, edited by Hanns Jürgen Küsters and Daniel Hofmann (Munich: R. Oldenbourg Verlag, 1998).

Diplomatie—Diplomatie für die deutsche Einheit: Dokumente des Auswärtigen Amts zu den deutsch-sowjetischen Beziehungen 1989/90, edited by Andreas Hilger (Munich: R. Oldenbourg Verlag, 2011).

Einheit Dokumente—Die Einheit: Das Auswärtige Amt, das DDR-Außenministerium und der Zwei-plus-Vier-Prozess, Institut für Zeitgeschichte, by Horst Möller, Ilse Dorothee Pautsch, Gregor Schöllgen, Hermann Wentker, and Andreas Wirsching, and edited by Heike Amos and Tim Geiger (Göttingen: Vandenhoeck & Ruprecht, 2015).

United Kingdom

TNA—The National Archives of the UK, Richmond. PREM is the acronym for the Prime Minister's Office files.

DBPO/Unification—Documents on British Policy Overseas, Series III, vol. VII, *German Unification 1989–1990*, edited by Patrick Salmon, Keith Hamilton, and Stephen Twigge (London: Routledge, 2010).

France

AD—Centre des Archives diplomatiques du ministère des Affaires étrangères, La Courneuve.

The papers of François Mitterrand are not generally open, but portions of them have been made available to several scholars, whose work from them is cited in our notes.

* * *

To help distinguish government documents from published materials, we have cited such documents with abbreviated dates (e.g., 30 Nov 89). Telegrams to or from American missions are cited by what the State Department calls message reference numbers, usually with subject and date of transmission. "Secto" means a message sent to Washington by the secretary of state's traveling party.

A "memcon" is a memorandum of a personal conversation; "telcon" is a memorandum of a telephone conversation.

Introduction: Catalytic Choices

1. David Childs, *The GDR: Moscow's German Ally*, 2nd ed. (London: Unwin Hyman, 1988), xii.

2. On Angela Merkel, the best overall biography so far is Gerd Langguth, *Angela Merkel* (Munich: DTB Verlag, 2007); and, for this period, see also Ralf Georg Reuth and Günther Lachmann, *Das erste Leben der Angela M.* (Munich: Piper Verlag, 2013). Merkel has not written a memoir, but a series of interviews with her given to Hugo Müller-Vogg were published as Angela Merkel, *Mein Weg* (Hamburg: Hoffmann und Campe, 2004). The best biographical studies of Merkel's early life available in English are Matthew Qvortrup, *Angela Merkel: Europe's Most Influential Leader* (New York: Overlook Duckworth, 2016); Mark Thompson and Ludmilla Lennartz, "The Making of Chancellor Merkel," *German Politics* 15 (2006): 99–110; and George Packer, "The Quiet German," *New Yorker*, December 1, 2014.

For specific quotes in the text: "meticulous" is from Merkel quoted in Herlinde Koelbl, *Spuren der Macht: Die Verwandlung des Menschen durch das Amt* (Munich: Knesebeck, 1999), 48; "people cried" is from Merkel, *Mein Weg*, 43. The school play story is in Reuth and Lachmann, *Das erste Leben*, 69–70, and Qvortrup, *Angela Merkel*, 58–61. Merkel tells her "chatterbox" story in Wolfgang Stock, *Angela Merkel: Eine politische Biographie* (Munich: Olzog, 2000), 49. Her husband's memory of how "she packed her bags" is from Qvortrup, *Angela Merkel*, 78. The department boss evaluation that "she is on to something" is from Langguth, *Angela Merkel*, 117.

On Vladimir Putin, the best biography so far for the early life is Steven Lee Myers, *The New Tsar: The Rise and Reign of Vladimir Putin* (New York: Knopf, 2015). On specific quotes, "two natures" is from Putin quoted by Roy Medvedev, in Allen Lynch, *Vladimir Putin and Russian Statecraft* (Washington, DC: Potomac Books, 2011), 9. Putin's memory of the movie and "one man's effort," along with his early experiences with intelligence work, are from Putin's own de facto memoir published shortly after he became Russia's president for the first time, a set of interviews interleaving interviews from his wife and a few close friends, in Vladimir Putin with Nataliya Gevorkyan, Natalya Timakova, and Andrei Kolesnilov, *First Person*, trans. Catherine Fitzpatrick (New York: PublicAffairs, 2000), 22, 41–42, 47, 49. A good overview of Putin's work in Dresden is Myers, *The New Tsar*, 38–47. The specific quotes about his experiences there and his wife's impressions are from Putin with Gevorkyan et al., *First Person*, 40, 68, 74, and 77. Putin's quoted remarks to his officemate and friend are from Myers, *The New Tsar*, 47.

3. John Gunther, "Inside England 1964," in *Procession* (New York: Harper & Row, 1965), 491.

4. For a brief entrée to how decision makers size up a situation as an interactive compound of value, reality, and action judgments, see Philip Zelikow, "Introduction: Three Judgments," in Zelikow, Ernest May, and the Harvard Suez Team, *Suez Deconstructed: An Interactive Study of Crisis, War, and Peacemaking* (Washington, DC: Brookings Institution Press, 2018), 1–8.

Quentin Skinner and others in the "Cambridge school" of political philosophy have similarly emphasized how the writings of famous thinkers like Thomas Hobbes or John Locke must be understood in a very specific original historical context. See, e.g., Skinner's collection of essays in *Visions of Politics*, vol. 1, *Regarding Method* (Cambridge: Cambridge University Press, 2002). R. R. Palmer emphasized that same point in his classic history *The Age of the Democratic Revolution: A Political History of Europe and America, 1760–1800* (Princeton, NJ: Princeton University Press, 2014 [orig. 1959 and 1964]), chapters 1–3.

5. Paraphrasing an expression Zelikow contributed to the 9/11 Commission, *Report* (New York: Norton, 2004), 339.

6. David Potter, *Lincoln and His Party in the Secession Crisis* (Baton Rouge: LSU Press, 1995 [reprinting the original 1942 book and its 1962 update]), 13 ("fallacy"); Potter, *The South and the Sectional Crisis* (Baton Rouge: LSU Press, 1968), 246 ("supreme task...imperfect eyes"). Edward L. Ayers, *In the Presence of Mine Enemies: War in the Heart of America, 1859–1863* (New York: Norton, 2003), 147. To describe such profound historical breakpoints, Ayers likes the term "deep contingency."

In natural history, Stephen Jay Gould helped popularize a different but analogous term: "punctuated equilibrium." Gould was more interested in the punctuations than in the equilibrium. "When we set our focus upon the level of detail that regulates most common questions about the history of life, contingency dominates and the predictability of general form recedes to an irrelevant background." Gould, *Wonderful Life: The Burgess Shale and the Nature of History* (New York: Norton, 1989), 289–90.

7. Genscher quoted in Richard Kiessler and Frank Elbe, *Ein runder Tisch mit scharfen Ecken: Der diplomatische Weg zur deutschen Einheit* (Baden-Baden: Nomos, 1993), 14–15; Timothy Garton Ash, *In Europe's Name: Germany and the Divided Continent* (New York: Random House, 1993), 343.

8. Karl Kaiser, *Deutschlands Vereinigung: Die internationalen Aspekte* (Bergisch Gladbach: Bastei Lübbe, 1991), 16 ("greatest triumph"); Alexander Bessmertnykh quoted in a 1991 interview in Michael Beschloss and Strobe Talbott, *At the Highest Levels: The Inside Story of the End of the Cold War* (Boston: Little, Brown, 1993), 240 ("most hated developments").

9. See, e.g., the interview excerpts with Helmut Kohl, Hans-Dietrich Genscher, Horst Teltschik, Eduard Shevardnadze, Vyacheslav Dashichev, Nikolai Portugalov, and Rainer Eppelmann in Ekkehard Kuhn, *Gorbatschow und die deutsche*

Einheit: Aussagen der wichtigsten russischen und deutschen Reteiligten (Bonn: Bouvier, 1993), 8–11.

10. Many historians might agree that the most significant catalytic episodes in world history since 1775 have been: (1) the revolutions that convulsed the Atlantic world and beyond, culminating in the settlements of 1814–15; (2) a series of civil and international wars around the world that began in about 1854 and subsided with the defeat of the Commune and the European settlements of 1871; (3) the period of global breakdown and war between 1911 and 1923; (4) the huge global struggles, that included the Second World War, between 1937 and 1954; and (5) the end of the Cold War and related developments in China, India, and other countries between 1988 and 1992.

11. Post-2006 trendline and "democratic recession" from Larry Diamond, "Is There a Crisis of Liberal Democracy?" *The American Interest*, October 13, 2017.

12. "Do You Hear Me Now?" was the title Stephen Hayes used for his post-election commentary in the *Weekly Standard*, November 11, 2016. "*What comes next?*" is from Condoleezza Rice, *Democracy: Stories from the Long Road to Freedom* (New York: Twelve, 2017), 439 (emphasis in original).

13. Since at the time we wished to avoid calling attention to Gorbachev's role in safeguarding his papers, in our 1995 book we referred to these papers that actually came from Gorbachev as coming from the young woman who delivered them to Stanford, Alexandra Bezymenskaya. We studied them in an uncataloged form. The papers were deposited with the Hoover Institution at Stanford, are cataloged, and have become available and useful to other researchers.

Chapter 1: The Renewal of the Free World

1. See John P. Diggins, *Up from Communism: Conservative Odysseys in American Intellectual History* (New York: Harper & Row, 1975), 161.

2. See Burnham, *The Managerial Revolution: What Is Happening in the World* (New York: John Day, 1941); and his less well-read but more mature reflections in *The Machiavellians: Defenders of Freedom* (New York: John Day, 1943), 269 ("belief in the myths"). The title *The Machiavellians* refers to the political thinkers whose ideas Burnham admired and dwells on. These were mainly

Italians—Gaetano Mosca, Vilfredo Pareto, Robert Michels, and Georges Sorel (who was French)—in addition to Burnham's admiration for the work of Machiavelli himself. The standard biography of Burnham is Daniel Kelly, *James Burnham and the Struggle for the World* (Wilmington, DE: ISI Books, 2002), and Burnham's is one of the four portraits in Diggins, *Up from Communism*. See also Samuel T. Francis, *Power and History: The Political Thought of James Burnham* (Lanham, MD: University Press of America, 1984).

3. For a sense of the prevailing expectations and pessimism among other leading thinkers of the period, see, e.g., Joseph Schumpeter, *Capitalism, Socialism, and Democracy* (New York: Harper & Row, either the 1st edition of 1942 or the 2nd edition of 1947); Karl Polanyi, *The Great Transformation* (New York: Farrar & Rinehart, 1944); or Friedrich Hayek, *The Road to Serfdom* (Chicago: University of Chicago Press, 1944).

4. Thomas Ricks, *Churchill and Orwell: The Fight for Freedom* (New York: Penguin, 2017), 44.

5. Orwell, "Inside the Whale" (1940), in Sonia Orwell and Ian Angus, eds., *The Collected Essays, Journalism and Letters*, vol. 1, *An Age Like This* (Boston: Nonpareil, 2000), 516.

6. Orwell, "James Burnham and the Managerial Revolution" (1946) and "Burnham's View of the Contemporary World Struggle" (1947), in Orwell and Angus, eds., *The Collected Essays, Journalism and Letters*, vol. 4, *In Front of Your Nose* (Boston: Nonpareil, 2000), 169, 170, 176, 325.

7. See Orwell, "James Burnham" and "Burnham's View," 173, 179–80, 324.

8. Intellectuals at the time recognized how much the novel was influenced and prompted by Burnham's work. "Whoever investigates the background of *1984* must pay particular attention to the work of James Burnham." William Steinhoff, *George Orwell and the Origins of 1984* (Ann Arbor: University of Michigan Press, 1975), 43. Steinhoff spends a chapter to prove that point.

9. Orwell, *Nineteen Eighty-Four*, quoted tellingly by an author who spent most of his career covering contemporary wars, Ricks, in *Churchill and Orwell*, 255–56.

10. Orwell, "Toward European Unity" (1947), in Orwell and Angus, eds., *Collected Essays*, vol. 4, 371 (emphasis added).

11. James Burnham, *Suicide of the West: An Essay on the Meaning and Destiny of Liberalism* (Chicago: Regnery, 1985 [orig. 1964]), 297. Burnham did not quite know what to do about ideals of liberty

and freedom. In his older work he had expected elites to rule. Yet, for America, he also emphasized ways to divide and separate power, by strengthening state government at the expense of the national/federal level, or by strengthening Congress against the presidency. But this created problems for his larger theory of managerial dictatorship of the superstate. As early as 1943 a perceptive critic had noticed that Burnham "runs away to Renaissance Florence, but Thomas Jefferson is right behind him. He hides himself among French Syndicalists, but James Madison plucks him by the sleeve." John Chamberlain, writing in the *New York Times* in 1943, quoted in Kelly, *James Burnham*, 111.

12. Placing "1968" in its global context, including the global conservative reactions, are Jeremi Suri, *Power and Protest: Global Revolution and the Rise of Détente* (Cambridge, MA: Harvard University Press, 2003); and Carole Fink, Philipp Gassert, and Detlef Junker, eds., *1968: The World Transformed* (Cambridge: Cambridge University Press, 1998).

13. See Milovan Djilas, *The New Class: An Analysis of the Communist System* (New York: Praeger, 1957). On the Cultural Revolution in China and its toll, Frank Dikötter, *The Cultural Revolution: A People's History, 1962–1976* (London: Bloomsbury, 2016).

14. In the 1960s and 1970s these elite theories were offered as an alternative to philosophies that emphasized a destabilizing "adversary culture." The elitists argued that such divisive and revolutionary ideas contributed little that was constructive to the real world of governance. Intellectuals should not try to become the new "high priests," one West German theorist argued. They should defer and let more competent "others do the work." On trends in more conservative social theory, partly in reaction to the influential work either from Marxists or thinkers like Jürgen Habermas, see, e.g., Chris Thornhill, *Political Theory in Modern Germany: An Introduction* (Cambridge, UK: Polity, 2000), and Michael King and Chris Thornhill, *Niklas Luhmann's Theory of Politics and Law* (New York: Palgrave Macmillan, 2003). "High priests" (an idiomatic translation of *Priestherrschaft*) is from a book by one of Luhmann's mentors, Helmut Schelsky, *Die Arbeit tun die anderen: Klassenkampf und Priestherrschaft der Intellektuellen* (Opladen: Westdeutscher Verlag, 1975).

15. Michel Crozier, Samuel Huntington, and Joji Watanuki, *The Crisis of Democracy: Report on the Governability of Democracies to the Trilateral Commission* (New York: NYU Press, 1975), 2.

16. Francis, *Power and History*, 97. Another *National Review* editor would eventually publish another book of prophecy with the title *Suicide of the West*. But this argument, published in 2018, is very different. Jonah Goldberg, *Suicide of the West: How the Rebirth of Tribalism, Populism, Nationalism, and Identity Politics Is Destroying American Democracy* (New York: Crown Forum, 2018); see also the reflections in Julius Krein, "James Burnham's Managerial Elite," *American Affairs* 1, no. 1 (Spring 2017).

17. On the application of civil rights laws, such as the laws against discrimination in private employment or voting rights, Zelikow participated in this directly as a civil rights lawyer during the late 1970s and early 1980s. On the ERA battle, the standard account is Jane Mansbridge, *Why We Lost the ERA* (Chicago: University of Chicago Press, 1986). The pivotal Supreme Court decision on the application of the Fourteenth Amendment to gender was *Craig v. Boren*, 429 U.S. 190 (1976).

18. Mikael Rask Madsen, "The Challenging Authority of the European Court of Human Rights: From Cold War Legal Diplomacy to the Brighton Declaration and Backlash," *Law and Contemporary Problems* 79 (2016): 141, 152; a useful survey of some of the European story is Patrick Pasture, "The Invention of European Human Rights," *History* 103, no. 356 (2018): 485–504.

19. There is a substantial literature on the movements in support of international human rights. These works often center on the evolution of transnational elites discussing and publicizing issues of human rights, for instance tracking groups like Amnesty International, which was certainly important. See, e.g., Kenneth Cmiel, "The Emergence of Human Rights Politics in the United States," *Journal of American History* 109, no. 1 (December 1999): 1231–50; or Michael Cotey Morgan, "The Seventies and the Rebirth of Human Rights," in Niall Ferguson, Charles Maier, Erez Manela, and Daniel Sargent, eds., *The Shock of the Global: The 1970s in Perspective* (Cambridge, MA: Harvard University Press, 2010), 237–50. For a more general survey, which does take a broader view of the human rights discourse, see the essays in Akira Iriye, Petra Goedde, and William Hitchcock, *The Human Rights Revolution: An International History* (New York: Oxford University Press, 2012).

These essays do not do quite enough to stress the wider domestic discourse about "rights" set off by decisions of the U.S. Supreme Court, such as the giant domestic controversies over the rights of criminal suspects, abortion, or press freedom, or the struggles over laws banning private employment discrimination. Also often overlooked is that these wrenching domestic arguments were occurring in Western Europe as well as in the United States.

　　In the aftermath of the shame and regret about the Vietnam War, it was natural for many Americans to turn to their discourse about "rights" as a way to reassert themselves in foreign policy as well. This is the point so ably stressed in Barbara Keys, *Reclaiming American Virtue: The Human Rights Revolution of the 1970s* (Cambridge, MA: Harvard University Press, 2014). What Keys seems to underplay is that the domestic debates about "rights," debates that were also roiling politics in Western Europe, had a much larger cultural impact in these societies than the debates about or specific assertions of "international" human rights norms in more traditional foreign policy settings. It is worth emphasizing that this transnational "rights" revolution flowered on a mass scale during the 1970s, not the 1960s. This happened on both sides of the Atlantic and began to cross the Pacific, affecting debates about laws and norms in Japan and South Korea.

20. Correctly stressing the West European leadership on this point, see Daniel Thomas, *The Helsinki Effect: International Norms, Human Rights, and the Demise of Communism* (Princeton, NJ: Princeton University Press, 2001); Angela Romano, *From Détente in Europe to European Détente: How the West Shaped the Helsinki CSCE* (Brussels: Peter Lang, 2009); Mark Gilbert, *Cold War Europe: The Politics of a Contested Continent* (Lanham, MD: Rowman & Littlefield, 2015), 185–91.

21. Samuel Huntington, *The Third Wave: Democratization in the Late Twentieth Century* (Norman: University of Oklahoma Press, 1993).

22. On the intellectual movement in Europe, see Michael Scott Christofferson, *French Intellectuals Against the Left: France's Antitotalitarian Moment* (New York: Berghahn, 2004); Jeffrey Herf, *War by Other Means: Soviet Power, West German Resistance, and the Battle of the Euromissiles* (New York: Free Press, 1991); and Jan-Werner Müller, "The Cold War and the Intellectual History of the Late Twentieth Century," in Melvyn Leffler

and Odd Arne Westad, eds., *The Cambridge History of the Cold War*, vol. 3, *Endings* (Cambridge: Cambridge University Press, 2010), 1–22. For "a kind of historical fool," W. L. Webb quoted in Tony Judt, *Postwar: A History of Europe Since 1945* (New York: Penguin, 2005), 559.

23. See generally Daniel Thomas, "Human Rights Ideas, the Demise of Communism, and the End of the Cold War," *Journal of Cold War Studies* 7, no. 2 (2005): 110–41.

24. Charles Maier, "'Malaise': The Crisis of Capitalism in the 1970s," in *The Shock of the Global*, 26–27.

25. Jeffry Frieden, *Global Capitalism: Its Fall and Rise in the Twentieth Century* (New York: Norton, 2006), 236 ("stabilize the business cycle").

26. Herman Van der Wee, *Prosperity and Upheaval: The World Economy 1945–1980*, trans. Robin Hogg and Max Hall (Berkeley: University of California Press, 1986), 380.

27. John Jackson quoted in Douglas Irwin, *Clashing over Commerce: A History of U.S. Trade Policy* (Chicago: University of Chicago Press, 2017), 614.

28. Although many of the key ideas about relying on international monetary discipline in a freer global financial system originated in Europe, the American role was critical in the early 1970s as President Nixon's treasury secretary, George Shultz, Shultz's successor William Simon (who also served President Gerald Ford), and a financial official who worked with both of them, Paul Volcker, successfully blocked various options to use capital and exchange controls to manage the crises of the early 1970s. Then some of the initiative to press for open financial markets shifted back again to Western Europe, as European central bankers developed their own approaches to stabilizing their exchange rates. The American role became crucial once more after Volcker took over the leadership of the Federal Reserve Board in 1979. See Eric Helleiner, *States and the Reemergence of Global Finance: From Bretton Woods to the 1990s* (Ithaca, NY: Cornell University Press, 1994), 65–67, 102–21, stressing the international financial aspects, and Greta Krippner, *Capitalizing on Crisis: The Political Origins of the Rise of Finance* (Cambridge, MA: Harvard University Press, 2011), stressing domestic deregulation of credit markets and then the U.S. reliance on borrowing, including international borrowing, to sustain continued deficits and high levels of consumption through the 1980s. An important

new work on this transition in global capitalism is Michael De Groot, "Disruption: Economic Globalization and the End of the Cold War Order in the 1970s" (PhD diss., University of Virginia, 2018).

Krippner also puts less emphasis on neoliberal ideas. She emphasizes a series of "ad hoc responses to crisis conditions" (p. 23). In the early 1980s these responses revealed, somewhat surprisingly, how readily the United States could borrow its way out of having to make the hard choices other countries faced. Krippner's work also ties into the work of historians like Louis Hyman, who have discussed how the U.S. financial system shifted from business lending into consumer and household lending, including the development of internationally marketable mortgage-based securities. Hyman, "American Debt, Global Capital: The Policy Origins of Securitization," in *The Shock of the Global*, 128–42.

29. See Kristina Spohr, *The Global Chancellor: Helmut Schmidt and the Reshaping of the International Order* (Oxford: Oxford University Press, 2016), 18–23; George Shultz, *Turmoil and Triumph: My Years as Secretary of State* (New York: Charles Scribner's Sons, 1993), 352 ("mistress").

30. Spohr, *The Global Chancellor*, 27–32.

31. Britain had already found itself forced to rely on outside finance, including bailout help from the International Monetary Fund, during a severe financial crisis in 1976. The resulting constraints on the Labour government then in power led to the strains and strikes that were the prelude to Margaret Thatcher's landmark electoral victory leading the Conservative Party in March 1979. On the significance of Britain's 1976 financial crisis, see Helleiner, *States and the Reemergence of Global Finance*, 124–30.

32. On the EMS and U.S. shifts, including Volcker's failed attempt in 1979–80 to try to regulate the Euromarket, see Daniel Gros and Niels Thygesen, *European Monetary Integration*, 2nd ed. (New York: Longman, 1998), 35–64; Helleiner, *States and the Reemergence of Global Finance*, 131–39; Peter Ludlow, *The Making of the European Monetary System: A Case Study in the Politics of the European Community* (Boston: Butterworth, 1982); and, emphasizing that the November 1978 improvisation was a key turning point in American policy, Daniel Sargent, *A Superpower Transformed: The Remaking of American Foreign Relations in the 1970s* (New York: Oxford University Press, 2015), 108–30, 273–85; along with

Krippner, *Capitalizing on Crisis*, 114–20. On November 1978 as a pivot point in the U.S. government, the best account of the whole episode, which calls out the work of a key deputy at Treasury, Anthony Solomon, is Stuart Eizenstat, *President Carter: The White House Years* (New York: St. Martin's Press, 2018), 327–51.

33. The notion of an inherent "trilemma" between national monetary autonomy, exchange rate stability, and free movement of capital in which governments can only have two of the three is associated with Robert Mundell and Marcus Fleming's work in the 1960s. For a reflective summary, see Maurice Obstfeld, Jay Shambaugh, and Alan Taylor, "The Trilemma in History: Trade-offs Among Exchange Rates, Monetary Policies, and Capital Mobility," *Review of Economics and Statistics* 87, no. 3 (2005): 423–38.

In effect, the "hard money" approach was returning global capitalism to the basic conceptual structure of the gold exchange standard system of the late nineteenth and early twentieth centuries. The new system, rather than base stability on the price of a mineral, based stability on the price of fiat money, its issuance controlled by the key issuers. As an approach to political economy the new system of regulated fiat money has many of the same virtues and problems that the gold exchange standard system once had—greater stability of prices and exchange rates, greater availability of global capital, and a heightened risk of severe financial crises.

34. Shultz, *Turmoil and Triumph*, 151.

35. "I did not appoint you": to Pierre Mauroy in the autumn of 1982, quoted in Philip Short, *A Taste for Intrigue: The Multiple Lives of François Mitterrand* (New York: Henry Holt, 2013), 374.

36. Rawi Abdelal, *Capital Rules: The Construction of Global Finance* (Cambridge, MA: Harvard University Press, 2007), 57 ("turning point"), 62–63 ("no Right"), quoting Pascal Lamy, who became the chief of staff to Jacques Delors during the Delors presidency of the European Commission.

37. On the stages of the French U-turn from 1982 to the summer of 1984 (when Fabius became prime minister and the Communists left the parliamentary coalition), see Wayne Northcutt, *Mitterrand: A Political Biography* (New York: Holmes & Meier, 1992), 116–69, and, emphasizing the key decisions in the second austerity package of March 1983, Helleiner, *States and the Reemergence of Global Finance*, 140–44. Richard Kuisel, *The French Way: How France Embraced and*

Rejected American Values and Power (Princeton, NJ: Princeton University Press, 2012), 25 ("that's what's chic").

38. Charles Moore, *Margaret Thatcher: The Authorized Biography*, vol. 2, *At Her Zenith: In London, Washington and Moscow* (New York: Vintage, 2015), 194.

39. See Vito Tanzi and Ludger Schuknecht, *Public Spending in the 20th Century: A Global Perspective* (Cambridge: Cambridge University Press, 2000); and Ludger Schuknecht and Vito Tanzi, "Reforming Public Expenditure in Industrialized Countries: Are There Trade-offs?," in Peter Wierts, Servaas Deroose, Elena Flores, and Alessandro Turrini, eds., *Fiscal Policy Surveillance in Europe* (Houndmills, UK: Palgrave Macmillan, 2006), 247–73.

40. William Niskanen quoted in Irwin, *Clashing over Commerce*, 574 ("ten-foot wall"). This account relies on ibid.; Barry Eichengreen, *Globalizing Capital: A History of the International Monetary System* (Princeton, NJ: Princeton University Press, 1996), 145–52; Yoichi Funabashi, *Managing the Dollar: From the Plaza to the Louvre* (Washington, DC: Institute for International Economics, 1988); Paul Volcker with Christine Harper, *Keeping At It: The Quest for Sound Money and Good Government* (New York: PublicAffairs, 2018); and C. Michael Aho and Marc Levinson, "The Economy After Reagan," *Foreign Affairs* 67, no. 2 (Winter 1988): 10–25.

41. For a similar argument, but focusing more on technological changes in commerce and the role of petrodollars in stimulating the global flows, see Hal Brands, *Making the Unipolar Moment: U.S. Foreign Policy and the Rise of the Post–Cold War Order* (Ithaca, NY: Cornell University Press, 2016), 54–57.

42. On the transition from Mao to Deng, see Richard Baum, *Burying Mao: The Age of Deng Xiaoping* (Princeton, NJ: Princeton University Press, 1994); on Deng's development of the reform agenda, see Ezra Vogel, *Deng Xiaoping and the Transformation of China* (Cambridge, MA: Harvard University Press, 2011), 118–19, 218 ("backward"), 223 ("completely different"), 228 ("superiority of our system"). For "few parallels," Julian Gewirtz, *Unlikely Partners: Chinese Reformers, Western Economists, and the Making of Global China* (Cambridge, MA: Harvard University Press, 2017), 3.

43. Vogel, *Deng Xiaoping*, 242 ("emancipate"), 256 (Lord Ye's view of dragons), 262–64 (on the March 1979 crackdown), 344 ("this one simple gesture," quoting Orville Schell).

44. David Reynolds, *One World Divisible: A Global History Since 1945* (New York: Norton, 2000), 512 ("a very antiestablishment revolution"); see generally Walter Isaacson, *The Innovators: How a Group of Hackers, Geniuses, and Geeks Created the Digital Revolution* (New York: Simon & Schuster, 2014).

45. "The Computer Moves In," *Time*, December 26, 1982.

46. From a creator of Czechoslovakia's Ondra computer, made by Tesla (a Czech acronym, not the twentieth-century inventor or twenty-first-century company), quoted in Karen Dawisha, *Eastern Europe, Gorbachev, and Reform: The Great Challenge*, 2nd ed. (Cambridge: Cambridge University Press, 1990), 160.

47. The best biography of Kohl is now Hans-Peter Schwarz, *Helmut Kohl: Eine Politische Biographie* (Munich: Deutsche Verlags-Anstalt, 2012), 611 ("center").

48. On Mitterrand, the best overall biographies are Franz-Olivier Giesbert, *François Mitterrand, une vie* (Paris: Éditions du Seuil, 1996); Jean Lacouture, *Mitterrand: Une histoire de Français*, and for this period vol. 2, *Les vertiges du sommet* (Paris: Éditions du Seuil, 1998); and (in English) Short, *A Taste for Intrigue*.

49. Charles Grant, *Delors: Inside the House that Jacques Built* (London: Nicholas Brealey, 1994), 56–58.

50. Moore, *At Her Zenith*, 392 ("half-admiringly"); Grant, *Delors*, 68 ("cool"). On Delors's critical role as "the pragmatic visionary," see Helen Drake, *Jacques Delors: Perspectives on a European Leader* (London: Routledge, 2002), 78–112.

51. On Cockfield's role as a key causal factor in the Single Market story, see Christopher Lord, "Lord Cockfield: A European Commissioner as a Political Entrepreneur," in Kevin Theakston, ed., *Bureaucrats and Leadership* (London: Macmillan, 2000), 151–70, 153 ("massively detailed"); Drake, *Jacques Delors*, 86 ("a coherent whole"); and Cockfield's own account in *The European Union: Creating the Single Market* (London: Wiley Chancery Law, 1994), esp. 23–59. On his appointment and Thatcher's evolving attitudes, see Moore, *At Her Zenith*, 390–94.

52. Moore judges that in giving way to the Single Market's requirements, Thatcher was not only deceived a bit about the momentum of European integration, she was also "self-deceiving. For the Single Market to function, which she wanted, individual states could not be allowed to impose

their own regulations on imports from the rest of the EU.... So when she complained later, she was in effect repudiating what she herself had driven forward." Ibid., 394.

53. The evolution of British and U.S. attitudes during the crisis is charted expertly, with access to key evidence on both sides, in Charles Moore, *Margaret Thatcher: The Authorized Biography*, vol. 1, *From Grantham to the Falklands* (New York: Knopf, 2013), 665–744.

54. Vogel, *Deng Xiaoping*, 315.

55. Michael Green, *By More Than Providence: Grand Strategy and American Power in the Asia Pacific Since 1783* (New York: Columbia University Press, 2017), 389. Green regards Reagan's first secretary of state, Alexander Haig, as a source of friction on Asia policy. He argues that Haig's 1982 successor, George Shultz, was the most capable American secretary of state on Asia policy in American history, leading an exceptionally strong team of lower-level officials.

56. Diego Ruiz Palmer, quoted in Gordon Barrass, *The Great Cold War: A Journey Through the Hall of Mirrors* (Stanford, CA: Stanford University Press, 2009), 193.

57. For a review based on East bloc archives, see Vojtech Mastny, "Imagining War in Europe: Soviet Strategic Planning," in Mastny, Sven Holtsmark, and Andreas Wenger, eds., *War Plans and Alliances in the Cold War: Threat Perceptions in the East and West* (New York: Routledge, 2006), 15–45; the quote is from Mastny's summary of his argument in the introduction, 3.

58. See, for example, the interviews with former lieutenant general Geli Batenin and former colonel general Andrian Danilevich in John Hines, chief editor, *Soviet Intentions 1965–1985*, vol. 2, *Soviet Post–Cold War Testimonial Evidence*, BDM Corporation report to the Office of the Secretary of Defense Net Assessment director, September 1995, excised version released in 2009 and available from the National Security Archive at https://nsarchive2.gwu.edu/nukevault/ebb285/. The quote "hold all of Europe hostage" is from a 1992 interview with Danilevich (at p. 33 of the report); he was the main author of the authoritative three-volume Soviet strategy guidance on "deep operations."

59. These agents were Dmitri Polyakov and Ryszard Kuklinski. Polyakov was arrested and executed in 1988, having been betrayed by Soviet agents working inside the CIA and the FBI (Aldrich Ames and Robert Hanssen). In December 1981,

just before Poland declared martial law, Kuklinski was extracted from Poland with CIA assistance and lived out his life in the United States.

60. Barrass, *The Great Cold War*, 193. Barrass was a member of Britain's Joint Intelligence Committee and headed the Cabinet Office's Assessments Staff during the last years of the Cold War.

61. The best account of the origins of the Euromissile confrontation is now Kristina Spohr Readman, "Conflict and Cooperation in Intra-Alliance Nuclear Politics: Western Europe, the United States, and the Genesis of NATO's Dual-Track Decision, 1977–1979," *Journal of Cold War Studies* 13, no. 2 (2011): 39–89.

62. William Perry, at the time a Carter administration defense official who was one of the fathers of the "offset" strategy, discusses the plan in *The Role of Technology in Meeting the Challenges of the 1980s* (Stanford, CA: Arms Control and Disarmament Program, Stanford University, 1982). An authoritative historical review is Edward Keefer, *Harold Brown: Offsetting the Soviet Military Challenge, 1977–1981* (Washington, DC: Historical Office, Office of the Secretary of Defense, 2017), esp. 575–600.

63. Giesbert, *François Mitterrand, une vie*, 401.

64. In his memoir, Genscher calls attention to the impact of these contrasting messages from Mitterrand, Soviet foreign minister Andrei Gromyko, and the G-7 summit statement (meeting in Williamsburg, Virginia). Hans-Dietrich Genscher, *Rebuilding a House Divided*, trans. Thomas Thornton (New York: Broadway Books, 1998), 163–65.

65. See the revealing transcript of the May 1983 Soviet Politburo meeting published in "More Documents from the Russian Archives," *Cold War International History Project Bulletin* 4 (Fall 1994): 77–80; see also Jonathan Haslam, *The Soviet Union and the Politics of Nuclear Weapons in Europe, 1969–81: The Problem of the SS-20* (London: Macmillan, 1989).

66. The best and most balanced overview of the Reagan administration's foreign policies around the world, one emphasizing a turn toward reassurance and the promotion of democratic change in East Asia, Latin America, and South Africa by the mid-to-late 1980s, is Brands, *Making the Unipolar Moment*; the most balanced summary of Reagan's strategy toward the Soviet Union is Melvyn Leffler, "Ronald Reagan and the Cold War: What Mattered Most," *Texas National Security Review* 1, no. 3 (2018): 76–89.

67. A foundational argument observing the rise of "post-materialism" was published in 1977. Ronald Inglehart, *The Silent Revolution: Changing Values and Political Styles Among Western Publics* (Princeton, NJ: Princeton University Press, 1977).

68. A balanced and well-informed summary of the 1983 war scare, including the Soviet alarm about the NATO command post exercise "Able Archer," is in Barrass, *The Great Cold War*, 278–303.

Chapter 2: Perestroika

1. Rodric Braithwaite, *Across the Moscow River: The World Turned Upside Down* (New Haven, CT: Yale University Press, 2002), 51–52, recounting a February 1980 discussion. Braithwaite was one of the diplomats; the other was Christopher Malaby.

2. Odom's note is quoted in Daniel Sargent, *A Superpower Transformed: The Remaking of American Foreign Relations in the 1970s* (New York: Oxford University Press, 2015), 295. Sargent has the document dated in September 1979 and does not give the author. On checking with Sargent, it was learned the document is actually from September 1980. We believe, and Sargent agrees, that Odom was its author.

3. The outstanding scholarly works in a large literature on Gorbachev are now William Taubman, *Gorbachev: His Life and Times* (New York: Norton, 2017); and Archie Brown, *The Gorbachev Factor* (New York: Oxford University Press, 1996); as well as Robert English, *Russia and the Idea of the West: Gorbachev, Intellectuals, and the End of the Cold War* (New York: Columbia University Press, 2000); and various essays by Vladislav Zubok, for instance in the relevant chapter of *A Failed Empire: The Soviet Union in the Cold War from Stalin to Gorbachev* (Chapel Hill: University of North Carolina Press, 2007), 278–321. Some of the best early short portraits of Gorbachev were offered by his aide Anatoly Chernyaev in "The Phenomenon of Gorbachev in the Context of Leadership," *International Affairs* (Moscow) (June 1993): 37–48, and by a Western journalist acquainted with Gorbachev, Robert Kaiser, in *Why Gorbachev Happened: His Triumphs, His Failure, and His Fall*, rev. ed. (New York: Simon & Schuster, 1991), 21–92. See also Anatoly Chernyaev, *Shest' let s Gorbachevym: Po dnevnikovym zapisyam* (Moscow: Progress Publishers, 1993); translated as *My Six Years with Gorbachev*, trans. and ed. Robert English and Elizabeth Tucker (University Park: Penn State University Press, 2000). On the German occupation and the deportations of the Karatchay, Kalmyks, and other peoples in the wake of the German retreat, see Michel Tatu, *Mikhail Gorbachev: The Origins of Perestroika*, trans. A. P. M. Bradley (Boulder, CO: East European Monographs, 1991), 6–10.

4. Gennadii Zoteev, in Michael Ellman and Vladimir Kontorovich, eds., *The Destruction of the Soviet Economic System: An Insiders' History* (Armonk, NY: M. E. Sharpe, 1998), 86.

5. "Let's be mature": in a 1986 Politburo meeting. Chris Miller, *The Struggle to Save the Soviet Economy: Mikhail Gorbachev and the Collapse of the USSR* (Chapel Hill: University of North Carolina Press, 2016), 88.

6. Vogel, *Deng Xiaoping*, 423–24.

7. Peter Nolan, *China's Rise, Russia's Fall: Politics, Economics and Planning in the Transition from Stalinism* (Houndmills, UK: Macmillan, 1995), 4; see also the kindred argument in Christopher Marsh, *Unparalleled Reforms: China's Rise, Russia's Fall, and the Interdependence of Transition* (Lanham, MD: Lexington Books, 2005).

8. This was, in fact, Eduard Shevardnadze's phrase in discussions with Gorbachev about the state of the Soviet Union in 1985. He describes the evolution of his thinking and that of other "new thinkers" in Eduard Shevardnadze, *Moi vybor: v zashchitu demokratii i svobody* (Moscow: Novosti, 1991), 193–220.

9. Miller, *The Struggle to Save the Soviet Economy*, 81.

10. Details are in ibid., 119–44. One apparent implication is that, as a Soviet economist put it, "Gorbachev would have needed the full support of the entire party structure" to implement the needed reforms. But that goes too far.

Deng and his allies never commanded that kind of unanimity. Their own leadership was riven by factions. Hence the unusual vertical alliances in the Chinese case, often in rivalry with another vertical alliance, each with their backers in Beijing. Deng's challenge, along with his closest allies like Hu Yaobang and Zhao Ziyang, was to juggle all the sides without crushing one or the other, while giving the experiments a chance to work.

One of Gorbachev's weaknesses may have been political. Perhaps he and his allies did not develop strong enough coalitions with allies at lower levels who could patiently try to develop workable policy designs. For example, another Chinese experimental innovation, the special economic zone, was also closely observed in the Soviet Union. A prime location to try this out would have been in Leningrad. There the local boss, Anatoly Sobchak, was interested and energetic. But movement there and in Vladivostok, another possible case, was delayed and hamstrung until it was too late. Miller has some suggestive evidence. Miller, *The Struggle to Save the Soviet Economy*, 107–18.

11. On the visit to Nizhnevartovsk, Michael Dobbs, *Down with Big Brother: The Fall of the Soviet Empire* (New York: Knopf, 1997), 134–36.

12. Andrei Grachev, *Gorbachev's Gamble: Soviet Foreign Policy and the End of the Cold War* (Malden, MA: Polity Press, 2008), 47.

13. Judith Goldstein and Robert Keohane, in their volume *Ideas and Foreign Policy: Beliefs, Institutions, and Political Change* (Ithaca, NY: Cornell University Press, 1993), put it this way: "Ideas help to order the world.... Insofar as ideas put blinders on people, reducing the number of conceivable alternatives, they serve as invisible switchmen, not only by turning action onto certain tracks rather than others... but also by obscuring the other tracks from the agent's view" (p. 12).

14. The debate between Stalin and his competitors for Lenin's throne has been largely obscured by the ruthless means that he used to weed out the opposition. But in this debate Stalin emphasized his theory for achieving "socialism in one country": That is, progress toward socialism in the USSR did not have to wait upon the achievement of worldwide revolution.

This debate about "socialism in one country" was perhaps the crucial ideological turning point for the Soviet Union's course in the post-Lenin era. The question was whether the Soviet Union could survive without a global proletarian revolution. This was more than a matter of academic debate; it would determine whether the Soviet Union made building socialism at home its highest priority or tried to foment revolution abroad.

The proponent of "permanent revolution," Lev Trotsky, while far more articulate and urbane, lacked a realistic plan for dealing with the Soviet Union's immediate circumstances of weakness and vulnerability in 1926–27. Depending as it did, even rhetorically, on revolutionary uprisings in the capitalist world, Trotsky's prescription simply did not accord with the world in which the Soviet Union found itself.

Stalin resolved any dilemma between the international movement and the Soviet Union's existence: "An internationalist is one who is ready to defend the USSR without reservation, without wavering, unconditionally; for the USSR is the base of the world revolutionary movement and this revolutionary movement cannot be defended unless the USSR is defended." J. V. Stalin, *Ob oppozitsii* (Moscow: Gosudarstvennoe Izdatel'stvo, 1928), 220–93. The Soviet Union would prepare to go it alone, but as a temporary condition until the revolution triumphed in the capitalist world and provided a more hospitable international environment. Martin Malia resurrected this debate in *The Soviet Tragedy: A History of Socialism in Russia, 1917–1991* (New York: Free Press, 1994). The implications of "socialism in one country" for Soviet foreign and military policy are discussed in Condoleezza Rice, "The Making of Soviet Strategy," in Peter Paret with Gordon Craig and Felix Gilbert, eds., *Makers of Modern Strategy: From Machiavelli to the Nuclear Age* (Princeton, NJ: Princeton University Press, 1986), 648–76.

15. Ed Hewett discussed the marginalization of the Soviet economy in Ed A. Hewett with Clifford G. Gaddy, *Open for Business: Russia's Return to the Global Economy* (Washington, DC: Brookings Institution Press, 1992), 1–32.

16. It is commonly believed in the United States that the CIA's supply of Stinger antiaircraft missiles to the Afghan resistance caused the Soviet decision to withdraw. The first use of Stinger missiles against Soviet forces was in September 1986. The Soviet decisions to withdraw were made successively between June 1985 and November 1986. See, e.g., William Odom, *The Collapse of the Soviet Military* (New Haven, CT: Yale University Press, 1998), 102–4. The Stingers may have been a prod to get it done, but probably no more than that.

17. Chernyaev, *My Six Years with Gorbachev*, 65 ("state within a state").

18. On Gorbachev's reaction to Chernobyl, Taubman, *Gorbachev*, 241; for the quoted comments at the April 1988 party conference, ibid., 356.

19. Chernyaev said he was always amazed at how much Moscow's specialists on America liked America while some Soviet experts on Germany (such as Bondarenko) seemed to dislike the Germans.

"Whatever their views," he said, "they respected the Germans but they did not like them." Rice interview with Chernyaev, Moscow, June 1994; letter from Chernyaev, February 1995.

20. Eduard Shevardnadze, *The Future Belongs to Freedom*, trans. Catherine Fitzpatrick (New York: Free Press, 1991), 13.

21. Quoted in Don Oberdorfer, *The Turn: From the Cold War to a New Era; The United States and the Soviet Union, 1983–1990* (New York: Poseidon Press, 1991), 119.

22. Both Yakovlev and Shevardnadze discuss these themes in detail in their written recollections. See Alexander Yakovlev, *Muki prochteniya byitiya: Perestroika—nadezhdyi real'nost* (Moscow: Novosti, 1991), esp. 73, 91; and Shevardnadze, *Moi vybor*, esp. 85–93. Yakovlev, in particular, links the confrontational division of the world along class lines to Stalinism. On the scholarly debates inside the USSR and the key scholars who contributed to the "new thinking," see the early account in Jeff Checkel, "Ideas, Institutions, and the Gorbachev Foreign Policy Revolution," *World Politics* 45 (January 1993): 271–300.

23. For a detailed review of the escalating conventional military rivalry in Europe during the late 1970s and 1980s, the role of technology, and the Soviet concepts for a conventional victory that would avoid use of nuclear weapons, see Diego Ruiz Palmer, "The NATO–Warsaw Pact Competition in the 1970s and 1980s: A Revolution in Military Affairs in the Making or the End of a Strategic Age?," *Cold War History* 14, no. 4 (2014): 533–73.

The then-chief of the Soviet General Staff, Marshal Nikolai Ogarkov, was a leader in publicizing the struggle for high ground in a "third revolution" in military affairs, a revolution in conventional military technology. Although the more politically sensitive Sergei F. Akhromeyev succeeded Ogarkov, his analysis of the general military balance was not very different. At the time of the Persian Gulf War in 1990, he told Rice that he suspected the United States of planning the war against Saddam Hussein that it had always intended to fight against Soviet military forces—one heavily dependent on the rapid transmission of information to independent weapons-carrying platforms at the front. He was right, of course.

24. Vitali Shlykov, former department chief of the Main Intelligence Administration of the General Staff, in Ellman and Kontorovich, eds.,

The Destruction of the Soviet Economic System, 43, 45.

25. The military wanted to look eager to get rid of nuclear weapons while assuring, as one general put it, that it "could hardly lead to any practical results in the foreseeable future." Odom, *Collapse of the Soviet Military*, 115–16, 128–29.

26. Major recent overviews of the reciprocal unwinding of superpower tension between 1985 and 1988, attending to moves on both sides, are Robert Service, *The End of the Cold War, 1985–1991* (New York: PublicAffairs, 2015) (the Reagan-Gorbachev period makes up most of this account); James Graham Wilson, *The Triumph of Improvisation: Gorbachev's Adaptability, Reagan's Engagement, and the End of the Cold War* (Ithaca, NY: Cornell University Press, 2014); and the summary in Melvyn Leffler, *For the Soul of Mankind: The United States, the Soviet Union, and the Cold War* (New York: Hill & Wang, 2007), 374–421.

27. The professional military opposed unilateral and asymmetrical arms control reductions. See Condoleezza Rice, "Is Gorbachev Changing the Rules of Defense Decision-Making?," *Journal of International Affairs* 42 (Spring 1989): 377–97.

28. Then a career diplomat, Zelikow was the initial political adviser on the U.S. CFE negotiating team as it formed and molded a NATO approach to the new negotiations in 1986 and 1987, first under Ambassador Robert Blackwill, then under Ambassador Stephen Ledogar.

29. Odom, *Collapse of the Soviet Military*, 137.

30. "The service sector": Ed A. Hewett quoted in Taubman, *Gorbachev*, 169; Yakovlev March 1988 memo quoted in ibid., 352.

31. In 1987, Gorbachev had read the writings of Nikolai Bukharin, a leading party figure of the 1920s and 1930s who had been executed by Stalin, prompted by Stephen Cohen's gift of his book on the debates of the Stalin era. Rice interview with Chernyaev, Moscow, June 1994. This is not the only instance in which Western scholarship helped reintroduce Russians to their own past.

32. Chernyaev, *Shest' let s Gorbachevym*, 184–86, 213–18. Gorbachev would later put his ideas into a series of speeches and articles. See, e.g., "Sosialisticheskaya ideya i revolutsionnaya perestroika," *Kommunist* 18 (December 1989): 3–20.

33. For an excellent summary, distilling much past work, see Archie Brown, "Did Gorbachev as General Secretary Become a Social Democrat?," *Europe-Asia Studies* 65, no. 2 (March 2013): 198–

230, which emphasizes the catalytic role of the Andreyeeva episode of the spring of 1988. Perestroika as "democratic socialism" from Aleksandr Galkin, in ibid., 204.

34. Chernyaev, *My Six Years with Gorbachev*, 92; "philosophically impoverished": Gorbachev to Chernyaev in 1988, quoted in Taubman, *Gorbachev*, 353.

35. On the internal political revolution during the first half of 1988, see Stephen Kotkin, *Armageddon Averted: The Soviet Collapse, 1970–2000* (New York: Oxford University Press, 2001), 73–83; Taubman, *Gorbachev*, 337–65; Zubok, *A Failed Empire*, 307–15. "Ultra-leftist loudmouths" is from Gorbachev to Chernyaev in January 1988, although Gorbachev still emphasized, "Conservatism is now the main obstacle." Taubman, *Gorbachev*, 342.

36. On Western Europe a key man was Valentin Falin, who had been the Soviet ambassador to West Germany during most of the 1970s. On Eastern Europe, Georgi Shakhnazarov was in the lead. On American matters there was Georgi Arbatov.

For background, see Mark Kramer, "The Role of the CPSU International Department in Soviet Foreign Relations and National Security Policy," in Frederic Fleron Jr., Erik Hoffmann, and Robbin Laird, eds., *Soviet Foreign Policy: Classic and Contemporary Issues* (New York: Aldine de Gruyter, 1991), 444–63.

37. See Odom, *Collapse of the Soviet Military*, 140–45; Taubman, *Gorbachev*, 418–20; Kramer, "The Demise of the Soviet Bloc," 383–85; and Chernyaev, *My Six Years with Gorbachev*, 193–97. Shevardnadze's suspicions about military implementation of the planned reductions are evident in the Politburo meeting on December 27–28, transcribed as doc. no. 35 in Svetlana Savranskaya, Thomas Blanton, and Vladislav Zubok, eds., *Masterpieces of History: The Peaceful End of the Cold War in Europe, 1989* (Budapest: Central European University Press, 2010) (hereinafter *Masterpieces of History*).

38. For the Soviet UN Mission's translation of excerpts from Gorbachev's speech, see "Excerpts from Speech to U.N. on Major Soviet Military Cuts," *New York Times*, December 8, 1988, p. A16. Our estimate of the 500,000 number as a one-seventh cut assumes about 3.5 million in the active-duty Soviet forces in 1988. This 3.5 million number does not include construction troops and similar auxiliaries. It also does not include KGB and Interior Ministry troops. On the size and

deployment of forces in Europe, as of the autumn of 1988, see International Institute for Strategic Studies (IISS), *The Military Balance 1988–1989* (London: IISS, 1988). The IISS annual tabulations were a respected standard reference at the time. This particular edition included (pp. 230–33) an analysis on the NATO–Warsaw Pact conventional force balance that briefly summarized the past decade's worth of expert quarrels in the West about how best to tally that balance.

39. Chernyaev, *Shest' let s Gorbachevym*, 255–60; Rice interview with Chernyaev, Moscow, June 1994.

40. Shevardnadze speech to the scientific-practical conference of the USSR Foreign Ministry, reprinted in *Pravda*, July 26, 1988, p. 4.

41. Yegor Ligachev speech reprinted in "Za delo—bez raskachki," *Pravda*, August 6, 1988, p. 2.

42. Mikhail Gorbachev, "Speech to Council of Europe," reprinted in *Pravda*, July 7, 1989, pp. 1–2.

43. Rice discussions with Gorbachev, Moscow, June 1994, and other informal discussions with Gorbachev while Rice was serving in the George H. W. Bush administration. Andrei Grachev, who entirely grasps the significance of the ideological shifts, also stresses this point. *Gorbachev's Gamble*, 73–75, agreeing with Jacques Lévesque, "The Emancipation of Eastern Europe," in Richard Herrmann and Richard Ned Lebow, eds., *Ending the Cold War: Interpretations, Causation, and the Study of International Relations* (New York: Palgrave Macmillan, 2004), 109.

44. The American notes (prepared by Rice) are Bush-Gorbachev, 3 Dec 89 (second expanded session held aboard the Soviet passenger liner *Maxim Gorkii*), Bush Library. Soviet notes from this session are published in Mikhail S. Gorbachev, *Gody trudnykh reshenii, 1985–1992: izbrannoye* (Moscow: Al'fa-Print, 1993), 176–79.

45. Some of the more interesting groundwork for this shift had been laid by Soviet academics almost a decade earlier. Among the more important participants in the debate were Oleg Bogomolov, Karen Brutents, and Yuriy Novopashin. On the scholarly debates that laid the basis for the revocation of the Brezhnev Doctrine and rejection of a segregated "socialist community of states," see Jonathan Valdez, *Internationalism and the Ideology of Soviet Influence in Eastern Europe* (Cambridge: Cambridge University Press, 1993).

46. The best work on the Soviet Union's earliest conceptions of CMEA remains Michael Kaser,

COMECON: Integration Problems of the Planned Economies, 2nd ed. (London: Oxford University Press, 1967).

47. To take a simple example of the effect of COCOM technology controls, the technology that permits multiple telephone lines on one instrument and that makes it possible to switch easily from one line to another was denied to the Soviet Union because it would have made it possible for the military quickly to establish alternative nodes of communication if the primary link was destroyed. Thus visitors to the offices of high-ranking Moscow officials often noticed that there were several telephones rather than several lines on one instrument, as is common in the West. It was often said that one could tell how important a Soviet official was by the number of phones on his desk.

48. Joseph Rothschild and Nancy Wingfield, *Return to Diversity: A Political History of East Central Europe Since World War II*, 3rd ed. (New York: Oxford University Press, 2000), 203.

49. "Polish disease": in Stephen Kotkin with Jan Gross, *Uncivil Society: 1989 and the Implosion of the Communist Establishment* (New York: Modern Library, 2009), 28; "millimeter by millimeter": Gerhard Schürer, October 1989, quoted in Charles Maier, *Dissolution: The Crisis of Communism and the End of East Germany* (Princeton, NJ: Princeton University Press, 1997), 60.

50. Michael De Groot sees a turning point in Soviet behavior in CMEA price decisions of 1975. See his "Disruption: Economic Globalization and the End of the Cold War Order in the 1970s" (PhD diss., University of Virginia, 2018); see also Fritz Bartel, "The Triumph of Broken Promises: Oil, Finance, and the End of the Cold War" (PhD diss., Cornell University, 2017). The Hungarian buses example is from Kotkin with Gross, *Uncivil Society*, 26, citing the work of Charles Gati.

51. Kotkin with Gross, *Uncivil Society*, 30–31.

52. In "Disruption," chapter 8, De Groot emphasizes this West German "Milliardenkredite" as a turning point in the terminal crisis of the East German regime. "We may sound very cynical": editorial in *PlanEcon*, April 1987, quoted in Fritz Bartel, "The Power of Omission: The IMF and the Democratic Transitions in Poland and Hungary," in Bernhard Blumenau, Jussi Hanhimäki, and Barbara Zanchetta, eds., *New Perspectives on the End of the Cold War: Unexpected Transformations?* (New York: Routledge, 2018), 203.

53. The critical period in the expansion of Soviet hard currency debt was in 1988 and 1989. At the end of 1990, Soviet and Western financial analysts calculated that the Soviet current account deficit in hard currencies, in foreign exchange, had swung from a surplus of almost $7 billion in 1987 to a deficit of $4 billion in 1989. The stock of short-term debt to foreign banks doubled from $9 billion at the end of 1987 to almost $18 billion by the end of 1989. By the end of 1989 the USSR had enough foreign exchange reserves left to finance about five months of foreign imports. IMF, World Bank, OECD, and EBRD, *A Study of the Soviet Economy*, February 1991, p. 40.

54. De Groot, "Disruption," 17.

55. State Department officials had opposed Bush's trip to Poland until they were overruled by Deputy Secretary of State John Whitehead. The recollection of Whitehead's intervention comes from Rice's discussion of the Bush trip with a State Department official in 1989.

56. Gregory Domber, *Empowering Revolution: America, Poland, and the End of the Cold War* (Chapel Hill: University of North Carolina Press, 2014), 200–205 (Bush quote is on 204, from Polish records of the meeting). Bush's trip was in September 1987; the Paris Club agreement was reached in December.

57. Bartel, "The Power of Omission," 214.

58. Domber, *Empowering Revolution*, 208–21 (the Brzezinski quote, in February 1988, is on 209).

59. Quoted in Seweryn Bialer and Joan Afferica, "The Genesis of Gorbachev's World," *Foreign Affairs* 64 (1985): 612. See also Ronald D. Asmus, J. F. Brown, and Keith Crane, *Soviet Foreign Policy and the Revolutions of 1989 in Eastern Europe* (Santa Monica, CA: Rand Corporation, 1991), 11.

60. For details, see Randall Stone, *Satellites and Commissars: Strategy and Conflict in the Politics of Soviet-bloc Trade* (Princeton, NJ: Princeton University Press, 1996).

61. Alex Pravda, "Moscow and Eastern Europe, 1988–1989: A Policy of Optimism and Caution," in Mark Kramer and Vit Smetana, eds., *Imposing, Maintaining, and Tearing Open the Iron Curtain: The Cold War and East-Central Europe, 1945–1989* (Lanham, MD: Lexington Books, 2014), 310 ("meager attention"). Mark Kramer carefully shows that Soviet policy toward the region did not begin to shift in any notable way until 1988. Kramer, "The Demise of the Soviet Bloc," in Kramer and Smetana, eds., *Iron Curtain*, 379–80.

62. Quoted in Kramer, "The Demise of the Soviet Bloc," 381.

63. Ibid., 385–91 (Shakhnazarov, Oct 88, quoted on 386).

64. Don Oberdorfer, "Thatcher: Gorbachev Has Ended Cold War," *Boston Globe*, November 18, 1988, p. 7; George Shultz, *Turmoil and Triumph: My Years as Secretary of State* (New York: Charles Scribner's Sons, 1993), 1131, 1138.

65. Robert Norris and Hans Kristensen, "Global Weapons Inventories, 1945–2010," *Bulletin of the Atomic Scientists*, July/August 2010, p. 82.

66. From a relatively dispassionate and bipartisan appraisal in Congressional Budget Office, *Budgetary and Military Effects of a Treaty Limiting Conventional Forces in Europe*, January 1990, p. 5, drafted by Frances Lussier.

67. Gorbachev address of December 31, 1988, quoted in Leffler, *For the Soul of Mankind*, 422.

68. Ronald Reagan, "Address to Members of the British Parliament," 8 Jun 82, in *Public Papers of the Presidents of the United States: Ronald Reagan* (Washington, DC: Government Printing Office, 1984), bk. 1, 742–48.

69. Address of Vice President George Bush at the Hofburg, Vienna, 21 Sep 83, in *Department of State Bulletin* 83 (November 1983): 19–23.

70. Address by Ronald Reagan, Berlin, 12 Jun 87, in *Public Papers of the Presidents of the United States: Ronald Reagan, 1987* (Washington, DC: Government Printing Office, 1989), bk. 1, 634–37; "showboating": Rozanne Ridgway Oral History, Association of Diplomatic Studies and Training, 2002, 124; Reagan-Shevardnadze memcon, 23 Sep 88, in *Foreign Relations of the United States, 1981–1988*, vol. 6 (Washington, DC: GPO, 2016), 1216–17. The language in Reagan's speech reportedly originated with a White House speechwriter, Peter Robinson. Lou Cannon, *President Reagan: The Role of a Lifetime* (New York: Simon & Schuster, 1991), 774. In her oral history, Ridgway added, "I have run into people who believe that it was that speech in 1987 that brought the Wall down. I tell them that I don't even want to discuss it, but will leave it to the historians. I did tell them that that speech did not bring the Wall down; in fact, in some respects, it threatened the process that eventually brought the Wall down. But I don't have much hope of making a dent in people who view history that way."

Reagan wrote that he offhandedly repeated the Berlin suggestion at the 1988 Moscow summit; see Ronald Reagan, *An American Life* (New York: Simon & Schuster, 1990), 705–7; Bob Spitz, *Reagan: An American Journey* (New York: Penguin, 2018), 721. Chernyaev found no mention of the subject in Soviet records of these talks. Letter from Chernyaev, February 1995.

In the policy world, Reagan's "Berlin initiative" became a working-level proposal to regularize Four Power controls. The State Department passed a proposal for talks to the Soviets six months after Reagan's speech. While Moscow debated its response, the East Germans weighed in with what a Soviet diplomat called their "100 percent negative attitude." Another ten months passed before the Soviet government replied to the Americans. That was that. The West did not return to the matter until the summer of 1989, after the Bush administration revived the issue during the president's visit to West Germany. See Igor Maximychev, "What 'German Policy' We Need," *International Affairs* (Moscow) (September 1991): 53, 58–60.

71. Shultz, *Turmoil and Triumph*, 1138.

72. Herbert Butterfield, *The Whig Interpretation of History*, 1st American ed. (New York: Scribner, 1951), 12.

73. Ibid., 39–40.

74. "Even Jesus Christ": in Shultz, *Turmoil and Triumph*, 1108, from the December 1988 meeting at Governors Island, New York.

Chapter 3: Hopes and Fears

1. Henry Kissinger, "A Memo to the Next President," *Newsweek* (international edition), September 19, 1988, p. 34.

2. Henry Kissinger, "The Challenge of a 'European Home,'" *Washington Post*, December 4, 1988.

3. Transcript of Politburo meeting, December 27–28, 1989, in *Masterpieces of History*, doc. no. 35, p. 337 (for the quote on Kissinger).

On the issue of just what the Soviets wanted to do next, or just what they wanted from the Americans, it is revealing to look at how *little* is said about that in Yakovlev's notes for Gorbachev to prepare him for this Politburo meeting. Yakovlev's lengthy memo is entirely devoted to abstract principles, for instance (which he underscores) that "the interdependence of the world means also the interconnectedness of all the processes of domestic development." But there is nothing in it about concrete policies. Yakovlev, "Notes for Presentation at the Politburo session," December 27, 1988, in National Security Archive Electronic Briefing Book No. 168, at nsarchive.gwu.edu.

4. Ross to Baker, "Thoughts on the 'Grand Design,'" 16 Dec 88, in Baker Papers, Box 1, Folder 4.

5. This account draws on both Kissinger's reports and the Soviet records of the meetings. Kissinger-Yakovlev memcon, 16 Jan 89; Kissinger-Gorbachev memcon, 17 Jan 89 (Soviet), in *Masterpieces of History*, docs. no. 36 and 37; Kissinger-Gorbachev memcon, 17 Jan 89, and Kissinger-Dobrynin memcon, 18 Jan 89 (Kissinger), in Baker Papers, Box 108, Folder 1. The material Kissinger quoted from Gorbachev is presented in Kissinger's memcon as being a verbatim quote. The same material is not in the available Soviet record.

The documents show that Kissinger's firm faxed his written memcons, probably to the White House (from indications in Bush Library records, where these reports have not yet been released), on January 21. Baker marked up his copies and carefully noted the discussions about the proposed Scowcroft-Dobrynin channel.

In his memoir, Dobrynin does not discuss this episode with Kissinger. Kissinger was in Moscow for a meeting of the Trilateral Commission, a private group of worthies that he cochaired along with former French president Valéry Giscard d'Estaing and former Japanese prime minister Yasuhiro Nakasone. These three men met separately with Gorbachev, who reported on this trilateral meeting to the Politburo. In that report he alluded to Kissinger with a pejorative Soviet diminutive, "*Kisa*." Report in *Masterpieces of History*, doc. no. 39.

6. Bush-Gorbachev memcon, 23 Jan 89, in George H. W. Bush Library, Memcons and Telcons online file, at https://bush41library.tamu.edu/archives/memcons-telcons (hereinafter Bush Library). This portion of the memcon is omitted from the Soviet record excerpted in *Masterpieces of History*, doc. no. 40.

A couple of months later Baker and his team alluded to Kissinger's ideas in a way that derided them as an idea for a "Yalta II." This episode further estranged Kissinger from both Bush and Baker and demolished any further role as a go-between. See Walter Isaacson, *Kissinger: A Biography* (New York: Simon & Schuster, 1992), 727–29; and Baker's view in James A. Baker III with Thomas DeFrank, *The Politics of Diplomacy: Revolution, War, and Peace 1989–1992* (New York: G. P. Putnam's Sons, 1995), 40.

7. Baker notes for meeting with Bush, "U.S.-Soviet Relations," February 1989, as marked up by Baker, in Baker Papers, Box 108, Folder 2. Ross has confirmed to us that he was the initial drafter of this paper and that these points were for a meeting with Bush. For an example of Bush commenting on Sakharov's warning, see Bush–Von Weizsaecker memcon, 24 Feb 89, Bush Library.

8. Based on Baker's handwritten notes from the Bush-Mulroney meeting, Baker Papers, Box 108, Folder 2 (emphasis in original), and the Bush-Mulroney memcon, 10 Feb 89, Bush Library. Baker put a few stars by his note of Mulroney's push for a major initiative. The official memcon does not include some of the material in Baker's notes from the meeting.

9. Bush explained his commitment to personal diplomacy in George Bush and Brent Scowcroft, *A World Transformed* (New York: Knopf, 1998), 60–61; his comment on Gorbachev is on 10.

10. See Dennis Ross interview, August 2001, and Robert Zoellick interview, January 2011, Bush 41 OHP. As of 2019 the Zoellick interview has not yet been publicly released. Zelikow helped conduct the interview and Zoellick granted him access to the transcript.

Although she did not do conventional policy strategy, Margaret Tutwiler was Baker's main adviser for handling the press, and much more. Baker's main deputy in the Reagan years had been Richard Darman; in the Bush administration Darman became the head of the Office of Management and Budget.

11. Ross interview, Bush 41 OHP. Zoellick held the post of counselor of the department, which since the 1930s had been a place where the secretary can put a deputy who has no formal portfolio. (This is the job Zelikow was given when Rice later became secretary of state in 2005.) Ross chose the post of director of policy planning. Zoellick, who had been working with Baker since 1985, tended to also be a kind of chief of staff for Baker, and had more regular contacts with the line bureaus of the department. The deputy secretary of state was Lawrence Eagleburger, a career diplomat close to Scowcroft and to Kissinger.

From the summer of 1989 onward, the European bureau was headed by Raymond Seitz and his deputy, James Dobbins. They developed an excellent working relationship with Baker. Seitz was a diplomat's diplomat, a man in whom grace and wit were joined to a keen, careful mind. Dobbins had recently been deputy chief of mission in Bonn and knew Germany well. More acerbic than Seitz, he had one of the quickest analytical minds in the Foreign Service. On this transition in the bureau, see James Dobbins, *Foreign Service: Five Decades on the Frontlines of American Diplomacy* (Washington, DC: Brookings Institution Press and Rand Corporation, 2017), 103–4.

12. The quote "seemed connected" (quoting Lamar Alexander) is from what is now the best biography of Bush as a person: Jon Meacham, *Destiny and Power: The American Odyssey of George Herbert Walker Bush* (New York: Random House, 2015). 356. The press, Bush wryly observed to his diary, "keep playing it up that [Baker's] always selfish, always looking after his own ass, always looking to be President, etc.,...but I have a lot of confidence in him." Ibid. On tennis and "no daylight," Baker oral history, 2011, Bush 41 OHP, 14.

13. The biography of Scowcroft is Bartholomew Sparrow, *The Strategist: Brent Scowcroft and the Call of National Security* (New York: PublicAffairs, 2015); on Scowcroft's views of the Reagan White House see also Engel, *When the World Seemed New*, 84. On Gates, see his memoir of this period in his public service, *From the Shadows* (New York: Simon & Schuster, 1996), 443–45 (for his confrontation with Shultz), 456–57 (which indicates some of his tension with Baker, whom he describes as a "real piece of work").

14. Scowcroft on Blackwill in Bush and Scowcroft, *A World Transformed*, 41.

15. Baker-Shevardnadze memcon, 7 Mar 89, Bush Library, NSC, Rice files, 89–90 Subject files. Zelikow was at this meeting.

16. Zoellick interview, Bush 41 OHP; see also Baker with DeFrank, *The Politics of Diplomacy*, 68.

17. Scowcroft to Bush, "Getting Ahead of Gorbachev," 1 Mar 89 (read on March 6 by Bush, who jotted a laconic "Interesting paper"), Scowcroft USSR Chron Files, Bush Library. It originated with a February 7 draft by Rice that Gates had liked. Scowcroft appears to have revised the memo, however, before it went forward to Bush a few weeks later, on March 1.

From Moscow, Ambassador Jack Matlock had sent in a set of three cables offering his and his embassy's assessment of Gorbachev's prospects and policy recommendations. The assessment of the situation in the USSR was perceptive. But the policy suggestions were even more conservative than Scowcroft's position. The lead summary was to stick with the traditional agenda. "We should continue negotiations for verifiable arms reductions but refuse to make these the centerpiece of the relationship. We should increase political

pressure on Moscow to end, once and for all, its military involvement in Central America and to scale back substantially its military presence in Cuba." Maybe, if all that went well, the United States might consider discussing multilateral cooperation and economic relations "based strictly on mutual profitability and reciprocal obligations." Moscow cable, "U.S.-Soviet Relations: Policy Opportunities," 22 Feb 89, in *Masterpieces of History*, doc. no. 47. The other two cables in the series are also reprinted as docs. 43 and 45.

18. Zelikow and Rice through Blackwill to Scowcroft, "Status of National Security Reviews on US-Soviet, US–East European, and US–West European Relations," 2 Mar 89, Blackwill Chron Files, Bush Library.

19. Baker with DeFrank, *The Politics of Diplomacy*, 68–69 ("academic theology"); Baker's March 8 meeting with Bush is discussed in ibid., 67–68, and his prepared notes for the Bush-Baker meeting, "Key Impressions from the Trip," are at Baker Papers, Box 108, Folder 3; Zelikow interviews with Baker, Houston, January 1995, and Zoellick, Washington, D.C., January 1995.

20. Frédéric Bozo, *Mitterrand, the End of the Cold War, and German Unification*, trans. Susan Emanuel (New York: Berghahn, 2009), 33.

21. Genscher proudly devotes a chapter of his memoirs to "the struggle against modernizing nuclear short-range missiles." With good cause, he claims a lead role in stopping this. Hans-Dietrich Genscher, *Rebuilding a House Divided*, trans. Thomas Thornton (New York: Broadway Books, 1997), chapter 9; it is also a chapter in the much longer original, *Erinnerungen* (Berlin: Siedler Verlag, 1995). On Thatcher pressing for "urgent" action on SNF, see Bush-Thatcher telcon, 23 Jan 89; for some of the tone of U.S.–West German handwringing, see also Bush-Lambsdorff memcon, 8 Feb 89; Bush-Schüble memcon, 9 Feb 89; Bush-Von Weizsaecker memcon, 24 Feb 89, all in Bush Library; Baker's notes from his meeting with Kohl, 13 Feb 89, and notes for discussions with Genscher and Defense Minister Gerhard Stoltenberg, Baker Papers, Box 108, Folder 2. Gorbachev's comment on Baker's "panic" was in a meeting with Soviet ambassadors to socialist countries, 3 Mar 89, in *Masterpieces of History*, doc. no. 51.

22. Taubman, *Gorbachev*, 440.

23. On the Polish crisis of 1980–81 as a turning point in Soviet reluctance to intervene, see Matthew Ouimet, *The Rise and Fall of the Brezhnev*

Doctrine in Soviet Foreign Policy (Chapel Hill: University of North Carolina Press, 2003).

24. Kramer, "The Demise of the Soviet Bloc," 387; Georgi Shakhnazarov, *Tsena svobody* (Moscow: Rossika-Zevs, 1993).

25. The best summary of this episode is Kramer, "The Demise of the Soviet Bloc," 387–91; see also Gorbachev-Károly Grósz [Hungarian party leader] memcon, 23–24 Mar 89, in *Masterpieces of History*, doc. no. 52.

26. See the instructions from Chernyaev to Zagladin, 4 Feb 89, in ibid., doc. no. 44.

27. See Michael R. Beschloss and Strobe Talbott, *At the Highest Levels: The Inside Story of the End of the Cold War* (Boston: Little, Brown, 1993), 14–17, 19–21, 45–46; and Thomas L. Friedman, "Baker, Outlining World View, Assesses Plan for Soviet Bloc," *New York Times*, March 28, 1989, p. A1; see also Rice through Blackwill to Scowcroft, "Your Meeting with the Executive Board of the Polish American Congress," 30 Mar 89, Scowcroft Files, USSR Chron Files, Bush Library.

28. For the speech, which was drafted principally by Rice, Dan Fried at State, speechwriter Mark Davis, and by Bush himself, see Bush address, Hamtramck, Michigan, 17 Apr 89, *Public Papers of the Presidents of the United States: George Bush, 1989* (Washington, DC: Government Printing Office, 1990), bk. 1, 432; see also the discussion of the speechwriting process (and the would-be assassin) in Bush and Scowcroft, *A World Transformed*, 50–52. Raymond Garthoff asserted that the timing of Bush's speech on the day Solidarity was legalized was a coincidence. *The Great Transition* (Washington, DC: Brookings Institution Press, 1994), 606. It was not. Bush's speech on this topic was planned in advance and timed to follow the Warsaw announcement of the Roundtable outcome. See also Robert Hutchings (who joined Blackwill's NSC staff later in the spring of 1989 to help on issues involving Eastern Europe and Germany), *American Diplomacy and the End of the Cold War* (Washington, DC: Woodrow Wilson Center Press, 1997), 39–40.

The Polish government agreed to hold free parliamentary elections in June. The Roundtable developed the procedures for these elections. The Hungarians followed this example after the shakeup of their government in June 1989, effectively creating a multiparty political system before fully free elections were held in March 1990. See Timothy Garton Ash, *The Magic Lantern: The Revolution of '89 Wit-*

nessed in Warsaw, Budapest, Berlin, and Prague (New York: Random House, 1990), 25–60; Bernard Gwertzman and Michael T. Kaufman, eds., *The Collapse of Communism*, rev. ed. (New York: Times Books, 1991), 3–40, 110–37, 161–63, 253–54.

29. Bush and Scowcroft, *A World Transformed*, 48–49. The new aid program, known as SEED (Support for Eastern European Democracies), was signed into law in November 1989. It became one among a number of bilateral and multilateral programs that Western countries started setting up in the second half of 1989.

30. Rice started work on the alternative paper in March, with the conceptual approach of looking beyond containment and imagining conditions in which the Soviet Union would be a cooperative partner. Elements of this paper then were worked into the Bush address, College Station, Texas, 12 May 89, in *Public Papers of the Presidents of the United States: George Bush, 1989*, bk. 1. The paper evolved into a formal national security directive, NSD-23 (23 Sep 89), which is what is quoted in the text. That document reflected further work by Scowcroft, Gates, Blackwill, and Rice, with some help from Ross. That directive came out months later, having gone through an interagency clearance process that hedged some of the detailed language, at which point U.S. leaders were regarding the NSD as a formality that had already been overtaken by events. There is a discussion of the paper in Bush and Scowcroft, *A World Transformed*, 40–41, that might be confusing this paper with another. Given the current state of declassification, it is hard to check.

31. Baker (2011), Bush 41 OHP, pp. 9–10. On Baker and Scowcroft silencing or distancing the White House from Cheney and Gates, see Baker, *Politics of Diplomacy*, 70, 75, 156–58; Gates, *From the Shadows*, 474, 480–81; Snider through Brooks and Blackwill for Scowcroft, "Secretary Cheney's Speech for Tomorrow Evening," 9 May 89 (with Scowcroft's note) in Scowcroft files, USSR Collapse files, Bush Library; Engel also discusses the Cheney speech incident in *When the World Seemed New*, 137–38.

On May 28, David Ignatius published a column, "Why Bob Gates Is the Eeyore of Sovietology," *Washington Post*, May 28, 1989, p. B2, that called him "someone capable of finding a dark lining in even the brightest cloud." Gates sent a note to Ignatius saying that "he thought of himself more as Winnie the Pooh." Robert Gates

Papers, Box 83, Folder 10, Swem Library, College of William and Mary.

The intelligence community (which included the defense intelligence agencies) had just issued a National Intelligence Estimate (which also went to Congress) that still had a more cautionary tone. Leading the "Key Judgments," it said, "For the foreseeable future, the USSR will remain the West's principal adversary." It described a Soviet desire, though, to shift the competition more "to a largely political and economic plane." NIE 11-4-89, "Soviet Policy Toward the West: The Gorbachev Challenge," 11 Apr 89, in Benjamin Fischer, ed., *At Cold War's End: US Intelligence on the Soviet Union and Eastern Europe, 1989–1991* (Washington, DC: CIA Historical Review Program, 1999), 229–32; the disagreements within the intelligence community about this estimate are itemized on 231.

32. Bush and Scowcroft, *A World Transformed*, 54. The Open Skies initiative led to negotiations that began in Ottawa in February 1990 (a meeting best known for the side discussions on Germany) and produced a 1992 treaty. The treaty gained thirty-five signatories. It entered into force in 2002, when Russia and the United States began conducting their first overflights. No territory could be placed off-limits.

The NSC staffers who had developed the idea (Blackwill and Zelikow) thought it had been important and ahead of its time in 1955. They believed its concept remained highly relevant in 1989. On the significance of the original 1955 proposal, see the interesting summary from one of its originators, Walt Rostow, in *Concept and Controversy* (Austin: University of Texas Press, 2003), 137–71. See also the context of "Glasnost and the Public Debate" on openness in the USSR, in Odom, *The Collapse of the Soviet Military*, chapter 8.

33. There is a large historical commentary about the so-called policy "pause" in the first half of 1989. The argument fits preconceptions, including partisan ones, about a supposedly much too cautious and unimaginative president. To be fair to the critics, however, the Bush team contributed to the impression, perhaps unavoidably, because of the ways they concealed what was going on, including from the disfavored holdover officials in their own administration. Engel, in *When the World Seemed New*, also has a "pause" chapter, a bit influenced by some of the factors we mention. He argues, though, that the "pause" seemed to be ending in March, which—six

weeks after Bush's inauguration—is not much of a pause. Engel believes the deliberations gave officials precious time to think anew and "in uncomfortable terms" (p. 135).

Most of the literature on the "pause" tends to ignore Baker, although he was actually driving most of the action in U.S.-Soviet relations. Baker's retrospective comment is that "we gave Gorbachev a little bit of grief because he couldn't figure out exactly what we were doing, but by May it was over. [He could see what the United States was doing.] After my meeting with Shevardnadze...in Vienna, and that may have been in March [March 7]...from about that time on [the United States was moving].... So do I think it cost the country anything? Absolutely not." Baker (2011), Bush 41 OHP, p. 4.

34. Tilo Schabert, *How World Politics Is Made: France and the Reunification of Germany*, trans. John Tyler Tuttle, ed. and abridged by Barry Cooper (Columbia: University of Missouri Press, 2009), 175, 178.

35. Quoted in ibid., 174; on the June 1988 agreement with Kohl, see 184. A French policy planner in the Foreign Ministry, Jean-Marie Guéhenno, had argued in April 1989 that "the Germany of 1989 does not find in the postwar political and strategic framework a dynamic response to its new ambitions. The apparent fluidity of the situation in the East further increases its impatience to be a full actor in international relations." "The Franco-German Relationship," 30 Apr 89, in Maurice Vaïsse and Christian Wenkel, eds., *La diplomatie française face à l'unification allemande* (Paris: Tallandier, 2011), 55–60.

36. Kenneth Dyson and Kevin Featherstone, *The Road to Maastricht: Negotiating Economic and Monetary Union* (Oxford: Oxford University Press, 1999), 170–71.

37. Harold James, *Making the European Monetary Union* (Cambridge, MA: Harvard University Press, 2012), 210–63; and Dyson and Featherstone, *Road to Maastricht*. The president of the Bundesbank during this period was Karl Otto Pöhl. The head of the Bank of England was Robin Leigh-Pemberton. The head of the Banque de France was Jacques de Larosière.

James was granted access to records of the European Committee of Central Bank Governors and Bundesbank records, including transcripts of meetings of the Delors committee. More details about the important roles of Genscher and Kohl are in Wilfried Loth, "Helmut Kohl und die Währungsunion," *Vierteljahrshefte für Zeitgeschichte* 61, no. 4 (2013): 455–63 (for this phase).

38. Dyson and Featherstone, *Road to Maastricht*, 186–87. The episode offers another good glimpse of the staff workings of the triumvirate. Mitterrand's key aide on these issues was Élisabeth Guigou, often working with Pascal Lamy on Delors's staff, and Joachim Bitterlich in the West German Chancellery.

39. Tommaso Padoa-Schioppa, *The Road to Monetary Union in Europe: The Emperor, the Kings, and the Genies* (Oxford: Oxford University Press, 2000), 117–18.

40. For Kohl's motives, Schwarz, *Helmut Kohl*, 518–20.

41. Blackwill to Zelikow, September 2018.

42. Bozo, *Mitterrand*, 46–47. The American memcons for these meetings are only partly open as of 2018. The lunch discussion of regional issues is declassified; an earlier discussion of European matters is not, but some of its contents along with Bush's views of Mitterrand are in *A World Transformed*, 74–78.

43. This initiative was announced in the speech Bush delivered in Mainz, Germany, on May 31. It was the seed that ultimately led to the creation of the CSCE's Office of Free Elections. Rice, having picked the idea up from Stephen Sestanovich, passed it on to Zelikow for inclusion in Bush's speech. For some context, especially the West German philosophical debate over whether CSCE norms should extend from individual liberties to matters of democratic governance, see Timothy Garton Ash, *In Europe's Name: Germany and the Divided Continent* (New York: Random House, 1993), 263–64.

44. Bush address, Boston, Massachusetts, 21 May 89, in *Public Papers of the Presidents of the United States: George Bush, 1989*, bk. 1; Rodman and Blackwill to Scowcroft, "Presidential Speech on Western Europe," 11 Apr 89, Zelikow files, Bush Library. Baker's warning is from his "Talking Points Cabinet Meeting," 23 Jan 89, Box 108, Baker Library.

45. Memcons, Bush-Delors, 30 May 89 (Brussels) and 14 Jun 89 (Washington), both at Bush Library.

46. The March 30 session, for example, had Bush, Vice President Dan Quayle, Baker and his deputy Lawrence Eagleburger, Scowcroft and his deputy Gates, Cheney, and chief of staff John Sununu. Later discussions would sometimes include others like Treasury Secretary Nicholas Brady or JCS

chairman William Crowe. The account of this meeting in Bush and Scowcroft, *A World Transformed*, 42–45, appears to draw on notes that have not yet been declassified.

47. Bush and Scowcroft, *A World Transformed*, 43; Gates remembered that "Cheney looked at Scowcroft as if he'd lost his mind." Gates, *From the Shadows*, 462. Scowcroft had been looking for more sympathetic analysis on his and Kissinger's troop withdrawal plan, including from a former Kissinger staffer, Peter Rodman. Rodman to Scowcroft, "Re: 'Kissinger Plan' for Central Europe," 14 Mar 89, in Scowcroft Files, USSR Chron Files, Bush Library (still classified).

48. On Baker's Moscow trip, Zelikow interview with Baker, Houston, January 1995; Soviet notes of Baker's meeting with Gorbachev on May 11 are published in Gorbachev, *Gody trudnykh reshenii, 1985–1992: izbrannoye*, 136–48. For the atmosphere surrounding Baker's trip to Moscow, see Beschloss and Talbott, *At the Highest Levels*, 61–68.

49. On the insight about linking the conventional and nuclear arms control problems, in which the Dutch foreign minister and West German defense minister also played important roles, see Baker, *The Politics of Diplomacy*, 82–83, 89–91; Bush and Scowcroft, *A World Transformed*, 45–46, 71–73.

Blackwill and Zelikow were familiar with the conventional arms control issues. In 1985–86, Blackwill had been the ambassador to the long-running predecessor negotiation, known as MBFR, that had been limited to Central Europe. Zelikow had worked for Blackwill on MBFR. Remaining there as the new negotiation, CFE, took shape, Zelikow became the political adviser during 1987 to the new U.S. ambassador, Stephen Ledogar.

50. The plan would cut Soviet foreign-deployed forces from about 565,000 to the new 275,000 limit. See IISS, *Military Balance 1988–89*. Oddly, Sparrow and Engel (relying on Sparrow) assert that the U.S. troop strength in Europe would be cut under this proposal by only 7,500, a number that Sparrow seems to have thought was 20 percent of the total U.S. troop strength in Europe (which was then about 320,000). *The Strategist*, 305; *When the World Seemed New*, 139.

To set the scene for the CFE arguments at the time: "In late 1988 in many NATO capitals (Ankara, London, Rome, and Washington, for example) NATO forces were considered too thin to maintain a credible conventional deterrent. Thus NATO could not afford to reduce any of its own forces even if facing a leaner [Warsaw Pact] force." Jane M. O. Sharp, *Striving for Military Stability in Europe* (London: Routledge, 2005), 37. (For details on the aircraft and helicopters issue, see also pp. 22, 52.) For background on CFE issues as of the spring of 1989, see Barry Blechman, William Durch, and Kevin O'Prey, *Regaining the High Ground* (New York: St. Martin's Press, 1990); Jonathan Dean, "Conventional Talks: A Good First Round," *Bulletin of the Atomic Scientists* 45, no. 8 (October 1989): 26–32; Richard Falkenrath, *Shaping Europe's Military Order* (Cambridge, MA: MIT Press, 1995), 29–48.

51. We recall the May 1989 debates in the U.S. government. Bush's meeting with Mitterrand occurred in the midst of these debates. Bush previewed his planned moves. Mitterrand very much approved. See also Baker, *Politics of Diplomacy*, 93–94; Gates, *From the Shadows*, 462–63; Don Oberdorfer, *The Turn: From the Cold War to a New Era; The United States and the Soviet Union, 1983–1990* (New York: Poseidon Press, 1991), 347–51; Baker's May 19 notes on a May 17 meeting on his copy of Zoellick to Baker, "NATO Summit—Possible Initiatives," 15 May 89.

52. "Some say we're cold warriors": Zelikow's notes of Bush's meeting with Italian prime minister Ciriaco De Mita, 27 May 1989, rendered slightly more formally in the memcon (2nd meeting), Bush Library.

53. Looking back after the treaty was concluded in 1990, it seemed evident that "by May 1989 the essential structural elements of the CFE treaty had been defined." Falkenrath, *Shaping Europe's Military Order*, 54; see also Blechman, Durch, and O'Prey, *Regaining the High Ground*, 65, 69.

54. On the "enthusiastic welcome" for Bush's initiatives from both the Bonn government and the opposition Social Democratic Party (SPD), see Dennis Bark and David Gress, *A History of West Germany: Democracy and Its Discontents*, 2nd ed. (Oxford: Blackwell, 1993), 575–77. Bush's reflections on the significance of the 1989 NATO summit for his presidency were related to Rice in 1993 discussions. For the Bush quote, see Oberdorfer, *The Turn*, 351.

55. Zelikow interview with Zoellick, Washington, DC, 1991.

56. Scowcroft to Bush, "The NATO Summit," 20 Mar 89. Any U.S. documents that are cited with-

out a public source, like this one, were accessed by Zelikow in 1991–94 in the preparation of the work that eventually became Philip Zelikow and Condoleezza Rice, *Germany Unified and Europe Transformed: A Study in Statecraft* (Cambridge, MA: Harvard University Press, paperback ed., 1997). We cited all our sources, including still-classified documents, and this has facilitated FOIA requests and more rapid declassification. But some of the original documents have not yet been released.

In this case Bush read the memo on March 26. He underscored and checked the paragraph about the priority to be attached to policy toward Germany. The NSC staff were thus effectively bypassing the formal review process, which had disagreed on this issue, among others. For more detail on the interagency differences about U.S. attitudes toward German unification, see Zelikow and Rice, *Germany Unified*, 25–26. The Bush comment is from a Zelikow interview with him in Houston, January 1995. For more on how U.S. intelligence saw the political situation in West Germany at the time, see National Intelligence Estimate 23-89W, "West Germany: A More Self-Assured Role," May 1989, in CIA FOIA files.

Bush eventually used the "commonwealth of free nations" phrase in his Mainz speech of May 31 and elaborated on it in a speech on U.S. relations with Europe delivered in Leiden on July 17. He used it again at the NATO summit on December 4. He used a similar phrase, simplified as a "commonwealth of freedom," in another speech delivered to the Czech Federal Assembly in Prague on November 17, 1990.

57. Arnaud de Borchgrave, "Bush 'Would Love' Reunited Germany," *Washington Times*, May 16, 1989, p. A1; on Bush's 1983 trip and quotes, Zelikow interview with Bush, Houston, January 1995. Bush discusses the powerful impressions made on him by an earlier February 1983 trip to Bavaria in the Federal Republic, in which he also formed an important friendship with then–West German defense minister Manfred Wörner, in Bush and Scowcroft, *A World Transformed*, 182–84.

At the same time, separately over at State, Zoellick was advising a receptive Baker "to get ahead of the curve" on the issue of German unification or Gorbachev "might grab it first." Zoellick to Baker, "NATO Summit—Possible Initiatives," 15 May 89; Zoellick, "Proposed

Agenda for Meeting with the President," 16 May 89, Box 115, Baker Library.

A few days before the de Borchgrave interview, Blackwill had written another memorandum for Bush on dealing with the West Germans. Blackwill urged again that the United States adopt this issue anew. In the context of renewed nuclear debates in NATO between Washington and Bonn, Blackwill argued that if the Western allies identified their interests more closely with Germany's national aspirations, it would be easier to persuade the German people to reciprocate by continuing to identify their nation's future with the Western alliance. See the proposed memo to Bush on "Dealing with the Germans," in Blackwill to Scowcroft, 11 May 89.

Blackwill's further advice in this May memo (following up on the earlier memo in March) cannot be causally linked to Bush's statement to de Borchgrave. Scowcroft held up this particular memo and did not endorse it on to Bush until August 7. Bush read and initialed the memo on September 9. That memo did arrive at another important time. Nine days later, Bush made another comment to the press about German unification, discussed in the next chapter.

58. Compare Bush's and Scowcroft's separate comments at the top and bottom of Bush and Scowcroft, *A World Transformed*, 188.

59. Pierre Favier and Michel Martin-Roland, *La Décennie Mitterrand*, vol. 3, *Les défis (1988–1991)* (Paris: Éditions du Seuil, 1996), 200 (from the French records); Bush and Scowcroft, *A World Transformed*, 77–78 (from the American records). Earlier that month, on May 3, Mitterrand had told his Council of Ministers, "That the Germans would want reunification is perfectly logical and normal. It is the job of our diplomacy to address such an irrepressible urge." Favier and Martin-Roland, *Les défis*, 200.

60. For a characteristic example, see the Bush–De Mita memcon (1st meeting), 27 May 89, Bush Library. Bush posed the question to Thatcher on June 1. Her response is not yet declassified in the American or British records.

61. *Public Papers of the Presidents of the United States: George Bush, 1989*, bk. 1, 638. Paragraph 26 of the NATO summit declaration, adopted on May 30, 1989, states, "We seek a state of peace in Europe in which the German people regains its unity through free self-determination" (ibid., 625).

62. Oberdorfer, *The Turn*, 351–52.

63. Address by Bush, Mainz, 31 May 89, in *Public Papers of the Presidents of the United States, 1989*, bk. 1, 650–54. The "Europe whole and free" phrase was coined by a State speechwriter on Ross's staff, Harvey Sicherman.

64. This was more traditional boilerplate. The drafts of the speech from Scowcroft's staff had suggested more radical phrases referring directly to German unification. Scowcroft did not want Bush to get ahead of what Kohl was saying. He "was concerned about unnecessarily stimulating German nationalism and took [such language] out." Bush and Scowcroft, *A World Transformed*, 83.

65. Bark and Gress, *History of West Germany*, 581.

66. Zelikow and Rice interview with Teltschik, Gütersloh, June 1992.

67. For Teltschik, see *General Anzeiger*, July 6, 1989, quoted by A. James McAdams in *Germany Divided: From the Wall to Reunification* (Princeton, NJ: Princeton University Press, 1993), 191–92. In the spring of 1988, leaders of the largest West German political party, the conservative Christian Democratic Union (CDU), almost amended their formal party platform to set aside, as one of them put it, "the old continuing assumption that the German question [had] to be on the agenda." Kohl's two top advisers on these issues in the Chancellery, Wolfgang Schäuble and Horst Teltschik, and the minister of inner-German affairs, Dorothee Wilms, had supported the push for change in the CDU platform. Unnamed "key author" of draft CDU policy statement quoted from 1988 interview with McAdams, *Germany Divided*, 191 n. 36. The original discussion paper produced by the CDU party commission would have downplayed the goal of political reunification, but the document finally adopted at the June 1988 Wiesbaden CDU party conference was wrested back to language mirroring the time-honored usage of the FRG's Basic Law. See Ash, *In Europe's Name*, 446–47; and Karl-Rudolf Korte, *Die Chance genutzt* (Frankfurt: Campus, 1994), 20 n. 11.

In February 1989 the head of the West German Chancellery, Wolfgang Schäuble, talked about the old hopes "that the unity of Germany could be achieved through the reunification of both German states in the not-too-distant future." But, he said, "we know today that these hopes [about a quick reunification] were illusory." It was clear by 1961 at the latest that for the time being there was "no way to overcome the German division."

What was left, given current realities, must be the preservation of the "substance of the nation," the "commonality of the Germans," which meant keeping open the "communication between the people." Schäuble address to the Evangelical Academy, Bad Boll, February 25, 1989, quoted in *Texte*, 47; see also the statement of the government's position by FRG inner-German minister Dorothee Wilms (CDU), address to the Friedrich-Ebert Stiftung, Bonn, January 24, 1989, quoted in ibid., 28.

68. Evident ambivalence and Kaiser quote in Marc Fisher, "The Unanswered 'German Question,'" *Washington Post*, July 27, 1989, p. A25.

69. The quote "far ahead" is from Zelikow and Rice interview with Teltschik, Gütersloh, June 1992. In an interesting work of evidentiary comparison by Alexander von Plato, *The End of the Cold War? Bush, Kohl, Gorbachev, and the Reunification of Germany*, trans. Edith Burley (New York: Palgrave Macmillan, 2015), he seems to give Americans credit for advancing the unification theme before the West Germans (pp. 12–13, 16), after attacking us for having said so in an exaggerated way, attributing to us the position "that the Americans had initiated the reunification and the leading CDU politicians were prepared to take reunification off the current CDU agenda" (p. 9). In his interviews he then confronted people like Genscher and Teltschik with such purported claims. They then bristled, including at us.

This method, however, invents friction where there was none. We had interviewed Teltschik and Genscher about these matters. We never believed or wrote that the United States "initiated the reunification," an inflammatory proposition.

Nor did we think that Kohl or Genscher were slow or backward on the matter, or trying "to take reunification off the current CDU agenda," another inflammatory phrasing (p. 9). As we document in note 67, CDU party leaders had their internal intraparty debates and had chosen to stay carefully within the prevailing party consensus until they decided to edge forward.

We describe their decisions to edge forward in chapter 4, decisions that we think began in the second half of 1989 and did so, for Kohl, *before* the opening of the wall. Our position, and Bush's, was that the West Germans should understand that the United States was ready to consider advancing this topic, if and when they

were. Within the U.S. government, that evident readiness was itself a large and controversial policy step.

70. On West German perceptions of America's "new orientation," see Kiessler and Elbe, *Ein runder Tisch mit scharfen Ecken*, 16–21. There was one suspected break in the partnership in November 1989, when Kohl surprised Washington with a major policy move that we will discuss in chapter 4. Washington came to realize that Kohl's secrecy had more to do with West German coalition politics than any difficulty with Washington.

71. Washington (Acland) to Defense Secretary George Younger, 7 Jul 89, in National Archives of the UK (TNA), PREM 19/3210; see also Bonn (Mallaby) to Sir J. Fretwell, 27 Jul 89, in Foreign and Commonwealth Office (FCO), *Documents on British Policy Overseas: Series III, Vol. VII—German Unification 1989–1990* (London: Routledge, 2010) (hereinafter *DBPO-Unification*), 20–23.

72. Blackwill raised the concern with British ambassador to NATO Michael Alexander. Alexander reported this in an informal letter to Patrick Wright, who shared the report with Foreign Secretary Major. Alexander to Wright, 18 Sep 89, in *DBPO-Unification*, 31–33.

73. On the internal Soviet discussions see Chernyaev, *Shest' let s Gorbachevym*, 262; letter to us from Chernyaev, February 1995; see also *Izvestiya*, October 16, 1988.

74. Gedmin, *The Hidden Hand*, 51–52; Sodaro, *Moscow, Germany, and the West*, 355–62. See the Bush-Kohl telcon, 15 Jun 89, and Bush-Genscher memcon (quoted in the text), 21 Jun 89, both at Bush Library.

75. Wjatscheslaw Kotschemassow, *Meine letzte Mission* (Berlin: Dietz, 1994), 121–29, 143–44, 148–55; Reinhold Andert and Wolfgang Herzberg, eds., *Der Sturz: Honecker im Kreuzverhör* (Berlin: Aufbau, 1990), 62; Zelikow interview with Chernyaev, Moscow, January 1994. On Soviet attitudes toward the GDR more broadly, see Charles Gati, *The Bloc That Failed: Soviet–East European Relations in Transition* (London: I. B. Tauris, 1990), 65–135; and J. F. Brown, *Surge to Freedom: The End of Communist Rule in Eastern Europe* (Durham, NC: Duke University Press, 1991), 48–70.

76. See the analysis of the various German and Soviet meeting records in Von Plato, *The End of the Cold War?*, 22–31.

77. Taubman, *Gorbachev*, 478.

78. The text is in *Masterpieces in History*, doc. no. 73.

79. Taubman, *Gorbachev*, 436–37 (quoting Gorbachev's comments at the Politburo meeting of May 11). Taubman sifts the evidence and sides with those who place accountability for the violence on party and military leaders in Georgia. The violence in Georgia took place against a background of prior national unrest. At the end of February and beginning of March 1988, Azerbaijani gangs had conducted horrific pogroms against Armenians, killing scores of people in the city of Sumgait. Troops slowly restored order, but Gorbachev was hesitant about declaring martial law. He sought political solutions. Ibid., 369–70.

80. Soviet memcon of Deng-Gorbachev meeting, 16 May 89, in Wilson Center Digital Archive; "Where is China's Gorbachev?": from editorial note in Zhang Liang, compiler, and Andrew Nathan and Perry Link, eds., *The Tiananmen Papers* (New York: PublicAffairs, 2001), 172.

81. From secret recollections later smuggled out of China, *Prisoner of the State: The Secret Journal of Zhao Ziyang*, trans. Bao Pu, Renee Chiang, and Adi Ignatius (New York: Simon & Schuster, 2009), 254–55.

82. Soviet memcon of Zhao-Gorbachev, 16 May 89, in Wilson Center Digital Archive.

83. Quotes are from minutes of Politburo Standing Committee meeting (at Deng's home), 17 May 89, in *Tiananmen Papers*, 189–90. See also the valuable additional evidence in Mary Sarotte, "China's Fear of Contagion: Tiananmen Square and the Power of the European Example," *International Security* 37, no. 2 (2012): 156–82. We do not share Sarotte's evident skepticism about the value of the *Tiananmen Papers* and the Zhao memoir.

84. Li Peng, in minutes of Politburo Standing Committee meeting, 6 Jun 89, in *Tiananmen Papers*, 421.

85. Sergey Radchenko, in Jeffrey Engel and Radchenko, "Beijing and Malta, 1989," in Kristina Spohr and David Reynolds, eds., *Transcending the Cold War: Summits, Statecraft, and the Dissolution of Bipolarity in Europe, 1970–1990* (Oxford: Oxford University Press, 2016), 196–97.

86. Politburo meeting, 4 Oct 89, quoted in ibid., 196.

87. For Scowcroft's comment on the press and Bush's style, Bush and Scowcroft, *A World Transformed*, 129.

88. Mitterrand-Bush, 13 Jul 89, blending the material about Mitterrand's statements from French records quoted in Favier and Martin-Roland, *Les défis*, 196, and the American memcon that Scowcroft prepared, at the Bush Library.

Bush's endorsement of Jaruzelski as the necessary leader at that moment followed the view of the able American ambassador in Warsaw, John Davis, who in June had secretly worked on this point with the Solidarity opposition; they also supported keeping Jaruzelski in place—for a time—for their own reasons. Domber, *Empowering Revolution*, 238–45, 263.

Mitterrand's discussion of "limits" may have been prompted by Gorbachev's complaint to Mitterrand that Bush had made statements in Poland calling for the withdrawal of all Soviet troops and for the restoration of Poland's 1939 borders. Gorbachev-Mitterrand memcon, 6 Jul 89, in *Masterpieces in History*, doc. no. 74. Bush had made an offhand comment about all Soviet troops leaving Poland in a press briefing before his departure to Europe, and regretted having said this publicly. He told Jaruzelski that he had only meant to say that perhaps someday all foreign troops might leave Europe. He asked him to be sure and pass this on to Gorbachev. Polish Foreign Ministry report on the earlier Bush-Jaruzelski meeting, 18 Jul 89, excerpted in *Masterpieces in History*, doc. no. 76. Bush had said nothing about the explosive topic of moving Poland back to its pre-1939 frontiers and was apparently unaware that anyone thought he had. Yet obviously someone had reported such an allegation to Gorbachev.

89. Ibid.

90. Engel, *When the World Seemed New*, 228–29.

91. Bush in Bush and Scowcroft, *A World Transformed*, 131.

92. Acland to Major, "The Making of Bush Foreign Policy: East-West and West-West Relations," 5 Sep 89 (this analysis was also shared with Thatcher), PREM 19/2682, TNA.

93. See, for example, Paul Kennedy, *The Rise and Fall of the Great Powers* (New York: Penguin, 1987); David Calleo, *Beyond American Hegemony* (New York: Basic Books, 1989); and Walter Russell Mead, *Mortal Splendor: The American Empire in Transition* (Boston: Houghton Mifflin, 1987) (remarking on American decline since the 1960s). "The American Century is over" is from Clyde Prestowitz in *Time*, July 4, 1988, p. 28.

94. Samuel P. Huntington, "The U.S.—Decline or Renewal?" *Foreign Affairs* 67, no. 2 (Winter 1988/89): 76–92.

95. Rice refers to the Gates memo to Bush in Rice to Scowcroft, "The Impact of Soviet Internal Dif-

ficulties on U.S.-Soviet Relations," 9 Aug 89, Master Chron for USSR Sep 89–Dec 89, Box 2, Bush Library. Hodnett's analysis was circulated formally in CIA SOVA, "Gorbachev's Domestic Gambles and Instability in the USSR," SOV 89-10077, Sep 89, available in Fischer, ed., *At Cold War's End*, 27–47.

The bulk of the U.S. intelligence community did not take such a radical view of Gorbachev's prospects. The conventional position expected him to muddle through. The disagreement was spotlighted a couple of months later in a National Intelligence Estimate. See NIE 11-18-89, "The Soviet System in Crisis: Prospects for the Next Two Years," November 1989, in ibid., esp. 55, 75 (vii and 18 in the original). We highlight the dire assessments from Hodnett/SOVA, representing CIA's Directorate of Intelligence, because they were more influential on Gates, Rice, Ross, and probably on Bush, Baker, and Scowcroft.

Chapter 4: The Pivot: A New Germany in a Different Europe

1. Dufourcq, "De l'Europe d'aujourd'hui à celle de demain," 20 Feb 89, quoted in Bozo, *Mitterrand*, 62.
2. Quoted from the original meeting records by Jacques Lévesque, *The Enigma of 1989: The USSR and the Liberation of Eastern Europe*, trans. Keith Martin (Berkeley: University of California Press, 1997), 120.
3. Ibid., 130–31.
4. For a useful Hungarian perspective on what they heard in their interactions with Western countries in the spring and summer of 1989, see László Borhi, "The International Context of Hungarian Transition, 1989: The View from Budapest," in Frédéric Bozo, Marie-Pierre Rey, N. Piers Ludlow, and Leopoldo Nuti, eds., *Europe and the End of the Cold War: A Reappraisal* (London: Routledge, 2008), 78–92.
5. See Klaus Bachmann, "Poland 1989: The Constrained Revolution," in Wolfgang Mueller, Michael Gehler, and Arnold Suppan, eds., *The Revolutions of 1989: A Handbook* (Vienna: Verlag der Österreichischen Akademie der Wissenschaften, 2015), 60–62, influenced by evidence supporting the analysis of the former Polish communist intellectual and party leader, Jerzy Wiatr.
6. "Most Solidarity Leaders": Warsaw 8512, "How to Elect Jaruzelski Without Voting for Him, and Will He Run?," 23 Jun 89, in National Security

Archive Electronic Briefing Book No. 42, ed. Gregory Domber. Domber has a good account of the U.S. efforts in Warsaw, including the role of Ambassador Davis. He describes Bush as seeking "stability," that he "slowed the pace of change" and sought "evolution" rather than revolution. *Empowering Revolution*, 208. Yet he also seems to agree that "another failed revolution could have set the clock back a decade in Eastern Europe and derailed Soviet reform." Ibid., 251.

7. A good brief summary of the formation of the Mazowiecki government in July–August 1989, informed by interviews with Mazowiecki, is Victor Sebestyen, *Revolution 1989: The Fall of the Soviet Empire* (New York: Vintage, 2010), 304–9.
8. Gorbachev's role during this crisis is traced in Kramer, "The Demise of the Soviet Bloc," 397–402.
9. See Lévesque, *Enigma*, 123–26.
10. See Domber, *Empowering Revolution*, 228–46; Engel, *When the World Seemed New*, 219–20. Engel, like others, recounts how frustrated Scowcroft and Blackwill were that they could not make larger commitments of U.S. aid at this point. Treasury Secretary Nicholas Brady is the usual villain. The essence of the argument is that the U.S. government lacked the vision that the Truman administration had, in 1947, to make a huge commitment. This argument naturally resonates with historians.

    Some U.S. officials, including both of us, underestimated the problems at the time. The skeptics had a point. The aid ideas actually required careful analysis. There were and are some serious problems with the Marshall Plan analogy. We and our NSC staff colleagues had not analyzed what was involved in standing up a really large aid program. Nor, back then, had we looked hard at the designs (like the use of counterpart funds) involved in past U.S. aid successes like the Marshall Plan. For an example of one such analysis, an extensive one that counseled "against a Marshall Plan for the East," see Barry Eichengreen and Marc Uzan, "The Marshall Plan: Economic Effects and Implications for Eastern Europe and the Former USSR," *Economic Policy* 7, no. 14 (1992): 14, 16.
11. On the creation and coordinating role of the G-24 among guiding governments and more important institutions, see Kohl to Bush, 28 Jun 89, in *Dokumente zur Deutschlandpolitik: Deutsche Einheit Sonderedition aus den Akten des*

Bundeskanzleramtes 1989/90, ed. Hanns Jürgen Küsters and Daniel Hofmann (Munich: R.
Oldenbourg Verlag, 1998), 320–23 (hereinafter
cited as *DzD-Einheit*); and Stephan Haggard
and Andrew Moravcsik, "The Political Economy of Financial Assistance to Eastern Europe,
1989–1991," in Robert Keohane, Joseph Nye,
and Stanley Hoffmann, eds., *After the Cold War:
International Institutions and State Strategies in
Europe, 1989–1991* (Cambridge, MA: Harvard
Center for International Affairs, 1993), 257–59.

On the background of the EC's involvement
and the Commission's energetic role in standing
up the G-24, see José Torreblanca, *The Reuniting
of Europe: Promises, Negotiations, and Compromises* (London: Routledge, 2001), 31–32; and on
the scale of food aid to Poland, Charlotte Benson
and Edward Clay, *Eastern Europe and the Former
Soviet Union: Economic Change, Social Welfare
and Aid* (London: Overseas Development Institute, 1992), Table 5.1, p. 40 (we assume a population of about thirty-eight million Poles in 1989).

12. Bartel, "The Power of Omission," 216 ("genuinely
radical").

13. The West European role in any major debt/aid/
reform effort in Eastern Europe was bound to be
crucial. Their banks held most East European
debt and the West European countries had the
most expertise on economic conditions in the
region. But the West European governments also
had not yet developed any substantial ideas about
what might be done. Emergency aid, like food aid
for Poland, was provided in significant amounts,
as we mentioned in the previous chapter. The
longer-term aid programs also began mounting
varied programs for technical assistance.

Recipient government policy planning had
been crucial in the development of the Marshall
Plan designs during 1947 and 1948. Rather than
a wrecked but basically capitalist system, manned
by people who knew how to run a capitalist system
and with viable institutions for private property
and banks, post-communist reformers confronted
a system organized on an entirely different basis.

At the beginning of September, Zoellick was
noting for Baker that the main source of money to
reform Eastern European economies would have
to come from the private sector. Recalling how
Western loan money had been wasted by the communist governments during the 1970s (especially
in Poland), he noted, "We must avoid the mistakes
of the 70s." "In sum, the Marshall Plan of the 90s

should rely on private capital and the help of those
[West European countries] who were rebuilt by
the first Marshall Plan." Baker/Zoellick note, "Re
Cabinet Meeting Presentation, September 5," 5
Sep 89, Box 108, Folder 9, Baker Papers.

14. On the Polish assistance arguments in Washing-
ton in the autumn of 1989 and the results, see
Condoleezza Rice, *Democracy: Stories from the
Long Road to Freedom* (New York: Twelve, 2017),
144–52; see also the brief material in Bush and
Scowcroft, *A World Transformed*, 138–40; and
Hutchings, *American Diplomacy and the End of
the Cold War*, 72–76.

15. The United States reallocated or appropriated about a billion dollars in grant money for
Poland by the end of 1989, joining a larger flow
of Western aid. See, e.g., Scowcroft to Bush, "Aid
to Poland," 18 Dec 89, in Scowcroft Files, Box
91125, Soviet Power Collapse in Eastern Europe
(December 1989–January 1990), Bush Library.

16. A good contemporary appraisal is Simon Johnson
and Marzena Kowalska, "Poland: The Political
Economy of Shock Therapy," in Stephan Haggard and Steven Webb, eds., *Voting for Reform*
(New York: Oxford University Press, for the
World Bank, 1994), 185–235. The Mazowiecki
government plan was developed under the leadership of its economics chief, Leszek Balcerowicz.
Among the most influential of the Western economic advisers to the Polish reformers in 1989
and 1990 were Jeffrey Sachs and David Lipton.
In addition to their substantive expertise, these
experts and a few others played a vital bridging
role between the Poles, the U.S. government, and
the international institutions. Thus, some of the
important strategic planning by the governments
occurred in this nongovernmental space.

17. Timothy Garton Ash, *The Magic Lantern: The
Revolution of '89 Witnessed in Warsaw, Budapest,
Berlin, and Prague* (New York: Vintage, 1999), 64.

18. Dieter Grosser, "Triebkräfte der Wiederver-
einigung," and Friedrich Kurz, "Ungarn 89," in
Grosser, Stephan Bierling, and Friedrich Kurz,
eds., *Die sieben Mythen der Wiedervereinigung:
Fakten und Analysen zu einem Prozeß ohne Alter-
native* (Munich: Ehrenwirth, 1991), 37–38, 123–
24, and 130 (for the quote from Prime Minister
Nemeth, interviewed by Kurz); Maximilian Graf,
"The Opening of the Austrian-Hungarian Bor-
der Revisited," in Blumenau, Hanhimäki, and
Zanchetta, eds., *New Perspectives on the End of the
Cold War*, 139 ("masterpiece").

19. Schabowski in an interview with Elizabeth Pond, quoted in Pond, *Beyond the Wall: Germany's Road to Unification* (Washington, DC: Brookings Institution Press, 1993), 90.

20. Lambert Der, originally for the *Greenville News-Piedmont*, 1990.

21. Kohl to Honecker, 14 Aug 89, *DzD-Einheit*, 355–56; see also Ralf Georg Reuth and Andreas Bonte, *Das Komplott: Wie es wirklich zur deutschen Einheit kam* (Munich: Piper, 1993), 56–58; "surprise": from Zelikow interview with Kastrup, Bonn, December 1994.

22. The Hungarian leaders pleaded for the West Germans to help them with their debts, including with the Americans and the IMF. The West Germans did what they could, including arrangements to encourage West German banks to extend significant further credit to the Hungarians. West German records are at *DzD-Einheit*, 377–82; Zelikow interviews with Genscher, Wachtberg-Pech, December 1994; Teltschik, Munich, December 1994; and Kastrup, Bonn, December 1994; Kiessler and Elbe, *Ein runder Tisch mit scharfen Ecken*, 30.

   Neither the refugee question nor the government's encouragement to West German banks are discussed in the West German records. Our interviewees heatedly denied a formal linkage between refugees and Hungarian debt help, but for more evidence on this point, see Andreas Rödder, *Deutschland einig Vaterland: Die Geschichte der Wiedervereinigung* (Munich: Beck, 2009), 74–75, and Hanns Jürgen Küsters and Daniel Hofmann, "Entscheidung für die deutsche Einheit: Einführung," *DzD-Einheit*, 44–45.

23. The literature on the East German revolution of 1989 is now quite strong. See, e.g., Charles Maier, *Dissolution: The Crisis of Communism and the End of East Germany* (Princeton, NJ: Princeton University Press, 1997); Ehrhart Neubert, *Geschichte der Opposition in der DDR 1949–1989* (Berlin: Ch. Links Verlag, 1998), 700–824; Walter Süß, *Staatssicherheit am Ende: Warum es den Mächtigen nicht gelang, 1989 eine Revolution zu verhindern* (Berlin: Links, 1999); Hans-Hermann Hertle, *Der Fall der Mauer: Die unbeabsichtigte Selbstauflösung des SED-Staates*, 2nd ed. (Opladen: Westdeutscher Verlag, 1999); Gareth Dale, *The East German Revolution of 1989* (Manchester: Manchester University Press, 2006); Konrad Jarausch, *The Rush to German Unity* (New York: Oxford University Press, 1994); Ilko-Sascha Kowalczuk, *Endspiel: Die Revolution von 1989 in der DDR* (Munich: Beck, 2009); Rödder, *Deutschland einig Vaterland*, 62–127; Mary Elise Sarotte, *The Collapse: The Accidental Opening of the Berlin Wall* (New York: Basic Books, 2014) (about much more than the opening of the wall); and Hannes Adomeit, *Imperial Overstretch: Germany in Soviet Policy from Stalin to Gorbachev*, 2nd ed. (Baden-Baden: Nomos, 2016), 463–535.

   Our earlier work has more detail on the play-by-play of international reactions to the GDR crisis as it unfolded, including the Soviet reactions. Zelikow and Rice, *Germany Unified and Europe Transformed*, 63–101.

24. A nice summary is in Mary Elise Sarotte, *1989: The Struggle to Create Post–Cold War Europe* (Princeton, NJ: Princeton University Press, 2009, with 2014 update), 19–20. "Garbage dump": quoted in Ilko-Sascha Kowalczuk, "The Revolution in Germany," in Frédéric Bozo, Andreas Rödder, and Mary Elise Sarotte, eds., *German Reunification: A Multinational History* (London: Routledge, 2017), 26; Robert Darnton, *Berlin Journal, 1989–1990* (New York: Norton, 1991), 11; see also 96–98. An excellent summary in English of the day's events in Leipzig, based on her direct reporting, is Elizabeth Pond, "The Day Leipzig's Residents Defied Their Masters," *Wall Street Journal* (Europe), October 7, 1994.

25. Krenz-Gorbachev memcon, 1 Nov 89, in Bundesarchiv, Abt. Potsdam, Ei-56320. Charles Maier originally helped us locate this document. This sensitive material on the GDR debt issues is not included in the excerpt from the Soviet record of this conversation that is published in the National Security Archive's online collection.

26. Minutes from the Politburo meeting, 3 Nov 89, quoted in Vladislav Zubok, "Gorbachev, German Reunification, and Soviet Demise," in Bozo et al., eds., *German Reunification*, 90.

27. The quotation appears in Igor Maximychev, "Possible 'Impossibilities,'" *International Affairs* (Moscow) (June 1993): 112–13, without an explanation of its origin. Maximychev, a top Soviet diplomat in the GDR, elaborated on the background of the quotation in an interview with Zelikow, Moscow, January 1994. See also Kotschemassow, *Meine letzte Mission*, 110 (placing "We will not forgive" on October 7). Gorbachev frequently called Kochemasov, unusual for a head of state. Ibid., 177.

28. Scowcroft, Gates, Blackwill, and Rice explicitly used alternative scenarios (rating the odds of the "violent crackdown" scenario at "less than 50 per cent," which is still a very high number) to draw out some of the policy implications. Scowcroft to Bush, "The Future of Perestroika and the European Order," Nov 89, Rice files, subject files 89–90, Malta summit papers (preparation), Bush Library.

    In February 1990, discussing why the Soviets should support NATO and EC options for Germany, the British ambassador in Moscow, Rodric Braithwaite, told Chernyaev that although he wanted perestroika to succeed, there was "at least a 30 per cent chance that it would not." This implied a 70 percent chance of success. Chernyaev replied "that he wished the odds [of success] were so good." Braithwaite, *Across the Moscow River*, 131.

29. Baker/Zoellick notes, "Re Cabinet Meeting Presentation," 5 Sep 89; and "Meeting with President, on September 6," Box 108, Folder 9, and Box 115, Folder 6, Baker Papers.

30. Bush and Scowcroft, *A World Transformed*, 154–55.

31. Bush's diary entry, 25 Nov 89, after a difficult meeting with Thatcher at Camp David, in ibid., 159.

32. Memcon of First Expanded Bilateral Session with Chairman Gorbachev, 2 Dec 89. This and other Malta summit memcons are in the Rice files, Soviet Union subject files, Malta summit memcons, Bush Library; see also the Soviet memcon of this meeting, published in Mikhail S. Gorbachev, *Gody trudnykh reshenii, 1985–1992: izbrannoye*, 173–76. For Bush's key briefing materials on Germany at Malta, see Presidential Briefing Book, "Presidential Presentations," 29 Nov 89. This book was prepared by Scowcroft, Rice, Ross, Blackwill, Zoellick, and Zelikow. It was distinct from the regular briefing materials and its contents were very closely held.

33. Greenspan memo for the record, 19 Oct 89, in Michael Boskin Files, Russian Trip 1990, Bush Library. Some of Greenspan's substantive suggestions were employed by Bush and Baker, who referred positively to the Fed chairman's visit. Baker had been following the issues closely. On October 4, he had offered his perspective on the Soviet economic future to the Senate Finance Committee; Zoellick had worked with him on the testimony.

34. Svetlana Savranskaya, ed., "The Diary of Anatoly Chernyaev, 1989," trans. Anna Melyakova (2009), 23 Oct 89, p. 45, donated to the National Security Archive and available at www.nsarchive.org (hereinafter cited as Chernyaev diary). Chernyaev's diary was also a source for the memoir he published in Russian, later abridged and translated into English (we have used both).

35. Chernyaev diary 1990 (2010), 2 Jan, p. 2; Taubman, *Gorbachev*, 498.

36. Scowcroft to Bush, "Objectives for US-Soviet Relations in 1990," Dec 89 (drafted mainly by Rice and Blackwill), Rice files, USSR subject files, US-Soviet Relations 1, Bush Library. Scowcroft called out, as a key priority for diplomacy, to help manage Soviet-German relations, since the German question was the one issue "that might cause Moscow to reassess its course in Eastern Europe, even bring Gorbachev down."

37. The Soviet military pressed Gorbachev and Shevardnadze to try and introduce naval arms control, the global control of naval size, as a whole new agenda for U.S.-Soviet arms control. Since the Soviet Union was not directly threatened by U.S. naval forces, other than by the nuclear missile submarines and sea-launched cruise missiles that were already on the table in the strategic nuclear talks, it is not easy to infer the reasons for this added push. The United States resisted it.

38. Chernyaev diary 1990, 2 Jan, p. 3. Chernyaev added, "There are more marshals and generals in Moscow alone than in the rest of the world combined! This is a political and social problem. It is fine that [Georgi] Arbatov and 'Ogonek' [a mass-circulation illustrated weekly magazine] are yelping at [defense minister] Yazov and [former army chief] Akhromeyev and tearing at their coattails, they're in a good spot! But what is it like for Gorbachev with this horde and armada!"

39. Teymuraz Stepanov, 13 Jan 90, quoted in Zubok, "Gorbachev, Germany, and Soviet Demise," 92.

40. Ibid.; see also Yakovlev's urging that Gorbachev lead another wave of revolutionary change, in Chernyaev diary 1990, 28 Jan, pp. 8–9.

41. For a critical analysis of Gorbachev's choice of indirect elections, see Archie Brown, *The Gorbachev Factor* (Oxford: Oxford University Press, 1996), 198–205; Brown, *Seven Years That Changed the World: Perestroika in Perspective* (Oxford: Oxford University Press, 2007), 209–10.

42. Excerpt from Thatcher-Gorbachev memcon, 23 Sep 89 (because he put his pen down, as Thatcher requested, Chernyaev added the material from his recollection when he wrote up his notes after the meeting). The record is in National Security Archive Electronic Briefing Book No. 422, ed. and trans. Svetlana Savranskaya. The British record of this part of the discussion, if any, has not yet been released. "What a woman!": Taubman, *Gorbachev*, 489.

43. Shevardnadze, "The Fate of the World Is Inseparable from the Fate of Our Perestroika," *Pravda*, September 27, 1989, pp. 4–5.

44. For instance, the day before Gorbachev's meeting with Krenz, President Carter's former national security adviser, Zbigniew Brzezinski, had told Yakovlev that "a united and powerful Germany would correspond neither to your interests nor to ours." Taubman, *Gorbachev*, 490.

45. Bonn 29066, 11 Sep 89. Seiters replied cautiously, urging that America only help knock down intellectual and spiritual walls between the two Germanys.

46. *Public Papers of the Presidents of the United States: George Bush, 1989*, bk. 2 (Washington, DC: Government Printing Office, 1990), 1221. The week before, Flora Lewis had advised the administration to "Go Slow on Germany," *New York Times*, September 12, 1989, p. A25.

47. The shift away from the old Ostpolitik consensus is evident, tracking the evolution of Kohl's position from the beginning of October to his government's statement on November 8. See Rödder, *Deutschland einig Vaterland*, 127–30; Schwarz, *Helmut Kohl*, 528–30.

48. Kohl-Bush telcon, 23 Oct 89, Bush Library. On the morning of Kohl's call, President Bush and other top officials had been briefed by intelligence analysts on "German Reunification: What Would Have to Happen?" They explained how many hurdles would have to be overcome. They feared that Bonn might agree to attenuate or even drop its NATO ties. On October 27 the briefing was circulated in the National Intelligence Daily and this version has been declassified in the CIA FOIA files. Having heard such a briefing, Bush might have been especially sensitive to Kohl's request. For the Bush interview, R. W. Apple Jr., "Possibility of a Reunited Germany Is No Cause for Alarm, Bush Says," *New York Times*, October 25, 1989, p. 1; see also p. A12. For other signs of Bush's thinking in this period, see Wörner-Bush memcon, 11 Oct 89, Bush Library.

49. See Bozo, *Mitterrand*, 98; Schabert, *How World Politics Is Made*, 220; and for a similarly philosophical approach suggested from the Foreign Ministry, Jacques Blot (head of the Quai's European office), "Reflections on the German question," 30 Oct 89, in Europe 1986–1990, Allemagne (Statut), Box 6122, Archives diplomatiques, Paris (hereinafter AD).

50. "Erklärung der Bundesregierung...," *Bulletin* (Bonn, Presse und Informationsamt der Bundesregierung), no. 123 (1989), p. 1053. For grudging acceptance of Kohl's line, even from SPD leader Vogel, see "Kohl: Die SED muss auf ihr Machtmonopol verzichten," *Frankfurter Allgemeine Zeitung*, November 9, 1989, p. 1. The editorial board of the *Washington Post* promptly criticized Kohl for his comments, warning against movement toward reunification. See "Toward German Reunification," *Washington Post*, November 9, 1989, p. A22.

51. EmbBerlin 8783, 8 Nov 89; see also the more detailed analysis in EmbBerlin 8764, "GDR Crisis: As the Plenum Meets, Can the SED Seize Its Slender Chance?," 8 Nov 89. West German ambassador to the United States Jürgen Ruhfus told Undersecretary of State Robert Kimmitt that Krenz was increasing his freedom to maneuver but confided that Bonn was pessimistic about a new SED government's chances for survival. The British ambassador to Washington, Antony Acland, said he was "nervous about something going very wrong." The State Department reported these remarks to President Bush. Eagleburger to President Bush (for his evening reading), 7 Nov 89.

52. When Krenz and Gorbachev discussed East German party figures, it was clear that Gorbachev had a good opinion of Modrow. But Gorbachev reserved his strongest praise for longtime party veteran Willi Stoph, who he had thought had done the best he could while working with Honecker. Both Gorbachev and Krenz blamed Günter Mittag for the GDR's deplorable economic problems. See memcon for Krenz-Gorbachev meeting, 1 Nov 89.

53. See memcon for Krenz-Gorbachev meeting; Krenz interview excerpt in Kuhn, *Gorbatschow und die deutsche Einheit*, 59.

54. Zelikow interviews with Tarasenko, Providence, June 1993, and Maximychev, Moscow, January 1994; Valentin Falin, *Politische Erinnerungen*, trans. Heddy Pross-Weerth (Munich: Droemer Knaur, 1993), 488–89. For variations on this account, see the excellent reconstruction in Igor

Maximytschew and Hans-Hermann Hertle, "Die Maueröffnung: Eine russisch-deutsche Trilogie," *Deutschland Archiv* 27 (November 1994): 1137–58; and Kotschemassow, *Meine letzte Mission*, 185–86; Igor Maximytschew, "Was ist bei euch los?," *Der Spiegel*, October 31, 1994, p. 43.

55. Maximychev, "End of the Berlin Wall," *International Affairs* (Moscow) (March 1991): 106–7 (based on numerous discussions with East German officials); and Maximytschew and Hertle, "Die Maueröffnung," 1146–48. Hertle expanded his account in his later book, *Der Fall der Mauer*.

56. In Bonn, for example, "there were no preparations or contingency plans for this situation, which had always been talked about, but in truth was considered most improbable. There was also no warning from the intelligence services." Kiessler and Elbe, *Ein runder Tisch mit scharfen Ecken*, 45. Kiessler and Elbe went on to criticize the West German intelligence service, the Bundesnachrichtendienst (BND), for having written reports that ignored the people of the GDR and focused only on the governing communist elite.

57. See Egon Krenz with Hartmut König and Gunter Rettner, *Wenn Mauern fallen* (Vienna: Paul Neff, 1990); Hans Modrow, *Aufbruch und Ende* (Hamburg: Konkret Literatur, 1991), 25; Heinrich Bortfeldt interview with Modrow, March 1993, in GDR Oral History Project, Hoover Institution, Box 2, pp. 15–16; Reuth and Bonte, *Das Komplott*, 160. Early accounts of the opening of the wall sometimes inaccurately assert that Gorbachev had approved the decision. The Soviet government had blessed a liberalization of travel laws but was taken aback like everyone else by what happened on the night of November 9–10.

58. Darnton, *Berlin Journal*, 85; see also Rödder, *Deutschland einig Vaterland*, 106–8; Sarotte, *The Collapse*, 93–119.

59. Schabowski, *Das Politburo*, 138–39. Unless otherwise cited, our account of the opening of the Berlin Wall is drawn from Krenz, *Wenn Mauern fallen*, 161–95; Schabowski, *Das Politburo*; Gedmin, *The Hidden Hand*, 109–10; Pond, *Beyond the Wall*, 132–34; Maximychev, "End of the Berlin Wall," 106–8; Maximytschew, "Was ist bei euch los?"; Kusmin, "Da wussten"; and Greenwald, *Berlin Witness*, 258–65. For the U.S. embassy's reporting of the events at the time, see EmbBerlin 8820, "GDR Plenum: Virtually Free Travel and Emigration in Force Immediately," 9 Nov 89; EmbBerlin 8823, "...And the Wall Came (Figuratively) Tumbling Down," 10 Nov 89.

60. Kohl-Gorbachev memcon, 11 Nov 89, *DzD-Einheit*, 515–17; an East German copy of the Soviet record of the call is in the German archives of the DDR (SAPMO), JIV 2/2A/3258K.

61. Hurd to Thatcher, "Eastern Europe," 17 Nov 89, in *DBPO-German Unification*, 128. For more details, see Zelikow and Rice, *Germany Unified and Europe Transformed*, 99–110.

62. FRG, *Texte zur Deutschlandpolitik*, ser. 3, vol. 7-1989 (Bonn: Deutscher Bundes-Verlag, 1990), 422–29.

63. On November 26 a group of thirty-one writers, respected reform Marxists, church figures, and opposition leaders all joined in a published appeal to their East German countrymen to "insist on GDR independence" and not to accept "a sell-out of our material and moral values and have the GDR eventually taken over by the Federal Republic." Within two weeks two hundred thousand people had signed this manifesto of "antifascist and humanist ideals." A prominent group of West German intellectuals responded with a parallel manifesto rejecting unification and dangerous nationalism. Jarausch, *The Rush to German Unity*, 67.

64. Zelikow interview with Teltschik, Munich, December 1994; on opinion, see *Der Spiegel*, November 20, 1989, pp. 16–17 (Emnid survey); Teltschik, *329 Tage*, 41 (ZDF Politbarometer survey); Lafontaine in *Süddeutsche Zeitung*, November 25–26, 1989, quoted in A. James McAdams, *Germany Divided: From the Wall to Reunification* (Princeton, NJ: Princeton University Press, 1993), 206 n. 74.

65. Schwarz, *Helmut Kohl*, 530–34, 533 ("*geht kaputt*"). See also Seiters-Krenz/Modrow memcon, 20 Nov 89, *DzD-Einheit*, 550–59. On Teltschik and his meeting with Nikolai Portugalov, see Teltschik, *329 Tage*, 43–44, and more generally on this episode, 41–58. Portugalov himself had publicly denounced unification only a few days earlier in an interview. He had not forgotten these words; he actually referred to this interview in his meeting with Teltschik. It is hard to avoid the conclusion that both sides to the conversation heard each other selectively. Novosti interview, "Two Systems, One Nation," in *Frankfurter Rundschau*, November 17, 1989, p. 2, in *FBIS-SOV* 89–222, November 20, 1989, 33–34.

66. Helmut Kohl, "Zehn-Punkte Programm zur überwindung der Teilung Deutschlands und Europas," in *Texte zur Deutschlandpolitik*, 426–33.

67. Teltschik, *329 Tage*, 58.

68. Ibid., 50–58. Unfortunately, probably because of a snarl in communicating the eleven-page message either in Bonn or in Washington, Kohl's message to Bush arrived at the end of the day, hours after the story had been broadcast all over the world.

69. Bush-Kohl telcon, 29 Nov 89, Bush Library.

70. *Public Papers of the Presidents of the United States: George Bush, 1989*, bk. 2, 1603. Bush was referring to his speeches at Boston University (May 21), in Mainz (May 31), and in Leiden (July 17).

71. It is important to note that, legally, the terms "reunification" and "unification" were not the same, though people frequently treat them as if they are. "Reunification" implied that the previous unified German state before Hitler began his conquests, the state that existed in 1937, might be brought back together. Indeed, the FRG itself defined reunification in its Basic Law by reference to the borders of Germany in 1937. For a prescient discussion of this point, see Karl Kaiser, "Unity for Germany, Not Reunification," *New York Times*, October 6, 1989, p. A31.

72. Bush-Mulroney dinner memcon, 29 Nov 89, Bush Library.

73. Julij A. Kwizinskij, *Vor dem Sturm: Erinnerungen eines Diplomaten*, trans. Hilde Ettinger and Helmut Ettinger (Berlin: Siedler, 1993), 16–17. For the explanation that Soviet inaction was a result of Gorbachev's hope that Krenz and Modrow would stabilize the situation, see Vyacheslav Dashichev, "On the Road to German Reunification: The View from Moscow," in *Soviet Foreign Policy, 1917–1991: A Retrospective*, ed. Gabriel Gorodetsky (London: Frank Cass, 1993), 170, 173.

74. Remarks of President Bush and Chairman Gorbachev and a question-and-answer session with reporters at Malta, December 3, 1989, in *Public Papers of the Presidents of the United States: George Bush, 1989*, bk. 2, 1877–78.

75. On Putin's experience, Lynch, *Vladimir Putin and Russian Statecraft*, 22–25. For the general situation, see *Krasnaya zvezda* and *Izvestiya*, December 5 and 6, 1989. For the reports on emergency measures taken by Soviet troops, see the same newspapers for December 8 and 9, 1989.

76. According to Shevardnadze's close aide, Sergei Tarasenko, and Chernyaev, the Soviet leadership was becoming worried that the real problem for them if Germany unified would be a witch hunt carried out against those who had "lost East Europe and Germany." Tarasenko claims that by the end of 1989, he and others knew that the unification of Germany was inevitable and were trying to figure out a strategy to keep this development from bringing down Gorbachev's government. Rice interviews with Tarasenko, Moscow, October 1991, and Chernyaev, Moscow, June 1994.

77. S. F. Akhromeyev and G. M. Kornienko [a former deputy foreign minister who retired in 1988], *Glazami marshala i diplomata* (Moscow: Mezhdunarodniye Otnosheniya, 1992), 253–54, 259.

78. This discussion is based on the Soviet memcon, Gorbachev-Genscher, 5 Dec 89, in Gorbachev papers provided to Stanford, and the West German memcons both for this meeting and for Genscher-Shevardnadze, 5 Dec 89, in Andreas Hilger, ed., *Diplomatie für die deutsche Einheit* (Munich: R. Oldenbourg Verlag, 2011), 73–82. See also Chernyaev, *Shest' let s Gorbachevym*, 306–9; Hans-Dietrich Genscher, *Erinnerungen* (Berlin: Siedler, 1995), 684–87. The "left no doubt" quotation is from Kiessler and Elbe, *Ein runder Tisch mit scharfen Ecken*, 70. Shevardnadze's reference to Hitler was in the context of an alleged German "diktat" in forcing the annexation of a neighbor. See also *Pravda*, December 6, 1989, p. 1, and *Izvestiya*, December 6, 1989, p. 4. Shevardnadze's public criticism of Genscher was especially sharp. On the hardening Soviet line, see the analysis sent urgently to Washington in Moscow 35285, "Soviet Concerns About Germany," 9 Dec 89.

79. Soviet memcon, Gorbachev-Mitterrand, 6 Dec 89, in Gorbachev papers provided to Stanford; for an account based on the French record, Schabert, *How World Politics Is Made*, 257.

80. Just after the wall opened, Kissinger told Bush he thought that, as unity became more likely, the Soviets would fall back to a choice between second and third options listed here. Bush and Scowcroft, *A World Transformed*, 191.

81. Védrine was specific in five dimensions: EC buildup; monetary union by deferring to German monetary policy preferences; EC openness toward all of Eastern Europe; a CFE treaty; and EC efforts to help reassure the Soviet Union. Schabert, *How World Politics Is Made*, 221–23. From the Quai, Blot had made a similar argument. "Reflections on the German Question," 30 Oct 89, Europe 1986–1990, Allemagne (Statut), Box 6122, AD.

82. Genscher, *Erinnerungen*, 679 ("most important"); the quotation from what Mitterrand told Genscher is from the West German memcon, Genscher-Mitterrand, 5 Dec 89 (the phrase at the end was quoted verbatim), in Hilger, *Diplomatie für die*

deutsche Einheit, 58. Schabert's reading of the French record is similar; see also Bozo, *Mitterrand*, 122.

Some French officials, like Guigou, deny any formal quid pro quo between EC decisions and French positions on unification. Ibid., 248. Others, like Caroline de Margerie, argued that the French "would not have dared" to push forward with the later stages of European unification without the fall of the Berlin Wall and "the shock of German unification." Quoted in Jean Lacouture, *Mitterrand: Une histoire de Français*, vol. 2, *Les vertiges du sommet* (Paris: Éditions du Seuil, 1998), 390. The record of what Mitterrand said in conversations like the one with Genscher, and what the Germans heard, seems to reinforce de Margerie's argument.

83. See the quotes from the French record, Mitterrand-Thatcher memcon, 20 Jan 90, in Schabert, *How World Politics Is Made*, 245–46. On musings about alternative alliance structures in No. 10 Downing Street, see Powell to Thatcher, "East/West Relations," 8 Dec 89, p. 3, PREM 19/2992, TNA.

84. Teltschik, *329 Tage*, 70 ("icy climate"); for the French side, see Bozo, *Mitterrand*, 129–32; on the Mitterrand-Thatcher discussions in Strasbourg, which developed no concrete common plan, Margaret Thatcher, *The Downing Street Years* (New York: HarperCollins, 1993), 796–97.

In early December, the Soviets made another move. They requested a Four Power meeting. The British and French agreed to this while they were in Strasbourg. The United States went along, insisting that the meeting would only discuss some Berlin issues.

Despite the December 11 meeting's modest content, the fact that it was held at all angered many West Germans. But one of the Soviet officials involved thought that the meeting had been the warning shot which "beyond all doubt, [was] one of the major conditions that enabled the revolution in the GDR to remain bloodless." The Americans had reasoned that the best way to defuse tensions at that moment was to do something to bring the Soviets down from the ceiling. Moscow needed an outlet for its anxiety. So, in fact, did Paris and London.

The meeting—as uncomfortable as it was for the Germans—may have served its purpose. The United States then refused repeated Soviet proposals to hold any more of them. Zelikow and Rice, *Germany Unified and Europe Transformed*, 140–41.

85. Mitterrand to Kohl, Latche, 7 Jan 90, quoted in Favier and Martin-Roland, *Les défis*, 257.

86. On November 13, Ross and Francis Fukuyama on Ross's staff suggested the articulation of "four principles which should frame our policy." They were: (1) The United States should support true German self-determination without endorsing any specific outcome; (2) unification must be consistent with Germany's membership in NATO and an integrated EC; (3) moves toward unity should be gradual, peaceful, and step-by-step; and (4) on the issue of postwar borders, all should respect "the principles adopted in the Helsinki Final Act recognizing the inviolability of frontiers in Europe, and allowing for the possibility of peaceful change." Baker made these points in his own pre-Malta press conference. Ross to Baker, "How to Approach the German Unity Issue," 13 Nov 89; transcript of Baker's pre-Malta press conference, 29 Nov 89, pp. 7–8; they led Teltschik's prompt report to Kohl, "Reaktionen aus den wichtigsten Hauptstädten auf Ihren 10-Punkte Plan," 30 Nov 89, *DzD-Einheit*, 574.

87. For the German account of this meeting, see Teltschik, *329 Tage*, 62–64; and see memcon Bush-Kohl at Château Stuyvenberg, Brussels, 3 Dec 89, Bush Library; the account that follows also draws on Zelikow interview with Scowcroft, Washington, DC, June 1991. See also Scowcroft to President Bush, "Scope Paper—Your Bilateral with Chancellor Kohl" (in-trip briefing materials).

88. On the road, Blackwill and Zoellick had worked on the earlier Baker formula and then the principals refined and approved it. The earlier Ross-Fukuyama formula had included a qualifier, "if there is unification." That phrase was dropped. An earlier State Department addendum saying the outcome must also be acceptable to Germany's neighbors had also been dropped. The language referring to Four Power rights was new, added because the embassy in Bonn had complained of Kohl's persistent failure to refer to these rights and because of the Americans' care to mention their legal obligation for Berlin and "Germany as a whole." See Bonn 37736, "Kohl's Ten-Point Program—Silence on the Role of the Four Powers," 1 Dec 89.

89. The text of the intervention, which had been prepared in Washington mainly by Blackwill and Zelikow, was subsequently released to the public. *Public Papers of the Presidents of the United States: George Bush, 1989*, bk. 2, 1644–47. Bush relayed

to Gorbachev his four principles on Germany. Bush to Gorbachev, 8 Dec 89.

90. Teltschik, *329 Tage*, 64–67; Zelikow interview with Blackwill, Cambridge, Mass., 1991.

91. Thatcher, *The Downing Street Years*, 795–96. Thatcher's views were growing further and further apart from those of her diplomats, who also sensed their loss of influence, and it would be months before she started heeding their advice.

92. Teltschik, *329 Tage*, 67.

93. See address of Secretary Baker, Berlin Press Club, 11 Dec 89, State Department transcript released to press. The speech was principally drafted by Zoellick.

94. Genscher had also mentioned some similar ideas to the Americans. See, for instance, Genscher-Bush memcon, 21 Nov 89, in Hilger, *Diplomatie für die deutsche Einheit*, 45; and the more abbreviated U.S. version of the memcon at the Bush Library. Kristina Spohr noticed this point in "Germany, America and the Shaping of Post–Cold War Europe: A Story of German International Emancipation Through Political Unification, 1989–90," *Cold War History* 15, no. 2 (2015): 221, 234.

95. Jean-Louis Bianco, Guigou, Védrine, and Mitterrand quoted in Schabert, *How World Politics Is Made*, 269–70; on the narrow vision for NATO, see Nicole Gnesotto, "The Future of the Military Alliances in Europe," 29 Nov 89, Allemagne files, Box 6123, AD.

96. Zoellick to Baker, 27 Nov 89, quoted (with emphasis apparently in original) in Sarotte, *1989*, 77.

97. Zelikow interview with Baker, Houston, January 1995, and Bush-Mitterrand memcon, St. Martin, 16 Dec 89, Bush Library.

98. The following account of the preparation of the speech was relayed to the authors in two interviews with the speech's principal drafter, Sergei Tarasenko, Moscow, October 1991, and Providence, Rhode Island, June 1993. Tarasenko was assisted by Teymuraz Stepanov from Shevardnadze's policy planning unit. Kvitsinsky also became involved in the speech drafting, along with the ministry's longtime German expert, Aleksandr Bondarenko.

99. Quotations from the speech are drawn from "Europe: A Time of Change—E. A. Shevardnadze's Speech at the European Parliament Political Commission," *Pravda*, December 20, 1989, p. 4; see Eduard Shevardnadze, *Moi vybor: v zashchitu demokratii i svobody* (Moscow: Novosti, 1991), 229–30.

100. The account of Genscher's reference to the *Bild* article was given to Zelikow by an official who was present. The article must have been Karl-Ludwig Günsche, "Schewardnadse: Sieben Bedingungen für die Einheit," *Bild-Zeitung*, December 20, 1989. It is conceivable that Genscher or his staff had some hand in this article, but there is no evidence for this. See also Kiessler and Elbe, *Ein runder Tisch mit scharfen Ecken*, 68–72.

101. Scowcroft to Bush, "U.S. Diplomacy for the New Europe," 22 Dec 89, Blackwill chron files, Bush Library. Blackwill and Zelikow had sent the draft to Scowcroft on December 19 with Blackwill's note that "I hope you like this memo. We over here believe it's important." Scowcroft agreed.

102. Gerd Langguth, *Angela Merkel: Aufstieg zur Macht* (Munich: Deutscher Taschenbuch, 2007), 124–34; Qvortrup, *Angela Merkel*, 111–21.

103. For more on the dreams of the civic groups, especially New Forum, see Sarotte, *1989*, 89–99.

104. Baker to President Bush (for his evening reading), 20 Dec 89. On Kohl's trip to the GDR, see Teltschik, *329 Tage*, 87–96.

105. Kiessler and Elbe, *Ein runder Tisch mit scharfen Ecken*, 47 (emphasis added). Elbe remembered Zoellick's reply.

106. The legal issue was whether the FRG had the capacity to settle the border with Poland. The Four Powers had reserved ultimate authority over the border of Germany in the Berlin declaration and Potsdam agreement of 1945. They reserved their rights in all subsequent agreements.

The West Germans had also argued, with support from the United States and Great Britain, that "Germany" still existed as a passive subject of international law, awaiting its eventual reestablishment as a unified state. Only such a reestablished Germany could conclude a final agreement on its borders.

The Polish and East German position, occasionally shared by the Soviets, was that "Germany" had been extinguished in 1945. The FRG and the GDR were its successors. These two states had declared their assent to the existing GDR-Polish border in the 1950 Treaty of Görlitz (GDR-Poland) and the 1970 Treaty of Warsaw (FRG-Poland). See, e.g., Wladyslaw Czaplinski, "The New Polish-German Treaties and the

Changing Political Structure of Europe," *American Journal of International Law* 86 (1992): 163, 164; Jochen Frowein, "Legal Problems of the German Ostpolitik," *International and Comparative Law Quarterly* 23 (1974): 105.

107. Zelikow and Rice, *Germany Unified and Europe Transformed*, 159; see also British ambassador Malaby's talk with Kohl, Bonn 92, "Call on Kohl: German Question," 25 Jan 90, in *DBPO-German Unification*, 222–24.

108. Blackwill to Scowcroft, "1990," 19 Jan 90, Blackwill papers, Box 2, German Reunification, Bush Library; Hutchings through Blackwill to Scowcroft, "Your Breakfast with Kissinger: Managing the German Question"; and Zelikow interviews with Baker, Houston, January 1995, and Zoellick, Washington, DC, January 1995.

109. Paris 139, "Call on Dumas: Developments in Europe," 2 Feb 90, in *DBPO-German Unification*, 246. On her copy of this cable, Thatcher noted her agreement with this pessimistic judgment. PREM 19/2998, TNA.

110. Washington 276, "Bilateral Discussion of German Issues," 2 Feb 90, in *DBPO-German Unification*, 243.

111. "Toad" refers to the happily reckless driver in Kenneth Grahame's *The Wind in the Willows*. Powell to Thatcher, "Germany: Meeting with Herr Teltschik," 9 Feb 90 (with Thatcher's annotations), in *DBPO-German Unification*, 274.

112. Rice to Blackwill, "Thinking about Germany," 23 Jan 90. Zoellick and Ross's views, at State, were similar. But as we will discuss, they believed the creation of the Two Plus Four process would be a proactive way to offer an outlet for Soviet concerns about German developments.

113. Zelikow and Rice, *Germany Unified and Europe Transformed*, 139–41, 146, 154–56; "open-ended negotiation": Scowcroft to Bush, "Mitterrand, the Germans, U.S.-EC Cooperation, and the CSCE," 15 Dec 89. In late December, Blackwill was so worried that the pace of unification might force America to accept such a Versailles-type peace conference that he even proposed that the United States might try to slow down unification in order to avoid this danger. Scowcroft did not agree. The United States would follow Kohl's lead on the pace. Hutchings through Blackwill to Scowcroft, "Responding to a Soviet Call for a German Peace Conference," n.d. (written in late Decem-

ber 1989). The memo contained a draft memo for Bush, which Scowcroft rejected. Zelikow interview with Scowcroft, Washington, DC, 1991. For more worries at the time among some staff members about how to negotiate the German issues, see Hutchings through Blackwill to Scowcroft, "Your Breakfast with Kissinger: Managing the German Question," 26 Jan 90, Blackwill papers, German Unification 1, Bush Library. At the same time, over at State, Zoellick and Ross were developing the Two Plus Four negotiating plan for Baker.

114. For details, see Zelikow and Rice, *Germany Unified and Europe Transformed*, 162–64; Chernyaev diary 1990, 28 Jan, p. 11. Compare Sarotte, *1989*, 100–102. She indicates that the only source for what happened is Chernyaev, but there are some nearly contemporary accounts of the discussions from Shakhnazarov and Falin. At this time Chernyaev's position on Germany did not quite reflect Shevardnadze's or Gorbachev's views.

115. Marc Fisher, "East German Offers Plan for Unity," *Washington Post*, February 2, 1990 ("united fatherland"). This East German–Soviet plan, announced on February 1, was the essential context to understand Gorbachev's positions when he met with Baker and Kohl eight and nine days later. Gorbachev explained the plan to Bush, Kohl, Mitterrand, and Thatcher. See, e.g., Gorbachev to Bush, 2 Feb 90; and Gorbachev to Thatcher, 2 Feb 90, PREM 19/2998, TNA.

On Modrow's talks with Gorbachev, see Modrow, *Aufbruch und Ende*, 120–23; Kotschemassow, *Meine letzte Mission*, 211–17; and interviews with Gorbachev, Modrow, and Manfred Gerlach excerpted in Kuhn, *Gorbatschow und die deutsche Einheit*, 100–103; TASS, "Shevardnadze Outlines Policy on German Unity," February 2, 1990, in *FBIS-SOV* 90–024, February 5, 1990, 33–35; Bericht des Bundesministerium für innerdeutsche Beziehungen, in *Materialen zur Deutschlandfragen* (Bonn: Kulturstiftung der deutschen Vertriebenen, 1989–1991), 243–44; "Rabochii visit G. Gysi v SSSR," *Vestnik*, February 28, 1990, pp. 4–5.

116. See Dieter Grosser, *Das Wagnis der Währungs-, Wirtschafts- und Sozialunion: Politische Zwänge im Konflikt mit ökonomischen Regeln* (Stuttgart: Deutsche Verlags-Anstalt, 1998), 183; Rödder, *Deutschland einig Vaterland*, 206–16; Teltschik, *329 Tage*, 122 et seq.; Powell, visiting on February 9, conveyed a vivid summary of the eco-

nomic union rush in his report, "Meeting with Herr Teltschik."

117. Grosser, *Das Wagnis*, 174–88, 177 ("riskiest").

118. See Modrow, *Aufbruch und Ende*, 127–36; Teltschik, *329 Tage*, 144–45.

119. See, for example, the East German interest in protecting the idea of "property pluralism" in a new German republic, in Sarotte, *1989*, 115.

120. An excellent summary of the arguments on Article 23 versus Article 146 can be found in "Grundgesetz oder 'neue Verfassung'?: Die Kontroverse über die Artikel 23 und 146 des Grundgesetzes," in Gerhart Maier, ed., *Die Wende in der DDR* (Bonn: Moeller-Druck, 1991), 73–83. Article 146 of the Basic Law did not itself require the convocation of a national assembly. It said only, "This Basic Law loses its validity on the day on which a constitution enters into force which has been adopted by the German people in a free decision." The name "Basic Law" itself originally had an interim quality, the implication being that it would eventually be superseded by a constitution. Since the West German government had maintained since 1950 that such a constitution would be prepared by an all-German, freely elected national assembly, Article 146 was interpreted as referring to this sequence of events. On the working group's early attraction to Article 23, see Teltschik, *329 Tage*, 128, 152–53.

121. See Henry Kissinger, "Delay Is the Most Dangerous Course," *Washington Post*, February 9, 1990, p. A27. Also raising some of the same questions was Flora Lewis, "Peace Before Power," *New York Times*, February 17, 1990, p. 27.

122. See Blackwill to Scowcroft, "Germany," 30 Jan 90. This memo attached a draft memo for Scowcroft to forward to President Bush, "A Strategy for German Unification," laying out the proposed policy. The blueprint (outlined in eight points) was in the draft memo to the president. A copy was also passed informally to Baker and Zoellick, all handled outside the normal paperwork system. We have been unable to determine when the "strategy" memo was actually forwarded by Scowcroft to Bush. We do know that Scowcroft agreed with it.

123. Zelikow interviews with Genscher, Wachtberg-Pech, December 1994, and with Kastrup, Bonn, December 1994; also Hans-Dietrich Genscher, "German Unity in the European Framework," Tutzing Protestant Academy, 31 Jan 90. Quota-

tions are from the English-language translation prepared for Genscher and passed by him to Baker when the two men met in Washington on February 2.

124. State 36191, "Baker/Genscher Meeting February 2," 3 Feb 90, Kanter files, Germany—March 1990, Bush Library (this was a readout that Zoellick, who was at the meeting, provided to Jim Dobbins, sent for Scowcroft and Blackwill, then in Munich, and for U.S. ambassador Vernon Walters to go over with Teltschik, who the United States guessed might not know what Genscher was doing).

At this time Genscher envisioned that both U.S. and Soviet forces might remain in Germany in some way for some time, as the alliances became part of "the all-European security structure." See, for example, Genscher-Hurd memcon, 6 Feb 90, in Institut für Zeitgeschichte, *Die Einheit: Das Auswärtige Amt, das DDR-Außenministerium und der Zwei-plus-Vier Prozess* (Göttingen: Vandenhoeck & Ruprecht, 2015) (hereinafter *Einheit Dokumente*), 231–32; the British account is at *DBPO-German Unification*, 262–63.

125. The Havel and Mazowiecki material, and the argument, is from Mary Elise Sarotte, "'His East European Allies Say They Want to Be in NATO': U.S. Foreign Policy, German Unification, and NATO's Role in European Security 1989–90," in Bozo et al., eds., *German Reunification*, 78–79.

126. Kiessler and Elbe, *Ein runder Tisch mit scharfen Ecken*, 80.

127. For details, see Zelikow and Rice, *Germany Unified and Europe Transformed*, 165–69 and the notes.

128. On Baker's CSCE plans, see "CSCE Summit," 22 Jan 90, in Box 115, Folder 7, Baker Papers; and on Genscher's agreement to the conditions, State 36191, "Baker/Genscher Meeting February 2," cited earlier.

129. Meanwhile, key British and American officials were also trying to improve their working relationships, outside the constraints of the Bush-Thatcher channel. As Genscher was coming to Washington, Zoellick and Blackwill opened a secret channel with British counterparts, meeting in Washington, to begin a more intensive sharing of ideas with an old ally that recently had seemed more distant. The channel was opened on January 29 (at American suggestion, according to the cable, although we believe Thatcher had also urged creation of such a

channel). Sir Patrick Wright (British permanent under-secretary at the FO) and Andrew Wood (British DCM in Washington) on the British side. See Washington 240, "Bilateral Discussion of German Issues," 30 Jan 90, in PREM 19/2998, TNA.

130. See Scowcroft to President Bush, "Trip Report," 4 Feb 90.

131. For Baker's plan, see the outline for Baker's meeting with President Bush, 31 Jan 90 (these outlines were usually prepared by Zoellick for Baker), Baker Papers. Baker's outline revealingly, erroneously, treats the concept of a "demilitarized" eastern Germany as identical to Genscher's suggestion that the former GDR remain outside NATO. For Scowcroft's advice, see Scowcroft to President Bush, "Message to Kohl," 8 Feb 90 (drafted by Blackwill and Zelikow).

132. Ibid. The message to Kohl went out on February 9. Bush, Baker, and Scowcroft had decided to use this NSC staff draft instead of an alternative approach, drafted by the European bureau of the State Department, in which the former GDR would be protected not by NATO but by new promises to defend this part of Germany that would be given outside of the NATO treaty, by the United States, Britain, and France. Blackwill to Scowcroft, "State Department Draft Message to Kohl," 8 Feb 90. The previous day Blackwill and Zelikow had drafted for Scowcroft an analysis of the complete spectrum of possible German affiliations to NATO and outcomes for the U.S. security presence. See "German Unity: Variations on the Theme," 8 Feb 90 (a copy was passed to Zoellick after his return to Washington).

Even before Bush's letter went to Kohl, the NSC staff briefed the British on their proposed formula for NATO in a unified Germany. Practically overnight, the British government prepared its own analysis for Thatcher of all the possible options. The Foreign Office and Thatcher immediately agreed that the formula the United States had chosen was best. They emphasized that the United States needed to preserve its military commitment on the ground in Germany. For Thatcher's decision and the attached analyses, see the set of documents from Wall to Powell, on to Powell's reply, "Germany and NATO," 9 and 10 Feb 90, *DBPO-German Unification*, 281–86.

133. *Public Papers of the Presidents of the United States: George Bush, 1990*, bk. 1 (Washington, DC: Government Printing Office, 1991), 266.

134. Baker-Shevardnadze memcon, "Second One-on-One," 9 Feb 90, pp. 3, 8 (Ross was the notetaker), released in full in 2016, State FOIA Case M-2015-11816.

135. Baker-Gorbachev memcon (U.S.), Kremlin, 9 Feb 90. The Soviet record is similar.

136. Kristina Spohr, "Precluded or Precedent-Setting? The 'NATO Enlargement Question' in the Triangular Bonn-Washington-Moscow Diplomacy of 1990–1991," *Journal of Cold War Studies* 14, no. 4 (Fall 2012): 4–54; see also Spohr, "Germany, America and the Shaping of Post–Cold War Europe," 235–41.

137. Much of the debate about the February "no extension" positions thus make the argument seem stronger by simply omitting any mention of how Genscher had explained his own alternative plan. For instance, Joshua Itzkowitz Shifrinson spends three pages describing the Genscher-Baker discussions and assurances without mentioning, even in the footnotes, the CSCE or "cooperative security structures" half of Genscher's design. Shifrinson, "Deal or No Deal? The End of the Cold War and the U.S. Offer to Limit NATO Expansion," *International Security* 40, no. 4 (2016): 7, 22–25.

Sarotte does spell out this counterfactual. *1989*, 197–99. The issue then becomes one of whether the alternative design was viable. To analyze that, she or others would have to explain how this new structure might have worked and why it would have been plausible, even to the Soviet Union. The Soviet government did end up developing an alternative design during the spring, but it had some distinctive features of its own, especially to manage German military power.

It would have been hard for leaders of major powers to have endorsed Genscher's alternative structure without seriously considering its design. For instance, one can assume that in such a "cooperative" system, defense guarantees would no longer be sought or offered, but that assumption must be analyzed. If, on the other hand, the participants would seek security guarantees from each other, it cannot be assumed that the United States would have made security guarantees for an all-European collective security system, that U.S. troops would have remained in Europe after NATO was taken down, or that other European countries would have sought Soviet security guarantees as part of such a system.

138. See "Debate Speech by Ye. K. Ligachev," *Pravda*, February 7, 1990, p. 6; "Speeches in the Discussion of the Report [to the Central Committee]," *Pravda*, February 7, 1990, pp. 5–6. The letter is reprinted in Ligachev's memoir, Yegor K. Ligachev, *Zagadka Gorbacheva* (Novosibirsk: Interbook, 1992), 98–99.

139. Shifrinson quotes this Gorbachev response, but he leaves out that last Gorbachev sentence, "But don't ask me to give you a bottom line right now." Shifrinson, "Deal or No Deal?," 23. The full exchange was as follows:

> *Baker*: Let's assume for the moment that unification is going to take place. Assuming that, would you prefer a united Germany outside of NATO that is independent and has no US forces or would you prefer a unified Germany with ties to NATO and assurances that there would be no extension of NATO's current jurisdiction eastward?
>
> *Gorbachev*: Well I am giving thought to all these options. Soon we are going to have a seminar among our political leadership to talk about all these options. Certainly any extension of the zone of NATO is unacceptable.
>
> *Baker*: I agree.
>
> *Gorbachev*: Also, I believe that the presence of US troops could be very constructive and be positive in the situation as it evolves. Let me say that the approach you have outlined is a very possible one. We don't really want to see a replay of Versailles, where the Germans were able to arm themselves. The lessons of the past tell us that Germany must stay within European structures. This is especially true given its enormous economic capabilities and what that can mean for its military potential. The best way to constrain that process is to ensure that Germany is contained within European structures. What you have said to me about your approach and your preference is very realistic. So let's think about that. But don't ask me to give you a bottom line right now. (Baker-Gorbachev memcon, 9 Feb 90,

released in full in 2016, State FOIA Case M-2015-11816, p. 9.)

The exchange shows that Baker is still adhering to the Genscher formula. It also shows that the whole discussion is about how best to handle Germany—and whether U.S. forces should stay there.

This kind of intense exchange would go on in coming months. Each side's position continued to evolve. Kohl, Mitterrand, and Thatcher would all also weigh in with Gorbachev about this topic.

As Gorbachev suggested, the Soviet side considered "all these options" and would later go into much more detail about its preferred stand. The U.S. position on how to define Germany's NATO status also changed (in fact, later that same day Baker realized that his president had a different view than the one he had agreed to with Genscher). To help Gorbachev accept the Germany/NATO position, in May 1990 Baker would spell out a set of nine assurances that we discuss in the next chapter. These previewed the ultimate agreement Gorbachev hashed out with Kohl, codified in NATO actions, the Final Settlement on Germany, the pan-European CFE process, and the pan-European CSCE process. The U.S. and other governments followed through on all nine of Baker's assurances.

140. Bush-Wörner memcon, Camp David, 10 Feb 90, Bush Library (the memcon in the official records is incorrectly dated).

141. See Teltschik, *329 Tage*, 142–43; the venomous comments about Teltschik are in Kiessler and Elbe, *Ein runder Tisch mit scharfen Ecken*, 98.

142. Sarotte, *1989*, 113 (saying, in response to Kohl's NATO offer, that Gorbachev had agreed "Germany could unify") and, in her 2014 update, 222 (saying that, in response to Kohl's NATO offer, Gorbachev had agreed to Kohl's plan for economic and monetary union). She thus argues that there was a quid pro quo, but Gorbachev just did not lock it in. Sarotte, "Not One Inch Eastward? Bush, Baker, Kohl, Genscher, Gorbachev, and the Origin of Russian Resentment Toward NATO Enlargement in February 1990," *Diplomatic History* 34, no. 1 (2010): 119, 131. In her book and in her article, Sarotte does not mention the Gorbachev-Modrow work, in which Gorbachev had just helped prepare an alternative conception of German unification that he

had just praised to Kohl, Bush, and others. Shifrinson also repeatedly asserts that Gorbachev's assent to unification was a quid pro quo for the Baker/Kohl assurances. He also omits any mention of the Modrow-Gorbachev unification plan. Shifrinson, "Deal or No Deal?," 15, 25.

On February 10, Gorbachev knew that Kohl was proposing negotiations for a currency and economic union and that Kohl hoped this process would happen sometime after the March elections. Gorbachev and Modrow's plan had its own conception of economic union (for instance, one of the other two among the three options in Waigel's list that we mentioned earlier). Gorbachev chose to let the Germans work this out for themselves, without Soviet intervention. Kohl was quite relieved that Gorbachev did not plan to intervene in the imminent inter-German negotiations to discuss the form or timing of possible negotiations about economic and monetary union. But, as his subsequent actions would show, it is wrong to construe Gorbachev's reluctance to intervene in these inter-German talks as his abandonment of Modrow. It is also wrong to then construe this supposed choice as a quid pro quo for a NATO proposal about which Gorbachev was also studiously noncommittal.

143. For example, Valentin Falin blasted both the Bush and Genscher formulas for suggesting NATO membership for a united Germany; see interview with Rudolf Augstein, *Der Spiegel*, February 19, 1990, pp. 168–72. He could not have picked a more prominent way to do this in the West German elite press. For Bondarenko's public effort to set the record straight from the Foreign Ministry, see A. P. Bondarenko, "The Truth Is This," *Trud*, February 18, 1990, p. 3, in *FBIS-SOV* 90–040, February 28, 1990, pp. 23–24. The Soviet government organized an extraordinary collective statement of its Foreign Ministry. See TASS International Service (Moscow), "Foreign Ministry Collegium Statement on Germany," February 24, 1990, in *FBIS-SOV* 90–038, February 26, 1990, p. 1. Tarasenko confirmed that the collegium statement was intended as a "slap at Kohl." Zelikow interview, Providence, June 1993.

144. Gorbachev-Modrow memcon, 12 Feb 90, in Gorbachev papers provided to Stanford.

145. This was not some bureaucratic boilerplate. Chernyaev himself drafted this *Pravda* statement for Gorbachev. Chernyaev diary 1990, 25 Feb, p. 14. For the statement, Moscow Domestic Service, "Gorbachev Discusses German Reunification," February 21, 1990, in *FBIS-SOV* 90–035, 21 Feb 90, pp. 50–53.

146. On the internal West German arguments, see Zelikow and Rice, *Germany Unified and Europe Transformed*, 203–4; and Spohr, "Precluded or Precedent-Setting?," 33–36.

147. The "honest and unadorned" and "historic bargain" quotes are from Scowcroft to Bush, "Meetings with German Chancellor Helmut Kohl," 22 Feb 90, Rice files, 1989–90 subject files, Bush Library (drafted by Zelikow with Blackwill). Zoellick had given Blackwill suggested guidance on the Two Plus Four approach to use in this briefing for Bush. Details in Zelikow and Rice, *Germany Unified and Europe Transformed*, 211–12, 431 n. 30.

148. For a recent account of the French withdrawal in 1966, see Timothy Andrews Sayle, *Enduring Alliance: A History of NATO and the Postwar Global Order* (Ithaca, NY: Cornell University Press, 2019), 125–27. France formally rejoined NATO's military command in 2009.

149. Bush-Kohl memcon, Camp David, 24–25 Feb 90, Bush Library; also *DzD-Einheit*, 860–77; Bush-Kohl press conference, 25 Feb 90, Bush Library; Baker to Genscher, State 63344, "Message to Genscher," 28 Feb 90; see also Dobbins through Kimmitt and Bartholomew to Baker, "NATO and German Unification: Message to Genscher," 27 Feb 90.

150. In his May 1989 proposal Bush had suggested setting a ceiling on U.S. and Soviet stationed troop strength of no more than 275,000. That then meant about a 15 percent cut in U.S. forces and a withdrawal of more than half of stationed Soviet forces. To respond to the momentous events of late 1989, Bush was presented with three new alternatives. His Defense and military leaders wanted to stick with 275,000. So did Baker, until CFE was signed. The NSC staff recommended dropping now to 200,000. Bush chose the NSC staff position. The final number was 195,000 as a common ceiling for American and Soviet forces in Central and Eastern Europe, and 225,000 for Europe overall, by 1994. See Scowcroft to President Bush, "CFE Reductions," 16 Jan 90, attaching separate memos from Cheney, Scowcroft, and Baker. The NSC staff approach that was ultimately adopted was crafted by Blackwill and Zelikow with Arnold Kanter and Heather Wilson from Kanter's defense and arms control

directorate in the NSC staff, then refined by Scowcroft.

151. Under the revised ceilings the United States and the Soviet Union would be limited to 195,000 military personnel in Central Europe (defined to include the two Germanys, the Benelux countries, Denmark, Poland, Czechoslovakia, and Hungary). The Americans would have the right to station an additional 30,000 troops elsewhere in Europe (e.g., Great Britain or Italy). The Soviets had no troops stationed in Europe outside the central zone, so they were given no such extra entitlement. Zelikow participated in these negotiations; see also Zelikow through Blackwill to Scowcroft, "Impressions from the Ottawa Conference," 14 Feb 90.

152. Mitterrand interview, "German Reunification: Interview with President Mitterrand," February 14, 1990; English translation provided to the U.S. government by the French embassy. Interestingly, the embassy chose to delete some of the more disturbing parts of the interview in the translation they gave to the Americans. The complete text of the press interview was reported and commented on in Paris 5018, "President Mitterrand on Architecture: Is the French President Afraid of History After All?," 14 Feb 90.

153. Based on Zelikow's notes at the meeting.

154. See Kiessler and Elbe, *Ein runder Tisch mit scharfen Ecken*, 99–100; Shevardnadze, *Moi vybor*, 225–27, 231–33. The background of the Two Plus Four was well described in the detailed background press briefings conducted by Zoellick and Ross at the time. See PA transcript, "Background Briefing by Senior Administration Officials," 12 Feb 90, pp. 5–8 (Zoellick is the briefer in the cited portion); PA transcript, "Department of State Background Briefing on Results of Ottawa Ministerial," 14 Feb 90 ("First Official" is Ross; "Second Official" is Zoellick).

155. Based on Zelikow's notes of the meeting, echoed in other sources. On Thatcher's support for the Two Plus Four design (although the British preferred to call it "Four plus Two"), see Powell to Wall, "German Reunification," 15 Feb 90, *DBPO-German Unification*, 297–98.

The United States then turned to the task of structuring the Two Plus Four talks so that, as Scowcroft warned Bush, "we do not mismanage what will arguably be the most important set of talks for the West in the postwar period."

Scowcroft to Bush, "Preparing for the Six Power German Peace Conference," 15 Feb 90 (drafted principally by Rice); see also Robert Blackwill, "German Unification and American Diplomacy," *Aussenpolitik* 45, no. 3 (1994): 211, 214–15. Three tasks were then vital. First, commit the West Germans and other allies to a common position on the details of the security issues that would soon be so contentious. Second, delay. The Two Plus Four should start work very slowly, while German unification was happening very quickly. Third, when the Two Plus Four started up, the subjects for discussion should be "as limited as possible—dealing only with the legal issues related to the end of Four Power rights, the consequences of the absorption of the GDR into the FRG, and the issue of what becomes of forces on the territory of Germany's eastern half." Zoellick had already begun to think of the Two Plus Four as a "steering committee" with a narrow mandate. Kohl and Genscher and their teams also liked the American approach, and it prevailed in the discussions to prepare the talks.

156. For the Shevardnadze statement in Ottawa, see *Pravda*, February 16, 1990, p. 5.

157. Gorbachev in *Pravda*, March 5, 1990; Shevardnadze, published in an East German magazine aimed at the East German audience, in TASS, "Shevardnadze Discusses German Unity in Interview," March 7, 1990, in *FBIS-SOV* 90–046, March 8, 1990, pp. 37–40. On Gorbachev's meeting with Modrow, see Modrow, *Aufbruch und Ende*, 137–41.

All of this was closely followed in diplomatic and intelligence reports. U.S. ambassador Jack Matlock, for example, analyzed—in Moscow 8648, "Soviets Move Publicly to 'Put the Brakes' on German Rush for Unification," 14 Mar 90—that "to Moscow, the rush toward German unification is not unlike a large Mercedes barreling down the autobahn showing little regard for public safety.... Moscow is sending the message that unless Kohl (and others) are prepared to meet the Soviets part-way, Germany's journey to reunification could be far lengthier and slower than expected."

158. See Hans-Dietrich Genscher, "German Unity as a Contribution to European Stability," *Nordsee-Zeitung*, March 3, 1990. By SPD centrists we mean figures like Willy Brandt, Horst Ehmke, and Dietrich Stobbe. Opposed to NATO membership were the party's chancellor candidate Oskar Lafontaine and Egon Bahr. The SPD had

prepared a party platform calling for the dissolution of both alliances. See Scowcroft to President Bush, "SPD Thinking on a United Germany" (probably the last week of March); Baker to Bush (for his evening reading), 7 Mar 90.

159. See the joint "Erklärung zum Weg zur deutschen Einheit" issued by both SPD parties, February 19, 1990, in *Materialen zu Deutschlandfragen*, 192–93. The SPD joint statement also called for much earlier external intervention by the Four Powers in the unification process, envisioning a conference in the second half of April that would also include all of Germany's neighbors, whose views would "be dealt with as a matter of the highest priority."

160. Teltschik, *329 Tage*, 173.

161. The election day's cover of *Der Spiegel* read simply: "Kohl's Triumph." Among the best contemporary accounts of the campaign and election are "Es gibt keine mehr," *Der Spiegel*, March 19, 1990, pp. 20–33; Timothy Garton Ash, "The East German Surprise," *New York Review of Books*, April 26, 1990, p. 14; Jarausch, *The Rush to German Unity*, 115–28; Pond, *Beyond the Wall*, 199–201; Martin Mantzke, "Eine Republik auf Abruf: Die DDR nach den Wahlen vom 18. März 1990," *Europa-Archiv*, April 25, 1990, p. 287; Maier, *Die Wende in der DDR*, 83–88; and Daniel Hamilton, *After the Revolution: The New Political Landscape in East Germany* (Washington, DC: American Institute for Contemporary German Studies, 1990), 14–18, 42–43.

162. Secto 2017, "Memorandum for the President: Namibia, March 20," 20 Mar 90 (sent from Windhoek).

163. This was an important theme when Bush called Gorbachev to brief him directly on his talks with Kohl. Bush-Gorbachev telcon, 28 Feb 90, Bush Library.

Chapter 5: The Designs for a New Europe

1. Powell to Thatcher, "Seminar on British Defence Policy," 21 Jan 90, in PREM 19/2992, TNA. Thatcher marked up and appears to have agreed with Powell's argument. See also Francis Fukuyama, "The End of History?," *The National Interest*, no. 16 (Summer 1989): 3–18. Fukuyama regarded liberalism as the durable synthesis, after the defeat of fascism and communism. He worked in 1989–90 for Ross on Baker's Policy Planning Staff, but his much-publicized philosophical argument antedated and was unrelated to his State Department service.

2. See generally Kristina Spohr, *Post Wall, Post Square: Rebuilding the World After 1989* (London: William Collins, 2019), chapter 5.

3. Thomas Banchoff, "German Policy Towards the European Union: The Effects of Historical Memory," *German Politics* 6, no. 1 (1997): 60–76, focuses on Kohl's historical understanding.

4. To piece together the story of the origins of the political union, compare the good accounts in Werner Weidenfeld with Peter Wagner and Elke Bruck, *Außenpolitik für die deutsche Einheit* (Stuttgart: Deutsche Verlags-Anstalt, 1998), 384–414, 403 ("garbage heap"), 405 ("federalist excesses"); with Dyson and Featherstone, *The Road to Maastricht*, 204–9, 375–78; and with Bozo, *Mitterrand*, 235–37 (emphasizing Guigou's role in late March); see also, appearing to kick off the main action, Hartmann-Ludewig-Delors memcon, Paris, 16 Feb 90, *DzD-Einheit*, 852–53. In the workings of the triumvirate Delors often was closer to Kohl than he was to Mitterrand. Delors's aide, Pascal Lamy, could usually get his work done at the Elysée by working through Guigou (rather than Jacques Attali). Joachim Bitterlich was a key aide for Kohl, along with Teltschik. The foreign ministries became intensely involved in the last stage of the process, with Genscher and Dumas working well together, as usual.

5. See the summary in Andrew Moravcsik, *The Choice for Europe: Social Purpose and State Power from Messina to Maastricht* (Ithaca, NY: Cornell University Press, 1998), 447–57, 384–85, Table 6.2.

6. Dyson and Featherstone, *The Road to Maastricht*, xi.

7. Chernyaev diary 1990, entries for 22 and 30 Apr, pp. 25, 27.

8. This summary draws from Rice's recollections; Bush and Scowcroft, *A World Transformed*, 222–29; Baker, *The Politics of Diplomacy*, 239–44; Bozo, *Mitterrand*, 240–41. The use of Lugar as an intermediary arose from an American debate about whether the United States should pressure the Lithuanians to go along with the German and French initiative. Gates, Blackwill, and Rice were opposed. They argued that Washington should not leave its fingerprints on an effort to dissuade the Baltic states from seeking independence. Scowcroft, Baker, and Ross, however, believed that the Americans could send an "indirect" message to the Lithuanians that they wanted

to see a resolution. "When progress stopped," Don Oberdorfer, *The Turn: from the Cold War to a New Era; The United States and the Soviet Union, 1983–1990* (New York: Simon & Schuster, 1991), 404 (from Oberdorfer interview with Rice).

9. On the historical evolution of conventional wisdom about the Sverdlovsk issue, up to a point, see Michael Gordin, "The Anthrax Solution: The Sverdlovsk Incident and the Resolution of a Biological Weapons Controversy," *Journal of the History of Biology* 30, no. 3 (1997): 441–80. When Gordin wrote this article he did not know about the information that Soviet leaders of the BW program had already provided, from late 1989 onward, to the U.S. and British governments.

10. The first key defector, in October 1989, was Vladimir Pasechnik. Later there were other defectors and sources. The head of the Soviet biological weapons program, and Pasechnik's supervisor, was Ken Alibek. In 1989, Alibek joined in the cover-ups, external and internal. In 1992, Alibek defected to the United States. He has since published a memoir about his work and his defection: *Biohazard* (New York: Random House, 1999). The best overall account of the Soviet biological weapons story is now Milton Leitenberg and Raymond Zilinskas, *The Soviet Biological Weapons Program: A History* (Cambridge, MA: Harvard University Press, 2012). For more on the origins of the Soviet program, see Raymond Zilinskas, *The Soviet Biological Weapons Program and Its Legacy in Today's Russia* (Washington, DC: National Defense University Occasional Paper 11, July 2016); see also the valuable narrative in David Hoffman, *The Dead Hand: The Untold Story of the Cold War Arms Race and Its Dangerous Legacy* (New York: Doubleday, 2009), 327–57. The Soviet program leaders, like Alibek, appear to have assumed that the United States and Britain also had large clandestine BW programs. They were profoundly shocked when they learned, including through Soviet site visits in the United States, that this was not true and that the Americans and British had actually complied with the BWC.

The 1990s-era memoirs, including that of the U.S. ambassador, Matlock, leave out any discussion of these BW issues. The British ambassador in Moscow published his memoir in 2002, after the Soviet defector identities and information had been made public, and he gave some information about this. Braithwaite, *Across the Moscow River*, 141–43, but Braithwaite did not feel able to discuss other details that have since come out.

11. Some British officials apparently wanted to publicize all that was known and have a public confrontation with the Soviet government. Bush and Thatcher, and their top aides, did not agree. See the sifting of the evidence on this in Leitenberg and Zilinskas, *The Soviet Biological Weapons Program*, 582–92 and their notes.

12. For the Matlock-Bessmertnykh discussion, ibid., 594–95. Leitenberg and Zilinskas have the best summary of the subsequent developments, including a substantial analysis puzzling over Gorbachev's handling of this issue. Ibid., 595-630. They are mistaken on a small factual point: They date the first Baker-Shevardnadze discussion of the BW issues on May 2. In fact, these discussions were on May 17, after the initial demarches at the lower level. Hoffman did the initial reporting on Gorbachev's recollection of his first discussion about the program with Bush. *The Dead Hand*, 350–51.

13. For the details of this diplomacy, see Zelikow and Rice, *Germany Unified and Europe Transformed*, 213, 217–22; Bozo, *Mitterrand*, 224–28; Weidenfeld, *Außenpolitik*, 484–91.

One great irony was that the issue was propelled by the inability of the FRG to sign a treaty on behalf of the future united Germany. But the FRG's March decision (formally announced on March 8) to unify by means of Article 23 made the point moot. If the FRG annexed the GDR, making it part of the existing Federal Republic, Bonn's past international legal obligations—including its 1970 treaty with Poland guaranteeing the borders—remained intact. As a legal matter, that would have been enough to bind a united Germany to recognition of the Polish border. See Zelikow and Rice, *Germany Unified and Europe Transformed*, 267, 435 n. 55, 451–52 nn. 30 and 31, 456 n. 9. But the issue was also about the political symbolism of reaffirming the border.

14. For variants of these Soviet positions, which were significantly guided by then–deputy foreign minister Yuli Kvitsinsky and the German expert Aleksandr Bondarenko, see Zelikow and Rice, *Germany Unified and Europe Transformed*, 248–49, 261, 264–65, 295–97.

15. An even earlier precedent for such military controls were those placed on Russia in 1856, in the Treaty of Paris that concluded the Crimean War and required the demilitarization of the Black Sea. Russian leaders had detested these restrictions. The Russians had finally cast off these controls in moves between 1866 and 1871—at the

time of Germany's first unification. See Stéphanie Burgaud, "1866: Why the Russian Bomb Did Not Explode," *International History Review* 40, no. 2 (2018): 253–72.

16. The proximate reason for the 1947 breakdown was disagreements among the Four Powers about the economic administration of occupied Germany. The Americans pressed their German disarmament plan but, amid the other quarrels, the Soviet government ignored it. Philip Zelikow, "George C. Marshall and the Moscow CFM Meeting of 1947," *Diplomacy and Statecraft* 8, no. 2 (1997): 97–124.

17. Rice and Zelikow to Blackwill, "Two Plus Four: The Next Phase," 10 May 90; Zoellick also made notes for himself around the same time, in his office files. He had discussed the issue with the West Germans and previewed it for Baker back in March. On that and also the difficult legal issue that would be confronted, effectively forcing the United States to adopt the kind of arguments that the Soviets had used in the 1950s during the Berlin crisis, see Zelikow and Rice, *Germany Unified and Europe Transformed*, 246, 448 n. 9.

    The British government disagreed internally on whether it was willing to let Four Power rights terminate. But Foreign Secretary Hurd and his team in London had about the same position as the Americans did. They pushed back hard against concerns voiced in No. 10 and from their ambassador in Bonn, and insisted that the British should let their rights lapse when Germany unified. See Weston to Wall, 18 May 90, answering Powell to Wall that day, reacting to Bonn 634, "German Unification: The Timetable Accelerates," 17 May 90, in *DBPO-German Unification*, 390–94; see also the earlier Foreign Office analysis by Hurd's policy planner, Robert Cooper, on "The Soviet Veto in the Two plus Four Talks," 6 Apr 90, in ibid., 371–72.

18. On the Hurd-Kohl meeting, see Teltschik, *329 Tage*, 235; Bonn (U.S. embassy) 15540, "Hurd's May 15 Visit to Bonn," 16 May 90.

19. Zelikow and Rice, *Germany Unified and Europe Transformed*, 236.

20. On the details of this diplomacy, with the approach effectively settled among the Americans and West Germans in June 1990, see Zelikow and Rice, *Germany Unified and Europe Transformed*, 239, 267–68, 274–75, 306–7, 308, 323, 333.

21. On the eventual scale and cost of German CFE compliance, Celeste Wallander, *Mortal Friends,*

Best Enemies: German-Russian Cooperation After the Cold War (Ithaca, NY: Cornell University Press, 1999), 104, 110.

22. CFE 1A was more formally called the Concluding Act of the Negotiation on Personnel Strength of Conventional Armed Forces in Europe, signed in Helsinki in July 1992. In that agreement, Germany reduced its ceiling to 345,000. France, which had about three-quarters of Germany's population, had a ceiling of 325,000. With nearly double Germany's population, Russia was granted a disproportionately large ceiling of 1.45 million, more than four times the German total. Ukraine, with about one-third the population of Russia, was granted a ceiling of 450,000.

23. Kohl-Bush memcons, Washington, 17 May 90, Bush Library; Teltschik, *329 Tage*, 236–39; *DzD-Einheit*, 1126–27 (in which the records of the three meetings run together). The small discussion seeking the "honest opinion" was just with Bush, Kohl, Scowcroft, Teltschik, and the interpreters (the 10:00 to 11:30 meeting), on which the American record is more detailed than the German one, although the essence of the exchange is clear in all the sources. During April and early May, Bush had just completed another set of summit meetings with Thatcher and Mitterrand and Wörner, in addition to his talks with Kohl.

24. Bush address, Oklahoma State University, 4 May 90, Bush Library.

25. Kohl-Mitterrand memcon, Latche (near the coast in the French Pyrenees), 4 Jan 90, *DzD-Einheit*, 685.

26. The account that follows is drawn from Teltschik, *329 Tage*, 221, 226–28, 230–35.

27. The discussion that follows is drawn from ibid., pp. 237–38; Bush-Kohl memcon, 17 May 90, Bush Library.

28. For the Zoellick-Ross drafted presentation on Germany that Baker took into his meeting with Gorbachev, see briefing paper, "One-on-One Points: Gorbachev Meeting," n.d. For Baker's summary to Bush on his meeting with Gorbachev, see Secto 7015 (from Moscow), "Memorandum for the President: Moscow, May 18," 19 May 90. For Chernyaev's vehement private dissent, see Chernyaev diary 1990, 5 May, p. 29.

29. Scowcroft to Bush, "A Strategic Choice: Do We Give Aid to the Soviet Union?," 25 May 90, in Rice files, Soviet Union/USSR Subject Files, US-USSR Soviet Relations (2), Bush Library. The memo was drafted principally by Rice, working with Blackwill and Gates. It was highly classified

at the time and handled outside of the normal paperwork system.

30. Quoted in Bozo, *Mitterrand*, 253.

31. The language appears in "Principle I" of the "Principles Guiding Relations between Participating States" in "Basket I" of the Helsinki Final Act of 1975, dealing with security questions: "[The participating states] also have the right to belong or not to belong to international organizations, to be or not to be a party to bilateral or multilateral treaties including the right to be or not to be a party to treaties of alliance; they also have the right to neutrality." Within the American government Zoellick had seized on this principle months earlier as a way to strengthen the West's position, since the CSCE document, though not legally binding on signatories, was one of the few bodies of principles clearly agreed to by both sides.

32. Central Committee staff to members of the Politburo, "O svazi otnosheniyakh c vostochnymevropa," May 1990, in Center for the Storage of Contemporary Documentation (TsKhSD), Moscow.

33. The German government has long had relatively broad authority to guarantee export-related loans, combined (not coincidentally) with close relationships between top government and banking leaders. An example is their "Hermes cover" program. In the U.S. government the strongest export credit guarantee authorities are confined to agricultural exports. The G-7 governments could help fund and try to persuade the international financial institutions to make loans, led by the IMF. This would require Soviet membership in the IMF, a process that began getting under way, precariously, in late 1990, and would then lead to setting policy conditions in order to get credit.

34. See Bush and Scowcroft, *A World Transformed*, 276–78.

35. See Oberdorfer, *The Turn*, 414–15; Beschloss and Talbott, *At the Highest Levels*, 217–18 (both sources are accurate on this episode, based on interviews with participants).

36. We have been unable to locate a memcon for this May 31 afternnon meeting in the American archives, but there are extensive quotes in Bush and Scowcroft, *A World Transformed*, 281–83. When in doubt we have relied on their language. Part of the Soviet memcon is quoted in Chernyaev, *Shest' let s Gorbachevym*, 348. Other details in the discussion that follows are drawn

from Zelikow's interviews with participants at the meeting (Chernyaev, Blackwill, and Zoellick); Zoellick's and Blackwill's handwritten notes from the meeting; and the memoir of another participant, Valentin Falin, *Politische Erinnerungen*, trans. Heddy Pross-Weerth (Munich: Droemer Knaur, 1993), 492–93.

37. Bush stayed close to a prepared presentation titled "The Future of Europe: Germany, NATO, CFE, and CSCE." His talking points were drafted by Ross and Rice, then edited and refined by Blackwill, Zoellick, and Zelikow.

38. Rice interview with Chernyaev, Moscow, June 1994.

39. The conversation was recorded by CNN, with Gorbachev and the congressmen apparently unaware that the TV cameras were broadcasting it live to the world—and to Bush, who was watching in the Oval Office. Oberdorfer, *The Turn*, 418–19; Beschloss and Talbott, *At the Highest Levels*, 221–22.

40. Based on our understanding of the discussion at the time. As far as we know, there is no written record of the Bush-Gorbachev side discussions at Camp David about economic aid or about biological weapons.

41. See Teltschik, *329 Tage*, 255–58; Bush-Kohl and Bush-Thatcher telcons, 3 Jun 90, Bush-Mitterrand telcon, 5 Jun 90, Bush Library. The written messages were sent out on June 4. Bush did tell both Kohl and Thatcher about the private discussions of economic aid. The letter to Thatcher did not mention Bush's discussion of the biological weapons problem with Gorbachev. Some of those discussions were handled directly between Scowcroft and Charles Powell. Thatcher was kept up to date on the BW discussions and she followed up on the subject with Gorbachev when she went to Moscow later that month.

42. Hannes Adomeit, "Gorbachev, German Unification and the Collapse of Empire," *Post-Soviet Affairs* 10 (August–September 1994): 197, 229 n. 28; Zelikow interview with Chernyaev, Moscow, January 1994.

43. Julij Kwizinskij, *Vor dem Sturm*, 16 ("surrealistic jumble"). One of the more complete summaries of the developed Soviet alternative emerged from the lengthy Genscher-Shevardnadze talks in Brest-Litovsk on 11 Jun 90. The memcon is in Hilger, *Diplomatie*, doc. 35, see pp. 175–77; and summarized in Dieter Kastrup's report on the talks to NATO ambassadors, 13 Jun, in *Einheit*

Dokumente, doc. 112, esp. pp. 559–60. Shevardnadze's examples of the disputes that a CSCE conflict prevention center might address are from Genscher's recounting of his May 23 meeting with Shevardnadze to Baker a couple of days later. Ibid., doc. 102, p. 510.

44. See Zelikow and Rice, *Germany Unified and Europe Transformed*, 244, 293. However, in mid-June 1990 the Soviet government did table ideas for a proposed NATO–Warsaw Pact joint declaration that would create a joint pan-European collective military alliance open to all thirty-five CSCE states. The same draft also included multilateral peacekeeping forces "to maintain peace between East and West," but it required that NATO drop its own mutual defense obligations. It also called for withdrawal of all U.S. forces, including nuclear forces, from Germany as Soviet forces left. It also required withdrawal of naval and air forces from Europe that might be used for "surprise offensive actions and large-scale operations" based in Europe. The United States and other NATO allies regarded this proposal as so obnoxious as to be nonnegotiable. The West Germans and British hoped to salvage the joint declaration idea if it could be made dull and substance-free.

Top Soviet officials never really explained their arguments for how such a pan-European military alliance would work. We believe this particular laundry list of ideas had not been seriously considered, but instead was tabled as a set of straw positions to slow down the diplomatic process. Ibid., 310–11.

45. Baker to Bush (sent as Secto 6013 from Bonn), "My Meeting with Shevardnadze," 5 May 90; Baker made a similar point six weeks later, in June, after another tough meeting with Shevardnadze; on that and the context, see Zelikow and Rice, *Germany Unified and Europe Transformed*, 303. "Demonic" is from a comment Genscher made in Kohl-Bush memcons, 17 May 90, Bush Library.

46. For the details of the American work, pre-summit allied consultations, and the summit itself, see Zelikow and Rice, *Germany Unified and Europe Transformed*, 238–40, 303–24. In addition to the sources cited there, Ross's handwritten notes of the pre-summit meeting with Bush in Kennebunkport (which Zelikow attended) are available in Box 109, Folder 3, Baker Papers. For the summit itself, the practically verbatim records of the head of state meetings at the London NATO summit, North Atlantic Council, 5 and 6 Jul 90, C-VR(90)36, Parts I and II, are now opened in the NATO Archives, available online.

47. On the origins of the diplomatic liaison mission move, see Zelikow and Rice, *Germany Unified and Europe Transformed*, 304, 460 n. 36. Sarotte emphasizes a memo that one of Ross's staffers, Harvey Sicherman, wrote on March 12 arguing that East European countries might want some sort of cooperation with NATO and the EC to ease their dilemma of being between Germany and Russia. Mary Sarotte, "Perpetuating U.S. Preeminence: The 1990 Deals to 'Bribe the Soviets Out' and Move NATO In," *International Security* 35, no. 1 (2010): 110, 118. Sicherman's memo was one among various ideas circulating in March and April that led us to come up with the liaison missions initiative, which we presented to Blackwill and Scowcroft in April, then to the interagency European Strategy Steering Group (which included Ross and Zoellick), which endorsed it. It thus became part of the U.S.-proposed NATO offer accepted by NATO leaders—an offer made to the Soviet government as well as to other former Warsaw Pact member states. Led by Delors, who favored this, the EC had started its own efforts to reach out to the East European states.

48. Eduard Shevardnadze, *Moi vybor: zashchitu demokratii i svobody* (Moscow: Novosti, 1991), 239; "Comments by Soviets on NATO," *New York Times*, July 7, 1990, p. 5; TASS, "Shevardnadze on NATO Communique," July 6, 1990, in *FBIS-SOV* 90–131, July 9, 1990; see also Chernyaev's satisfied comment in his 1990 diary, 9 Jul, p. 39.

49. Hans Klein, *Es begann im Kaukasus: Der entscheidende Schritt in die Einheit Deutschlands* (Berlin: Ullstein, 1991), 234–35 ("Never in my life"). Details of the diplomacy, based on American, German, and Soviet sources, plus surrounding context, are at Zelikow and Rice, *Germany Unified and Europe Transformed*. Both of us participated in the Two Plus Four talks. A fine narrative summary of this diplomatic endgame is Kristina Spohr, *Post Wall, Post Square*, chapter 4.

50. The nine points were:

1. limiting the Bundeswehr in CFE II [this was actually done in 1990 without waiting for CFE II];
2. accelerating SNF negotiations [Bush jumped over the negotiations in September 1991 with

a unilateral withdrawal of practically all such weapons, which Gorbachev reciprocated];

3. ensuring that the Germans would not develop, possess, or acquire either nuclear, biological, or chemical weapons [this was done in the Final Settlement];

4. keeping NATO forces out of the GDR for a transition period [also done, with further details discussed in Soviet–West German talks];

5. developing a transition period for Soviet forces to leave the GDR [worked out between West Germans and Soviets];

6. adapting NATO politically and militarily [accomplished both in word and deed in 1990 and 1991];

7. getting an agreement on the Polish-German border [done in the manner we discussed above];

8. institutionalizing and developing CSCE [done in the 1990 Charter of Paris and the 1992 Helsinki CSCE summit, with solid Soviet, then Russian, participation]; and

9. developing economic relations with the Germans, while ensuring that GDR economic obligations to the USSR would be fulfilled [also worked out between the Soviets and Germans].

As Baker recalled, "Gorbachev took copious notes as I went through the list and made clear he approved of it very much." Where Gorbachev still balked at that time, in mid-May, was the acceptance of a unified Germany in NATO. Baker, *The Politics of Diplomacy*, 250–51.

Citing "insights from international relations theory," Shifrinson has argued that the United States made "informal assurances" not to extend NATO and that it made a "false promise of accommodation" of Soviet interests. The promise was false, he asserts, because, in 1990, the United States and its allies hoped to preserve NATO and because, in 1990, the door to possible future NATO enlargement was "left ajar." Thus "the United States was insincere when offering the Soviet Union informal assurances against NATO expansion." "Deal or No Deal?," 34, 38, 40.

The context of the "left ajar" quote provides a more accurate snapshot of U.S. views not only in 1990, but also onward until 1993, after the Soviet Union had disintegrated. At the end of October 1990, Zelikow briefed Gates on the state of play, in the European Strategy Steering Group, on the question of: "Should the US and NATO now

signal to the new democracies of Eastern Europe NATO's readiness to contemplate their future membership?"

Zelikow reported that "all agencies agree that East European governments should not be invited to join NATO anytime in the immediate future. There is general satisfaction with the way the State paper ended up handling the issue of Eastern Europe [page numbers given]. However, OSD [Cheney's civilian aides] and State's Policy Planning Staff (and possibly Zoellick) would like to keep the door ajar and not give the East Europeans the impression that NATO is forever a closed club." The rest of State preferred to just be "inscrutable," treating the issue "as premature and not on the table, while of course reserving our options as the political situation in Europe evolves." Zelikow through Gompert and Kanter to Gates, "Your Meeting of the European Strategy Steering Group," 26 Oct 90, pp. 4–5, Wilson files, Bush Library. This reserved stance was precisely the approach that had animated our "liaison missions" proposal that NATO had adopted in July 1990, which then led to the 1991 creation of the NACC.

There were no "informal assurances" to scuttle or settle NATO's future contours, one way or another. The American sources, which we know well, do not say different. Perhaps more to the point, the other governments so centrally involved, like the Soviet and West German governments, also did not believe at the time that they had struck such an agreement, formally or informally. Those who did the work were professionals who knew what they were agreeing to, or not.

Bush, Baker, Kohl, and Genscher actually worked conscientiously and in good faith to accommodate Soviet and Russian security concerns. Those looking for informal assurances meant to accommodate such concerns can readily find them: Baker presented his list of nine assurances to Gorbachev in May 1990, a list circulated and discussed among allied governments, and repeatedly stressed in the subsequent diplomacy.

51. Blackwill's July 25 remarks were reported by a British embassy attendee a week later. *DBPO-German Unification*, 470 n. 9.

52. On the last-minute tensions, centered on a quarrel among the Western allies over how to delimit allowable foreign troop movements in the former GDR, a blowup that the West Germans blamed on the British, details are in Zelikow and Rice,

Germany Unified and Europe Transformed, 359–62. See, for the amusing British version of the story, Weston to Mallaby, "Two Plus Four: The End Game," 17 Sep 90, in *DBPO-German Unification*, 466–71.

53. See, e.g., Scowcroft's comments in Bush and Scowcroft, *A World Transformed*, 297–98.

54. The metaphor of a "bribe" is vivid because it sounds corrupt. E.g., Sarotte, "Perpetuating U.S. Preeminence: The 1990 Deals to 'Bribe the Soviets Out' and Move NATO In." Sarotte attributes the original "bribe" expression to Gates, and she applies it liberally, even to moves like the London NATO summit. There was nothing corrupt about this bargain. Gorbachev displayed integrity in office. In the case of the Soviet troop maintenance and withdrawal costs, he had a legitimate case that, for several reasons, was better addressed to the German side. The German money included, for example, items like money for construction of more than forty-five thousand apartments for returning troops, itself only a fraction of the Soviet military housing problem. Odom, *The Collapse of the Soviet Military*, 279.

55. Chernyaev diary 1990, entries for July 14 and 15 [there is a typo in the month given for the July 14 entry], p. 41.

56. Grosser, *Das Wagnis*, 433. West German grants related to Soviet troop withdrawal totaled about DM 15 billion, or about $9 billion. German Finance Ministry, "Deutsche Unterstützungmaßnahmen für den Reformprozeß in der UdSSR," 12 Apr 91, in ibid., 432–33.

57. As of April 1991, the German credit guarantees totaled DM 24.7 billion (including balance of payments credits and portions of EC credits) and the Germans carried a balance of DM 16.9 billion in transferable rubles. Ibid.

58. On this point, see, e.g., Stanley Fischer, "Stabilization and Economic Reform in Russia," *Brookings Papers on Economic Activity*, no. 1 (1992): 84–85 (comparing Soviet export income to a Soviet foreign debt of $80 billion by the end of 1991).

59. Baker, *Politics of Diplomacy*, 529.

60. Zelikow participated in the work on these NATO operations. In the case of the movement of the U.S. VII Corps, the procedures for large international movements of military forces had been put in place with standing NATO agreements (called STANAGs) and rehearsed in more than twenty REFORGER exercises practicing movement of American forces in Europe, as well as movements that had already begun to withdraw U.S. forces from Europe to comply with the soon-to-be-signed CFE treaty.

61. The other occasion when foreign troops were deployed into Israel to aid its defense was during the Suez War of 1956, when French forces, mainly aircraft, were secretly deployed to Israel and operated from Israeli bases.

62. David Gompert, "The United States and Yugoslavia's Wars," in Richard Ullman, ed., *The World and Yugoslavia's Wars* (New York: Council on Foreign Relations, 1996), 122; see also, including on the prescient, gloomily detached November 1990 intelligence estimate, Hutchings, *American Diplomacy and the End of the Cold War*, 305–6.

63. Dumas, in Pierre Favier and Michel Martin-Roland, *La décennie Mitterrand*, vol. 4, *Les déchirements (1991–1995)* (Paris: Seuil, 1999), 197.

64. Bush and Scowcroft, *A World Transformed*, 268, discussing the exchanges with Mitterrand about NATO's future at the April 1990 Key Largo summit.

65. The French views in this period are well summarized in Bozo, *Mitterrand*, 245–82. French troops in Germany were there as part of alliance defense, but not under NATO's integrated military command, which France had left in 1966 (when NATO headquarters left Paris and moved to its present home on the outskirts of Brussels).

66. Bozo, *Mitterrand*, 346, 390; for the best overall analysis of the argument in the early 1990s, compare the account in Bozo with Kori Schake, "NATO After the Cold War, 1991–1995: Institutional Competition and the Collapse of the French Alternative," *Contemporary European History* 7, no. 3 (1998): 379–407.

67. Short, *A Taste for Intrigue*, 514; Favier and Martin-Roland, *Les déchirements*, 168–69, 201–19.

68. For a succinct overview of why it took ten years to sort all of this out, see Jolyon Howorth, "The EU, NATO, and the Origins of CFSP and ESDP," in Frédéric Bozo, Marie-Pierre Rey, N. Piers Ludlow, and Leopoldo Nuti, eds., *Europe and the End of the Cold War: A Reappraisal* (London: Routledge, 2008), 259–70.

69. Zara Steiner, *The Lights That Failed: European International History 1919–1933* (Oxford: Oxford University Press, 2005), 355.

70. Quotes are from the Kohl-Mitterrand memcon, Latche, 4 Jan 90, *DzD-Einheit*, 687; Kohl-Mitterrand dinner memcon, 15 Feb 90, in ibid., 850. In their January conversation, Mitterrand

observed that if Gorbachev could be a candidate for the office of a European president he would have a better chance of being elected than in the Soviet Union. Ibid., 689.

71. Frédéric Bozo, "The Failure of a Grand Design: Mitterrand's European Confederation, 1989–1991," *Contemporary European History* 17, no. 3 (2008): 391–412; and see Vojtech Mastny, "Eastern Europe and the Early Prospects for EC/EU and NATO Membership," *Cold War History* 9, no. 2 (2009): 203, 209, 213 (on the conception and fate of Mitterrand's concept).

72. Genscher had suggested ten ideas for building up the CSCE in his January 31 Tutzing speech. On the formative staff work in the U.S. government, see Zelikow and Rice, *Germany Unified and Europe Transformed*, 443 n. 105 and 305–6.

73. Compare the CSCE ideas Shevardnadze presented to Genscher in Münster on June 18 with the ideas Baker presented confidentially to Shevardnadze in Berlin on June 22 (previewing what America hoped its allies would agree to at the upcoming London summit). Ibid., 293 (on Münster), 302 (on Berlin); see also Genscher-Shevardnadze memcon, Münster, 18 Jun 90, in Hilger, *Diplomatie*, docs. 37 and 38, esp. pp. 200, 203–4, 213.

74. The CFE treaty was much more impactful for the Soviet military than any nuclear arms control agreement. It had a significant political impact in Soviet domestic politics too, since Gorbachev and Shevardnadze had to use their waning authority to push this through. Those two leaders may not have been fully aware of the measures being taken to circumvent the treaty's restrictions (there is an analogy in the biological weapons story). The CFE treaty would have halved Soviet armored equipment west of the Urals. Before the treaty came into effect, the Soviet military began massive movements of such equipment into Asia, moves probably put in motion during 1989 and well under way by the time the treaty was signed in November 1990. Other more flagrant measures to circumvent CFE limits (for instance by turning army units into "naval infantry") became a subject of acrimonious negotiations at the end of 1990 and during 1991. See Zelikow and Rice, *Germany Unified and Europe Transformed*, 261, 449–50 n. 19.

75. See Stuart Croft, "Ratification of CFE and Agreement on CFE 1A," in Croft, ed., *The Conventional Armed Forces in Europe Treaty: The Cold War Endgame* (Aldershot, UK: Dartmouth, 1994), 241–63; Wallander, *Mortal Friends, Best Enemies*, 104–7, is a good summary and recounts the German and Russian views of the process. CFE 1A also kept the promise that Germany's national limits would become part of a system in which all the other participants accepted such limits.

76. Pál Dunay, "On the (Continuing, Residual) Relevance of the CFE Regime," *Helsinki Monitor*, no. 4 (2004): 263, 264. Dunay was writing before Russia suspended its participation in the CFE system at the end of 2007. See also the overview of the emergent European security system, from a former U.S. diplomat, in Jenonne Walker, *Security and Arms Control in Post-Confrontation Europe*, SIPRI Research Report (New York: Oxford University Press, 1994).

On the difficult negotiation of the 1996 "flank" limits, see the German and Russian views in Wallander, *Mortal Friends, Best Enemies*, 107–10. On the evolution of Russian views about CFE during the 1990s and 2000s, see Mark Wilcox, "Russia and the Treaty on Conventional Armed Forces in Europe (CFE Treaty)—A Paradigm Change?," *Journal of Slavic Military Studies* 24 (2011): 567–81.

77. State Department paper for Baker, "CSCE Summit," 22 Jan 90, Box 115, Folder 7, Baker Papers. The economic preparatory conference was held in Bonn in March–April 1990.

78. Mikhail Gorbachev, *Memoirs* (New York: Doubleday, 1996), 548.

Chapter 6: The Designs for a Commonwealth of Free Nations

1. Sir T. Smith, *De Republica Anglorum* (1583), quoted in the *Oxford English Dictionary*, "commonwealth," definition 2.

2. Bush address to the Brazilian Congress, 3 Dec 90, *Public Papers of the Presidents of the United States: George Bush, 1990*, bk. 2, 1738.

3. Baker with DeFrank, *The Politics of Diplomacy*, 138–42.

4. Chernyaev diary 1990, 21 Aug, p. 44; Taubman, *Gorbachev*, 526 ("gravediggers").

5. Chernyaev diary 1990, 21 Aug, p. 46.

6. Moscow 23603, "Looking into the Abyss: The Possible Collapse of the Soviet Union and What We Should Be Doing About It," 13 Jul 90; and Scowcroft to Bush, "Turmoil in the Soviet Union

and U.S. Policy," n.d., possibly 18 Aug 90, both in Rice files, USSR subject files, USSR Political, Bush Library.

7. Scowcroft to Bush (drafted by Rice), "Your Meeting with Gorbachev in Helsinki," n.d. Sep 90, Scowcroft files, USSR Collapse files, U.S.-Soviet Chron, USSR Collapse: U.S.-Soviet Relations Thru 1991, Bush Library; for the analogous perspective of the American ambassador in Moscow, see also Jack Matlock, *Autopsy on an Empire* (New York: Random House, 1995), 406–9.

8. Bush-Gorbachev afternoon meeting memcon, 9 Sep 90, Bush Library (Rice was the notetaker); and (including "None of the Soviets asked") Burns through Rice for Scowcroft, "Results of Presidential Business Development Mission to the USSR," 20 Sep 90, Scowcroft files, USSR Collapse, Box 12, Bush Library.

9. Chernyaev diary 1990, 18 Sep, p. 53, quoting Abel Aganbegyan and Shatalin.

10. Chernyaev has an especially thoughtful reconstruction and reflection on Gorbachev's choice. *My Six Years with Gorbachev*, 284–95; see also Taubman, *Gorbachev*, 521–30, 530 ("worst"); Anders Åslund, *Russia's Capitalist Revolution: Why Market Reform Succeeded and Democracy Failed* (Washington, DC: Peterson Institute for International Economics, 2007), 61–62.

   Peter Reddaway and Dmitri Glinski make the curious argument that it was the IMF and Western interests that helped derail the "500-day plan." *The Tragedy of Russia's Reforms: Market Bolshevism Against Democracy* (Washington, DC: U.S. Institute of Peace, 2001), 176. In fact, at the time, reporters following this were told, "Officials at the IMF, who were commissioned at the July Houston economic summit to come up with recommendations on how the Soviet economy might be helped, welcome the new [500-day] initiative. For the first time, they see recognition in Moscow of the need for drastic change. Until now, says one official, 'it wasn't even possible to engage in a policy debate because there was nothing to bite on.'" Hobart Rowen, "The Soviet Union Needs IMF, Bank," *Washington Post*, September 23, 1990. The IMF's positive interest was echoed at the White House, at State, and from Matlock in Moscow.

11. French Foreign Ministry, "Internal Situation of the USSR: Troubled Times," and "Internal Evolution of the USSR: What Possibilities for the Next Two Years," both briefing memos for Gorbachev's upcoming visit to Paris, 24 Oct 90, in Europe 1986–1990, URSS, Box 6686, AD.

12. Scowcroft offers his perspective on Shevardnadze's role and Gorbachev's temporizing in Bush and Scowcroft, *A World Transformed*, 493–95; "By the turn": Braithwaite, *Across the Moscow River*, 199.

13. Matlock, *Autopsy on an Empire*, 451.

14. Yeltsin quoted in Odom, *Collapse of the Soviet Military*, 270; Matlock, *Autopsy on an Empire*, 471 ("zigs and zags").

15. The "prerevolutionary" quote comes from Scowcroft in *A World Transformed*, 499 (referring to assessments in March 1991); see the comments on Yavlinsky, new prime minister Pavlov, and Yevgeny Primakov, in Chernyaev diary 1991, 17 May, pp. 58–59. On the Yavlinsky-Allison idea and the G-7 meeting in London, see Taubman, *Gorbachev*, 590–95.

16. Baker's marked-up notes for his meeting with Shevardnadze (now seeing him as a friend and adviser), 6 May 91, Box 110, Folder 4, Baker Papers.

17. Baker, "Points for Meeting with Primakov, et al," 28 and 29 May 91, Box 110, Folder 4, Baker Papers; and Gates, *From the Shadows*, 503.

18. Chernyaev diary 1991, 21 Jun, p. 72.

19. Ibid., 6 Jul, p. 79.

20. Bush and Scowcroft, *A World Transformed*, 503–9.

21. Chernyaev diary 1991, 23 Jul, p. 91; "we simply did not know enough": Bush in *A World Transformed*, 540; see also the discussions in Chernyaev, *My Six Years with Gorbachev*, 385–89.

22. The best general account of the breakup of the Soviet Union in the second half of 1991 is Serhii Plokhy, *The Last Empire: The Final Days of the Soviet Union* (New York: Basic Books, 2014).

23. On the origins of the work, see also Gates, *From the Shadows*, 526–27.

24. For the state of the Gorbachev-Yeltsin-Kravchuk work on the new Union treaty, along with U.S. views and Bush's Kiev visit, a balanced synthesis is Plokhy, *The Last Empire*, 24–69.

   On the START treaty, Plokhy approvingly quotes Strobe Talbott's comment, immediately after the Bush-Gorbachev Moscow summit that "the U.S.S.R. has conceded so much and the U.S. reciprocated so little [in the START treaty] for a simple reason: the Gorbachev revolution is history's greatest fire sale" (p. 15).

   START codified an overall equality in U.S. and Soviet strategic nuclear delivery vehicles and weapons. The supposed great Soviet concessions were that it gave up too much on land-based ICBMs while not getting enough reductions in U.S. bombers and submarine-launched weapons.

Perhaps Gorbachev was more farsighted about what the Soviet Union really needed than were his critics. It is hard to imagine that, even a year later, in 1992, Plokhy or Talbott would wish that Gorbachev had stalled the treaty or held out, just to ensure that his government could deploy, within its overall total, more heavy or mobile ICBMs.

25. Putin quoted in Plokhy, *The Last Empire*, 120–21.
26. On the early September arguments and Baker's five principles, see Bush and Scowcroft, *A World Transformed*, 540–44; Baker, *The Politics of Diplomacy*, 524–26; Dick Cheney with Liz Cheney, *In My Time: A Personal and Political Memoir* (New York: Simon & Schuster, 2011), 232; Gates, *From the Shadows*, 529–30; "Secretary Baker's Five Principles Guiding U.S. Policy Toward the Soviet Union," 4 Sep 91, Box 110, Folder 8, Baker Papers. "Set the philosophical": from a memo to Baker by Andrew Carpendale and John Hannah (on Ross's staff), in Baker, *Politics of Diplomacy*, 525.
27. The 35,000 number is from Robert Norris and Hans Kristensen, "Global Nuclear Weapons Inventories, 1945–2010," *Bulletin of the Atomic Scientists* 66, no. 4 (2010): 77, 82. Their comparable estimate for the U.S. stockpile in 1991 is 19,000. At the time, outsiders, like the Harvard group working on this, estimated the Soviet number at 27,000. Kurt Campbell, Ashton Carter, Steven Miller, and Charles Zraket, *Soviet Nuclear Fission: Control of the Nuclear Arsenal in a Disintegrating Soviet Union* (Cambridge, MA: Harvard CSIA, November 1991), which also has a good breakdown of weapons distribution (pp. 16–22). The Cheney quote is from Graham Allison, "What Happened to the Soviet Superpower's Nuclear Arsenal? Clues for the Nuclear Security Summit," Harvard Kennedy School Belfer Center paper, March 2012, p. 1.
28. See Bush and Scowcroft, *A World Transformed*, 545–46; Cheney, *In My Time*, 233–34; Chernyaev, *My Six Years with Gorbachev*, 390. The Soviet total was 14,000 weapons redeployed to Russia, many of them then dismantled. Allison, "What Happened," 4.
29. Zbigniew Brzezinski, "The Premature Partnership," *Foreign Affairs* 73, no. 2 (1994); Mearsheimer, "The Case for a Ukrainian Nuclear Deterrent," *Foreign Affairs* 72, no. 3 (1993).
30. See, e.g., how Undersecretary of State Reginald Bartholomew was addressing the "Russia-only" nuclear issue in Yakovlev-Bartholomew (undersecretary of state) memcon, 8 Oct 91,

in "Nunn-Lugar Revisited," National Security Archive Electronic Briefing Book No. 447, ed. Tom Blanton and Svetlana Savranskaya, with Anna Melyakova, doc. no. 5. The National Security Archive documentary sets are an essential resource on the cooperative denuclearization process of the 1990s. See their Electronic Briefing Books Nos. 447, 491, 528, and 571.
31. On the unofficial work with Ukrainians during late 1991, see Zelikow to Allison et al., "Harvard Discussion with Kravchuk on Nuclear Weapons," 30 Sep 91 (relayed by Allison to Hewett); Hewett to Scowcroft, "Ukrainian Approach to Defense Matters," 8 Nov 91 (relaying debrief of Zelikow's Geneva talks with Ukrainian officials), both in National Security Archive Electronic Briefing Book No. 447. A Harvard group then journeyed to Kiev in December to continue the discussions. After that, the USSR ceased to exist, the U.S. government recognized the Ukrainian government, and U.S. officials took over the work.

Ukraine appeared to agree to give up nuclear weapons on its territory in the December 1991 Minsk agreements with Yeltsin creating the Commonwealth of Independent States and ending the Soviet Union. Yeltsin so informed Bush. Yeltsin-Bush telcon, 23 Dec 91, Bush Library. It is still hard to tell whether Ukraine's later reluctance during 1992 and 1993 was a choice to tear up that Minsk deal, or was a bargaining strategy, or both.
32. See Wallander, *Mortal Friends, Best Enemies*, 110–15, 123, and n. 37.
33. Bush-Nazarbayev memcon, 19 May 92, Bush Library (small meeting from 11 to 12).
34. An excellent analysis is Mariana Budjeryn, "Was Ukraine's Nuclear Disarmament a Blunder?," *World Affairs* 179, no. 2 (2016): 9–20.
35. A good overview of the post-Soviet nuclear and biological legacy and the remarkable effort to cope with it is Hoffman, *The Dead Hand*, part III.
36. Paul Bernstein and Jason Wood, *The Origins of Nunn-Lugar and Cooperative Threat Reduction* (Washington, DC: NDU Press, 2010), 5. The special election, which sent an electric shock through American politics, was Democrat Harris Wofford's November 1991 victory over a veteran Republican, Richard Thornburgh.
37. Ibid., 5–7; Hoffman, *The Dead Hand*, 380–85; the November 1991 Harvard report was Campbell, Carter, Miller, and Zraket, *Soviet Nuclear*

Fission; the follow-on was Graham Allison, Ashton Carter, Steven Miller, and Philip Zelikow, eds., *Cooperative Denuclearization: From Pledges to Deeds* (Cambridge, MA: Harvard CSIA, January 1993).

38. Bush to Kravchuk, 4 Dec 92, in National Security Archive Electronic Briefing Book 447, doc. no. 36.

39. See Ashton Carter and William Perry, *Preventive Defense: A New Security Strategy for America* (Washington, DC: Brookings Institution Press, 2000); William Perry, *My Journey at the Nuclear Brink* (Stanford, CA: Stanford University Press, 2015), 77–102; see also William Potter and John Shields, "Lessons from the Nunn-Lugar Cooperative Threat Reduction Program," *Asia-Pacific Review* 4, no. 1 (1997): 35–56; and on total spending, the tables in Mary Beth Nikitin and Amy Woolf, "The Evolution of Cooperative Threat Reduction: Issues for Congress," CRS Report, June 2014.

40. In the first few years, 1989–92, the main multilateral aid institutions were the IMF, the World Bank, the European Bank for Reconstruction and Development (EBRD), and the EC. Much of this work was coordinated through the G-24 process created in July 1989, which we discussed in chapter 3, and the EC's "PHARE" (Pologne/Hongrie, Assistance à la reconstruction économique) program. Poland was the major early recipient of aid and debt relief. Most food aid was distributed through bilateral channels, by the EC and the United States. Poland again received most of the early deliveries, but significant deliveries also went to the Soviet Union, Romania, and Bulgaria during 1990 and 1991. During 1992 the scope of aid of many kinds was dramatically expanding across Eastern Europe and the now-former Soviet Union.

Working with the Bush administration, the U.S. Congress appropriated American bilateral aid in two major stages, first in the Support for Eastern European Democracies (SEED) Act of 1989 and then by the FREEDOM Support Act (FSA) of 1992. The United States also provided significant assistance from Defense Department funds for denuclearization of the former Soviet Union, mainly in the Nunn-Lugar legislation.

41. Ivan T. Berend, *From the Soviet Bloc to the European Union: The Economic and Social Transformation of Central and Eastern Europe Since 1973* (Cambridge: Cambridge University Press, 2009), 201–2.

42. Philipp Ther, *Europe Since 1989: A History*, trans. Charlotte Hughes-Kreuzmüller (Princeton, NJ: Princeton University Press, 2016), 82.

43. The Marshall Plan system was fashioned in 1947–48. It operated from 1948 to 1952. A group of European governments got together to develop an elaborate European Recovery Program, working with the Americans. The quotes are from Benn Steil, *The Marshall Plan: Dawn of the Cold War* (New York: Simon & Schuster, 2018), 372; see also the similar diagnosis of what worked about the Marshall Plan in Barry Eichengreen and Marc Uzan, "Economic Effects and Implications for Europe and the USSR," *Economic Policy* 7, no. 14 (1992): 13–75.

44. A recent, detailed comparative reexamination of the data by experts working in the region is James Roaf, Ruben Atoyan, Bikas Joshi, Krzysztof Krogulski, and an IMF Staff Team, *25 Years of Transition: Post-Communist Europe and the IMF* (Washington, DC: International Monetary Fund, 2014). Their measures of inequality use GINI coefficients.

45. The Marlboro example is from Åslund, *Russia's Capitalist Revolution*, 53. The Sukhoi/aluminum example is from Pierre Lorrain, in Allen Lynch, *How Russia Is Not Ruled: Reflections on Russian Political Development* (Cambridge: Cambridge University Press, 2005), chapter 2, section IX.

46. Joel Hellman, "Winners Take All: The Politics of Partial Reform in Postcommunist Transitions," *World Politics* 50, no. 2 (1998): 203, 204–5 (emphasis in original).

47. The best-known exponent of "gradualism" was the Nobel laureate economist Joseph Stiglitz, attacking the "Washington consensus" in the finger-pointing after the 1997–98 financial crises in Asia and Russia, not long before he was dismissed in 1999 from his position as chief economist of the World Bank. See Sebastian Mallaby, *The World's Banker* (New York: Penguin, 2004), 193–95, 266–68. For a careful exposition and analysis of this alternative gradualist viewpoint, including the China analogy, from experts who worked in Eastern Europe and Russia, see Marek Dabrowski, Stanislaw Gomulka, and Jacek Rostowski, *Whence Reform? A Critique of the Stiglitz Perspective* (London: LSE Centre for Economic Performance, 2000).

48. On the slow rise of the catchall use of "neoliberalism" as "the linguistic omnivore of our times, a neologism that threatens to swallow up all the other words around it," see Daniel Rodgers,

"The Uses and Abuses of 'Neoliberalism',", *Dissent*, Winter 2018, at www.dissentmagazine.org/article/uses-and-abuses-neoliberalism-debate.

49. Reddaway and Glinski, *The Tragedy of Russia's Reforms*, 663 n. 44. Their book is a valuably detailed account of the events inside Russia during the turbulent 1990s. It is not as reliable in its account of U.S. or international policy.

50. John Williamson, "From Reform Agenda to Damaged Brand Name," *Finance and Development*, September 2003, pp. 11–13. The term "silent revolution" was one used in the early 1990s by IMF managing director Michel Camdessus to refer generally to economic liberalization, including the liberalization of international capital flows.

51. James Boughton, *Tearing Down Walls: The International Monetary Fund 1990–1999* (Washington, DC: IMF, 2012), liii.

52. Lipton, foreword in Roaf et al., *25 Years of Transition*, ix. The transformation process for the IMF and World Bank had already begun during the 1980s, because of the economic transitions we described in chapter 1. They were rapidly processing key lessons. For a snapshot in October 1990, see Vittorio Corbo, Fabrizio Coricelli, and Jan Bossak, eds., *Reforming Central and Eastern European Economies: Initial Results and Challenges* (Washington, DC: World Bank, 1991) (William Easterly offered an especially prescient paper on the dangers of partial reform).

53. Stanley Fischer, Ratna Sahay, and Carlos Vegh, "Stabilization and Growth in Transition Economies: The Early Experience," *Journal of Economic Perspectives* 10, no. 2 (1996): 45, 46.

54. Boughton, *Tearing Down Walls*, 14. Leading this charge was IMF managing director Camdessus and his senior deputy, Stanley Fischer.

55. Anders Åslund, Peter Boone, and Simon Johnson, "How to Stabilize: Lessons from Post-communist Countries," *Brookings Papers on Economic Activity*, no. 1 (1996): 217–313, quotes are from 227.

56. A sympathetic but balanced portrait of Yeltsin in the 1992 transition, including the rise and fall of Gaidar and Yeltsin's juggling of the political factions, is Timothy Colton, *Yeltsin: A Life* (New York: Basic Books, 2008), 211–46. A vivid depiction of how one of Gaidar's advisers saw the Russian economic situation at the time is Jeffrey Sachs, "Russia's Economic Prospects," *Bulletin of the American Academy of Arts and Sciences* 48, no. 3 (1994): 45–63.

57. Yegor Gaidar, *Days of Defeat and Victory*, trans. Jane Miller (Seattle: University of Washington Press, 1999 [orig. 1996]), 51; Åslund, *Russia's Capitalist Revolution*, 118; for more on the underlying political weakness of Gaidar and the factions he represented, see Michael McFaul, *Russia's Unfinished Revolution: Political Change from Gorbachev to Putin* (Ithaca, NY: Cornell University Press, 2001), 162–83.

58. Both of us left the White House in March 1991—Zelikow to return to the State Department and then, later that year, leaving government for a professorship at Harvard; Rice to return to her professorship at Stanford from which she had been on leave. Rice's successor as Bush and Scowcroft's chief adviser on Soviet affairs was Ed Hewett, an expert on the Soviet economy. Hewett fell ill in 1992 and passed away, much too soon, in January 1993. Blackwill had left in July 1990, eventually replaced by David Gompert.

59. Bush-Kohl memcon, small group session, 22 Mar 92, Bush Library.

60. To see both sides of this work, compare the section III on Soviet humanitarian aid in Baker's markup of "Proposed Agenda for Meeting with the President," 25 Oct 91, Box 115, Folder 8, Baker Papers, with the almost desperate exchanges about this with Gorbachev and Chernyaev shortly afterward in Madrid, with Baker urging the Soviets to grab this money while they could (he had struggled to get it) and Chernyaev depressed by his government's lassitude in grabbing it. Chernyaev diary 1991, 2 and 3 Nov, pp. 145–46, 156.

61. See "Soviets," 4 Dec 91, and "Soviet Points for Meeting with the President," 10 Dec 91, both in Box 115, Folder 8, Baker Papers.

62. Braithwaite, *Across the Moscow River*, 308.

63. Edward Brau, "External Financial Assistance: The Record and Issues," in Daniel Citrin and Ashok Lahiri, eds., *Policy Experiences and Issues in the Baltics, Russia, and Other Countries of the Former Soviet Union* (Washington, DC: IMF, 1995), 110 and Table 7.5.

64. See Baker, *The Politics of Diplomacy*, 654–58. The bill was the FREEDOM Support Act. For more on the role of Nunn and Lugar in this effort, and their work with Baker, which joined with their efforts to provide aid for denuclearization, see Bernstein and Wood, *Origins of Nunn-Lugar*, 9–10.

65. Gaidar, *Days of Defeat and Victory*, 153 (writing about Russia's macroeconomic stabilization program, not the foreign fund to support it, though the two were supposed to be linked). Although

the material in Braithwaite, *Across the Moscow River* (pp. 308–15), and Baker's memoir is suggestive, there is not yet a satisfactory account of just what happened in the work on the planned IMF stabilization fund for Russia during 1992.

66. E.g., on the 1993–94 developments, Angela Stent, *Russia and Germany Reborn: Unification, the Soviet Collapse, and the New Europe* (Princeton, NJ: Princeton University Press, 1999), 175–76.

67. On the real world of post-Soviet political and economic "informal practices," Alena Ledeneva, *How Russia Really Works: The Informal Practices That Shaped Post-Soviet Politics and Business* (Ithaca, NY: Cornell University Press, 2006), is a good place to start. Comparative economic studies since the late 2000s generally do not regard Russia and Ukraine as cases where radical reform was effectively adopted. A political scientist, also focusing on the failures of democratic political reform, concluded that "gradualism, rather than shock therapy, best characterizes economic policy in post-Soviet Russia." M. Steven Fish, *Democracy Derailed in Russia: The Failure of Open Politics* (Cambridge: Cambridge University Press, 2005), 159–60.

The IMF does not generally involve itself much in issues of privatization. Such problems of microeconomic technical assistance are more in the province of the World Bank, or organizations like the EBRD, or national governments and the contractors or consultants they hire. The IMF does attend closely to macroeconomic stabilization and central bank management. Their people believe the technical assistance on these topics did prove valuable to Russians in 1999 and after, once the government restored fiscal and financial discipline.

68. Miller, *The Struggle to Save the Soviet Economy*, 160–64. Miller also perceptively observes that in the Soviet and post-Soviet case the powerful interest groups, including the military-security complex, blocked the tough reforms. In China, partly because of its underdevelopment and Deng's firmer control, such obstacles were either not as difficult or they were overcome. Ibid., 177–83.

69. See Boughton, *Tearing Down Walls*, 297–334; and the drier account from a participant, John Odling-Smee, "The IMF and Russia in the 1990s," *IMF Staff Papers* 53, no. 1 (2006): 151, 159–63, 165–72.

70. Ledeneva, *How Russia Really Works*, 1 ("rarely operates").

71. The most balanced, archivally based account of the common ruble zone controversy is Boughton, *Tearing Down Walls*, 353–61; for an example of a more critical view, see Brigitte Granville, "The IMF and the Ruble Zone: Response to Odling-Smee and Pastor," *Comparative Economic Studies* 54, no. 4 (2002): 59–80; for an acknowledgment of the criticism's validity from one of the protagonists, see Odling-Smee, "The IMF and Russia in the 1990s," 165 n. 25. "Why hold down the budget deficit": Vitold Fokin quoted in Gaidar, *Days of Defeat and Victory*, 154.

72. Boughton, *Tearing Down Walls*, 312–13, 324–26. After another crash of the ruble in 1994, the Russian government had climbed back in 1995–96 and set the strong ruble, but then fell off the wagon in 1996–98, foreseeably setting up conditions for a major crisis. In November 1996, Gaidar predicted to Fischer that if the IMF did not enforce tough conditionality, "everything will blow up in one-and-a-half years" (p. 319). The catalyst for the 1998 crash came out of Asia. Still, it is notable that Gaidar's prediction was off by only about a month.

73. Gaidar, *Days of Defeat and Victory*, 154 ("soft"); Boughton, *Tearing Down Walls*, 372 ("We made all possible mistakes").

74. See Boughton, *Tearing Down Walls*, 373–79; and Anders Åslund, *How Ukraine Became a Market Economy and Democracy* (Washington, DC: Peterson Institute of International Economics, 2009).

75. For an example of the emerging critique coming out of work in the developing world, see Robert Klitgaard, *Tropical Gangsters: One Man's Experience with Development and Decadence in Deepest Africa* (New York: Basic Books, 1991), an appraisal of microeconomic technical and infrastructure assistance later crystallized in the influential report by the World Bank, *Assessing Aid* (New York: Oxford University Press, 1998); see also Steven Radelet, *Challenging Foreign Aid* (Washington, DC: Center for Global Development, 2003), 1–18. Arguments emphasizing the centrality of local policy choices and the frequently counterproductive effects of outside project aid in fueling local corruption and predation, associated with then-controversial works by experts like William Easterly in the early 2000s, now enjoy wide acceptance. For the most recent synthesis of his argument, see Easterly, *The Tyranny of Experts: Economists, Dictators, and the Forgotten Rights of the Poor* (New York: Basic

Books, 2014); and, for an example of the emerging scholarly consensus, Daron Acemoglu and James Robinson, *Why Nations Fail: The Origins of Power, Prosperity, and Poverty* (New York: Crown, 2012).

76. For an understandably angry but useful set of illustrations, mainly focusing on problems in technical assistance in Poland early on and in Russia later, with a particular focus on the scandal involving a group at Harvard, see Janine Wedel, *Collision and Collusion: The Strange Case of Western Aid to Eastern Europe*, updated ed. (New York: St. Martin's Griffin, 2001).

77. Randall Schweller, book review in *Political Science Quarterly* 115, no. 2 (2000): 315.

78. A good contemporary account of the historical evolution in East European views, free from knowing what would happen later, is Andrew Cottey, *East-Central Europe After the Cold War: Poland, the Czech Republic, Slovakia, and Hungary in Search of Security* (New York: St. Martin's, 1995).

79. Zoellick-Kastrup telcon (debriefing on Baker's meeting), 23 May 90, in *Einheit Dokumente*, doc. 101, p. 506 (Baker on Gorbachev not joking); Baker-Genscher memcon, Washington, 25 May 90, in ibid., doc. 102, p. 509 (Genscher's reply).

80. Based on discussions with former Clinton administration officials and records of the Clinton-Yeltsin exchanges. On those, see Clinton-Yeltsin telcon, 22 Dec 93, Clinton Library, Mandatory Review case 2015-0782-M (on Yeltsin and Wörner); Clinton-Yeltsin memcon from dinner in Moscow, 14 Jan 94 (on the concert or "cartel"-like approach and "Russia is not yet ready"), quoted in Ronald Asmus, *Opening NATO's Door: How the Alliance Remade Itself for a New Era* (New York: Columbia University Press, 2002), 67 (this memcon does not yet appear to have been declassified); Clinton-Yeltsin memcon for second one-on-one meeting, 28 Sep 94 (which also does not yet seem to have been declassified), in ibid., 90; Clinton-Yeltsin telcon, 27 Apr 95, Clinton Library (indicating Yeltsin's assent to the two-track approach); Clinton-Yeltsin memcon, summary of one-on-one meeting, Moscow, 10 May 95, Clinton Library (concentrating on delaying enlargement until the end of the 1990s, or at least for a year and a half to two years, until after the 1996 election). In the May 1995 meeting, Yeltsin's alternative to NATO enlargement was no longer Russian membership, which was no longer being mentioned at all, it was that "Russia will give every state that wants to join NATO a guarantee that we won't infringe on its security."

81. Wałęsa quoted in epigraph for Joanna Gorska, *Dealing with a Juggernaut: Analyzing Poland's Policy Toward Russia, 1989–2009* (Lanham, MD: Lexington, 2010).

82. Krzysztof Skubiszewski writing in 1999, quoted in Asmus, *Opening NATO's Door*, 6–7. NATO secretary-general Wörner made it clear that, at first, the door was not yet open to new members. Mastny, "Eastern Europe and the Early Prospects," 212–13.

83. Mastny, "Eastern Europe and the Early Prospects," 213.

84. Clinton remarks, Brussels, 9 Jan 94, quoted in Asmus, *Opening NATO's Door*, 65. Asmus offers the leading history of the enlargement process during the 1990s. It does a good job of presenting non-American perspectives as well. His well-documented conclusion about the turning point lines up with the analysis from a European perspective in Jonathan Eyal, "NATO's Enlargement: Anatomy of a Decision," *International Affairs* 73, no. 4 (1997): 695–719.

85. Theo Sommer, "The Problems of Enlargement," in Anton Bebler, ed., *The Challenge of NATO Enlargement* (Westport, CT: Praeger, 1999), 37.

86. Asmus's account of Deputy Secretary of State Strobe Talbott's exploratory trip to Paris and Berlin at the beginning of 1997 nicely encapsulates the core positions in Europe, even after nearly four years of debate. *Opening NATO's Door*, 183–88.

87. The main changes reflect the positive evolution of the NATO versus EU argument (including the rise of the "Euro-Atlantic" adjective instead of just "Atlantic") and the discussion of enlargement. For an upbeat comparative analysis, see Paul Cornish, "A Strategic Concept for the Twenty-First Century," *Defense Analysis* 15, no. 3 (1999): 241–60.

In 1997–98, State Department officials were urging that NATO be reformed to work with the Europeans to tackle problems outside of Europe, with an OSCE setting norms to promote democracy. E.g., Asmus, *Opening NATO's Door*, 278–79. The memos essentially duplicated the memos their predecessors had written in 1990–91, seeming to forget that all these things (out-of-area efforts, Europe-wide democracy promotion with organizations like the OSCE) had not only been advocated before, but had been adopted and began happening on a rather large scale in

1990–92. It is not a tale of partisan differences, more of the institutional amnesia endemic in the American government.

During the mid-1990s there was a noisy public debate about the initial NATO enlargement. This debate served various political purposes on both sides of the Atlantic, and in Russia. The two of us were not involved much in it. Rice, who was provost of Stanford at the time, did not engage in it but generally supported NATO enlargement. Although Zelikow believed the 1990 diplomacy had left the issue of future enlargement open, he thought both sides of the enlargement debate were exaggerating its immediacy and importance, neglecting more burning issues in the Balkans and elsewhere. For instance, his essay "The Masque of Institutions," *Survival* 38, no. 1 (Spring 1996): 6–18.

88. Joseph Stiglitz, from a 2007 column, and "actually determined," both from Berend, *From the Soviet Bloc to the European Union*, 100–101.

89. For a mid-1990s glimpse at the converging criteria of both institutions, see Anton Bebler, "A Research Note on Eligibility for NATO Membership," in Bebler, ed., *The Challenge of NATO Enlargement*, 49–57.

90. Berend, *From the Soviet Bloc to the European Union*, 101.

91. Asmus, *Opening NATO's Door*, 247–48. Asmus was a key State official on the Baltic enlargement issues from the beginning. He details the strength and influence of Albright's and Talbott's views during the formative debates of 1997.

On NATO enlargement to the Baltic countries, at the time (July 1997), Asmus summarized the U.S. political divisions. "Right-wing Republicans want to bring them in now, Bush Republicans and Democratic defense hawks say never; Democratic internationalists such as you [Talbott] and me say yes in principle but not now; and liberal Democratic arms controllers say it is not worth risking the arms control agenda with Moscow because of the Baltic issue." Ibid., 231.

92. Those who study the Gulf War diplomatic records of 1990–91 will find plenty of evidence of the enormous effort expended, amid great strain, to keep the United States and Soviet Union together in the political coalition, including the compromises made in the conduct of the diplomacy. The best analytical summary, from a core participant, is Dennis Ross, *Statecraft: And How to Restore America's Standing in the World* (New York: Farrar, Straus & Giroux, 2008), 77–96.

93. "I have never met": Clinton-Yeltsin telcon, 19 Apr 99, p. 2, Clinton Library; "there will not be": Clinton-Yeltsin telcon, 24 Mar 99, p. 3, Clinton Library; see generally Talbott, *The Russia Hand*, 298–349.

94. For a balanced appraisal, see Michael Green, *By More Than Providence: Grand Strategy and American Power in the Asia Pacific Since 1783* (New York: Columbia University Press, 2017), 425–52.

95. Thomas Zeiler, *Free Trade Free World: The Advent of GATT* (Chapel Hill: University of North Carolina Press, 1999), 196.

96. In North America, they built on the U.S.-Canada deal that Baker had forged in 1988 and worked with new leaders in Mexico to create a 1990 initiative for a North American Free Trade Agreement (NAFTA). Reagan and Baker had originally hoped for a hemispheric-wide initiative. Mexico was a start, but the initiative had to come from the Mexican side. It came in February 1990 from Mexican president Carlos Salinas de Gortari. The United States, Mexico, and Canada began the negotiations in 1991 and wrapped them up in August 1992.

NAFTA was a touchstone for debate in America, a major point for the populist third candidate in the 1992 presidential race, Ross Perot. The Clinton administration had a major decision to make about NAFTA. It decided to proceed with the agreement, after negotiating some side agreements with Mexico. Clinton faced off mainly against his own party in Congress in "the most epic trade-policy battle in Congress since the end of World War II." He won largely with Republican votes, but Bush might not have been able to carry the necessary margin of Democrats. Clinton did.

There is still great debate about the effects of NAFTA. Beyond the economic statistics, what it did most fundamentally is that "it connected Mexico to North America.... NAFTA's orientation toward North America, and the opening of Mexican society, were definitely part of Mexico's transition to democracy." Robert Zoellick, "An Architecture of U.S. Strategy After the Cold War," in Melvyn Leffler and Jeffrey Legro, eds., *In Uncertain Times: American Foreign Policy After the Berlin Wall and 9/11* (Ithaca, NY: Cornell University Press, 2011), 34.

97. Irwin, *Clashing over Commerce*, chapter 13.

98. Zoellick, "An Architecture of U.S. Strategy," 38–40.

99. See David Autor, David Dorn, and Gordon Hanson, "The China Syndrome: Local Labor Market Effects of Import Competition in the United States," *American Economic Review* 103, no. 6 (2013): 2121–68; Katherine Eriksson, Katheryn Russ, Jay Shambaugh, and Minfei Xu, "Trade Shocks and the Shifting Landscape of U.S. Manufacturing," NBER Working Paper 25646, 8 March 2019.

100. On Saddam's motives, using captured Iraqi records, see Hal Brands and David Palkki, "'Conspiring Bastards': Saddam Hussein's Strategic View of the United States," *Diplomatic History* 36, no. 3 (2012): 625–59, 627 ("strangle Iraq"); Emily Meierding, "Dismantling the Oil Wars Myth," *Security Studies* 25, no. 2 (2016): 258–88; for similar conclusions without using the same Iraqi records, see F. Gregory Gause III, "Iraq's Decisions to Go to War, 1980 and 1990," *Middle East Journal* 56, no. 1 (2002): 47–70; and the commentary in Kevin Woods, David Palkki, and Mark Stout, eds., *The Saddam Tapes: The Inner Workings of a Tyrant's Regime, 1978–2001* (Cambridge: Cambridge University Press, 2011). This outlook can be compared to the actual record of the prewar American policy toward Iraq described in Zachary Karabell and Philip Zelikow, "Iraq, 1988–1990: Unexpectedly Heading Toward War," in Ernest May and Zelikow, eds., *Dealing with Dictators: Dilemmas of U.S. Diplomacy and Intelligence Analysis, 1945–1990* (Cambridge, MA: MIT Press, 2006), 167–202.

101. Baker, *The Politics of Diplomacy*, 276.

102. See, for example, Warren Kimball, *The Juggler: Franklin Roosevelt as Wartime Statesman* (Princeton, NJ: Princeton University Press, 1991), 95–99, 195–97.

103. On the coalition work in this crisis, see the instructive summary in Ross, *Statecraft*, 77–99; see also Spohr, *Post Wall, Post Square*, chapter 6; Engel, *When the World Seemed New*, chapters 18 and 19.

104. Quoted in Michael Watkins and Susan Rosegrant, *Breakthrough International Negotiation: How Great Negotiators Transformed the World's Toughest Post–Cold War Conflicts* (San Francisco: Jossey-Bass, 2001), 195.

105. "To make war": from war cabinet meeting, 5 Aug 90, in Favier and Martin-Roland, *Les défis*, 443–44; Jacques Attali, *Verbatim*, vol. 3 (Paris: Fayard, 1995), 551–53, 556–61 (cabinet meeting, 9 Aug 90, "false brothers"); Short, *A Taste for Intrigue*, 499 ("happy few"). Mitter-

rand would have entirely appreciated the irony of quoting Shakespeare's phrase, spoken by an English king on the eve of a battle against the French.

In April 1991, Mitterrand expressed his regret to Bush that the war had not continued longer, so that Saddam Hussein could have been toppled from power. Ibid., 500 (date in Short's notes, provided separately to the authors). We mention this to indicate the strength of Mitterrand's views, although we believe this option was not viable. For a summary of the reasons why, see Baker on "the marching-to-Baghdad canard," in *The Politics of Diplomacy*, 436–38.

106. Scowcroft in Bush and Scowcroft, *A World Transformed*, 400.

107. Charles Krauthammer, "The Unipolar Moment," *Foreign Affairs* 70, no. 1 (1990/91): 23–33, adapted from a lecture he delivered in September 1990.

108. Bush address to Congress on the Persian Gulf crisis and the federal budget deficit, 11 Sep 90, quoted in the perceptive essay by Jeffrey Engel, "A Better World...but Don't Get Carried Away: The Foreign Policy of George H. W. Bush Twenty Years On," *Diplomatic History* 34, no. 1 (2010): 25, 33.

109. Ibid., 23.

110. Chernyaev diary 1991, 25 Feb, p. 32.

Chapter 7: New Challenges Evolve

1. Bush-Gorbachev memcon, 25 Dec 91, Bush Library.

2. Jan-Werner Müller, *What Is Populism?* (Philadelphia: University of Pennsylvania Press, 2016).

3. Ironically, the 5 percent threshold had been set as Basic Law in Germany after World War II in order to prevent far-right political parties from rising to power the same way the National Socialist German Workers' Party had gained a foothold in the 1924 and 1928 elections for the Reichstag.

4. "While [AfD] scored on average 11% in west Germany, it got 21.5% in east Germany, almost twice as much." Cas Mudde, "What the Stunning Success of AfD Means for Germany and Europe," *Guardian*, September 24, 2017.

5. Stalin wielded national communist parties as a "fifth column." The aim was to assert communist influence abroad through support for indigenous communist movements. See Kevin McDermott and Jeremy Agnew, *The Comintern: A History of International Communism from Lenin to Stalin* (London: Palgrave, 1997); or older studies such as

William Henry Chamberlin, "Russians Against Stalin." *Russian Review* 11, no. 1 (1952): 16–23.

6. Quoted in Condoleezza Rice, *No Higher Honor: A Memoir of My Years in Washington* (New York: Crown, 2011), 715–16.

7. Amid a large literature, the best transatlantic overview is now Adam Tooze, *Crashed: How a Decade of Financial Crises Changed the World* (New York: Viking, 2018); see John Taylor, "Government as a Cause of the 2008 Financial Crisis: A Reassessment After 10 Years," October 19, 2018, at www.hoover.org/sites/default/files/research/docs/govt_as_cause_of_crisis-a_reassement_10 .pdf; and the panel discussion of Taylor, George Shultz, Niall Ferguson, Caroline Hoxby, Darrell Duffie, and John Cochrane, Hoover Institution, December 7, 2018, at www.hoover.org/sites/default/files/hauck_-_revisiting_the_financial _crisis.pdf.

8. Dinara Bayazitova and Anil Shivdasani, "Assessing TARP," *Review of Financial Studies* 25, no. 2 (2011): 377–407; Daniel Drezner, *The System Worked: How the World Stopped Another Great Depression* (New York: Oxford University Press, 2014); Eric Helleiner, *The Status Quo Crisis: Global Financial Governance After the 2008 Meltdown* (New York: Oxford University Press, 2014); and David Wessel, *In Fed We Trust: Ben Bernanke's War on the Great Panic* (New York: Crown, 2010).

9. The meeting is described further in Rice, *No Higher Honor*, 716.

10. A good summary of the G-20's development during the global financial crisis is Adam Tooze, *Crashed*, 265–75. Tooze does not discuss the Sarkozy-Bush meeting at Camp David.

11. Quoted in Tony Paterson, "Greece Debt Crisis: German-Greek Relations Slump Further After Der Spiegel Magazine Cover Prompts Controversy," *Independent* (UK), July 14, 2015.

12. Quoted in Anthony Faiola and Stephanie Kirchner, "Greece Bailout Revives Image of the 'Cruel German,'" *Washington Post*, July 16, 2015.

13. Quote from June 29 press conference by Angela Merkel in Anton Troianovski, "Germany's Angela Merkel Takes Firm Stance on Greek Bailout," *Wall Street Journal*, June 29, 2015.

14. For the "no" camp see Dani Rodrik, "Populism and the Economics of Globalization," *Journal of International Business Policy* 1 (2018): 12–33; Janan Ganesh, "Populism Was Not Sparked by the Financial Crisis," *Financial Times*, August 29, 2018; Greg Ip, "No, the Financial Crisis Didn't Spawn Populism," *Wall Street Journal*, September 18, 2018.

For the "yes" camp, see Manuel Funke, Moritz Schularick, and Christoph Trebesch, "The Financial Crisis Is Still Empowering Far-Right Populists," *Foreign Affairs*, Online Snapshot, September 13, 2018; Fareed Zakaria, "Populism on the March," *Foreign Affairs* 95, no. 6 (2016); Larry Elliott, "Populism Is the Result of Global Economic Failure," *Financial Times*, March 26, 2017; and Philip Stephens, "Populism Is the True Legacy of the Global Financial Crisis," *Financial Times*, August 29, 2018.

15. Shultz at the Hoover panel discussion, December 7, 2018, p. 3.

16. The history of European migration is laid out further in Rita Chin, *The Crisis of Multiculturalism in Europe: A History* (Princeton, NJ: Princeton University Press, 2017).

17. "Thirty years ago, many Europeans saw multiculturalism—the embrace of an inclusive, diverse society—as an answer to Europe's social problems....As a political tool, multiculturalism has functioned as not merely a response to diversity but also a means of constraining it." Kenan Malik, "The Failure of European Multiculturalism," *Foreign Affairs* 94, no. 2 (2015).

18. While the United Kingdom, for instance, can trace the election of the first British-Indian member of Parliament to 1892, the diversity of Parliament did not begin to grow in earnest until the 1987 and 1992 parliamentary elections. In 1987, four minority members won their elections, including three Afro-Caribbean British and one British Indian. In 1992, three more minority members won, including two British Indians and one British Sri Lankan. See Muhammad Anwar, "The Participation of Ethnic Minorities in British Politics," *Journal of Ethnic and Migration Studies* 27, no. 3 (2001): 533–49.

19. Ruben Atoyan, Lone Christiansen, Allan Dizioli, Christian Ebeke, Nadeem Ilahi, Anna Ilyina, Gil Mehrez, Haonan Qu, Faezeh Raei, Alaina Rhee, and Daria Zakharova, "Emigration and Its Economic Impact on Eastern Europe," International Monetary Fund, July 2016. Other work by Ivan Krastev in *After Europe* (Philadelphia: University of Pennsylvania Press, 2017), 47, 50–51, finds that Polish émigrés between 2005 and 2014 were twice as likely to have a college education as the general population, and during this period, approximately one-third of young college graduates in Latvia had emigrated to the West.

20. Statistic in Valentina Romei, "Eastern Europe Has the Largest Population Loss in Modern History," *Financial Times,* May 27, 2016.

21. Statistic from "EU Thumbs-Up for 'Polish Plumber,'" BBC, November 18, 2008.

22. By 2015, approximately 2.9 million displaced migrants were in Jordan, 2.8 million were in Yemen, and 2.8 million were in Turkey. See "Middle East Migrant Population More Than Doubles Since 2005," Pew Research Center (2016).

23. Patrick Kingsley, "Migration to Europe Is Down Sharply. So Is It Still a Crisis?," *New York Times,* June 27, 2018; "Briefing: Illegal Immigration in the EU: Facts and Figures," *European Parliament* (April 2015): 1–4.

24. Hungary suspended the rule on June 23, 2015, announcing that it would not take back refugees once they had traveled through the country. See "Defying EU, Hungary Suspends Rules on Asylum-Seekers," Reuters, June 23, 2015.

25. For more on the linguistic history of this phrase and how it came to haunt Angela Merkel during the refugee crisis, see Joyce Marie Mushaben, "Wir Schaffen Das! Angela Merkel and the European Refugee Crisis," *German Politics* 26, no. 4 (2017): 516–33.

26. Merkel quoted in "Merkel the Bold," *Economist,* September 5, 2015; Pope Francis quote in Anthony Faiola and Michael Birnbaum, "Pope Calls on Europe's Catholics to Take in Refugees," *Washington Post,* September 6, 2015.

27. Obama quote from his speech to the United Nations on September 20, 2016; "gaps": Paul Ryan quoted in Jennifer Steinhauer, "Senate Blocks Bill on Tougher Refugee Screening," *New York Times,* January 20, 2016; 33,000 figure in Philip Connor and Jens Manuel Krogstad, "For the First Time, U.S. Resettles Fewer Refugees Than the Rest of the World," Pew Research Center (2017).

28. For further reading on Viktor Orbán, we suggest Paul Lendvai, *Orbán: Europe's New Strongman* (Oxford: Oxford University Press, 2017). Scholars situate events in Hungary since 1989 as part of a larger populist trend in Central and Eastern Europe. See Umut Korkut, *Liberalization Challenges in Hungary: Elitism, Progressivism, and Populism* (Houndmills, UK: Palgrave Macmillan, 2012); Jacques Rupnik, "Hungary's Illiberal Turn: How Things Went Wrong," *Journal of Democracy* 23, no. 3 (2012): 132–37; and Janos Kornai, "Hungary's U-Turn: Retreating

from Democracy," *Journal of Democracy* 26, no. 3 (2015): 34–48.

29. Stephan Faris, "Power Hungary: How Viktor Orban Became Europe's New Strongman," Bloomberg, January 22, 2015. These results match similar polls cited in "End of Communism Cheered, but Now with More Reservations," Pew Research Center (November 2, 2009), and "Hungary Dissatisfied with Democracy, but Not Its Ideals," Pew Research Center (April 7, 2010).

30. "European Elections Database," Norsk Senter for Forskningsdata, n.d.

31. Scholars who examine Putin and Orbán are divided on whether this is a fair comparison. For arguments in the "no" camp, see Péter Krekó and Zsolt Enyedi, "Explaining Eastern Europe: Orbán's Laboratory of Illiberalism," *Journal of Democracy* 28, no. 3 (2018): 39–51; Mitchell Orenstein, Péter Krekó, and Attila Juhaz, "The Hungarian Putin?," *Foreign Affairs,* Online Snapshot, February 8, 2015. For arguments in the "yes" camp, see András Simonyi, "Putin, Erdogan and Orbán: Band of Brothers?," *New Perspectives Quarterly* 31, no. 4 (2014): 33–35.

32. Our interpretation of what transpired in Hungary between 1989 and 2016 complements a growing set of work in the comparative institutions literature. See James Dawson and Sean Haley, "East Central Europe: The Fading Mirage of the 'Liberal Consensus,'" *Journal of Democracy* 27, no. 1 (2016): 20–34; Aron Buzogány, "Illiberal Democracy in Hungary: Authoritarian Diffusion or Domestic Causation?," *Democratization* 24, no. 7 (2017): 1307–25; Matthijs Bogaards "De-democratization in Hungary: Diffusely Defective Democracy," *Democratization* 25, no. 8 (2018): 1481–99.

33. Orbán speech, 26 Jul 14, in Hungarian Government online archives, 2010–14.

34. Quoted in "Migrant Crisis 'a German Problem'—Hungary's Orban," BBC, September 3, 2015.

35. Statistics from "Country Report Poland 2018" in "Assessment of Progress on Structural Reforms, Prevention and Correction of Macroeconomic Imbalances, and Results of In-depth Reviews Under Regulation (EU) No 1176/2011," Commission Staff Working Document, European Commission, March 7, 2018, pp. 1–46.

36. See Aleksandra Wisniewska, "Unemployment in Poland to Hit 25-Year Low," *Financial Times,* August 19, 2016.

37. A longer version of this story can be found in Condoleezza Rice, *Democracy: Stories from the*

Long Road to Freedom (New York: Twelve, 2017), 159–64.

38. Megan Specia, "Nationalist March Dominates Poland's Independence Day," *New York Times*, November 11, 2017.

39. According to Jordan Kyle and Limor Gultchin, "Populists in Power Around the World," Tony Blair Institute for Global Change (n.d.), populist leaders came into power in eight Central and Eastern European countries between 1990 and 2018: Belarus (Alexander Lukashenko), Bulgaria (Boyko Borisov), the Czech Republic (Andrej Babiš), Hungary (Viktor Orbán), Poland (Law and Justice Party), Russia (Vladimir Putin), Serbia (Aleksandar Vučić) and Slovakia (Robert Fico).

40. From "Facts on the Living Situation," German Federal Statistics Office, October 1, 2018; and "The East-West Divide Is Diminishing, but Differences Still Remain," The Local.de, October 2, 2018.

41. See Sabine Rennefanz, "East Germans Are Still Different," *Guardian*, September 30, 2010; Kate Connolly, "German Reunification 25 Years On: How Different Are East and West Really," *Guardian*, October 2, 2015; Ben Knight, "East Germans Still Victims of 'Cultural Colonialism' by the West," *DW*, November 1, 2017.

42. Chrupalla quoted in "Why Is the Former East Germany Tilting Populist?," *Der Spiegel*, November 17, 2017.

43. "Emmanuel Macron Speech, European Parliament," French Elysée, April 7, 2018.

44. In the months before the referendum, the margin of support for "Remain" over "Leave" was in the double digits. A September 28, 2015, poll by ComRes, for example, found 55 percent for "Remain" and 37 percent for "Leave." In February 2016, polls still reported marginal support for "Remain" in the upper single digits. However, polls began to tighten as voters made up their minds, and a small shift toward the "Leave" campaign began to emerge. Survey results conducted and released by YouGov, Opinium, and TNS the day before the referendum, predicted, on average, a 51 percent vote for "Remain" and 49 percent vote for "Leave." More analysis on pre-Brexit polling can be found by Peter Barnes, "EU Referendum Poll Tracker," BBC (2016).

45. For one insider elite reaction to Brexit, see Craig Oliver's *Unleashing Demons: The Inside Story of Brexit* (London: Hodder & Stoughton, 2017). Oliver was David Cameron's communications director from 2011 to 2016.

46. "Leave" won with 51.9 percent of the vote; "Remain" secured 48.1 percent.

47. For a longer history on events leading up to this referendum, see Harold Clarke, Matthew Goodwin, and Paul Whiteley, *Brexit: Why Britain Voted to Leave the European Union* (Cambridge: Cambridge University Press, 2017).

48. For more, see Michael Lewis-Beck and Daniel S. Morey, "The French 'Petit Oui': The Maastricht Treaty and the French Voting Agenda," *Journal of Interdisciplinary History* 38, no. 1 (2007): 65–87.

49. Thomas Bräuninger, Tanja Cornelius, Thomas König, and Thomas Schuster, *The Dynamics of European Integration: A Constitutional Analysis of the Amsterdam Treaty* (Manchester: Manchester University Press, 2001).

50. "HR Key Figures—Staff Members," European Commission (2018), and "Structure of the College of Commissioners," European Commission (2018). The latter document outlines the twenty-eight members of the European Commission as the president, high representative on foreign policy and security policy, first vice president, four additional vice presidents, and twenty-one commissioners.

51. Matthew Dalton, "EU Corks Its Plan to Limit Olive Oil," *Wall Street Journal*, May 23, 2013.

52. For samples of the argument, see Andrew Moravcsik, "Reassessing Legitimacy in the European Union," *JCMS: Journal of Common Market Studies* 40, no. 4 (2002): 603–24; and Moravcsik, "Is There a 'Democratic Deficit' in World Politics? A Framework for Analysis," *Government and Opposition* 39, no. 2 (2004): 336–63; Andreas Follesdal and Simon Hix, "Why There Is a Democratic Deficit in the EU: A Response to Majone and Moravcsik," *JCMS: Journal of Common Market Studies* 44, no. 3 (2006): 533–62; and Mathias Koenig–Archibugi, "The Democratic Deficit of EU Foreign and Security Policy," *International Spectator* 37, no. 4 (2002): 61–73.

53. These results come from the annual Eurobarometer question that asked respondents to holistically decide if their country had "on balance benefited or not from being a member of the EU." The perceived benefits of EU membership peaked in 1991 at 71 percent. Similar Eurobarometer questions aimed at trust in EU institutions and whether the EU was perceived as a positive force or not saw slightly different results. The EU's positive image peaked in 2007 at 52 percent. Trust in the EU peaked in 2007 at 57 percent.

See "Major Changes in European Public Opinion Regarding European Union, Exploratory Study," Public Opinion Monitoring Series, European Parliament Research Service (November 2016), 13–14.

The Eurobarometer results reveal that the perceived benefits of EU membership declined in 1993–94, around the escalation of the Bosnian war, again in 2003–4 around the start of the Iraqi insurgency, and in 2009–10 as the severity of the Eurozone debt crisis began to reveal itself. See ibid., 13–17.

54. The failure of France and the Netherlands to approve the EU Constitution highlighted the growing Euroskeptic movements within these countries. As mentioned earlier in this chapter, fears of the "Polish plumber" became a rallying cry for populist movements to mobilize support against increased integration and the European Union. The efforts worked. For more, see Mabel Berezin, "Appropriating the 'No': The French National Front, the Vote on the Constitution, and the 'New' April 21," *PS: Political Science and Politics* 39, no. 2 (2006): 269–72; Lewis-Beck and Morey, "The French 'Petit Oui'; and Matt Qvortrup, "The Three Referendums on the European Constitution Treaty in 2005," *Political Quarterly* 77, no. 1 (2006): 89–97.

55. Specifically, ten countries—the Czech Republic, Cyprus, Estonia, Hungary, Latvia, Lithuania, Malta, Poland, Slovakia, and Slovenia—joined the EU in 2004. Two more countries—Bulgaria and Romania—joined the EU in 2007, and Croatia joined in 2013.

56. For more on the EU's efforts to construct important symbols to deepen integration, see Michael Bruter, "On What Citizens Mean by Feeling 'European': Perceptions of News, Symbols and Borderless-ness," *Journal of Ethnic and Migration Studies* 30, no. 1 (2004): 21–39; and Ian Manners, "Symbolism in European Integration," *Comparative European Politics* 9, no. 3 (2011): 243–68.

57. These results come from the annual Eurobarometer question that asked respondents whether they identify according to their nationality, their nationality and their European identity, or just their European identity. Self-identity as solely "European" peaked in 1994, shortly after the Maastricht Treaty and the formal creation of the European Union in 1993. Since then, individuals have been less likely to identify as European. See "Major Changes in European Public Opinion Regarding European Union, Exploratory Study," Public Opinion Monitoring Series, European Parliament Research Service (November 2016), 38.

58. Edward Lawler, "Affective Attachments to Nested Groups: A Choice-Process Theory," *American Sociological Review* 57, no. 3 (1992): 327–39.

59. Ronald Inglehart, "Cognitive Mobilization and European Identity," *Comparative Politics* 3, no. 1 (1970): 45–70. According to Inglehart, technological developments and innovations have increased the overall welfare of individuals, satisfying their "materialist" needs for economic and physical security. This has opened space for a new set of "post-materialist" values to emerge in developed countries. Building on Abraham Maslow's hierarchy of needs, Inglehart defines post-materialist values as those further up in the hierarchy. These values emphasize personal freedoms and a sense of belonging.

60. "Confidence in Institutions," Gallup Historical Trends Polling; see "Congress Less Popular Than Cockroaches, Traffic Jams," Public Policy Polling (January 8, 2013). The poll found at the time that Congress's favorability rating was 9 percent. This was smaller than the favorability ratings for cockroaches (43 percent favorable), Genghis Khan (37 percent favorable), and traffic jams (34 percent favorable).

61. "Income Inequality and the Great Recession," U.S. Congress Joint Economic Committee (Washington, DC: Government Printing Office, 2010), 1–11.

62. For a longer development of this, see "The American Experience," in Rice, *Democracy*, 25–67.

63. Francis Fukuyama, *Identity: The Demand for Dignity and the Politics of Resentment* (New York: Farrar, Straus & Giroux, 2018), 159.

64. Richard Rorty, "A Cultural Left," in *Achieving Our Country* (Cambridge, MA: Harvard University Press, 1999).

65. "For if you turn out to be living in an evil empire (rather than, as you had been told, a democracy fighting an evil empire), then you have no responsibility to your country; you are accountable only to humanity. If what your government and your teachers are saying is all part of the same Orwellian monologue—if the differences between the Harvard faculty and the military-industrial complex, or between Lyndon Johnson and Barry Goldwater, are negligible—then you have a responsibility to make a revolution." Ibid.

66. See Ronald Inglehart and Pippa Norris, *Cultural Backlash: Trump, Brexit, and Authoritarian*

Populism (Cambridge: Cambridge University Press, 2019).

67. Quotes from essay discussion by Isaiah Singleton (Oakland) and Annays Yacaman (Chicago) in *American Creed*, prod. Randy Bean and Dan Soles, Citizen Film, 2018.

68. Clark Murdock, Kelley Sayler, and Ryan Crotty, "The Defense Budget's Double Whammy: Drawing Down While Hollowing Out from Within," Center for Strategic and International Studies (October 18, 2012), 1.

69. Bill Adair, "Peace Dividend Began with a Bush," Poynter Institute Politifact Organization (January 24, 2008).

70. Appendix, "UN Security Council–Authorized Military Operations, 1950–2007," in Adam Roberts and Dominik Zaum, *Selective Security: War and the United Nations Security Council Since 1945*, Adelphi Paper no. 395 (London: IISS, 2008).

71. The meeting is described more fully in Rice, *No Higher Honor*, 62–63.

72. Other research focusing on the unique post-9/11 relationship between the two powers is Caroline Kennedy-Pipe and Stephen Welch, "Russia and the United States After 9/11," *Terrorism and Political Violence* 17, no. 1–2 (2005): 79–291; and Kari Roberts, "Empire Envy: Russia-US Relations Post 9/11," *Journal of Military and Strategic Studies* 6, no. 4 (2004): 1–23.

73. For more on these connections, including the activities of Chechen Al Qaeda affiliates the International Islamic Peacekeeping Brigade and the Caucasus Emirate, see Gordon Hahn, *The Caucasus Emirate Mujahedin: Global Jihadism in Russia's North Caucasus and Beyond* (Jefferson, NC: McFarland, 2014); and Emil Souleimanov, "The Caucasus Emirate: Genealogy of an Islamist Insurgency," *Middle East Policy* 18, no. 4 (2011): 155–68.

74. See 9/11 Commission, *Report* (New York: Norton, 2004), 165–66.

75. The Department of Homeland Security is responsible for overseeing counterterrorism, border security, immigration and customs enforcement, and disaster response programs. The homeland security adviser comments and helps coordinate local state responses on these issues. The military command for the continental United States includes the creation of a new combatant command center, "Northern Command." It provides military support and is responsible for defending the United States against an external invasion. The director of national intelligence (DNI) grew out of the 9/11 Commission report as a way to coordinate activities within the intelligence community and mitigate the risk of future intelligence failures. The National Counterterrorism Center also formed on the recommendations of the report as a government organization designed to improve the government's ability to detect and disrupt future terrorist attacks.

76. Bush, "Address to a Joint Session of Congress and the American People," White House Archives, 20 Sep 01.

77. Rice, *No Higher Honor*, 79.

78. The Iraq war is discussed extensively in Rice, *No Higher Honor*, and again in her later book, *Democracy*, 273–330. Zelikow's first duty as counselor of the State Department, a deputy to Rice, in February 2005, was to join a group heading to Iraq to critique what was going on, the first of many such trips during the next few years.

79. Ibid., 215.

80. The foundational resolutions against Iran were UNSC 1696 (July 2006) and 1737 (December 2006). The foundational resolutions against North Korea were UNSC 1695 (July 2006) and 1718 (October 2006).

81. C. J. Chivers and Mark Landler, "Putin to Suspend Pact with NATO," *New York Times*, April 27, 2007.

82. Quoted in Rice, *No Higher Honor*, 578.

83. Putin's reference to Ukraine as a "made-up country" and the Bucharest summit are described in Condoleezza Rice, *Democracy*, 115–17; and Rice, *No Higher Honor*, 673–74.

84. The words "you are with us or against us" were first mentioned in the Bush statement to a Joint Session of Congress, 20 Sep 01.

85. See UN Development Program and Arab Fund for Economic and Social Development, *Arab Human Development Report 2002: Creating Opportunities for Future Generations* (New York: UNDP, 2002).

86. Scholars argue that Russia's reaction to the color revolutions varied according to the states involved, but the Russians primarily saw the events as undermining *blizhneye zarubezhiye*, or Russia's ability to influence foreign policy "near abroad." For a longer take on this argument, see Lincoln Mitchell, *The Color Revolutions* (Philadelphia: University of Pennsylvania Press, 2012).

87. Rice, *No Higher Honor*, 360.

88. For more, see Rice, *Democracy*, 97–98; and Michael McFaul, *From Cold War to Hot Peace*

(Boston: Houghton Mifflin Harcourt, 2018), 23–50.

89. Quoted in Jeffrey Goldberg, "The Obama Doctrine," *Atlantic*, April 2016.

90. Quoted in Jack McCallum, "Lord of the Rings," *Sports Illustrated*, February 18, 1991.

91. See Miklós Hadas, "The Olympics and the Cold War: An Eastern European Perspective," in Alan Bairner and Gyozo Molnar, eds., *The Politics of the Olympics: A Survey* (London: Routledge, 2010).

Epilogue: To Build a Better World

1. John Barnes, "Lord Cockfield," *Independent* (UK), January 20, 2007.

2. Zelikow was a managing director of a group, Rework America, that developed a comprehensive set of specific ideas. Rework America, *America's Moment: Creating Opportunity in the Connected Age* (New York: W. W. Norton, 2015). Sponsored in part by the Markle Foundation, Rework America's "Skillful" initiative is now piloting projects in dozens of states. Rice has continued to work on education policy and to foster civic conversations about American aspirations, an "American Creed." E.g., Condoleezza Rice & Joel Klein, "Education keeps America safe," CNN (2012); and, working with the American Library Association, Jason Reynolds, "Can Dialogue Help Americans Overcome the Red and Blue Divide? Some Say Yes," *WYSO Excursions* [Dayton, OH] (2019).

3. Eighty percent of Russia's exports are in oil, gas, and minerals; 65 percent of its budget is dependent on this sector. This information is drawn from Fiona Hill, "Putin, Yukos, and Russia," Brookings Institution, December 1, 2004.

4. Kori Schake, *Safe Passage: The Transition from British to American Hegemony* (Cambridge, MA: Harvard University Press, 2017).

5. Quoted in Simon Denyer, "Move Over, America. China Now Presents as the Model 'Blazing a New Trail' for the World," *Washington Post*, October 19, 2017. Reagan was invoking the expression coined by John Winthrop as inspiration and warning to the colonists founding a settlement in the New World that would become America.

6. James Dobbins, Howard Shatz, and Ali Wyne, "Russia Is a Rogue, Not a Peer; China Is a Peer, Not a Rogue," *Rand Perspective*, October 2018, p. 12; see generally Peter Frankopan, *The New Silk Roads: The Present and Future of the World* (New York: Knopf, 2019); Parag Khanna, *The Future Is Asian: Global Order in the Twenty-First Century* (New York: Simon & Schuster, 2019); and Bruno Maçães, *Belt and Road: A Chinese World Order* (London: Hurst, 2018).

7. See John Darwin, *The Empire Project: The Rise and Fall of the British World System, 1830–1970* (Cambridge: Cambridge University Press, 2009).

8. Nicholas Casey and Clifford Krauss, "It Doesn't Matter if Ecuador Can Afford This Dam. China Still Gets Paid," *New York Times*, December 24, 2018.

9. See, for example, the debate between Stephen Biddle and Ivan Oelrich, "Future Warfare in the Western Pacific: Chinese Antiaccess/Area Denial, U.S. AirSea Battle, and Command of the Commons in East Asia," *International Security* 41, no. 1 (2016): 7–48; and Andrew S. Erickson, Evan Braden Montgomery, Craig Neuman, Stephen Biddle, and Ivan Oelrich, "Correspondence: How Good Are China's Antiaccess/Area-Denial Capabilities?," *International Security* 41, no. 4 (2017): 202–13.

10. John Deutch, "Is Innovation China's New Great Leap Forward," *MIT Issues in Science and Technology*, Summer 2018.

11. The reference to thirty-four million Chinese men is from Simon Denyer and Annie Gowen, "Too Many Men," *Washington Post*, April 18, 2018.

12. Address in *Vital Speeches of the Day*, vol. 9 (1943), 674–76; an audio recording is available online from the CBC Archives. Although most of this speech was drafted by Robert Sherwood and Samuel Rosenman, the quoted passage was written by Roosevelt himself. Samuel Rosenman, *Working with Roosevelt* (London: Rupert Hart-Davis, 1952), 356.

Index

About the Authors

PHILIP ZELIKOW holds chaired professorships in history and in governance, both at the University of Virginia. A former attorney and career diplomat, his scholarship focuses on critical episodes in American and world history. He has also served at all levels of American government, including policy work in each of the five administrations from Reagan through Obama.

CONDOLEEZZA RICE was the sixty-sixth U.S. secretary of state and the first black woman to hold that office. Prior to that, she was the first woman to serve as national security adviser. She is a professor at Stanford University and cofounder of RiceHadleyGates LLC. Rice is the *New York Times* bestselling author of *No Higher Honor: A Memoir of My Years in Washington* (2011), *Extraordinary, Ordinary People: A Memoir of Family* (2010), *Democracy: Stories from the Long Road to Freedom* (2017), and *Political Risk: How Businesses and Organizations Can Anticipate Global Insecurity* (2018).